To Peter and Minda—wishing you every happiness

Microsoft®

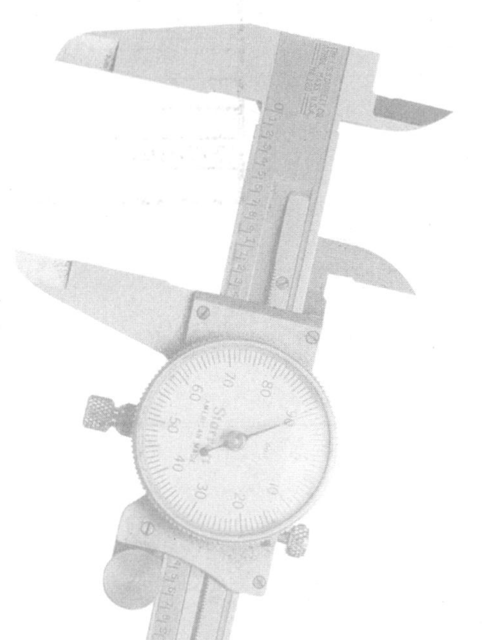

2

Second Edition

BUILDING MICROSOFT® ASP.NET APPLICATIONS FOR MOBILE DEVICES

Andy Wigley

Peter Roxburgh

Microsoft® .net

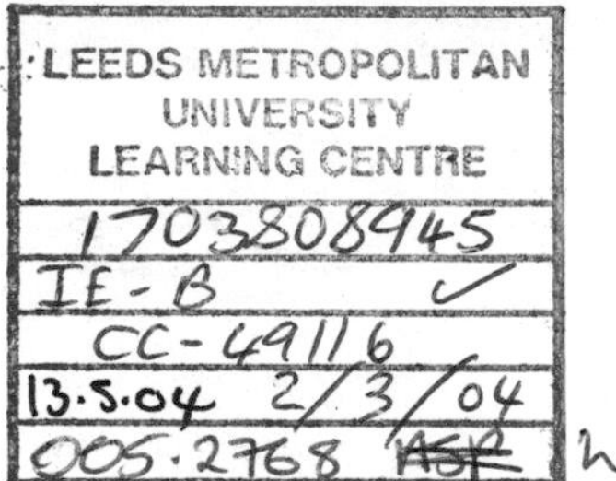

PUBLISHED BY
Microsoft Press
A Division of Microsoft Corporation
One Microsoft Way
Redmond, Washington 98052-6399

Library of Congress Cataloging-in-Publication Data pending.

Printed and bound in the United States of America.

1 2 3 4 5 6 7 8 9 QWE 8 7 6 5 4 3

Distributed in Canada by H.B. Fenn and Company Ltd.

A CIP catalogue record for this book is available from the British Library.

Microsoft Press books are available through booksellers and distributors worldwide. For further information about international editions, contact your local Microsoft Corporation office or contact Microsoft Press International directly at fax (425) 936-7329. Visit our Web site at www.microsoft.com/mspress. Send comments to *mspinput@microsoft.com*.

Acquisitions Editor: Anne Hamilton
Project Editor: Kathleen Atkins
Technical Editor: Allen Jones

Body Part No. X09-45921

Table of Contents

Acknowledgments

All authors are perfectionists. Although I'm proud of the first edition of this book, doing a second edition has allowed me not only to write about the cool new stuff in the products but also to fix the things about the first edition I didn't like. I'm grateful for the opportunity to write this book, and thanks for that goes to my commissioning editor at Microsoft Press, Anne Hamilton.

Warm thanks to my project editor, Kathleen Atkins, who is not only a great editor but also an excellent photographer. She took the photograph of me that accompanies the biography at the back of this book. Thanks to the very thorough technical editing of Allen Jones, who has contributed hugely to making my garbled technical explanations understandable and to getting the sample code into shape. Thanks also to all the other excellent people on the Microsoft Press team: Jennifer Harris, Joel Panchot, Julie Hatley—and apologies to anyone else I've missed.

In the Microsoft ASP.NET product group, thanks to Susan Chory, Andres Sanabria, and Matthew Gibbs for their help and support—and thank you for a great product! At Content Master, thanks to my colleagues, who remain a pleasure to work with, but particularly to David Glanville, my project manager and provider of weary sighs as I overran on the time estimates for this book yet again. (Hey, we don't write these things for profit, do we? It's just for FUN!)

The final paragraph of acknowledgments is always thanks to the author's family. Well, it should be the *first* paragraph (but I don't quite feel able to break with tradition). I give heartfelt thanks to the center of my world, my wonderful wife, Caroline, who provides me with support and encouragement, but more particularly, love and companionship. And thanks to my wonderful daughters, Frances and Claire: I thought teenagers were meant to be awful, but you two are really great.

Introduction

A few weeks ago, I got my hands on my first Microsoft Windows Powered Smartphone. It's a beautiful device and a great phone, but the first thing I noticed (and the first thing anyone else I show it to notices) is that it has a large, high-definition color screen. It's a far cry from the three-line black-and-white text screens that everyone was using when the first edition of this book came out.

I expect that everyone will have mobile devices with large, color screens before long. When you use the browser on these devices, you get a readable amount of information displayed, instead of having to scroll continuously through it. The color and high definition make it pleasurable to the eye. These kinds of browsers could not be used on mobile communications networks until recently because of the limited bandwidth, but over the last year, faster GPRS and CDMA2000 networks have been launched throughout the world. Faster networks and bigger color displays mean that you can create richer, more compelling Web content for mobile browsers, which results in a more usable, more satisfying user experience. The mobile Web is beginning to come of age.

I don't believe that the three-line monochrome browser is doomed, although I expect it will be seen less often on consumer communications devices. However, Internet connectivity is turning up in more and more unlikely places, so monochrome microbrowsers might still turn up in cars, on household appliances, and on portable electronic gadgets.

The pace of change in mobile device technology is as fast as any other computing sector, if not faster. It's nearly a year since the first version of what is now called ASP.NET Mobile Controls was launched (previously called the Microsoft Mobile Internet Toolkit). In that time, we've seen smart new devices such as the Microsoft Smartphone appear, and we've also seen a migration of lower-end devices from Wireless Application Protocol (WAP) 1.1 to WAP 2.0, which introduces a brand new markup language, Extensible HyperText Markup Language-Mobile Profile (XHTML-MP). ASP.NET Mobile Controls have handled these developments comfortably. Microsoft has released configuration updates throughout the year, adding support for these new devices and markup language and demonstrating how *extensible* this technology really is. You can develop applications for these new devices using exactly the same techniques you used for WAP 1.1 devices. The powerful abstract model the developer works with hides the details of the underlying devices, allowing you to get on with creating great applications. If you wanted to sum up the capabilities of this technology, you'd say it is extensible, adaptable, and customizable.

Time for Enterprise Mobility Applications?

There's momentum building from different directions that makes me believe that we'll see a huge increase in the implementation of mobility solutions in the enterprise. The devices are getting cheaper, and they have better capabilities. The telecommunications networks are getting faster, and with the spread of Wi-Fi (802.11 wireless LAN) throughout the workplace and at hot spots in public places such as airports, railway stations, and coffee shops, enterprises can be confident that if they equip their personnel with capable devices such as a Pocket PC Phone Edition PDA with integrated Wi-Fi, they'll never be far from a wireless network connection with decent bandwidth. If you develop mobile Web applications, your users can access them from the browser in the device over Wi-Fi when they are in a location where that's available. When users can't connect to a wireless LAN, they can connect to a GPRS or CDMA2000 network operated by a phone network operator. (GPRS and CDMA2000 connections are sometimes known as *WWAN*—wireless wide area network—to distinguish them from *WLAN*, which is the proper term for Wi-Fi.)

So, good devices and good networks. However, the key ingredient from an enterprise point of view is good software. Microsoft continues to make huge investments in mobility technology. The Microsoft Windows CE operating system that drives Pocket PC and Windows Powered Smartphone devices continues to develop and gain new capabilities. The latest version is called Windows CE .NET and includes support for the .NET Compact Framework, which is a "light" version of the .NET Runtime for handheld devices. Using Microsoft Visual Studio .NET 2003, you can build .NET applications that run on handheld devices, but only those that support the runtime, which currently are Pocket PC and Windows CE .NET devices. To reach the majority of browser-equipped mobile devices, you need ASP.NET Mobile Controls. Again using Visual Studio .NET 2003, you can build applications that run not on the device, but on the Web server, and that send markup to the browser on the device. The difference is "rich" vs. "reach." The .NET Compact Framework is about rich client applications running on only some mobile devices; ASP.NET Mobile Controls are about mobile Web applications that work with the majority of mobile devices.

With Visual Studio .NET, developers use a single integrated development environment to build applications for each of these scenarios. Needless to say, building ASP.NET applications requires a different skill set than building Windows Forms applications that run on the device, but they're both built on top of the .NET Framework, so there's a lot of commonality that can make a developer's skills more transferable between these different disciplines.

Who Is This Book For?

We've organized this book to serve two distinct audiences. The first group is wireless developers who already have experience developing for handheld devices. You might be new to Microsoft development and probably haven't yet used Visual Studio .NET. We've written Chapter 1, Chapter 2, and Chapter 3 primarily with you in mind; they introduce ASP.NET and Visual Studio .NET and walk you through the development of some mobile Web applications. Chapter 3 explains the essential information you'll need to understand to work with mobile Web Forms.

The second audience is those who already have experience working with the .NET Framework and Visual Studio .NET. If you've used ASP.NET before, you'll want to skim the first three chapters to get acquainted with the Mobile Internet Designer but then dive straight into Chapter 4 to begin working with the mobile controls.

Regardless of your background, you need to be familiar with object-oriented programming. The .NET Framework and everything built on it is completely object-oriented. ASP.NET Mobile Controls are classes, just like everything else in ASP.NET, and you need to understand about classes, methods, properties, and inheritance to make full use of the mobile controls and the .NET Framework.

Perhaps surprisingly, you don't need to be familiar with HyperText Markup Language (HTML) or Wireless Markup Language (WML). More important is familiarity with a programming language such as Microsoft Visual Basic or Microsoft Visual C#. We want to stress that you're writing object-oriented programs that just happen to output markup. It's quite possible to write very sophisticated ASP.NET Mobile Controls applications without ever having to dirty your hands with device-specific markup. Later on, some familiarity with HTML, WML, or XHTML can be useful if you want to customize your application for specific handheld devices. One of the things you can do with the Templates feature is send "raw" markup directly to the device. Advanced developers who want to develop their own controls must, of course, be completely familiar with the markup languages the devices use.

All the code examples in this book are written in C#, the programming language Microsoft developed concurrently with the .NET Framework. Our hope is that Visual Basic developers won't feel alienated by this focus on C#. In fact, C# code and Visual Basic code are structurally very similar, and apart from the obvious language syntax differences, the C# samples should be very readable to a Visual Basic .NET developer. On the Web site for this book, you'll find all the sample code from this book, with versions in C# and Visual Basic .NET. The only exceptions to this are the custom control examples in Chapter 21 and Chapter 22. These are only in C#, not because you can't use Visual Basic (or any other language the .NET Framework supports), but because we didn't have time to write the code!

What's in This Book?

In Chapter 1, we set the scene by describing the challenges facing mobile Web application developers and explaining how ASP.NET Mobile Controls resolve many of those issues. In Chapter 2, we continue the introductory theme, giving you a brief tour of Visual Studio .NET, focusing on the capabilities introduced by ASP.NET Mobile Controls. We show you the Mobile Internet Designer, which allows you to design your application using a drag-and-drop GUI editor, dragging mobile controls from the Toolbox and dropping them onto a mobile Web Forms page.

Chapter 3 is in many ways the most important chapter in this book. It gives you a grounding in the important basics of ASP.NET Mobile Controls application development. This chapter is essential reading if you're new to ASP.NET, explaining how the request-response interactions between client and server are handled and how actions performed by the user of the mobile device translate into events, which you trap in your code in the server. It's also important if you already have experience with ASP.NET as you'll learn much about the differences between ASP.NET Web Forms and ASP.NET mobile Web Forms.

Chapter 4, Chapter 5, Chapter 6, and Chapter 7 take you through each of the standard mobile controls. The intention here was to provide a handy mini-reference to each control so that you can find out—in one place—how to include a control in a mobile Web Forms page using Extensible Markup Language (XML) syntax and how to access the properties and methods of the control in your code. Each control includes one or more sample applications demonstrating how to use it.

In Chapter 8, Chapter 9, and Chapter 10, we explain the features of ASP.NET Mobile Controls that allow you to enhance the presentation of an application. These features can be categorized into three distinct areas of functionality: styles, property overrides, and templates. Through styles, you can define colors and fonts to apply to the output of controls, which will be honored on those browsers that support them. Property overrides allow you to customize your application so that for specific models or types of client devices, different values are assigned to control properties. Templates are a powerful feature, allowing you to customize the way a list control is displayed or to insert device-specific markup into the output sent to a particular device.

Chapters 11 through 18 describe all the other areas of functionality that you will use as a mobile Web developer. Topics include an introduction to data handling with Microsoft ADO.NET, testing and debugging using Visual Studio .NET and mobile device emulators, good design practice and internationalizing your application, handling state management, packaging and deploying your application, and writing secure ASP.NET applications.

The last four chapters in this book, Chapters 19 through 22, describe the extensibility capabilities of ASP.NET Mobile Controls. Chapter 19 describes how to extend support in ASP.NET Mobile Controls to new devices. You can wait until Microsoft issues an update that supports your new device, or you can add support yourself with the help of this chapter. Most of the material in these four chapters is for the advanced developer, although Chapter 20 describes user controls, which you can use to easily develop reusable visual components for mobile Web applications. Chapter 21 and Chapter 22 address the authoring of custom mobile controls in code.

What Do I Need to Use This Book?

You'll need the following software to work through the samples in this book:

- Microsoft Visual Studio .NET 2003, or Microsoft Visual Studio .NET 2002 and the Microsoft Mobile Internet Toolkit 1.0. (Download the Mobile Internet Toolkit from *http://msdn.microsoft.com/library/default.asp?url=/downloads/list/netdevmit.asp*.)
- Microsoft Windows 2000, Microsoft Windows XP, or Microsoft .NET Server

The minimum hardware specification for your development PC is a Pentium II-class processor, 450 MHz with a minimum of 128 MB (Windows 2000) or 256 MB (Windows XP or Windows .NET Server) of RAM. You'll need around 5 GB of free hard disk space to install Visual Studio .NET 2003.

Visual Studio .NET 2003 includes emulators of a Windows CE .NET and a Pocket PC 2003 device. You can use the browsers on these emulated devices for testing, so a real handheld device is not essential. You can also perform initial testing of applications using Microsoft Internet Explorer. See Chapter 16 for details of emulators from other sources that you can use for testing.

Sample Code

Most of the sample code in this book is written in C#. Many readers will prefer to use Visual Basic, so we have implemented samples in Visual Basic as well and made all of them, both the C# and the Visual Basic samples, available for download from this book's Web site. We hope that Visual Basic .NET developers will download the samples and refer to those when reading the text. Fortunately, in .NET, the differences between languages are not as pronounced as they used to be. C# and Visual Basic .NET applications are structurally similar—only the language syntax changes—so descriptions in the text that describe how to use a programming technique in C# should be understandable to someone referring to the Visual Basic version of a sample.

You can download the samples from *http://www.microsoft.com/mspress/books/6709.asp*. Click the companion content link in the More Information box on the right side of this page to bring up the companion content Web page. This page has the link to download the sample code. See the instructions on that site for how to install the samples on your own PC. Check this site for corrections and updates to the book as well.

Installing the MSDE .NET Framework Samples Database

Some of the samples in Chapter 11 use the pubs database, which installs with the Microsoft .NET Framework SDK QuickStart samples. You don't need to install the SQL Server product on your development system because the setup for the .NET Framework QuickStart samples will install the Microsoft SQL Server Desktop Engine (MSDE), a stand-alone database server, if necessary.

To install the MSDE server and the sample databases, go to the C:\Program Files\Microsoft Visual Studio .NET 2003\SDK\v1.1 folder, and double-click StartHere.htm. The Microsoft .NET Framework SDK welcome page is displayed. Click on the QuickStarts, Tutorials, And Samples link. If you haven't already installed the .NET Framework QuickStart samples, the page that is displayed shows two steps you must perform to install the samples on your computer. First click Step 1: Install The .NET Framework Samples Database. When the database has been set up, click Step 2: Set Up The QuickStarts to install all the sample databases and set up the .NET Framework QuickStart tutorials.

> **Warning** After you've installed the MSDE, be sure to install the latest service pack. Service Pack 3 or later is necessary to ensure that your system does not get infected with the Slammer virus. See *http://msdn.microsoft.com/netframework/downloads/updates/sdkfix/default.asp* for details.

Using the Samples with Visual Studio .NET 2002

The samples have been developed using Visual Studio .NET 2003. You can't open the supplied project and solution files with Visual Studio .NET 2002. If you're using Visual Studio .NET 2002 and the Mobile Internet Toolkit 1.0, all the supplied sample code will still work, however. For any sample you want to use, you'll have to create a new ASP.NET mobile Web application in Visual Studio .NET 2002 and then navigate to the project folder and replace the .aspx, .aspx.cs (or .aspx.vb), Web.config, and (if supplied) global.asax and global.asax.cs (or .asax.vb) files with those supplied in the sample. There should be no code changes required to get the sample to work.

Support

Every effort has been made to ensure the accuracy of this book and the contents of the companion content. Microsoft Press provides corrections for books and companion content through the World Wide Web at the following address:

http://www.microsoft.com/mspress/support

To connect directly to the Microsoft Press Knowledge Base and enter a query, go to:

http://www.microsoft.com/mspress/support/search.asp

If you have comments, questions, or ideas regarding this book or the companion content or questions that aren't answered by querying the Knowledge Base, please send them by e-mail to Microsoft Press at:

mspinput@microsoft.com

or by postal mail to:

Microsoft Press
Attn: Microsoft ASP.NET Mobile Devices Editor
One Microsoft Way
Redmond, WA 98052-6399

Please note that product support is not offered through the preceding mail address. For product support information, please visit the Microsoft Support Web site at:

http://support.microsoft.com

1

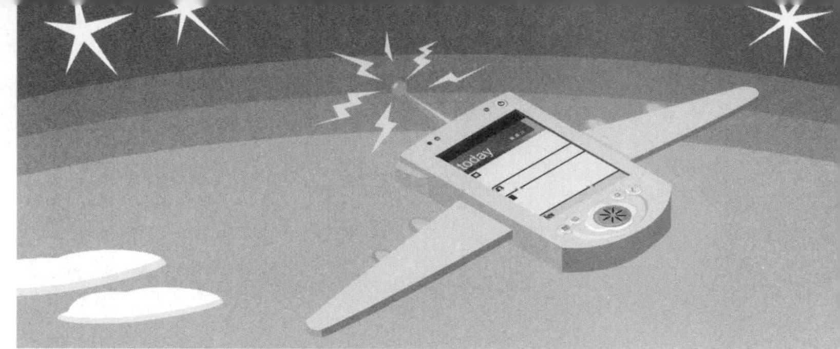

Introducing Microsoft ASP.NET for the Mobile Web

Consider this scenario: Caroline, software engineer extraordinaire at A. Datum Corporation, is in trouble. After a few high-profile successes, she earns recognition as a key employee. Her technical director becomes interested in wireless Internet devices and asks her to build a mobile Web site that allows field personnel to access their company data remotely. Figure 1-1 illustrates the challenge Caroline faces.

After some initial research, Caroline decides Wireless Application Protocol (WAP) is the best approach. Handsets are available, and industry support looks solid. Then the first headache appears: Caroline has to learn a new markup language. She knows Hypertext Markup Language (HTML), but she finds WAP's Wireless Markup Language (WML) so different that she discards her first few efforts until she succeeds in working out how the "cards and decks" structure of a WML page works and figures out how to present meaningful content in such a small display area. Although she wasn't naïve enough to assume that an existing HTML Web site would transfer wholesale to a small device, she's surprised by the difficulty she has creating a workable application given the device's small display and limited text-input capabilities. Eventually the application takes shape, written using Microsoft Active Server Pages (ASP)—meaning that Caroline had to refresh her knowledge of Microsoft Visual Basic Scripting Edition (VBScript) and write all the code required to output the appropriate WML markup for her Web pages.

Figure 1-1 Designers of mobile applications face a bewildering number of choices.

Soon the prototype is ready for beta testing, and Caroline is quite pleased with it. However, the testers report that the application is confusing and unintuitive, which surprises Caroline, who carefully considered its usability. After investigation, Caroline, who had used an emulation of a Nokia phone for testing, learns that her users were working with Openwave browsers. Although both devices conform to WML 1.1 specifications, the WML markup that offers the best usability on each browser differs slightly.

Caroline encounters even more problems. Field personnel at A. Datum Corporation's other main location don't have a network operator providing WAP handsets in their metropolitan area. However, their network operator does offer a mobile Internet service called M-mode service, which uses a different markup language, compact HTML (cHTML). In addition, some of the prototype testers, despite seeing the potential of the service, have recently acquired new two-way pagers, which offer text mobile Internet service—and now they want to access the company data through the service their new pagers offer. Furthermore, the field service managers recently received personal organizers with HTML browsers operating over wireless modems, and they don't want to carry a WAP device as well. The technical director, looking a little disappointed, thanks Caroline for her efforts and walks away scribbling on her indispensable personal digital assistant (PDA), which is—of course—equipped with wireless Internet access, but not for WML.

At this point, Caroline quits the business in disgust and pursues her long-time ambition of guiding outdoor expeditions. Once in the mountains, she finds with some relief that there are no computers in sight and that she can't get mobile data coverage because of the surrounding peaks. Sometimes, however, lying in her sleeping bag, she misses the excitement of software development and thinks back on the mobile project she led at A. Datum Corporation. She realizes that the project would have succeeded if she'd had the following capabilities:

- A way to write one application that, when run, automatically generates the correct markup for all major mobile browsers
- A runtime smart enough to send not only valid markup, but also markup that actually yields optimum usability on a particular manufacturer's browser
- A presentation optimized for each type of browser—so that if, for example, the browser supports color, the browser will use color as appropriate
- The ability to lay out the user interface in a graphical user interface (GUI) editor
- The ability to code in a proper object-oriented manner so that it's possible to cleanly isolate user interface elements from application logic
- Application logic that can be coded in a major language such as Microsoft Visual Basic .NET, C++, C#, or even COBOL, with full access to data and the facilities of the underlying operating system
- The ability to customize the user interface for any specific device
- An extensible system that easily supports the next generation of mobile devices on the market as well as their applications

These are features that ASP.NET Mobile Controls offer to overcome the obstacles to a successful implementation that Caroline faced.

A Solution for the Wireless Muddle

ASP.NET Mobile Controls provide a solution for the "wireless muddle" that caused so many problems for the developer in the preceding scenario. Wireless developers have to cope with a confusing variety of different devices—small or large devices with different-size screens, in color or monochrome, and that require one of the HTML, cHTML, WML, or XHTML markup languages, and quite often a specific "dialect" of one of those. Since the first edition of this book came out early in 2002, the situation has gotten more confusing! At that time, WAP/WML 1.1 browsers were commonplace in Europe, cHTML 1.0 browsers were predominant in Japan, and Pocket PCs and Palm devices using an HTML 3.2 browser were the favored handheld devices for businesses. A year later, you can walk into a shop of any of the major mobile network operators and be faced with mobile phones with WML 1.1 or WML 1.3 browsers, Pocket PC Phone Edition and Microsoft Smartphone devices with HTML browsers, and smartphones with WAP 2.0 browsers that require XHTML Mobile Profile (XHTML-MP) markup, which is the successor to WML. Japanese i-mode technology, already a huge success in Japan, is now being offered by operators in Europe and North America. PDAs and higher-end Smartphones usually have HTML 3.2 browsers, although the version of Pocket Internet Explorer included in the latest release of Microsoft's operating system for handheld devices, Microsoft Windows CE .NET, accepts HTML 4.0 markup.

How then do you create an application that works with a significant number of these devices? If you're lucky and you can control which devices are issued to your users, you can standardize on one device and one technology. Few of us will have that luxury, however. Even if you build an application for one specific device, the speed of technological change in this industry means that you will quite likely be looking at a major rewrite a year down the line, when you want to take advantage of a new generation of handheld devices.

The answer is to make the technology on the client device an irrelevance—or to put it another way, to use middleware on the Web server that takes care of worrying about the specific requirements of a particular client device on your behalf. You develop a single application using ASP.NET Mobile Controls, deploy it to a Windows Web server running Internet Information Services (IIS) and the Microsoft .NET Framework, and that application works with over 200 different kinds of mobile devices from many different vendors, each with its own specific requirements of markup language and screen size, as illustrated in Figure 1-2. Microsoft regularly releases Device Update packs for ASP.NET Mobile Controls that add support for still more handheld devices.

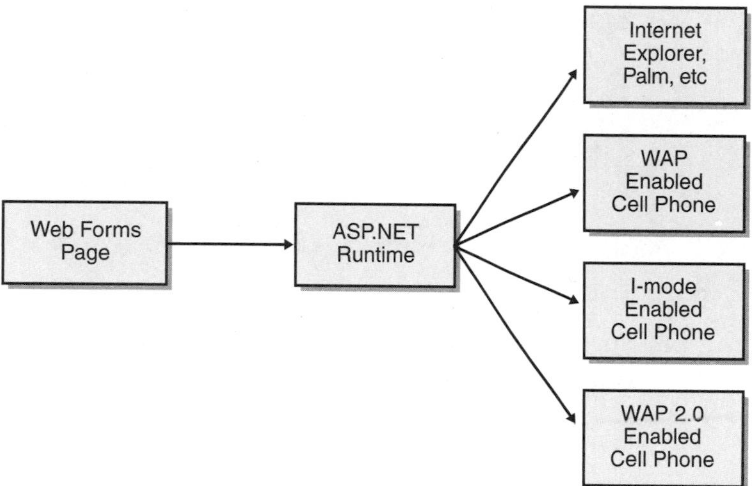

Figure 1-2 The ASP.NET Mobile Controls use adaptive rendering to support over 200 different handheld devices from a single application.

Developing with Mobile Web Forms

You use ASP.NET Web Forms to build Web pages for HTML PC clients. ASP.NET mobile Web Forms allow you to build pages for mobile clients, regardless of the markup languages they support.

Abstracting the Mobile Device User Interface

In ASP.NET, the developer works with an abstraction of a user interface, with objects representing the fundamental components of a visual display, such as text labels and input boxes. It's the runtime's responsibility to take this abstract representation and turn it into device-specific markup. ASP.NET provides mobile Web Forms controls that, like standard Web Forms controls, represent individual components of the user interface. You simply define a user interface using mobile controls within a page, and ASP.NET delivers the content in the markup language that's appropriate to the device requesting the page. ASP.NET Web Forms controls are programmable objects, but you define the layout of the controls in your user interface by creating a text file containing Extensible Markup Language (XML) that represents the controls. For example, a simple "Hello, World" application is implemented as a mobile Form control containing a mobile Label control. The label has the value *"Hello, World"*, as shown in Listing 1-1.

```
<%@ Page Language="vb" Inherits="System.Web.UI.MobileControls.MobilePage" %>
<%@ Register TagPrefix="mobile" Namespace="System.Web.UI.MobileControls"
    Assembly="System.Web.Mobile" %>

<mobile:Form id="Form1" runat="server">
   <mobile:Label id="Label1" runat="server">Hello, World</mobile:Label>
</mobile:Form>
```

Listing 1-1 ASP.NET mobile Web Forms code for a "Hello, World" application.

The first time a client requests this page from your Web server, the ASP.NET page compiler parses the contents of the mobile Web Forms page and dynamically builds an application that it then caches for future requests for the same page. When the application is run, it examines the Hypertext Transfer Protocol (HTTP) headers sent with the request to determine what kind of device is making the request and what kind of markup the device requires. The application then generates the appropriate markup in the response that it sends back to the client.

Even wireless devices that support the same markup languages can require subtly different markup to best provide a certain functionality. For example, when providing navigation links within WML 1.1 applications, Nokia devices achieve best usability with a WML *a* (anchor) element, whereas Openwave browsers usually achieve best results with a *do* element. Writing code for each specific task on every specific device would be an enormous undertaking. Using the ASP.NET mobile controls, you can simply place a Link control on a mobile Web Forms page, and the runtime automatically renders the correct elements for any given wireless device.

Using Mobile Web Forms Controls

The mobile controls supplied with ASP.NET are a special type of Web Forms control. You can use all the mobile controls without worrying about the capabilities of the requesting device. It might help to think of the set of mobile controls as falling into three categories:

- **Core controls** These controls are mobile versions of standard ASP.NET controls. Some examples of these controls include TextBox, Label, and Image. In addition, ASP.NET provides a number of special features, such as the Calendar control.
- **Server validation controls** More than a third of the controls have something to do with validating user input. Validation controls help simplify code and can be used to prevent users entering incorrect

data—they provide a vast amount of functionality in just a few simple elements. For example, with these controls, you can validate a field to ensure that it fits the following criteria:

- ❑ Follows a specific input format, such as a date, or some custom format that you define
- ❑ Contains a value of a particular data type, such as a string
- ❑ Contains some value—in other words, isn't blank

- **Mobile-only controls** These controls offer functionality that applies only to mobile clients. Examples of these controls include PhoneCall and DeviceSpecific.
- **DeviceSpecific/Choice constructs** These constructs allow you to customize your application for specific devices—for example, to set the property of a control to one value on one device, and differently on others. Each construct consists of a DeviceSpecific element and one or more Choice child elements. You use the Choice element to reference device filters, which test the capabilities of the requesting device. If the Choice element evaluates to *true*, that choice applies to the current request. For example, a device filter can test whether a client requires a monochromatic or a color image, and then your application delivers the appropriate image to that client.
- **Templates** The Form, Panel, List, and ObjectList controls support templates. These controls use DeviceSpecific/Choice constructs to target specific devices with specific content, which you define in a template. This content can be device-specific markup or ASP.NET mobile controls. With some controls, such as List, you can override the default output, whereas with others, such as Form, you can insert whole new sections of content that renders in addition to the default markup.

Working with Mobile Web Forms Using .NET Tools

You can easily construct mobile Web Forms in your favorite text editor, such as Microsoft Notepad. Alternatively, integrated development environments (IDEs) such as Microsoft Visual Studio .NET give you powerful facilities for developing mobile Web applications, including the Mobile Internet Designer, a GUI editor for mobile Web Forms. This allows you to use a drag-and-drop graphical editor to create the XML that defines the layout of your mobile Web Forms and set properties of mobile controls. In Chapter 2, we'll examine how to use Visual Studio .NET to create mobile applications.

Implementing Code

An ASP.NET application combines the XML that describes the mobile controls used in the user interface with code that acts on those controls and that implements the functionality of your application. You can code an ASP.NET application in one of two ways: embed the code within a page, or provide the code in a separate file. Implementing code within the body of a page is simple. You must first declare the language you want to use. You then delimit any sections of code with either *script* tags or an ASP.NET script delimiter—namely, <% %>. The following example shows how to implement code within the body of a Web Forms page:

```
<script language="C#">
    class DoNothing {
        public void DoesNothing() {;}
    }
</script>
```

The alternative method of coding an ASP.NET application—providing code in a separate file—is known as the *code-behind technique*. Coding behind is often a better method of implementing code than using inline code, because it provides a clean separation between the layout of the graphical elements contained in the mobile Web Forms page and the application logic contained in the code-behind module. Implementing the code-behind technique is simple. If you're using Visual Studio .NET, the IDE automatically stores your code in a file separate from the controls. If you're creating your own projects using a text editor, you write your code and save it as a normal class file with that language's standard file extension, such as .vb for Visual Basic .NET or .cs for Microsoft Visual C#. To use the code, you insert a special tag at the start of the .aspx page, which declares that the page inherits from the class that you created. Programmatically, this simply means that the .aspx page inherits the methods and properties you program in the code-behind classes, logically becoming a part of that page. We'll examine the structure of an ASP.NET mobile Web application in more detail in Chapter 3.

> **Note** A mobile Web Forms page is a particular representation of a .NET class object. When a page inherits from another object, it inherits the properties and methods of that object. In addition, you can often override the inherited properties and methods. Inheritance is one of the key principles of both object-oriented programming and programming within the .NET Framework. (We'll examine inheritance more fully in Chapter 3.)

Consuming Events

Mobile Web Forms controls fire events, which methods in your code can trap and act upon. An example of such an event is when a user clicks a button displayed within a page. When a user clicks this button, the mobile Command control in your application running on the server raises an event. This event is trapped by an event handler method that you write in your application; the method then carries out some function such as displaying an acknowledgment to the user. You can access all the properties of the mobile Web Forms controls in your application through this event-driven model. Therefore, you can dynamically change what the application displays to the user, make controls visible and invisible, access and display data, and perform any of the other functions required in your application. You can even dynamically create new mobile controls at run time and load them into your mobile Web Forms pages. This allows you to build very efficient applications that are responsive to user actions.

Building Mobile Solutions with Microsoft .NET

ASP.NET applications run on a Windows server that has IIS and the .NET Framework installed. Figure 1-3 shows an outline of the .NET Framework.

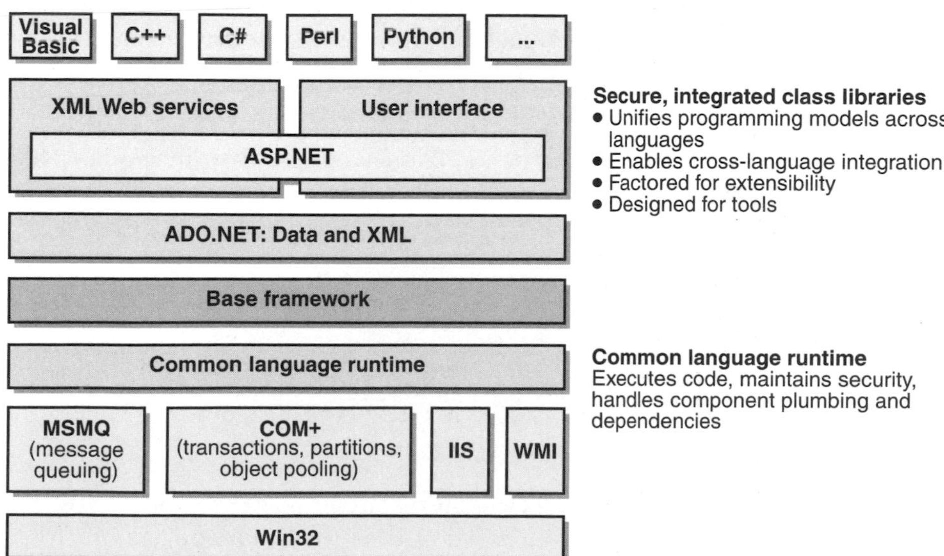

Figure 1-3 The .NET Framework provides a common infrastructure for loosely coupled objects and emphasizes the development of applications that exploit the Internet.

The .NET Framework consists of two main parts:

- **Base Class Libraries (BCL)** A huge collection of classes used by developers to build applications. Different parts of these libraries are used to develop XML Web services, to build Windows Forms applications to run on PCs, to access the Windows file system, to perform I/O, and of course to build Web applications.
- **.NET Common Language Runtime** A comprehensive runtime responsible for executing .NET applications on a computer. .NET common language runtimes are available for Windows, of course, but various companies are working on implementations for other platforms, such as Linux.

Once developers master the skills required, .NET makes them more productive than they were using earlier technologies. In particular, developers can build rich client applications using Windows Forms that run on PCs on which the .NET Framework has been installed. However, this clearly isn't an option for constrained mobile devices such as cell phones, which do not have the persistent storage to store the libraries, nor the CPU power or an operating system capable of running the common language runtime.

In early 2003, Microsoft released three significant products:

- Microsoft .NET Framework 1.1 is a new version of the common language runtime and BCL, improving on the capabilities of the first version, released a year earlier.
- Microsoft .NET Compact Framework 1.0 is a lightweight version of the BCL and .NET common language runtime targeted at higher-end handheld devices (smart devices) such as Pocket PCs.
- Microsoft Visual Studio .NET 2003 is a new version of the IDE that allows you to build PC applications for .NET Framework 1.1 and smart device applications using .NET Compact Framework 1.0. See my book *Microsoft .NET Compact Framework (Core Reference)* (Microsoft Press, 2003) for details of programming using the .NET Compact Framework.

The ASP.NET mobile controls aren't intended for devices that support a sophisticated runtime, however. Rather than *rich* applications for PC or Pocket PC clients, their emphasis is on *reach*, ensuring delivery of the application to the widest range of client devices that are not PCs. Their primary goal is to enable the delivery of ASP.NET applications to mobile devices that use any WML, cHTML, HTML, or XHTML-MP browser. The ASP.NET mobile controls do this by extending the .NET Framework classes with new classes such as *MobilePage*. These classes descend from the other ASP.NET classes and have the capability to deliver the required markup for the target browser. Offering full integration into the Visual Studio .NET IDE, the ASP.NET mobile controls provide mobile developers with a powerful tool for building applications. Not only is Visual Studio .NET flexible and extensible, but it also encourages the production of good, clean, object-oriented applications.

The ASP.NET mobile controls are a fully integrated part of .NET Framework 1.1. You can install .NET Framework 1.1 and 1.0 on the same computer and run applications targeting each of them side-by-side. However, if for some reason you must work with .NET Framework 1.0, you will find that the ASP.NET mobile controls are not integrated into that version. You must download and install the Microsoft Mobile Internet Toolkit on your development computer and also on the Web server where your application will run. Go to *http://www.asp.net*, and click on the Mobile tab on that page for a download link for the Mobile Internet Toolkit, which also integrates support for building ASP.NET mobile Web Forms applications into Visual Studio .NET 2002. (That capability is fully integrated into Visual Studio .NET 2003.)

Whether you use .NET Framework 1.0 with the Mobile Internet Toolkit or .NET Framework 1.1, you still need to ensure that you have the latest Device Update packs. Microsoft releases Device Update packs at intervals to configure support for new devices. Device Update 2, published in October 2002, increases the count of officially supported devices to 201. (Go to *http://www.asp.net* and click on the Mobile tab on that page for information about Device Update packs and a list of supported devices.) Device Update 2 is significant because it adds support for a new family of mobile device browsers, those requiring XHTML-MP markup, in addition to the existing support for HTML, cHTML, and WML browsers. XHTML-MP will supercede WML in WAP-enabled devices.

> **Note** You can use a device that is not officially supported in the Device Update pack, but you'll have to configure support for the device yourself. You'll learn how to add this support in Chapter 19.

A Powerful Solution for Mobile Web Application Development

Microsoft's ASP.NET Mobile Controls provide a powerful solution for mobile Web developers. With this technology, you can build mobile Web applications using ASP.NET and a skill set similar to that needed to build applications for PC browsers. The runtime and control classes generate the markup a client requires as well as the optimum markup a particular model of browser requires. Consequently, you can concentrate on creating an application that solves a business problem rather than spend your time wrestling with interoperability issues.

ASP.NET is a fully integrated member of the Microsoft developer tools family. Undeniably, in the past, some C++ and Visual Basic developers regarded ASP development as unworthy of their talents—an unfair criticism if you look at the sophistication and complexity of some applications developed with ASP. ASP.NET, on the other hand, isn't constrained by scripting languages that offer limited functionality or by requiring callable objects to support particular interfaces so that the poor, disadvantaged scripting clients can use them. The full facilities that the .NET Framework and its associated technologies offer are available to any ASP.NET application, just as they are to any Windows GUI application.

As computing power is delivered to increasing numbers of devices throughout the world, application developers are required to work on delivering applications for new devices and scenarios undreamed of a few years ago. The need is greater than ever for enabling technologies such as the .NET Framework and ASP.NET Mobile Controls. With these tools, developers can apply their skills to widely differing application areas, without wasting development time handling arcane issues such as differing client browser implementations.

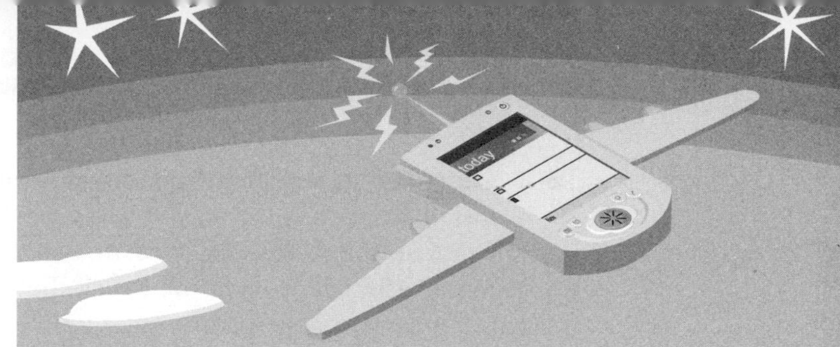

2

Getting Started

In this chapter, we'll provide you with an overview of the mobile Web application development process. We'll systematically guide you through some simple applications built using Microsoft Visual Studio .NET and the Mobile Internet Designer (the GUI editor for mobile Web applications), and we'll introduce you to the features of Visual Studio .NET.

We'll start the chapter by outlining the system requirements for development platforms and showing you how to create your first mobile Web applications. You'll then discover how to test your application with Microsoft Internet Explorer as well as with a tool that emulates a mobile device. Finally, we'll look at some of the basic design issues you'll face when developing Web applications for handheld devices.

Setting Up Your Development System

To develop ASP.NET mobile Web applications, you'll need access to a computer with the following configuration:

- **Microsoft Windows XP Professional, Microsoft Windows 2000 Professional, or Microsoft Windows 2000 Server with Service Pack 2 or later** Microsoft Windows XP is the newest version of the world's most popular operating system. If you're using Windows XP, you'll need to develop on the Professional Edition, which includes Internet Information Services (IIS).

- **Microsoft Internet Information Services (IIS) 5.0 or later** To install IIS in Windows 2000, click Start, Settings, and then Control Panel. In Windows XP, click Start, and then Control Panel. Click Add/Remove Programs, and then click the Add/Remove Windows Components button. Select the Internet Information Services (IIS) check box to enable IIS on your system. Complete the IIS install by clicking Next and providing any Windows media requested by the subsequent installation process.
- **Microsoft .NET Framework** You can download the .NET Framework from the MSDN Web site at *http://msdn.microsoft.com/netframework/downloads*. If you install Visual Studio .NET, the .NET Framework is installed at the same time.
- **Microsoft Visual Studio .NET** Strictly speaking, Visual Studio .NET isn't essential for developing mobile Web applications. You can create mobile Web Forms applications using a text editor and the command-line compilation tools on a computer with the .NET Framework and Mobile Internet Toolkit installed. However, an integrated development environment (IDE) such as Visual Studio .NET is indispensable for efficient development. You can also use the free ASP.NET development IDE, Microsoft ASP.NET Web Matrix, which you can download from *http://www.asp.net/webmatrix/*. The illustrations in this book show Visual Studio .NET 2003.
- **Mobile Internet Toolkit** If you've installed .NET Framework version 1.1 or Visual Studio .NET 2003 (which installs .NET Framework 1.1 during the Component Update phase of installation), the ASP.NET mobile controls are already installed. However, if you're working with .NET Framework version 1.0 or Visual Studio .NET 2002, you must download the Mobile Internet Toolkit and device updates from *http://www.asp.net/download.aspx*.

> **Note** ASP.NET Mobile Controls is the new name for the Mobile Internet Toolkit. If you're using Visual Studio .NET 2002 for development and deploying to systems with .NET Framework 1.0, you need to install the Mobile Internet Toolkit on both. If you're using Visual Studio .NET 2003 and deploying applications to Web servers with .NET Framework 1.1, you don't need to install anything else, as the ASP.NET mobile controls are a fully integrated part of .NET Framework 1.1.

> There's very little difference between ASP.NET Mobile Controls and the Mobile Internet Toolkit. The techniques and descriptions in this book apply to either version, but we'll refer to the product using the new name, ASP.NET Mobile Controls. We'll describe any differences between the two versions where they occur.

If you want, you can develop applications using Visual Studio .NET on your development workstation but locate your applications on a different Web server. In this configuration, your development system must be running Microsoft Windows NT 4 Service Pack 6a, Windows 2000 Service Pack 2, or Windows XP and must have either Visual Studio .NET 2003 or Visual Studio .NET 2002 plus the Mobile Internet Toolkit installed. The Web server must be running Microsoft Windows 2000, Microsoft Windows Server 2003, or Microsoft Windows XP and must be running IIS version 5.0 or later. It must also have either the .NET Framework 1.1 installed or the .NET Framework 1.0 plus the Mobile Internet Toolkit. The easy way to configure a separate Web server is to install Visual Studio .NET, proceed through the Windows Component Update phase, and then clear all options apart from server components prior to the installation of Visual Studio .NET. In addition, you'll need administrative access to the Web server.

By default, Visual Studio .NET expects to create Web projects on a Web server running on the development system, which you can access using URLs that begin with *http://localhost*. The examples we'll give in this chapter assume this configuration.

The minimum computer specification recommended for Visual Studio .NET 2002 or 2003 development on Windows XP Professional is a Pentium II 450-MHz machine with 160 MB of RAM. However, we recommend at least a Pentium III 733-MHz machine with 256 MB of RAM. Like many IDEs, Visual Studio .NET provides a wealth of information, so for effective development we advise using at least a 17-inch monitor.

In addition, you'll need either some mobile devices or software emulations of them to thoroughly test your applications. Visual Studio .NET integrates Internet Explorer for easy testing of Web applications, which is a useful tool for the early stages of mobile Web application development. The multiple browser support of ASP.NET with the Mobile Internet Toolkit means that Internet Explorer is just as valid a client browser as a Wireless Application Protocol (WAP) browser or Pocket Internet Explorer. However, you'll also need to test your applications on the intended target devices. You'll learn more about mobile device emulators and using them for testing later in this chapter, in the section "Testing with a Mobile Phone Emulator."

Which Version of the .NET Framework and ASP.NET Mobile Controls Should You Use?

At the time of this writing, two versions of the .NET Framework are available: version 1.0, released in February 2002, and version 1.1, released in January 2003. To use the ASP.NET mobile controls with version 1.0, you must download the Mobile Internet Toolkit from the MSDN Web site or from *http://www.asp.net*. You must install these on your development computer and also on the production Web server where your application is deployed. If you install Visual Studio .NET 2002, you install .NET Framework 1.0 during the Component Update phase of the installation.

The .NET Framework version 1.1 includes the ASP.NET mobile controls as an integral part. You use Visual Studio .NET 2003 to develop applications that use this version of the .NET Framework. Production Web servers must have .NET Framework 1.1 installed on them.

The two versions of the .NET Framework work side by side, so you can run applications developed to use version 1.0 and applications targeting version 1.1 on the same computer. Similarly, you can install Visual Studio .NET 2002 and Visual Studio .NET 2003 on the same development computer.

There is very little difference between the ASP.NET mobile controls included in the Mobile Internet Toolkit for .NET Framework 1.0, and those included in .NET Framework 1.1. The major impact is in deployment. To deploy an ASP.NET mobile controls application developed for version 1.1, only .NET Framework 1.1 needs to be installed on the Web server. If you have developed an application for version 1.0, the Web server must have .NET Framework 1.0 and the Mobile Internet Toolkit installed. If you have the choice, develop applications with .NET Framework 1.1 to simplify application deployment.

Creating Your First Mobile Web Applications

Visual Studio .NET is a complete development environment for authors of .NET Framework applications. Its graphical designer enables you to select mobile Web Forms controls from the Toolbox and then drag and drop them into position on mobile Web Forms. You can use any .NET-compliant language to code program logic, and the integrated editing and compilation facilities make producing accurate code much easier. Visual Studio .NET also features an integrated Web browser for testing, end-to-end debugging facilities, and powerful project file management, making it an indispensable tool for the mobile Web application developer.

Creating a Mobile Web Project with Visual Studio .NET

To create a project, you can click the Get Started option on the Start page and then click the New Project button. You can also create a project by clicking the File menu, pointing to New, and then clicking Project on the drop-down menu. The New Project dialog box appears, as shown in Figure 2-1.

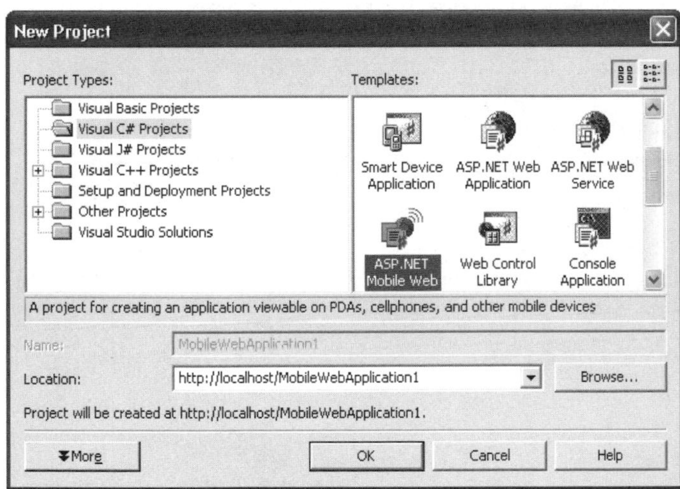

Figure 2-1 The New Project dialog box

The left pane of the New Project dialog box allows you to select the project type. This pane offers one project type for each .NET language you've installed; the standard options are Microsoft Visual Basic, Visual C#, Visual J#, and Visual C++. Once you select your preferred language, the templates displayed in the right-hand pane change to reflect that language. All the languages offer similar options and allow you to create Web applications, as well as options to create other standard solutions such as Windows applications, class libraries, or Web services. Currently, Mobile Web Application templates are offered for the Visual Basic, Visual C#, and Visual J# languages.

It doesn't matter which language you choose for your first project, since the application won't require you to write code. Therefore, unless you have a preference, we suggest that you choose Visual C#. Click the ASP.NET Mobile Web

Application option to highlight it, and then replace the suggested project name MobileWebApplication1 with the name **MyFirstMobileApp**. To do this, change the Location of the project from *http://localhost/MobileWebApplication1* to *http://localhost/MyFirstMobileApp*. Visual Studio .NET updates the grayed out project name according to the location you enter.

Notice that below the Location text box Visual Studio .NET shows where it will create the project, in this case at the location *http://localhost/MyFirstMobileApp* of the Web server on your development machine. When you click OK, the Create New Web dialog box appears, informing you that Visual Studio .NET is creating the new Web application at *http://localhost/MyFirstMobileApp*.

Visual Studio .NET now updates its various dialog boxes with information relevant to your project. The default layout will look like Figure 2-2.

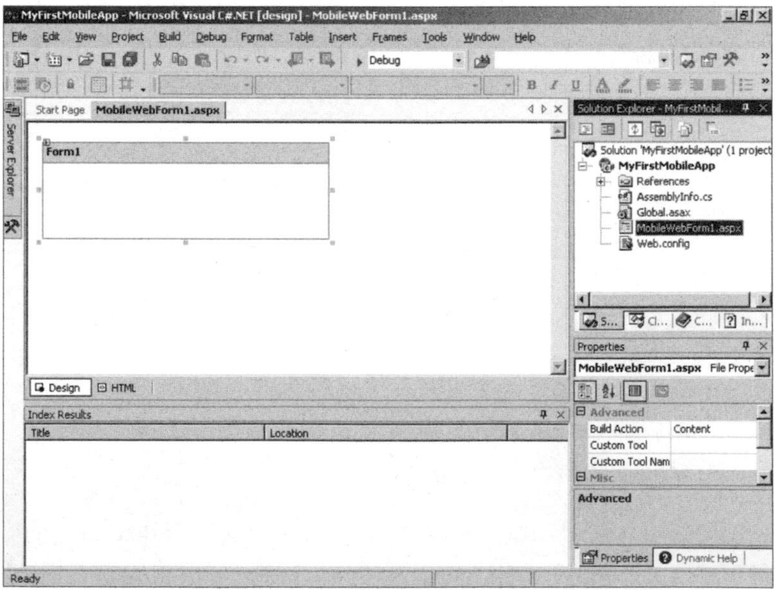

Figure 2-2 Mobile project development environment

The main view is a tabbed view, which displays all the files that you're currently working on, positioned one behind another. An asterisk next to the filename on the tab indicates that the file has been modified but hasn't been saved to disk yet.

Whenever you create a mobile Web application, the New Project Wizard creates your project with the name you specified and creates in it a number of files, including MobileWebForm1.aspx, which defines a mobile Web Forms page. This file is currently open and visible in the Mobile Internet Designer, which provides a GUI for designing mobile Web Forms.

Using Solution Explorer and the Properties Dialog Box

In Visual Studio .NET, on the upper-right side of your screen, you'll see Solution Explorer. This window lists all the files in your project. If you click the MobileWebForm1.aspx file listed there, the Properties dialog box on the lower-right side of your screen updates to reflect the properties of the currently selected object—that is, the MobileWebForm1.aspx file. This is a standard feature of Visual Studio .NET. Whenever you select an object, whether it's a user interface control you've dragged onto the design area of your mobile Web Forms, a file in Solution Explorer, or any other object listed on screen, the Properties dialog box updates so that you can easily change that object's properties.

Although not essential, it's a good idea to change the name of the mobile Web Forms file. When a browser accesses a Web application—mobile or otherwise—it does so by specifying that application's URL. The URL of the application you're creating is currently *http://localhost/MyFirstMobileApp/MobileWebForm1.aspx*.

You can also let users access the application by specifying the URL's shorter form, *http://localhost/MyFirstMobileApp*, thus enhancing the application's usability. To enable this functionality, you must change the name of the first file users will access to one of the standard default document names that IIS recognizes. The standard IIS default document names are Default.htm, Default.asp, Iisstart.asp, or Default.aspx.

If IIS receives a request for a URL that doesn't specify a document, it will search the directory that stores Web site files for a file with a default document name. If IIS finds such a default document, it processes the document and returns the results to the caller; otherwise, it returns a Hypertext Transfer Protocol (HTTP) status code 404 (page not found). Giving your primary mobile Web Forms page one of the default document names makes it easier for users to remember the shorter name for your Web site; that way, they no longer have to include a nonintuitive document name such as MobileWebForm1.aspx within a request.

Click MobileWebForm1.aspx in Solution Explorer to select it. In the Properties pane, locate the *File Name* property and change it to **default.aspx**. Figure 2-3 shows the result.

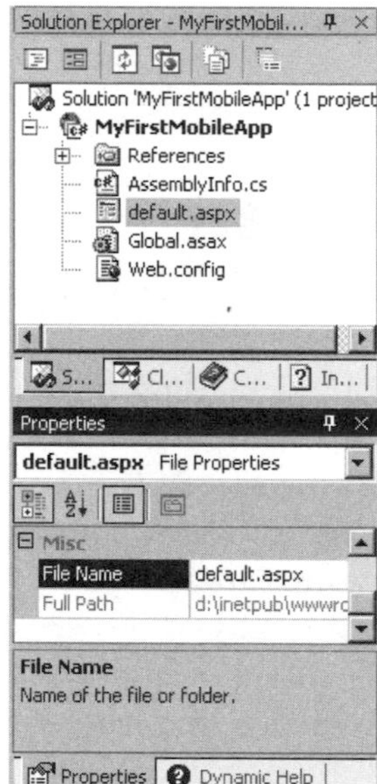

Figure 2-3 Setting file properties

> **Note** You could leave the name of your mobile Web Forms page as MobileWebForm1.aspx and configure IIS so that it recognizes that name as a default document. (Consult the IIS documentation for details on how to do this.) However, a better approach is to change the filename to one of the standard default document names; if you don't, the target Web server will require this additional configuration step when you deploy your application.

Building the User Interface with the Toolbox

The project that Visual Studio .NET created will build and run. Of course, the application currently does nothing. You'll now add a mobile control to the mobile Web Forms page so that your application displays a simple text message.

The Toolbox displays all the mobile Web Forms controls that you can use when designing your Web Forms. You can access the Toolbox by holding the mouse cursor over the Toolbox tab at the left margin of the screen. By default, this window is set to Auto Hide—it stays hidden until needed rather than taking up valuable screen space. If you right-click on the Toolbox when it is visible, you can set or clear the List View option. When set to List View, the controls are presented in a list showing their full name; when List View is disabled, only an icon is displayed for each control. As you move your mouse over each control, a ToolTip displays the control name. The Toolbox is divided into a number of tabs, each containing related controls, as shown in Figure 2-4.

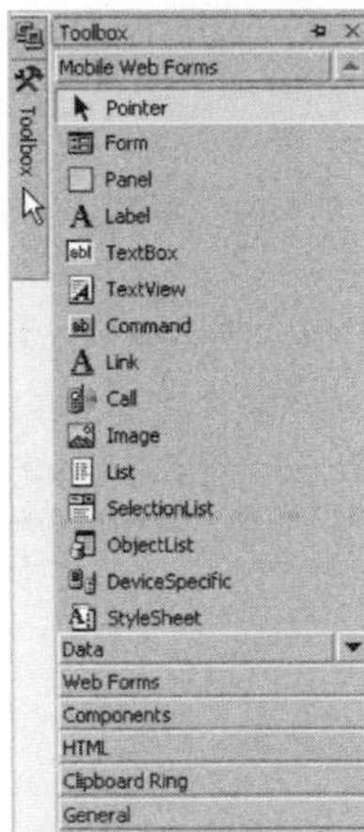

Figure 2-4 The mobile Web Forms Toolbox

Select the compartment labeled Mobile Web Forms, which contains the standard mobile controls, such as the Label, TextBox, Command, and Image controls and the validation controls. You'll learn about these controls in more detail in Chapters 4 and 5.

An A icon denotes the Label control. You can click this control and drag it onto the mobile Web Forms page. Notice that the Properties window now shows the properties of the Label control, which has an *ID* value of *Label1* and a *Text* property value of *Label*.

In the Properties window, change the *Text* property to something more meaningful, such as the venerable **Hello World**. Doing so updates the text displayed on the Label control shown in the Design view accordingly.

Building and Running Your Application

Visual Studio .NET offers many ways to build an application. Over time, you'll probably develop a preference or find yourself using certain methods at certain junctures. You can use one of the following methods to build your project:

- Go to Solution Explorer, right-click the solution name, and click Build on the pop-up menu.

- Right-click the MyFirstMobileApp project line immediately below the solution name, and then click Build Solution.
- Click the Build menu, and then click Build.
- Simply choose to run the application in Debug mode by clicking the Start button in Visual Studio .NET, which automatically initiates a build before running it.

The project will then compile, and you'll see the build output display at the bottom of the screen, including details of any compilation errors.

To test your application, you can click the Debug menu and then select Start or click the Start button on the standard toolbar. Internet Explorer starts and calls the IIS server to access your application, just as an external Web client would. Figure 2-5 shows MyFirstMobileApp running in Internet Explorer.

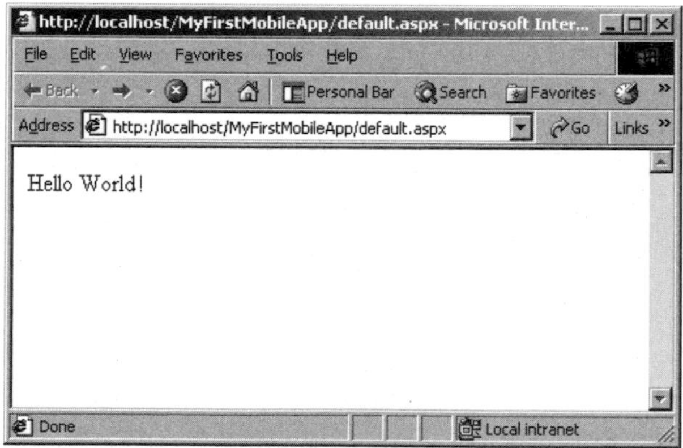

Figure 2-5 Testing the application with Internet Explorer

While Internet Explorer is active, Visual Studio .NET is running in Debug mode. Therefore, after you view the output from the application, close Internet Explorer to return Visual Studio .NET to Design mode.

Testing with a Mobile Phone Emulator

You'll find Internet Explorer an adequate development tool for performing the initial testing of an application's functionality. However, one of the most powerful features of the ASP.NET mobile controls is that they can render your application on different client browsers, each with its own capabilities and possibly even requiring a completely different markup language.

You should test your application on devices that are likely to access it in the real world. You use the mobile Web Forms controls in your applications to carry out some function on a mobile device; however, the actual physical appearance might differ from device to device. Furthermore, the ASP.NET mobile controls allow you to customize your application to introduce device-specific behavior. For example, when you use the mobile Image control, you should supply images appropriate to each browser. In other words, you should supply GIF files for HTML browsers, color JPG or PNG files for advanced WAP browsers, and monochrome WBMP format graphics for older WAP devices. Clearly, it is crucial that you test your application on the different devices that are likely to access it.

Purchasing the actual mobile devices so that you can test your application with mobile clients can be an expensive undertaking. Fortunately, a cheaper option exists: installing software *emulators* (sometimes called *simulators*) on your development system. In Chapter 16, we'll look at how to get and use emulators in more detail, but to get you started, in this section we'll show you how to set up the Openwave simulator.

Setting Up the Openwave Simulator

Openwave is the company formed from the merger of Phone.com and Software.com. Phone.com was itself formerly known as Unwired Planet, which was responsible for devising the Handheld Device Markup Language (HDML) for mobile devices, a predecessor of Wireless Markup Language (WML). Many of the world's Internet-enabled phones use Openwave mobile browser software. The ASP.NET mobile controls include support for devices from Alcatel, Motorola, Samsung, Sanyo, Siemens, Panasonic, Casio, Denso, Hitachi, Kyocera, LG, and many others, all of which use the Openwave browser—or its predecessor, the UP.Browser. Openwave has always been a good friend to developers, and many have cut their teeth with WAP development using the Openwave Software Development Kit (SDK). This kit includes a phone simulator, which you can use to test mobile Web applications.

You can download the Openwave SDK free of charge from *http://developer.openwave.com/download/index.html*. At the time of this writing, Openwave had recently released the Openwave SDK 6.1, which targets developers building applications for devices with XHTML Mobile Profile 1.0 with cascading style sheets (CSS) for the Openwave Mobile Browser 6.1. However, we recommend that you download SDK 4.1.1, which includes a simulator with the UP.Browser V4.1, a WML 1.1 browser included with many devices in current use. ASP.NET mobile controls fully support this browser.

After you install the SDK, click the UP.SDK 4.1.1–UP.Simulator shortcut in the UPSDK411 entry in your Programs or All Programs menu, and you'll see a phone image similar to the one shown in Figure 2-6.

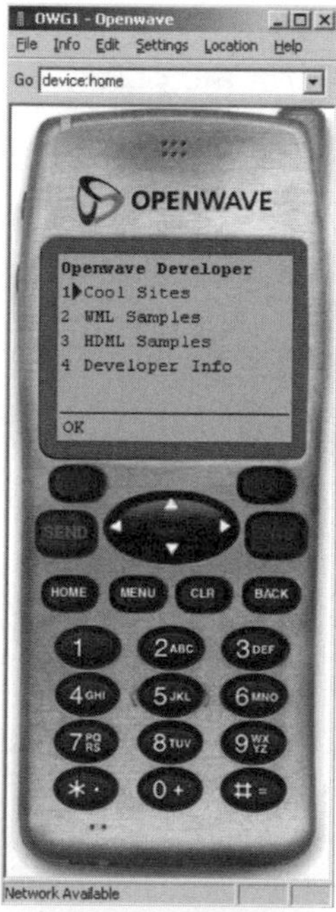

Figure 2-6 The Openwave simulator

The phone image allows you to test mobile applications on a simulated mobile phone that accepts WML 1.1 markup. You can use this instead of or in addition to the integrated Internet Explorer browser.

Using the Simulator for Testing

During development, you can view a mobile Web Forms page in the Openwave simulator by entering the URL of the start page in the Go drop-down box, as shown in Figure 2-7.

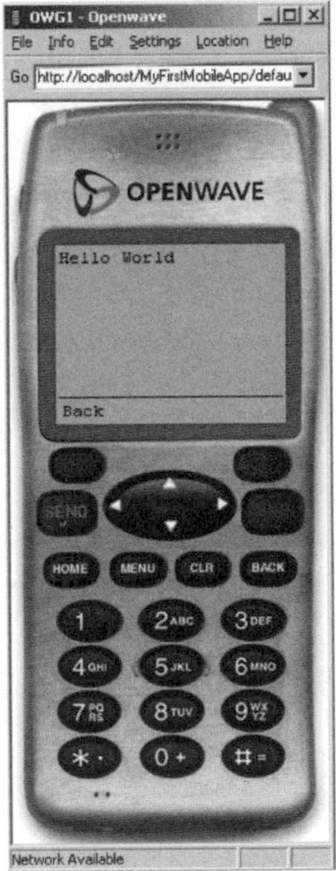

Figure 2-7 Testing a mobile Web application with the Openwave simulator

Figure 2-8 shows the functions of the Openwave simulator buttons.

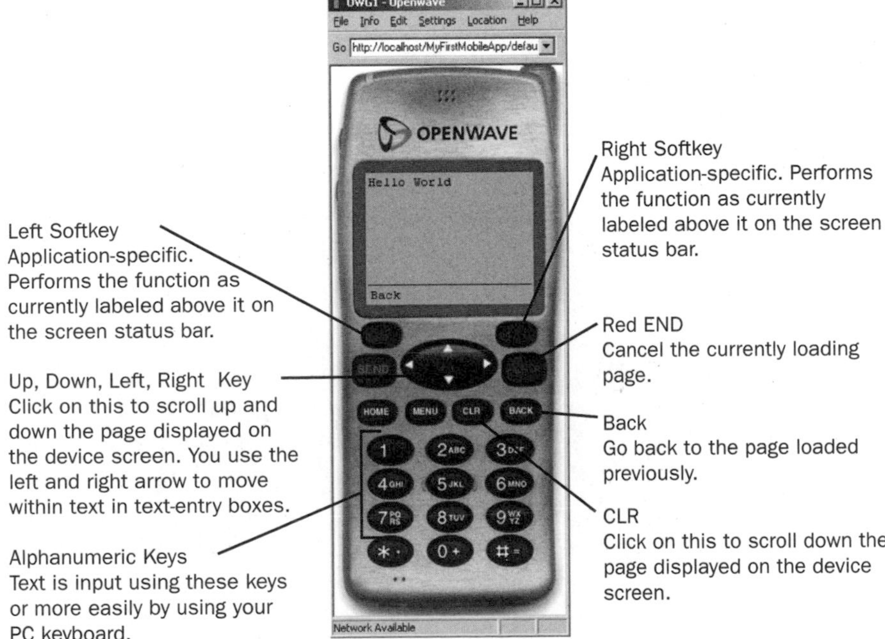

Figure 2-8 Openwave simulator button functions

Actual WAP devices always connect to the Internet via a special proxy, called a *WAP gateway*. This gateway acts as an important bridge between the wireless WAP protocols used by the phone and the HTTP over TCP/IP used by the wired Web. When you test with a real device, you must configure it to connect via a WAP gateway, operated by your wireless service provider, or in some cases, by your company. Fortunately, the Openwave simulator includes gateway functionality within it, so you don't have to worry about this when testing on your own workstation. The default configuration for the simulator is to connect directly to a server using HTTP protocols over the wired Web. To check that your simulator is configured like this, click the Settings menu of the Openwave simulator and then click UP.Link Settings. Check the HTTP Direct check box, as shown in Figure 2-9.

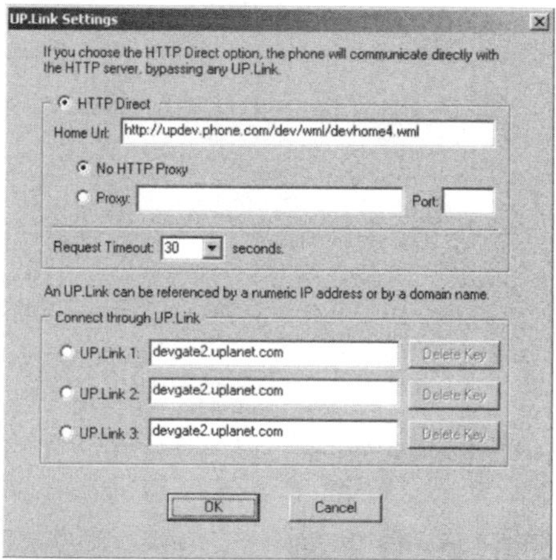

Figure 2-9 Configure the Openwave simulator for direct HTTP access to your development server

Working with the Mobile Internet Designer

The MyFirstMobileApp project you just created introduced you to the power Visual Studio .NET and the Mobile Internet Designer have to develop mobile Web applications. The Mobile Internet Designer allows you to graphically lay out your mobile Web Forms pages. However, the layout possibilities are more limited than those offered by a full WYSIWYG graphical Web page designer, such as a designer you'd use with ASP.NET Web Forms targeted at desktop clients. For example, the Mobile Internet Designer doesn't offer grid layout. As a result, you can't position controls at specific coordinates. Each control in a mobile Web Forms page displayed in the Mobile Internet Designer is shown positioned directly beneath the previous control, as though in a list; the controls aren't resizable.

These restrictions reflect the limited display capabilities of the target devices. Remember that you're working with an *abstraction* of the mobile device application. Your application is rendered differently for each target device. ASP.NET mobile controls allow you to concentrate on the functionality you want to deliver without worrying about the specific markup language a particular device requires. Mobile device capabilities differ substantially in characteristics such as color support or screen size. Consequently, the visual representation of the controls you place on a mobile Web Forms page signifies the intended functionality, not the exact appearance.

The Mobile Web Forms Page and Form Control

As you saw earlier, when you use the New Project dialog box to build a new mobile Web solution, you create a single file with an .aspx extension. This file defines a mobile Web Forms page. Simple applications typically contain a single Web Forms page, although there's nothing stopping you from building mobile Web applications that consist of many mobile Web Forms pages.

> **Note** Many people confuse the terms *mobile Web Forms page* and *mobile Form control*. A mobile Web Forms page is the .aspx file that contains one or more mobile Form controls. A mobile Form control is itself a mobile control and contains other mobile controls.

Within a mobile Web Forms page, you might have one or more mobile Form controls. The New Project wizard creates a single Form control in your application, which you can see in the Design window when you create a new project. Figure 2-10 shows what this mobile control looks like.

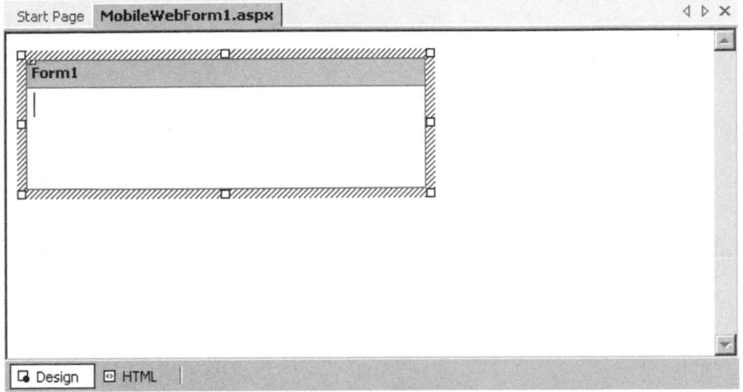

Figure 2-10 The mobile Form control within a mobile Web Forms page

You can use the Form control to group other standard controls and contain them. A Form control is the outermost container for other controls in a mobile page. You can't nest a mobile Form control within another Form control; however, a mobile Web Forms page can contain multiple Form controls.

Usually, a Form control is rendered as a single screen on a target device, but the runtime might split the contents of a Form control across multiple screens if the Form control contains too much content to be displayed in one go on the particular client device that is making the call. From the developer's perspective, it's more accurate to describe a Form control as a container for a named, logical grouping of controls. The Form control can be set to paginate the output so that the data sent for each page doesn't exceed the limitations of the receiving device. For example, if you've placed a large number of controls inside a Form control or a control that is capable of displaying a large amount of output, such as the TextView control, the output from those controls can end up being displayed on different display pages on smaller devices. You'll learn more about pagination in Chapter 8.

Positioning Controls on Web Forms

Unlike standard ASP.NET Web Forms, which you use to build applications for desktop browsers, the Mobile Internet Designer, used to lay out mobile Web Forms, doesn't offer a grid for placing mobile controls. Instead, the Mobile Internet Designer lets you position controls only from the top down. To illustrate this, this section shows you how to create a new project with a selection of controls.

Using the MyFirstMobileApp solution that you created earlier, click on the Toolbox tab to open it, and drag two Label controls and a TextBox control onto the Form control. Notice that the Mobile Internet Designer does not allow you to position new controls alongside any existing ones and only allows you to place controls in a top down list. See the sidebar "Limited Layout Possibilities" for an explanation of this behavior.

If you click any of the controls you've just placed on the Form control, or on the Form control's title bar, some small squares will appear at the four corners and in the middle of each side. Those of you familiar with Visual Studio .NET will recognize these squares; they indicate anchor points that you can click with the mouse and then drag to resize the control. However, this isn't possible with mobile Web Forms controls. Remember that mobile controls are just design objects that enable you to create the functionality of an application. A mobile control's actual appearance differs from one type of target device to another, and some of the more complex controls might differ in appearance substantially. In this context, resizing controls on a design palette has no relevance.

Limited Layout Possibilities

You can order mobile controls only in a top-down list, and you can't control the vertical spacing between them. This might seem a little strange, particularly to those developers who are used to graphical Web application designers. But remember that with the ASP.NET mobile controls, you're working with control objects that represent distinct pieces of user interface functionality—in other words, such an object is an abstraction of the user interface rather than a WYSIWYG representation of the finished result.

Mobile devices tend to have very small displays, and the scope for artistic expression on your user interface is unfortunately very small. The main purpose of the ASP.NET mobile controls is to make it easy to build applications that run on mobile devices using various client browsers. Developers of ASP.NET applications targeted at desktop browsers using full Web Forms work with the visual appearance of the form in mind. Mobile Web developers concentrate more on the functionality of the application and—with some exceptions, as you will see in Chapter 9 and Chapter 10—leave the presentation to the runtime and the target browser.

Many wireless developers are already familiar with this idea. In general, mobile phone displays don't have a screen size that allows complex layouts or a mouse-like navigation device.

When designing a mobile Web Forms page, you can use the mouse to drag controls to a new location within the Form control. If you want to move a control above an existing one, you must drop it immediately to the left of or above the existing control. To position a control below an existing one, you must drop it just to the right of or below the existing control.

Working with Multiple Form Controls

Very few mobile Web applications consist of a single transaction with a user. You could conceivably write a very simple service using a single Form control—for example, a mobile Web site that simply returns the number of cans remaining in the computerized vending machine on the first floor of your office. However, in practice, most applications consist of a number of discrete pieces of functionality, each of which you can logically represent with one or more Form controls containing the required mobile controls, which can all be contained within the same mobile Web Forms page.

To introduce you to structuring your application into multiple Form controls, this discussion shows you how to build a simple application that uses three forms. To do so, execute the following steps:

1. Create a new mobile project, and name it MultipleForms.
2. As before, rename the MobileWebForm1.aspx file default.aspx to enhance usability.
3. Within the Mobile Internet Designer, drag two additional Form controls from the Mobile Web Forms Toolbox to the mobile Web Forms page.
4. Drag a Label control onto each of the Form controls. Click the Label control on Form1 to access the properties in the Properties window. Set the *Text* property to **This Is Form1**, and select a title from the options offered for the *StyleReference* property. This causes the application to render the text with emphasis. Repeat this operation with the Label controls on the other two forms, but set the *Text* property as appropriate for each form.
5. Drag two Link controls onto the first Form. The Link control is a simple navigation control, usually rendered as a hyperlink. You must set two key properties on a Link control: the *Text* property, which describes the purpose of the link to the user, and the *NavigateUrl* property, which indicates the target destination. Figure 2-11 shows how the Design window should now look.

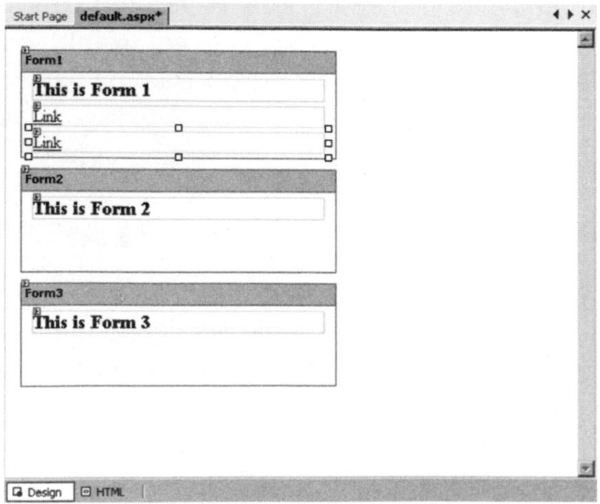

Figure 2-11 The Design window in Visual Studio .NET

6. Click the first Link control, and set the *Text* property to **Go To Form 2**. Now select the *NavigateUrl* property and click the drop-down list to view a list of options, as shown in Figure 2-12.

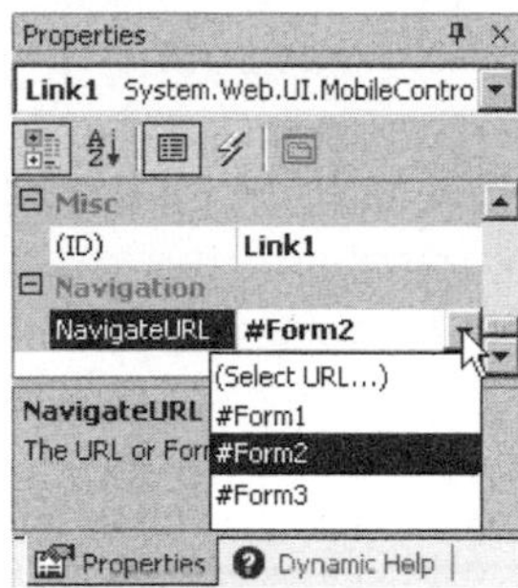

Figure 2-12 The drop-down list of the *NavigateUrl* property

7. The Link control can navigate to any accessible URL, or it can navigate within the current application. To enter a URL, click the (Select URL…) option in the list. To specify a destination within the current application, be sure that the *NavigateUrl* property starts with a pound sign (#) followed by the *ID* of a Form control. The valid destinations are *#Form1*, *#Form2*, and *#Form3*. Select **#Form2** for this first Link control.

8. Click the second Link control, and set the *Text* property to **Go To Form 3** and the *NavigateUrl* property to **#Form3**.

That's it! Now click the Start button in the Visual Studio .NET toolbar to build and run your application in your chosen browser.

Control ID Naming Conventions

In the MultipleForms example presented in the section "Working with Multiple Form Controls," you use the *ID* for each Form Visual Studio .NET supplied. Since the *ID* is a property like any other, you're free to change it. The only requirement is that each control must have a unique *ID*.

Every time you add a new control to a Web Forms page, Visual Studio .NET assigns it a name consisting of the control type followed by a numeric suffix, such as Form1 or Form2. Many developers prefer to change these IDs to names that are more meaningful and that indicate the control's function within the application. For example, you might name a Label control that displays a city name CityNameLabel. Think back to the two Link controls used in our MultipleForms sample application. Meaningful names for these two controls could be LinkToForm2 and LinkToForm3. Such a name immediately indicates the purpose of the control. In a real application, the Form controls would also have meaningful names describing their purpose.

As you'll see in Chapter 3, you'll frequently write code that will access the properties and methods of controls. If you use meaningful control names, your application code will be more precise, readable, and clear.

Backward and Forward Navigation in Mobile Web Applications

In the MultipleForms sample application you just built, two obvious, named links appear on the first Form control. These Link controls provide your applications with forward navigation. In a real application, you'd expect users to execute a specific part of the application and then exit or return to the entry screen to make further selections. In our sample application, you didn't place Link controls on the second and third Web Forms linking back to Form1. However, your application does have built-in backward navigation support: Internet Explorer achieves such backward navigation support by using the built-in Back button, and all the major desktop Web browsers offer this functionality.

When it comes to mobile devices, however, experienced wireless developers know that backward navigation support isn't built into all browsers. Pocket Internet Explorer displays a Back control at the foot of the page. Some mobile phone browsers (such as the Openwave WML browser) hardwire one of the soft keys under the phone screen so that the back function is always available. Other browsers (such as the Nokia WML browser) require you to program backward navigation support into the WML markup.

Fortunately, using the ASP.NET mobile controls saves you from having to worry about such idiosyncrasies. The ASP.NET Runtime delivers the required markup to each of the supported client devices to ensure that backward navigation is always available. Application developers can concentrate on the functionality of the application, knowing that it will behave consistently on supported client devices.

You can enhance the usability of certain applications by employing Link controls to deliver more explicit backward navigation, rather than relying on the default implementation.

There's one other consideration of standard navigation options you should be aware of: Internet Explorer and other major desktop browsers offer a Forward navigation button that enables the user to return to a page from which they just backed out. However, mobile browsers don't offer this option. Small browsers can't retain such a detailed record of a user's navigation. Whenever a user leaves a page via backward navigation, the browser removes any references to that page from its history, keeping no record that the user ever visited the page. Consequently, a mobile user can't undo a backward navigation by accessing a built-in forward function.

Device-Specific Rendering of Complex Controls

The Calendar control is one of the more complex ASP.NET mobile controls. This control illustrates how the user interface of a mobile control can differ from one mobile client to another. The following steps create an application that allows a user to enter the preferred date for an appointment:

1. Create a new mobile project, and name it Scheduler. You might want to rename the mobile Web Forms file default.aspx, as you did earlier.
2. Drag a Label control and a Calendar control from the Toolbox to Form1.
3. Set the *Title* property of the Form1 control to **Appointments**, a suitable title for this page. Remember to keep such titles short—they have to fit on a single line of a mobile phone display.
4. Set the *Text* property of the label to **Choose preferred:**.
5. Click the Start button in the toolbar to run the application within Internet Explorer.

> **Note** Don't expect the page title to be displayed on all client devices. Internet Explorer on a PC and Pocket Internet Explorer on the Microsoft Smartphone displays this property in the title bar, and Nokia and Ericsson phones display it at the head of the screen. If you don't specify a title, the Ericsson R380 displays an ugly *<No Title>* legend at the head of the screen. However, Pocket Internet Explorer on the Pocket PC and phones using the Openwave browser don't display the page title at all. If the title text is vital to your application, use a Label control. Even if your device *doesn't* support page titles, it's good practice to give your pages appropriate names. You never know when things might change.

If you run this application with Internet Explorer, with Pocket Internet Explorer on a Pocket PC, or on a mobile phone, the difference in appearance will be quite striking. Figures 2-13 and 2-14 show this difference. Internet Explorer and Pocket Internet Explorer render this appointment application as a calendar grid. But on a mobile phone, the appearance is quite different. Clearly, a grid isn't possible on such a small display; instead, the user either types in a date directly or steps through a number of selection options to choose the desired date.

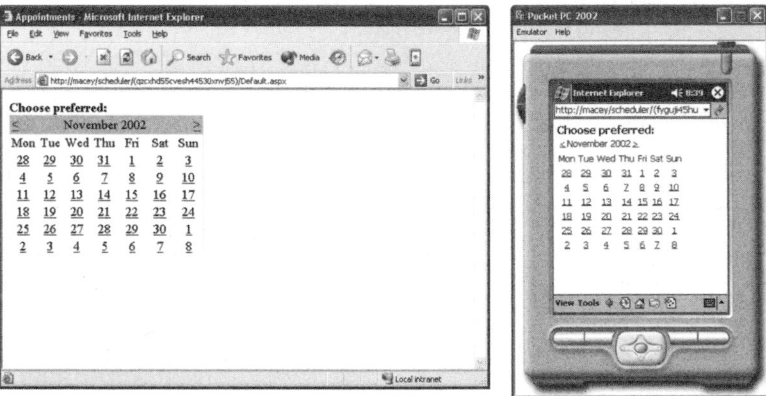

Figure 2-13 The Calendar control in Internet Explorer and Pocket Internet Explorer

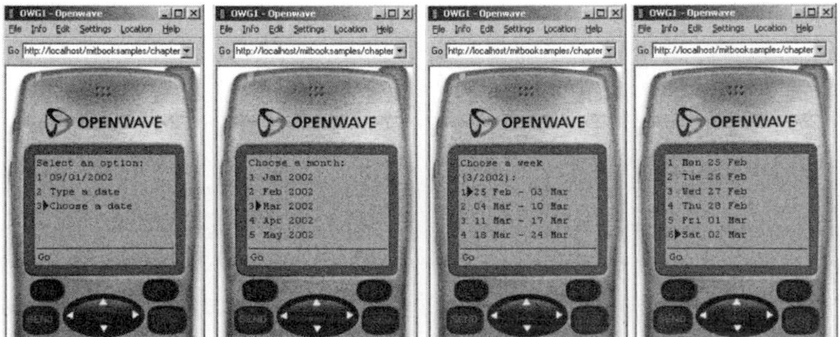

Figure 2-14 The Calendar control on a mobile phone

Despite the obvious differences in appearance, the Calendar control's functionality—its ability to select a date—remains unchanged, regardless of the mobile device you use to access it. Sophisticated controls like this handle the details of delivering functionality to the user so that you don't have to waste valuable time worrying about it. That's not to say you can't dictate the appearance of controls on different platforms. (You can, as you'll see in Chapter 9.) However, you might find a control's default rendering appropriate for many applications.

Basic Design Principles

It might seem strange to discuss design in a chapter called "Getting Started." But because handheld devices all have small screens and limited input capabilities that present special design difficulties for mobile Web applications, it's important to keep these design issues in mind from the very beginning

Consider the following poem, which is a haiku, an ancient form of poetry originating in Japan. A haiku consists of three lines—the first line contains five syllables, the second line contains seven syllables, and the third line contains five. Haiku is challenging to write in part because of its brevity. A haiku should express simple, clear images, and its concise message should be easily understood.

My house has burnt down.

Now I own a better view

Of the rising moon.

—Matsuo Bashö (1644–1694)

Try to evoke the spirit of haiku in your mobile applications: be simple, clear, and concise. If your applications read like poetry, you can consider yourself a very fine software engineer!

When you are designing and building applications for mobile devices, keep in mind five general guidelines. First, be economical with screen display space. If mobile phones with smaller screens will access your application, the viewable area could be as small as four lines, each containing 12 characters. Consequently, you should keep text as short as possible without sacrificing clarity. You might want to provide terse prompts on a small-screen device and fuller descriptions on other devices. In Chapter 9, we'll describe a useful technique for providing prompts appropriate to each particular client's display screen: implementing device filters that can be used in DeviceSpecific/Choice constructs to test whether the requesting client has a small display area.

The second design guideline is to use graphics sparingly in your mobile Web applications. You should consider your use of graphics carefully for the same reasons you must be economical with screen display space. In addition to consuming valuable display space, the overuse of graphics can cause your application to perform poorly. First-generation WAP-enabled mobile phones operate over a wireless link at only 9.6 Kbps. More important, wireless communications links exhibit higher *latency* (the delay network entities introduce when delivering a message) than wired communications links. This increased latency is often a few seconds, and every graphic you display on your Web page causes an additional round-trip to the server. Although the industry is rapidly upgrading wireless communications capabilities, this latency promises to remain an issue for many devices.

> **Tip** Be sure to specify a meaningful *AlternateText* parameter with any image, because many devices allow users to disable image display to improve performance. Carefully size the images that you use to fit the display screen so that they don't shrink or stretch to fit—and therefore, distort.

The third guideline is to limit the amount of input you require of your users. Mobile device manufacturers have yet to solve the problem of how to provide easy-to-use, reliable input to a handheld device. The only devices that offer input comparable to that of a PC are personal digital assistants (PDAs) and mobile phones that support plug-in portable keyboards. Most PDA devices support input using a stylus, using handwriting recognition or a virtual keyboard display. Most mobile phones allow input through the alphanumeric phone keys. Figure 2-15 highlights the input support of several mobile devices.

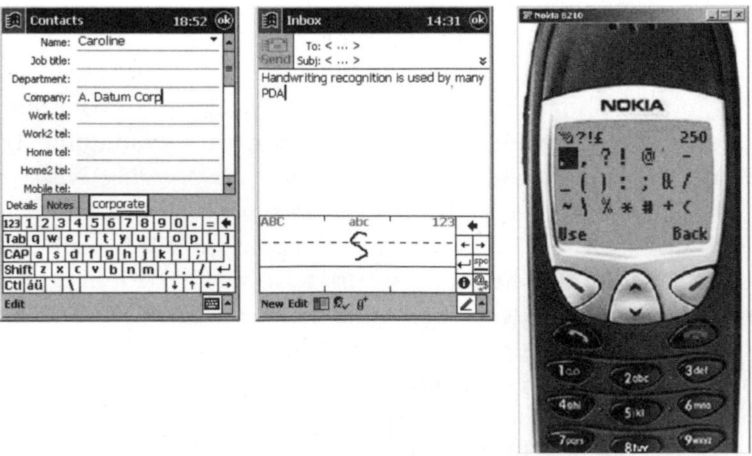

Figure 2-15 Various ways to input text on a mobile device, all of which are more difficult than using a PC keyboard

Whatever handheld device you're targeting, your users won't appreciate having to enter a lot of information. Try to keep the data requested to the minimum needed to complete the application's function. If the architecture of your application allows it, you might want to let users register preferences or certain information about themselves, perhaps through a PC-accessible Web site. You can store this information on your back-end servers and then offer default inputs on the mobile device based on those preferences when applicable.

The fourth design guideline is to keep individual pieces of functionality short and concise. In the spirit of haiku, keep mobile transactions as brief as possible. This guideline varies somewhat depending on the application, but in general, mobile devices will likely serve remote users who have a small window of time available to access information or perform a transaction. Your traveling users and your business's mobile personnel won't appreciate lengthy, tedious procedures. Short, snappy applications add real value to a busy person's day!

And finally, learn how to use the customization features of the ASP.NET mobile controls to provide a richer interface on devices that support such capabilities. Chapter 9 describes how to use property overrides and templates, and Chapter 10 describes how to use the List and ObjectList control templates. But keep your priorities in order. When working with an abstraction of a mobile device, as you do with the ASP.NET mobile controls, concentrate on the bare functionality of the application. You should focus on presentation only after the application is functioning correctly.

The default output of the ASP.NET mobile controls yields good results on monochrome devices with limited displays, such as mobile phones with WML 1.1 browsers, color devices such as the Pocket PC, and large-display smart phones such as the Microsoft Smartphone or Nokia Communicator. Figure 2-16 shows some of the PDAs and smart phones that are rapidly gaining acceptance among corporate users as effective devices for mobile solutions. The larger display and color support of the latter devices allow you to create much more visually appealing applications. You can take full advantage of their presentation capabilities by using the customization features of the ASP.NET mobile controls. Such capabilities will make working with your applications more pleasurable for your users.

Figure 2-16 PDAs and smart phones are becoming increasingly popular for business applications.

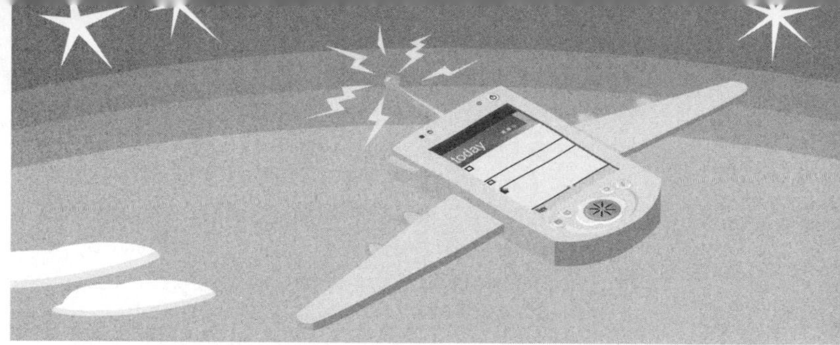

3

Programming ASP.NET Mobile Web Forms

In Chapter 2, you learned how to build simple mobile Web applications. In this chapter, you'll learn how a Microsoft ASP.NET application operates so that you can work effectively with .aspx pages and code-behind modules. You'll learn how to manipulate the methods and properties of mobile Web Forms controls in code and how to respond to the events those controls raise. You'll also learn how ASP.NET maintains state information across multiple request-response interactions between client and server. And finally, you'll learn how to use the classes of the Microsoft .NET Framework base class libraries and how to build mobile Web applications with command-line tools.

We've organized this chapter into a discussion of five sample applications. These sample applications guide you through the programming fundamentals, which you'll need to understand to write ASP.NET mobile Web Forms applications. The first four sample applications use the Microsoft Visual Studio .NET integrated development environment (IDE); however, the principles we'll examine also apply if you choose to employ an alternative IDE. The final sample application uses command-line tools and offers greater insight into how the components of a mobile Web application fit together.

Throughout this chapter, sidebars present more detailed explanations and information that will be of interest to the more experienced developer, but beginners are advised to ignore the sidebars until they have gained more experience with Visual Studio .NET and ASP.NET. Once a beginner has worked through the sample applications, he or she should have mastered the basic skills needed to create ASP.NET mobile Web applications

We've written the majority of code examples in this book in C#, which was designed from the ground up to fully exploit the .NET Framework. Programmers can use C# to build rich client applications, XML Web services, and Web applications. C and C++ programmers will find the syntax familiar, but for detailed coverage refer to the .NET Framework SDK documentation.

Understanding .aspx Files and Code-Behind Modules

In Chapter 2, you created applications that consisted only of controls dragged out of the Visual Studio.NET Toolbox and positioned on a mobile Web Forms control. Of course, these simple examples are not representative of real applications. In reality, your applications consist not only of controls dragged onto a form, but also code that runs on the server to perform some function and then displays the results using the mobile controls. To demonstrate how you run code in your application, we'll create a simple application that displays a command button. When the user clicks the command button, the form displays the current time. We'll program this in two different ways: using code-behind files and then using inline code.

The Code-Behind Technique

With the code-behind technique, you place your application's mobile controls in an .aspx file and you store the application's code in a separate file. The code file usually has the extension .aspx.cs for C# files, and .aspx.vb for Microsoft Visual Basic .NET files.

Create a new ASP.NET mobile Web project, named Time. Drag a Label control and a Command control from the Toolbox onto the Form1 control, which will display the time. Clear the *Text* property of the Label control. Set the *Text* property of the Command control to Update Time. If you now double-click the Command control, Visual Studio .NET opens an editing window on a different file which is the code-behind module for the application, with the cursor positioned in the *Command1_Click* method that it has created for you. This method executes every time the user clicks the command button. Enter the following code in the *Command1_Click* method:

```
private void Command1_Click(object sender, System.EventArgs e)
{
    Label1.Text = DateTime.Now.ToString("T");
}
```

This code uses the *Now* method of the .NET Framework *System.DateTime* class to get the current date and time and then converts that information to a string using the *ToString* method. The *"T"* format modifier ensures that the return string contains just the time portion of the *DateTime* object. Build and run this application to verify that it works correctly.

Notice that the file containing the program code that Visual Studio .NET displays is named MobileWebForm1.aspx.cs and that it contains a complete class definition. The Design view that was displayed by the Mobile Internet Designer when you first opened the project is a view of a file named MobileWebForm1.aspx.

Working with Controls in the Code-Behind Class

The code-behind version of the Time application sets the *Text* property of *Label1* with the following code:

```
protected System.Web.UI.MobileControls.Label Label1;
⋮
private void Command1_Click(object sender, System.EventArgs e)
{
    Label1.Text = DateTime.Now.ToString("T");
}
```

The *Label1* object is declared as a data member of the class of type *System.Web.UI.MobileControls.Label*. If you look at the Design view of the .aspx file, the Properties window of the same Label control reveals that Visual Studio .NET has set the *ID* property of the label to Label1.

To manipulate a mobile control in class methods in the code-behind module, you must include in that class a reference to the mobile control using the same name as the *ID* assigned to the control in the .aspx file. This reference must be declared using the *protected* modifier, which is similar to a *private* class member but is accessible to descendant classes. As you'll learn in the next section, the .aspx file actually defines a class that is a descendant of the class in the code-behind file, so this modifier is necessary to tie the two parts together. Listings 3-1 and 3-2 demonstrate how to use this modifier.

> **Note** When you drag a control onto a form using the Mobile Internet Designer, Visual Studio .NET automatically adds the required object declarations for the control to your code-behind class.

```
using System;

namespace Time
{
    public class MobileWebForm1 : System.Web.UI.MobileControls.MobilePage
    {
        protected System.Web.UI.MobileControls.Label Label1;
        protected System.Web.UI.MobileControls.Command Command1;

        override protected void OnInit(EventArgs e)
        {
            this.Command1.Click +=
                new System.EventHandler(this.Command1_Click);
        }

        private void Command1_Click(object sender, System.EventArgs e)
        {
            Label1.Text = DateTime.Now.ToString("T");
        }
    }
}
```

Listing 3-1 C# example that declares a class member for manipulating visual controls from the parent class

```
Public Class MobileWebForm1
    Inherits System.Web.UI.MobileControls.MobilePage

    Protected Label1 As System.Web.UI.MobileControls.Label
    Protected WithEvents Command1 As System.Web.UI.MobileControls.Command

    Private Sub Command1_Click(ByVal sender As System.Object, _
                          ByVal e As System.EventArgs) Handles Command1.Click

        Label1.Text = DateTime.Now.ToString("T")
    End Sub
End Class
```

Listing 3-2 Visual Basic .NET example that declares a class member for manipulating visual controls from the parent class

Design and HTML Views

Before we consider the inline coding technique for creating ASP.NET mobile Web Forms, let's look more closely at the .aspx file for the code-behind version. Understanding this file will help you to understand the difference between the two techniques.

On the taskbar at the bottom of the Design window for MobileWebForm1.aspx in the Time application, you'll see two view options: Design and HTML. Select HTML view (shown in Figure 3-1).

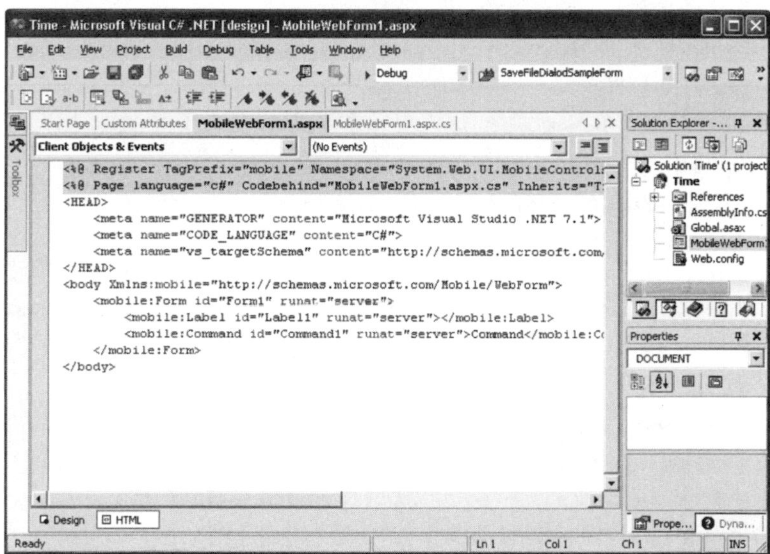

Figure 3-1 The MobileWebForm1.aspx mobile Web Forms page in HTML view

The Design and HTML views offer alternative ways to view the same file. In Design view, you drag visual representations of the mobile controls from the Toolbox onto a mobile Web Forms page. Whenever you drop a control onto a Form, Visual Studio .NET writes XML representing that control into the .aspx file. The visual display of mobile controls that you see in the Design view is simply a visual representation of the XML stored in the .aspx file. When you save the .aspx file, you're not saving a complex document with embedded graphical objects, you're actually saving a simple text file in ASP.NET server control syntax, which is the text shown when you select HTML view. In fact, *Source view* might be a more appropriate name than *HTML view*, since the text you are looking at is not HTML at all, but XML, but Microsoft uses the latter term because ASP.NET is a successor to Microsoft Active Server Pages (ASP) and ASP developers are accustomed to working with the HTML view.

The two lines of code at the top of the HTML view in Figure 3-1 are ASP.NET page *directives*, which specify settings that ASP.NET compilers must use when processing the page. The *@ Page* directive defines page-specific attributes that the ASP.NET page parser and compiler use. Some of the more important attributes are described here:

- ***language="c#"*** This directive tells the ASP.NET runtime to compile any inline code included within the page as C#. For example, code included in the page might appear as inline rendering (code enclosed by *<% %>* or *<%= %>* tags) or as code-declaration blocks (code within *<script>* and *</script>* tags), as described in the next section.
- ***Codebehind="MobileWebForm1.aspx.cs"*** As an alternative to inline code—or in addition to it—ASP.NET allows you to place code logic in an alternative file, the code-behind file. The *Codebehind="MobileWebForm1.aspx.cs"* declaration tells the runtime where to find this code. Visual Studio .NET always creates a code-behind module for a mobile Web Forms page.
- ***Inherits="Time.MobileWebForm1"*** Although not a program module in the traditional sense, the source in the .aspx file actually defines a .NET class, which inherits from a class defined in its code-behind module. Every mobile Web Forms page must inherit from the .NET *MobilePage* class or a class that derives from it. The class that the ASP.NET page compiler constructs from this page inherits from the *Time.MobileWebForm1* class, which is the class defined in the code-behind module.

The second line of the mobile Web Forms page that Visual Studio .NET generated reads as follows:

```
<%@ Register TagPrefix="mobile" Namespace="System.Web.UI.MobileControls"
    Assembly="System.Web.Mobile" %>
```

This syntax simply tells the ASP.NET runtime that when it compiles the page for display, any server control tags using the prefix *mobile* (such as *<mobile:Form…>* and *<mobile:Label…>*) represent controls found in the *System.Web.UI.MobileControls* namespace, within the *System.Web.Mobile* assembly. (An *assembly* is the .NET name for a compiled file containing executable code, similar to an .exe or a .dll file. The *System.Web.Mobile.dll* assembly contains the Mobile Internet Controls Runtime and all the mobile Web Forms controls.)

Below the heading lines, you'll see the following syntax contained in the *<body>* element:

```
<mobile:Form id=Form1 runat="server">
    <mobile:Label id="Label1" runat="server"></mobile:Label>
    <mobile:Command id="Command1" runat="server">Update Time</mobile:Command>
</mobile:Form>
```

An XML element represents each control that you place on a mobile Web Forms page. The start tag for the mobile Form control is *<mobile:Form ...>*, and the end tag is *</mobile:Form>*. The elements for the Label control and the Command control are enclosed within the Form control's tags. The syntax you use for this XML representation of visual controls is called *ASP.NET server control syntax* and it is also known as the *persistence format*.

When you drag a control from the Toolbox onto the Form control using the Mobile Internet Designer, the designer records this action by writing the XML element for that control within the *Form* tags. The *Text* property of controls that you set through the Properties window appears here as the *value* of the XML element, which is the text positioned between a control's start and end tags. For example, if you use the Visual Studio .NET Properties window to set the *Text* property of the Label control to *"Hello World"*, the server control syntax for the Label control would look like this:

```
<mobile:Label id=Label1 runat="server">Hello World</mobile:Label>
```

The other way to represent properties in server control syntax is as XML *attributes*, which assign values to identifiers within a control's start tags using the form *property-name=value*. For example, you can set a control's *ID* property through an attribute, as shown here:

```
<mobile:Form id=Form1 runat="server"></mobile:Form>
```

The XML text, which represents the mobile controls, lies within the body of the document and is enclosed within the *<body>* and *</body>* tags. The three *<meta>* tags are additional metadata that Visual Studio .NET uses only at design time.

The Inline Coding Technique

When you use inline coding, program logic is in the same file as your mobile controls. You must work in the HTML View of a mobile Web Forms page. You can include inline code within mobile Web Forms pages in two ways. The first and perhaps most commonly used syntax is to delimit sections of code by using *<script>* tags. You can use a text editor to create a new version of the Time application using inline coding, as shown here:

```
<%@ Page Inherits="System.Web.UI.MobileControls.MobilePage" Language="C#"%>
<%@ Register TagPrefix="mobile" Namespace="System.Web.UI.MobileControls"
    Assembly="System.Web.Mobile" %>

<script language="C#" runat="server">
    public void DisplayCurrentTime(Object sender, EventArgs e)
    {
```

```
        Label1.Text=DateTime.Now.ToString("T");
    }
</script>
<mobile:Form runat="server">
    <mobile:Label runat="server" id="Label1" text=""/>
    <mobile:Command runat="server" text="Update Time" id="Command1"
        onClick="DisplayCurrentTime"/>
</mobile:Form>
```

Most of this code is similar to that shown in the HTML view of the Time application you created in Visual Studio .NET. However, the section enclosed by the lines containing the *<script>* tags is new. The first of these *<script>* tags declares that the following section is script rather than mobile Web Forms controls. This element has two attributes: the *Language* attribute states that the code is written in C#, and the *runat* attribute states that code should execute on the server.

The inline code consists of the three lines that are between the *<script>* and *</script>* tags. This C# code displays the current time in the *Label1* control. If you look at the line further down that begins with *<mobile:Command*, you'll see that the Command control has an event attribute named *onClick*. This attribute's value is the name of the inline code method that executes when the command button's *onClick* event fires.

Save the code to a file named InlineTime.aspx, and place it in the root directory of your Internet Information Services (IIS) server (in \inetpub\wwwroot). If you access the URL *http://localhost/InlineTime.aspx* from a browser, you'll see an application that behaves the same as the Time application you created in Visual Studio .NET.

Language Choice

You can code a code-behind module in any of the more than 20 .NET languages available from Microsoft and other suppliers, because you must compile it into a separate assembly before deploying your application and put the resulting dynamic-link library (DLL) into your application's /bin directory.

You have less flexibility with inline code that you include in *<script>* … *</script>* blocks in an .aspx file. This file is compiled at run time by the ASP.NET page compiler, and the compiler understands only Visual Basic .NET, C#, J#, or Microsoft JScript .NET.

Inline Coding with Data-Binding Statements

Data binding, the second way of providing inline code, is a little more complex than placing blocks of code inside *<script>* tags. You can include data-binding statements anywhere within your mobile Web Forms page. The binding takes the form *<%# InlineCode %>*, where *InlineCode* can be one of the following items:

- The name of a property or collection in the code-behind module
- An expression, which the runtime evaluates
- A call to a method in the code-behind module

When the runtime loads the Web Forms page, it evaluates any expressions, makes any method calls, and then writes the results—along within any property or collection values—to the requesting device.

This method of inline coding is particularly useful when you're working with templates and list controls. In Chapter 9, Chapter 10, and Chapter 11, we'll discuss the data binding technique more fully, in the context of the more advanced scenarios in which it's used.

> **Note** ASP developers might wonder whether they can use the *<% ... %>* syntax to include inline code within a mobile Web Forms page. When using ASP.NET mobile Web Forms, you can't use this syntax. The closest syntax is that used for data binding. ASP developers might be interested to know that ASP.NET does support the use of this syntax in nonmobile projects, but unlike in ASP, it's *illegal* to declare a method or a class within these delimiters.

The *MobilePage* Class

The example we used in the previous section, called The Inline Coding Technique, begins with the following *@ Page* statement:

```
<%@ Page Inherits="System.Web.UI.MobileControls.MobilePage" Language="C#"%>
```

Notice that there is no *Codebehind* attribute naming a code-behind module and the *Inherits* attribute states that this Web Forms page inherits from *System.Web.UI.MobileControls.MobilePage* rather than from a class in a code-behind module. If you look again at the code-behind module for the first version of the Time application you created in this chapter, you'll notice that the class defined in that module inherits from *MobilePage*. Figure 3-2 compares the inheritance trees for ASP.NET mobile Web Forms using inline coding to those using a code-behind module. In fact, more classes are involved than are shown here—the *MobilePage* class itself inherits from *System.Web.UI.Page*, which is the class that implements an ASP.NET Web Forms control targeting desktop browsers.

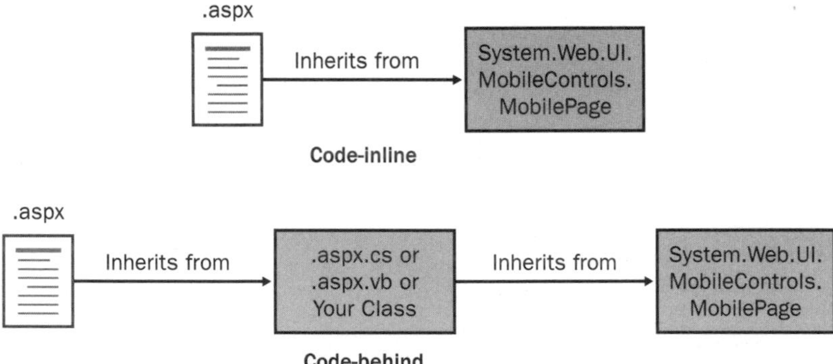

Figure 3-2 Inheritance for a single file ASP.NET Mobile Web Forms application compared to an application using a code-behind module

Although it doesn't appear anything like a class definition written in a programming language like C# or Visual Basic .NET, the text in the .aspx file is also a class definition. The first time a client calls an ASP.NET application, the ASP.NET runtime parses the .aspx file and builds a .NET class from it, which it then compiles into a .NET assembly. (Subsequent calls to the same application use a cached version of the generated assembly, so the compilation process does not need to be repeated.) As explained in the section "Design and HTML Views," earlier in this chapter, the ASP.NET server control syntax maps directly to control classes, and attributes and values define properties of those controls. The ASP.NET page compiler creates a class containing instances of the mobile controls that you dragged onto the mobile Web Forms control when you designed it—such as a mobile Web Forms control containing a mobile Label control and a mobile Command control, as in the sample Time application. The ASP.NET runtime executes the compiled assembly to generate the markup that is sent back to the client.

Properties of the *MobilePage* Class

The *MobilePage* class is the base class for all mobile Web Forms pages. The *MobilePage* class provides a number of properties that you can use in your applications. Table 3-1 describes some of the more commonly used properties.

Look up the *MobilePage* class in the .NET Framework SDK documentation for details of all the properties available to you.

Table 3-1 Commonly Used *MobilePage* Class Properties

Property	Description
ActiveForm	Sets or gets the currently active Form control. Mobile Web Forms often contain more than one Form control. The *ActiveForm* property specifies which Form control is displayed to the user.
Device	Provides access to the *MobileCapabilities* object for the current requesting device. See Chapter 9 for details of how to make use of the *MobileCapabilities* object.
HiddenVariables	Returns a dictionary of hidden variables in which data associated with the mobile Web Forms page can be stored.
IsPostBack	This property returns False the very first time an application runs the code in your application, but True on each subsequent post-back. See the next example application in this chapter for an example of its use.
ViewState	Provides access to a dictionary structure, which is useful for persisting variables in a *MobilePage*-derived class across different requests (as shown in the section "Programming State Management in ASP.NET," later in this chapter). The *ViewState* property is saved on the Web server so that token round-trips between the client and *ViewState* can be tracked and restored on subsequent requests.

A run-time error occurs if a compiled instance of *MobilePage*—in other words, your mobile Web application—doesn't contain any Form controls. A mobile Web Forms page must contain at least one Form control.

Using Events and Event Handlers

In this next application, you'll expand on the simple Hello World-style mobile Web Forms page that you created in Chapter 2 to build a Hello Universe mobile Web application. Although simple, this application illustrates a number of important features of building .NET mobile Web applications, including these:

- Using the code-behind technique
- Capturing events fired by mobile controls
- Dynamically altering the properties of controls within Web Forms
- Working with the object-oriented features of .NET applications

To get started, create a new project using the Mobile Web Forms Application template in Microsoft Visual C#. Create the GUI by dragging a label and a Command control onto Form1 from the Toolbox. Figure 3-3 shows how the form should look.

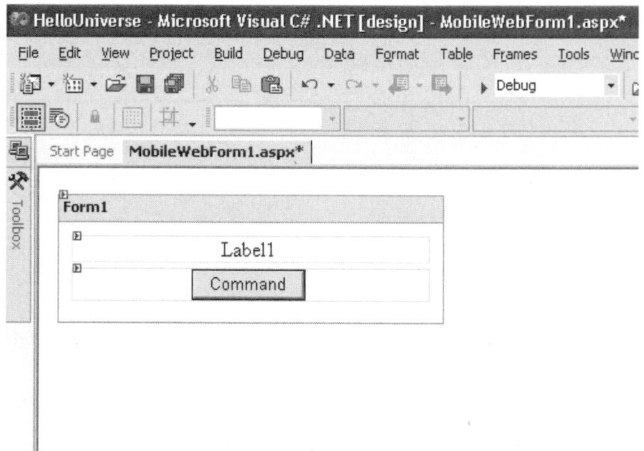

Figure 3-3 Creating the user interface in the Design window

> **Tip** If you set the *Alignment* property of the Command and Label controls to *Center*, the controls will align centrally.

Currently, the application doesn't do anything. To fix this, you'll implement code that sets the *Text* properties of the controls when the page loads, and which changes the Label text to *"Hello Universe"* and hides the Command control when a user clicks the Upgrade Now! button. This is a good example of how to work with the event-driven model of a mobile Web application.

In an event-driven program, a specific block of code executes when a specific event occurs, such as a user selecting an item from a menu. In fact, all code you'll write in a mobile Web Forms page is in the form of an event handler—code that executes when a particular event occurs. Figure 3-4 illustrates what happens within the execution of an event-driven program.

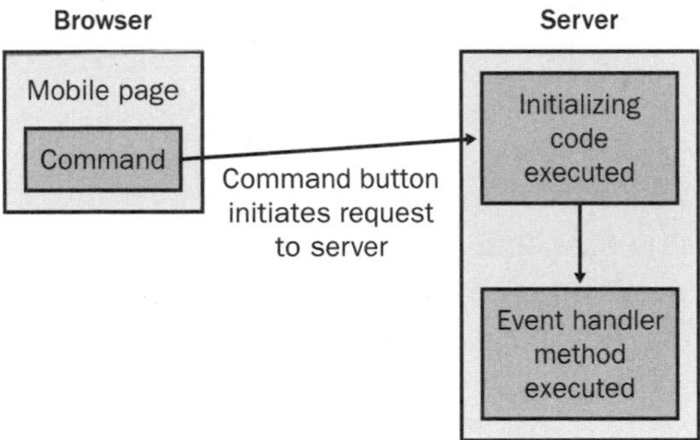

Figure 3-4 Execution flow within an event-driven program

Most mobile controls trigger events, some as the result of a user interaction such as clicking a button, and others as the result of an external action. All controls inherit from the *System.Web.UI.Control* class. This class implements a number of events, such as *Init*, which fires when the server control initializes, and *Load*, which fires when the control loads into the *MobilePage* object. Individual controls can implement additional events that are appropriate to their function.

You can write code to trap events fired by any of the controls in your application. The ASP.NET mobile controls are all examples of ASP.NET *server* controls, meaning that they are programmable objects that you can manipulate in code running on the Web server. Writing code to handle events fired by ASP.NET server controls differs from developing desktop Windows Forms applications and, to a certain extent, from older Web development technologies such as ASP. In a Microsoft Windows Forms desktop application, when a user clicks a button, the *Click* event is raised immediately. In an ASP.NET Web application, the user clicks a button displayed in the Web browser on the remote client, but this only causes certain data to be posted back to the Web server with the next *HTTP* request. It's only after the data that's posted back is analysed on the server that the control class in your server-side code raises the event and your application can handle it.

To create the method called whenever the *Click* event of the Command control fires, double-click the Command control shown in the Design window of your mobile Web Forms page. Visual Studio .NET displays a view of the code-behind module, which has the same name as your .aspx file, but with the suffix *.cs*. Visual Studio .NET automatically creates the event handler method for the control you double-clicked. In this case, the method is *Command1_Click*, and it looks like this:

```
private void Command1_Click(object sender, System.EventArgs e)
```

The runtime calls the *Command1_Click* method whenever the component with the *Command1* ID fires a *Click* event. This event method takes two arguments:

- The object that fired the event (in this case, the *sender* object).
- An object that contains data specific to the event. In the preceding code, this object takes the type *System.EventArgs*, which is the type used if the event doesn't generate any control-specific data. Most mobile Web Forms controls raise events that don't generate any control-specific data, so they typically take an argument of the type *System.EventArgs*. Other events, such as those associated with the AdRotator control, do generate data, and so they take different object types. For example, the AdRotator control takes an argument of the type *System.Web.UI.WebControls.AdCreatedEventArgs*, and the ObjectList control takes an argument of the type *System.Web.UI.ObjectListCommandEventArgs*.

Before coding the *Click event* handler, add the following code to the *Page_Load* method in the code-behind module:

```
protected void Page_Load(object sender, System.EventArgs e)
{
    if (!IsPostBack)
    {
        Label1.Text = "Hello World";
        Command1.Text = "Upgrade Now!";
    }
}
```

You might notice that this method takes similar arguments to the the *Click* event handler. Like the *Command1_Click* method, the *Page_Load* method handles an event. However, this event isn't directly associated with an action performed by the user such as the *Click* event of the Command control. Instead, this event is raised by the MobilePage. Whenever the browser on the remote mobile device posts data back to the server, the entire mobile Web Forms page object reloads, whereupon it raises the *Load* event. The *Load* event may be handled by an event handler such as the *Page_Load* method in this application.

The code in the *Page_Load* method tests the *IsPostBack* property of the MobilePage. The *IsPostBack* property is a Boolean value that indicates whether this is the first time the application is processing the page. If the *IsPostBack* property is *false*, as it is the first time this code executes when the user accesses the application the very first time, the code within the method simply initializes the text properties of the Label and Command controls. (Of course, you would normally do this by setting properties using the Mobile Internet Designer, but it's just as valid to set properties such as this in your application logic.) After the first call to the page, *IsPostBack* is *true,* so the contents of the *if* statement won't be executed. The code ensures that the controls are initialized only when the page first loads and the Text properties are not reset to their starting values on subsequent postbacks.

Now return to the *Click* event handler. The code you'll now write will change the text display on the label in the form from *"Hello World"* to *"Hello Universe"* and will hide the Command control after the user has clicked it. Edit the *Command1_Click* method so that it now reads this way:

```
private void Command1_Click(object sender, System.EventArgs e )
{
    Label1.Text = "Hello Universe";
    Command1.Visible = false
}
```

This application is now complete. You just need to build and deploy it. Build the project by selecting Build Solution from the Build menu. If you've made any errors writing the code, you'll see build errors in the Task List. The error tasks detail the names of the affected files, the line numbers of the errors, and error descriptions. Now that you've built the application, you can view it in the test browser. The left screen in Figure 3-5 shows how the output will initially appear if you're using the Openwave simulator. When you click the Upgrade Now! link, the display changes to the one shown on the right.

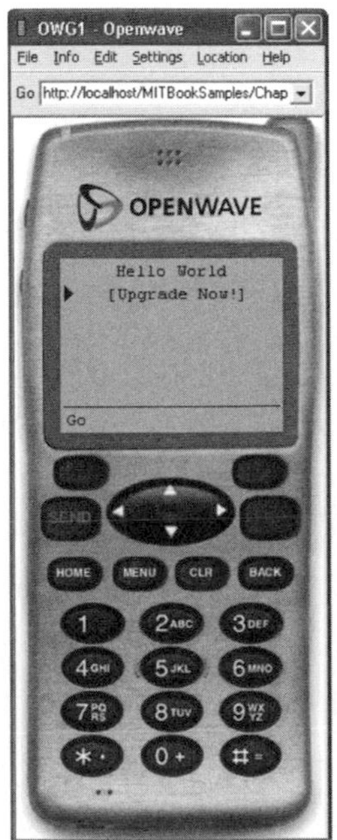

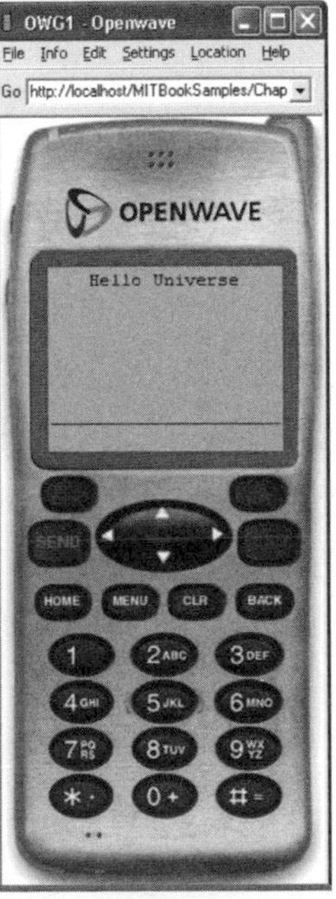

Figure 3-5 The first page of the application and the application page after you've clicked the Upgrade Now! link

Wiring Up Events and Event Handlers

In the Hello Universe application, you use event handler methods without too much concern for how the actual events and their respective handler methods connect. Both Visual Studio .NET and the .NET Framework hide the details of this connection from you, so you don't really need to follow what's going on behind the scenes.

Wiring Up Primary Event Handlers in Visual Studio .NET

If you use Visual Studio .NET, you don't generally need to worry about wiring up events and event handlers because the IDE inserts the necessary code in the code-behind module automatically. You can just double-click on a control shown in the Mobile Internet Designer, and it will automatically wire up the "primary" event for that control. For example, if you double-click on a Command control, Visual Studio .NET automatically inserts the code into your code-behind module to wire up the *Click* event for the Command control. It's worth understanding the code that Visual Studio .NET creates because you can use the same technique in code you write.

The class in the code-behind module overrides the *OnInit* event handler method of its parent which executes when the mobile Web Forms page initializes, and this method contains the code that wires up the event handlers. For the Hello Universe application, *OnInit* wires up the *Click* event handler with the following code:

```
Command1.Click += new System.EventHandler(this.Command1_Click);
```

This code declares a new delegate of type *System.EventHandler*, passing the address of the *Command1_Click* method as the event handler method to execute. As the += operator suggests, this delegate is added to a collection, because you can, if you want, execute more than one event handler method when the *Command1* object raises the *Click* event. The event handler method can be declared using the *private* access modifier.

Visual Basic .NET provides two alternative ways of wiring up the event handlers at run time. The equivalent of the C# example just given is to use the *AddHandler* keyword, as shown here:

```
AddHandler Command1.Click, Me.Command1_Click
```

The other technique is to use the *Handles* keyword in the event handler declaration itself. The control declaration must be declared with the *WithEvents* keyword, as follows:

```
Protected WithEvents Command1 As System.Web.UI.MobileControls.Command
⋮
Private Sub Command1_Click(ByVal sender As System.Object, _
    ByVal e As System.EventArgs) Handles Command1.Click
    ⋮
End Sub
```

Wiring Up Secondary Event Handlers in Visual Studio .NET

If you want to wire up an event handler for one of the other events of a control, double-clicking on the control in the Mobile Internet Designer won't help you. For example, double-clicking on the Command control wires up the *Click* event, but perhaps you want to write an event handler for the *PreRender* event? The technique for doing this differs between C# and Visual Basic .NET projects.

In C#, click on the control in the Mobile Internet Designer to select it, then click the lightning flash icon at the top of the Properties window. This displays a list of all the events for that control. Simply type in the name of the event handler method you want to create in the box next to the event, or double-click there to accept the default name. Visual Studio.NET adds the required code to wire up the event into the *OnInit* method, just as it does for the primary event, and creates the event handler method in your code-behind class.

In Visual Basic .NET, you don't wire up event handlers through the Properties window. Instead, open the code-behind module in the code editor and click the left-hand dropdown list at the top of the page. Select the control for which you want to create an event, then select the required event in the right-hand dropdown list. Visual Studio .NET inserts the required code to wire up the event into your code-behind module and creates the event handler function for you to complete.

Wiring Up Event Handlers Using Server Control Syntax

If you are writing applications using a text editor, rather than Visual Studio .NET, you can wire up event handlers using server control syntax:

```
<%@ Register TagPrefix="mobile" Namespace… %>
<%@ Page Language="vb" AutoEventWireup="false" … %>

<mobile:Form id="Form1" runat="server">
    <mobile:Command id="Command1" OnClick="Command1_Click" runat="server">
        Command
    </mobile:Command>
</mobile:Form>
```

If you use this technique, the event handler method named must be either declared in a *<script>* ... *</script>* block within the .aspx file, or as a *public* method in the code-behind module.

Wiring Up Events with the AutoEventWireup Attribute

As a final alternative, you can request that the runtime automatically wire up the events and event handlers. To do this, you must give the *AutoEventWireup* attribute of the *@ Page* directive (located at the top of your .aspx file) a value of *true*. (The default is *false*.) Here's an example:

```
<%@ Page language="c#" codebehind="MobileWebForm1.aspx.cs" inherits="Examp
le.MobileWebForm1.aspx" AutoEventWireup="true" %>
```

You don't need to wire up your event handlers in any of the ways described earlier, because the runtime does the wiring up automatically if it finds methods with expected names, such as *Page_Load* or *Command1_Click*. The disadvantage of this technique is that your event handler methods must have predictable names. If you wire up the event handlers explicitly, you could handle the *Click* event of the control with the ID *Command1* with a method named *ThisCoolMethodHandlesTheClickEvent*, but with `AutoEventWireup="true"`, the method must be named *Command1_Click*.

Programming State Management in ASP.NET

In this next sample application, you'll build on the concepts illustrated in the previous example and enhance the Scheduler mobile Web application that you created in Chapter 2. This application also highlights these features of building mobile Web applications:

- The common language runtime
- Control-class relationships
- Class member persistence

The Scheduler application you built in Chapter 2 featured a calendar from which a user could select a date. Now you'll rewrite Scheduler to perform the following tasks:

- Accept a date that the user selects
- Echo the chosen date to the user
- Switch to a Thank You screen at the end

You'll create this application from scratch using the Visual Studio IDE, and you'll build the project the same way you did in the previous applications in this chapter.

The original Scheduler application contained only a Calendar control. You'll now build a more complex GUI that consists of two Form controls. The first Form contains a Label with the text "Select Appointment Date", a Calendar, and a Command control with the legend "Book Now!" The second Form contains a label with the text "Thank you for using this application!" Figure 3-6 shows how the finished result will look.

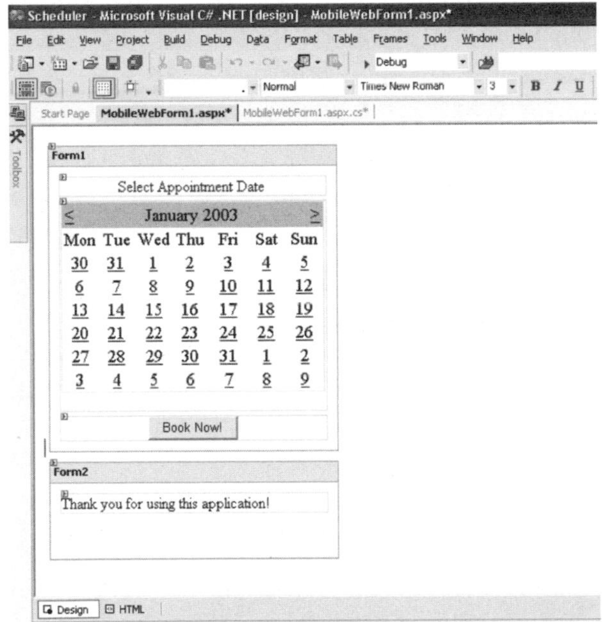

Figure 3-6 The Scheduler application with Form, Label, Calendar, and Command controls

Double-click the Command control to create the event handler for the *Click* event in the code-behind module. Now type the following switch statement in the *Command1_Click* method body, and also declare a private class member named *pageCount*, as shown here:

```
// Declare and initialize an integer private to this class.
private int pageCount=0;

private void Command1_Click(object sender, System.EventArgs e )
{
    pageCount++;
    switch (pageCount)
    {
```

```
        case 1: ConfirmDates();
            break;
        case 2: RenderFinalPage();
            break;
        default: break;
    }
}
```

This code determines a course of action that depends on the value of *pageCount*, which represents the number of times a user accesses the application. We'll explain this variable in the next section. The two private methods, *ConfirmDates* and *RenderFinalPage*, called from the *Command1_Click* method, alter the properties of the page's controls. Now type the two private methods into your code, after the *Command1_Click* method, as shown here:

```
private void ConfirmDates()
{
    Calendar1.Visible=false;
    Command1.Text="Ok";
    Label1.Text="Your Appointment: "
      + Calendar1.SelectedDate.ToShortDateString();
}

private void RenderFinalPage()
{
    ActiveForm = Form2;
}
```

In the Hello Universe application, you wrote code that changed the *Text* property of a Label control. The *ConfirmDates* method you've just written changes the *Visible* property of the Calendar control. You can set this property to *True* to make a control visible on the display page, or *False* to hide it. The *RenderFinalPage* method sets the *ActiveForm* property of the page (a property inherited from the *MobilePage* base class) to Form2, so that the Thank You page displays.

Persisting Class Members

Look again at the *Command1_Click* method. You've probably noticed that the *Switch* statement in the *Command1_Click* method evaluates the value of *pageCount*. You might expect the program to increment *pageCount* at each call of the *Command1_Click* method, as shown here:

```
private void Command1_Click(object sender, System.EventArgs e)
{
    pageCount++;
    switch (pageCount)
```

```
        {
            case 1: ConfirmDates();
                break;
            case 2: RenderFinalPage();
                break;
            default:
                break;
        }
    }
```

As you might also expect, when you run this application and click the Command button for the first time, the *Command1_Click* method executes, *pageCount* increments to *1*, and the *ConfirmDates* method runs, making the calendar invisible and displaying the selected date. The second time you click the button, you might expect the *pageCount* variable to increment to *2*, causing the *RenderFinalPage* method to execute. However, you find the *RenderFinalPage* method does *not* get called, and if you use the debugger, you'll find that the *pageCount* variable doesn't increment between clicks of the button. Why? The answer illustrates a feature of ASP.NET that often trips up the unwary: Web applications consist of a series of interactions between a Web server and a browser. These interactions are self-contained and essentially stateless, a process that is illustrated in Figure 3-7.

Every time control passes back to the server from the client browser, the runtime starts up the application. After sending the response to the client, the runtime destroys the application. Before it destroys it, the ASP.NET runtime saves state information so that each time the runtime re-creates the application and the controls it contains, the classes in the application and the controls are restored to the same state they had at the end of the previous request. ASP.NET controls know how to operate in this environment, save their state at the end of each request, and restore their state again at the beginning of the subsequent request, so for example, if you set the *Text* property of a Label control in code, the Label control remembers that value across subsequent requests. However, if you add any properties of your own to the class, you must make the effort to maintain state information across invocations. The simple answer is that *pageCount* never increments higher than 1 because it doesn't persist between server round-trips.

A number of methods for storing data between server round-trips exist—for example, using the ASP.NET Session or Application objects. (You'll learn more about these methods in Chapter 12.) In this example, you'll use the *ViewState* property of the *MobilePage* class. The *ViewState* property returns a dictionary of information that you can use to maintain data over multiple requests for the same page. The ASP.NET runtime persists the property's values by storing them on disk at the server and sending a session key to the client that is returned with the next *HTTP* request and that the runtime uses to locate and restore the correct persisted *ViewState* property.

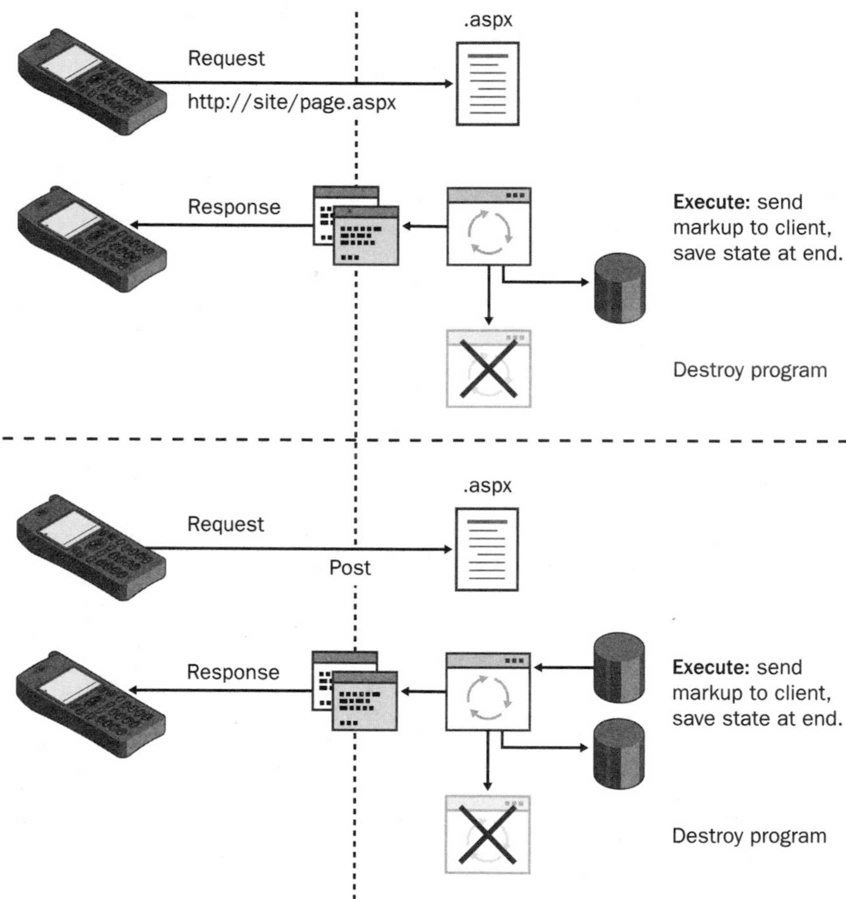

Figure 3-7 An ASP.NET application is destroyed after each response, and runs again to service the next request.

The following code uses the *ViewState* property to store the value of *pageCount* between server round-trips. This code declares *pageCount* as a public property of the class and provides appropriate *get* and *set* accessors:

```
public int pageCount
{
    get
    {
        // Initialize pageCount if not found
        if (ViewState["pageCount"] == null)
            ViewState["pageCount"] = 0;
        return (int)ViewState["pageCount"];
    }
    set
```

```
        {
            ViewState["pageCount"] = value;
        }
    }
```

When accessed by the *Command1_Click* method for the first time, the *get* accessor initializes *pageCount* to zero and returns that value. In subsequent *get* requests, the *pageCount* property returns the *pageCount* value stored within the *ViewState* object.

Building and Testing the Application

Figure 3-8 shows how the appointment selection page of your application should look when you're using the Openwave emulator. Remember that the Calendar control might render very differently on other devices. In this instance, when you click the Calendar link, a new page appears, showing the date and two options for selection: Type A Date and Choose A Date (depicted in Figure 3-9). Or if you select an appointment date from the appointment selection page and then click the Book Now! button, the screen will display the date of your appointment, as shown in Figure 3-10. Finally, if you click the OK button on the appointment selection page, the application loads its Thank You page.

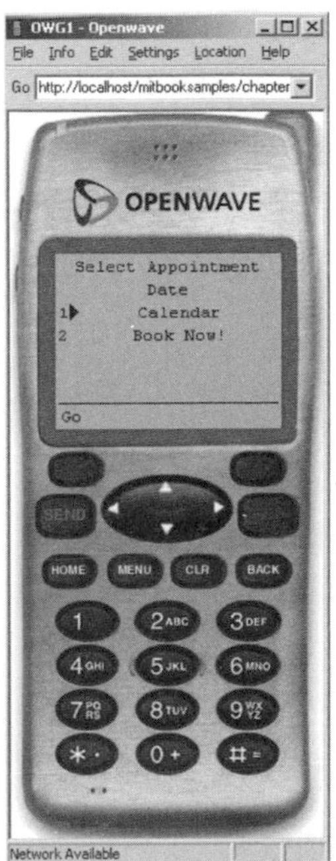

Figure 3-8 Openwave simulator displaying the Scheduler's appointment selection page

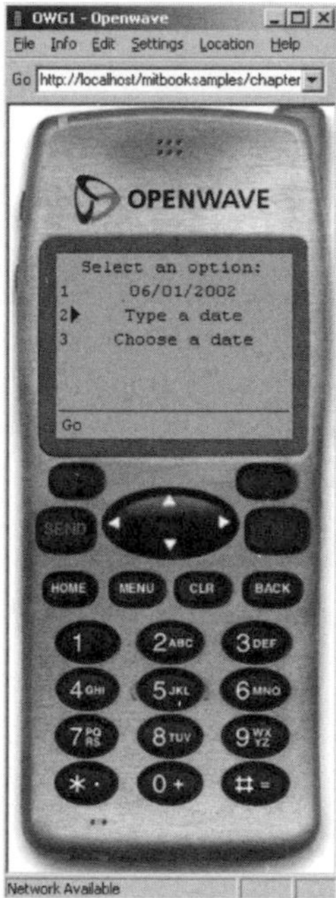

Figure 3-9 The first of the application's calendar pages

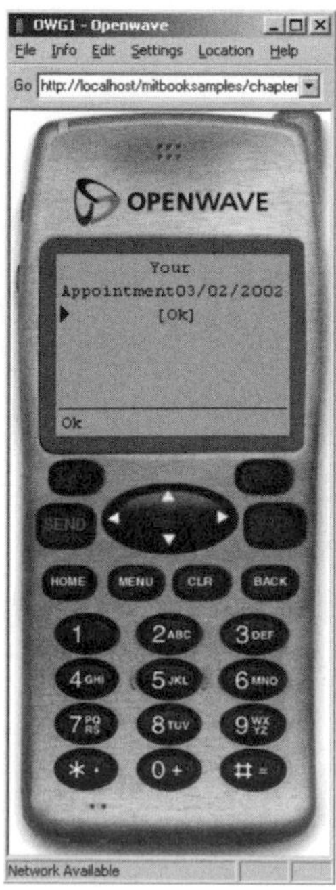

Figure 3-10 The application confirming an appointment date

Accessing .NET Framework Classes

This application builds on the application you created in the preceding section. In this application, you'll use classes provided by the .NET Framework to write the date that the user chooses to a local file. This example application also introduces *application lifetime* and *garbage collection*.

This example uses exactly the same GUI that we used in the previous application. You can copy the previous solution to a new project named SchedulerPlus by clicking Copy Project in the Project menu, or you can just continue working with the previous solution.

This application starts with the same code as the preceding application. However, when the user enters a date, your new application will write the date to a local file.

To create this functionality, double-click the Command control to display the *Command1_Click* method in the code-behind module. You'll keep the code that you wrote in the previous application, and you'll add a new method that writes data to a local file and call that method from the *ConfirmDates* method.

This new method, which we'll write in a minute, will use the *FileStream* and *StreamWriter* .NET Framework classes to write to a file. Whenever you refer to these classes in code, you could use their full names, including the namespace, of *System.IO.FileStream* and *System.IO.StreamWriter*. However, to make your code easier to read and more concise, you can import the *System.IO* namespace into your code module. To import the *System.IO* namespace, add *using System.IO* to your code, like so:

```
using System.Web.UI.MobileControls;
using System.Web.UI.WebControls;
using System.Web.UI.HtmlControls;
using System.IO; //import System.IO namespace
```

Now you can refer to classes in the *System.IO* namespace using just the class name, without prefixing them with the namespace name.

> **Tip** You can use the *using* directive to assign an alias to a namespace. That way, you can reference any types of the namespace by using its reference. For example, you can reference the namespace *System.Web.UI.MobileControls* as *MobileControls* by typing **using System.Web.UI.MobileControls = MobileControls;** into your code.

The new method, called *WriteFile*, writes data to a local file. Add this method to your code after the *ConfirmDates* method:

```
private void WriteFile()
{
    FileStream fs = new FileStream(
        Request.PhysicalApplicationPath + "header.log",
        FileMode.Append,
        FileAccess.Write);
    StreamWriter w = new StreamWriter(fs);
    w.WriteLine("Appointment log entry ("
        + DateTime.Now.ToString("f") + "):");
    w.WriteLine(Calendar1.SelectedDate.ToShortDateString());
    w.Flush();
    w.Close();
}
```

> **Note** In a real-life situation, you wouldn't implement the code as shown here. Instead, you'd place the code in a *try-catch-finally* construct to handle any errors. In this instance, we've dispensed with the error-handling code to make the code sample easier to understand.

This method creates two objects that are instances of the *FileStream* and *StreamWriter* classes. Unlike the classes of mobile Web Forms controls, these two classes aren't part of the ASP.NET mobile controls. Instead, they're part of the underlying .NET Framework class library.

The .NET Framework provides a large number of classes on which you can build Web applications, mobile controls, and XML Web services. Some of the classes, such as classes for working with lists of objects in dictionaries and classes that act as wrappers around primitive data types, increase your productivity. Other classes provide system-level functionality, such as the I/O tasks this sample application demonstrates.

The first line of code in the *WriteFile* method creates a new *FileStream* object. You can use the *FileStream* class to read and write buffered input or output to a file. In our code example, *FileStream* takes three parameters, the first being the name of the local file to which the program will write data. The second parameter is a member of the *FileMode* enumeration, which you can use to dictate how the file should be opened. In this case, we use the value *FileMode.Append*. If the file exists, data is appended to its contents; otherwise, the runtime creates a new file. The final parameter is a member of the *FileAccess* enumeration and determines the type of access permitted to the file. In this instance, the code gives the file write-only access.

The second line of the code creates a *StreamWriter* object, which is an object you use to write a stream of characters to a stream, such as the *FileStream* used here to access the file.

The third and fourth lines of the code write data to the file. The *WriteLine* method writes the specified information, a carriage return (*"\r"*), and a linefeed (*"\n"*) to the local file. If we had wanted to write information without a line terminator, we would have used the *Write* method. Once the information is written to the local file, we call the *Flush* and *Close* methods of the *StreamWriter* instance. The *Flush* method clears any buffers for the *StreamWriter* object, thus causing any buffered data to be written to the output stream. The *Close* method simply closes the current *StreamWriter* instance and its underlying output stream.

You can use the following code snippet to retrieve the current time on the local system and display it in your local time zone format:

```
DateTime.Now.ToString("f")
```

The *DateTime* class is also a .NET Framework class. The *WriteFile* code calls the *DateTime* class's *Now* property, which is a *static* member (*Shared* in Visual Basic .NET), so it's not necessary to create an instance of the *DateTime* class first.

> **Note** This sample demonstrates writing to the local file system. The default security restrictions on ASP.NET applications allow you to write to the application directory, as we show here, but not elsewhere in the host computer file system. If you want to write to other directories, you must set up an appropriate access control list (ACL) on the target file or directory to give the ASP.NET account the authorization to write there. (By default, ASP.NET applications run under the *aspnet* Windows user ID.)

After the *WriteFile* method writes out the time, it formats the date the user has set in the calendar control as a short date string (for example, mm/dd/yy) and writes that to the file:

```
w.WriteLine(Calendar1.SelectedDate.ToShortDateString());
```

Finally, modify the *ConfirmDates* method to call the new *WriteFile* method, as shown here:

```
private void ConfirmDates()
{
    WriteFile();
    Calendar1.Visible=false;
    Command1.Text="Ok";
    Label1.Text="Your Appointment: "
        + Calendar1.SelectedDate.ToShortDateString();
}
```

Garbage Collection

ASP.NET controls are objects that have properties and methods, just like any other objects in the .NET Framework. If you're an experienced programmer, you might be wondering what happens to all the memory used for the objects that you create in ASP.NET applications such as the *FileStream* and *StreamWriter* objects created in the *WriteFile* method in the example application. The answer is that the garbage collector in the common language runtime cleans them up automatically when your application has finished with them.

Garbage collection is a process that the runtime performs to free memory. By controlling how memory is allocated and freed, the runtime can help prevent memory leaks caused by programming errors.

Building and Testing the Application

You can now build the project the same way you did in the previous sample applications. Once you've built the application, view it in the browser of your choice. This application should be identical in appearance to the Scheduler application you developed in the preceding section, "Programming State Management in ASP.NET." However, this application will have written to a log file on the server from which it was run. (This server might be your local development machine.) Check the server's file system to confirm that this application has successfully created a log file to which it has written the appointment information.

Understanding the Application Life Cycle

We've touched on how garbage collection and class member persistence are managed within the ASP.NET framework. They might not operate as you had expected because of the life cycle of a Web application. This life cycle is predominantly influenced by the effectively stateless Hypertext Transfer Protocol (HTTP).

Figure 3-7 illustrated the life cycle of an ASP.NET Web Forms page, and Figure 3-11 also illustrates the client-server interactions between a Web application—in this instance, the SchedulerPlus application—and a mobile client. The first stage of the process occurs when the client posts the form data to the server. When the server receives the request, a sequence of processing events occurs, which commences with the *configuration state*. This first step involves reading and restoring values from *ViewState* that were persisted at the end of the previous request, such as this application's *pageCount* class member, and properties of the mobile controls such as the value of the Label control's *Text* property. Once the runtime restores these values, it invokes the *event handling state*. The application then raises page and control events and calls any event handlers that you've implemented, which in this application means calling the *Command1_Click* method.

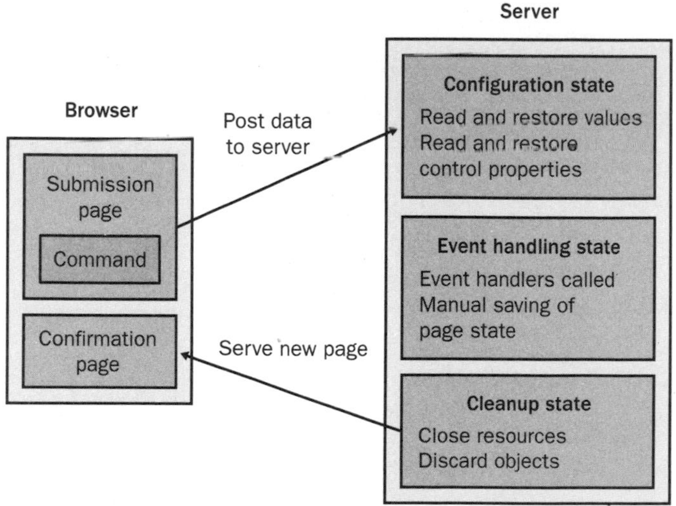

Figure 3-11 The client-server interactions between a Web application and a mobile client

Next the application saves the new state of the controls and page and renders the new output to send in the response to the client. The final step in the sequence is the *cleanup state*, in which the application closes any resources (such as log files) and discards any objects. Once this is complete, the server sends the new page to the client and, significantly, doesn't retain any of the page's information. However, ASP.NET does maintain control state between invocations, which effectively masks the fact that the code is instantiating the Web Forms page on every call back to the server. Therefore, the next time application control passes back to the server (for example, the next time the program posts data from the Web browser), the runtime repeats the whole process of re-creating the page on the server.

Writing Applications with a Text Editor

In this last example, you'll build a small application that displays the current time and allows the user to click a button to update the display. This application introduces you to writing Web applications with command-line tools, using the .NET Framework SDK. Although you're unlikely to write real-world applications in this way, knowing how the command-line approach works will help you understand the process by which Visual Studio .NET helps you construct a mobile Web application. This example also places code in a code-behind file and overrides the *Page_Load* method.

Building the User Interface

In this example, you'll use your favorite text editor—for example, Microsoft Notepad—to create the mobile application. You'll write the text that represents the server controls directly into the source file of the mobile Web Forms page, rather than using the drag-and-drop facility that Visual Studio .NET offers.

Create a new file named ClockGUI.aspx, and save it in a subdirectory of the IIS document root directory named TicToc, (c:\inetpub\wwwroot\). The new file commences with the following two lines:

```
<%@ Page Inherits="MSPress.MobWeb.TicToc.ClockGUI"
    Codebehind="ClockGUI.aspx.cs"
    Language="C#" AutoEventWireup="true" %>
<%@ Register TagPrefix="mobile" Namespace="System.Web.UI.MobileControls"
    Assembly="System.Web.Mobile" %>
```

We discussed the meaning of these two lines earlier in this chapter; however, the first line requires further explanation. This line is a page directive that has four attributes: *Inherits*, *Codebehind*, *Language*, and *AutoEventWireup*.

The value of the *Inherits* attribute states that this page inherits from the *ClockGUI* class in the *MSPress.MobWeb.TicToc* namespace. Thus, the page inherits properties and methods from the *ClockGUI* class. The value of the *Codebehind* attribute indicates the name of the module containing this class. In this example, the file containing the *ClockGUI* class is ClockGUI.aspx.cs, which we'll create in the next section. The third attribute specifies the language that the code-behind module is written with. In this example, the code is written in C#. The *AutoEventWireup* attribute is set to *true*, so event handlers such as *Page_Load* and *Command1_Click* will be called automatically, without having to be explicitly wired up.

Now that you've referenced the code-behind file and ensured that you can access its methods, you can write the source code that represents the visual elements of the application. These elements consist of a single Web Forms control that contains two other mobile controls, a Label and a Command. Use the following code for the GUI:

```
<mobile:Form runat="server" method="post">
    <mobile:label runat="server" id="Label1" alignment="center"/>
    <mobile:command runat="server" text="Update Time"
            id="Command1" alignment="center"/>
</mobile:Form>
```

You probably recognize this Form design as being the same as in the first application you created in this chapter. Notice that the Label control doesn't have a *Text* attribute value defined here; you'll set that attribute in the code-behind module.

Creating the Code-Behind Module

Now that you've completed the GUI, save and then close the file. Create a new file named ClockGUI.aspx.cs, and type the following code. Then save the file in the TicToc application directory you created earlier.

```
using System;

namespace MSPress.MobWeb.TicToc
{
    public class ClockGUI : System.Web.UI.MobileControls.MobilePage
    {
        protected System.Web.UI.MobileControls.Label Label1;

        protected void Page_Load(object sender, System.EventArgs e)
        {
            Label1.Text=DateTime.Now.ToString("T");
        }
    }
}
```

Notice that this code is far more succinct than the code generated for a similar project by Visual Studio .NET would be. There are two main reasons for this. First, Visual Studio .NET creates some code for its own use, to support the Mobile Internet Designer and other Visual Studio .NET features. Because this code module won't be developed or debugged in Visual Studio .NET, the application doesn't need to include these superfluous methods. Second, Visual Studio .NET inserts *using* statements for the most common programming namespaces that you're likely to use, although not many are required for simple applications.

The code example consists of one class that contains just one method. Two statements we have yet to discuss appear before the class definition. The first statement follows:

```
using System;
```

This statement tells the runtime that this file uses types of the *System* namespace, which every .NET application must include as a minimum. These types include a wide variety of classes that contain the following programming elements:

- Definitions of commonly used value types and reference types
- Events and event handlers
- Processing exceptions

Here's the second statement that appears outside the class boundaries:

```
namespace MSPress.MobWeb.TicToc
```

This statement defines a namespace named *MSPress.MobWeb.TicToc* within the code-behind module. A namespace enables you to organize your code and ensure that it has a globally unique name. Consequently, each class that you create doesn't stand in isolation; instead, it belongs to a given namespace. The following scenario might help you better understand the benefits of using namespaces.

Consider an application that uses methods declared in two different libraries, *A* and *B*. Both libraries define a class named *C* which your application needs to use. If both of these libraries use the same namespace, a naming clash will occur and it will be impossible to decide which class *C* the application should use. However, if both libraries define a different namespace, we can fully qualify the name of class *C* in each library. In this example, to create an instance of the class *C* in library *A*, the application would use the fully qualified type name of *ANameSpace.C*, while the class *C* in library *B* is defined by the fully qualified type name *BNameSpace.C*.

If you neglect to declare a namespace within a file, the file will still have a namespace. This namespace is a default that the .NET environment creates on your behalf. However, relying on default namespaces can easily result in confused, tangled, and unusable code. You should consider omitting namespace declarations only in the *very* simplest applications.

Namespaces

All the samples in this book that use a code-behind module explicitly declare the namespace that the class in the code-behind module belongs to. If no namespace is declared, ASP.NET compiles the classes into a default namespace that matches the name of the virtual directory where the application is installed—in other words, the application name. In your own applications, it's better to explicitly declare the namespace to avoid naming clashes between similar-named objects in different applications. Visual Studio .NET always generates C# code modules that include a namespace declaration. In Visual Basic .NET projects, the code-behind module generated by Visual Studio .NET does not include a namespace declaration (although you can add one if you want); the namespace used is defined in the project properties.

When you create a project in Visual Studio .NET, the namespace for your application is derived from the application name. For example, the code for the application at *http://localhost/Time* is created in the *Time* namespace. For most production applications, you'll want to use a more meaningful namespace, perhaps derived from your company name. For example, most of the samples in this book are in the *MSPress.MobWeb.{sampleName}* namespace.

To change the namespace of a Visual Studio .NET project, right-click on the project name in Solution Explorer and select Properties. Change the namespace in the Project properties to the required value. You could then edit the four file names in which the namespace is explicitly stated: MobileWebForm1.aspx, MobileWebForm1.aspx.cs, Global.asax, and Global.asax.cs. A quicker way is simply to use Solution Explorer to delete MobileWebForm1.aspx and Global.asax from the project and then right-click on the project name and choose Add New. Choose a new Mobile Web Form item and a new Global Application Class item from those offered. This re-creates the required files in the correct namespace.

The class definition, shown here, follows the two statements just described:

```
public class ClockGUI : System.Web.UI.MobileControls.MobilePage
```

The class definition declares a class named *ClockGUI* that has *public* visibility. The syntax indicates that this class is derived from *System.Web.UI.MobileControls.MobilePage* and therefore inherits its characteristics and behavior. All mobile Web Forms pages must inherit directly or indirectly from *MobilePage*.

The first line of the class declares a class member, as shown here:

```
protected System.Web.UI.MobileControls.Label Label1;
```

This declarations represents the mobile Label control.

The *Page_Load* method of the class reads:

```
protected void Page_Load(object sender, System.EventArgs e)
{
    Label1.Text=DateTime.Now.ToString("T");
}
```

Whenever the browser on the remote mobile device posts back to the server, the entire mobile Web Forms page object reloads, whereupon it raises the *Load* event. The *Load* event may be handled by an event handler such as the *Page_Load* method in this application. This code updates the Label to display the correct time. Note that even though this application does not contain a *Command1_Click* event handler, when the user clicks on the Command button, it still causes a post back to the server.

> **Note** There is no code to explicitly wire up the *Page_Load* event handler in this application. This is because the *AutoEventWireUp* attribute is set to *True* in the declarations at the head of the .aspx page, so event handlers using 'standard' names such as *Page_Load* or *Command1_Click* get called automatically, without any extra coding steps being required to wire up these events.
>
> Refer to the sidebar called "Wiring Up Events and Event Handlers," earlier in this chapter, for more details on different techniques for wiring up event handlers.

Building and Testing the Application

Now that you've written all the code for this application, you just need to build and test it. If this application consisted simply of an .aspx file, you could call it from a browser and it would compile at run time. In this instance, the application consists of an .aspx file and a code-behind module, which means that you can't simply call the application from a browser. Instead, you must compile the code-behind module and save it to the bin directory, which is a subdirectory of your application's directory.

To compile the code-behind module, follow these steps:

1. Set the path environment variable so that it references the directory containing csc.exe (the C# compiler).
2. Open a Command prompt, and change to your application's directory.
3. Create a new directory, and name it bin.
4. Type the following command, which compiles the code-behind module:

```
csc /t:library /reference:System.Web.Mobile.dll
/out:bin/ClockGUI.dll ClockGUI.aspx.cs
```

> **Tip** You'll need to configure the directory containing your ASP.NET application as an application directory in IIS. To do this, find your application's directory using Internet Services Manager, right-click the directory, select Properties, and then click the Create button in the Application Settings section of the Directory tab. If you use Visual Studio .NET to create you applications, it will automatically configure IIS on your behalf.

That's it! You've compiled the code-behind module, and you can now call your application from a browser. But before you do that, let's look at the command you typed to compile the code-behind module. The command you called to invoke the C# compiler, *csc*, took three switches:

- **/t:library** Instructs the compiler to output a library (DLL) rather than another type, such as an executable (EXE), which is the default operation.
- **/reference:System.Web.Mobile.dll** Instructs the compiler to reference the System.Web.Mobile.dll. The compiler needs this reference so that it can compile code that uses the ASP.NET mobile controls.
- **/out:bin/ClockGUI.dll** Instructs the compiler where to output the DLL. In this case, we create the ClockGUI.dll and place it in the bin directory.

To run the application, simply call ClockGUI.aspx from a browser. Every time the application loads, the *Page_Load* method of the code-behind module executes and the display updates to show the current time. Figure 3-12 shows the result.

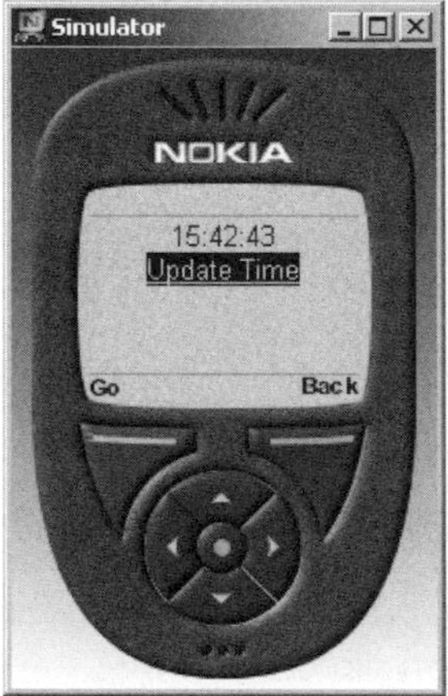

Figure 3-12 The TicToc application, displaying the updated time

4

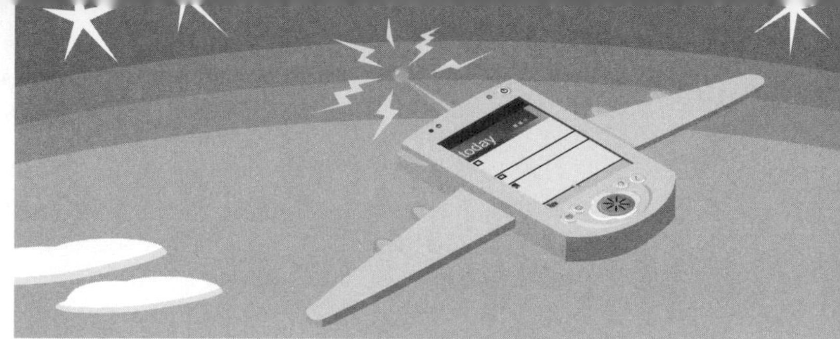

Programming the Standard Controls

In this chapter, we'll describe some of the standard ASP.NET mobile controls and demonstrate how to use the most important properties, methods, and events of the associated mobile control class. In addition, we'll show you how to use Microsoft ASP.NET server control syntax in a mobile Web Forms page to define a control's properties.

The container and core controls are the focus of this chapter. In Chapter 5, we'll deal with the special-purpose and validation controls; in Chapter 6, we'll discuss the list controls; and in Chapter 7, we'll look at some additional controls that you can download from the Microsoft ASP.NET Web site. These four chapters aren't intended to be an exhaustive reference of all the properties, methods, and events of each control class. For that, you'll need to consult the online documentation for the ASP.NET mobile controls. However, these chapters do demonstrate how to program the controls to perform the most common tasks.

How to Use the Control Descriptions

In this chapter, and in Chapter 5, Chapter 6, and Chapter 7, we describe the individual ASP.NET mobile controls. If you search for any of the ASP.NET mobile controls in the online reference documentation supplied with Visual Studio .NET or the Microsoft .NET Framework SDK, you'll find two descriptions—one in the "Control Reference" section and one in the "Classes" section. These are different ways of describing the same ASP.NET mobile control class. The control reference documentation describes how to set properties of the class in an .aspx file using ASP.NET server control syntax. The class documentation describes how to work with the controls in code. See Chapter 3 for a description of how ASP.NET uses server control syntax and how to work with controls in code.

In these chapters, you'll find a single description of each control that serves as a useful reference to the most important characteristics of each control, whether declaring them in server control syntax or manipulating them in code. The "Syntax" section shows you how to represent the control in an .aspx page using ASP.NET server control syntax. The "Properties and Events" section provides details of the most significant properties and events of the control, both *declarative* properties, which are those that can be set using attributes in server control syntax and which can also be set in code, and *nondeclarative* properties that can be set only in code. The "Using the *{controlName}* Control" section gives a short example demonstrating how to use the control in an application.

> **Note** Chapter 4, Chapter 5, Chapter 6, and Chapter 7 don't constitute an exhaustive reference to every event and property of each control. Instead, we have concentrated on those events and properties you're most likely to use. The "Classes Reference" section of the Microsoft ASP.NET mobile controls documentation gives a complete description of the methods, events, and properties of each mobile control class.

We've written each example in these chapters as a mobile Web Forms page (an .aspx file) and, where relevant, a code-behind module (an .aspx.cs file). We used the C# language for all the examples shown in these chapters. However, on the Web site for this book, you can download the examples in both Microsoft Visual C# .NET and Microsoft Visual Basic .NET. See the Introduction of this book for details of how to download and use the sample code for this book.

Introducing the Controls: Class Hierarchy

In Chapter 3, we introduced you to the programming techniques for mobile Web Forms. A mobile Web Forms page consists of a source file containing directives (such as the *@Page* directive) and Extensible Markup Language (XML) format code representing the ASP.NET mobile controls, which are the visual elements of your mobile Web Forms page. This XML representing the server controls is in *server control syntax* (sometimes referred to in the product documentation as the *persistence format*). Figure 4-1 shows a partial class hierarchy of the mobile controls.

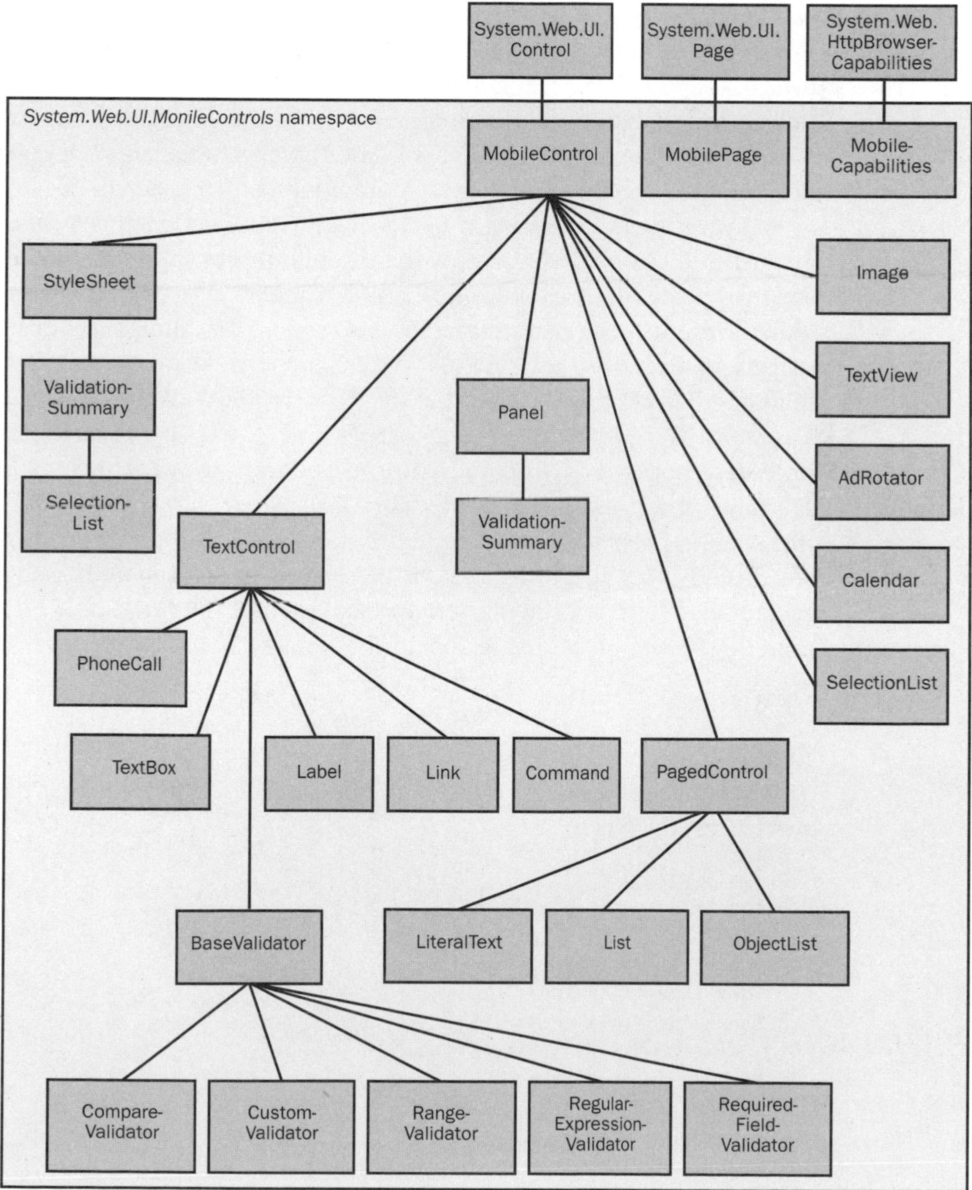

Figure 4-1 The top-level hierarchy of the mobile controls

Common Mobile Controls Behavior

All the mobile Web Forms control classes descend from, and inherit much of their behavior and characteristics from, the *System.Web.UI.MobileControl* base class (which itself inherits from *System.Web.UI.Control*). In this and the following three chapters, we'll discuss each of the mobile controls, describing their unique capabilities. Because these controls inherit certain aspects of their behavior—primarily style and context—from the *MobileControl* base class, we won't bother repeating these capabilities and features in every control's definition. Instead, we'll describe these common characteristics here.

Every control contains a *System.Web.UI.MobileControls.Style* object. However, this *Style* object is not exposed through public members. Instead, for each style property, the MobileControl has a publicly accessible property that internally references the privately contained style. For example, every mobile control exposes a *Font* property, which is actually a property of the privately contained *Style* object. (Note that the *Font* property of the *Style* object exposes a *System.Web.UI.WebControls.FontInfo* object, which has *Bold*, *Italic*, *Name*, and *Size* properties.). In code, you can get and set properties of the contained *FontInfo* object using the syntax *Font.Italic*. However, in ASP.NET server control syntax, properties of contained objects such as the *FontInfo* object can be set directly through attributes of the server control syntax by using a ContainedObject-Property notation. For example, set the *Italic* property of the contained *FontInfo* object using the attribute name *Font-Italic*:

```
<mobile:Label Font-Italic="True" Text="Some text"></ mobile:Label>
```

Syntax

You set the common properties of the mobile controls using the following server control syntax:

```
<mobile:aMobileControl
    runat="server"
    id="id"
    BreakAfter=="{True|False}"
    Font-Name="fontName"
    Font-Size="{NotSet|Normal|Small|Large}"
    Font-Bold="{NotSet|False|True}"
    Font-Italic="{NotSet|False|True}"
    ForeColor="foregroundColor"
    BackColor="backgroundColor"
    Alignment="{NotSet|Left|Center|Right}"
    StyleReference="styleReference"
    Visible="{True|False}"
    Wrapping="{NotSet|Wrap|NoWrap}"
```

```
<!-- Events -->
OnDataBinding="EventHandlerMethodName"
OnDisposed="EventHandlerMethodName"
OnInit="EventHandlerMethodName"
OnLoad="EventHandlerMethodName"
OnPreRender="EventHandlerMethodName"
OnUnLoad="EventHandlerMethodName"
```

The meaning of individual properties is given in Table 4-1 in the next section, and the meaning of the events is given in Table 4-2.

Common Properties and Events

Table 4-1 shows a subset of the properties that all mobile controls possess, including the style attributes and other important properties you will use frequently. The Property column lists the property name you use to set these *MobileControl* class properties in code. The property name is generally the same as the attribute name listed in the "Syntax" section, apart from exceptions already mentioned, such as subproperties of the *Font* property.

Table 4-1 Properties Common to All Mobile Controls

Property	Values	Description
Alignment	*Alignment.NotSet* | *Left* | *Center* | *Right*	Alignment of the control in the display. If *NotSet*, *Alignment* is inherited from the parent container control (the Form or Panel control within which the control is positioned). If the alignment isn't defined in any containing control, the default is left-aligned.
BackColor	*None* | hexadecimal RGB values | standard HTML color identifiers | color constants	The background color used for the control. The default is *Color.Empty*, meaning the system default applies. Unlike other properties, *BackColor* is not inherited from its container control.
BreakAfter	*True* | *False*	The default is *True*, which means that a trailing break is rendered after the control. Set to *False* to request that the following control or literal text is rendered on the same line. Note that the runtime might not observe this property setting if it results in an inappropriate layout on a particular device.
Font.Name	Valid font name	This property contains the name of the specified font used to display text in the control. The default font name is an empty string, indicating that the Font used is inherited from its containing control. If the font name isn't defined in any containing control, the default is the system font of the server.

Table 4-1 Properties Common to All Mobile Controls

Property	Values	Description
Font.Size	*FontSize.NotSet* | *Normal* | *Small* | *Large*	The font will be rendered using the requested size, subject to the capabilities of the client device. If the value is set to *NotSet*, the property is inherited from the container control.
Font.Bold	*BooleanOption.NotSet* | *False* | *True*	Specifies whether the text is boldface. If *NotSet*, the property is inherited from the container control.
Font.Italic	*BooleanOption.NotSet* | *False* | *True*	Specifies whether the text is italic. If *NotSet*, the property is inherited from the container control.
ForeColor	*None* | hexadecimal RGB values | standard HTML color identifiers | color constants	The color used for text display in the control. If *None*, the color is inherited from the container control. If no container specifies the *ForeColor* property, the system default applies.
ID	String value	If you assign an ID to the control in the server control syntax, you can use the ID to refer to the control in your code-behind module. If you don't assign an ID, the system supplies one. The Microsoft Visual Studio .NET Mobile Internet Designer always assigns an ID to controls when you drag them from the Toolbox onto a form.
Style-Reference	*Null* | named style	Styles are named collections of style attributes stored in a style sheet. (You'll learn more about styles and style sheets in Chapter 8.) Three system-defined styles exist: *title*, in which the text of the control is presented with emphasis, typically a boldface and large font size; *subcommand*, which uses a small font size to deemphasize the text; and *error*, which appears in a red font on those devices that support color.
UniqueID	*System-assigned value*	This is a nondeclarative property. The system generates this value when it processes the page to assign a unique name to every control in the page. The generated name consists of the *ID* property of the control, preceded by the *ID*s of any containing controls that are Naming Containers, for example *MyList:ctrl0:Label1*. (See Chapter 9 for a description of naming containers.)

Table 4-1 Properties Common to All Mobile Controls

Property	Values	Description
Visible	*True | False*	A control that isn't visible still exists as a programmable object on the page, but it isn't rendered to the client device.
Wrapping	*Wrapping. NotSet | Wrap | NoWrap*	Determines whether the text wraps onto the next line. If wrapping is disabled, the text will extend beyond the right screen margin. Browsers such as Pocket Internet Explorer allow you to scroll to the right to read wide text. Many Wireless Markup Language (WML) browsers allow right-scrolling using keypad buttons or apply *marquee scrolling*, meaning that the line in question automatically scrolls across and then back so that the user can read it. If the property is set to *NotSet*, the value is inherited from the container control.

Many of the style properties have a default value of *NotSet*. Controls inherit many of their style attributes from any container control. Therefore, if you set a foreground color on a Form control, all the controls it contains will inherit that foreground color. However, defining a control style attribute directly overrides any inheritance. The value *NotSet* indicates that the control will inherit the property value, and this value is displayed in the Properties window in Visual Studio .NET or returned when you query a style property value in code, so you can easily determine whether the control's style is inherited or is set explicitly.

Style attributes of a control can also be set differently on different client devices by using DeviceSpecific/Choice constructs or by using templates on the controls that support them. These techniques allow you to apply device-specific behavior to your application at run time so that specific types of requesting devices use different style attributes from others. For example, you might want to display a different font size or text color on an HTML browser than you do on a compact HTML (cHTML) device. You'll learn more about both these techniques in Chapter 9.

Table 4-2 Events Common to All Mobile Controls

Event	Description
DataBinding	Occurs when the control binds to a data source.
Disposed	Occurs when a control is released from memory, which is the last stage of the server control life cycle when an ASP.NET page is requested.
Init	Occurs when the control is initialized, which is the first step in its life cycle. When the *Init* event occurs, *ViewState* has not been restored yet (*ViewState* stores properties of the control saved at the end of the previous request), so you should not try to access properties of another control in an event handler for this event.
Load	Occurs when the control is loaded into the *MobilePage* object. You can access *ViewState* information and other controls in the mobile page from this event.
PreRender	Occurs when the control is about to render to its containing *MobilePage* object.
Unload	Occurs when the control is unloaded from memory.

Event handlers for all these events take two arguments: an argument of type *Object* that identifies the sending control, and an argument of type *System.EventArgs*:

```
EventHandlerMethodname(Object sender, EventArgs e)
```

Note The different ways in which you can wire up event handlers to events was described in the topic Wiring up Event handlers and Events in Chapter 3. One possible technique is to use ASP.NET server control syntax, for example:

```
<mobile:aMobileControl
    runat="server"
    id="id"
    OnLoad="methodName"
    ⋮
```

> The "Syntax" section for each mobile control in Chapter 4 through Chapter 7 includes events in the list of valid attributes to show how you would wire up the event using server control syntax. However, be aware that if you use Visual Studio .NET to create your ASP.NET mobile Web applications, it does not use server control syntax to wire up event handlers, but instead wires them up in code. Refer to Chapter 3 for an explanation of the different methods of wiring up event handlers.

Container Controls

Two container controls allow you to group other controls. The Form control, which is the outermost container control, enables you to group controls into programmatic units. This grouping doesn't necessarily determine the final rendering of the controls, as you'll learn when we examine the Form control in this section. The Panel control is a convenient way of grouping controls within a form. Controls placed within a form or panel inherit style properties from their container, unless specifically overridden by the controls. The Panel control is a convenient way of applying common style properties to the group of controls contained within it. Figure 4-2 shows the class hierarchy of the Form and Panel container controls.

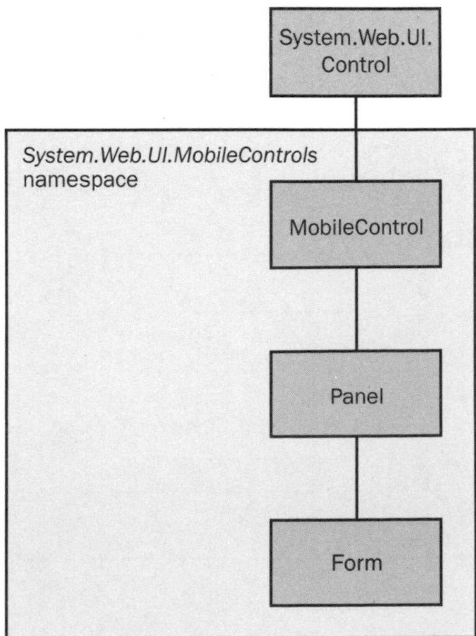

Figure 4-2 Class hierarchy of container controls

Containment Rules

Container controls provide a powerful means of structuring your Web application. However, you must understand the containment rules to which they adhere. As you've learned, all mobile Web Forms pages derive from the *MobilePage* class, which itself derives from the ASP.NET *Page* class. Therefore, every mobile Web Forms page is a valid *MobilePage* object. Each *MobilePage* object must contain one or more Form controls, which, as we've mentioned, you use to group controls into programmatically accessible objects.

A mobile Web Forms page can contain more than one Form control; however, you can't nest (or overlap) these controls. Each Form control can contain one or more mobile controls. These mobile controls can be of any type except other Form controls or style sheets. You can include zero or more Panel controls within a Form control; you can place other mobile controls inside a Panel control, thus allowing you to group controls within the Form. Unlike Form controls, you can nest Panel controls. For example, Panel control A can contain Panel control B, and Panel control B can contain Panel control C.

Figure 4-3 shows the relationships of the container controls and demonstrates how they can be nested.

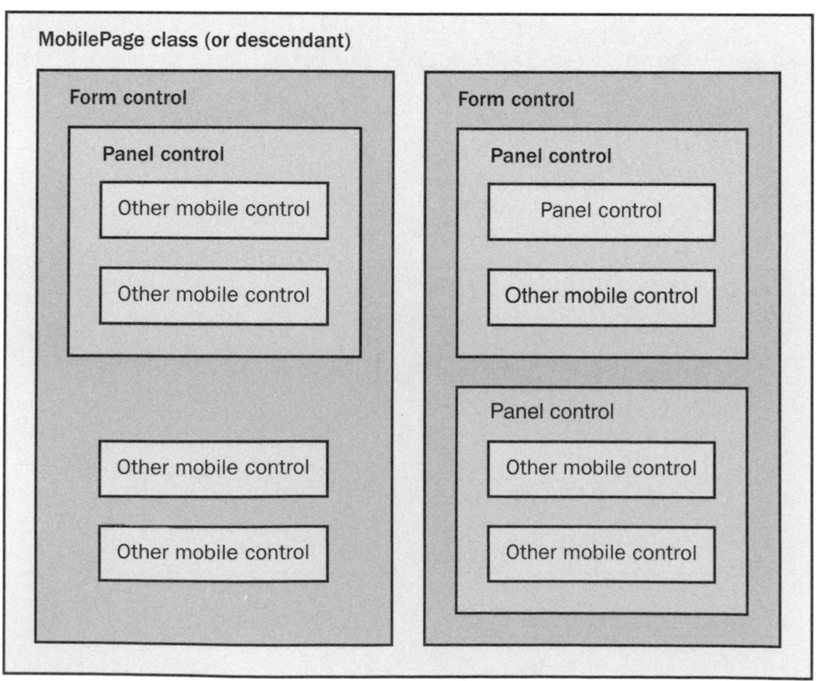

Figure 4-3 Nesting Panel and Form controls

Form Controls

A Form control is the outermost container that resides within a *MobilePage* object. Each mobile Web Forms page must have one or more Form controls that in turn contain one or more mobile controls. Although you can't nest Form controls, you can use multiple forms within a single page, as Figure 4-4 shows.

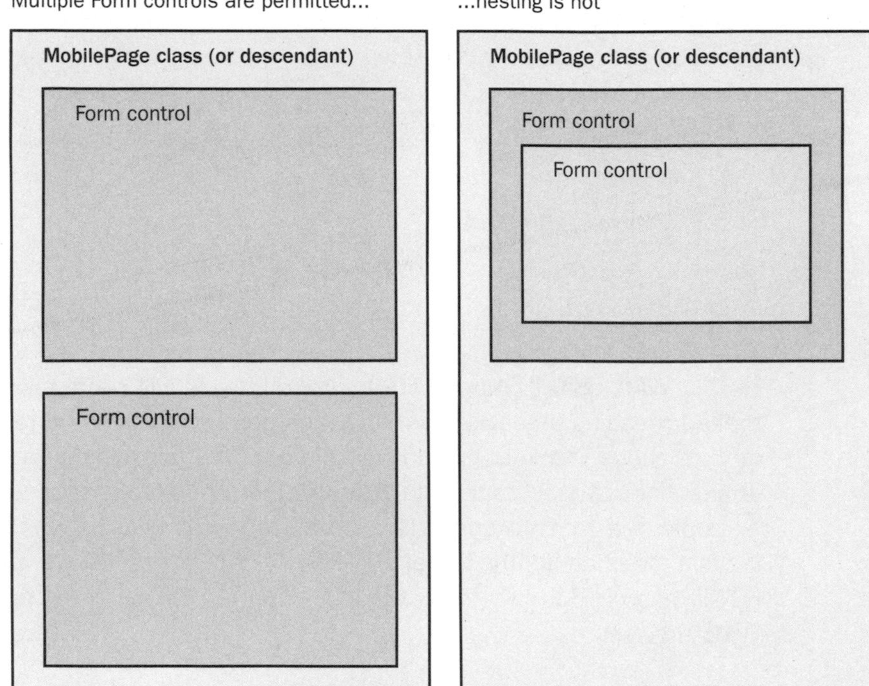

Figure 4-4 Using the Form control

In addition to containing mobile controls, a Form control can contain literal text—that is, text outside the mobile controls. For example, in the Mobile Internet Designer, you can type literal text directly into the Form control. You can format the text by using formatting tags, which Table 4-3 describes.

Table 4-3 Text Formatting Tags Used Within a Form Control

Tag	Description
<p> ...</p>	Places the enclosed text in a paragraph
* * or * *	Inserts a line break
<b> ... </b>	Makes the enclosed text boldface

Table 4-3 Text Formatting Tags Used Within a Form Control

Tag	Description
<i> ... </i>	Italicizes the enclosed text
<a href='url of resource'>Link - Text</a>	Inserts a hyperlink to another resource

When you use the tags in this table to display literal text, you can nest tags, but each set of tags must be enclosed completely by another. Server control syntax in a mobile Web Forms page adheres to XML structural rules. For example, the following code is valid:

```
<b><i>Hello World</i></b>
```

But the following code is invalid:

```
<b><i>Hello World</b></i>
```

> **Note** WML, HTML, and cHTML programmers will be familiar with these formatting tags. However, the tags don't specifically correlate to any of these markup languages. Rather, the formatting tags are abstractions of their counterparts in the three markup languages. For example, the runtime converts a break tag (*
*) to the break tag that's appropriate for the target platform. A *
* tag will be delivered to HTML and cHTML browsers, while a *
* tag will be delivered to a WML browser.

> **Warning** You can't use formatting tags within a mobile control element to format the text that it displays. Formatting tags can be used only where literal text is permitted. For example, the code `<mobile:Label runat="server"><b>Hello World</b></mobile:Label>` isn't valid and therefore won't compile. To format the text contained within a mobile control element, you must use the control's properties.

Syntax

You code the Form control in server control syntax as shown in the following listing. (See Table 4-4 for more details on these properties.) Note that *Action* and *Method* affect the way in which data is transmitted from the client to the server. In most circumstances, you don't need to change these from the default values. *Paginate* is an important property that specifies whether the display of a form can be split across multiple display screens—if the requesting client is unable to handle the complete contents of the form in one go. The Child controls entry at the bottom of the listing identifies where you would place the server control syntax defining the controls within the Form.

```
<mobile:Form
    runat="server"
    id="id"
    Font-Name="fontName"
    Font-Size="{NotSet|Normal|Small|Large}"
    Font-Bold="{NotSet|False|True}"
    Font-Italic="{NotSet|False|True}"
    ForeColor="foregroundColor"
    BackColor="backgroundColor"
    Alignment="{NotSet|Left|Center|Right}"
    StyleReference="styleReference"
    Visible="{True|False}"
    Wrapping="{NotSet|Wrap|NoWrap}"

    Action="url"
    Method="{Post|Get}"
    OnActivate="onActivateHandler"
    OnDeactivate="onDeactivateHandler"
    Paginate="{True|False}"
    PagerStyle-NextPageText="text"
    PagerStyle-PageLabel="text"
    PagerStyle-StyleReference="styleReference"
    Title="formTitle">
Child controls
</mobile:Form>
```

Properties

Table 4-4 lists the most important properties of the Form control. You set these properties either in server control syntax as described above or in code. The *Type* column describes the type of the property when setting or getting the property in code. Refer to the Syntax section above for valid values when setting the property in server control syntax. *CurrentPage* and *PageCount* are read-only properties that are set at run time as a result of pagination. You can't set them in server control syntax.

The controls contained within a Form control represent a single, addressable unit. However, this doesn't mean that the Form control will be displayed within a single unit on the client's browser. This is because the runtime adapts the output display to suit the target device by using *pagination*—meaning that the runtime breaks the output into smaller chunks. For example, a form collecting a user's personal details might split into a number of parts on a mobile phone to accommodate the phone's limited display capabilities. In contrast, the same form might appear as a single page on a device with a larger screen, such as a Pocket PC.

Table 4-4 Significant Properties of the Form Control

Property	Type	Description
Action	*String*	The URL to which the form is submitted on a *Post* or a *Get*. The default is an empty string, which means the form does a postback to the same URL from which it was loaded. Has the same meaning as *Action* in HTML.
ControlToPaginate	*Control*	The *ControlToPaginate* property is used to allow a single control on a form to paginate, even when the form's *Paginate* property is set to false. This allows individual controls to be paginated instead of the entire form.
CurrentPage	*Integer*	Returns the index of the current page, once pagination occurs.
Method	*System.Web.UI.MobileControls.FormMethod enumeration: Post | Get*	The HTTP request method for a postback, which is either *Post* or *Get*. The default value is *FormMethod.Post*.
PageCount	*Integer*	Returns the number of pages a form is broken into when pagination occurs.
PagerStyle	*System.Web.UI.MobileControls.PagerStyle* object	Sets or returns a *PagerStyle* object that specifies the text displayed and styles applied to the navigation prompts. The system automatically generates Next/Previous navigation as a result of pagination. Refer to Chapter 8 for details about usage.
Paginate	*True | False*	Boolean value of *True* or *False* that specifies whether pagination is permissible.
Title	*String*	The title of the form. Depending on the browser, this title can appear in a title bar, as a page heading, or not at all.

By default, the Form control doesn't paginate content. If you're testing an application on a small device and the device reports an error when attempting to load your Web page, the rendered size of the form might have exceeded the device's capacity. If this happens, enabling pagination might cure the problem. To disable pagination and thus ensure that the form's contents render as a single unit, you must set the *Paginate* property to *False*. Even if you disable pagination for the form, you can specifically enable it for one of the form's individual controls by setting the form's *ControlToPaginate* property to the ID of the control that you do want to paginate. This strategy might be appropriate for controls capable of displaying large quantities of output, such as any of the list controls or TextView.

The Form control has a number of events, including *Activate*, *Deactivate*, and *Paginated*. The *Activate* event occurs when a form becomes active, which can happen in the following instances:

- A form is first requested.
- A form is activated programmatically.
- A user follows a link to a form.

The *Deactivate* event occurs when the current form becomes inactive, as in the following instances:

- The user follows a link to a form, the current form is deactivated, and the new form is activated.
- A new form is activated programmatically, and the current form is deactivated.

The *Paginated* event occurs when form pagination completes, which happens prior to rendering each request. After this event occurs, the *CurrentPage* property of the form contains the actual number of display pages for the form.

The Form control supports *HeaderTemplate*, *FooterTemplate*, and *ScriptTemplate*, templates that can be used to provide device-specific markup in the rendered form. Chapter 9 describes the usage of these templates.

Using the Form Control

Listing 4-1 displays a label and a link in a Form control. A second Form control displays a message. When the user clicks the link, the first form deactivates and the second form activates. The second form, which has a label, demonstrates how to use literal text in the Form control context.

```
<%@ Register TagPrefix="mobile"
    Namespace="System.Web.UI.MobileControls"
    Assembly="System.Web.Mobile" %>
<%@ Page language="c#"
    Inherits="System.Web.UI.MobileControls.MobilePage" %>

<mobile:Form id="Form1" runat="server">
    <mobile:Label id="Label1" runat="server">
        Form 1
    </mobile:Label>
    <mobile:Link id="Link1" runat="server" NavigateUrl="#Form2">
        Link
    </mobile:Link>
</mobile:Form>

<mobile:Form id="Form2" runat="server">
    <b>
        <i>Phew, you made it!</i>
    </b>
    <br>
    <mobile:Label id="Label2" runat="server">
        Form 2
    </mobile:Label>
</mobile:Form>
```

Listing 4-1 Source code for FormExample.aspx

Figure 4-5 shows the output of both forms on the Nokia simulator.

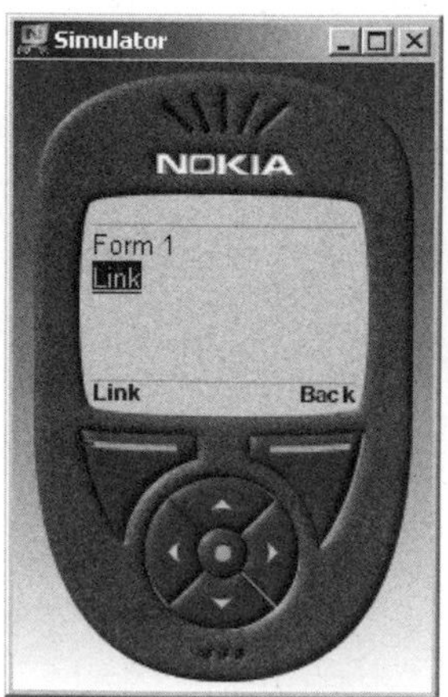

Figure 4-5 Output of the Form control example

Panel Controls

Panel controls don't have any visual appearance, but are used to logically group mobile controls. A Form control can contain zero or more Panel controls, and a Panel control can contain any mixture of controls, including other Panel controls but excluding Form controls. Unlike the grouping constructs you might have used before, Panel controls don't dictate the layout of the controls; the target platform always determines the control layout.

Syntax

You code the Panel control in server control syntax, as shown in the following listing. This control has no visual representation or events, but it possesses a number of properties that apply to the contained child controls through style inheritance. Apart from the common properties, *Paginate* is the only noteworthy property.

```
<mobile:Panel
    runat="server"
    id="id"
    BreakAfter=="{True|False}"
    Font-Name="fontName"
    Font-Size="{NotSet|Normal|Small|Large}"
    Font-Bold="{NotSet|False|True}"
    Font-Italic="{NotSet|False|True}"
    ForeColor="foregroundColor"
    BackColor="backgroundColor"
    Alignment="{NotSet|Left|Center|Right}"
    StyleReference="styleReference"
    Visible="{True|False}"
    Wrapping="{NotSet|Wrap|NoWrap}"

    Paginate="{True|False}" >
Child controls
</mobile:Panel>
```

Properties

Refer to Table 4-1 for details about how the common properties shown in the server control syntax work. These properties dictate the appearance of any text between the *<mobile:Panel></mobile:Panel>* tags and any child controls (controls contained within the panel). For example, if you set the value of *Font-Bold* to *True*, the panel's child controls will inherit this property and thus render the text in boldface. Not surprisingly, this behavior is device specific. For example, setting the *ForeColor* property to *Red* won't yield red text on a WML 1.1 browser because these browsers don't support color.

If you want to set style properties differently on specific devices, you can use a DeviceSpecific/Choice construct. The Panel control also supports the *ContentTemplate* template, which allows you to send arbitrary device-specific markup to a particular type of client. You'll learn more about the use of DeviceSpecific/Choice constructs and templates in Chapter 9.

The *Paginate* property is a hint to the runtime that it should try to keep the contained controls together when paginating. By default, this property is *True*. But if you set the *Paginate* property of the enclosing Form control to *False*, the *Paginate* property of the Panel control is ignored. When you enable pagination for the Form control and request pagination for an enclosed Panel control, the runtime attempts to keep the enclosed controls together on a "best-effort" basis.

Using the Panel Control

Listing 4-2 displays four Label controls. The first two labels appear within a Panel control. This panel also contains a panel, which contains two additional labels. The code sets font attributes for the panels but not the labels. When the code runs, the labels inherit the display characteristics of the panels. Therefore, all four labels are displayed in boldface and the last two labels are displayed in italics.

```
<%@ Register TagPrefix="mobile"
    Namespace="System.Web.UI.MobileControls"
    Assembly="System.Web.Mobile" %>
<%@ Page language="c#"
    Inherits="System.Web.UI.MobileControls.MobilePage" %>

<mobile:Form id="Form1" runat="server">
    <mobile:Panel id="Panel1"
    runat="server"
    Font-Bold="True">
        <mobile:Label id="Label1" runat="server">
            Label 1 Panel 1
        </mobile:Label>
        <mobile:Label id="Label2" runat="server">
            Label 2 Panel 1
        </mobile:Label>
        <mobile:Panel id="Panel2"
        runat="server"
        Font-Italic="True">
            <mobile:Label id="Label3" runat="server">
                Label 1 Panel 2
            </mobile:Label>
            <mobile:Label id="Label4" runat="server">
                Label 2 Panel 2
            </mobile:Label>
        </mobile:Panel>
    </mobile:Panel>
</mobile:Form>
```

Listing 4-2 Source for PanelExample.aspx

Figure 4-6 shows how these four labels will appear in the Nokia simulator.

Figure 4-6 Output of the Panel control example

Core Controls

In this section, we'll examine the basic navigation controls: the Command control, the Link control, and—when used as a link—the Image control, and controls that affect simple output operations (the Label, TextView, and Image controls) and straightforward input (the TextBox control).

Your applications will largely consist of a user interface comprised of these controls and set in the Form and Panel container controls. Figure 4-7 shows the class hierarchy of the core controls.

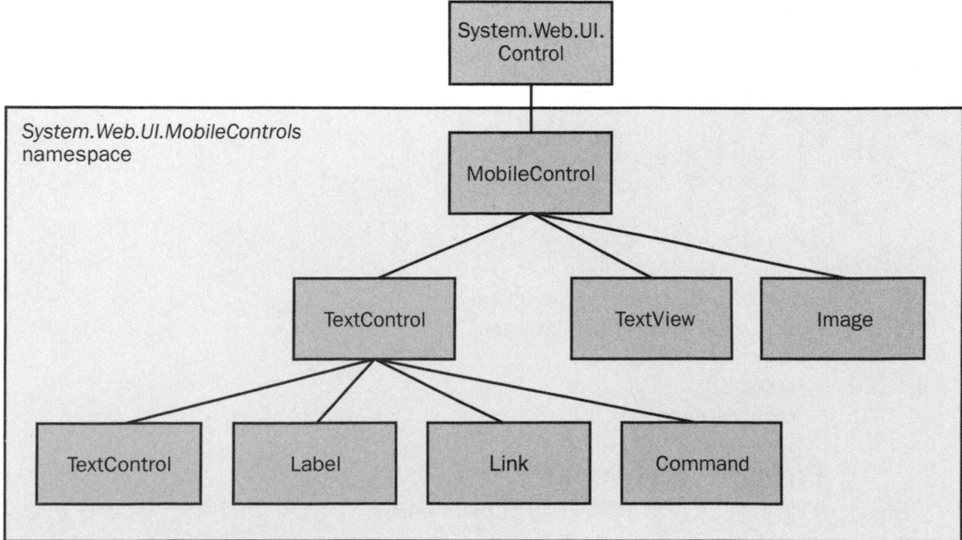

Figure 4-7 Class hierarchy of the core controls

Command Controls

The Command control allows you to invoke a postback so that user input is transferred back to the server. Once control passes back to the server, the runtime invokes event handler routines that enable you to implement user interface logic. Although this control differs in appearance on different target platforms and in different contexts, it usually appears as a button on HTML browsers and as a hyperlink on WML browsers.

Syntax

You code the Command control in server control syntax as shown in the following listing. This control always causes a postback, regardless of whether you've specified an event handler in the *OnClick* or *OnItemCommand* property. *CausesValidation* is useful only when the Command control is on the same form as one of the Validator controls (described in Chapter 5). You use *CommandName* and *CommandArgument* only when you specify an *OnItemCommand* event handler.

```
<mobile:Command
    runat="server"
    id="id"
    Alignment="{NotSet|Left|Centre|Right}"
    BackColor="backgroundColor"
    BreakAfter=="{True|False}"
    Font-Bold="{NotSet|False|True}"
    Font-Italic="{NotSet|False|True}"
    Font-Name="fontName"
    Font-Size="{NotSet|Normal|Small|Large}"
    ForeColor="foregroundColor"
    StyleReference="StyleReference"
    Visible="{True|False}"
    Wrapping="{NotSet|Wrap|NoWrap}"

    CausesValidation="{True|False}"
    CommandArgument="commandArgument"
    CommandName="commandName"
    ImageUrl="softkeyLabel"
    OnClick="clickEventHandler"
    OnItemCommand="commandEventhandler"
    SoftkeyLabel="softkeyLabel"
    Text="Text">
TextContent
</mobile:Command>
```

Properties and Events

The Command control inherits the common properties and events from the *MobileControl* class. (See Tables 4-1 and 4-2.) Table 4-5 describes the usage of the other properties and events of this control. The *Type* column describes the type of the property when setting or getting the property in code. Refer to the preceding "Syntax" section for valid values when setting the property in server control syntax.

Table 4-5 Significant Properties and Events of the Command Control

Property/Event	Type	Description
CausesValidation	*True | False*	This property is useful only when the Command control is placed in the same form as a CompareValidator, CustomValidator, RangeValidator, RegularExpressionValidator, or RequiredFieldValidator control. By default, any validator controls are triggered when a Command control causes a postback to the server. If you have a form containing validator controls, you might want to place one Command control that causes the validator controls to trigger (*CausesValidation="True"*) and another that performs some subsidiary function, such as showing more data, but that isn't intended to signify closure of the form or submission of the form contents. In the latter case, set *CausesValidation* to *False*.
CommandArgument	*String*	Value of the *CommandArgument* property of the *CommandEventArgs* object delivered to an *OnItemCommand* event handler.
CommandName	*String*	Value of the *CommandName* property of the *CommandEventArgs* object delivered to an *OnItemCommand* event handler.
Format	*System.Web.UI.MobileControls.CommandFormat enumeration: Button | Link*	Default rendering of a Command control is as a button on HTML browsers and as a link on WML browsers. You force rendering as a Link control on all devices by setting this property to *CommandFormat.Link*, but this is effective only if the device supports JavaScript.
ImageUrl	*String*	When the Command control is rendered as a button, set this property to the URL of an image source to render it as an image button. Ignore this property for those devices that don't support image buttons, such as WML browsers. You can also specify picture symbols or picture characters on those devices that support them. See the description of the *ImageUrl* property of the Image control in Table 4-6 for details.

Table 4-5 Significant Properties and Events of the Command Control

Property/Event	Type	Description
Click (Event)	Event handler method name	Specifies the name of an event handler method. When a user clicks or invokes a Command control, the control returns to the server. The runtime calls the event handler method specified as the value of this property. The method must have the signature *EventHandlerMethodName(Object sender, System.EventArgs e)*. The *System.EventArgs* argument contains no useful data.
ItemCommand (Event)	Event handler method name	As with the *Click* event, this parameter specifies an event handler method. At the server, the runtime calls the *ItemCommand* event handler after the *Click* event handler. The method must have the signature *EventHandlerMethodName(Object sender, System.Web.UI.WebControls. CommandEventArgs e)*. You can specify values to be inserted into the *CommandEventArgs* argument of the event handler using the *CommandName* and *CommandArgument* properties of the Command control. Unlike the *Click* event, this event bubbles up to parent controls. (We'll explain event bubbling shortly.)
SoftkeyLabel	*String*	Certain mobile devices, such as mobile phones with Openwave WML browsers, enable users to press a softkey under the screen to select a hyperlink. You set this property to override the default label displayed for this softkey. By default, this property is an empty string, which equates to a Go label on browsers that support this feature.
Text	*String*	You can designate the text to be displayed for the link either by using the *Text* attribute or by specifying the text as the content of the *<Control>* element. If you specify both, when the control is rendered, the attribute takes precedence. However, setting the *Text* property programmatically overrides any existing setting.

If a user has completed some input fields, you can use the Command control to perform further processing based on that input. Typically, the Command control appears as a button on HTML browsers and as a hyperlink or softkey button on WML browsers. As with the Link control, you shouldn't make assumptions about the rendering of a Command control. For example, helpful prompts to the user (such as *Click The Link Below*) might not be appropriate on all client platforms. You don't have to specify an event handler with this control. Even if you don't specify an event handler, activating this control will still cause a postback to the server, allowing the runtime to fire any events associated with controls that don't themselves trigger postback, such as the TextBox or SelectionList controls.

The Command control raises two events that you can trap in event handlers. The simplest is the *OnClick* event handler, which passes no useful values in its *System.EventArgs* argument. The *OnItemCommand* event offers more flexibility. When the code calls the event handler associated with an *ItemCommand* event, the handler passes a *CommandEventArgs* object as an argument. This object has two properties, *CommandName* and *CommandValue*, which you can set using the *CommandName* and *CommandArgument* properties of the Command control. This allows you to create a form that offers two or more Command controls, providing different options to the user. Each control specifies the same *ItemCommand* event handler method but has different *CommandArgument* and *CommandName* attributes. This enables you to determine in your event handler code which button the user has pressed, as shown in Listing 4-3.

The *ItemCommand* event also supports something called *event bubbling*. In normal usage, you write event handler routines that execute as a direct result of something happening to a control. In complex applications, however, you might have a design that uses templating features of a control such as List, providing a richer user interface or additional functionality for more capable client devices. Rather than write event handlers for the *ItemCommand* event of the child Command controls in the template, you can let the event bubble up to the parent control (the List control), and handle the event in the *ItemCommand* event handler of the List control. The topic "Event Handling for Controls Embedded in Templates" in Chapter 10 gives more information on event bubbling.

Using the Command Control

When run, the code in Listing 4-3 and Listing 4-4 displays a Form containing three Command controls, all using the same *OnItemCommand* event handler. Each Command control has a different *CommandName* property so that you can determine which control activated the event handler method.

```
<%@ Register TagPrefix="mobile" Namespace="System.Web.UI.MobileControls"
    Assembly="System.Web.Mobile" %>
<%@ Page language="c#" Codebehind="CommandExample.aspx.cs"
    Inherits="MSPress.MobWeb.CmdEx.MyWebForm" %>

<mobile:Form id="Form1" runat="server">
<mobile:Command id="Command1" runat="server" CommandName="RED"
    OnItemCommand="Command_SelectEvent" BackColor="Red">
    Red
</mobile:Command>
<mobile:Command id="Command2" runat="server" CommandName="BLUE"
    OnItemCommand="Command_SelectEvent" BackColor="Blue" ForeColor="White">
    Blue
</mobile:Command>
<mobile:Command id="Command3" runat="server" CommandName="GREEN"
    OnItemCommand="Command_SelectEvent" BackColor="Lime">
    Green
</mobile:Command>
<mobile:Label id="Message" runat="server"></mobile:Label> </mobile:Form>
```

Listing 4-3 Source for CommandExample.aspx

```
using System;
using System.Web.UI.WebControls;

namespace MSPress.MobWeb.CmdEx
{
    public class MyWebForm :
        System.Web.UI.MobileControls.MobilePage
    {
        protected System.Web.UI.MobileControls.Label Message;

        protected void Command_SelectEvent(
            Object sender, CommandEventArgs e)
        {
            if(e.CommandName=="RED")
                Message.Text="You selected the Red option";
            else if(e.CommandName=="BLUE")
                Message.Text="You selected the Blue option";
            else
                // Catchall case
                Message.Text="You selected the Green option";
        }
    }
}
```

Listing 4-4 The code-behind module CommandExample.aspx.cs

Image Controls

The Image control allows you to display graphics files. This control presents unique problems to the developer because of the differing graphics formats supported by different handheld devices. Even within devices that support the same formats, screen display size constraints often dictate that a graphic of one size might not be appropriate for another device. Although the Image control is programmed in the same way regardless of which clients will access your application, in most cases, you'll have to supply graphics in multiple formats and use DeviceSpecific/Choice constructs and property overrides to send the correct format to each client.

> **Tip** The DynamicImage control described in Chapter 7 is a useful alternative to the standard Image control. It has the ability to take an image and dynamically convert it to the preferred image format of the requesting device. The DynamicImage control makes it easier to work with graphics when an application will be accessed by clients requiring different graphics file formats.

Syntax

You code the Image control in server control syntax as shown in the following listing. *ImageUrl* specifies the location of the graphics file that is displayed or the identity of an icon or a symbol resident in the device. If you set the *NavigateUrl* property, the image functions as a link to that location.

```
<mobile:Image
    runat="server"
    id="id"
    Alignment="{NotSet|Left|Centre|Right}"
    BackColor="backgroundColor"
    BreakAfter=="{True|False}"
    Font-Bold="{NotSet|False|True}"
    Font-Italic="{NotSet|False|True}"
    Font-Name="fontName"
    Font-Size="{NotSet|Normal|Small|Large}"
    ForeColor="foregroundColor"
    StyleReference="StyleReference"
    Visible="{True|False}"
    Wrapping="{NotSet|Wrap|NoWrap}"
```

```
    AlternateText="AltText"
    ImageUrl="masterImageSource"
    NavigateUrl="targetURL"
    SoftkeyLabel="softkeyLabel">
Optional DeviceSpecific/Choice construct here.
</mobile:Image>
```

Properties

Table 4-6 lists the most important properties of the Image control. The *Type* column describes the type of the property when setting or getting the property in code. Refer to the preceding "Syntax" section for valid values when setting the property in server control syntax.

Table 4-6 Significant Properties of the Image Control

Property	Type	Description
AlternateText	*String*	Specifies the text to be displayed on devices that don't support graphics files. This text is also displayed when the page first appears to the user, while the server retrieves the image file.
ImageURL	*String*	URL of the graphics file you're using. You can use a relative URL if the image file resides in the same directory or a subdirectory of the application. (For example, just use the name *filename.gif* if the image file resides in the same directory as the application files.) Or you can use a full URL to a different location. Alternatively, you can specify *ImageURL* in the form *symbol:image*, where *image* indicates a device-resident glyph. See the section "Using Device-Resident Glyphs," later in this chapter, for more details.
NavigateURL	*String*	If you set this property, the image becomes a hyperlink. When the user activates the image, the program flow jumps to the form or resource specified in *NavigateURL*. If the value of *NavigateURL* begins with a pound sign (#), the application interprets the rest of the value as the ID of a Form control on the same mobile Web Forms page. Otherwise, the application interprets the value as the URI of a resource.

Table 4-7 lists the support that different mobile platforms provide for the various graphics file formats.

Table 4-7 Mobile Platform Support for Graphics Files

File Extension	Type	Where Found
.gif	Graphics Interchange Format	HTML browsers such as Pocket Internet Explorer and Microsoft Mobile Explorer support GIF files. Pocket PCs feature a usable screen size of 240 pixels wide by 320 pixels high, although they support a virtual screen size of twice that. Some i-mode phones support 256-color GIF files. The maximum size of a GIF image is 94 by 72 pixels. Palm OS devices that feature Web Clipping support both GIF and JPEG graphics. The typical usable screen size on such devices is 153 pixels wide by 144 pixels high.
.jpg	JPEG files	Supported on HTML browsers such as Pocket Internet Explorer and Microsoft Mobile Explorer; also supported by the Palm Web Clipping system as described for GIF files.
.wbmp	Wireless Bitmap (monochrome graphics)	All WML 1.1–compliant WAP devices must support Wireless Bitmap (WBMP) image files. The majority of WAP-enabled mobile phones support this format, as do RIM BlackBerry devices and other personal digital assistants (PDAs) equipped with a WML browser. Usable screen dimensions on a WAP mobile phone range from 90 by 40 pixels on smaller devices to 310 by 100 pixels on landscape-oriented devices such as the Ericsson R380. RIM devices using the GoAmerica browser have a usable screen size of 64 by 132 pixels on smaller devices. Palm devices using a WAP browser and larger RIM devices support up to 160 by 160 pixels.
.png	Portable Network Graphics	In time, this format might come to replace GIF files in general usage. WAP-enabled devices that support WML version 1.2 and offer color must support Portable Network Graphics (PNG) format. However, support for this format is rare, so you should check your device capabilities before attempting to use it.

Even within a particular genre of browser (such as the HTML browsers), your application might have to provide different graphics files if you want to support both small mobile devices and those with a larger screen. Consequently, you'll usually use this control with a DeviceSpecific/Choice construct, using the Property Override feature to set an alternative value for the *ImageURL* property if the requesting device is of a particular type. You'll learn more about property overrides, DeviceSpecific/Choice constructs, and device filters in Chapter 9.

Using the Image Control

Consider Listing 4-5, which doesn't specify a value for the *ImageUrl* property within the *<mobile:Image …>* tag. However, based on the Web.config file shown in Listing 4-6, if the target device supports HTML 3.2 (device filter *isHTML32* is *True*), a property override applies to set *ImageUrl* to *Northwind.gif*. If the device supports WML version 1.1, *ImageUrl* is set to *Northwind.wbmp*. If no device filter matches, *ImageUrl* doesn't have a value, so the *AlternateText* string is displayed instead of a graphics file.

```
<%@ Page Inherits="System.Web.UI.MobileControls.MobilePage"
    Language="c#" %>
<%@ Register TagPrefix="mobile"
    Namespace="System.Web.UI.MobileControls"
    Assembly="System.Web.Mobile" %>

<mobile:Form runat="server">
  <mobile:Image runat="server" id="Image1"
        AlternateText="Northwind Corp.">
    <DeviceSpecific>
      <Choice Filter="isHTML32"
        ImageUrl="Northwind.gif"/>
      <Choice Filter="isWML11"
        ImageUrl="Northwind.wbmp"/>
    </DeviceSpecific>
  </mobile:Image>
</mobile:Form>
```

Listing 4-5 ImageExample.aspx, showing the use of choice filters and the Image control

```
<?xml version="1.0" encoding="utf-8" ?>
<configuration>
  <system.web>
    <deviceFilters>
        <!-- Markup Languages -->
        <filter name="isHTML32"
                compare="preferredRenderingType" argument="html32" />
        <filter name="isWML11"
                compare="preferredRenderingType" argument="wml11" />
    </deviceFilters>
 </system.web>
</configuration>
```

Listing 4-6 Web.config containing the device filters required by Image-Example.aspx

As with other mobile controls, if you set the *BreakAfter* property to *False*, the runtime attempts to render the image without a trailing line break, subject to it being able to lay out the page as requested in the client's available display space. This allows you to insert an image inline with text or other images. Note, however, that certain WML browsers, such as the Nokia 7110, always display images on their own line, with a following line break enforced by the browser.

Using Device-Resident Glyphs

As was described in Table 4-6, you can specify the *ImageURL* property in the form *symbol:0000*, where the *0000* decimal code is a valid identifier for a device-resident glyph, or icon. Many of these glyphs are available on i-mode devices. For example, *symbol: 63648* is a glyph depicting cloudy weather. (See *http://www.nttdocomo.co.jp/english/i/tag/emoji/index.html* for an online reference.) If you're developing applications for J-Phone devices (devices available on the SkyWeb network in Japan), you use glyphs with the syntax *symbol:X00*, where *X* is the group picture character *G*, *E*, or *F*, and *00* is the hexadecimal picture character code for the glyph.

Many WML 1.1 browsers also support device-resident icons. To use these icons, you must specify the icon name. For example, *symbol:cloudy* indicates a cloud icon on an Openwave browser. Unfortunately, the icons available are device-specific, so you must consult the device documentation for details about supported glyphs. To use them, you must use DeviceSpecific/Choice constructs to identify the major browsers, and you must apply a property override for the *ImageUrl* property to set it to the appropriate symbol name for that browser. (See Listing 4-7 for an example.) You should always ensure that you specify a suitable text alternative by using the *AlternateText* property for devices that you don't cover. Listing 4-7 shows a form that displays two images. The first image specifies a graphic (cloudy.jpg) and alternative text (Cloudy!) that will appear if the graphic can't be displayed. If the device is an Openwave UP.Browser V4.x, you can use a DeviceSpecific/Choice construct with the *isUP4x* device filter that overrides the *ImageURL* property and instead specifies a device-resident icon called *cloud*.

By default, the second Image control specifies a graphic named MSNlogo-small.gif. However, a DeviceSpecific/Choice construct overrides this graphic if the browser is Pocket Internet Explorer (device filter *isPocketIE*)—in this case, the code uses the larger MSNlogo.gif. This control also links to the MSN Web site. Listing 4-8 shows the device filter entries you must have in your Web.config for this example.

```
<%@ Register TagPrefix="mobile"
    Namespace="System.Web.UI.MobileControls"
    Assembly="System.Web.Mobile" %>
<%@ Page Inherits="System.Web.UI.MobileControls.MobilePage"
    Language="c#" %>

<mobile:Form runat="server">
    <mobile:Label runat="server">
        The Weather today will be...</mobile:Label>
    <mobile:Image runat="server"
                  AlternateText="Cloudy!"
                  ImageUrl="cloudy.jpg">
        <DeviceSpecific>
            <Choice ImageUrl="symbol:cloud" Filter="isUP4x">
            </Choice>
        </DeviceSpecific>
    </mobile:Image>
    <br>
    <mobile:Image runat="server"
                  AlternateText="GoTo MSN"
                  ImageUrl="MSNlogosmall.gif"
                  NavigateUrl="http://mobile.msn.com">
        <DeviceSpecific>
            <Choice ImageUrl="MSNlogo.gif" Filter="isPocketIE">
            </Choice>
        </DeviceSpecific>
    </mobile:Image>
</mobile:Form>
```

Listing 4-7 Source for ImageGlyphExample.aspx

```
<?xml version="1.0" encoding="utf-8" ?>
<configuration>
  <system.web>
    <deviceFilters>
        <!-- Device Browsers -->
        <filter name="isGoAmerica"
            compare="browser" argument="Go.Web" />
        <filter name="isMME" compare="browser"
            argument="Microsoft Mobile Explorer" />
        <filter name="isMyPalm" compare="browser" argument="MyPalm" />
        <filter name="isPocketIE" compare="browser" argument="Pocket IE" />
        <filter name="isUP3x"
            compare="type" argument="Phone.com 3.x Browser" />
        <filter name="isUP4x"
            compare="type" argument="Phone.com 4.x Browser" />
```

Listing 4-8 Web.config containing the device filters required by ImageGlyphExample.aspx

```
    </deviceFilters>
  </system.web>
</configuration>
```

Figure 4-8 shows the results of running this code. On Pocket Internet Explorer, the cloudy.jpg graphic is displayed with the large MSN link. On the Openwave V4.1 simulator, the device-resident icon is displayed for the first image, but because the device doesn't support GIF files, it uses the alternative text for the second image. The Nokia simulator supports the JPEG of the first image, and it also supports GIFs, so it displays the small MSN logo for the second image.

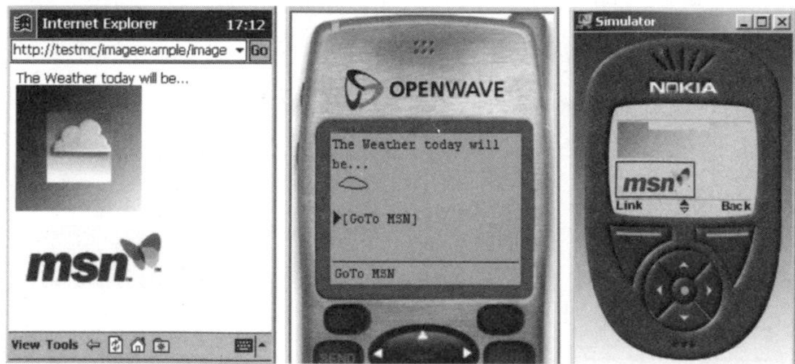

Figure 4-8 Image control output on Pocket Internet Explorer, Openwave simulator, and Nokia simulator

Label Controls

The Label control allows you to place small, read-only text strings on the output device screen. We've already used it a number of times in this book.

Syntax

You code the Label control in server control syntax, as shown here. Apart from the common properties, *Text* is the only property of note.

```
<mobile:Label
    runat="server"
    id="id"
    Alignment="{NotSet|Left|Centre|Right}"
    BackColor="backgroundColor"
    BreakAfter=="{True|False}"
    Font-Bold="{NotSet|False|True}"
    Font-Italic="{NotSet|False|True}"
    Font-Name="fontName"
    Font-Size="{NotSet|Normal|Small|Large}"
```

```
    ForeColor="foregroundColor"
    StyleReference="StyleReference"
    Visible="{True|False}"
    Wrapping="{NotSet|Wrap|NoWrap}"

    Text="Text">
TextContent
</mobile:Label>
```

The text that the Label control generates will be displayed on all output devices and will include the requested style attributes if the target device supports them.

You must place the Label control within a Form or Panel container control, or within the template of a templated control. (You'll learn more about control templates in Chapter 9.)

Properties

The Label control inherits the common properties and events from the *MobileControl* class, as listed in Table 4-1 and Table 4-2, and exposes the *Text* property, as described in Table 4-8.

Table 4-8 Significant Property of the Label Control

Property	Type	Description
Text	*String*	You can designate the text to be displayed either by setting the *Text* attribute or by specifying the text as the content of the *<Label>* element. If you specify both, when the control is rendered, the attribute takes precedence. However, setting the *Text* property programmatically overrides any existing setting.

As an alternative to using the Label control, you can enter text directly onto the background of a Form control in the Mobile Internet Designer (or switch to HTML View and type literal text between the *<mobile:Form>* and *</mobile:Form>* tags). However, the Label control lets you change the text at run time; the Form control does not. If you set the *Wrapping* attribute on either of these controls to *Wrap*, the text will wrap onto the next display line. For large blocks of text, you should use the TextView control, which offers built-in pagination support. We'll discuss the TextView control later in this chapter.

Using the Label Control

Listing 4-9 defines the properties of a Label control named Label1 solely within the .aspx file. The code in Listing 4-10 sets the properties of a second label, named Label2.

```
<%@ Register TagPrefix="mobile"
    Namespace="System.Web.UI.MobileControls"
    Assembly="System.Web.Mobile" %>
<%@ Page Inherits="MSPress.MobWeb.LblEx.MyWebForm" AutoEventWireup="False"
    Language="c#"  CodeBehind="LabelExample.aspx.cs" %>

<mobile:Form runat="server" id="Form1">
    <mobile:Label id="Label1" runat="server"
        StyleReference="title"
        Alignment="Center">
        Centered Title
    </mobile:Label>
    <mobile:Label id="Label2" runat="server"></mobile:Label>
</mobile:Form>
```

Listing 4-9 Source for LabelExample.aspx

```
using System;
using System.Web.UI.MobileControls;

namespace MSPress.MobWeb.LblEx
{
    public class MyWebForm : System.Web.UI.MobileControls.MobilePage
    {
        protected System.Web.UI.MobileControls.Label Label2;

        override protected void OnInit(EventArgs e)
        {
            InitializeComponent();
            base.OnInit(e);
        }

        private void InitializeComponent()
        {
            this.Load += new System.EventHandler(this.Page_Load);
        }

        protected void Page_Load(Object sender, EventArgs e)
        {
            Label2.Text = "This was set in code";
            Label2.Font.Italic = BooleanOption.True;
        }
    }
}
```

Listing 4-10 Code-behind module LabelExample.aspx.cs

Figure 4-9 shows the output of this application in Microsoft Internet Explorer and in the Openwave simulator.

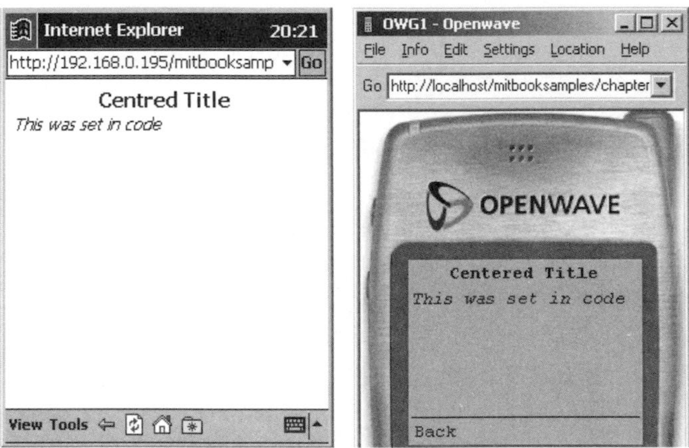

Figure 4-9 Output from the Label control examples

Link Controls

The Link control allows you to place a hyperlink on a page in order to link to another Form control or to an arbitrary Internet resource such as a URL.

Syntax

The Link control is represented in server control syntax as shown in the following listing. *NavigateUrl* is the most significant property. You can set this property to the ID of a Form control within your application, in which case, Link causes a postback to the server and control remains within your application. If you set *NavigateUrl* to the URL of some other resource, the client browser fetches from that resource and the execution of your application on that client ends.

```
<mobile:Link
    runat="server"
    id="id"
    Alignment="{NotSet|Left|Centre|Right}"
    BackColor="backgroundColor"
    BreakAfter=="{True|False}"
    Font-Bold="{NotSet|False|True}"
    Font-Italic="{NotSet|False|True}"
    Font-Name="fontName"
    Font-Size="{NotSet|Normal|Small|Large}"
    ForeColor="foregroundColor"
    StyleReference="StyleReference"
    Visible="{True|False}"
    Wrapping="{NotSet|Wrap|NoWrap}"
```

```
    NavigateUrl="target"
    SoftkeyLabel="softkeyLabel"
    Text="Text">
TextContent
</mobile:Link>
```

Properties

The Link control inherits the common properties from the *MobileControl* class (again, refer back to Table 4-1) and uses the *Text* property, as described in Table 4-9. The server control syntax doesn't expose any events.

Table 4-9 Significant Properties of the Link Control

Property	Type	Description
NavigateUrl	*String*	If the value of the *NavigateUrl* property begins with a pound sign (#), the code interprets the rest of the value as the ID of a Form control on the same mobile Web Forms page. Otherwise, the code interprets the value as the resource's *Uniform Resource Identifier* (URI). A URI is the identification of any content on the Internet. The most common form of URI is a Web address, which is a subset of URI, called a *Uniform Resource Locator* (URL).
SoftkeyLabel	*String*	Certain mobile devices, such as Nokia mobile phones with WML browsers, enable users to press a softkey under the screen to select a hyperlink. You set this property to override the default label displayed for this softkey. By default, this property is set to a blank string, which equates to a Go label on browsers that support this feature.
Text	*String*	You can designate the text to be displayed for the link either by using the *Text* attribute or by specifying the text as the content of the *<Link>* element. If you specify both, when the control is rendered, the attribute takes precedence. However, setting the *Text* property programmatically overrides any existing setting.

When a user selects the Link, the browser navigates to the resource that you have specified in the *NavigateUrl* property. You can use this control to allow the user to move between different Form controls within your application or to the URI of a resource on the Web.

The way a user selects a hyperlink differs between HTML and WML browsers. On HTML browsers, a user can click the link using a pointing device, such as a mouse or a stylus. But on WML browsers, the user usually selects the link by pressing a softkey or by selecting the link from a menu. (Mobile phones with WML browsers often have two softkeys, which are programmable buttons positioned beneath the display screen.) Therefore, if you're targeting your application at multiple browsers, you shouldn't supply your users with text prompts such as *Click the link below*, because the link below might actually be a softkey, or it might not even be below!

Using the Link Control

The first form shown in Listing 4-11 contains three links. The first two of these links access the other two forms, and the third link accesses a different application—the MSN Mobile service.

```
<%@ Register TagPrefix="mobile"
    Namespace="System.Web.UI.MobileControls"
    Assembly="System.Web.Mobile" %>
<%@ Page Inherits="System.Web.UI.MobileControls.MobilePage"
    Language="c#" %>

<mobile:Form runat="server" id="Form1">
    <mobile:Link id="Link1" runat="server"
                 SoftkeyLabel="->Hello"
                 NavigateURL="#Form2">
        GoTo Hello
    </mobile:Link>
    <mobile:Link id="Link2" runat="server"
                 SoftkeyLabel="->Bye"
                 NavigateURL="#Form3">
        GoTo Goodbye
    </mobile:Link>
    <mobile:Link id="Link3" runat="server"
                 StyleReference="subcommand" SoftkeyLabel="MSN"
                 NavigateURL="http://mobile.msn.com">
        MSN Mobile
    </mobile:Link>
</mobile:Form>

<mobile:Form id="Form2" runat="server">
    <B><I>Hello!</I></B>
</mobile:Form>

<mobile:Form id="Form3" runat="server">
    <B><I>Goodbye</I></B>
</mobile:Form>
```

Listing 4-11 Source code for LinkExample.aspx

Figure 4-10 shows how the page appears on two mobile devices, demonstrating how the *SoftkeyLabel* property is used on a WML browser.

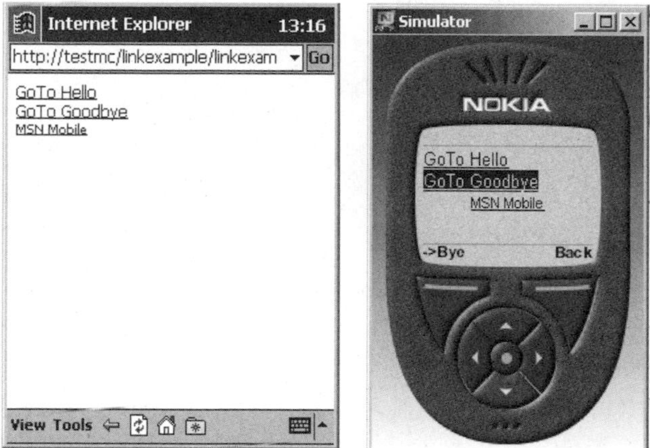

Figure 4-10 Links on the Pocket PC and the Nokia simulator

TextBox Controls

The TextBox control enables single-line input. Using this control, you can either display an initial default value or allow user input to modify or replace that initial value.

Syntax

You code the TextBox control in server control syntax, as shown in the following listing. Only the most commonly used attributes are listed. The common style attributes, such as *Font-**, *BackColor* and *ForeColor*, are ignored when the TextBox control is rendered, so they're not listed here. The *wmlFormat* attribute is a custom attribute used for defining the *Format* property of the WML *<input>* element. To use this attribute, custom attributes must be enabled, as described later in this section.

```
<mobile:TextBox
    runat="server"
    id="id"
    Alignment="{NotSet|Left|Centre|Right}"
    BreakAfter=="{True|False}"
    StyleReference="StyleReference"
    Visible="{True|False}"
    Wrapping="{NotSet|Wrap|NoWrap}"
```

```
    MaxLength="maxlength"
    Numeric="{True|False}"
    Password="{True|False}"
    OnTextChanged="textChangedEventHandler"
    Size="textBoxLength"
    Text="Text"
    Title="Text"
    WmlFormat="formatMask">
TextContent
</mobile:TextBox>
```

Properties

In addition to the common properties, methods, and events that the TextBox control inherits from the *MobileControl* class (as listed in Table 4-1 and Table 4-2), it contains the properties described in Table 4-10. The *Type* column describes the type of the property when setting or getting the property in code. Refer to the preceding "Syntax" section for valid values when setting the property in server control syntax.

Table 4-10 Significant Properties of the TextBox Control

Property	Type	Description
MaxLength	*Integer*	Sets or gets the maximum length allowed for the input text. Default is 0, which means that no limit exists.
Numeric	*True|False*	Sets or gets whether the input is to be forced to be numeric. This property has no effect with HTML browsers. When used with WML browsers, this property enforces numeric input on the device. On mobile phones, the browser usually switches the input mode of the phone keys from alphanumeric to numeric only.
Password	*True|False*	Sets or gets whether the input is accepted in a password style—that is, asterisks or another character masks the characters a user enters so that they're not readable.
Size	*Integer*	Desired length, in characters, of the rendered TextBox control. If you don't specify this property, the code uses a default length that's suitable for the target device. If the text the user enters exceeds the rendered control size, the input scrolls to allow further input.

Table 4-10 Significant Properties of the TextBox Control

Property	Type	Description
Text	*String*	This property is blank by default. You can designate the text to display either by using the *Text* attribute or by specifying the text as the content of the <*TextBox*> element. If you specify both, when the TextBox control is rendered, the *Text* attribute takes precedence. However, setting the *Text* property programmatically overrides any text defined through server control syntax.
Title	*String*	This property is ignored for HTML browsers. On WML browsers (for example, the Ericsson R320), *Title* can be used as a prompt. On the R320, if you don't specify *Title*, the browser supplies a default prompt of *Input*.
TextChanged (Event)	Event handler method name	Specifies the name of an event handler routine. When a user changes the text in the TextBox control and the changed value posts back to the server, the code calls the event handler routine specified as the value of this attribute. The routine must be of the type *EventHandlerMethodName(Object sender, System.EventArgs e)*.
wmlFormat	*String*	WML markup allows input to be constrained according to an input mask. For example, an input mask of *NNNNNN* forces the input to be exactly six numeric characters. For information about what formats can be applied, consult a WML language reference. This is a custom attribute, so custom attributes must be enabled to specify this attribute in server control syntax.

You can supply a default value to be displayed in the TextBox control by setting the *Text* property or by specifying the text as the content of this element. However, it's possible to supply a value that exceeds the maximum length you've set using the *MaxLength* property. The *MaxLength* property limits the length of the value the user can enter, but if he or she accepts the default value that you've provided, the text passed back to your program can exceed this length.

The *TextChanged* event allows you to specify the name of an event handler method that the code calls when a user changes the value of the *Text* property. The TextBox control doesn't itself trigger a postback, so when the user changes the text in a TextBox control, the event isn't raised immediately. The

Form control still must contain a control that does trigger postback, such as a Command control to post the changes back to the server.

The TextBox control is rendered in the appropriate style for the input box on each target platform. This control can't contain any other controls.

> **Warning** If you want devices with WML browsers to access your application, you can't use the same ID property for TextBox controls that reside on different mobile Web Forms pages within the *same* application—in other words, controls that are fetched from the same Web site. For example, your application could start in one .aspx file and contain a link that at some point transfers execution to a second .aspx file. Each Web Forms page might contain a TextBox control with the ID *TextBox1*. This is programmatically correct because each *TextBox1* ID exists in a different ASP.NET class and therefore has a different fully qualified name.
>
> However, pages with controls of the same name can lead to unexpected behavior on some WML version 1.1 browsers. Values entered in a WML *<input>* element are stored in variables, which in turn are stored in a browser cache. Because the runtime uses the ID of the TextBox control to derive the variable name, TextBox controls that use the same ID will use the same variable. When some WML 1.1 browsers encounter an *<input>* element that uses the same variable name that was used by another *<input>* element in a card from the same site, they display the cached value that was entered in the first *<input>* element as the default value for the second.

Using Custom Attributes

Custom attributes, such as the *wmlFormat* property mentioned in the preceding section, differ from the primary attributes of a control. You enable custom attributes in one of two ways:

- Set an attribute for the *<mobileControls>* section in the application Web.config file, which applies to all pages in the application, as shown here:

```
<configuration>
    <system.web>
        ⋮
        <mobileControls allowCustomAttributes="True" />
```

```
        ⋮
    </system.web>
</configuration>
```

- Set the *AllowCustomAttributes* property of the *MobilePage* object to *True* in code. This setting applies to all controls on the page, as shown here:

```
private void Page_Load(object sender, System.EventArgs e)
{
    this.AllowCustomAttributes = true;
    ⋮
}
```

If you don't enable custom attributes, you'll get a parsing error when you attempt to use the *wmlFormat* attribute. Be careful when custom attributes are enabled, however, because any misspellings of standard attributes will no longer be detected during parsing. For example, the misspelled *Alignmet* attribute will be saved as a custom attribute of that name—the parser doesn't report it as an error.

Using the TextBox Control

In Listing 4-12 and Listing 4-13, the user enters a password, reenters it to confirm it then clicks OK, which causes the entry to post to the server and makes a call to the *TextChanged* event handler, which compares the two password entries. If the entries don't match, an error message appears and the user must reenter the password, as shown in Figure 4-11. Be aware that you can achieve this kind of field validation more effectively by using the CompareValidator control, which we'll discuss in Chapter 5.

```
<%@ Register TagPrefix="mobile"
    Namespace="System.Web.UI.MobileControls"
    Assembly="System.Web.Mobile" %>
<%@ Page Inherits="MSPress.MobWeb.TBEx.MyWebForm" AutoEventWireup="False"
    Language="c#" CodeBehind="TextBoxExample.aspx.cs" %>

<mobile:Form runat="server" id="Form1" title="Confirm Password">
    <mobile:Label runat="server" id="Label1">
        Enter new password</mobile:Label>
    <mobile:Label runat="server" id="Label2" Visible="False"/>
    <mobile:TextBox runat="server" id="TextBox1"
                    Password="True">
    </mobile:TextBox>
    <mobile:Label runat="server" id="Label3">
        Confirm password
```

Listing 4-12 Source code for TextBoxExample.aspx

```
    </mobile:Label>
    <mobile:TextBox runat="server" id="TextBox2"
                    Password="True"/>
    <mobile:Label runat="server" id="Label4"/>
    <mobile:Command runat="server" id="cmdButton">OK</mobile:Command>
</mobile:Form>
```

```
using System;
using System.Web.UI.MobileControls;

namespace MSPress.MobWeb.TBEx
{
    public class MyWebForm : System.Web.UI.MobileControls.MobilePage
    {
        protected System.Web.UI.MobileControls.Label Label1;
        protected System.Web.UI.MobileControls.Label Label2;
        protected System.Web.UI.MobileControls.Label Label3;
        protected System.Web.UI.MobileControls.Label Label4;
        protected System.Web.UI.MobileControls.TextBox TextBox1;
        protected System.Web.UI.MobileControls.Command cmdButton;
        protected System.Web.UI.MobileControls.Form Form1;
        protected System.Web.UI.MobileControls.TextBox TextBox2;

        override protected void OnInit(EventArgs e)
        {
            InitializeComponent();
            base.OnInit(e);
        }

        private void InitializeComponent()
        {
            this.TextBox2.TextChanged +=
                new System.EventHandler(this.Verify_OnTextChanged);
            this.cmdButton.Click +=
                new System.EventHandler(this.cmdButton_Click);

        }

        protected void Verify_OnTextChanged(Object sender, EventArgs e)
        {
            if (TextBox1.Text != TextBox2.Text)
            {
                Label2.Visible = true;
                Label2.StyleReference = "error";
```

Listing 4-13 Code-behind file TextBoxExample.aspx.cs

```
                Label2.Text = "No match - please reenter";
            }
        }

        protected void cmdButton_Click(Object sender, EventArgs e)
        {
            if (TextBox1.Text == TextBox2.Text)
            {
                Label1.Visible = false;
                Label2.Visible = false;
                Label3.Visible = false;
                TextBox1.Visible = false;
                TextBox2.Visible = false;
                Label4.Text = "Confirmed - Thanks";
            }
        }
    }
}
```

Figure 4-11 Output generated by the TextBox control sample

TextView Controls

The TextView control allows you to display text that's too long for the Label control. Unlike Label, TextView supports internal pagination, so very long blocks of text are split across multiple display pages when the enclosing Form control has pagination enabled. TextView also supports embedded markup tags, in the same way as literal text on a Form control. (See Table 4-3 for details of the allowable tags.)

Syntax

In server control syntax, you code the TextView control like this:

```
<mobile:TextView
    runat="server"
    id="id"
    Alignment="{NotSet|Left|Centre|Right}"
    BackColor="backgroundColor"
    BreakAfter=="{True|False}"
    Font-Bold="{NotSet|False|True}"
    Font-Italic="{NotSet|False|True}"
    Font-Name="fontName"
    Font-Size="{NotSet|Normal|Small|Large}"
    ForeColor="foregroundColor"
    StyleReference="StyleReference"
    Visible="{True|False}"
    Wrapping="{NotSet|Wrap|NoWrap}"

    Text="Text">
TextContent
</mobile:TextView>
```

Properties

The significant property of the TextView control is the Text property. Table 4-11 describes the use of this property.

Table 4-11 Significant Property of the TextView Control

Property	Type	Description
Text	*String*	This is blank by default. You can designate the text to be displayed either by using the *Text* attribute or by specifying the text as the content of the *<TextView>* element. If you specify both the content and the attribute, the element's content takes precedence at run time. However, setting the *Text* property programmatically overrides any text defined through server control syntax.

The TextView control allows you to display larger amounts of text. As Table 4-11 shows, you can specify the text that you want to display in ASP.NET server control syntax using the *Text* attribute or the TextView element content. However, you'll probably specify the content you want to display programmatically, by setting the *Text* property of the *TextView* class.

The text content you display in the control can include literal text as well as certain markup elements such as *
*, *<i>* and so on. This behavior is the same as literal text in a Form control. (Refer to Table 4-3 for details of the markup elements you can use.)

With Visual Studio .NET, you don't have to code the text directly into the HTML view of the mobile Web Forms page. Instead, you can click the TextView control in Design view and then click the ellipsis (...) button adjacent to the *Text* property in the Properties window.

Doing so opens the text editor shown in Figure 4-12. When you enter text in this editor, don't type in the literal tags (for example, **<b>This text is in boldface</b>**). If you do, the tags will be treated as literal text—they will appear on the target device and won't format the text. Instead, use the Bold, Italic, and Anchor buttons at the top of the text editor screen.

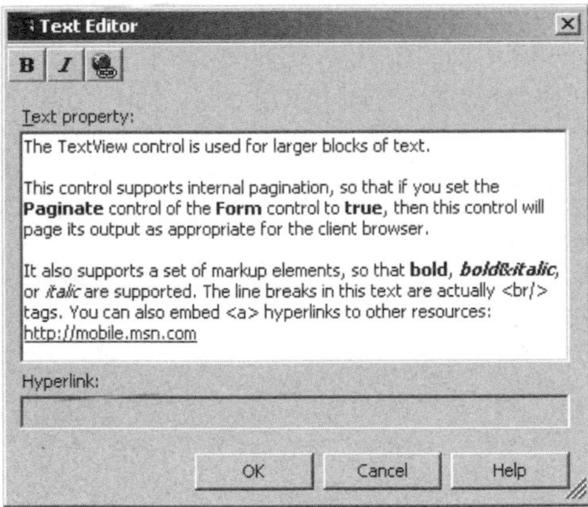

Figure 4-12 Visual Studio .NET text editor for the TextView control

The TextView control supports internal pagination, which means it can split its content across multiple display screens if the *Form.Paginate* property is set to *True* in the enclosing Form control. The Form control will then ensure that any text that's too big to display on a single screen of a particular device gets split onto multiple screens. The Mobile Internet Controls Runtime will provide the necessary navigation support.

Using the TextView Control

Listing 4-14 displays the text as literal text within the server control syntax of the mobile Web Forms page.

```
<%@ Page language="c#"
    Inherits="System.Web.UI.MobileControls.MobilePage" %>
<%@ Register TagPrefix="mobile"
    Namespace="System.Web.UI.MobileControls"
    Assembly="System.Web.Mobile" %>

<mobile:Form runat="server" id="Form1" Paginate="True">
    <mobile:Label id="Label1" runat="server" StyleReference="title"
                  Alignment="Center">
        TextView In Use
    </mobile:Label>
    <mobile:TextView id="TextView1" runat="server">
        The TextView control is used for larger blocks of text.
        <br />
        <br />
        This control supports internal pagination so that if you set
        the <b>Paginate</b> control of the <b>Form</b> control to
        <b>true</b>, this control will page its output as
        appropriate for the client browser.<br />
        <br />
        It also supports a set of markup elements so that <b>bold</b>,
        <b><i>bold&amp;italic</i></b>, or <i>italic </i>are supported.
        The line breaks in this text are actually &lt;br/&gt; tags.
        You can also embed &lt;a&gt; hyperlinks to other resources:
        <br />
        <a href='http://mobile.msn.com'>http://mobile.msn.com</a>
    </mobile:TextView>
</mobile:Form>
```

Listing 4-14 Source code for TextViewExample.aspx

Figure 4-13 shows how this text would appear on both a Pocket PC and the Openwave simulator.

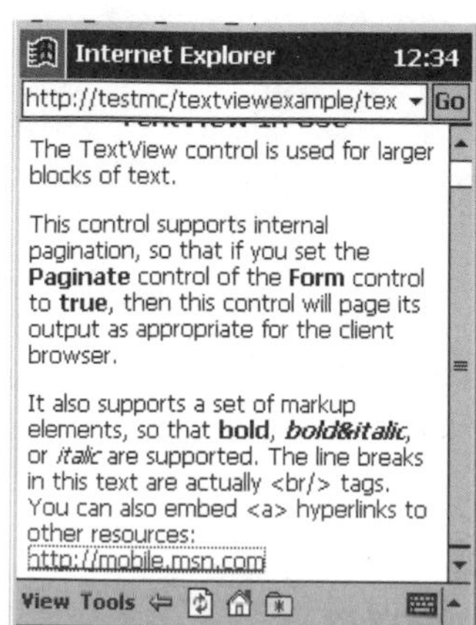

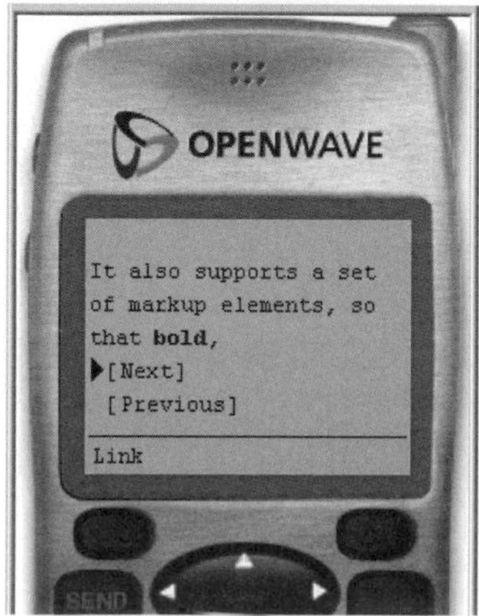

Figure 4-13 Larger blocks of text displayed on two mobile devices

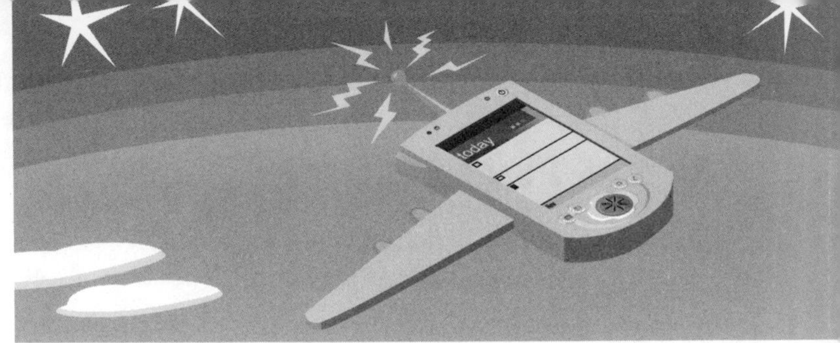

5

Special-Purpose Controls and Validation Controls

In this chapter, we describe two groups of controls: special-purpose controls and validation controls. These controls aren't necessarily commonplace—that is, you won't use them in every application—but they do provide neat solutions to specific problems that mobile Web application developers sometimes face.

The special-purpose controls are

- Calendar
- PhoneCall
- AdRotator

The validation controls group consists of

- CompareValidator
- CustomValidator
- RangeValidator
- RegularExpressionValidator
- RequiredFieldValidator
- ValidationSummary

Special-Purpose Controls

ASP.NET mobile controls supplies three special-purpose controls to assist you in building feature-rich mobile Web applications: Calendar, PhoneCall, and AdRotator, shown in Figure 5-1.

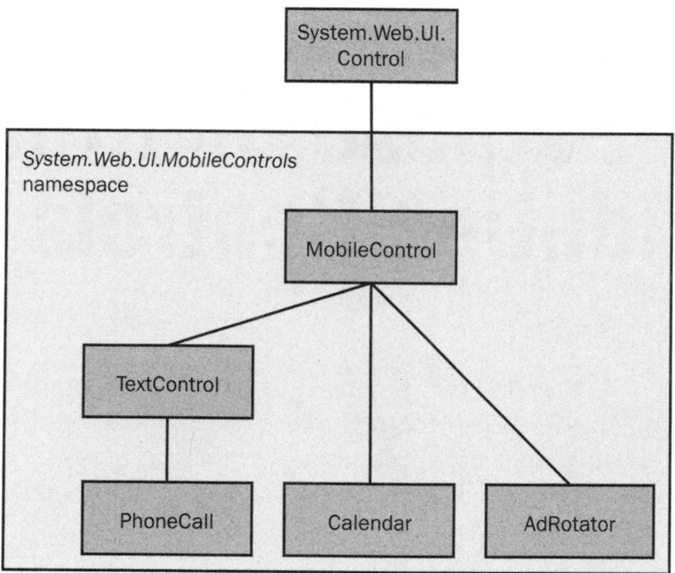

Figure 5-1 Class hierarchy of the special-purpose controls

The Calendar control allows a user to select a date. It renders the date differently on HTML and Wireless Markup Language (WML) browsers, allowing for any display and input limitations of mobile phone devices. The PhoneCall control allows your application to initiate a voice call on mobile phones or supply a visual prompt on devices that don't support telephony. The AdRotator control allows you to display banner advertisements in different graphical formats to suit the display capabilities of the target device.

Calendar Control

The Calendar control allows you to easily integrate date-selection functionality into a mobile Web application. This control provides an interface from which a user can select an individual day from any calendar month of any year—past, present, or future. The control also provides a number of modes that determine what range of dates the user can select. For example, the user could select a single day, a week, or an entire month.

The standard Microsoft ASP.NET Calendar control presents the user with a graphical representation of a single month. However, this representation isn't possible on some mobile devices because of the limited size of their display area. Instead, the mobile Calendar control will appear differently to suit the display characteristics of the target device. For example, a desktop HTML browser might present a full calendar, whereas a mobile phone with a WML browser might present a hierarchy of links, as Figure 5-2 illustrates.

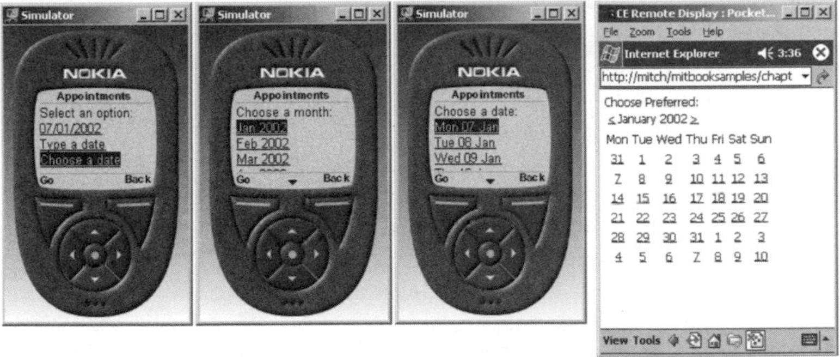

Figure 5-2 The Calendar control on a WML browser and an HTML browser

Every time a user selects a date from the Calendar control, the remote form makes an HTTP Post back to the server, so you do not need to place an additional control on the Form that performs a postback, such as a Command control.

Syntax

You code the Calendar control in server control syntax using the properties and values shown in the following listing. See Table 5-1 below for information on the meaning of the properties.

When you're defining dates as a string, as you do when setting the *SelectedDate* or *VisibleDateMonth* properties in server control syntax, the rules that apply are the same as those for the *System.DateTime.Parse* method. This means that the string is parsed according to the cultural-specific norms. For example, in U.S. English, *"03/02/2003"*, *"2003-03-02"*, *"2 Mar 2003"*, and *"2 March 2003"* all parse to a *DateTime* object set to the 2nd March, 2003. See Chapter 14 for details of how to define a particular culture for your mobile Web forms page.

```
<mobile:Calendar
    runat="server"
    id="id"
    BreakAfter="{True|False}"
    Font-Name="fontName"
    Font-Size="{NotSet|Normal|Small|Large}"
    Font-Bold="{NotSet|False|True}"
    Font-Italic="{NotSet|False|True}"
    ForeColor="foregroundColor"
    BackColor="backgroundColor"
    Alignment="{NotSet|Left|Center|Right}"
    StyleReference="styleReference"
    Visible="{True|False}"
    Wrapping="{NotSet|Wrap|NoWrap}"

    CalendarEntryText="prompt string"
    FirstDayOfWeek="{Default|Sunday|Monday|Tuesday|Wednesday|
        Thursday|Friday|Saturday|Sunday}"
    OnSelectionChanged="selectionChangedHandler"
    SelectedDate="selectedDate"
    SelectionMode="{None|Day|DayWeek|DayWeekMonth}"
    ShowDayHeader="{True|False}"
    VisibleDate="visibleDateMonth"
/>
```

Properties

Table 5-1 shows the most significant properties of the Calendar control. The Description column describes the usage of the property whether used in server control syntax, or when programming the class in code. The Type column describes the type of the property when setting or getting the property in code. Refer to the preceding “Syntax” section for valid values when setting the property in server control syntax. Note, however, that this table doesn’t list the properties and events that the Calendar control inherits from the *MobileControl* class. (See Table 4-1 and Table 4-2 for that information.)

The Calendar control observes the setting of the *BreakAfter* property (inherited from *MobileControl*) only on HTML browsers. On WML and compact HTML (cHTML) browsers, the calendar is displayed as a link within the mobile page. The default text of this link is *Calendar*, or its localized equivalent; you override this default by using the *CalendarEntryText* property.

Table 5-1 Significant Properties and Events of the Calendar Control

Property	Type	Description
CalendarEntry-Text	*String*	Sets or gets the text used on WML and cHTML devices for the link to enter the Calendar control.
FirstDayOfWeek	*System.Web.UI.Web-Controls.FirstDayOf-Week* enumeration (for example, *First-DayOfWeek.Friday*)	The first day of the week on which a list of the days of the week begins. Possible values are one of the *System.Web.UI.Web-Controls.FirstDayOfWeek* enumeration values (for example, *FirstDayOfWeek.Friday*). The default value is *FirstDayOfWeek.Default* which establishes the first day from the server's locale settings.
SelectedDate	*DateTime* object	Sets or gets the date selected in the control. This date is highlighted when the browser renders the control. On browsers that don't show the calendar graphically, the selected date appears as a subheading that precedes the date-selection options. The default value is today's date.
SelectedDates	Collection of *DateTime* objects	Gets the currently selected dates returned as a *SelectedDatesCollection* object. In code, you can use the *Add* and *Clear* methods to modify the dates in this collection. This property is not valid in server control syntax.
SelectionMode	*System.Web.UI. WebControls. Calendar-SelectionMode* enumeration: *None|Day|Day-Week|DayWeek-Month*	Controls the date units that the user can select. If this property is set to *None*, no date is selectable. If it's set to *Day*, individual days are selectable. *DayWeek* allows the user to select an individual day or week and *Day-WeekMonth* allows the user to select an individual day, week, or month.
ShowDayHeader	*True|False*	Accepts a Boolean value of *True* or *False* that indicates whether the display accompanies dates with an indication of the day of the week.
VisibleDate	*DateTime* object	Controls which month is displayed to the user when the browser renders the calendar. You can use any day in the month because only the month and year values of the *DateTime* object are used.

Table 5-1 Significant Properties and Events of the Calendar Control

Property	Type	Description
WebCalendar	*System.Web.UI.WebControls.Calendar* (Get only)	A *MobileControls.Calendar* object wraps an instance of *System.Web.UI.WebControls.Calendar*, which is exposed through this property. Use this property to set properties of the wrapped *WebControls.Calendar* instance. Consult the *WebControls.Calendar* documentation in the .NET Framework SDK documentation for details of the properties available. If you set any properties of the underlying WebCalendar control, they will take effect only with HTML and cHTML clients.
SelectionChanged (Event)	Event handler method name	Specifies the event handler to call when a user changes the dates selected in the control.

The Calendar control has one event, *SelectionChanged*. The event fires each time the user selects a date. Listings 5-1 and 5-2 in the following section show how the *SelectionChange* event is used in a mobile Web application.

Using the Calendar Control

Listings 5-1 and 5-2 display the code for a calendar from which the user can select individual days or weeks. When the user makes a selection, the *SelectionChanged* event fires and the application makes an HTTP Post to the server. On the server, the event handler sets the value of the current form's label to match the date the user selected.

```
<%@ Register TagPrefix="mobile"
    Namespace="System.Web.UI.MobileControls"
    Assembly="System.Web.Mobile" %>
<%@ Page language="c#" Codebehind="CalendarExample.aspx.cs"
    Inherits="MSPress.MobWeb.CalEx.CalendarExampleMobileWebForm" %>

<mobile:Form id="Form1" runat="server">
    <mobile:Calendar id="Calendar1" runat="server"
        SelectedDate="2001-07-21"
        SelectionMode="DayWeek"
        Alignment="Center"
```

Listing 5-1 Source for CalendarExample.aspx

```
        OnSelectionChanged="Calendar1_SelectionChanged">
    </mobile:Calendar>
    <mobile:Label id="Label1" runat="server" Alignment="Center"/>
</mobile:Form>
```

```
using System;
using System.Web.UI.MobileControls;

namespace MSPress.MobWeb.CalEx
{
    public class CalendarExampleMobileWebForm :
        System.Web.UI.MobileControls.MobilePage
    {
        protected System.Web.UI.MobileControls.Calendar Calendar1;
        protected System.Web.UI.MobileControls.Form Form1;
        protected System.Web.UI.MobileControls.Label Label1;

        override protected void OnInit(EventArgs e)
        {
            InitializeComponent();
            base.OnInit(e);
        }

        private void InitializeComponent()
        {
            this.Calendar1.SelectionChanged +=
                new System.EventHandler(this. Calendar1_SelectionChanged);
        }

        protected void Calendar1_SelectionChanged(
            object sender,
            System.EventArgs e)
        {
            Label1.Text=Calendar1.SelectedDate.ToShortDateString();
        }
    }
}
```

Listing 5-2 Code-behind file CalendarExample.aspx.cs

When the form data posts back to the server, the code assigns *Label1* the selected date, which is then displayed to the user. Figure 5-3 shows an Openwave simulator displaying calendar options and the label with the selected date.

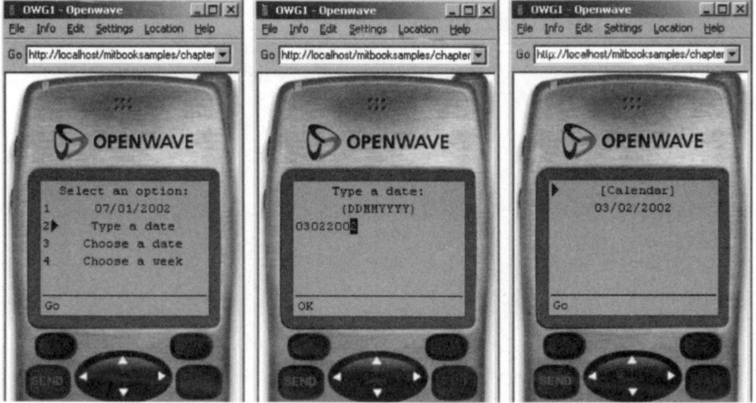

Figure 5-3 Output from the Calendar control example in the Openwave simulator

PhoneCall Control

Mobile data services increase the functionality of mobile phones and allow the user to access information in ways that simply weren't possible in the past. For example, a mobile phone with access to mobile data services can access ASP.NET Web sites written using the ASP.NET mobile controls. The possibilities for mobile Internet services are seemingly unlimited. With all this new functionality, it's sometimes easy to overlook the primary use of mobile phones. They really are quite suitable for making voice calls! The PhoneCall control allows you to easily take advantage of a mobile phone's voice call capabilities.

Mobile phones offer two main options for programmatically initiating voice calls:

- Full programmatic access that automatically initiates a voice call, although the device might ask the user whether he or she wants to make the call
- A Use Number option that allows a user to optionally call a number within a page, regardless of whether the phone displays that number to the user

The PhoneCall control uses automatic call initiation if the mobile phone supports this. Otherwise, the control displays a link that the user can select. Selecting the link can initiate the call or prompt the user about whether to do so. Figure 5-4 shows this latter option.

Figure 5-4 The Nokia Use Number option

Syntax

You code the PhoneCall control in server control syntax using the properties and values shown in the following listing. See Table 5-2 for descriptions of the purpose of the properties.

```
<mobile:PhoneCall
    runat="server"
    id="id"
    BreakAfter="{True|False}"
    Font-Name="fontName"
    Font-Size="{NotSet|Normal|Small|Large}"
    Font-Bold="{NotSet|False|True}"
    Font-Italic="{NotSet|False|True}"
    ForeColor="foregroundColor"
    BackColor="backgroundColor"
    Alignment="{NotSet|Left|Center|Right}"
    StyleReference="styleReference"
    Text="text"
    Visible="{True|False}"
    Wrapping="{NotSet|Wrap|NoWrap}"

    AlternateFormat="alternateText"
    AlternateURL="targetURL"
    PhoneNumber="phoneNumber"
    SoftkeyLabel="text"
    Text="text">
innerText
</mobile:PhoneCall>
```

Properties

Table 5-2 shows the noninherited properties of the PhoneCall control. The properties and events inherited from the *MobileControl* base class are shown in Table 4-1 and Table 4-2.

Table 5-2 Significant Properties of the PhoneCall Control

Property	Type	Description
AlternateFormat	*String*	The format of the message displayed on devices that can't make voice calls. The string you supply can include two placeholders, *{0}* and *{1}*. The *Text* property is displayed in place of the *{0}* placeholder, and the *PhoneNumber* property is displayed in place of the *{1}* placeholder. The default value for this property is "*{0} {1}*". You can change the value to display a custom message. For example, *Call support on {1}* will display *Call support on* followed by the value of the *PhoneNumber* property.
AlternateURL	*String*	The absolute or relative URL of the page to access if the device can't make calls or the user doesn't want to make a call.
PhoneNumber	*String*	The phone number to call, formatted as *country code | national number | short number*. You can format the number's sections, including any of these characters: left parenthesis [( ] right parenthesis [ )] period [.] hyphen [-] space [ ] The country code is optional, but if specified, it must be prefixed with a plus sign (+). If a short number is used, it must be prefixed with a pound sign (#). On i-mode devices, the number must begin with a zero or #.
SoftkeyLabel	*String*	On certain WML browsers, a softkey beneath the display screen can be pressed to initiate the call. This property sets the prompt displayed above the softkey. Keep this prompt to around seven characters or less.
Text	*String*	Specifies the message displayed on the link to initiate a call.

Using the PhoneCall Control

The code in Listing 5-3 prompts the user to press a link, which initiates a call to customer support.

```
<%@ Page Inherits="System.Web.UI.MobileControls.MobilePage"
    Language="c#"%>
<%@ Register TagPrefix="mobile"
    Namespace="System.Web.UI.MobileControls"
    Assembly="System.Web.Mobile" %>

<mobile:Form id="Form1" runat="server">
    <mobile:PhoneCall runat="server"
        AlternateFormat="Call {0} on {1}"
        AlternateURL="http://www.northwindtraders.com"
        phoneNumber="123-456-7890"
        Text="Northwind Traders">
    </mobile:PhoneCall>
</mobile:Form>
```

Listing 5-3 Source for PhoneCallExample.aspx

When the page loads, one of two events occurs, depending on the capabilities of the mobile phone. In the first instance, a call automatically initiates to the phone number 123-456-7890, although the phone might first prompt the user about whether he or she wants to make the call. The alternative event displays the phone number to the user, who can then initiate a call either by using a Use Number option or manually entering the phone number with the phone's keypad. Figure 5-4 illustrates both scenarios.

AdRotator Control

Current Internet marketing strategies require that advertisements rotate frequently to give the maximum number of people as many viewings as possible. But rotating advertisements is often a time-consuming, awkward practice. Microsoft addressed this issue in Active Server Pages (ASP) by supplying an AdRotator component. ASP.NET greatly improves upon this component; it's now much simpler to use.

The AdRotator control provides an advertisement rotation service that you can easily insert into a mobile Web Forms page. This mobile control enables you to provide graphical advertisements that match the graphics formats the target device supports. An XML configuration file references the source graphics files. The XML file must comply with a prespecified format. Table 5-3 shows the permissible elements, and Listing 5-4 offers an example of such an XML configuration file.

Table 5-3 XML Configuration File Elements for AdRotator

Attribute	Description
Advertisements	The root element of the configuration file. Only one *<Advertisements>* element can exist in a file.
Ad	The child of the root element. This attribute contains information pertaining to each advertisement.
ImageUrl	The relative or absolute path to the image to be displayed.
MonoImageUrl	The relative or absolute path to the monochrome image to be displayed. Typically, this is a WBMP file for WML browsers.
NavigateUrl	The absolute or relative URL of the page that is displayed when the user presses the advertisement link.
AlternateText	The text that is displayed if the target device can't display the image.
Keyword	Represents the advertisement category. This attribute allows you to categorize advertisements—for example, as hardware or software.
Impressions	Determines how many times a given advertisement is displayed compared to the other advertisements in the configuration file.

> **Warning** The names of the XML elements in the advertisement configuration file are case sensitive. For example, *<ImageUrl>* is a valid XML element name, but *<ImageURL>* isn't.

```
<?xml version="1.0"?>
<Advertisements>
    <Ad>
        <ImageUrl>ColorImage.gif</ImageUrl>
        <MonoImageUrl>Northwind.wbmp</MonoImageUrl>
        <NavigateUrl>http://northwindtraders.com</NavigateUrl>
        <AlternateText>Buy this!</AlternateText>
        <Keyword>Software</Keyword>
        <Impressions>2</Impressions>
    </Ad>
    <Ad>
         <!---Another advertisement defined here -->
    </Ad>
</Advertisements>
```

Listing 5-4 Advertisements.xml

Syntax

You code the AdRotator control in server control syntax using the properties and values shown in the following listing. See Table 5-4 for descriptions of the purpose of the properties.

```
<mobile:AdRotator
    runat="server"
    id="id"
    Font-Name="fontName"
    Font-Size="{NotSet|Normal|Small|Large}"
    Font-Bold="{NotSet|False|True}"
    Font-Italic="{NotSet|False|True}"
    ForeColor="foregroundColor"
    BackColor="backgroundColor"
    Alignment="{NotSet|Left|Center|Right}"
    StyleReference="styleReference"
    Visible="{True|False}"
    Wrapping="{NotSet|Wrap|NoWrap}"

    AdvertisementFile="relativeURL"
    ImageKey="XML element"
    KeywordFilter="keywordFilter"
    NavigateUrlKey="XML element"
    OnAdCreated="clickHandler">
<!--DeviceSpecific/Choice construct (optional)-->
</mobile:AdRotator>
```

Properties

Table 5-4 explains the noninherited properties of the AdRotator control. See Table 4-1 and Table 4-2 for details of those properties and events that are inherited from MobileControl. The Type column describes the type of the property when setting or getting the property in code. Refer to the preceding "Syntax" section for valid values when setting the property in server control syntax.

Table 5-4 Significant Properties and Events of the AdRotator Control

Property or Event	Type	Description
Advertisement-File	*String*	The absolute or relative URL to the XML advertisement configuration file. The XML file must reside within the same Web site as your application. We strongly recommend that you place the file within the same Web application. This property can specify an absolute path or a path relative to the location of the mobile page or user control that contains the AdRotator control.

Table 5-4 Significant Properties and Events of the AdRotator Control

Property or Event	Type	Description
ImageKey	*String*	The XML element name in the Advertisement file that contains the URL of the image to be displayed. The default value is *"ImageUrl"*, which means that the <*ImageUrl*> element in the XML file contains the URL of the image. This property is often used within DeviceSpecific/Choice constructs so that a different XML element specifies the image to be used on certain client devices, as shown in Listing 5-5 in the following section.
KeywordFilter	*String*	The keyword used to filter the advertisement categories. *KeywordFilter* allows you to select categories of advertisements from the named configuration file to use in the application. For example, if you set the value of this property to software and the advertisement configuration file contains <*Ad*> elements for both software and hardware, only the software elements will be displayed.
NavigateUrlKey	*String*	The XML element name in the Advertisement file that contains the URL to which the user is transferred when he or she selects an advertisement. The default value is *NavigateUrl*, which means that <*NavigateUrl*> element in the XML file is used. This property is often used within DeviceSpecific/Choice constructs so that a different destination URL is used on certain client devices.
AdCreated (Event)	Event handler method	The runtime raises this event each time it selects an advertisement for display. The event handler has the signature *Method(Object sender, System.Web.UI.WebControls.AdCreatedArgs e)*. The *AdCreatedArgs* object contains *AdProperties*, *AlternateText*, *ImageUrl*, and *NavigateUrl* properties that describe the advertisement to be displayed.

Using the AdRotator control

Listings 5-5, 5-6, and 5-7 use the AdRotator control to display an advertisement to users.

```
<%@ Page Inherits="System.Web.UI.MobileControls.MobilePage"
    Language="c#" %>
<%@ Register TagPrefix="mobile"
    Namespace="System.Web.UI.MobileControls"
    Assembly="System.Web.Mobile"  %>
```

Listing 5-5 Source for AdRotatorExample.aspx

```
<mobile:Form id="Form1" runat="server">
    <mobile:AdRotator id="AdRotator1" runat="server"
        AdvertisementFile="AdConfig.xml">
        <DeviceSpecific>
            <Choice Filter="isWML11"
                ImageKey="WAPImageUrl"
                NavigateUrlKey="WAPNavigateUrl"/>
        </DeviceSpecific>
    </mobile:AdRotator>
</mobile:Form>
```

```
<?xml version="1.0" encoding="utf-8" ?>
<Advertisements>
    <Ad>
        <ImageUrl>ad1.gif</ImageUrl>
        <WAPImageUrl>ad1.wbmp</WAPImageUrl>
        <NavigateUrl>http://www.microsoft.com/net</NavigateUrl>
        <WAPNavigateUrl>http://news.wirelessdevnet.com/</WAPNavigateUrl>
        <AlternateText>Info on .NET</AlternateText>
        <Keyword>Complus</Keyword>
        <Impressions>2</Impressions>
    </Ad>
    <Ad>
        <ImageUrl>ad2.gif</ImageUrl>
        <WAPImageUrl>ad2.wbmp</WAPImageUrl>
        <NavigateUrl>http://msdn.microsoft.com</NavigateUrl>
        <WAPNavigateUrl>http://news.wirelessdevnet.com/</WAPNavigateUrl>
        <AlternateText>MSDN Developer Support</AlternateText>
        <Keyword>Support</Keyword>
        <Impressions>1</Impressions>
    </Ad>
</Advertisements>
```

Listing 5-6 Configuration file AdConfig.xml

```
<?xml version="1.0" encoding="utf-8" ?>
<configuration>
  <system.web>
    ⋮
    <deviceFilters>
        <filter name="isWML11"
                compare="preferredRenderingType"
                argument="wml11" />
    </deviceFilters>
  </system.web>
</configuration>
```

Listing 5-7 Web.config containing the isWML11 device filter required by this example

> **Note** If you use Microsoft Visual Studio .NET to build your application, you must add the XML advertisement configuration file and the graphics files to the current project. To add a file to an open project, go to the File menu and click Add Existing Item. In the Add Existing Item dialog box, select the file you want to add and click the Open button.

Validation Controls

Form validation is an essential part of any mobile Web application. You perform validation for a number of reasons—among them, ensuring that your code meets these conditions:

- Form fields are completed.
- Values correspond to a particular format, such as an e-mail address.
- Two fields contain the same value—for example, when a user enters his or her password and confirms it.

Traditionally, performing these tasks has required server-side programming, which often requires extensive use of complex regular expressions. If you've worked with regular expressions before, you know how troublesome programming them can be.

ASP.NET offers a new, flexible method of performing form validation: using server validation controls. These controls allow you to perform complex validation tasks by simply inserting server validation control tags in your Web Forms page. The controls enable actions that range from straightforward checking of field completion to comparing user input against regular expressions. Figure 5-5 shows the class hierarchy of the mobile validation controls.

You use the RequiredFieldValidator control to ensure that a user cannot exit a Form until they have entered a value in some other control, such as a TextBox. The CompareValidator control is used to compare the values in two other controls on the page, for example TextBox1.Text == TextBox2.Text, and allow the user to leave the Form only if the comparison statement evaluates *True*. The RangeValidator control verifies that the user has entered a value into an entry field that lies between limit values that you specify. The RegularExpressionValidator control allows you to check that the value of a field conforms to a given character pattern, for example that it is a valid e-mail address, a ZIP code, or a social security number. The CustomValidator control allows you to write your own validation method; during page validation, your custom validation method is used alongside all the standard validation controls. The ValidationSummary control is used to amalgamate the output from all the validation controls on a Web Forms page so that the error messages can be presented together, rather then singly.

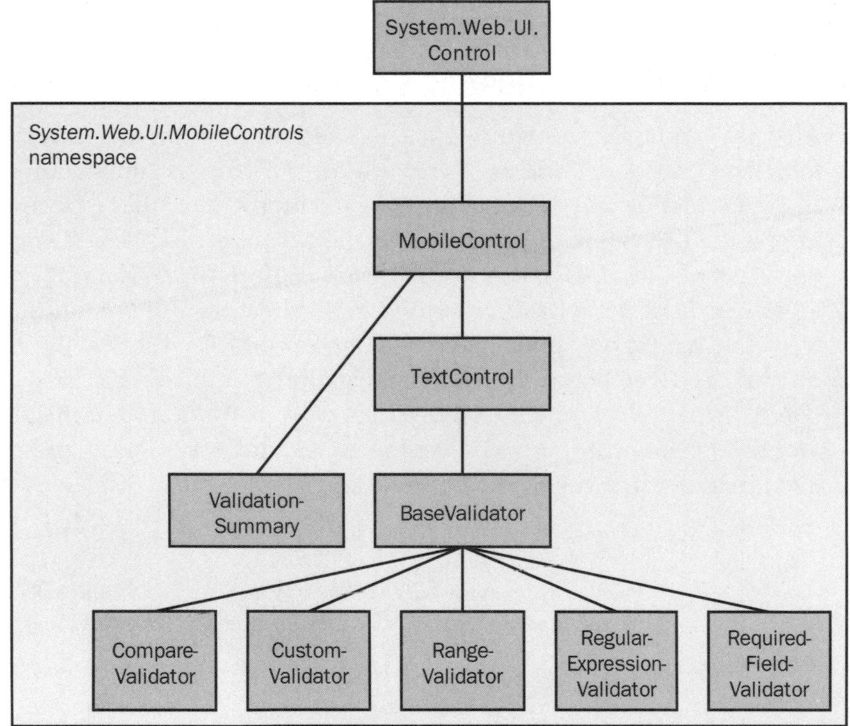

Figure 5-5 Class hierarchy of the server validation controls

The mobile validation controls provide functionality similar to a set of ASP.NET controls intended for validating desktop client input. However, unlike the ASP.NET controls, which might add Microsoft JScript to the Web page sent to desktop browsers to perform client-side validation, the mobile validation controls *never* execute on the client. Instead, they execute on the server, after the client posts the form data. If the data is invalid, you can program against this result or allow ASP.NET to return the page to the user for correction.

> **Note** Server validation controls used within mobile Web applications always execute on the server. However, in standard ASP.NET, you can execute some of the validation controls on the client by using client-side script. You can't do this with mobile applications, even if you know that a client supports client-side script.

Common Behavior of the Validation Controls

All the Validation controls, except ValidationSummary, inherit from *System.Web.UI.MobileControls.BaseValidator*. The most important property is *IsValid* which is *true* if the control's validation criteria have been satisfied, or *false* if the user's input has failed validation. The *System.Web.UI.Page* class (parent class of the *MobilePage* class) also has the *IsValid* property, which is the logical AND of the *IsValid* property of all validation controls on the page.

The typical way of using the Validation controls, is to test the *IsValid* property of the *Page* before allowing navigation away from the page being validated. To get a reference to the parent *System.Web.UI.Page* instance, use the *MobilePage.Page* property. The following example is a Command control *Click* event handler in a class derived from MobilePage:

```
protected void Command1_Click(object sender, System.EventArgs e)
{
    // Move onto second Form only if input on first page has
    // passed validation by all the validation controls on the page
    if (Page.IsValid)
    {
        ActiveForm = Form2;
    }
}
```

With logic such as this, the Form with the validation controls on it now redisplays, but this time with error messages displayed by each of the validation controls that have detected a validation error.

Validation controls display error messages in two ways; either at the position where you placed the validation control on the Form, or in the display of a ValidationSummary control. You define the error message that displays at the control position using the *Text* property. You define the error message that goes into the ValidationSummary control display using the *ErrorMessage* property. If you have not set the *Text* property, then *ErrorMessage* is used for the control error message as well. You can turn off the display of the message at the position of the control, so that the message only appears in the ValidationSummary control, by setting the *Display* property to *None*. Error messages display next to the validation controls if the *Display* property is set to *Static* or *Dynamic*.

> **Note** *Display.Static* and *Display.Dynamic* behave the same way in the ASP.NET mobile controls. This enumeration is inherited from the ASP.NET versions targeted at desktop browsers, and these values cause different behavior depending on whether the client browser supports client-side scripting or not.
>
> With the mobile controls, no client-side validation takes place, so the behavior of *Display.Static* and *Display.Dynamic* is the same: an error message displays when a validation error occurs.

By default, the validation controls use *StyleReference="error"* to format the error message, which on an HTML browser displays the associated error message in red. You can use the style properties inherited from *MobileControl* to alter this behavior.

If the *Visible* property of a validation control is *False*, it doesn't just mean that the error message isn't displayed—it means that the control doesn't perform validation.

The use of the common properties inherited from the *BaseValidator* class is summarized in Table 5-5.

Table 5-5 Common Properties of the Validation Controls

Property	Type	Description
ControlTo-Validate	*String*	The *ID* of the control to validate.
Display	*System.Web.UI.WebControls.ValidatorDisplay enumeration: None | Static | Dynamic*	The display behavior of the control. If this property is set to *Dynamic* or *Static*, an error message is displayed when a validation error occurs. If *Display* is set to *None*, error messages won't be displayed by the RequiredFieldvalidator control, but they will still appear in the output from the ValidationSummary control (discussed later in this chapter).

Table 5-5 Common Properties of the Validation Controls

Property	Type	Description
ErrorMessage	*String*	The message displayed in the output of the ValidationSummary control. If the *Text* property is blank and *Display* isn't set to *None*, this value is displayed next to the control being validated in the event of an error.
IsValid	*True | False*	Indicates whether the data is valid.
Text	*String*	The message displayed in the event of an error. If this property has no value, the control displays the *ErrorMessage* value instead. The *Text* property isn't included in the ValidationSummary control's output; use *ErrorMessage* for this purpose.

RequiredFieldValidator Control

The RequiredFieldValidator control, the simplest of the validation controls, is the one you'll use most frequently. This control simply checks whether a user has entered a value for an input control.

Syntax

You code the RequiredFieldValidator control in server control syntax using the properties and values shown in the following listing. See Table 5-6 for descriptions of the purpose of the properties listed here.

```
<mobile:RequiredFieldValidator
    runat="server"
    id="id"
    BreakAfter="{True|False}"
    Font-Name="fontName"
    Font-Size="{NotSet|Normal|Small|Large}"
    Font-Bold="{NotSet|False|True}"
    Font-Italic="{NotSet|False|True}"
    ForeColor="foregroundColor"
    BackColor="backgroundColor"
    Alignment="{NotSet|Left|Center|Right}"
    StyleReference="styleReference"
    Visible="{True|False}"
    Wrapping="{NotSet|Wrap|NoWrap}"

    ControlToValidate="IdOfTargetControl"
    Display="{None|Static|Dynamic}"
```

```
    ErrorMessage="ErrorTextForSummary"
    InitialValue="initialValueInTheControl"
    Text="ErrorText">
innerText
</mobile:RequiredFieldValidator>
```

Properties

Table 5-6 shows the unique properties that the RequiredFieldValidator control doesn't inherit from the *MobileControl* class. (See Table 4-1 for details of those properties that are inherited from MobileControl.) The Type column describes the type of the property when setting or getting the property in code. Refer to the preceding "Syntax" section for valid values when setting the property in server control syntax.

Table 5-6 Significant Properties of the RequiredFieldValidator Control

Property	Type	Description
ControlTo-Validate	*String*	The *ID* of the control to validate. This property inherits from the *BaseValidator* class. See Table 5-5 for details.
Display	*ValidatorDisplay. None|Static|Dynamic*	This property inherits from the *BaseValidator* class. See Table 5-5 for details.
ErrorMessage	*String*	This property inherits from the *BaseValidator* class. See Table 5-5 for details.
InitialValue	*String*	The initial value of the control. The RequiredFieldValidator control compares the value submitted to the server with this value. If the two values are the same, the control assumes that the required field is incomplete.
IsValid	*True|False*	This property inherits from the *BaseValidator* class. See Table 5-5 for details.
Text	*String*	This property inherits from the *BaseValidator* class. See Table 5-5 for details.

Using the RequiredFieldValidator Control

Listings 5-8 and 5-9 prompt the user to enter his or her name into a form. When the form data posts to the server, the RequiredFieldValidator control validates the *userName* field.

```
<%@ Page Inherits="MSPress.MobWeb.ReqEx.RequiredExample"
    CodeBehind="RequiredExample.aspx.cs"
    Language="C#"%>
<%@ Register TagPrefix="mobile"
    Namespace="System.Web.UI.MobileControls"
    Assembly="System.Web.Mobile"  %>

<mobile:Form id="Form1" runat="server">
    <mobile:Label id="Label1" runat="server">
        Your name:
    </mobile:Label>
    <mobile:TextBox id="userName" runat="server"/>
    <mobile:RequiredFieldValidator id="RequiredFieldValidator1"
        runat="server"
        Display="Dynamic"
        ErrorMessage="Your name is required! "
        ControlToValidate="userName"/>
    <mobile:Command id="Command1" OnClick="Command1_Click" runat="server">
        Submit
    </mobile:Command>
</mobile:Form>

<mobile:Form id="Form2" runat="server">
    <mobile:Label id="Label2" runat="server">
        Input validated OK.
    </mobile:Label>
</mobile:Form>
```

Listing 5-8 Source file RequiredExample.aspx

```
using System;

namespace MSPress.MobWeb.ReqEx
{
    public class RequiredExample : System.Web.UI.MobileControls.MobilePage
    {
        protected System.Web.UI.MobileControls.Label Label1;
        protected System.Web.UI.MobileControls.TextBox userName;
        protected System.Web.UI.MobileControls.RequiredFieldValidator
            RequiredFieldValidator1;
        protected System.Web.UI.MobileControls.Command Command1;
        protected System.Web.UI.MobileControls.Form Form1;
        protected System.Web.UI.MobileControls.Label Label2;
        protected System.Web.UI.MobileControls.Form Form2;
```

Listing 5-9 Code-behind file RequiredExample.aspx.cs

```
        override protected void OnInit(EventArgs e)
        {
            InitializeComponent();
            base.OnInit(e);
        }

        private void InitializeComponent()
        {
            this.Command1.Click +=
                new System.EventHandler(this. Command1_Click);
        }

        protected void Command1_Click(object sender, System.EventArgs e)
        {
            if (Page.IsValid)
            {
                ActiveForm = Form2;
            }
        }
    }
}
```

When the user accesses the Web Forms page and doesn't enter a value in the *name* field, the application marks the page as invalid. Figure 5-6 shows the message Pocket Internet Explorer displays when this happens.

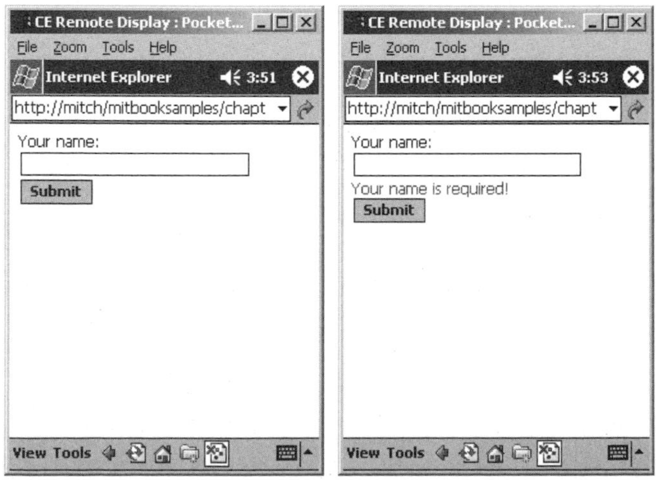

Figure 5-6 Input page and returned page with missing field

CompareValidator Control

The CompareValidator control allows you to compare the values of two input controls.

Syntax

You code the CompareValidator control in server control syntax using the properties and values shown in the following listing. See Table 5-7 for descriptions of the properties listed here.

```
<mobile:CompareValidator
    runat="server"
    id="id"
    BreakAfter="{True|False}"
    Font-Name="fontName"
    Font-Size="{NotSet|Normal|Small|Large}"
    Font-Bold="{NotSet|False|True}"
    Font-Italic="{NotSet|False|True}"
    ForeColor="foregroundColor"
    BackColor="backgroundColor"
    Alignment="{NotSet|Left|Center|Right}"
    StyleReference="styleReference"
    Visible="{True|False}"
    Wrapping="{NotSet|Wrap|NoWrap}"

    ControlToCompare="IdOfControl"
    ControlToValidate="IdOfTargetControl"
    Display="{None|Static|Dynamic}"
    ErrorMessage="ErrorTextForSummary"
    Operator="{DataTypeCheck|Equal|GreaterThan|
        GreaterThanEqual|LessThan|
        LessThanEqual|NotEqual}"
    Text="errorText"
    Type="{Currency|DateTime|Double|Integer|String}"
    ValueToCompare="Value">
innerText
</mobile:CompareValidator>
```

Properties

Table 5-7 lists the properties the CompareValidator control doesn't inherit from the *MobileControl* class. (See Table 4-1 for details of those properties that are inherited from *MobileControl*.) The Type column describes the type of the property when setting or getting the property in code. Refer to the preceding "Syntax" section for valid values when setting the property in server control syntax.

Table 5-7 Significant Properties of the CompareValidator Control

Property	Type	Description
ControlTo-Validate	*String*	The *ID* of the control to validate. This property inherits from the *BaseValidator* class. See Table 5-5 for details.
ControlTo-Compare	*String*	The ID of the control to compare. Set this property if you want to compare the *Text* property of the *ControlToValidate* control to the *Text* property of another control. If you want to do the comparison against a fixed value rather than the value of another control, use *ValueToCompare*.
Display	*ValidatorDisplay. None* | *Static* | *Dynamic*	This property inherits from the *BaseValidator* class. See Table 5-5 for details.
ErrorMessage	*String*	This property inherits from the *BaseValidator* class. See Table 5-5 for details.
IsValid	*True* | *False*	This property inherits from the *BaseValidator* class. See Table 5-5 for details.
Operator	*System.Web.UI.Web-Controls.Validation-CompareOperator* enumeration: *DataTypeCheck* | *Equal* | *GreaterThan* | *GreaterThanEqual* | *LessThan* | *LessThan-Equal* | *NotEqual*	The operator that compares the control values. Use *DataTypeCheck* to ensure that the data types for the *ControlToValidate* and *ControlTo-Compare* properties are both of the type set in the *Type* attribute. The other comparison operators function as though *ControlToValidate* is on the left side of the operator, and *ControlTo-Compare* is on the right.
Text	*String*	This property inherits from the *BaseValidator* class. See Table 5-5 for details.
Type	*System.Web.UI.Web-Controls.Validation-DataType* enumeration: *String* | *Integer* | *Double* | *Date* | *Currency*	Sets or gets the data type of the two values being compared. The values are implicitly converted to the specified data type before the comparison is made. If the types can't be converted, the validation fails.
ValueTo-Compare	*String*	Set this property if you want to compare the *Text* property of the *ControlToValidate* control to a constant value rather than the *Text* property of another control (use *ControlToCompare* instead of *ValueToCompare* for that). If you set both the *ValueToCompare* and *ControlToCompare* properties, *ControlToCompare* takes precedence.

Using the CompareValidator Control

Listings 5-10 and 5-11 prompt the user to enter his or her password and then reenter it in a second TextBox control. When the form data posts to the server, the CompareValidator control validates the fields to check that they have the same value.

```
<%@ Page Inherits="MSPress.MobWeb.CmpEx.CompareExample"
    CodeBehind="CompareExample.aspx.cs"
    Language="C#"%>
<%@ Register TagPrefix="mobile"
    Namespace="System.Web.UI.MobileControls"
    Assembly="System.Web.Mobile" %>

<mobile:Form id="Form1" runat="server">
    <mobile:Label runat="server">
        Your Password
    </mobile:Label>
    <mobile:TextBox id="password1" runat="server" password="true"/>
    <mobile:Label runat="server">
        Retype password
    </mobile:Label>
    <mobile:TextBox id="password2" runat="server" password="true"/>
    <mobile:CompareValidator id="CompareValidator1"
        Type="String"
        Operator="Equal"
        runat="server"
        ErrorMessage="Passwords do not match!"
        ControlToCompare="password1"
        ControlToValidate="password2"/>
    <mobile:Command id="Command1"
        OnClick="Command1_Click" runat="server">
        Submit
    </mobile:Command>
</mobile:Form>

<mobile:Form id="Form2" runat="server">
    <mobile:Label runat="server">
        Passwords match!
    </mobile:Label>
</mobile:Form>
```

Listing 5-10 Source file CompareExample.aspx

```
using System;

namespace MSPress.MobWeb.CmpEx
{
    public class CompareExample : System.Web.UI.MobileControls.MobilePage
    {
        protected System.Web.UI.MobileControls.Label Label1;
        protected System.Web.UI.MobileControls.TextBox password1;
        protected System.Web.UI.MobileControls.Label Label2;
        protected System.Web.UI.MobileControls.TextBox password2;
        protected System.Web.UI.MobileControls.CompareValidator
            CompareValidator1;
        protected System.Web.UI.MobileControls.Command Command1;
        protected System.Web.UI.MobileControls.Form Form1;
        protected System.Web.UI.MobileControls.Label Label3;
        protected System.Web.UI.MobileControls.Form Form2;

        override protected void OnInit(EventArgs e)
        {
            InitializeComponent();
            base.OnInit(e);
        }

        private void InitializeComponent()
        {
            this.Command1.Click +=
                new System.EventHandler(this. Command1_Click);
        }
        protected void Command1_Click(object sender, System.EventArgs e)
        {
            if (Page.IsValid)
            {
                ActiveForm = Form2;
            }
        }
    }
}
```

Listing 5-11 Code-behind file CompareExample.aspx.cs

Figure 5-7 shows the password input page and the page returned when the two passwords the user enters don't match.

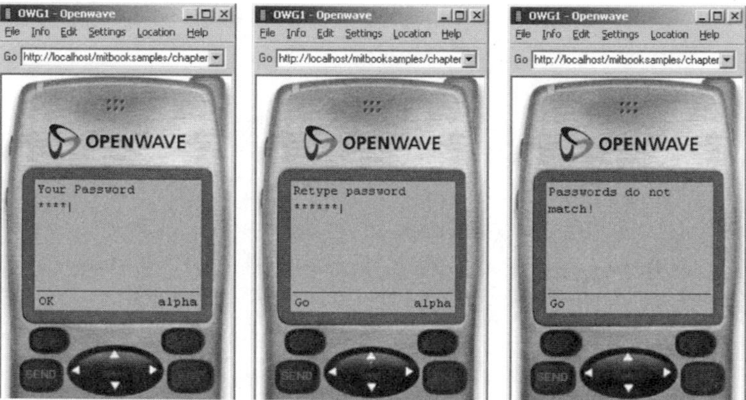

Figure 5-7 Password input page and returned page, which contains the error message

RangeValidator Control

The RangeValidator control allows you to test whether a value falls within a specified range.

Syntax

You code the RangeValidator control in server control syntax using the properties and values shown in the following listing. See Table 5-8 for descriptions of the properties listed here.

```
<mobile:RangeValidator
    runat="server"
    id="id"
    BreakAfter="{True|False}"
    Font-Name="fontName"
    Font-Size="{NotSet|Normal|Small|Large}"
    Font-Bold="{NotSet|False|True}"
    Font-Italic="{NotSet|False|True}"
    ForeColor="foregroundColor"
    BackColor="backgroundColor"
    Alignment="{NotSet|Left|Center|Right}"
    StyleReference="styleReference"
    Visible="{True|False}"
    Wrapping="{NotSet|Wrap|NoWrap}"

    ControlToValidate="IdOfTargetControl"
    Display="{None|Static|Dynamic}"
    ErrorMessage="ErrorTextForSummary"
    MinimumValue="minValue"
    MaximumValue="maxValue"
```

```
    Text="errorText"
    Type="{Currency|DateTime|Double|Integer|String}">
innerText
</mobile:RangeValidator>
```

Properties

Table 5-8 shows the significant properties of the RangeValidator control. (See Table 4-1 for details of those properties that are inherited from *MobileControl*.) The Type column describes the type of the property when setting or getting the property in code. Refer to the preceding "Syntax" section for valid values when setting the property in server control syntax.

Table 5-8 Significant Properties of the RangeValidator Control

Property	Type	Description
ControlTo-Validate	*String*	The *ID* of the control to validate. This property inherits from the *BaseValidator* class. See Table 5-5 for details.
Display	*Validator-Display.None|Static|Dynamic*	This property inherits from the *BaseValidator* class. See Table 5-5 for details.
ErrorMessage	*String*	This property inherits from the *BaseValidator* class. See Table 5-5 for details.
IsValid	*True|False*	This property inherits from the *BaseValidator* class. See Table 5-5 for details.
MinimumValue	*String*	The minimum value of the *ControlToValidate* that will successfully validate.
MaximumValue	*String*	The maximum value of the *ControlToValidate* property that will successfully validate. Both *MinimumValue* and *MaximumValue* are required properties.
Type	*System.Web.UI. WebControls. Validation-DataType* enumeration: *String|Integer|Double|Date|Currency*	Sets or gets the data type of the value being validated. The Text property of the control being validated and the values of the *MinimumValue* and *MaximumValue* properties are implicitly converted to the specified data type before the comparison is made. If they can't be converted, the validation fails.
Text	*String*	This property inherits from the *BaseValidator* class. See Table 5-5 for details.

When the RangeValidator control compares two strings, it does so by alphabetic precedence. For example, if the *MinimumValue* property has the value *ABRA* and the *MaximumValue* is *CADABRA* and the control to be validated contains the single character string *B*, the validation succeeds because *B* would appear after ABRA in an alphabetical sorted list, but before CADABRA. Similarly, *ABS* validates successfully against the range of *ABRA* to *CADABRA*. However, *AB* fails because it would come before *ABRA* in an alphabetical sorted list.

You should bear in mind two caveats when working with fields and user input:

- If the user submits a blank field, the RangeValidator control will deem that field valid. To ensure that the user enters a value for a field and that the value is of a given data type, use the RequiredFieldValidator control as well as the RangeValidator control.
- If the user submits a floating-point number when the syntax calls for an integer, the RangeValidator control will deem that input invalid. If you want to allow the user to enter a floating-point number, specify the value *Double* for the *Type* controls property.

Using the RangeValidator Control

Listings 5-12 and 5-13 prompt the user to enter his or her birthday in a TextBox control in a form. Part of the initialization of the RangeValidator control happens in the *Page_Load* method, where the *MaximumValue* is set to 21 years before today's date. When the form data posts to the server, the RangeValidator control checks whether the value indicates that the user is at least 21 years old.

```
<%@ Page Inherits="MSPress.MobWeb.RgeEx.RangeExample"
    CodeBehind="RangeExample.aspx.cs"
    Language="C#" AutoEventWireup="False" %>
<%@ Register TagPrefix="mobile"
    Namespace="System.Web.UI.MobileControls"
    Assembly="System.Web.Mobile" %>

<mobile:Form id="Form1" runat="server">
    <mobile:Label runat="server">
        Date of birth:
    </mobile:Label>
    <mobile:TextBox id="dob" runat="server"></mobile:TextBox>
    <mobile:RangeValidator id="RangeValidator1" runat="server"
        MinimumValue="01/01/1900"
```

Listing 5-12 Source file RangeExample.aspx

```
        ControlToValidate="dob"
        ErrorMessage="Sorry, you are not 21.">
    </mobile:RangeValidator>
    <mobile:Command id="Command1" runat="server" text="Submit">
    </mobile:Command>
</mobile:Form>

<mobile:Form id="Form2" runat="server">
    <mobile:Label id="Label2" runat="server">
        Welcome, you are over 21.
    </mobile:Label>
</mobile:Form>
```

```
using System;

namespace MSPress.MobWeb.RgeEx
{
    public class RangeExample : System.Web.UI.MobileControls.MobilePage
    {
        protected System.Web.UI.MobileControls.RangeValidator
            RangeValidator1;
        protected System.Web.UI.MobileControls.Label Label1;
        protected System.Web.UI.MobileControls.TextBox dob;
        protected System.Web.UI.MobileControls.Command Command1;
        protected System.Web.UI.MobileControls.Form Form1;
        protected System.Web.UI.MobileControls.Label Label2;
        protected System.Web.UI.MobileControls.Form Form2;

        override protected void OnInit(EventArgs e)
        {
            InitializeComponent();
            base.OnInit(e);
        }

        private void InitializeComponent()
        {
            this.Load += new System.EventHandler(this.Page_Load);
            this.Command1.Click +=
                new System.EventHandler(this. Command1_Click);
        }

        protected void Command1_Click(object sender, System.EventArgs e)
        {
            if (Page.IsValid)
```

Listing 5-13 Code-behind file RangeExample.aspx.cs

```
            {
                ActiveForm = Form2;
            }
        }

        private void Page_Load(object sender, System.EventArgs e)
        {
            DateTime now = DateTime.Now;
            DateTime dt21yearsago =
                new DateTime(now.Year - 21, now.Month, now.Day, 0, 0, 0);
            RangeValidator1.MaximumValue =
                dt21yearsago.ToShortDateString();
            RangeValidator1.Type =
                System.Web.UI.WebControls.ValidationDataType.Date;
        }
    }
}
```

Figure 5-8 shows the birthday input field and the message that appears if the user isn't 21.

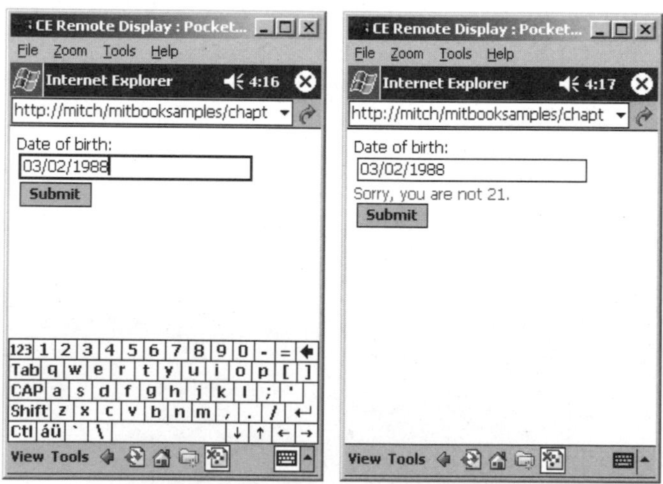

Figure 5-8 Output from RangeValidator example

RegularExpressionValidator Control

The RegularExpressionValidator control allows you to check that the value of a field conforms to a given character pattern. For example, you can use this control to validate an e-mail address, a ZIP code, or a social security number. This control is more complex than the validation controls we've discussed so far. It will help if you're familiar with regular expression syntax; however, working with this validation control is still significantly simpler than programming with traditional regular expressions.

Syntax

You code the RegularExpressionValidator control in server control syntax using the properties and values shown in the following listing. See Table 5-9 for descriptions of the properties listed here.

```
<mobile:RegularExpresssionValidator
    runat="server"
    id="id"
    BreakAfter="{True|False}"
    Font-Name="fontName"
    Font-Size="{NotSet|Normal|Small|Large}"
    Font-Bold="{NotSet|False|True}"
    Font-Italic="{NotSet|False|True}"
    ForeColor="foregroundColor"
    BackColor="backgroundColor"
    Alignment="{NotSet|Left|Center|Right}"
    StyleReference="styleReference"
    Visible="{True|False}"
    Wrapping="{NotSet|Wrap|NoWrap}"

    ControlToValidate="IdOfTargetControl"
    Display="{None|Static|Dynamic}"
    ErrorMessage="ErrorTextForSummary"
    Text="ErrorText">
    ValidationExpression="regexp" >
innerText
</mobile:RegularExpressionValidator>
```

Properties

Table 5-9 lists the properties the RegularExpressionValidator control doesn't inherit from the *MobileControl* class. (See Table 4-1 for details of those properties that are inherited from *MobileControl*.) The Type column describes the type of the property when setting or getting the property in code. Refer to the preceding "Syntax" section for valid values when setting the property in server control syntax.

Table 5-9 Significant Properties of the RegularExpressionValidator Control

Property	Type	Description
ControlToValidate	*String*	The *ID* of the control to validate. This property inherits from the *BaseValidator* class. See Table 5-5 for details.
Display	*ValidatorDisplay.None* | *Static* | *Dynamic*	This property inherits from the *BaseValidator* class. See Table 5-5 for details.
ErrorMessage	*String*	This property inherits from the *BaseValidator* class. See Table 5-5 for details.
IsValid	*True* | *False*	This property inherits from the *BaseValidator* class. See Table 5-5 for details.
Text	*String*	This property inherits from the *BaseValidator* class. See Table 5-5 for details.
ValidationExpression	*String*	The regular expression against which to validate the *ControlToValidate* property.

Using Regular Expressions in Microsoft Visual Studio .NET

Constructing regular expressions can be daunting. However, Visual Studio .NET helps by providing a selection of prewritten, commonly used expressions. You can find these expressions in the Regular Expression Editor, which you can access by dragging a RegularExpressionValidator control onto a Form, then pressing the … button next to the *ValidationExpression* property shown in the Properties window. This displays the Regular Expression Editor window where you can select a prebuilt expression or enter a custom regular expression.

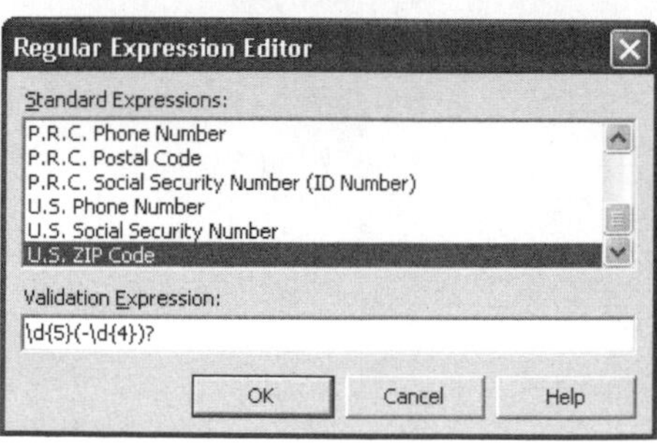

Using the RegularExpressionValidator Control

Regular expression syntax is a large topic that's beyond the scope of this book. However, Listings 5-14 and 5-15 demonstrate a common use of regular expression validation: confirming a ZIP code. The regular expression for this is "*\d{5}(-\d{4})?*" which means that the entered text must consist of five digits, followed by an optional portion of a dash followed by four digits. For detailed information about regular expression syntax, refer to the *System.Text.RegularExpressions.Regex* class in the Visual Studio .NET documentation.

```
<%@ Page Inherits="MSPress.MobWeb.RegEx.RegularExample"
    CodeBehind="RegularExample.aspx.cs" Language="c#"%>
<%@ Register TagPrefix="mobile"
    Namespace="System.Web.UI.MobileControls"
    Assembly="System.Web.Mobile" %>

<mobile:Form id="Form1" runat="server">
    <mobile:Label runat="server">
        ZIP Code
    </mobile:Label>
    <mobile:TextBox id="zip" runat="server"/>
    <mobile:Command id="Command1" runat="server" OnClick="Command1_Click">
        Submit
    </mobile:Command>
    <mobile:RegularExpressionValidator
        id="RegularExpressionValidator1"
        runat="server"
        ErrorMessage="Invalid ZIP Code"
        ControlToValidate="zip" ValidationExpression="\d{5}(-\d{4})?"/>
</mobile:Form>

<mobile:Form id="Form2" runat="server">
    <mobile:Label runat="server">
        Valid ZIP Code
    </mobile:Label>
</mobile:Form>
```

Listing 5-14 Source file RegularExample.aspx

```
using System;

namespace MSPress.MobWeb.RegEx
{
    public class RegularExample : System.Web.UI.MobileControls.MobilePage
    {
        protected System.Web.UI.MobileControls.Label Label1;
```

Listing 5-15 Code-behind file RegularExample.aspx.cs

```
        protected System.Web.UI.MobileControls.TextBox zip;
        protected System.Web.UI.MobileControls.Command Command1;
        protected System.Web.UI.MobileControls.RegularExpressionValidator
                       RegularExpressionValidator1;
        protected System.Web.UI.MobileControls.Form Form1;
        protected System.Web.UI.MobileControls.Label Label2;
        protected System.Web.UI.MobileControls.Form Form2;

        override protected void OnInit(EventArgs e)
        {
            InitializeComponent();
            base.OnInit(e);
        }

        private void InitializeComponent()
        {
            this.Command1.Click +=
                new System.EventHandler(this. Command1_Click);
        }

        protected void Command1_Click(object sender, System.EventArgs e)
        {
            if (Page.IsValid)
            {
                ActiveForm = Form2;
            }
        }
    }
}
```

With a minor adjustment, you can also use Listings 5-12 and 5-13 to validate an e-mail address. The only change you need to make to the .aspx file just shown is to give the *ValidationExpression* attribute of the RegularExpressionValidator control a different value. Change the value of the *ValidationExpression* attribute to the following:

```
\w+([-+.]\w+)*@\w+([-.]\w+)*\.\w+([-.]\w+)*
```

This expression forces the input to be a grouping of any number of word characters (*\w+*, which means anything from the ranges A–Z, a–z, or 0–9) separated by -, +, or . characters ([-+.]) followed by more word characters, with that group repeated zero or more times (the (…)* construct). That part is followed by an @ character, after which there can be any number of words separated by – or ., but there must be at least a dot followed by a word.

> **Note** Like all other mobile controls, the RegularExpressionValidation control executes on the server rather than on the client. In contrast, the standard ASP.NET RegularExpressionValidation control used with desktop clients does support client-side execution.

CustomValidator Control

The CustomValidator control differs from the other validation controls because it doesn't directly provide validation functionality. Instead, this control allows you to create your own validation method, which it then references. In many ways, this control acts as a wrapper class, offering a way of implementing a validation method that operates in a consistent manner to the other validation controls.

Syntax

You use the *ControlToValidate*, *Display*, *ErrorMessage*, and *Text* properties in exactly the same way you do with all the other validation controls. An event handler for the *ServerValidate* event is required for this control. You can wire it up in server control syntax, or in code in the code-behind module. The following listing shows the server control syntax for the CustomValidator control.

```
<mobile:CustomValidator
    runat="server"
    id="id"
    BreakAfter="{True|False}"
    Font-Name="fontName"
    Font-Size="{NotSet|Normal|Small|Large}"
    Font-Bold="{NotSet|False|True}"
    Font-Italic="{NotSet|False|True}"
    ForeColor="foregroundColor"
    BackColor="backgroundColor"
    Alignment="{NotSet|Left|Center|Right}"
    StyleReference="styleReference"
    Text="ErrorText"
    Visible="{True|False}"
    Wrapping="{NotSet|Wrap|NoWrap}"

    ControlToValidate="IdOfTargetControl"
    Display="{None|Static|Dynamic}"
    ErrorMessage="ErrorTextForSummary"
```

```
    OnServerValidate="EventHandler"
    Text="ErrorText">
innerText
</mobile:CustomValidator>
```

Properties

Table 5-10 shows the properties the CustomValidator control doesn't inherit from the *MobileControl* class. (See Table 4-1 for details of those properties that are inherited from *MobileControl*.) The Type column describes the type of the property when setting or getting the property in code. Refer to the preceding "Syntax" section for valid values when you're setting the property in server control syntax.

Table 5-10 Significant Properties and Events of the CustomValidator Control

Property or Event	Type	Description
ControlToValidate	*String*	The *ID* of the control to validate. This property inherits from the *BaseValidator* class. See Table 5-5 for details.
Display	*Validator-Display.None* | *Static* | *Dynamic*	This property inherits from the *BaseValidator* class. See Table 5-5 for details.
ErrorMessage	*String*	This property inherits from the *BaseValidator* class. See Table 5-5 for details.
IsValid	*True* | *False*	This property inherits from the *BaseValidator* class. See Table 5-5 for details.
ServerValidate (Event)	Event handler method	The control raises this event when the page is validated on the server. The event handler receives a *ServerValidateEventArgs* parameter. The event handler must set the *IsValid* property of the *ServerValidateEventArgs* object to *true* if validation is successful.
Text	*String*	This property inherits from the *BaseValidator* class. See Table 5-5 for details.

The CustomValidator control has one event, *ServerValidate*. The control raises the event when the page passes to the server for validation. Set the *IsValid* property of the *ServerValidateEventArgs* to indicate validation success or failure, as in this example:

```
void ServerValidate (Object source, ServerValidateEventArgs args )
{
    args.IsValid=false;
```

```
    // Code to validate the user's input
    ⋮
    if (validationIsSuccessful)
        args.IsValid=true;
}
```

Using the CustomValidator Control

Listings 5-16 and 5-17 prompt the user to enter an integer in a form. When the form data posts to the server, the CustomValidator control validates the field to verify whether the value is a factor of 4.

```
<%@ Page Inherits="MSPress.MobWeb.CusEx.CustomExample"
    CodeBehind="CustomExample.aspx.cs"
    Language="C#"%>
<%@ Register TagPrefix="mobile"
    Namespace="System.Web.UI.MobileControls"
    Assembly="System.Web.Mobile" %>

<mobile:Form id="Form1" runat="server">
    <mobile:Label runat="server">
        Enter an integer
     </mobile:Label>
    <mobile:TextBox id="number" runat="server"/>
    <mobile:CustomValidator id="CustomValidator1"
        runat="server"
        ErrorMessage="Not a factor of four"
        ControlToValidate="number"
        OnServerValidate="ServerValidate"/>
    <mobile:Command id="Command1"
        OnClick="Command1_Click" runat="server">
        Submit
    </mobile:Command>
</mobile:Form>

<mobile:Form id="Form2" runat="server">
    <mobile:Label runat="server">
        A factor of four.
    </mobile:Label>
</mobile:Form>
```

Listing 5-16 Source file CustomExample.aspx

```
using System;
using System.Web.UI.WebControls;

namespace MSPress.MobWeb.CusEx
{
    public class CustomExample : System.Web.UI.MobileControls.MobilePage
```

Listing 5-17 Code-behind file CustomExample.aspx.cs

```
{
    protected System.Web.UI.MobileControls.Form Form2;
    protected System.Web.UI.MobileControls.Label Label1;
    protected System.Web.UI.MobileControls.CustomValidator
        CustomValidator1;
    protected System.Web.UI.MobileControls.Command Command1;
    protected System.Web.UI.MobileControls.Form Form1;
    protected System.Web.UI.MobileControls.Label Label2;
    protected System.Web.UI.MobileControls.TextBox number;
    override protected void OnInit(EventArgs e)
    {
        InitializeComponent();
        base.OnInit(e);
    }

    private void InitializeComponent()
    {
        this.Command1.Click +=
            new System.EventHandler(this.Command1_Click);
        this.CustomValidator1.ServerValidate +=
            new ServerValidateEventHandler(this.ServerValidate );
    }

    protected void Command1_Click(object sender, System.EventArgs e)
    {
        if (Page.IsValid)
        {
            ActiveForm = Form2;
        }
    }

    protected void ServerValidate (
        object source,
        ServerValidateEventArgs args)
    {
        args.IsValid=false;

        try
        {
            int x = Int32.Parse(number.Text);
            if (x % 4==0)
            {
                args.IsValid=true;
            }
        }
        catch(FormatException e)
```

```
                {
                    // Exception may be caused by
                    // non-integer input on HTML clients
                }
            }
        }
    }
```

ValidationSummary Control

The ValidationSummary control returns a summary of all the output from the validation controls a Web Forms page contains. This control's output can be very useful in a mobile application because it enables you to present error messages in a single block of text. You can therefore significantly improve the usability of an application on a device with limited display characteristics.

Syntax

You can place this control in the same Form control that contains the validation controls. After control has returned to the server and validation has taken place, the ValidationSummary control displays a list containing the *ErrorMessage* property value of each validation control for which *IsValid* is *False*.

Alternatively, place this control in a different Form control from the one that contains the validation controls. The *Click* event handler of the Command control that triggers validation should test the *Page.IsValid* property and set the *ActiveForm* property to the Form control containing the ValidationSummary control if *Page.IsValid* == *False*. In this case, you should set a value for the *BackLabel* property, typically something like *Retry*. When *BackLabel* has a value, the ValidationSummary control renders a link to return to the Form being validated, using the value of *BackLabel* as the link text, as shown in the code below, in Listings 5-18 and 5-19. The following listing shows the server control syntax for the ValidationSummary control.

```
<mobile:ValidationSummary
    runat="server"
    id="id"
    BreakAfter="{True|False}"
    Font-Name="fontName"
    Font-Size="{NotSet|Normal|Small|Large}"
    Font-Bold="{NotSet|False|True}"
    Font-Italic="{NotSet|False|True}"
    ForeColor="foregroundColor"
    BackColor="backgroundColor"
    Alignment="{NotSet|Left|Center|Right}"
    StyleReference="styleReference"
```

```
    Visible="{True|False}"
    Wrapping="{NotSet|Wrap|NoWrap}"

    BackLabel="BackLabel"
    FormToValidate="FormID"
    HeaderText="HeaderText">
</mobile:ValidationSummary>
```

Properties

Table 5-11 shows the three properties the ValidationSummary control doesn't inherit from the *MobileControl* class. (See Table 4-1 for details of those properties that are inherited from *MobileControl*.)

Table 5-11 Significant Properties of the ValidationSummary Control

Property	Type	Description
BackLabel	*String*	If this property has a value, it is used for the text of a link that takes the user back to the input Form control to try to reenter text.
FormToValidate	*String*	The *ID* of the form to validate.
HeaderText	*String*	The title that precedes the list of error messages on the validation page. This property is displayed at the head of the page in HTML renderings and preceding each error message in WML browsers.

> **Warning** The ValidationSummary control uses the value of the *ErrorMessage* property of each validation control. Each validation control also displays an inline error if its *Display* property isn't set to *None*. If the *Text* property of the validation control has a value, however, that value is displayed instead of the *ErrorMessage* property. The ValidationSummary control ignores the value of the *Text* attribute of the validation controls and always uses the *ErrorMessage* property in the validation summary.

Using the ValidationSummary Control

Listings 5-18 and 5-19 prompt the user to enter his or her name and password in a form. When the form data posts to the server, the ValidationSummary control provides a summary of all validation errors.

```
<%@ Page Inherits="MSPress.MobWeb.SumEx.SummaryExample"
    CodeBehind="SummaryExample.aspx.cs"
    Language="C#"%>
<%@ Register TagPrefix="mobile"
    Namespace="System.Web.UI.MobileControls"
    Assembly="System.Web.Mobile" %>

<mobile:Form id="Form1" runat="server">
    <mobile:Label id="Label1" runat="server">
        Your name:
    </mobile:Label>
    <mobile:TextBox id="userName" runat="server"/>
    <mobile:Label id="Label2" runat="server" >
        Password
    </mobile:Label>
    <mobile:TextBox id="password" runat="server" Password="True"/>
    <mobile:RequiredFieldValidator id="RequiredFieldValidator1"
        runat="server"
        ControlToValidate="userName"
        Display="None"
        ErrorMessage="Your name is required!"/>
    <mobile:RequiredFieldValidator id="RequiredFieldValidator2"
        runat="server"
        ControlToValidate="password"
        Display="None"
        ErrorMessage="A password is required!"/>
    <mobile:Command id="Command1" runat="server" OnClick="Command1_Click">
        Submit
    </mobile:Command>
</mobile:Form>

<mobile:Form id="Form2" runat="server">
    <mobile:ValidationSummary id="ValidationSummary1"
        runat="server"
        HeaderText="Missing Values:"
        FormToValidate="Form1"
        BackLabel="Retry"/>
</mobile:Form>

<mobile:Form id="Form3" runat="server">
    <mobile:Label runat="server">
        Error free submission.
    </mobile:Label>
</mobile:Form>
```

Listing 5-18 Source for SummaryExample.aspx

```
using System;

namespace MSPress.MobWeb.SumEx
{
    public class SummaryExample : System.Web.UI.MobileControls.MobilePage
    {
        protected System.Web.UI.MobileControls.Command Command1;
        protected System.Web.UI.MobileControls.Form Form2;
        protected System.Web.UI.MobileControls.Form Form3;

        override protected void OnInit(EventArgs e)
        {
            InitializeComponent();
            base.OnInit(e);
        }

        private void InitializeComponent()
        {
            this.Command1.Click +=
                new System.EventHandler(this.Command1_Click);
        }

        protected void Command1_Click(object sender, System.EventArgs e)
        {
            if (Page.IsValid)
            {
                ActiveForm = Form3;
            }
            else
            {
                ActiveForm = Form2;
            }
        }
    }
}
```

Listing 5-19 Code-behind file SummaryExample.aspx.cs

Figure 5-9 shows this summary displayed on the Nokia simulator.

Figure 5-9 ValidationSummary output showing multiple submission errors

Validation Controls Example

The validation scenarios we've presented so far have been rather limited. This next code sample is a bit more challenging. It demonstrates the type of validation you're likely to perform in a real mobile Web application.

Listings 5-20 and 5-21 display a form that collects information for an online charitable donation. When the user submits the form, full validation occurs. Figure 5-10 shows how this form will look if the user doesn't supply any data.

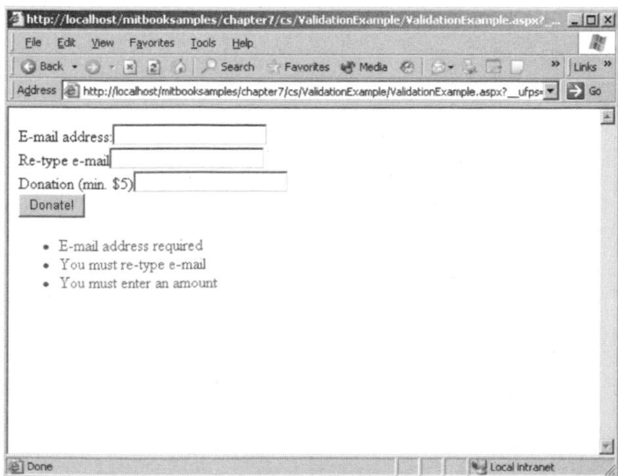

Figure 5-10 The page the validation controls example returns, indicating that the user made multiple submission errors

You should be aware of the following three issues when examining this sample application:

- Each input control uses multiple validation controls.
- The RequiredFieldValidator control validates each input control first.
- The program reports validation errors next to a control when the message is important; otherwise, the code places the message in the validation summary.

```
<%@ Page Inherits="MSPress.MobWeb.ValEx.ValidationExample"
    CodeBehind="ValidationExample.aspx.cs" Language="c#" %>
<%@ Register TagPrefix="mobile"
    Namespace="System.Web.UI.MobileControls"
    Assembly="System.Web.Mobile" %>

<mobile:Form id="Form1" runat="server">
    <mobile:Label runat="server" BreakAfter="false">
        E-mail address:
    </mobile:Label>
    <mobile:TextBox id="email1" runat="server"/>
    <mobile:RequiredFieldValidator id="RequiredFieldValidator1"
        runat="server"
        ErrorMessage="E-mail address required"
        ControlToValidate="email1"
        Display="None"/>
    <mobile:RegularExpressionValidator id="RegularExpressionValidator1"
        runat="server"
        ControlToValidate="email1"
        ValidationExpression="\w+([-+.]\w+)*@\w+([-.]\w+)*\.\w+([- .]\w+)*">
        Not a valid e-mail address
    </mobile:RegularExpressionValidator>

    <mobile:Label id="Label2" runat="server" BreakAfter="false">
        Re-type e-mail
    </mobile:Label>
    <mobile:TextBox id="email2" runat="server"/>
    <mobile:RequiredFieldValidator id="RequiredFieldValidator2"
        runat="server"
        ErrorMessage="You must re-type e-mail"
        ControlToValidate="email2"
        Display="None"/>
    <mobile:CompareValidator id="CompareValidator1"
        runat="server"
        ErrorMessage="E-mail addresses do not match. "
        ControlToValidate="email2"
        ControlToCompare="email1"
```

Listing 5-20 Source for ValidationExample.aspx

```
        Display="None"/>

    <mobile:Label id="Label3" runat="server" BreakAfter="false">
        Donation (min. $5)
    </mobile:Label>
    <mobile:TextBox id="donation" runat="server" Password="True"/>
    <mobile:RequiredFieldValidator id="RequiredFieldValidator3"
        runat="server"
        ErrorMessage="You must enter an amount"
        ControlToValidate="donation"
        Display="None"/>
    <!-- The RangeValidator Control requires that a maximum value is set.
        This value could represent the payment ceiling accepted by the
        online payment service provider -->
    <mobile:RangeValidator id="RangcValidator1"
        runat="server"
        ControlToValidate="donation"
        Type="Currency"
        MinimumValue="5"
        MaximumValue="1000">
    Minimum donation is $5
    </mobile:RangeValidator>

    <mobile:Command id="Command1" runat="server">
        Donate!
    </mobile:Command>
    <mobile:ValidationSummary id="ValidationSummary1"
        runat="server"
        FormToValidate="Form1"/>
</mobile:Form>

<mobile:Form id="Form2" runat="server">
    <mobile:Label id="Label4" runat="server">
        Thank you for donating.
    </mobile:Label>
</mobile:Form>
```

```
using System;

namespace MSPress.MobWeb.ValEx
{
    public class ValidationExample : System.Web.UI.MobileControls.MobilePage
    {
        protected System.Web.UI.MobileControls.Label Label1;
        protected System.Web.UI.MobileControls.TextBox email1;
        protected System.Web.UI.MobileControls.RequiredFieldValidator
```

Listing 5-21 Code-behind file ValidationExample.aspx.cs

```
            RequiredFieldValidator1;
        protected System.Web.UI.MobileControls.RegularExpressionValidator
            RegularExpressionValidator1;
        protected System.Web.UI.MobileControls.Label Label2;
        protected System.Web.UI.MobileControls.TextBox email2;
        protected System.Web.UI.MobileControls.RequiredFieldValidator
            RequiredFieldValidator2;
        protected System.Web.UI.MobileControls.CompareValidator
            CompareValidator1;
        protected System.Web.UI.MobileControls.Label Label3;
        protected System.Web.UI.MobileControls.TextBox donation;
        protected System.Web.UI.MobileControls.RequiredFieldValidator
            RequiredFieldValidator3;
        protected System.Web.UI.MobileControls.RangeValidator
            RangeValidator1;
        protected System.Web.UI.MobileControls.Command Command1;
        protected System.Web.UI.MobileControls.ValidationSummary
            ValidationSummary1;
        protected System.Web.UI.MobileControls.Form Form1;
        protected System.Web.UI.MobileControls.Label Label4;
        protected System.Web.UI.MobileControls.Form Form2;

        override protected void OnInit(EventArgs e)
        {
            InitializeComponent();
            base.OnInit(e);
        }

        private void InitializeComponent()
        {
            this.Command1.Click +=
                new System.EventHandler(this.Command1_Click);
        }

        protected void Command1_Click(object sender, System.EventArgs e)
        {
            if (Page.IsValid)
            {
                ActiveForm = Form2;
            }
        }
    }
}
```

6 Programming the List Controls

In this chapter, we'll describe the basic functionality of three controls that allow you to present a list of objects to the user: the SelectionList control, the List control, and the ObjectList control. As with the previous two chapters, for each control there is a "Syntax" section, which shows how you program the control using ASP.NET server control syntax. Also for each control is a "Properties and Events" section, which describes the usage of each of the properties and events of the control and gives information that will help you program the control in code. Finally, example applications are presented that demonstrate the different ways you can use these list controls. There are more examples for List controls than for other controls, reflecting their versatility. Figure 6-1 shows the class hierarchy of these three controls.

Of the three list controls, SelectionList is the simplest because it isn't able to paginate a long list across several display pages and therefore is suitable only for small lists. The SelectionList control is the only one of the three controls that accepts multiple selections. This control can be displayed as a drop-down list, as a set of radio buttons, and in other presentation formats for browsers with such support (including HTML browsers). The List control supports pagination, which means it supports long lists. It can render as a bulleted or numbered list (on browsers that support that) but it does not support the decorated forms (drop-down lists, etc.) that the SelectionList supports. However, you can customize the rendering of the List control using Templates, which we'll examine in Chapter 10.

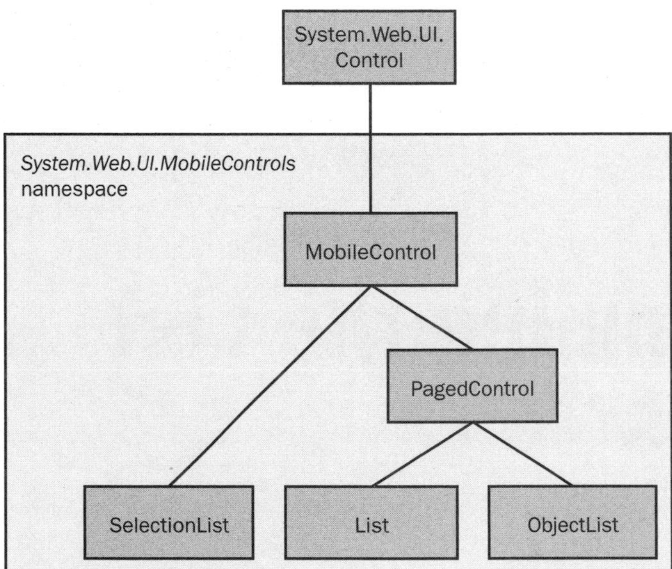

Figure 6-1 Class hierarchy of the list controls

The ObjectList control is the most sophisticated of the three list controls. The SelectionList and List controls allow you to define list items statically using server control syntax, but you can't do this with the ObjectList control; you must add list data programmatically by binding the list to a data source. The ObjectList allows you to display more than one field from the data item, whereas the other list controls only display a single item list. You can also display a customizable menu of options after a user selects a list item. The ObjectList control gives you the flexibility to develop responsive, interactive user interfaces.

The List and ObjectList controls are both *templated* controls, meaning that they offer great flexibility in how they are rendered on various devices. In Chapter 10, we'll describe this aspect of the two controls' behavior and provide more detail about advanced list programming techniques.

Table 6-1 summarizes the main capabilities of each list control.

Table 6-1 Capabilities of the List Controls

Capability	SelectionList	List	ObjectList
Renders as DropDown, ListBox, Radio, and so forth on HTML browsers	√		
Supports multiple selections	√		
Renders as a static, noninteractive list		√	√

Table 6-1 Capabilities of the List Controls

Capability	SelectionList	List	ObjectList
Renders as a bulleted or a numbered list		√	
Supports pagination of long lists		√	√
Declares display items statically	√	√	
Binds to data source	√	√	√
Displays two or more fields from data item*			√
Fires event on item selection	√†	√	√
Supports customizable menu links associated with each list item			√
Supports customizable rendering with templates		√	√

* Limited customization of what is displayed by any of the list controls is possible by implementing an ItemDataBind event handler. You can override the default display of a single field in the list and instead display a composite item made up of the contents of two or more fields. Chapter 9 examines this technique.

† The SelectionList requires another control on the same Form, such as a Command control, to trigger the postback from client to server before its SelectedIndexChanged event is fired.

Building Static or Data-Bound Lists

Before we examine each of the list controls separately, it's worth examining behavior that's common to all of them. The SelectionList and List controls allow you to define static list items, meaning that you define each item in the list using *<Item>* tags in server control syntax, or in code by creating *System.Web.UI.MobileControls.MobileListItem* objects and adding them to the *Items* collection of the control.

The alternative is to bind the control to a data source, so the values in the list are read from a *DataTable* or other .NET Framework data collection object, such as an *ArrayList*. All three list controls support data binding.

Defining Static List Items

You can use the *<Item>* tag with both the SelectionList control and the List control to define static list items in server control syntax. For example, look at this code:

```
<mobile:SelectionList SelectType="ListBox"
    id="SelectionList1" runat="server">
    <item Text="Dunes" Value="Posn:1 Pl:38 Pts:80"/>
    <item Text="Phoenix" Value="Posn:2 Pl:38 Pts:70"/>
    <item Text="Eagles" Value="Posn:3 Pl:38 Pts:69"/>
```

```
    <item Text="Zodiac" Value="Posn:4 Pl:38 Pts:68"/>
</mobile:SelectionList>
```

For an example application that uses this technique, see Listing 6-1 later in this chapter.

Visual Studio .NET provides a useful Item Editor you can use to define static list items, as shown in Figure 6-2. Access this editor by clicking the Property Builder link at the bottom of the Properties window. You can then define items in the Items view of the Properties dialog box.

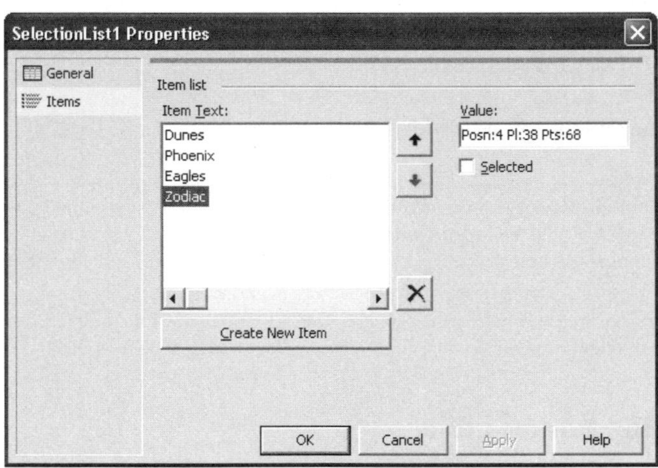

Figure 6-2 Using the SelectionList Properties dialog box to build a static list

When the ASP.NET runtime parses this server control syntax, it constructs *System.Mobile.UI.MobileControls.MobileListItem* objects, initializing the properties of the object using the *Text* and *Value* attributes of the *<Item>* tag, and it inserts the object into a *System.Mobile.UI.MobileControls.MobileListItemCollection* object, which you can access in code by getting the *Items* property of the SelectionList or List class. In fact, the following code is exactly equivalent to the server control syntax shown above; you could create static list items in code in this way, instead of defining them in server control syntax:

```
private void Page_Load(Object sender, EventArgs e)
{
    if (!IsPostBack)
    {
        SelectionList1.Items.Add(
            new MobileListItem("Dunes", "Posn:1 Pl:38 Pts:80"));
        SelectionList1.Items.Add(
            new MobileListItem ("Phoenix", "Posn:2 Pl:38 Pts:70"));
```

```
            SelectionList1.Items.Add(
                new MobileListItem ("Eagles", "Posn:3 Pl:38 Pts:69"));
            SelectionList1.Items.Add(
                new MobileListItem ("Zodiac", "Posn:4 Pl:38 Pts:68"));
        }
    }
```

Binding to a Data Collection

Instead of defining list items statically, you can bind the SelectionList control, the List control, and the ObjectList control to a data source. These controls support two types of data sources: *System.Collections.IEnumerable* and *System.ComponentModel.IListSource*. Many of the collection classes supplied in the Microsoft .NET Framework implement the *IEnumerator* interface and consequently support simple enumeration. Some examples from the *System.Collections* namespace include *Array*, *ArrayList*, *Hashtable*, and *ListDictionary*, as well as many of the collections associated with controls, such as *MobileListItemCollection* (used in the preceding code sample). To see the full list of classes that implement *IEnumerable*, click Help in Visual Studio .NET and search for *IEnumerable*. Statements such as C#'s *foreach* and Microsoft Visual Basic .NET's *For Each...Next* can iterate through an enumerable object.

You can also bind the list controls to *IListSource* data collections. Two .NET classes from the *System.Data* namespace implement this interface: *DataSet* and *DataTable*. These classes are related because a *DataSet* class is actually a collection of *DataTable* objects. The *DataSet* class is a major component of the Microsoft ADO.NET architecture and represents an in-memory cache of data retrieved from a database. When using a *DataSet* for the data source, you must always set the *SelectionList.DataMember* property to the name of the *DataTable* in the *DataSet* you want to use as the data source. You don't need to set the *DataMember* property when using an *IEnumerable* data source, however. In Chapter 11, we'll explore how you can use *DataSet* objects in your mobile applications.

When you databind a list control, you use the *DataSource* property to identify the source data collection. If your data source is a *DataSet*, you use the *DataMember* property to identify which *DataTable* inside the *DataSet* is the required data source. With the SelectionList and List controls, you use the *DataTextField* and *DataValueField* properties to identify the fields inside the data record to extract for the display value and the hidden value, respectively. The ObjectList uses the *LabelField* property to identify the field to display in the initial list. See the descriptions of the individual controls later in this chapter for more details on how to use these properties.

You can set these properties in server control syntax or in code. For example, you could set the name of the field to display in a SelectionList to be "Stats" and the field to supply the hidden value to be "TeamName" with the following server control syntax:

```
<mobile:SelectionList id="SelectionList1" runat="server"
    DataValueField="Stats" DataTextField="TeamName"
    SelectType="MultiSelectListBox">
</mobile:SelectionList>
```

In the code-behind module, you could define a simple class to store a data record, as you see in this example:

```
class TeamStats
{
    private String teamName, stats;

    public TeamStats(String teamName, String stats)
    {
        this.teamName = teamName;
        this.stats = stats;
    }

    public String TeamName { get { return this.teamName; } }
    public String Stats    { get { return this.stats; } }
}
```

Then, in the *Page_Load* event handler, create each of the data items and load them into an *ArrayList* object. Finally, set the *DataSource* property of the list control to be the *ArrayList* instance, and then call the *DataBind* method of the control to bind the control to the data:

```
    private void Page_Load(Object sender, EventArgs e)
    {
        if (!IsPostBack)
        {
            ArrayList array = new ArrayList();
            array.Add(new TeamStats("Dunes", "Posn:1 Pl:38 Pts:80"));
            array.Add(new TeamStats("Phoenix", "Posn:2 Pl:38 Pts:70"));
            array.Add(new TeamStats("Eagles", "Posn:3 Pl:38 Pts:69"));
            array.Add(new TeamStats("Zodiac", "Posn:4 Pl:38 Pts:68"));
            SelectionList1.DataSource = array;
            SelectionList1.DataBind();
        }
    }
```

See Listing 6-6 later in this chapter for the complete example application that uses this technique.

> **Important** The *DataBind* method is crucial to data binding. It's a common programming error to forget to call the method, whereupon your list control displays no data.
>
> You can call the method on a single control, as shown in this example, or you can call the *MobilePage.DataBind* method (in other words, substitute `this.DataBind()` for `SelectionList1.DataBind()` in the example just shown). This has the effect of calling *DataBind* for the page, but also for all controls contained within the page.

The SelectionList Control

As mentioned, this control is appropriate for displaying small lists of items. It doesn't support pagination of long lists, but it offers presentation options that allow you to render as drop-down lists, combo boxes, and radio buttons on devices that support them.

The SelectionList displays a list consisting of a single visible item, but there can also be a hidden value associated with each displayed item. You set the value of this item using the *Value* attribute of the *<Item>* element in server control syntax, or if the list is databound by specifying a field in the data source using the *DataValueField* property.

Syntax

The SelectionList control is used declaratively by means of the server control syntax shown in the following listing. Items that are displayed are either read from a data source, using the *DataMember*, *DataSource*, *DataTextField*, and *DataValueField* properties, or statically defined using *<Item>* tags. You can also add static items through code, as described in the section "Specifying a Static List," later in this chapter. The *SelectedIndex* property of this control is not shown here as it can't be set declaratively and can be set only in code. To select items declaratively, set the *Selected* attribute of the *<Item>* tag to *True*.

```
<mobile:SelectionList
   runat="server"
   id="id"
   Alignment="{NotSet|Left|Center|Right}"
   BackColor="backgroundColor"
   BreakAfter="{True|False}"
   Font-Bold="{NotSet|False|True}"
   Font-Italic="{NotSet|False|True}"
   Font-Name="fontName"
```

```
    Font-Size="{NotSet|Normal|Small|Large}"
    ForeColor="foregroundColor"
    StyleReference="StyleReference"
    Wrapping="{NotSet|Wrap|NoWrap}"

    DataMember="dataMember"
    DataSource="dataSource"
    DataTextField="DataTextField"
    DataValueField="DataValueField"
    SelectType="{DropDown|ListBox|Radio|MultiSelectListBox|CheckBox}"
    Title="String"
    OnItemDataBind="itemDataBindHandler"
    OnSelectedIndexChanged="selectedIndexChangedHandler">

        <!-- Optional statically declared list items -->
        <Item Text="Text" Value="Value" Selected="{True|False}"/>

</mobile:SelectionList>
```

Properties and Events

Table 6-2 describes the properties and events that you're most likely to use with the SelectionList control, but excludes those inherited from the *MobileControl* class. (See Table 4-1 and Table 4-2 for details of those properties that are inherited from *MobileControl*.) The *Type* column describes the type of the property when you're setting or getting the property in code. Refer to the preceding "Syntax" section for valid values when you're setting the property in server control syntax.

The *SelectedIndex* and *Selection* properties are set only after the user has made a selection from the list. You read the *SelectedIndex* property in code to determine the index number (zero-based) of the user's selection in the collection of items. The *Selection* property is similar but returns the *MobileListItem* object for the selected item rather than an index.

Table 6-2 Significant Properties and Events of the SelectionList Control

Property/Event	Type	Description
DataMember	*String*	Used only when the control is data bound to a *System.Data.DataSet* or *System.Data.DataTable* object. This attribute specifies the name of the table in the *DataSet* class to which the control should bind. (We'll describe these two classes later in this chapter.)
DataSource	*Object*	When the control is data bound, *DataSource* specifies the *DataSet* object or enumerated collection that is the data source.

Table 6-2 Significant Properties and Events of the SelectionList Control

Property/Event	Type	Description
DataTextField	*String*	When the control is data bound to either a *DataSet* class or an enumerated collection, *DataTextField* specifies the name of the field in the data source that appears in the list.
DataValueField	*String*	When the control is data bound to either a *DataSet* object or an enumerated collection, *DataValueField* specifies the name of the field in the data source that provides the hidden data value associated with each list item.
Items	*System.Web.UI.Mobile-Controls.MobileListItem-Collection*	Gives access to the *MobileListItemCollection* object, in which all the *System.Web.UI.Mobile-Controls.MobileListItem* objects that represent the list items are stored. You can programmatically manipulate the objects in this collection.
Rows	*Integer*	When the *SelectType* property is *ListBox* or *MultiSelectListBox*, *Rows* is used to set the number of visible rows when the control is rendered on HTML and cHTML browsers.
SelectedIndex	*Integer*	Returns or sets the index of the selected item. If the control is in multiple-selection mode, *SelectedIndex* returns the index of the first selected item.
Selection	*MobileListItem*	Returns the selected item (a *MobileListItem* object) or *null* if there is no selection.
SelectType	*System.Web.UI.MobileControls.ListSelectType* enumeration: *DropDown* | *ListBox* | *Radio* | *MultiSelectListBox* | *CheckBox*	This enumeration reflects the presentation style on the browsers that support it. *CheckBox* and *MultiSelectListBox* allow you to use the control to make multiple selections from the list. The other values enable only single selections. The default value is *DropDown*.
Title	*String*	Title string that is displayed on WML browsers, although it is not supported by all WML browsers.

Table 6-2 Significant Properties and Events of the SelectionList Control

Property/Event	Type	Description
ItemDataBind (event)	Event handler method	Set to the name of an event handler method of signature *OnItemDataBind(Object sender, ListDataBindEventArgs e)*. When the control is data bound, this event fires for each item that is added to the List. (See Chapter 10 for an example.)
SelectedIndexChanged (event)	Event handler method	If the SelectionList control executes in one of the single-selection modes, the application calls this event handler method when a user action causes the selected item to change. The event can fire only after a Command control has made a post to the server.

> **More Info** For more information about the commonly used properties inherited from the *MobileControl* class, refer to Table 4-1 in Chapter 4.

Using the SelectionList Control

You define the list items to display in the SelectionList control in ASP.NET server control syntax either using the *<Item>* element or by data binding to a single field of a data collection using the *DataSource*, *DataMember*, *DataTextField*, and *DataValueField* attributes, as outlined in the section "Building Static or Data-Bound Lists" at the beginning of this chapter.

When a user makes a selection in a SelectionList, the form on the client browser encodes the identity of the selected item or items and adds it to the data to be posted back to the server, where it is used by the ASP.NET runtime to update properties of the SelectionList such as *SelectedIndex*. However, the SelectionList control doesn't cause an automatic postback to the server when a user makes a selection. You must include a Command control on the same Form as a SelectionList control to post the user's selection to the server.

Specifying the Type of SelectionList

The SelectionList control allows the user to make single selections if you set the *SelectType* property to *DropDown*, *ListBox*, or *Radio*. You can enable multiple selections by using the *MultiSelectListBox* or *CheckBox* values of this attribute. In code, you can use the *SelectType* method of the *SelectionList* class to set or get the type of list to use. The *IsMultiSelect* property returns *true* if one of the multiple-selection styles is in use.

The names used for the values of the *SelectType* attribute reflect the way they are rendered on HTML browsers. WML browsers of version 1.2 and earlier don't support these GUI elements. On these devices, a selection list is rendered as a WML *<select>* element, which allows single-selection or multiple-selection options. On many WML browsers, you can select items either by navigating to an option and pressing a softkey or by pressing a number key to select a list item. (The second option is quicker.) Therefore, you should try to limit a SelectionList control to nine items or less so that all options can easily be displayed and each option can map to a key. Figure 6-3 offers some examples of selection list styles on a variety of browsers.

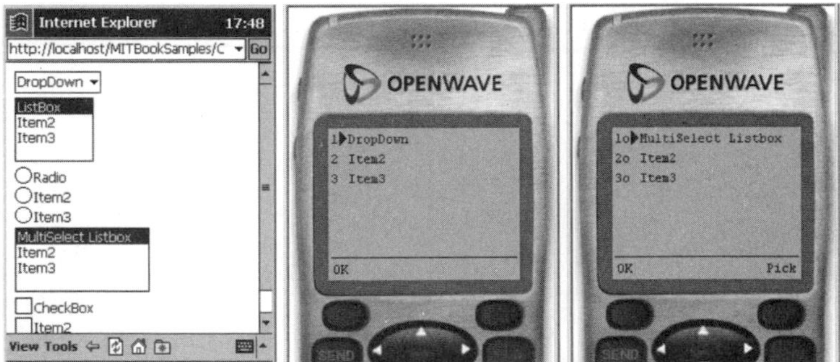

Figure 6-3 SelectionList control rendering styles on Pocket Internet Explorer as well as single-selection styles (middle) and multiple-selection styles (right) on an Openwave browser

Specifying a Static List

In a static list, list items are defined as string literals rather than read from a dynamic data source. To specify a static list of items, you must use the *<Item>* element, as shown here:

```
<Item Text="Text" Value="Value" Selected="{True|False}" />
```

The *Text* attribute specifies the item that is displayed to the user, whereas the *Value* attribute specifies a hidden associated value. Set *Selected* to *True* if you want that item to be preselected.

An associated *MobileListItemCollection* object stores items you've defined for a SelectionList control. When you define items statically, you're inserting *MobileListItem* objects into this collection. The *Items* property of the SelectionList control gives you access to this collection. You can use the methods of the *MobileListItemCollection* class to add to or remove items from the list. Consult the .NET Framework SDK reference documentation for details about *Add*, *Clear*, *Remove*, and other related methods of this class.

Identifying the Selection in a SelectionList Control

With single-selection styles, you can retrieve the display text of the selected item by fetching the *Selection.Name* property and the associated value using the *Selection.Value* property. In Listings 6-1 and 6-2, the user selects a single team from the list, and the Command control's *HandleTeamSelection* event handler uses the value associated with the selected item to set the text of *Label4* on the second form. Keep in mind that the SelectionList control always requires an accompanying Command control to generate the event that processes the user's choice.

```
<%@ Page Inherits="MSPress.MobWeb.SelListEx.ExampleWebForm" Language="c#"
    CodeBehind=" SingleSelectionListExample.aspx.cs"%>
<%@ Register TagPrefix="mobile"
    Namespace="System.Web.UI.MobileControls"
    Assembly="System.Web.Mobile" %>

<mobile:Form runat="server" id="Form1">
   <mobile:Label runat="server" StyleReference="title" id="Label1">
       Season 2003 results
   </mobile:Label>
   <mobile:Label runat="server" id="Label2">Select a team:</mobile:Label>
   <mobile:SelectionList SelectType="ListBox"
       id="SelectionList1" runat="server">
       <item Text="Dunes" Value="Posn:1 Pl:38 Pts:80"/>
       <item Text="Phoenix" Value="Posn:2 Pl:38 Pts:70"/>
       <item Text="Eagles" Value="Posn:3 Pl:38 Pts:69"/>
       <item Text="Zodiac" Value="Posn:4 Pl:38 Pts:68"/>
   </mobile:SelectionList>
   <mobile:Command runat="server" id="Command1">
       Get Stats!
    </mobile:Command>
</mobile:Form>

<mobile:Form runat="server" id="Form2">
   <mobile:Label runat="server" id="Label3">Team Full Stats:</mobile:Label>
   <mobile:Label runat="server" id="Label4"/>
</mobile:Form>
```

Listing 6-1 Source for SingleSelectionListExample.aspx

```
using System;

namespace MSPress.MobWeb.SelListEx
{
    public class ExampleWebForm : System.Web.UI.MobileControls.MobilePage
```

Listing 6-2 Code-behind file SingleSelectionListExample.aspx.cs

```
    {
        protected System.Web.UI.MobileControls.Label Label4;
        protected System.Web.UI.MobileControls.SelectionList SelectionList1;
        protected System.Web.UI.MobileControls.Command Command1;
        protected System.Web.UI.MobileControls.Form Form2;

        override protected void OnInit(EventArgs e)
        {
            InitializeComponent();
            base.OnInit(e);
        }

        private void InitializeComponent()
        {
            this.Command1.Click +=
                new System.EventHandler(this.HandleTeamSelection);
        }

        private void HandleTeamSelection(Object source, EventArgs args)
        {
            // Display the Stats page
            this.ActiveForm = Form2;
            String selectedTeamStats = SelectionList1.Selection.Value;
            Label4.Text = SelectionList1.Selection + ": "
                + selectedTeamStats;
        }
    }
}
```

Identifying Selections in a Multiple-Selection SelectionList Control

When you use one of the multiple-selection modes, you must test each *MobileListItem* object in the *MobileListItemCollection* collection to determine if it is selected. The *MobileListItemCollection* collection is accessible through the *Items* property of the SelectionList. Selected *MobileListItem* objects in the collection will have their *Selected* property set to *True*. Listings 6-3 and 6-4, which are variants of Listings 6-1 and 6-2, allow the user to make multiple selections and enable the statistics of each selection to be displayed in a TextView control. Within the *HandleMultiTeamSelection* event handler, the code retrieves the *Items* property and then tests each item in the collection to see whether its *Selected* property is *True*.

```
<%@ Page Inherits="MSPress.MobWeb.MultSelListEx.ExampleMobileWebForm"
    Language="c#" CodeBehind="multipleselectionlistexample.aspx.cs"%>
<%@ Register TagPrefix="mobile"
    Namespace="System.Web.UI.MobileControls"
```

Listing 6-3 Source for MultipleSelectionListExample.aspx

```
    Assembly="System.Web.Mobile" %>

<mobile:Form runat="server" id="Form1">
    <mobile:Label runat="server" StyleReference="title">
        Season 2003 results
    </mobile:Label>
    <mobile:Label runat="server">Select 2 or more teams:</mobile:Label>
    <mobile:SelectionList SelectType="MultiSelectListBox"
                          id="SelectionList1" runat="server">
        <item Text="Dunes" Value="Posn:1 Pl:38 Pts:80"/>
        <item Text="Phoenix" Value="Posn:2 Pl:38 Pts:70"/>
        <item Text="Eagles" Value="Posn:3 Pl:38 Pts:69"/>
        <item Text="Zodiac" Value="Posn:4 Pl:38 Pts:68"/>
    </mobile:SelectionList>
    <mobile:Command runat="server" id="Command1">
        Compare Stats!
    </mobile:Command>
</mobile:Form>

<mobile:Form runat="server" id="Form2">
    <mobile:Label runat="server">Teams Full Stats:</mobile:Label>
    <mobile:TextView runat="server" id="TextView1"/>
</mobile:Form>
```

```
using System;
using System.Web.UI.MobileControls;

namespace MSPress.MobWeb.MultSelListEx
{
    public class ExampleMobileWebForm :
        System.Web.UI.MobileControls.MobilePage
    {
        protected System.Web.UI.MobileControls.TextView TextView1;
        protected System.Web.UI.MobileControls.SelectionList SelectionList1;
        protected System.Web.UI.MobileControls.Command Command1;
        protected System.Web.UI.MobileControls.Form Form2;
        override protected void OnInit(EventArgs e)
        {
            InitializeComponent();
            base.OnInit(e);
        }

        private void InitializeComponent()
        {
            this.Command1.Click +=
```

Listing 6-4 Code-behind module MultipleSelectionListExample.aspx.cs

```
                new System.EventHandler(this.HandleMultiTeamSelection);
        }

        protected void HandleMultiTeamSelection(Object source,EventArgs args)
        {
            this.ActiveForm = Form2;
            // Get the list items collection.
            MobileListItemCollection colItems = SelectionList1.Items;
            String strDisplaytext = "";
            foreach (MobileListItem item in colItems)
            {
                if (item.Selected)
                {
                  strDisplaytext += (item.Text + ": " + item.Value + "<BR>");
                }
            }
            TextView1.Text = strDisplaytext;
        }
    }
}
```

Figure 6-4 shows multiple selection on a WAP simulator (left) and the result (right).

Figure 6-4 Output from the multiple-selection list example

Binding to a Data Collection

Instead of defining list items statically, you can bind the SelectionList control (and the other list controls) to a data source, as outlined in the topic "Building Static or Data-Bound Lists" at the beginning of this chapter.

Listings 6-5 and 6-6 create a simple *ArrayList* collection to use as the data source for a SelectionList control. In the code-behind module, we create a simple class named *TeamStats,* in which we store the details about a single team. In the *Page_Load* event handler, we create *TeamStats* objects and load them into an *ArrayList* collection. The SelectionList control is data bound to that *ArrayList*. The output from this sample looks identical to that of the *MultipleSelectionListExample* sample shown earlier.

```
<%@ Page Inherits="MSPress.MobWeb.DBListEx.ExampleWebForm" Language="c#"
    CodeBehind="DataboundListExample.aspx.cs" AutoEventWireup="False" %>
<%@ Register TagPrefix="mobile"
    Namespace="System.Web.UI.MobileControls"
    Assembly="System.Web.Mobile" %>

<mobile:Form runat="server" id="Form1">
    <mobile:Label id="Label1" runat="server" StyleReference="title">
        Season 2003 results
    </mobile:Label>
    <mobile:Label id="Label2" runat="server">
        Select 2 or more teams:
    </mobile:Label>
    <mobile:SelectionList id="SelectionList1" runat="server"
        DataValueField="Stats" DataTextField="TeamName"
        SelectType="MultiSelectListBox">
    </mobile:SelectionList>
    <mobile:Command id="Command1" runat="server">
        Compare Stats!
    </mobile:Command>
</mobile:Form>

<mobile:Form runat="server" id="Form2">
    <mobile:Label id="Label3" runat="server">Teams Full Stats:</mobile:Label>
    <mobile:TextView id="TextView1" runat="server"></mobile:TextView>
</mobile:Form>
```

Listing 6-5 Source for DataboundListExample.aspx

```
using System;
using System.Collections;
using System.Web.UI.MobileControls;

namespace MSPress.MobWeb.DBListEx
```

Listing 6-6 Code-behind file DataboundListExample.aspx.cs

```
{
    public class ExampleWebForm : System.Web.UI.MobileControls.MobilePage
    {
        protected System.Web.UI.MobileControls.TextView TextView1;
        protected System.Web.UI.MobileControls.SelectionList SelectionList1;
        protected System.Web.UI.MobileControls.Command Command1;
        protected System.Web.UI.MobileControls.Form Form2;

        override protected void OnInit(EventArgs e)
        {
            InitializeComponent();
            base.OnInit(e);
        }

        private void InitializeComponent()
        {
            this.Load += new System.EventHandler(this.Page_Load);
            this.Command1.Click +=
                new System.EventHandler(this.HandleMultiTeamSelection);
        }
        private void Page_Load(Object sender, EventArgs e)
        {
            if (!IsPostBack)
            {
                ArrayList array = new ArrayList();
                array.Add(new TeamStats("Dunes", "Posn:1 Pl:38 Pts:80"));
                array.Add(new TeamStats("Phoenix", "Posn:2 Pl:38 Pts:70"));
                array.Add(new TeamStats("Eagles", "Posn:3 Pl:38 Pts:69"));
                array.Add(new TeamStats("Zodiac", "Posn:4 Pl:38 Pts:68"));
                SelectionList1.DataSource = array;
                SelectionList1.DataBind();
            }
        }
        private void HandleMultiTeamSelection(
            Object source, EventArgs args)
        {
            this.ActiveForm = Form2;

            // Get the list items collection.
            MobileListItemCollection colItems = SelectionList1.Items;
            String strDisplaytext = "";
            foreach (MobileListItem item in colItems)
            {
                if (item.Selected)
                {
```

```
                strDisplaytext += (item.Text + ": " + item.Value +
                "<br/>");
            }
        }
        TextView1.Text= strDisplaytext;
    }
}

class TeamStats
{
    private String teamName, stats;

    public TeamStats(String teamName, String stats)
    {
        this.teamName = teamName;
        this.stats = stats;
    }

    public String TeamName { get { return this.teamName; } }
    public String Stats    { get { return this.stats; } }
}
}
```

The List Control

The List control is very similar to the SelectionList control, but it supports internal paging and is therefore appropriate for displaying larger lists of items. You can use the List control for non-interactive display lists or for interactive selection lists. In the interactive mode, the control only allows selection of a single item (unlike the SelectionList which allows multiple items to be selected), but its *ItemCommand* event, which fires when the user selects a list item, causes a postback from the client to the server. Therefore, you don't need an additional Command control for the user interaction to generate an event at the server. The List control also supports templating, which makes it flexible and suitable for implementing device-specific behavior. You'll learn more about using templates with the List control in Chapter 10.

Syntax

The List control is always rendered with a trailing break, overriding any setting of the *BreakAfter* property. The *LoadItems* event and the *ItemCount* property are inherited from the *PagedControl* parent class; you use these only when you implement custom pagination. (See the section “Custom Pagination,” later in the chapter, for more details.) You code the List control in server control syntax using the properties and values shown in the following listing.

```
<mobile:List
   runat="server"
   id="id"
   Alignment="{NotSet|Left|Center|Right}"
   BackColor="backgroundColor"
   Font-Bold="{NotSet|False|True}"
   Font-Italic="{NotSet|False|True}"
   Font-Name="fontName"
   Font-Size="{NotSet|Normal|Small|Large}"
   ForeColor="foregroundColor"
   StyleReference="StyleReference"
   Wrapping="{NotSet|Wrap|NoWrap}"

   DataMember="dataMember"
   DataSource="dataSource"
   DataTextField="DataTextField"
   DataValueField="DataValueField"
   Decoration="{None|Bulleted|Numbered}"
   ItemsAsLinks="{False|True}"
   ItemCount="itemCount"
   OnItemDataBind="onItemDataBindHandler"
   OnItemCommand="onItemCommandHandler"
   OnLoadItems="loadItemsHandler">

   <!-- Optional statically declared list items -->
   <Item Text="Text" Value="Value" Selected="{True|False}" />

</mobile:List>
```

Properties and Events

Table 6-3 lists the primary properties and events of the List control but excludes those inherited from the *MobileControl* class. (See Table 4-1 and Table 4-2 for details of those properties that are inherited from MobileControl.) The *Type* column describes the type of the property when you're setting or getting the property in code. Refer to the preceding “Syntax” section for valid values when setting the property in server control syntax.

Table 6-3 Significant Properties and Events of the List Control

Property/ Event	Type	Description
DataMember	*String*	Used only when the control is data bound to a *DataSet* or *DataTable* object. This attribute specifies the name of the table in the *DataSet* object to which the control should bind.
DataSource	*Object*	When the control is data bound, *DataSource* identifies the collection object or *DataSet* that is the data source.
DataTextField	*String*	When the control is data bound, either to a *DataSet* object or to an enumerated collection, *DataTextField* specifies the name of the field in the data source that is displayed in the list.
DataValueField	*String*	When the control is data bound, either to a *DataSet* object or to an enumerated collection, *DataValueField* specifies the name of the field in the data source that provides the hidden data value associated with each item in the list.
Decoration	*System.Web.UI.MobileControls.ListDecoration* enumeration: *None* | *Bulleted* | *Numbered*	On HTML browsers, *Decoration* dictates the presentation style used. Default is *ListDecoration.None*.
ItemsAsLinks	*False* | *True*	Used in special cases in which you use the *Text* value of each list item for the hyperlink text and the value is a valid URI. When you select *ItemsAsLinks*, the client directly calls the specified resource, meaning that the code can't deliver any selection events. Consequently, setting this attribute to *True* overrides the *OnItemCommand* property.
ItemCount	*Integer*	You use this property with custom pagination. *ItemCount* specifies the total number of items in the source dataset. To use custom pagination, you must set the *Form.Paginate* property to *True*.

Table 6-3 Significant Properties and Events of the List Control

Property/ Event	Type	Description
ItemCommand (event)	Event handler method name	Specifies the event handler to call when a user selects an item in the list—except when you've specified *ItemsAsLinks*, as described above.
LoadItems (event)	Event handler method name	Required when you've specified an *ItemCount* property, thus enabling custom pagination. The code calls this event handler each time the runtime requires new data. This allows you to pass data to the control in chunks.

Using the List Control

As mentioned at the beginning of this section, you can use the List control in two ways:

- **Non-interactive mode** In this mode, items are rendered as a simple display list. The user can't select any items. On HTML browsers, the list is rendered in the style indicated by the *Decoration* property. For this mode, do not define an *ItemCommand* event handler.
- **Interactive mode** This mode activates if you define an *ItemCommand* event handler. In this case, the *Text* value of each list item is rendered as a selectable link that calls the *ItemCommand* event handler when the user activates it.

Setting *ItemsAsLinks* to *True* creates a unique situation that overrides this behavior. This attribute causes the list to be rendered as a set of hyperlinks. The *Text* property of each list item becomes the hyperlink text, while the *Value* property identifies the destination. When the user selects such a link, the client calls for a resource at the URL specified, meaning that the code doesn't make a call to the *ItemCommand* event handler.

You can use the List control with the *<Item>* tag with both the statically defined list items by using the *<Item>* element or by data binding to a single field of a data collection using the *DataMember*, *DataSource*, *DataTextField*, and *DataValueField* elements. You program these features for the List control the same way you do for the SelectionList control. Refer to the section "The SelectionList Control" earlier in this chapter for details.

Trapping User Selections

When you use the *ItemCommand* property to specify an event handler to call when the user selects a list item, the List control operates just like a SelectionList control in single-selection mode. Although the List control doesn't support the same presentation options as SelectionList, it does support pagination for large lists. In addition, the List control causes a postback from the client to the server, rather than requiring an accompanying Command control, as the SelectionList control does.

The second argument of the *ItemCommand* event handler is a *System.Web.UI.MobileControls.ListCommandEventArgs* object, which contains a *ListItem* property that identifies the item that the user selects. Listings 6-7 and 6-8 depict a new version of the team statistics example we used earlier to demonstrate the SelectionList control in single-selection mode. However, here we've updated the code to use the *ItemCommand* functionality of the List control.

```
<%@ Page Inherits="MSPress.MobWeb.ListItmCmd.MyWebForm" Language="c#"
    CodeBehind="ListItemCommandExample.aspx.cs"%>
<%@ Register TagPrefix="mobile"
    Namespace="System.Web.UI.MobileControls"
    Assembly="System.Web.Mobile" %>

<mobile:Form runat="server" id="Form1">
    <mobile:Label runat="server" id="Label1" StyleReference="title">
        Season 2003 results
    </mobile:Label>
    <mobile:Label runat="server" id="Label2">Select a team:</mobile:Label>
    <mobile:List runat="server" id="List1">
        <item Text="Dunes" Value="Posn:1 Pl:38 Pts:80"/>
        <item Text="Phoenix" Value="Posn:2 Pl:38 Pts:70"/>
        <item Text="Eagles" Value="Posn:3 Pl:38 Pts:69"/>
        <item Text="Zodiac" Value="Posn:4 Pl:38 Pts:68"/>
    </mobile:List>
</mobile:Form>

<mobile:Form runat="server" id="Form2">
    <mobile:Label runat="server" id="Label3" StyleReference="title">
        Team Full Stats:
    </mobile:Label>
    <mobile:Label runat="server" id="Label4" />
</mobile:Form>
```

Listing 6-7 Source for ListItemCommandExample.aspx

```
using System;
using System.Web.UI.MobileControls;

namespace MSPress.MobWeb.ListItmCmd
{
    public class MyWebForm : System.Web.UI.MobileControls.MobilePage
    {
        protected System.Web.UI.MobileControls.List List1;
        protected System.Web.UI.MobileControls.Label Label4;
        protected System.Web.UI.MobileControls.Form  Form2;

        override protected void OnInit(EventArgs e)
        {
            InitializeComponent();
            base.OnInit(e);
        }

        private void InitializeComponent()
        {
             this.List1.ItemCommand += new
                    ListCommandEventHandler(this.ClickTeamSelection);
        }

        private void ClickTeamSelection(
            Object source,
            ListCommandEventArgs args)
        {
            // Display the Stats page
            this.ActiveForm = Form2;
            String strSelectedTeamStats = args.ListItem.Value;
            Label4.Text = args.ListItem.Text
                               + ": " + strSelectedTeamStats;
        }
    }
}
```

Listing 6-8 Code-behind file ListItemCommandExample.aspx.cs

Instead of requiring a separate Command control to post results to the server, each item in the list is now a link, as Figure 6-5 illustrates.

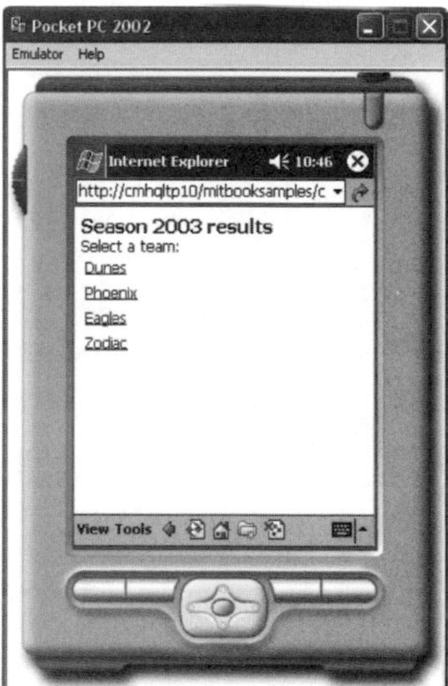

Figure 6-5 List control example output

Automatic Pagination

As shown in Figure 6-1, unlike the SelectionList control, the List control derives from the *PagedControl* class. This gives the List control support for internal pagination. To use this feature, you must supply all the data to the control up front and set the *Paginate* property of the enclosing Form control to *True*.

If you enable automatic pagination, the Mobile Internet Controls Runtime will insert page breaks between controls to split the output over the necessary number of screens, depending on the client's capabilities. For controls that support internal pagination, such as the List and ObjectList controls, automatic pagination permits the runtime to insert page breaks between list items.

Custom Pagination

Instead of supplying all the data up front, you can pass data to the control on demand each time a new display page builds. You can activate custom pagination by setting the *ItemCount* property to the total number of items that can be displayed across all pages. The control paginates as though it had all the data, even though you didn't supply any data initially. Then, as each page is constructed, the control raises the *LoadItems* event that you can trap in code in your event handler. In your event handler, you can fetch the data and supply the next page of items to the control for display. This technique can yield performance benefits when the list is very large or in situations where the computational effort required is high.

Your *LoadItems* event handler method takes a parameter of type *System.Web.UI.MobileControls.LoadItemsEventArgs*. This object has two properties that specify how much data to return:

- ***ItemIndex*** The index of the first item
- ***ItemCount*** The number of items to return

For example, if *ItemCount* is 10 and *ItemIndex* is 50, the event handler must supply 10 items starting from (and including) the 50th record in the data source. You build the items that you want to display as objects of type *MobileListItem*, and you add them to the *Items* collection of the List control, as Listings 6-9 and 6-10 demonstrate. In this example, the code creates an array of *TeamStats* objects that provides the data source. Keep in mind that a real application would probably be getting data from a database or some external data source. Each time the application requires more display data, it calls the *LoadTeams* event handler.

> **Important** Clear the *Items* collection of the *List* object each time the application makes a call, as this sample does in the first line of the LoadItems method; otherwise, the runtime will attempt to display the same items it showed in the previous screen as well as the ones you've added to the collection.

```
<%@ Page Inherits="MSPress.MobWeb.CusPag.ExampleWebForm" Language="c#"
    CodeBehind="CustomPaginationExample.aspx.cs" AutoEventWireup= "False" %>
<%@ Register TagPrefix="mobile"
    Namespace="System.Web.UI.MobileControls"
    Assembly="System.Web.Mobile" %>

<mobile:Form runat="server" id="Form1" paginate="true">
    <mobile:Label runat="server" StyleReference="title">
        Season 2003 results</mobile:Label>
    <mobile:List id="List1" runat="server"></mobile:List>
</mobile:Form>
```

Listing 6-9 Source for CustomPaginationExample.aspx

```
using System;
using System.Collections;
using System.Web.UI.MobileControls;

namespace MSPress.MobWeb.CusPag
{
    public class ExampleWebForm : System.Web.UI.MobileControls.MobilePage
    {
        private TeamStats[] _premierTable;

        protected System.Web.UI.MobileControls.List List1;

        public ExampleWebForm()
        {
            // In the constructor, create the data source we will use.
            _premierTable = new TeamStats[16];
            _premierTable[0] = new TeamStats("Dunes",    "Pts:80");
            _premierTable[1] = new TeamStats("Phoenix",  "Pts:70");
            _premierTable[2] = new TeamStats("Eagles",   "Pts:69");
            _premierTable[3] = new TeamStats("Zodiac",   "Pts:68");
            _premierTable[4] = new TeamStats("Arches",   "Pts:66");
            _premierTable[5] = new TeamStats("Chows",    "Pts:61");
            _premierTable[6] = new TeamStats("Creation", "Pts:57");
            _premierTable[7] = new TeamStats("Illusion", "Pts:54");
            _premierTable[8] = new TeamStats("Torpedo",  "Pts:52");
            _premierTable[9] = new TeamStats("Generals", "Pts:52");
            _premierTable[10] = new TeamStats("Reaction","Pts:51");
            _premierTable[11] = new TeamStats("Peanuts", "Pts:49");
            _premierTable[12] = new TeamStats("Caverns", "Pts:48");
            _premierTable[13] = new TeamStats("Eclipse", "Pts:42");
            _premierTable[14] = new TeamStats("Dragons", "Pts:42");
            _premierTable[15] = new TeamStats("Cosmos",  "Pts:42");    }

        override protected void OnInit(EventArgs e)
        {
            InitializeComponent();
            base.OnInit(e);
        }

        private void InitializeComponent()
        {
               this.Load += new System.EventHandler(this.Page_Load);
             this.List1.LoadItems +=
                   new LoadItemsEventHandler(this.LoadTeams);
        }
```

Listing 6-10 Code-behind file CustomPaginationExample.aspx.cs

```
        private void Page_Load(Object sender, EventArgs e)
        {
            // Tell the List how many items it can expect by the time
            // it has asked for them all.
            List1.ItemCount = _premierTable.Length;
        }

        private void LoadTeams(Object source, LoadItemsEventArgs args)
        {
            List1.Items.Clear();
            //  The LoadItemsEventArgs tells us which items and how many.
            for (int i = 0; i < args.ItemCount; i++)
            {
                // Get the relevant item from the array;
                // Create a MobileListItem.
                int intTablePosn = args.ItemIndex + i;
                MobileListItem lstItem = new MobileListItem(
                    string.Format("{0} {1}",intTablePosn+1,
                        _premierTable[intTablePosn].TeamName),
                   _premierTable[intTablePosn].Stats);

               // Add the item to the Items collection of the List control.
               List1.Items.Add(lstItem);
            }
        }
    }

    class TeamStats
    {
        private String teamName, stats;

        public TeamStats(String teamName, String stats)
        {
            this.teamName = teamName;
            this.stats = stats;
        }

        public String TeamName
        { get { return this.teamName; } }

        public String Stats
        { get { return this.stats; } }
    }
}
```

If you run the code in these two listings with Internet Explorer, all the items will be displayed on a single screen. However, using a device with a small display screen causes the output to paginate, as Figure 6-6 shows.

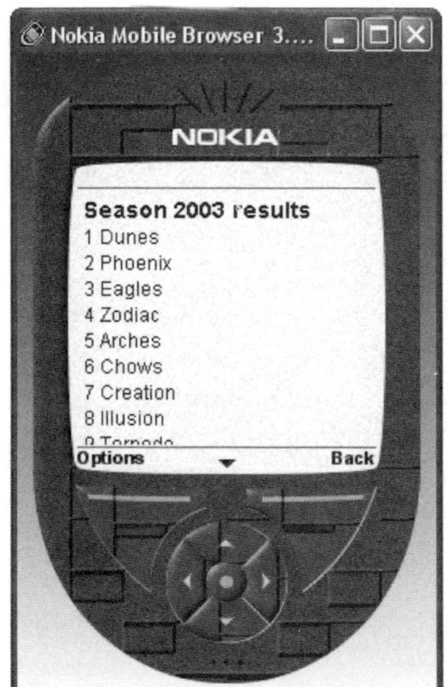

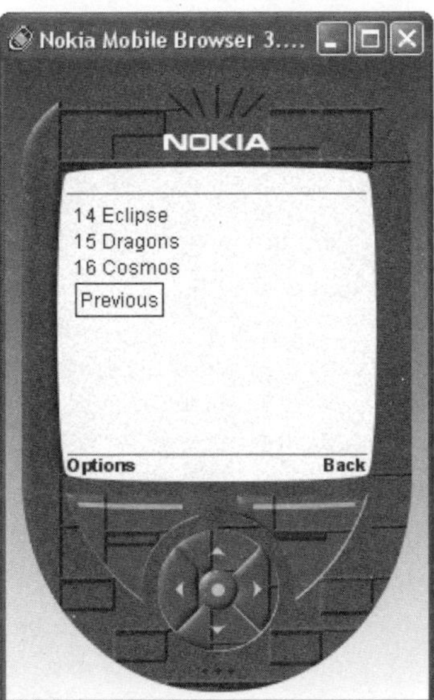

Figure 6-6 Custom pagination in action on the Nokia Simulator

> **Tip** You can override the default text for the Next and Previous buttons used for navigation by setting the *NextPageText* and *PrevPageText* properties of the Form control's *PagerStyle* object, as shown here:
>
> ```
> this.Form1.PagerStyle.NextPageText = "->";
> ```

The ObjectList Control

The ObjectList control is a very flexible control. Its primary purpose is to display a single field from the data source to the user as the initial list of items, and then when the user selects an item, it displays many more fields from the selected data record (the detail display). In addition, the ObjectList control offers much more flexibility in the commands that you can associate with each item. When it displays the detail view, it can also display a menu of options which you can customize to offer unique menu options depending on which item from the initial list the user selected. You can choose to display all the fields in the data record, or a subset of the fields.

Like the List control, the ObjectList control supports internal paging, meaning that it's useful for displaying larger lists of items. The ObjectList control also supports templating, making it very flexible and able to implement device-specific behavior. (You'll learn more about templating in Chapter 10.) Unlike the SelectionList and List controls, you can't supply the data of an ObjectList control as static data items; instead, the ObjectList must be data bound.

Syntax

The following listing shows the server control syntax used to code the ObjectList control. The *LoadItems* event and *ItemCount* property are inherited from the *PagedControl* parent class; you use these only when you implement custom pagination. (See the section "Custom Pagination," earlier in this chapter, for more details.) *<Field>* items are used to explicitly declare named fields from the source data set to display. Usually, you use these if you have *AutoGenerateFields* set to *False*, although you can use them together (see Table 6-4 below for more information on these properties). You use *<Command>* tags to declare item commands that are displayed along with the details of a selected item. (See the section "Providing More Than One Command for Each Item," later in this chapter.)

```
<mobile:ObjectList
   runat="server"
   id="id"
   Alignment="{NotSet|Left|Center|Right}"
   BackColor="backgroundColor"
   Font-Bold="{NotSet|False|True}"
   Font-Italic="{NotSet|False|True}"
   Font-Name="fontName"
   Font-Size="{NotSet|Normal|Small|Large}"
   ForeColor="foregroundColor"
   StyleReference="StyleReference"
   Wrapping="{NotSet|Wrap|NoWrap}"

   AutoGenerateFields="{True|False}"
   CommandStyle="StyleReference"
   DataMember="dataMember"
   DataSource="dataSource"
   DefaultCommand="onDefaultCommandHandler"
   ItemCount="itemCount"
   LabelField="fieldname"
   LabelStyle="StyleReference"
   OnItemDataBind="onItemDataBindHandler"
   OnItemCommand="onItemCommandHandler"
   OnLoadItems="loadItemsHandler">
   OnShowItemCommands="onShowItemCommandsHandler"
   TableFields="tableFields">
```

```
    <!-- Optional explicitly declared fields -->
    <Field
        id="id"
        Title="titleText"
        DataField="value"
        FormatString="formatString"
        Visible="{True|False}" />
    </Field>

    <!-- Optional explicitly declared commands -->
    <Command Name="CommandName" Text="CommandText" />

</mobile:ObjectList>
```

Properties and Events

Table 6-4 describes the most significant properties and events of the ObjectList control but excludes those inherited from the *MobileControl* class. (See Table 4-1 and Table 4-2 for details of those properties that are inherited from *MobileControl*.) The *Type* column describes the type of the property when setting or getting the property in code. Refer to the preceding "Syntax" section for valid values when setting the property in server control syntax.

Table 6-4 Significant Properties and Events of the ObjectList Control

Property/ Event	Type	Description
AllFields	*System.Web.UI. MobileControls. ObjectListField-Collection*	This property returns an *ObjectListFieldCollection* object, which contains a *System.Web.UI.MobileControls.ObjectListField* object for each data source field added to the ObjectList control, whether automatically generated or explicitly defined (through a *<Field>* tag or added in code through the *Fields* property). This collection is available only after data binding. You can't add or remove fields from this collection; however, you can manipulate the properties of the contained fields.
AutoGenerateFields	*True | False*	Configures the control to displays all the fields from the source *DataSet* object. Field labels (displayed on the details screen) default to the *FieldName* property. You'll need to set the *LabelField* property so that the application uses the correct field as the primary list index.

Table 6-4 Significant Properties and Events of the ObjectList Control

Property/ Event	Type	Description
BackCommandText	*String*	Sets or gets the text used for the navigation link to return from the Details view to the List view. Default is "Back" (or localized equivalent).
Commands	*System.Web.UI. MobileControls. ObjectList-Command-Collection*	Returns the *ObjectListCommandCollection* object. There is an *ObjectListCommand* object in this collection for each item command that you define using <*Command*> tags or that you add in code. See the section "Providing Different Commands for Different List Items," later in this chapter, for an example of manipulating this collection.
Command-Style	Valid *Style* in *StyleSheet*	Sets the style used to display item commands on the client device. This property is not persisted between client requests, so you must set it on every request. The easiest way to do this is to define it in server control syntax.
DataMember	*String*	Used only when the control is data bound to a *DataSet* or *DataTable* object. This property specifies the name of the table in the *DataSet* to which the control should bind.
DataSource	*Object*	The *DataSet* object or enumerated collection that is the data source.
DefaultCommand	*String*	By default, the list displays the value of the field specified by the *LabelField* property as a hyperlink. Selecting the link takes the user to another screen that displays additional fields for that item. However, if the code defines a *DefaultCommand* property, selecting an item from the list invokes the *OnItemCommand* event handler with this property's value. You can still access the item details through a More or More Details link, which appears alongside links for any other *item* commands you might have defined. (See the *ItemCommand* description in this table for more information.)
Details	*System.Web.UI. MobileControls. Panel*	Gets the Panel control that is used to display the item details. This property is particularly useful when you've implemented an <*ItemDetailsTemplate*> and want to set properties of a control that you've placed in the template. To locate the control, you use this syntax: `ObjectList1.Details.FindControl("controlID")`

Table 6-4 Significant Properties and Events of the ObjectList Control

Property/ Event	Type	Description
DetailsCommandText	*String*	Sets or gets the text used for the link that displays the Details view. *DetailsCommandText* is used only on WML browsers.
Fields	*ObjectListFieldCollection*	Similar to *AllFields*. *Fields* returns an *ObjectListFieldCollection* object, which contains an *ObjectListField* object for each data source field added to the ObjectList control that has been explicitly defined (through a *<Field>* tag or added in code through the *Fields* property). Unlike the *AllFields* collection which is read-only, you can add or remove fields from this collection using methods of the *ObjectListFieldCollection* object.
ItemCount	*Integer*	You use this property with custom pagination. It specifies the total number of items in the source dataset. To use custom pagination, you must set the *Form.Paginate* property to *True*.
LabelField	*String*	Specifies the name of the field in the data source you'll use as the primary index. The primary index provides the list from which users make their initial selection. The *LabelFieldIndex* property does the same thing but by specifying the index into the *AllFields* collection.
LabelStyle	*String*	Sets the style used to display the header label. *LabelStyle* isn't persisted between client requests, so you must set it on every request. The easiest way to do this is to define it in server control syntax.
MoreText	*String*	Sets or gets the text used for the More link on HTML browsers. See the description of the *TableFields* property for situations where a More link is displayed.
SelectedIndex	*Integer*	Gets or sets the index of the selected item.
Selection	*System.Web.UI.MobileControls.ObjectListItem*	Gets the selected item or *null* if there is no selection.

Table 6-4 Significant Properties and Events of the ObjectList Control

Property/ Event	Type	Description
TableFields	*String*; a list of field names separated by semicolons	If you don't specify *TableFields* (the default), the application presents the list as a single column that consists solely of the value contained in the field specified by the *LabelField* property. If you specify a *DefaultCommand* property and the device supports tables, that single column will consist of both the value of the *LabelField* property and a More link. If you define the *TableFields* property, the application presents each item in the list in a table (if the device supports tables), with the columns defined by the fields identified in this property. A More column allows access to a view that shows all the fields for the item.
ViewMode	*System.Web.UI. MobileControls. ObjectListViewMode* enumeration: *List* | *Commands* | *Details*	Allows you to set the desired *ObjectList* views displayed. *List* view is the initial item list. The *Details* view shows the details of the selected item. The *Commands* view is displayed only on small-screen browsers such as those on mobile phones and is the first screen displayed after the user has made a selection; it displays a menu of options consisting of any item commands (such as those you have defined with *<Command>* tags) plus a link to the Details view (as shown on the right-hand image in Figure 6-9). The user must make a selection from the list the ObjectList first displays before you are allowed to set the *ViewMode* property to *Commands* or *Details*.
Item-Command (Event)	Event handler method name	Specifies the event handler the code calls when the user selects a command associated with an item's detail display. You define commands using the *<Command>* element or by manipulating the collection exposed through the *Commands* property. The event handler method must have a signature of *eventHandlerMethodName(object source, System.Web.UI.MobileControls. ObjectListCommand-EventArgs e).*

Table 6-4 Significant Properties and Events of the ObjectList Control

Property/ Event	Type	Description
LoadItems (Event)	Event handler method name	Required when you specify an *ItemCount* property, thus enabling custom pagination. The application calls this event handler each time the runtime requires new data. This allows you to pass display data to the control as needed, rather than passing all of the data up front.
ShowItem-Commands (Event)	Event handler method name	Specifies the event handler to call when the detail of an item must be displayed and the application is formulating the command links to display alongside the details (such as those defined using <*Command*> tags). In this event handler, you can create or delete commands, thus building a list of commands specific to the item to be displayed.

Using the ObjectList Control

Like the List control, the ObjectList control supports internal pagination. The List control allows you to define items statically or add them programmatically, and you can bind it to a dataset. The ObjectList control, however, must be bound to a data source.

As mentioned, the ObjectList control offers many more capabilities than the List control. Here is a list of the things you can do with the ObjectList control that you can't do with the other list controls:

- **Displaying multiple fields from the data source** The List control and SelectionList control can display only a single field from the source.
- **Displaying the items in a table, rather than in a single-column list** The initial list can display more than one field from the source, but this is supported only on HTML browsers.
- **Providing more than one command for each item** The List control can handle only a single command action, which it applies to all items. The ObjectList control can do this too, but it also offers a number of command options associated with each item.
- **Providing different commands for different list items** This capability is similar to a context menu that you can program to display a different set of item commands to users, depending on which list item they select.

- **Displaying a single field, with multiple fields as a secondary function** Although displaying the details of a selected item is no longer the list's primary purpose, it's still available to users as a secondary function.

In the following sections, you'll learn how to implement each of these scenarios.

Displaying Multiple Fields from the Data Source

The data records in the data source to which you bind the ObjectList consists of a number of fields. One of the fields is displayed as the *Label* field—that is, the field that is displayed as a link in the initial list. When the user selects an item in the initial list, the application directs him or her to a second screen that displays the full set of fields for the item, as Figure 6-7 shows.

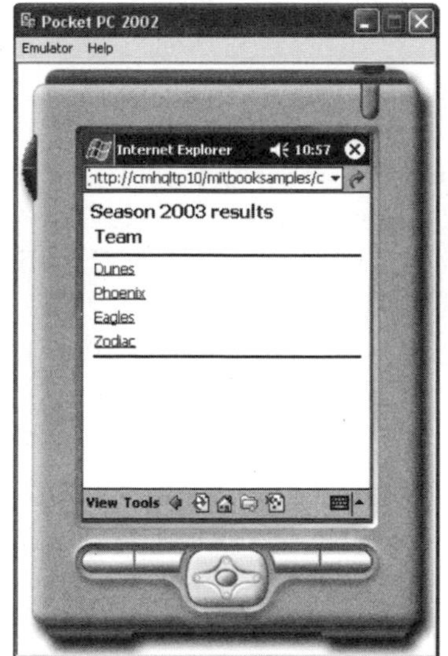

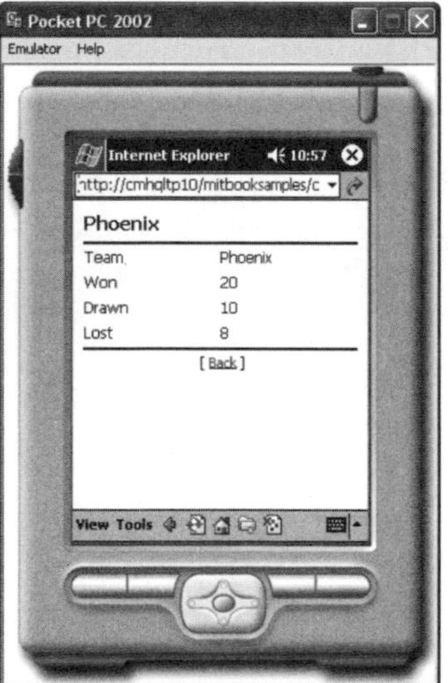

Figure 6-7 Using the ObjectList control to display multiple fields of an item in a dataset. Selecting an item shows all its fields.

You have two ways to select which fields will be displayed. First, you can set the *AutoGenerateFields* property to *true*. (This is the default.) This setting takes each field in the source *DataSet* and displays it, using the field name as the label. One of the fields will be the *Label* field, which will be displayed as the initial link. Often, this won't be the field you want as the initial link. Therefore, you must set the *LabelField* property to the name of the field that you want to use as the primary selection field.

The second way you can select the fields to be displayed is by setting the *AutoGenerateFields* property to *false*. Instead of automatically generating the fields to be displayed, you define them yourself. The easiest way to do this is to define these fields statically in the mobile Web Forms page by using the field declaration syntax, as you can see in the following example:

```
<Field
    id="Teamname"          <!-- Programmatic ID of field -->
    Title="Team"           <!-- Label text -->
    DataField="TeamName" <!-- Field name -->
    FormatString=""        <!-- ToString() format string -->
    Visible="true" />      <!-- true or false -->
</Field>
```

The *Title* attribute specifies a label to use instead of the *FieldName*, the *DataField* attribute specifies which source field to use, and the *Visible* attribute enables and disables a particular field's display. By default, the field is displayed by calling its *ToString* method with no format modifier. If this isn't suitable, use *FormatString* to specify an alternative conversion. *FormatString* uses the rules defined by the *System.String.Format* method. For example, to format a numeric value as a currency string, set the *FormatString* attribute to *"{0:c}"*.Consult the Microsoft .NET Framework SDK documentation for details.

Whether you let the display fields generate automatically or you define them yourself in the .aspx file, the result is a collection of field definitions stored in an *ObjectListFieldsCollection* object. You can retrieve this collection by using the *AllFields* property of the *ObjectList* class, accessing the *ObjectListField* objects from the collection, and then manipulating the properties.

For example, the following code fragment shows how to set the *Visible* property of the *ObjectListField* object for the *Played* field:

```
foreach (ObjectListField oblFld in myObjectList.AllFields)
{
    if (oblFld.DataField == "Played") oblFld.Visible = false;
}
```

You can also access the *ObjectListField* object directly if you know the index for the collection of the field you want, as shown here:

```
myObjectList.AllFields[3].Visible = false;
```

Listings 6-11 and 6-12 show an *ObjectList* object that's bound to a control that's bound to a data collection stored in an *ArrayList* object. The *TeamStats* class defines the data records this sample uses and has seven properties. The *LabelField* property is the *TeamName* field, which is displayed as the primary index for the user. You could set the *AutoGenerateFields* property to *true* and display all the properties of the source data record (a *TeamStats* instance), but instead, the sample explicitly declares *<Field>* items to display the *TeamName*, *Won*, *Drawn*, *Lost*, and *Points* properties of the source.

```
<%@ Page Inherits="MSPress.MobWeb.ObjListEx.MyWebForm" Language="c#"
    CodeBehind="ObjectListExample.aspx.cs" AutoEventWireup="False"  %>
<%@ Register TagPrefix="mobile"
    Namespace="System.Web.UI.MobileControls"
    Assembly="System.Web.Mobile" %>

<mobile:Form runat="server" >
    <mobile:Label runat="server" StyleReference="title">
        Season 2003 results</mobile:Label>
    <mobile:ObjectList id="ObjectList1" runat="server">
        AutoGenerateFields="false">
        <Field Title="Team" DataField="TeamName"></Field>
        <Field Title="Won" DataField="Won"></Field>
        <Field Title="Drawn" DataField="Drawn"></Field>
        <Field Title="Lost" DataField="Lost"></Field>
        <Field Title="Pts" DataField="Points" Visible="false"></Field>
    </mobile:ObjectList>
</mobile:Form>
```

Listing 6-11 Source for ObjectListExample.aspx

```
using System;
using System.Collections;
using System.Web.UI.MobileControls;

namespace MSPress.MobWeb.ObjListEx
{
    public class MyWebForm : System.Web.UI.MobileControls.MobilePage
    {
        protected ObjectList ObjectList1;

        override protected void OnInit(EventArgs e)
        {
            InitializeComponent();
            base.OnInit(e);
        }

        private void InitializeComponent()
        {
                this.Load += new System.EventHandler(this.Page_Load);
        }

        private void Page_Load(Object sender, EventArgs e)
```

Listing 6-12 Code-behind module ObjectListExample.aspx.cs

```
        {
            if (!IsPostBack)
            {
                ArrayList array = new ArrayList();
                array.Add(new TeamStats("Dunes",1,38,24,8,6,80));
                array.Add(new TeamStats("Phoenix",2,38,20,10,8,70));
                array.Add(new TeamStats("Eagles",3,38,20,9,9,69));
                array.Add(new TeamStats("Zodiac",4,38,20,8,10,68));

                ObjectList1.DataSource = array;
                ObjectList1.LabelField = "TeamName";
                ObjectList1.DataBind();
            }
        }
    }

    class TeamStats
    {
        private String  _teamName;
        private int _position, _played, _won, _drawn, _lost, _points;

        public TeamStats(String teamName,
            int position,
            int played,
            int won,
            int drawn,
            int lost,
            int points)
        {
            this._teamName = teamName;
            this._position = position;
            this._played = played;
            this._won = won;
            this._drawn = drawn;
            this._lost = lost;
            this._points = points;
        }

        public String TeamName { get { return this._teamName; } }
        public int    Position { get { return this._position; } }
        public int    Played   { get { return this._played; } }
        public int    Won      { get { return this._won; } }
        public int    Drawn    { get { return this._drawn; } }
        public int    Lost     { get { return this._lost; } }
        public int    Points   { get { return this._points; } }
    }
}
```

Displaying the Items in a Table

The *TableFields* property defines which fields appear in the initial list. By default, this property is a blank string, meaning that it will display only the field the *LabelField* property indicates. If you provide a list of field names separated by semicolons, the runtime will attempt to render a table displaying the requested fields, subject to the client's ability to support tables. This will override any *LabelField* setting. Furthermore, the first field in the list becomes the link—either to show all the item fields or, if you specify a *DefaultCommand* property, to invoke the *OnItemCommand* event handler for the default command. Figure 6-8 offers an example of the output.

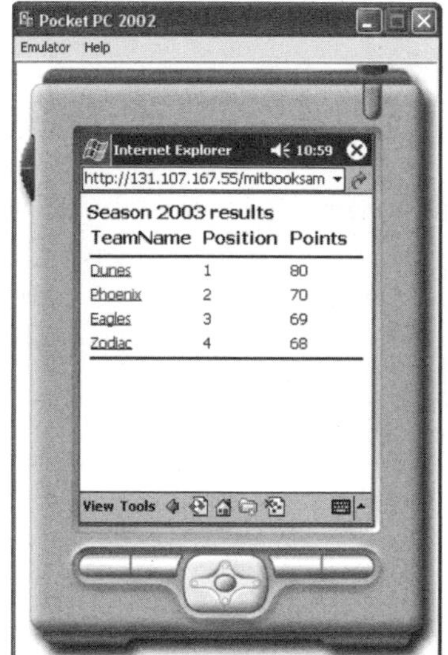

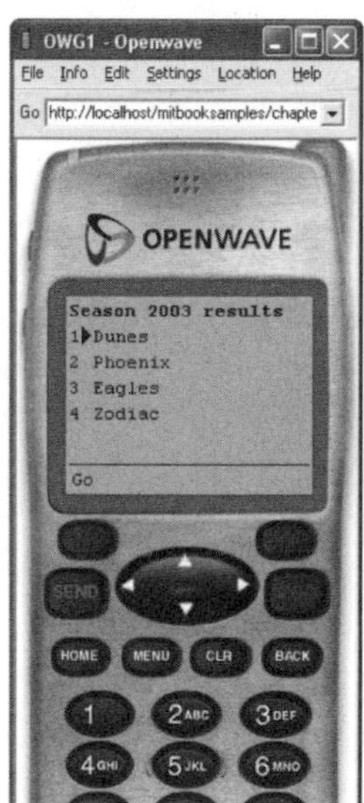

Figure 6-8 An HTML browser supports table output, but a WML browser displays a single-column list. In both cases, all fields are displayed when you select the link.

The code-behind module for the .aspx file shown in Listing 6-13 is identical to that shown in Listing 6-12, apart from the change of the namespace to *MSPress.MobWeb.ObjListTblEx*, so we don't show it here.

```
<%@ Page Inherits="MSPress.MobWeb.ObjListTblEx.MyWebForm" Language="c#"
    CodeBehind="ObjectListTableExample.aspx.cs" AutoEventWireup="False" %>
<%@ Register TagPrefix="mobile" Namespace="System.Web.UI.MobileControls"
    Assembly="System.Web.Mobile" %>

<mobile:Form runat="server"
```

Listing 6-13 Source for ObjectListTableExample.aspx

```
    <mobile:Label runat="server" StyleReference="title">
        Season 2003 results</mobile:Label>
    <mobile:ObjectList id="ObjectList1"
                       runat="server"
                       AutoGenerateFields="true"
                       TableFields="TeamName;Position;Points">
    </mobile:ObjectList>
</mobile:Form>
```

Providing More Than One Command for Each Item

The List control allows only a single command for each item. The List control raises the *ItemCommand* event when the user selects an item from the list.

The ObjectList control allows you to associate as many commands as you want with each item (we'll call them *item commands*). After the user selects an item from the initial list, the control displays all the other properties of the item. On HTML browsers, any item commands that you specify will be displayed at the foot of that page. On WML browsers, the item commands appear on an intermediate page, which is displayed after the user selects an item. Figure 6-9 illustrates this. (The code for this example is shown in Listings 6-14 and 6-15.)

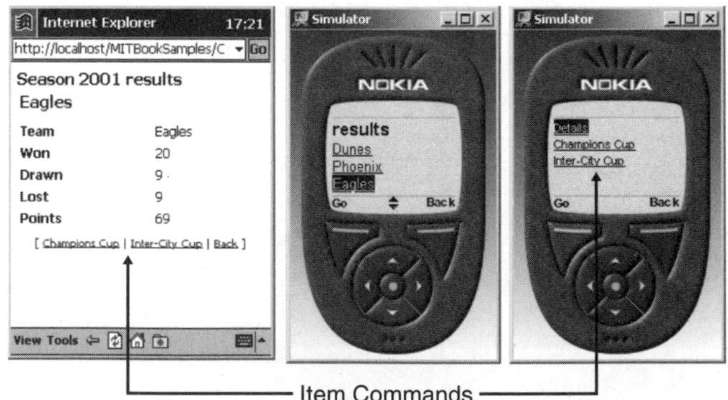

Figure 6-9 ObjectList item commands appear below the details page on a Pocket PC but on an intermediate page (after the user selects an item) on the Nokia June 2000 simulator.

You can specify item commands using the optional *<Command>* element. The following example displays a link with the text "Champions Cup" and sets the name associated with this command to "ChampsCup." (You can access this value in your event handler method.)

```
<Command Name="ChampsCup" Text="Champions Cup"/>
```

You must specify the event handler method to call in the *ItemCommand* property. In the event handler, you can determine which command item the user selects by getting the *CommandName* property of the *ObjectListCommandEventArgs* argument.

When you define item commands using the *<Command>* element, the runtime builds *ObjectListCommand* objects and places them in an *ObjectListCommandsCollection* object. You can access this collection through the *Commands* property of the *ObjectList* class in code and add, remove, or modify the item command objects it contains. For more details on working with this collection, see the section "Providing Different Commands for Different List Items," later in this chapter.

Listings 6-14 and 6-15 improve on the previous example. In Listing 6-15, the *TeamStats* class that defines our data source records now has two additional fields, *ChampionsCup* and *InterCup*, which record the success of a team in two fictional knock-out cup competitions. In the *<Field>* definitions in ObjectListItemCommandsExample.aspx (Listing 6-14), the application loads these two new fields into the control. However, we've set the *Visible* property to *False*, so these fields don't appear on the main page.

On Pocket Internet Explorer, selecting a team from the initial list will lead a user to the team's page. This screen now contains two new commands, in addition to the standard Back button. When the user selects either the Champions Cup or the Inter-City Cup command, the code calls the *Team_OnItemCommand* event handler. There the code tests the *CommandName* property to determine which option the user chose. The code also sets the label on the form *Form2* with the result for the requested competition (retrieved from the *ObjectListItem* object passed in the parameter) or the string *Did not compete* if the source property is *null*.

```
<%@ Page Inherits="MSPress.MobWeb.ObjListCmdsEx.MyWebForm" Language="c#"
    CodeBehind="ObjectListItemCommandsExample.aspx.cs"
    AutoEventWireup="False" %>
<%@ Register TagPrefix="mobile"
    Namespace="System.Web.UI.MobileControls"
    Assembly="System.Web.Mobile" %>

<mobile:Form runat="server" id="Form1">
    <mobile:Label runat="server" StyleReference="title">
        Season 2003 results</mobile:Label>
    <mobile:ObjectList id="ObjectList1" runat="server"
                       AutoGenerateFields="false"
                       LabelField="TeamName">
        <Field Title="Team" DataField="TeamName"></Field>
```

Listing 6-14 Source for ObjectListItemCommandsExample.aspx

```
        <Field Title="Won" DataField="Won"></Field>
        <Field Title="Drawn" DataField="Drawn"></Field>
        <Field Title="Lost" DataField="Lost"></Field>
        <Field Title="Points" DataField="Points"></Field>
        <Field Title="Champs. Cup" DataField="ChampionsCup"
               Visible="false">
        </Field>
        <Field Title="Inter-City Cup" DataField="InterCup" Visible="false">
        </Field>
        <Command Name="ChampsCup" Text="Champions Cup"/>
        <Command Name="InterCityCup" Text="Inter-City Cup"/>
    </mobile:ObjectList>
</mobile:Form>

<mobile:Form runat="server" id="Form2">
    <mobile:Label runat="server" StyleReference="title">
        Season 2003 European Results</mobile:Label>
    <mobile:Label runat="server" id="Label1"/>
    <mobile:Link runat="server" NavigateUrl="#Form1">
        Back
    </mobile:Link>
</mobile:Form>
```

```
using System;
using System.Collections;
using System.Web.UI.MobileControls;

namespace MSPress.MobWeb.ObjListCmdsEx
{
    public class MyWebForm : System.Web.UI.MobileControls.MobilePage
    {
        protected ObjectList ObjectList1;
        protected Form       Form2;
        protected Label      Label1;

        override protected void OnInit(EventArgs e)
        {
            InitializeComponent();
            base.OnInit(e);
        }

        private void InitializeComponent()
        {
            this.Load += new System.EventHandler(this.Page_Load);
            this.ObjectList1.ItemCommand +=
```

Listing 6-15 Code-behind file ObjectListItemCommandsExample.aspx.cs

```
            new ObjectListCommandEventHandler(this.Team_OnItemCommand);
    }

    private void Page_Load(Object sender, EventArgs e)
    {
        if (!IsPostBack)
        {
            ArrayList array = new ArrayList();
            array.Add(new TeamStats("Dunes",1,38,24,8,6,80,
                                        "Quarter Finals",""));
            array.Add(new TeamStats("Phoenix",2,38,20,10,8,70,
                                        "Quarter Finals",""));
            array.Add(new TeamStats("Eagles",3,38,20,9,9,69,
                                        "","Winners"));
            array.Add(new TeamStats("Zodiac",4,38,20,8,10,68,
                                        "Semi Finals",""));

            ObjectList1.DataSource = array;
            ObjectList1.LabelField = "TeamName";
            ObjectList1.DataBind();
        }
    }

    private void Team_OnItemCommand(
        Object sender,
        ObjectListCommandEventArgs e)
    {
        Label1.Text = "Did Not Compete"; //Default
        this.ActiveForm = Form2;

        if (e.CommandName == "ChampsCup")
        {
            // Set the label to the Champions Cup result.
            if (e.ListItem["ChampionsCup"] != "")
                Label1.Text = "Champions Cup: " +
                    e.ListItem["ChampionsCup"];
        }
        else if (e.CommandName == "InterCityCup")
        {
            // Set the label to the Inter-City Cup result.
            if (e.ListItem["InterCup"] != "")
                Label1.Text = " Inter-City Cup: " +
                    e.ListItem["InterCup"];
        }
    }
}

class TeamStats
```

```
    {
        private String  _teamName;
        private int _position, _played, _won, _drawn, _lost, _points;
        private String  _champsCup, _interCup;

        public TeamStats(String teamName,
            int position,
            int played,
            int won,
            int drawn,
            int lost,
            int points,
            String championsCup,
            String interCup)
        {
            this._teamName = teamName;
            this._position = position;
            this._played = played;
            this._won = won;
            this._drawn = drawn;
            this._lost = lost;
            this._points = points;
            this._champsCup = championsCup;
            this._interCup= interCup;
        }

        public String TeamName { get { return this._teamName; }}
        public int    Position { get { return this._position; }}
        public int    Played   { get { return this._played; }}
        public int    Won      { get { return this._won; }}
        public int    Drawn    { get { return this._drawn; }}
        public int    Lost     { get { return this._lost; }}
        public int    Points   { get { return this._points; }}
        public String ChampionsCup { get { return this._champsCup; }}
        public String InterCup{ get { return this._interCup; }}
    }
}
```

Providing Different Commands for Different List Items

By default, the *<Command>* element defines item commands that appear on the details page whichever item in the list the user selects. However, you can customize the item commands that are displayed so that when a user selects a particular item in the list, fewer item commands are displayed, or you can create additional item commands to display just for that data item.

You do this by specifying an event handler for the *ShowItemCommands* event. The ObjectList control raises this event before the item commands are displayed. A *ShowItemCommands* event handler takes an argument of type *ObjectListShowCommandsEventArgs* that has two properties:

- ***Commands*** This is the same collection of commands that you might have specified using the *<Command>* element, which is of type *ObjectListCommandsCollection*. You can use the *Add*, *AddAt*, *Remove*, and *RemoveAt* methods to manipulate this collection. Any changes you make apply only to the current item and don't affect the available commands collection should the user make subsequent selections.
- ***ListItem*** This returns the item that the user selects.

Listings 6-16 and 6-17 improve on the previous example. When the displayed item already appears as the top list item, the application removes the Team Before command from the item commands collection. Likewise, when the bottom item is displayed, the code removes the Team Below command. The only changes from the previous example are the wiring up of the *ShowItemCommands* event handler in Listing 6-17 to the event handler (called *SetItemCommands*), which implements the logic just described. Now the "Champions Cup" and "Inter Cup" item commands are displayed only if the team entered the competition (and if the *ChampionsCup* or *InterCup* fields in the source data item are not null).

```
<%@ Page Inherits="MSPress.MobWeb.ObjListShowItems.MyWebForm" Language="c#"
    CodeBehind="ObjectListOnShowItemsExample.aspx.cs"
    AutoEventWireup="False" %>
<%@ Register TagPrefix="mobile"
    Namespace="System.Web.UI.MobileControls"
    Assembly="System.Web.Mobile" %>

<mobile:Form runat="server" id="Form1">
    <mobile:Label runat="server" StyleReference="title">
        Season 2003 results</mobile:Label>
    <mobile:ObjectList id="ObjectList1" runat="server"
                       AutoGenerateFields="true"
                       LabelField="TeamName">
        <Command Name="ChampsCup" Text="Champions Cup"/>
        <Command Name="InterCityCup" Text="Inter-City Cup"/>
    </mobile:ObjectList>
</mobile:Form>

<mobile:Form runat="server" id="Form2">
    <mobile:Label runat="server" StyleReference="title" id="Label1"/>
    <mobile:Label runat="server" id="Label2"/>
    <mobile:Link runat="server" NavigateUrl="#Form1">
        Back
    </mobile:Link>
</mobile:Form>
```

Listing 6-16 Source for ObjectListOnShowItemsExample.aspx

```
using System;
using System.Collections;
using System.Web.UI.MobileControls;

namespace MSPress.MobWeb.ObjListShowItems
{
    public class MyWebForm : System.Web.UI.MobileControls.MobilePage
    {
        protected ObjectList ObjectList1;
        protected Form       Form2;
        protected Label      Label1;
        protected Label      Label2;

        override protected void OnInit(EventArgs e)
        {
            InitializeComponent();
            base.OnInit(e);
        }

        private void InitializeComponent()
        {
             this.Load += new System.EventHandler(this.Page_Load);
             this.ObjectList1.ItemCommand += new
                    ObjectListCommandEventHandler(this.Team_OnItemCommand);
             this.ObjectList1.ShowItemCommands += new
                    ObjectListShowCommandsEventHandler(this.SetItemCommands);
        }

        private void Page_Load(Object sender, EventArgs e)
        {
            // Not shown
            // As in previous example
        }

        private void Team_OnItemCommand(
            Object sender,
            ObjectListCommandEventArgs e)
        {
            this.ActiveForm = Form2;

            if (e.CommandName == "ChampsCup")
            {
                // Set the label to the Champions Cup result.
                Label1.Text = "Champions Cup 2003";
                Label2.Text = e.ListItem["ChampionsCup"];
            }
```

Listing 6-17 Code-behind file ObjectListOnShowItemsExample.aspx.cs

```
        else if (e.CommandName == "InterCityCup")
        {
            // Set the label to the Inter-City Cup result.
            Label1.Text = "Inter-City Cup 2003";
            Label2.Text = e.ListItem["InterCup"];
        }
    }

    private void SetItemCommands(
        Object sender,
        ObjectListShowCommandsEventArgs  e)
    {
        // Remove either the Champions Cup or Inter-City Cup
        // command if the team didn't compete (if field is blank).
        if (e.ListItem["ChampionsCup"] == "")
            e.Commands.Remove("ChampsCup");

        if (e.ListItem["InterCup"] == "")
            e.Commands.Remove("InterCityCup");
    }
}

class TeamStats
{
    private String  _teamName;
    private int _position, _played, _won, _drawn, _lost, _points;
    private String  _champsCup, _interCup;

    public TeamStats(String teamName,
        int position,
        int played,
        int won,
        int drawn,
        int lost,
        int points,
        String championsCup,
        String interCup)
    {
        this._teamName = teamName;
        this._position = position;
        this._played = played;
        this._won = won;
        this._drawn = drawn;
        this._lost = lost;
        this._points = points;
        this._champsCup = championsCup;
        this._interCup= interCup;
    }
```

```
        public String TeamName { get { return this._teamName; }}
        public int    Position { get { return this._position; }}
        public int    Played   { get { return this._played; }}
        public int    Won      { get { return this._won; }}
        public int    Drawn    { get { return this._drawn; }}
        public int    Lost     { get { return this._lost; }}
        public int    Points   { get { return this._points; }}
        public String ChampionsCup { get { return this._champsCup; }}
        public String InterCup{ get { return this._interCup; }}
    }
}
```

Displaying a Single Field, with Multiple Fields as a Secondary Function

In this usage of the ObjectList control, the list is displayed the same way as it appears with a List control. Therefore, selecting an item from the list causes an event handler method to execute.

If you select more than one field to display from the data source, the control still renders a user interface that allows the user to view these fields, but this is no longer the list's primary purpose. A More link is displayed on the same line as the selection item (in HTML browsers), or a Details option is displayed on a subsidiary screen after the user makes the initial selection (in WML browsers). The extra fields can be viewed by users to give them additional information about the main list item to help them make the correct selection. Figure 6-10 shows both these scenarios.

Figure 6-10 In Pocket Internet Explorer, selecting an item from the list raises the *ItemCommand* event with a CommandName defined by the *DefaultCommand* property, which in this example displays another Form (the center image). The user can click the More link on the first screen to access the details display (right-hand image).

To enable this behavior, set the *DefaultCommand* property to a unique command name and the *ItemCommand* event to the name of an event handler routine. This is the same event handler that manages item commands, as described in the previous example. For the default command, the code makes a call to the *ItemCommand* event handler with the argument's *CommandName* property set to the name you define in the *DefaultCommand* property.

One word of caution: if you decide to use the *DefaultCommand* property, you must always repeat the default command as one of the item commands that you designate with the *<Command>* element. For example, this code segment offers the *TeamPoints* command both as the *DefaultCommand* property and as a *<Command>* item command:

```
<mobile:ObjectList id="oblTeamList" runat="server"
    OnItemCommand="Team_OnItemCommand"
    DefaultCommand="TeamPoints"
    LabelField="TeamName">
    <Command Name="TeamPoints" Text="Points"/>
    <Command Name="TeamAbove" Text="Team Above"/>
    <Command Name="TeamBelow" Text="Team Below"/>
</mobile:ObjectList>
```

On HTML browsers, the list item (in this example, *TeamName*) is rendered as a link that, when invoked, raises the *ItemCommand* event for the *DefaultCommand* property. Furthermore, a More link on the same line grants access to the other fields, as Figure 6-10 shows. On a small WML browser, the list item isn't rendered in this way. Instead, when the user selects a list item, the control displays a second screen containing only the item commands. If you don't duplicate the *DefaultCommand* option in your *<Command>* item commands, the user of a WML browser never sees a link to your *DefaultCommand* option.

Another word of caution: On an HTML browser, selecting an item from the list invokes the *DefaultCommand* action, which may well display a new Form control. But as Figure 6-10 shows, the item commands are displayed only on the details page (the right-hand image in Figure 6-10), but not on the page that displays when the user selects an item in the list (which is a Form you design yourself and not built-in functionality of the ObjectList control, an example of which is shown in the center image in Figure 6-10). By default, the user doesn't get to see the item commands unless he or she clicks the More link (now only a secondary function of the ObjectList control) to get to the details page. If the item commands provide functionality that is crucial to your application and you need to ensure that that functionality is available to your users after they select an item in the list, you must put standard mobile Command controls onto the form the user sees after they select an item. Program the Command controls to implement the same functionality as the item commands you defined in the ObjectList.

today

7

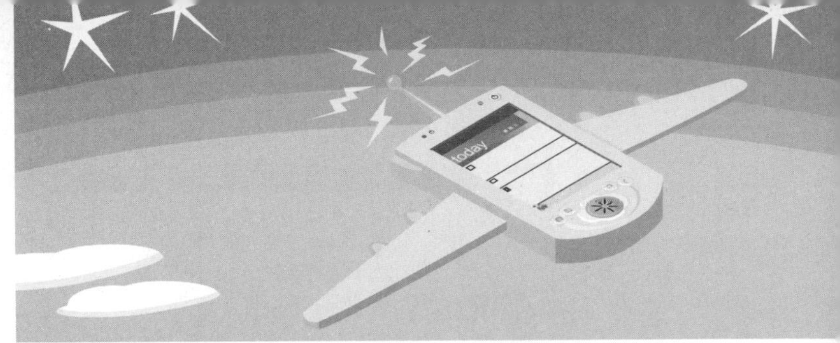

Using the Downloadable Controls

In this chapter, we'll take a look at three mobile controls that have been built by members of the mobile developer community to supplement the standard controls included in Microsoft ASP.NET Mobile Controls. The three controls described in this chapter, MobileCheckbox, MobileMultiLineInput, and MobileDynamicImage are available from the Microsoft ASP.NET Web site (*http://www.asp.net*). Over time, other custom controls will be made available from this and other sources, or you can write your own controls, a topic that we'll address in Chapter 21 and Chapter 22.

Using the Custom Controls

The controls described in this chapter are all available from the Microsoft ASP.NET Web site, at *http://www.asp.net*. The Microsoft ASP.NET Web site provides a vast amount of information about ASP.NET for desktop and mobile browsers, including a control gallery of custom controls. Click the Control Gallery tab on the main page, and then click the Mobile Controls link to navigate to the controls, as shown in Figure 7-1.

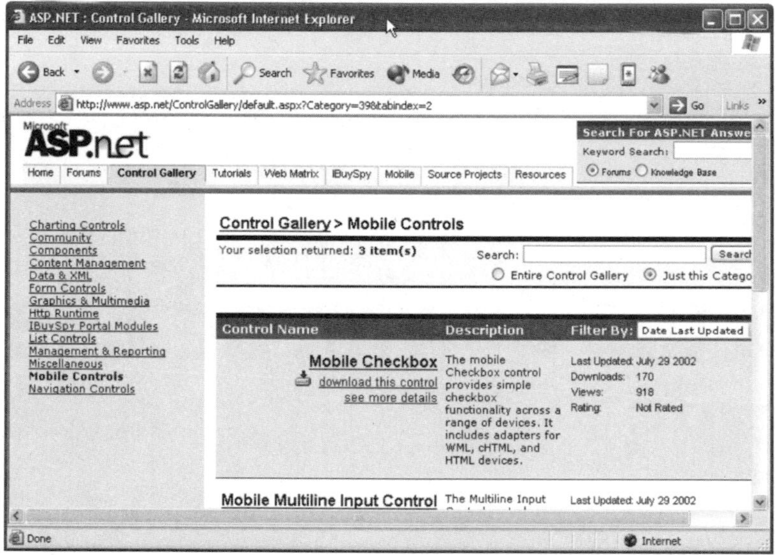

Figure 7-1 Custom mobile controls are downloadable from *http://www.asp.net* and other sources on the Web.

Download the zipped controls and read their installation instructions. Copy the assembly for each control to an accessible directory; the supplied installation instructions suggest the C:\Inetpub\wwwroot\bin directory, which is a good location if you only want to install the custom controls on your own development machine. (C:\Inetpub\wwwroot\bin is not a standard directory created when you install IIS on your computer, so you'll need to create it if this is where you want to install the custom controls.) Alternatively, if you want to make the controls available to a group of developers, you could copy them into a directory on a network share.

All three controls work with both Microsoft .NET Framework 1.0/Mobile Internet Toolkit 1.0 and Microsoft .NET Framework 1.1.

Adding the Controls to the Toolbox

If you're using Microsoft Visual Studio .NET, it's a good idea to add the custom controls to the Toolbox. You can then drag a custom control from the Toolbox onto your Web Form page just as you would any other control; Visual Studio .NET will automatically take care of much of the additional configuration steps you must perform to make use of a custom control.

To add a custom control to the Toolbox, follow these steps:

1. Open a Mobile Web Application project in Design mode.
2. Right-click on the Toolbox, and select Add/Remove Items… as shown in Figure 7-2.

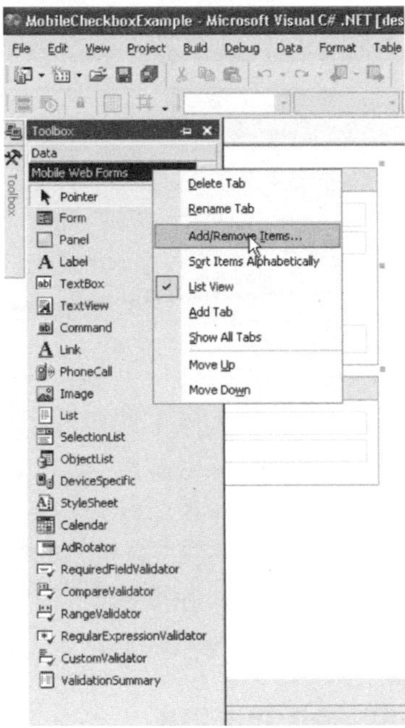

Figure 7-2 Customizing the Toolbox

3. In the Customize Toolbox window, select the .NET Framework Components tab.
4. Browse for the compiled control—for example, c:\inetpub\wwwroot\bin\MobileDynamicImage.dll.
5. In the Open dialog, select the control and click Open. The control is added to the .NET Framework Components list, as shown in Figure 7-3. Click OK to confirm the addition.

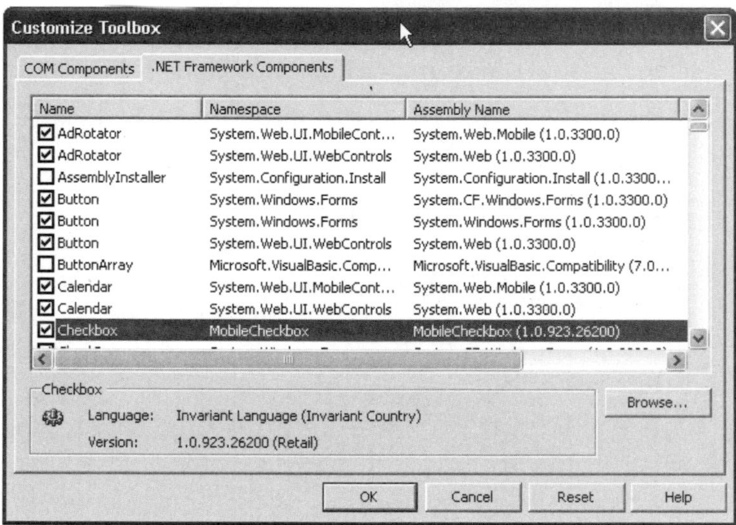

Figure 7-3 Selecting the assembly containing the custom

If you move the custom controls from the directory where you originally installed them to a new location, you will have to remove these controls from the Visual Studio .NET Toolbox and add them again so that the Visual Studio .NET Toolbox knows where to find the control assemblies when you drag one of these controls onto a project.

Copying the Control Assembly to Your Application

If you have customized the Visual Studio .NET Toolbox so that it includes one or more of the custom controls, you can now drag the custom controls from the Toolbox onto a Web Forms page, just as you do with other controls. Visual Studio .NET adds the required declarations to your .aspx file and copies the control assembly (for example, MobileCheckbox.dll) into the /bin directory of your application. Visual Studio .NET also adds a reference to the control's assembly to your project, which is required for the project to compile correctly.

If you're not using Visual Studio .NET or you have not customized the Toolbox, you must manually copy the assembly into your application's /bin directory and then add a reference to the head of the .aspx file, as shown here for the MobileCheckbox:

```
<%@ Register TagPrefix="mobCB" Namespace="MobileCheckbox"
    Assembly="MobileCheckbox" %>
```

You can then use the MobileCheckbox control in server control syntax, by specifying the *TagPrefix* you just defined (*mobCB* in this example) followed by the name of the control class (*Checkbox* for the MobileCheckbox control), as shown here. We describe the complete server control syntax for the MobileCheckbox in the next section.

```
<mobCB:Checkbox id="Checkbox1" runat="server" …></mobCB:Checkbox>
```

You must also add a reference to the control assembly to your Visual Studio .NET project by right-clicking on the project in Solution Explorer, selecting Add Reference, clicking the Browse button, and then navigating to the control assembly (for example, MobileCheckbox.dll) in your application /bin directory.

Configuring Your Application to Use Custom Controls

You must ensure that any required configuration changes are made to the *<mobileControls>* section of your ASP.NET application's web.config configuration file. (See the section "Configuring Your Application" for each control described in this chapter for more details about the precise configuration required by each control.) You can make the configuration changes in the application's Web.config file (located in the application directory) so that the change applies only to that application. (The Web.config file that Visual Studio .NET generates for you already contains a *<mobileControls>* section, so be sure to merge this new XML into that section instead of creating a new *<mobileControls>* section, which will cause a run-time error.)

Instead of making the changes in each application, you can do this just once in the machine.config file in *drive:*\\Windows\Microsoft.NET*version*\CONFIG. This saves you having to make the change in the Web.config file of every mobile Web project that uses the controls but is not recommended because it can cause difficulties when you're deploying an application to a production Web server. It's much easier to make the configuration changes in the application Web.config file because this file ships with the application instead of trying to alter the machine.config file of a production Web server. If you make an error in a server's machine.config file, you can stop all ASP.NET applications on that server from operating!

The MobileCheckbox Control

The MobileCheckbox control, written by Mike Bohlander of Microsoft, implements simple check box functionality. MobileCheckbox is supplied with device adapter functionality to allow it to operate on HTML, cHTML, and WML browsers. Figure 7-4 shows how the control looks on the HTML browser used on the Microsoft Smartphone and on a WML browser.

Figure 7-4 MobileCheckbox control shown on an HTML browser and a WML browser

Configuring Your Application

You must configure your application to use the new device adapters for the MobileCheckbox control, as described in the section "Configuring Your Application to Use Custom Controls" earlier in this chapter. Add the following *<device>* configuration XML inside the *<mobileControls>* tags in an application's web.config configuration file:

```
<configuration>
  <system.web>
    <mobileControls>
```

```
      <device name="MobileCheckboxHtmlDeviceAdapter"
          inheritsFrom="HtmlDeviceAdapters">
        <control name="MobileCheckbox.Checkbox,MobileCheckbox"
          adapter="MobileCheckbox.HtmlCheckboxAdapter,MobileCheckbox"/>
      </device>
      <device name="MobileCheckboxWmlDeviceAdapter"
          inheritsFrom="WmlDeviceAdapters">
        <control name="MobileCheckbox.Checkbox,MobileCheckbox"
          adapter="MobileCheckbox.WmlCheckboxAdapter,MobileCheckbox"/>
      </device>
      <device name="MobileCheckboxChtmlDeviceAdapter"
          inheritsFrom="ChtmlDeviceAdapters">
        <control name="MobileCheckbox.Checkbox,MobileCheckbox"
          adapter="MobileCheckbox.ChtmlCheckboxAdapter,MobileCheckbox"/>
      </device>

    </mobileControls>
  </system.web>
</configuration>
```

Syntax

The MobileCheckbox control is used declaratively, as shown in the following code:

```
<%@ Register TagPrefix="mobCB" Namespace="MobileCheckbox"
    Assembly="MobileCheckbox" %>

<mobCB:Checkbox
   runat="server"
   id="id"
   Alignment="{NotSet|Left|Center|Right}"
   BackColor="backgroundColor"
   BreakAfter="{True|False}"
   Font-Bold="{NotSet|False|True}"
   Font-Italic="{NotSet|False|True}"
   Font-Name="fontName"
   Font-Size="{NotSet|Normal|Small|Large}"
   ForeColor="foregroundColor"
   StyleReference="StyleReference"
   Wrapping="{NotSet|Wrap|NoWrap}"

   AutoPostBack="{True|False}"
   Checked="{True|False}"
   OnCheckedChanged="EventHandlerMethodName"
   TextAlign="{Left|Right}"
   Text="LabelText"
</mobCB:Checkbox>
```

Properties

Table 7-1 describes the properties and events you're most likely to use with the MobileCheckbox control.

Table 7-1 Significant Properties and Events of the MobileCheckbox Control

Property/ Event	Type	Description
AutoPostBack	*True* | *False*	Gets or sets a value indicating whether the MobileCheckbox state is automatically posted back to the server when the control is clicked. Default is *False*. This property applies only to HTML browsers. If *AutoPostBack* is *false*, then you must have another control on the same Form to make the postback to the server, such as a Command control.
Checked	*True* | *False*	Gets or sets a value indicating whether the MobileCheckbox control is initially checked. Default is *False*.
TextAlign	*System.Web.UI.Web-Controls.TextAlign* enumeration: *Left* | *Right*	Use this property to specify the alignment of the text label associated with the MobileCheckbox control. You can specify whether the text label appears to the right or left of the check box. Default is *Left*. Use the *Text* property to specify the label text.
Text	*String*	Use this property to set or get the text label associated with the MobileCheckbox control.
Checked-Changed (Event)	Event handler method	Set to the name of an event handler method of signature *OnChecked-Changed(Object sender, EventArgs e)*. This event fires when the *Checked* property of the Checkbox changes.

> **More Info** For more information about the commonly used properties and events inherited from the *MobileControl* class, refer to Table 4-1 and Table 4-2 in Chapter 4.

Using the MobileCheckbox Control

The example application shown in Listings 7-1 and 7-2 uses the MobileCheckbox control to implement a true/false quiz game. The application produces the output shown earlier in Figure 7-4.

```
<%@ Register TagPrefix="cc1" Namespace="MobileCheckbox"
    Assembly="MobileCheckbox" %>
<%@ Page language="c#" Codebehind="default.aspx.cs"
    Inherits="MSPress.MobWeb.CheckboxEx._default"
    AutoEventWireup="false" %>
<%@ Register TagPrefix="mobile" Namespace="System.Web.UI.MobileControls"
    Assembly="System.Web.Mobile" %>

<mobile:Form id="Form1" runat="server" title="Facts about Wales">
    <mobile:Label id="Label3" runat="server" StyleReference="title">
        Facts about Wales:</mobile:Label>
    <mobile:Label id="Label2" runat="server">
        True or False?:</mobile:Label>
    <cc1:Checkbox id="Checkbox1" runat="server"
        Text="Capital is Cardiff"></cc1:Checkbox>
    <cc1:Checkbox id="Checkbox2" runat="server"
        Text="Highest mountain is Snowdon"></cc1:Checkbox>
    <cc1:Checkbox id="Checkbox3" runat="server"
        Text="Favorite sport is rugby"></cc1:Checkbox>
    <mobile:Command id="Command1" runat="server">Next</mobile:Command>
</mobile:Form>

<mobile:Form id="Form2" runat="server" title="Result">
    <mobile:Label id="Label1" runat="server"
        StyleReference="title">Result</mobile:Label>
    <mobile:Label id="result" runat="server">Label</mobile:Label>
</mobile:Form>
```

Listing 7-1 Source for default.aspx in MobileCheckboxExample

```
using System;
using System.Web.UI.MobileControls;

namespace MSPress.MobWeb.CheckboxEx
{
    public class _default : System.Web.UI.MobileControls.MobilePage
    {
        protected MobileCheckbox.Checkbox Checkbox1;
        protected System.Web.UI.MobileControls.Command Command1;
        protected System.Web.UI.MobileControls.Form Form2;
```

Listing 7-2 Code-behind file default.aspx.cs in MobileCheckboxExample

```
        protected MobileCheckbox.Checkbox Checkbox2;
        protected MobileCheckbox.Checkbox Checkbox3;
        protected System.Web.UI.MobileControls.Label result;
        protected System.Web.UI.MobileControls.Form Form1;

        override protected void OnInit(EventArgs e)
        {
            InitializeComponent();
            base.OnInit(e);
        }

        private void InitializeComponent()
        {
            this.Command1.Click +=
                new System.EventHandler(this.Command1_Click);
        }

        private void Command1_Click(object sender, System.EventArgs e)
        {
            int correct = 0;
            if (Checkbox1.Checked) correct++;
            if (Checkbox2.Checked) correct++;
            if (Checkbox3.Checked) correct++;

            result.Text = "You got " + correct.ToString() + " correct";

            ActiveForm = Form2;
        }
    }
}
```

The MobileMultiLineInput Control

The MobileMultiLineInput control, written by Bogdan Popp of Microsoft, derives from the standard mobile TextBox control and implements multiline input functionality on mobile browsers. Applications that require large amounts of text input, such as mobile chat and message boards, can benefit from this control. In WML and cHTML, the MobileMultiLineInput control will be rendered as a text box using the *<input>* tag; in HTML, it will be rendered as a multiline text box using the *<textarea>* tag. Figure 7-5 shows the control rendered on an HTML browser and a WML browser.

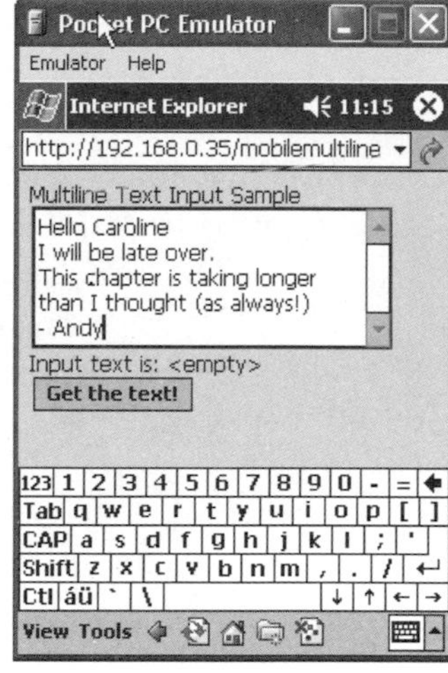

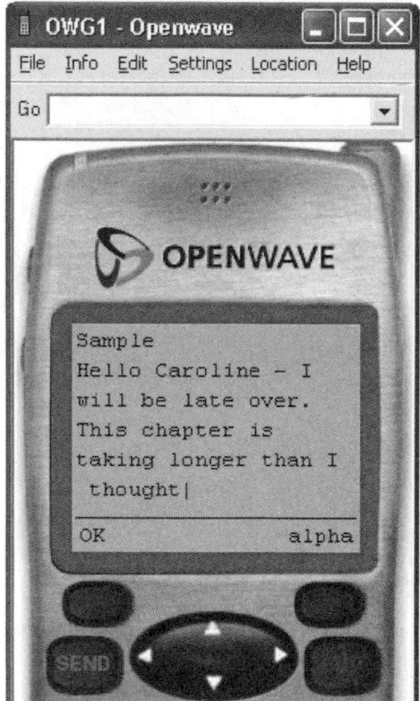

Figure 7-5 The MobileMultiLineInput control shown on an HTML browser and a WML browser

> **Tip** Think carefully before designing a mobile application that allows or encourages large amounts of user input. Pocket PCs with an add-on keyboard and devices such as BlackBerry RIM devices that have a thumb keyboard allow entry of text fairly easily, but on standard PDAs and particularly mobile phones, data entry can be awkward and frustrating for the user.

The MobileMultiLineInput control provides a good demonstration of how to take advantage of the ASP.NET mobile controls extensibility model. The download for the MobileMultiLineInput control includes full source code that shows how to author a new device adapter and associate it with a control. A device adapter is a class that works in tandem with a control class, which is responsible for the rendering of the control on a particular class of mobile device, such as WML browsers. See Chapter 22 for more about device adapters and the authoring of custom controls.

Currently there is no Visual Studio .NET design support for this sample, so if for example you set the *Rows* property to a new value, the visualization of the control in the Mobile Internet Designer display doesn't resize to reflect this.

Installation

The MobileMultiLineInput control is supplied uncompiled. You must unzip the files and then execute the supplied Make.bat file to build the control. You must include the directory in which the C# compiler is located in your *path* environment variable—the easiest way to achieve this is to run the Visual Studio .NET Command Prompt from the Visual Studio .NET program group on your Start menu.

Copy the compiled executable MLIC.dll to the directory where you keep your ASP.NET custom controls, as explained in "Using the Custom Controls" earlier in this chapter.

If you're using Visual Studio .NET, you can add the new control to the Toolbox, as described in "Adding the Controls to the Toolbox" earlier in this chapter.

Configuring Your Application

You must configure your application to use the new device adapter for the MobileMultiLineInput control, as described in the section "Configuring Your Application to Use Custom Controls" earlier in this chapter. Add the following *<assembly>* and *<device>* configuration XML inside an application configuration file:

```
<configuration>
    <system.web>
        <compilation debug="true">
            <assemblies>
                <add assembly="MLIC" />
            </assemblies>
        </compilation>
        <mobileControls>
            <device name="MMITTextInputHtmlDeviceAdapter"
                inheritsFrom="HtmlDeviceAdapters">
                <control name="MMIT_Sample.MultiLineInput,MLIC"
                    adapter="MMIT_Sample.HtmlMultiLineInputAdapter,MLIC"/>
            </device>
        </mobileControls>
    </system.web>
</configuration>
```

Syntax

The MobileMultiLineInput control includes many properties inherited from the standard mobile TextBox control, with the addition of the *Rows* and *Cols* properties, as shown here:

```
<%@ Register TagPrefix="mobMLI" Namespace="MMIT_Sample"
    Assembly="MLIC" %>

<mobMLI:MultiLineInput
    runat="server"
    id="id"
    Alignment="{NotSet|Left|Center|Right}"
    BackColor="backgroundColor"
    Font-Bold="{NotSet|False|True}"
    Font-Italic="{NotSet|False|True}"
    Font-Name="fontName"
    Font-Size="{NotSet|Normal|Small|Large}"
    ForeColor="foregroundColor"
    StyleReference="StyleReference"
    Wrapping="{NotSet|Wrap|NoWrap}"

    MaxLength="maxlength"
    Numeric="{True|False}"
    Password="{True|False}"
    OnTextChanged="textChangedEventHandler"
    Size="textBoxLength"
    Text="Text"
    Title="Text"

    Rows="{number of rows}"
    Cols="{number of columns}" >

</mobMLI:MultiLineInput>
```

Properties

Table 7-2 describes the unique properties of the MobileMultiLineInput control. See Table 4-10 for a description of the properties inherited from the TextBox control.

Table 7-2 Properties of the MobileMultiLineInput Control

Property	Type	Description
Rows	*Integer*	Indicates the number of rows that will be rendered for this control. Default is *0*. This property applies only to HTML browsers.
Cols	*Integer*	Indicates the number of columns that will be rendered for this control. Default is *0*. This property applies only to HTML browsers.

Using the MobileMultiLineInput Control

The sample application shown in Listings 7-3 and 7-4 allows input of five lines of 25 characters on HTML browsers. The application's output was shown earlier, in Figure 7-5. On WML and cHTML browsers, multiple lines of input are allowed, but you can't limit the line length or number of lines as you can on an HTML browser. Use the *MaxLength* property (supported by all browsers) to limit the total length of the input.

> **Warning** One of the aims of this control is to illustrate how to develop custom controls, so it is not perfect. This control currently crashes if the user enters text that includes carriage return characters in it. To fix this limitation, a new version of the control must be written that inherits from MobileControl and would require custom device adapters to be written to render it. The source code that is supplied with the MobileMultiLineInput control will help guide you. See Chapter 22 for details of how to write a custom control that inherits from MobileControl and how to write device adapters.

```
<%@ Register TagPrefix="cc1" Namespace="MMIT_Sample" Assembly="MLIC" %>
<%@ Page language="c#" Codebehind="default.aspx.cs"
    Inherits="MSPress.MobWeb.MLICExample._default"
    AutoEventWireup="false" %>
<%@ Register TagPrefix="mobile" Namespace="System.Web.UI.MobileControls"
    Assembly="System.Web.Mobile " %>

<mobile:Form id="Form1" runat="server" BackColor="PaleTurquoise">
    <mobile:Label id="1" runat="server"
        text="Multiline Text Input Sample"></mobile:Label>
```

Listing 7-3 Source for default.aspx in MultiLineInputExample

```
    <cc1:MultiLineInput id="MultiLineInput1" runat="server"
        Cols="25" Rows="5" MaxLength="125"></cc1:MultiLineInput>
    <mobile:Label id="Result" runat="server"
        Text="Input text is: <empty>"></mobile:Label>
    <mobile:Command id="Command1" runat="server"
        Text="Get the text!"></mobile:Command>
</mobile:Form>
```

```
using System;
using System.Web.UI.MobileControls;

namespace MSPress.MobWeb.MLICExample
{
    public class _default : System.Web.UI.MobileControls.MobilePage
    {
        protected MMIT_Sample.MultiLineInput MultiLineInput1;
        protected System.Web.UI.MobileControls.Label Result;
        protected System.Web.UI.MobileControls.Command Command1;

        override protected void OnInit(EventArgs e)
        {
            InitializeComponent();
            base.OnInit(e);
        }

        private void InitializeComponent()
        {
            this.Command1.Click +=
                new System.EventHandler(this.Command1_Click);
        }

        private void Command1_Click(object sender, System.EventArgs e)
        {
            Result.Text = "Input text is: "+ MultiLineInput1.Text;
        }
    }
}
```

Listing 7-4 Code-behind module default.aspx.cs in MultiLineInputExample

The MobileDynamicImage Control

MobileDynamicImage is a fantastic control created by Joseph Croney of Microsoft that goes a long way toward solving a major development headache of mobile developers. Using ASP.NET mobile controls, you can build mobile Web applications in a device-independent manner. The only area in which you're forced to program for specific devices is when you're using images. HTML browsers usually support GIF and JPG graphics; WAP browsers support WBMP and, in some cases, PNG format graphics. You couldn't create one graphic and use it across all devices because there is no single consistent format that works on all devices. The MobileDynamicImage control solves this problem, as it allows you to take one graphic and render it at run time in the graphics format supported by the requesting device.

The MobileDynamicImage control derives from the standard mobile Image control and extends that control by adding support for dynamically created images that will be rendered on mobile devices. The MobileDynamicImage control converts images to the appropriate image format and resizes the images based on the device screen size. It has the following features:

- Automatically determines correct image type for the device and converts appropriately
- Supports GIF, JPEG, WBMP, and PNG image formats
- Automatically resizes images to fit the mobile device's screen
- Caches dynamically created images so that they are created only once
- Supports three dithering techniques for converting color images to black and white
- Provides full Visual Studio .NET design support, including Design Time View and a Property Builder and Preview windows, as shown in Figure 7-6

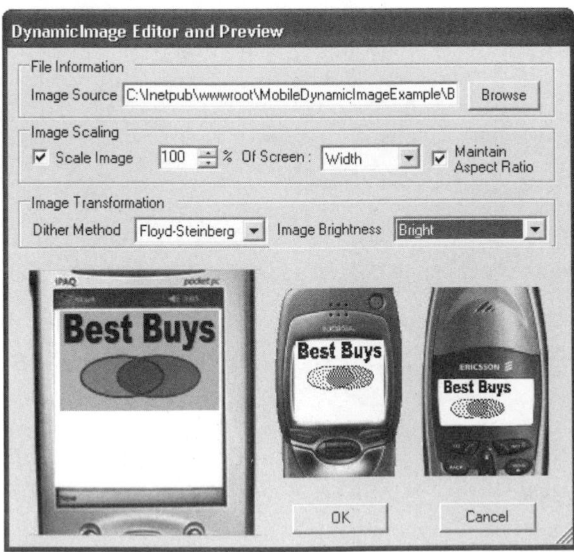

Figure 7-6 MobileDynamicImage control Property Builder and Preview

- Supports source images referenced by Web location, and will load and convert
- Allows temporary image save location to be specified in machine.config or Web.config

Installation

Download the zipped control from the Microsoft ASP.NET Web site, unzip it and copy the files MobileDynamicImage.dll and JCroneyImageUtilites.dll to the directory where you keep your ASP.NET custom controls, as explained in "Using the Custom Controls" earlier in this chapter. If you're using Visual Studio .NET, you can add the new control to the Toolbox, as described earlier in "Adding the Controls to the Toolbox."

Configuring Your Application

There are no new device adapter classes for the MobileDynamicImage control, so there are no configuration changes required in the *<mobileControls>* element of your Web.config file, unlike the MobileCheckbox control. The MobileDynamicImage control extends the standard mobile Image control, so it inherits the configuration and device adapters of its parent.

By default, the MobileDynamicImage control writes files in a directory below the application directory named \DynamicImages. You must set security permissions on the application directory to allow the ASP.NET account write access (the name of the account that runs ASP.NET applications is *ASPNET* in default configurations).

However, it is advised that you select an alternative virtual directory where images can be saved. To do so, from the Control Panel, open Internet Information Services Manager. Right-click on the Default Web Site entry, choose New, and select Virtual Directory. Create a folder in which to save the images—for example, C:\inetpub\wwwroot\dynimg, which maps to the URL *http://Myserver/dynimg* where *Myserver* is the name of your machine. You must then define two configuration settings in an *<appSettings>* section of the Web.config or machine.config file to redirect the location where images are created to this new virtual directory, as follows:

```
<appSettings>
    <add key="MobileDynamicImagePath" value="c:\inetpub\wwwroot\dynimg\" />
    <add key="MobileDynamicImageURL" value="http://Myserver/dynimg/" />
</appSettings>
```

These two settings have the following meaning:

- ***MobileDynamicImagePath*** This string value defines the physical path to the directory where the dynamic image should be stored. You must set security permissions on this folder to grant the ASP.NET account write access. If *MobileDynamicImagePath* is specified, *MobileDynamicImageURL* must also be specified (see below).
- ***MobileDynamicImageURL*** The URL that is mapped to the virtual directory mapping specified in the *MobileDynamicImagePath* and configured in IIS.

Syntax

The MobileDynamicImage control possesses many properties inherited from *System.Web.UI.MobileControls.Image*, with the addition of some unique properties, as shown here:

```
<%@ Register TagPrefix="mobDI" Namespace="MobileDynamicImage"
    Assembly=" MobileDynamicImage" %>

<mobDI:MobileDynamicImage
    runat="server"
    id="id"
    Alignment="{NotSet|Left|Centre|Right}"
    BackColor="backgroundColor"
    BreakAfter="{True|False}"
    Font-Bold="{NotSet|False|True}"
    Font-Italic="{NotSet|False|True}"
    Font-Name="fontName"
    Font-Size="{NotSet|Normal|Small|Large}"
    ForeColor="foregroundColor"
    StyleReference="StyleReference"
    Visible="{True|False}"
    Wrapping="{NotSet|Wrap|NoWrap}"

    AlternateText="AltText"
    ImageUrl="masterImageSource"
    NavigateUrl="targetURL"
    SoftkeyLabel="softkeyLabel"

    AutoConvert="{True|False}"
    AutoSizeImage="{True|False}"
    DynamicImageSource="string"
    ScalePercent="{0-100}"
    ScaleBasedOn="{ScreenWidth|ScreenHeight}"
    ImageBrightness=
        "{Auto|Very_Light|Light|Medium|Dark|Very_Dark}"
```

```
    ImageDitherMethod="{ThreshHold|Matrix|Floyd_Steinberg}"
    MaintainAspectRatio="{True|False}" >
</mobDI:MobileDynamicImage >
```

Properties

The MobileDynamicImage control extends the standard mobile Image control, from which it inherits many properties. See Chapter 4 for a description of the standard Image control. Table 7-3 describes the unique properties of the MobileDynamicImage control.

Table 7-3 Properties of the MobileDynamicImage Control

Property	Type	Description
AutoConvert	*True* | *False*	If *True*, the image will be dynamically set to the proper format; otherwise, the image will be treated as a normal Image control using the *ImageUrl* property for the path to the source image. Default is *True*.
AutoSizeImage	*True* | *False*	If *True*, the image will be resized to the dimensions of the device based on the *Scale-BasedOn* and *ScalePercent* properties. Default is *True*.
DynamicImageSource	*String*	The path to the source image, or the Web address of the image.
ScalePercent	*Integer*	Value in the range 0 – 100. If *AutoSizeImage* is set to *True*, the image will be resized using this percent of the *ScaleBasedOn* property.
ScaleBasedOn	*MobileDynamicImage.Scale-BasedOnType* enumeration: *ScreenWidth* | *ScreenHeight*	If *AutoSizeImage* is set to *True*, the image will be resized based on this and the *Scale-Percent* property. For example, if this value is set to *Screen-Width*, and *ScalePercent* is set to *50*, the image will be resized to 50 percent of the screen width.

Table 7-3 Properties of the MobileDynamicImage Control

Property	Type	Description
ImageBrightness	*MobileDynamicImage. Brightness* enumeration: *Auto* | *Very_Light* | *Light* | *Medium* | *Dark* | *Very_Dark*	Indicates the brightness of the source image. Can be used to tweak dithering.
ImageDitherMethod	*MobileDynamicImage. DitherMethod* enumeration: *ThreshHold* | *Matrix* | *Floyd_Steinberg*	The dithering technique used for the image. Photos work best with *Floyd_Steinberg*, logos might look better using *ThreshHold* or *Matrix*.
MaintainAspectRatio	*True* | *False*	If set to *True*, the Mobile-DynamicImage control resizes the image keeping the ratio of height to width the same, avoiding introducing horizontal or vertical distortion. Default is *True*.

The *DynamicImagePath* property specifies the path to the source image or the Web address (the URL) of the image. Note that if a physical path is used, the source image is fetched only if a converted image of the required image format is not already available. Converted images are cached to be used for future requests. However, if a Web address is specified, a Web request will be made for the image, and the image will be reformatted and resized for the device on every request, meaning that performance is not as good as when the *DynamicImagePath* property specifies the physical path.

Using the MobileDynamicImage Control

The MobileDynamicImage control is very easy to use. If you're using Visual Studio .NET, just use the built-in Visual Designer support to enter the path or URL to an image into the *DynamicImageSource* property and you can see what the image looks like. At runtime, the image is automatically converted to a graphics format supported by the requesting client.

Some skill is required to get the best results. Photos and other detailed images always look great on an HTML browser; however, you can't expect a detailed image to convert well if the client is a monochrome WAP device with a small screen. In this case, it's better to use a source image that is clear, simple, and has good contrast. You might still want to use two images—a detailed color image for PDAs and high-end smart phones, and a simpler, high-contrast image for small-screen devices. You can use the Property Overrides feature described in Chapter 9 to choose between the source images depending on the screen size of the requesting client device.

Figure 7-7 shows how a single JPG image appears on a color display with an HTML browser and on a monochrome WAP device.

Figure 7-7 A single JPG rendered as a black-and-white WBMP for a WAP device (left) and resized to fit on an HTML browser (right)

Listing 7-5 shows the .aspx file for this demonstration. This example does not have a code-behind module.

```
<%@ Register TagPrefix="mobile" Namespace="System.Web.UI.MobileControls"
    Assembly="System.Web.Mobile" %>
<%@ Page language="c#"
    Inherits="System.Web.UI.MobileControls.MobilePage %>
<%@ Register TagPrefix="cc1" Namespace="MobileDynamicImage"
    Assembly="MobileDynamicImage" %>
```

Listing 7-5 Source for default.aspx in MobileDynamicImageExample

```
<mobile:Form id="Form1" runat="server">
    <cc1:DynamicImage id="DynamicImage1" runat="server"
        ImageBrightness="Light" ImageDitherMethod="Floyd_Steinberg"
        DynamicImageSource=
           "C:\Inetpub\wwwroot\MobileDynamicImageExample\BestBuys1.JPG">
    </cc1:DynamicImage>
</mobile:Form>
```

8

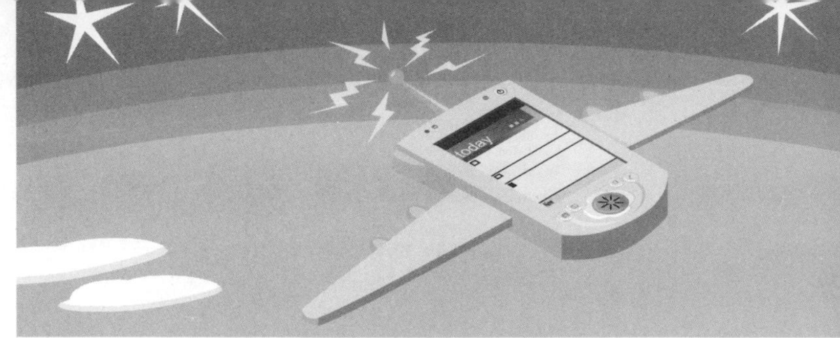

Programming Styles and Style Sheets

In this chapter, you'll learn how to use the style capabilities of the Microsoft ASP.NET Mobile Controls to make your application more visually appealing and to apply specific styles to specific devices. You'll use styles and StyleSheet controls to apply a named collection of style attributes to your applications. These features give you great flexibility in the way you present your mobile Web Forms controls on specific mobile devices.

Using Mobile Control Style Properties and the StyleSheet Control

Styles provide you with a convenient means for setting the display characteristics of mobile controls in such a way that you take full advantage of the display capabilities of individual client browsers. Every mobile control has a number of style properties that you can set to alter the foreground and background color, the font and font size, and the type of emphasis used. In general, HTML browsers support all these properties. The less capable Wireless Markup Language (WML) browsers apply these properties on a "best fit" basis.

For example, you can specify that page titles be displayed in a particular color, which will be used on devices that support color but ignored on monochrome devices. You also can define more complex display attributes—for instance, you can specify that a control renders text italicized, centered, and in the Verdana font. Figure 8-1 shows Label controls that use some of these style properties.

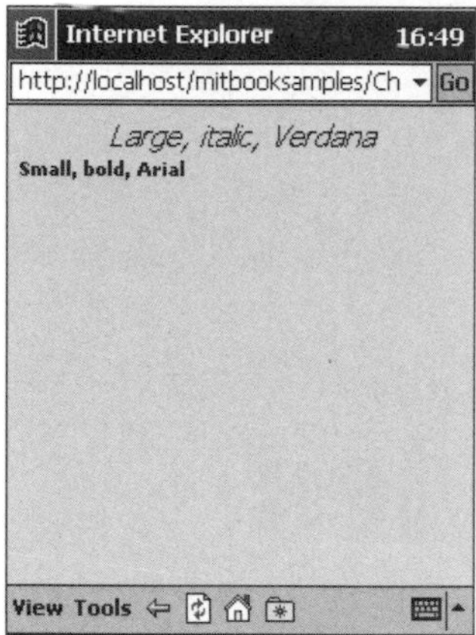

Figure 8-1 Use of style properties in Microsoft Pocket Internet Explorer

ASP.NET provides a number of ways you can apply style information to mobile controls. The simplest method is to set the style properties of the control itself. This technique allows you to quickly define an individual control's display characteristics within a mobile Web Forms page. However, if you set the style properties of several controls within a mobile Web Forms page, the code can become bloated and maintaining the page can be time-consuming. This is because you have to manually update the style attributes of every control, which is a very tedious task.

Using style sheets can help you overcome the limitations of working with individual style properties. Style sheets enable you to define one or more styles, where each style is a collection of style properties that you can then reuse. For example, in a style sheet you can specify that a named style such as *h1* represents text that appears in boldface and italic. You can then set the *StyleReference* property of any control to the style *h1*, rather than set the control's individual properties. Thus, the control is rendered according to the properties that the style sheet defines. By altering the style sheet definitions, each control that uses a style defined in the style sheet will automatically update to reflect changes in appearance.

> **Note** In addition to defining your own styles, you can set the *StyleReference* property of a control to any of the three predefined styles provided by the ASP.NET mobile controls. These styles provide formatting for common usage scenarios, such as error messages. The three styles are *title*, which is displayed in a large bold font size; *subcommand*, which is displayed centered and in a small font size; and *error*, which is displayed in red and in a small font size.

You can further enhance your use of style properties by using external style sheets. You can define and store external style sheets in a separate file that you can reference from your mobile Web Forms page. This approach to style sheet deployment allows you to reuse the styles in multiple controls and multiple Web Forms pages.

Using Style Properties

Every mobile control has a number of style properties inherited from the *MobileControl* base class. Table 8-1 describes these style properties.

Table 8-1 Style Properties Inherited from the *MobileControl* Class

Property	Allowed Values	Description
Alignment	*NotSet* | *Left* | *Center* | *Right*	The alignment of the control, specified using members of the *System.Web.UI.MobileControls.Alignment* enumeration.
BackColor	HTML color name or RGB value expressed in hexadecimal notation preceded by a number sign (#)	The color displayed behind the text of a control on devices that support color. You define the color either as an HTML color name or as an RGB value expressed in hexadecimal notation. Table 8-2 lists the standard HTML color names and RGB values.
Font	Read-only	The *Font* property of a mobile control exposes a *System.Web.UI.WebControls.FontInfo* object that encapsulates the style-related properties of the control. The *FontInfo* object has *Name*, *Size*, *Bold*, and *Italic* properties. In server control syntax, you set these properties using the *Font-Property* syntax—for example, *Font-Name* and *Font-Bold*.
Font.Name	*String* specifying the font name	The font used to render the text on devices that support multiple fonts. This property can be an exact font name, such as Arial Narrow, or it can be a font family name, such as Arial. Using a font family name allows the browser to determine which font to select from the given family. Therefore, this approach yields better font support on wireless clients. *Font.Name* is equivalent to a controls *Font-Name* attribute in server control syntax.
Font.Size	*NotSet* | *Normal* | *Small* | *Large*	The size of the text, specified using members of the *System.Web.UI.MobileControls.FontSize* enumeration. The default value is *NotSet*. Note that the size is relative and that not all devices support text of different sizes. *Font.Size* is equivalent to a controls *Font-Size* property in server control syntax.

Table 8-1 Style Properties Inherited from the *MobileControl* Class

Property	Allowed Values	Description
Font.Bold	*NotSet* | *True* | *False*	Configured using members of the *System.Web.UI.MobileControls.BooleanOption* enumeration. When set to *True*, the text is boldface. The default value is *NotSet*. *Font.Bold* is equivalent to a controls *Font-Bold* attribute in server control syntax.
Font.Italic	*NotSet* | *True* | *False*	Configured using members of the *System.Web.UI.MobileControls.BooleanOption* enumeration. When set to *True*, the text is italicized. The default value is *NotSet*. *Font.Italic* is equivalent to a controls *Font-Italic* attribute in server control syntax.
ForeColor	HTML color name or RGB value expressed in hexadecimal notation preceded by a number sign (#)	The color of the text displayed on devices that support color. You define the color either as an HTML color name or as an RGB value expressed in hexadecimal notation. Table 8-2 lists the standard HTML color names and RGB values.
Wrapping	*NotSet* | *Wrap* | *NoWrap*	Controls wrapping of text using members of the *System.Web.UI.MobileControls.Wrapping* enumeration. When set to *Wrap*, the text wraps onto the next line if it exceeds the available display area. This property can be particularly useful on devices with small display areas, because some of these devices don't support side-scrolling. The default value is *NotSet*.

Unlike desktop HTML browsers, wireless devices that support color can have a very limited palette. Using RGB colors allows you to define approximately 16.5 million colors. If a browser doesn't support the color that you define, it will attempt to substitute that color with the closest color it does support. This substitution can yield some strange and unexpected results, which can often degrade an application's usability. When using color for generic wireless clients, we suggest you restrict your palette to the 16 main colors that HTML supports. Table 8-2 shows these 16 colors and their equivalent hexadecimal values.

Table 8-2 Standard HTML Colors

HTML Color	Hexadecimal Value
Aqua	#00FFFF
Black	#000000
Blue	#0000FF

Table 8-2 Standard HTML Colors

HTML Color	Hexadecimal Value
Fuchsia	#FF00FF
Gray	#808080
Green	#008000
Lime	#00FF00
Maroon	#800000
Navy	#000080
Olive	#808000
Purple	#800080
Red	#FF0000
Silver	#C0C0C0
Teal	#008080
White	#FFFFFF
Yellow	#FFFF00

Inheriting Style Properties

Controls that reside within a container control (the Form or the Panel control) inherit the style properties of the container control. Similarly, when you set a style property on a list control (the SelectionList, List, or ObjectList), each display element in the list inherits the style property of the list.

The Form and Panel controls serve as containers for other mobile controls. Because these controls form part of the Web page, they have no visual appearance. For more information about these two controls, refer to Chapter 4. Although Form and Panel have no physical characteristics, they do support style properties. Once you set style properties on a container control, they will apply to all contained child controls, as Figure 8-2 illustrates.

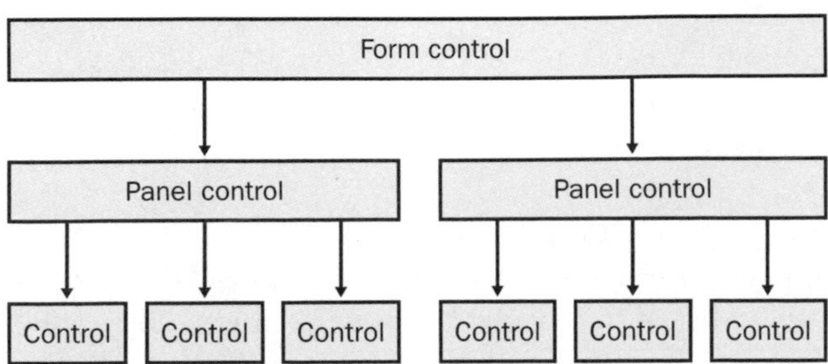

Figure 8-2 Style property inheritance of the container controls

When run, Listing 8-1 demonstrates the inheritance of the container controls' style properties. This code sets the Form control's style properties, which then apply to all child controls. However, the second Panel control overrides these properties by declaring its own properties, which apply to all of its child controls.

```
<%@ Page language="c#"
    Inherits="System.Web.UI.MobileControls.MobilePage" %>
<%@ Register TagPrefix="mobile"
    Namespace="System.Web.UI.MobileControls"
    Assembly="System.Web.Mobile" %>

<mobile:Form id="Form1"
    runat="server"
    Font-Bold="True"
    Font-Size="Large"
    Alignment="Center">
    <mobile:Label id="Label1" runat="server">
        Form level defines properties
    </mobile:Label>
    <mobile:Label id="Label2" runat="server">****</mobile:Label>
    <mobile:Panel id="Panel1" runat="server">
        <mobile:Label id="Label4" runat="server">
            Panel 1 inherits form properties
        </mobile:Label>
        <mobile:Label id="Label5" runat="server">****</mobile:Label>
    </mobile:Panel>
    <mobile:Panel id="Panel2"
        runat="server"
        Font-Bold="False"
        Font-Size="Normal"
        Font-Italic="True">
        <mobile:Label id="Label6" runat="server" Alignment="Right">
            Panel 2 overrides form properties
        </mobile:Label>
    </mobile:Panel>
</mobile:Form>
```

Listing 8-1 Style property inheritance of the container controls from StyleInheritanceContainerExample.aspx

The same rules of style property inheritance that we showed for the container controls apply to the list controls. For example, Listing 8-2 consists of a form with two lists—a list of fruit and a list of vegetables. The code sets the style properties for the Form control and all the list controls. Thus, all the items in the list inherit these properties. The list controls set the font size to differentiate among the lists. These font sizes then apply to each item in each list.

```
<%@ Page language="c#"
    Inherits="System.Web.UI.MobileControls.MobilePage" %>
<%@ Register TagPrefix="mobile"
    Namespace="System.Web.UI.MobileControls"
    Assembly="System.Web.Mobile" %>

<mobile:Form id="Form1"
    runat="server"
    Alignment="Center"
    Font-Italic="True">
    <mobile:List id="List1" runat="server" Font-Size="Small">
        <Item Value="apples" Text="apples"></Item>
        <Item Value="oranges" Text="oranges"></Item>
        <Item Value="bananas" Text="bananas"></Item>
    </mobile:List>
    <mobile:List id="List2" runat="server" Font-Size="Large">
        <Item Value="cabbage" Text="cabbage"></Item>
        <Item Value="zucchini" Text="lettuce"></Item>
        <Item Value="tomatoes" Text="tomatoes"></Item>
    </mobile:List>
</mobile:Form>
```

Listing 8-2 StyleInheritanceListExample.aspx—style property inheritance of the list controls

Figure 8-3 shows how the output of this application appears when accessed from the Pocket Internet Explorer HTML browser and from the Nokia simulator accessing WML content.

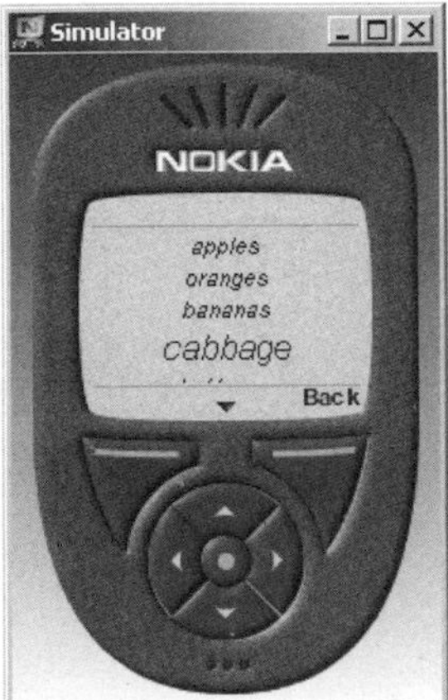

Figure 8-3 Output of Listing 8-2

Using the StyleSheet Control

The example we've just looked at set individual style properties of mobile controls. Instead of setting style properties individually, you can define a collection of style properties in a named style, which you store in a style sheet. Style sheets give you a reusable, efficient way to define style properties. Mobile controls can simply use these styles by referring to the name of a style in a style sheet.

You can define a style sheet in an .aspx file within *<mobile:StyleSheet>...</mobile:StyleSheet>* tags. Allowing any control within that mobile Web Forms page to use the styles defined in the style sheet. Alternatively, you can store the style sheet in a separate .ascx file, allowing controls in any mobile Web Forms page to use it. You'll learn how to do this in the section "Attaching an External Style Sheet" later in this chapter. Your choice of technique depends on the particular mobile Web Forms page you're working with. For example, you would store corporate style guidelines for fonts used on all company Web sites in an external file so that multiple Web Forms can reuse them. In contrast, you would store styles for an individual list appearing in a single file in the same .aspx file as the list, to ease code maintenance and improve its readability.

You can further enhance the power of style sheets by defining styles that include DeviceSpecific/Choice constructs. Style settings contained within a DeviceSpecific/Choice construct apply to a specific type of device and consequently can exploit unique display characteristics of that device. Using device-specific styles allows you to define how a heading might appear on a WML device, differently on an HTML browser, and so forth. Furthermore, device-specific styles can be used to contain templates that are used with the templated controls, which are the list and container controls. Templates are extremely flexible, allowing you to do such things as include an AdRotator control at the head of every page or format an HTML page as an HTML table. See the section "Defining Templates Within Style Sheets" in Chapter 9 for more information.

Using the Default Style Sheet

As mentioned, the ASP.NET mobile controls supply a default style sheet that provides you with three predefined styles: *error*, *subcommand*, and *title*.

To reference a predefined style or any style in a style sheet that you create yourself, you simply assign the name of the style to the *StyleReference* property of a control. Listing 8-3 shows three labels, each of which references one of the predefined styles.

```
<%@ Page language="c#"
    Inherits="System.Web.UI.MobileControls.MobilePage" %>
<%@ Register TagPrefix="mobile"
    Namespace="System.Web.UI.MobileControls"
    Assembly="System.Web.Mobile" %>

<mobile:Form id="Form1" runat="server">
    <mobile:Label id="Label1" runat="server" StyleReference="error">
        Error
    </mobile:Label>
    <mobile:Label id="Label2" runat="server"
        StyleReference="subcommand">Subcommand</mobile:Label>
    <mobile:Label id="Label3" runat="server" StyleReference="title">
        Title
    </mobile:Label>
</mobile:Form>
```

Listing 8-3 PredefinedStylesExample.aspx—using predefined styles

Figure 8-4 shows the output this code yields.

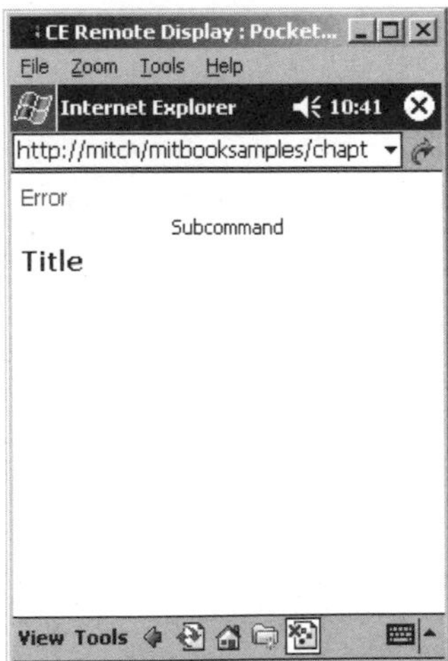

Figure 8-4 Output from Listing 8-3

Creating a Style Sheet

You construct a style sheet by using individual *<Style>* elements that define each named style and its properties within a StyleSheet control. Here's the general syntax of a style sheet:

```
<mobile:StyleSheet runat="server">
    <Style Name="Header" Font-Size="Large" Alignment="Center"/>
```

```
    <Style Name="SubHead" Font-Size="Normal" Alignment="Left"/>
</StyleSheet>
```

You can include only one style sheet in each .aspx file, and you must place it within the page container itself—you can't place a StyleSheet control in any other mobile control, for example inside a Form control.

The StyleSheet control inherits from the *System.Web.UI.MobileControls.MobileControl* class, and so inherits all of the properties of MobileControl. This implies that you can set style attributes for the StyleSheet control itself. However, the runtime *completely ignores* any style attributes that you set for the StyleSheet control—for example, *<mobile:Stylesheet Font-Bold="True"/>*. Attributes of the StyleSheet control are not inherited by any of the control's child elements either. Here's the server control syntax for the StyleSheet control:

```
<mobile:Stylesheet
    runat="server"
    id="id"
    ReferencePath="externalReferencePath">
    <!-- Style definitions here -->
    <Style name="style-name">
        ⋮
    </Style>
</mobile:Stylesheet>
```

You'll use the *ReferencePath* attribute when working with external style sheets. (You'll learn more about external style sheets later in this section.)

The properties of the *<Style>* element that you use to define individual styles follow:

```
<Style
    Name="uniqueStyleName"
    Font-Name="fontName"
    Font-Size={NotSet|Normal|Small|Large}
    Font-Bold={NotSet|False|True}
    Font-Italic="{NotSet|False|True}
    ForeColor="foregroundColor"
    BackColor="backgroundColor"
    Alignment={NotSet|Left|Center|Right}
    StyleReference="styleReference"
    Wrapping={NotSet|Wrap|NoWrap}>

    <!-- Optional Device-Specific choices here -->
    <DeviceSpecific>
        <Choice Filter="deviceFilterName">
            ⋮
        </Choice>
        <Choice> <!-- This is the default choice -->
```

```
            ⋮
        </Choice>
    </DeviceSpecific>
</Style>
```

The *Name* attribute represents a unique name that mobile controls use to reference a style. This element also has a *StyleReference* attribute, which might not seem sensible at first. However, *<Style>* elements can inherit style attributes from other styles and then extend or override these attributes. For example, the following code shows two styles, one of which inherits from the other. When the code runs, *h2* inherits the attributes of *h1* but overrides the *Font-Size* attribute.

```
<StyleSheet runat="Server">
    <Style name="h1" Font-Size="Large" Alignment="Center"/>
    <Style name="h2" StyleReference="h1" Font-Size="Normal"/>
</StyleSheet>
```

> **Tip** When naming styles, use names that relate to the function of a particular style rather than its appearance. For example, if you create a style to represent a page title, you might name it *title* or *bigBoldCenter*. If you use the latter name, as soon as one of the style's properties changes, the name becomes meaningless. But if you use the former name, it will continue to describe the function of the style.

Listing 8-4 presents a more detailed example of creating and consuming style sheets. The style sheet in the code defines three styles. Two of these, *BodyText* and *Head*, are unique styles. However, the *SubHead* style inherits the properties of the *Head* style and then overrides some of them.

```
<%@ Page language="c#"
    Inherits="System.Web.UI.MobileControls.MobilePage" %>
<%@ Register TagPrefix="mobile"
    Namespace="System.Web.UI.MobileControls"
    Assembly="System.Web.Mobile" %>

<mobile:Form id="Form1" runat="server">
    <mobile:Label id="Label1" runat="server" StyleReference="Head">
        Using Styles
    </mobile:Label>
```

Listing 8-4 Main form from CreatingConsumingStyleSheets-Example.aspx

```
    <mobile:Label id="Label2" runat="server" StyleReference="SubHead">
        Inheritance
    </mobile:Label>
    <mobile:TextView id="TextView1"
        runat="server"
        StyleReference="BodyText">
        This text uses the BodyText style. The subheading uses the
        SubHead style, which inherits properties from the Head
        style.
    </mobile:TextView>
</mobile:Form>

<mobile:StyleSheet id="StyleSheet1" runat="server">
    <Style Name="Head"
        Font-Size="Large" Font-Bold="True" Alignment="Center" />
    <Style Name="SubHead"
        StyleReference="Head" Font-Size="Normal" Alignment="Left" />
    <Style Name="BodyText" Font-Italic="True" />
</mobile:StyleSheet>
```

Figure 8-5 shows how the output of this code will look in a browser.

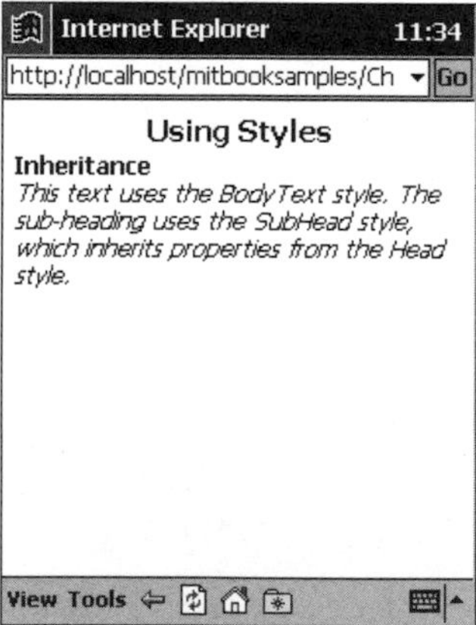

Figure 8-5 Output of Listing 8-4 shown in an HTML browser

Applying Device-Specific Styles

On many occasions, you'll want to apply different styles to controls that are relevant only when your application runs on specific client device. In fact, if you don't use different styles on different devices, your applications will appear dull and uninspiring. Imagine how unsatisfying output written to suit a WML browser would look on a desktop HTML browser!

The simplest way to define styles for richer clients is to take full advantage of the style attributes that the controls and *<Style>* elements offer. For example, if you set the background color of a control to red, the runtime won't generate markup requesting that color for devices that don't support color.

Unfortunately, this solution works only in simple scenarios. Consider the use of font sizes: Many WML browsers do support different font sizes. However, with limited screen size, using the larger fonts is often undesirable. In contrast, HTML-based handhelds and i-mode mobile phones generally have larger screen sizes, so using larger fonts is quite acceptable. In such instances, you can't use the simplistic approach to delivering client-specific styles we just outlined. You need an alternative method of applying styles.

Styles used in conjunction with DeviceSpecific/Choice filters allow you to specify different styles for particular browsers or types of browsers. We'll explore DeviceSpecific/Choice filters in detail in the section "Device-Specific Customization with Property Overrides" in Chapter 9. But for now, here's a quick summary: DeviceSpecific/Choice filters allow you to test, or query, the capabilities of a target device. You can then set properties to different values if the test is passed. Listing 8-5 tests whether the client is a WML browser. If it is, the *Header* style is rendered with the *Font-Size* property set to *"Normal"*. In all other circumstances, the *Header* style is rendered using the default properties of the style, in this case using *Font-Size="Large"*.

```
<%@ Page language="c#"
    Inherits="System.Web.UI.MobileControls.MobilePage" %>
<%@ Register TagPrefix="mobile"
    Namespace="System.Web.UI.MobileControls"
    Assembly="System.Web.Mobile" %>

<mobile:Form id="Form1" runat="server">
    <mobile:Label id="Label1" runat="server" StyleReference="Header">
        Device Specific
    </mobile:Label>
    <mobile:TextView id="TextView1" runat="server">
        The heading is shown normal sized on WML browsers and large on
        all other browsers.
    </mobile:TextView>
</mobile:Form>

<mobile:StyleSheet id="StyleSheet1" runat="server">
    <Style Name="Header"
        Font-Size="Large"
```

Listing 8-5 Using styles with choice filters in StylesChoiceFilters-Example.aspx

```
        Font-Bold="True"
        Alignment="Center">
        <DeviceSpecific>
            <Choice Filter="isWML11" Font-Size="Normal"></Choice>
        </DeviceSpecific>
    </Style>
</mobile:StyleSheet>
```

Figure 8-6 shows the output of Listing 8-5 on the two types of browser.

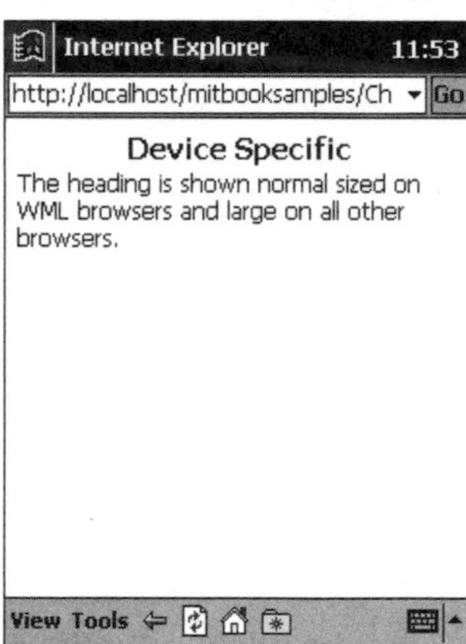

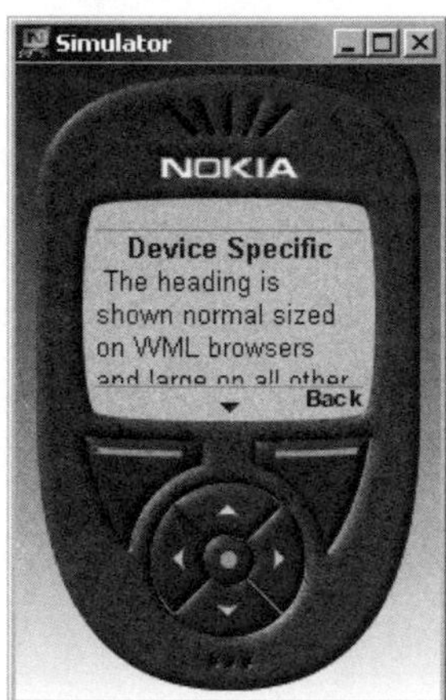

Figure 8-6 Output of Listing 8-5 shown in an HTML browser and a Nokia WML browser

Tip In Listing 8-5, the style named *"Header"* defines the default style using attributes of the *<Style>* tag: *Font-Size= "Large"*, *Font-Bold="True"*, and *Alignment= "Center"*. If the choice filter *"isWML11"* is true, the value of *Font-Size* is overridden and set to *"Normal"*.

An alternative way of defining the default properties is to use a default choice statement; that is one without a Filter attribute. The following code is exactly equivalent to the Style definition in Listing 8-5:

```
<Style Name="Header"
    <DeviceSpecific>
        <Choice Filter="isWML11" Font-Size="Normal"></Choice>
        <Choice Font-Size="Large" Font-Bold="True"
            Alignment="Center"></Choice> <!-- Default -->
    </DeviceSpecific>
</Style>
```

You can further enhance styles by using DeviceSpecific/Choice filters with *template sets*. Template sets gather a collection of styles, each targeting a different device, into a single named style. Using template sets is a relatively complex topic that you'll learn more about in Chapter 9.

Attaching an External Style Sheet

When you want to apply a set of styles to multiple mobile Web Forms pages, it's inappropriate to include the StyleSheet control within a page. If you want to update the style sheet, you need to manually update it in every page that you're targeting. ASP.NET provides a solution to this problem: it allows you to externalize your style sheets by saving them in a file separate from the mobile Web Forms page. Any of your mobile Web Forms pages can then use this external style sheet simply by referencing it.

Creating an external style sheet To create an external style sheet, you must first create a user control. Within that control, you can code a single StyleSheet control with as many *<Style>* elements as you require. User controls provide a simple means to encapsulate controls and their logic in a single file. (You'll find more information about this topic in Chapter 20.) For the purpose of creating an external style sheet, a user control is simply a file with an .ascx extension, the *@ Register* directive (common to all mobile Web Forms pages), an *@ Control* declaration instead of the normal *@ Page*, and a single StyleSheet control. Listing 8-6 shows an example of an external style sheet.

```
<%@ Control language="c#"
    Inherits="System.Web.UI.MobileControls.MobileUserControl" %>
<%@ Register TagPrefix="mobile"
    Namespace="System.Web.UI.MobileControls"
    Assembly="System.Web.Mobile" %>

<mobile:StyleSheet id="StyleSheet1" runat="server">
    <Style Font-Bold="True" Font-Italic="True" Name="Heading"/>
</mobile:StyleSheet>
```

Listing 8-6 ExternalStyle1.ascx—user control acting as an external style sheet

Consuming an external style sheet To use an external style sheet, you must insert a StyleSheet control into your mobile Web Forms page and set its *Reference* property to the location of the external style sheet. You can then reference the styles that the style sheet contains as though they were within the mobile Web Forms page. Listing 8-7 shows a mobile Web Forms page that references the external style sheet shown in Listing 8-6, and sets the style of a label to a style that the external style sheet defines.

```
<%@ Page language="c#"
    Inherits="System.Web.UI.MobileControls.MobilePage" %>
<%@ Register TagPrefix="mobile"
    Namespace="System.Web.UI.MobileControls"
    Assembly="System.Web.Mobile" %>

<mobile:Form id="Form1" runat="server">
    <mobile:Label id="Label1" runat="server" StyleReference="Heading">
        Label
    </mobile:Label>
</mobile:Form>

<mobile:StyleSheet id="StyleSheet1"
    runat="server"
    ReferencePath="ExternalStyle1.ascx"/>
```

Listing 8-7 Using an external style sheet in ExternalStyleSheet-Example.aspx

> **Note** If you're using Microsoft Visual Studio .NET, you'll find that external style sheets behave differently than style sheets embedded directly into a mobile Web Forms page in two respects. First, styles specified in an external style sheet aren't rendered during design time, meaning that controls referencing them won't appear formatted in Design view. Second, the styles will not appear on your controls in the drop-down StyleReference list provided in the Properties window.

Pagination and Styles

ASP.NET mobile Web applications can automatically paginate if the amount of output to be displayed is too much for the client device. For example, a list of 20 items would be displayed in its entirety on a large screen Pocket PC but would be paginated over three screens on a mobile phone with a four-line display. When the output is paginated, ASP.NET automatically renders Next and Previous functions on the phone navigation buttons or displays Next and Previous buttons on the screen of an HTML browser, allowing the user to page backward and forward through the contents, as shown in Figure 8-7.

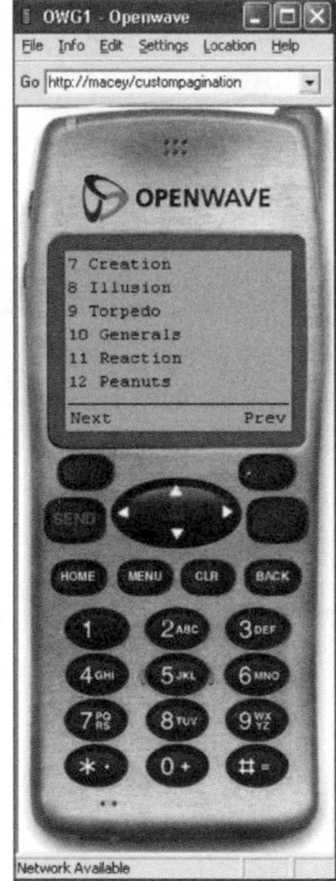

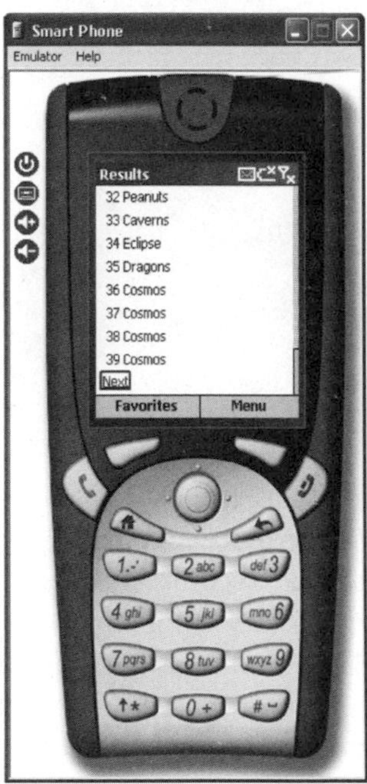

Figure 8-7 A paginated mobile Web Forms application with Navigation buttons added—WML browser (left) and HTML browser (right)

To enable this capability, set the *Paginate* property of the Form control to *true*. (The default is *false*.) You can control the style and text used for the Next and Previous pagination controls using the *PagerStyle* property of the Form control. This exposes an object of type *System.Web.UI.MobileControls.PagerStyle* which inherits from *MobileControl*, and so possesses all the properties described in Table 8-1. It also has a number of properties that relate to pagination which are described in Table 8-3.

Table 8-3 Pagination Properties of the *PagerStyle* Object

Property	Allowed Values	Description
NextPageText	*String*	The text for the Next navigation prompt; defaults to "Next".
PageLabel	*String*	The text for the label of the current page; default to an empty string "". A more complete description of this property immediately follows this table.

Table 8-3 Pagination Properties of the *PagerStyle* Object

Property	Allowed Values	Description
PreviousPageText	*String*	The text for the Previous navigation prompt; defaults to "Previous".
StyleReference	*String*	The name of a PagerStyle object in a style sheet that is used to set the pagination style properties. PagerStyle objects are defined in style sheets in a similar manner to Style objects, but use the <PagerStyle> tag instead of the <Style> tag.

The *PageLabel* property allows you to define a title for each page of the paginated Form. The property can have a value that's a mixture of text and format specifiers. There are two format specifiers: *{0}* for the current page number, and *{1}* for the total number of pages. For example, the value *{0} of {1}* will display the text *1 of 3* on the first page of a Form that displays as three pages.

You can set these properties in code or in server control syntax. To set these properties in server control syntax, you use *contained object notation*, in which a child object is separated from its parent by a dash, as in the following example:

```
<mobile:Form PagerStyle-NextPageText="More" PagerStyle-Font-Bold="True"…
```

Using Pager Styles in Style Sheets

The *StyleReference* property of the *PagerStyle* object allows you to reference a *PagerStyle* object stored in a StyleSheet control in the .aspx file or stored externally in an external style sheet, instead of setting pagination properties directly on the Form control. For example, if you had a *PagerStyle* called *"myPagerStyle"* defined in a style sheet, you would program a Form to use that *PagerStyle* using the following server control syntax:

```
<mobile:Form PagerStyle-StyleReference="myPagerStyle" …
```

The *<PagerStyle>* element defines pagination style information for the pagination of a mobile Web Forms page. The following syntax shows the attributes associated with this element:

```
<PagerStyle id="id"
    StyleReference="styleControlReference"
    Font-Size="{NotSet|Normal|Small|Large}"
    Font-Name="fontName"
    Font-Bold="{NotSet|False|True}"
    Font-Italic="{NotSet|False|True}"
    ForeColor="color"
```

```
Alignment="{NotSet|Left|Center|Right}"
BackColor="color"
Wrapping="{NotSet|Wrap|NoWrap}"
NextPageText="nextPageText"
PreviousPageText="previousPageText"
PageLabel="pageLabel" />
```

You can use the *<PagerStyle>* element only within a StyleSheet control. You can, however, have a mixture of *<PagerStyle>* elements and *<Style>* elements within a single style sheet.

Working with Styles in Visual Studio .NET

The Visual Studio .NET integrated development environment (IDE) offers some powerful assistance with building style sheets and applying choice filters to these styles. So far, this chapter has demonstrated how you write style sheets using ASP.NET server control syntax. However, this entails working in the HTML view of your mobile Web Forms application and writing the XML text directly, which isn't the most effective use of the IDE. Throughout this section, we'll describe how you can use the tools in Visual Studio .NET to tackle the most common tasks associated with creating style sheets.

The Styles Editor

When you place a mobile StyleSheet control on a mobile Web Forms page, you can access a style editor in Design view that makes creating new styles straightforward. To access this editor, right-click the StyleSheet control and then click Edit Styles on the context menu to reveal the Styles Editor dialog box. Figure 8-8 shows how this editor looks.

The upper-left corner of this dialog box contains a Style Types list box. The list box shows all the available style types, of which there should be two: *PagerStyle* and *Style*. As you'll recall, we discussed these two styles earlier in this chapter. To create a new style, you must select the style type you want and then click the right arrow (>) button. A new entry will appear in the dialog box's Defined Styles list. This style has a default name, which is *Style1* in the first instance. That's all it takes to successfully create a new style! Now you simply need to define its properties.

To define the style properties, you must set the property values in the Properties window, found in the lower-right corner of the dialog box. As you set each property, the Sample view to the left of the Properties window updates, showing the visual appearance of the style. When you finish setting the style properties, simply click the OK button to complete the style definition.

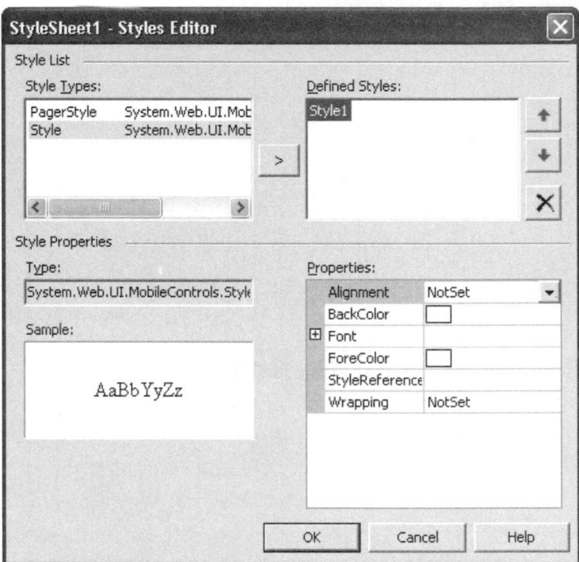

Figure 8-8 The Styles Editor dialog box

Using Cascading Style Sheets (CSS)

Cascading Style Sheets (CSS) are another way of defining style definitions. The World Wide Web Consortium (W3C) has actively promoted CSS on the Web for use with all desktop and mobile browsers. CSS is often used to define styles for Web pages targeted at Web browsers that support HTML 4.0 or later, such as recent versions of Microsoft Internet Explorer or Netscape. CSS is not supported by WML browsers used in WAP-enabled mobile phones, by cHTML browsers used on i-mode phones, or by HTML 3.2 browsers used on Pocket PC 2002 and similar PDAs.

However, CSS is supported by browsers that support Extensible HTML Mobile Profile (XHTML-MP), which is the markup language of the newest generation of mobile Web browsers. You must install Device Update 2 or later to add support for XHTML-MP to ASP.NET, which you can download by following the links from the Mobile page at *http://www.asp.net*. There are two versions of Device Update 2; one for Visual Studio.NET 2002/Mobile Internet Toolkit and one for Visual Studio .NET 2003. Device Update 2 updates device configuration files to support many new devices, including some that have XHTML-MP browsers, and also installs new assemblies that contain the device adapters that perform the runtime rendering of mobile controls into XHTML markup. See Chapter 22 for more information about device adapters.

What Is XHTML?

Extensible HTML (XHTML) represents the evolution of HTML, using HTML-like tags and syntax, but imposing the strict rules common to all XML languages. XHTML 1.0 is a W3C recommendation (see *http://www.w3.org/TR/xhtml1*) and implements an XML-compliant version of HTML 4.01.

XHTML Basic

XHTML Basic is a subset of XHTML 1.0, which defines a document type that is rich enough to be used for content authoring and precise document layout but can be used on different classes of device, such as desktop PCs, PDAs, and mobile handsets. It includes everything in XHTML 1.0 apart from those features that are suitable only for large-screen devices, such as frames. XHTML Basic is defined in the XHTML 1.0 recommendation.

XHTML Mobile Profile

The WAP Forum, which is the industry body responsible for defining WAP specifications, took the XHTML Basic specification and specialized it for use in mobile browsers by adding the following elements: *<hr>*, *<b>*, *<i>*, *<big>*, *<small>*, and *<style>*. XHTML-MP also permits the use of the *Style* attribute in all elements. XHTML-MP has been sanctioned by the W3C and is the markup language used by WAP 2.0 devices; it supercedes WML 1.0, which was the markup language used by WAP 1.0 devices.

XHTML-MP and WAP CSS

Unlike WML, which embeds style information in the application, XHTML-MP uses CSS to define presentation. The WAP Forum defined WAP CSS, which is a subset of CSS suitable for devices with small screens. (You can download the specification, called "WAP CSS Specification 1.0," from the WAP Forum Web site at *http://www.wapforum.org*.)

The big failing of WML is that it does not define rules for the visual display of elements on the page, which has led to interoperability problems between browsers from different suppliers. XHTML-MP and WAP CSS are a huge improvement in layout control and consistency, alleviating most interoperability problems.

Managing Cascading Style Sheets

When an XHTML-MP client accesses an ASP.NET mobile Web application, the runtime takes all the *Style* properties defined for the control and dynamically constructs a CSS style sheet that it sends to the device as a part of the response. By default, the mobile controls store dynamically-generated CSS style sheets in session state. Your application must not disable session state if you want to use dynamically generated CSS style sheets. Session state is disabled if you include *EnableSessionState = False* in the *@ Page* directive at the head of your .aspx file, or if you have *<sessionStatemode="Off"...>* in the application Web.config file.

You can get improved performance if you cache dynamic style sheets in the application cache. The application cache is shared by all instances of your Web application, so the style sheet is created only the very first time your application runs after IIS is started on the Web server; thereafter, the cached version is available. The version in the cache is also automatically invalidated if you change any style properties requiring the generation of a new CSS style sheet. To enable this, set the *XhtmlCssStore* element value to *application* in the Web.config file, as follows:

```
<appSettings>
   <add key="XhtmlCssStore" value="application" />
</appSettings>
```

See Chapter 12 for more information about using the application cache.

Programming your own CSS Style Sheet

ASP.NET Mobile Controls supports clients with browsers that require XHTML-MP and CSS style sheets automatically, without your needing to carry out any additional programming effort. It reads the style properties that you have defined on the mobile controls and automatically generates the appropriate CSS style sheet to send to the client browser. All you need to do is ensure that you have installed Device Update 2 on your development computer and on your Web server, as previously explained.

If you don't want to use the dynamically generated style sheet and decide to create your own, ASP.NET Mobile Controls allows you to do this. To add a CSS style sheet to your Visual Studio .NET project, right-click on your project in Solution Explorer, click Add, then Add New Item, and then choose the Style Sheet template from the Add New Item window. When you edit the CSS style sheet, Visual Studio .NET displays the built-in CSS style sheet editor which can help you with this task. However, remember that the CSS style sheet editor is intended for building style sheets for desktop browsers, so do check the WAP CSS specification to ensure that you don't use features that are supported only on desktop browsers.

Programming CSS style sheets is too large a topic to cover in detail here. Visual Studio .NET includes good documentation on how to do this, and there are plenty of resources on the Web that can help. However, the following is a simple example of a CSS style sheet which sets the style attributes of a style named *style1* to boldface, large size, and the color green:

```
.style1
{
    font-weight: bold;
    font-size: large;
    color: green;
}
```

The correct name for a style in a CSS style sheet is a *CSS Class*; the example just shown defines a CSS class called *style1*.

CSS Custom Attributes

To use your own CSS style sheet, you must use custom attributes. You're used to using standard attributes, such as *Font-Bold* or *ID*, when programming server control syntax for the mobile controls. You use custom attributes in exactly the same way as standard attributes, except that custom attributes are not recognized as valid syntax by the ASP.NET page parser until you enable them. The way in which you enable custom attributes is described in the next section.

To support CSS style sheets, you can use the custom attributes described in Table 8-4 with any ASP.NET mobile control.

Table 8-4 MobileControl Custom Attributes for XHTML

Attribute	Description
CssClass	The CSS class (the style name) within the CSS file associated with the control.
CssLocation	The URL to the physical location of the CSS file for the page.
CssCommandClass	The CSS class in a physical CSS file to control an ObjectList command link style. Use this attribute with the ObjectList control to set the style used for Item commands.
CssLabelClass	The CSS class in a physical CSS file to control an ObjectList label style. Use this attribute with the ObjectList control to set the style used for field headings.
CssPagerClass	The CSS class in a physical CSS file to control the style of the pagination prompts. Use this attribute with the Form control.

For example, the following simple style sheet, default.css, sets the style attributes of a CSS class named *style1* to boldface, large size, and the color green.

```
.style1
{
    font-weight: bold;
    font-size: large;
    color: green;
}
```

In server control syntax, you use the *CssLocation* custom attribute to specify the path to the CSS style sheet file and use the *CssClass* custom attribute to use a style in the style sheet on a control:

```
<mobile:form id="Form1" runat="server" csslocation="default.css">
    <mobile:label id="Label1" runat="server">
        Label with no style
    </mobile:label>
    <mobile:label id="Label2" runat="server" cssclass="style1">
        Label using CSS style
    </mobile:label>
</mobile:form>
```

> **Tip** The real power of CSS is the ability to develop different style sheets for different devices. You can use the Property Override technique, described in Chapter 9, to override the values of the *CssLocation* and/or *CssClass* attributes for specific devices, allowing you to use different external style sheets or different styles within a style sheet according to the type of the requesting client device.

Enabling Custom Attributes

To enable the use of custom attributes, you must set the *AllowCustomAttributes* property of the MobilePage to *true*. There are two ways of doing this:

- You can set this property for your application in the Web.config file using the *allowCustomAttributes* attribute of the *mobileControls* tag, as shown in the following example:

  ```
  <system.web>
     <mobileControls allowCustomAttributes="true" />
  </system.web>
  ```

- Alternatively, you can set the *AllowCustomAttributes* property of the MobilePage in code, for example in the *Page_Load* event handler in the code behind module of your mobile Web Forms page:

```
private void Page_Load(object sender, System.EventArgs e)
{
    this.AllowCustomAttributes = true;
⋮
}
```

Be careful when custom attributes are enabled, however, because any misspellings of standard attributes will no longer be detected during parsing by the ASP.NET runtime. For example, the misspelled *Alignmet* attribute will be saved as a custom attribute of that name—the parser doesn't report it as an error.

today

9

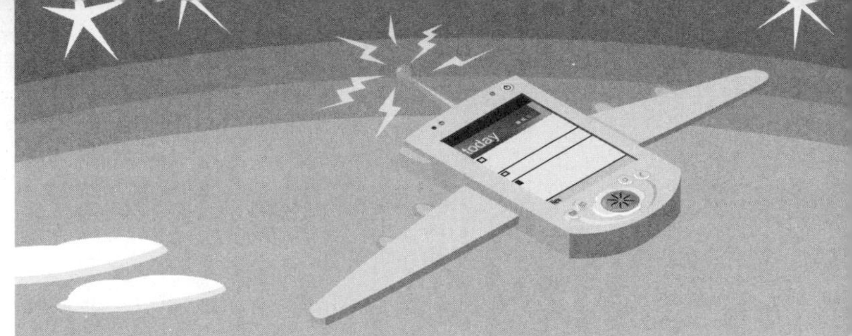

Customizing with Property Overrides and Templates

In this chapter, you'll learn how to customize your applications for a particular client device and how to customize the Form and Panel controls using templates. You'll use property overrides to set control properties that apply to a specific subset of client devices. You'll use the template features of the Form and Panel controls to override the default rendering of these controls, which allows you to include device-specific markup in the content sent to the client. These features give you great flexibility in the way you present your mobile Web Forms controls on specific mobile devices.

Customization Overview

Property overrides and templates are both techniques for customizing your application for different mobile devices. You apply either of these customization techniques to a mobile control in an .aspx page using a section of server control syntax called a *DeviceSpecific/Choice construct*. This construct allows you to identify particular client devices or particular groups of client devices. For example, the following server control syntax is for a Label control, which has a DeviceSpecific/Choice construct which identifies HTML browsers:

```
<mobile:Label id="Label1" runat="server"
    Text="Default text">
    <DeviceSpecific>
        <Choice Filter="isHTML32"
```

```
                Text="Text for selected devices" >
            </Choice>
        </DeviceSpecific>
    </mobile:Label>
```

The *Filter="isHTML32"* attribute applies a *Device Filter*. This device filter is called *isHTML32* and identifies client devices that have HTML 3.2 browsers. For those devices identified by Choice device filters, the contents of the *<Choice>...</Choice>* elements are applied, which might be a Property Override or a Template. In the example just shown, the *<Choice>* element applies a property override for the *Text* property of the Label.

We'll look at how you define device filters first in this chapter. Before we do that, let's take a high-level overview of Property Overrides and Templates to see how and when they would be used.

Property Overrides

By design, the Microsoft ASP.NET mobile controls allow you to develop applications for a broad range of mobile devices. These devices share the characteristics of being small, portable, and able to connect to the Internet. Despite their similarities, however, these devices can also differ substantially. For instance, color support, screen display size, input capabilities, and markup language support can differ widely among mobile clients. Applications you develop using the ASP.NET mobile controls operate on all supported mobile devices, and the properties you set on any mobile control apply to all those devices. However, you'll sometimes want to override the default rendering of your application on a particular device. A typical example is that you might show shorter strings on mobile devices that have smaller display areas and longer strings on other devices. Property Overrides is a technique that allows you to set properties of mobile controls to different values on different devices.

Templates

The Form, Panel, List, and ObjectList mobile controls are *templated* controls. Templates are the most powerful tool you have for customizing the appearance and/or content of your application. The Form and Panel controls allow you to define items such as a header or footer within the template. This content is then inserted into the rendered page and displayed at the top (the header) and the bottom (the footer) of each display page. In the case of the List and ObjectList controls, templates allow you to completely override the appearance of the control's content. (We focus on the Form and Panel controls in this chapter and examine List and ObjectList templates in Chapter 10.) The template can contain ASP.NET controls or literal text. The literal text is inserted into the rendered page sent to the client; this literal text you write could be the markup that the client browser understands. An example of the application of this technique is to use the Form control templates to inject HTML markup into the response sent to HTML clients which formats the page as an HTML table, taking advantage of all the inherent formatting flexibility of HTML.

Writing Device Filters

The *<Choice>* element in a DeviceSpecific/Choice construct relies on knowledge of the mobile device's capabilities. When a client browser requests a mobile ASP.NET page, the Hypertext Transfer Protocol (HTTP) headers sent with the request contain identifying information. The Mobile Internet Controls Runtime uses this information to construct a *System.Web.Mobile.MobileCapabilities* object, which is attached to the client's request. The device filters work by testing read-only properties of the *MobileCapabilities* object. A typical example of a device filter is one that identifies all browsers that accept HTML 3.2 markup; to do this, the device filter identifies all requests for which the *PreferredRenderingType* property of the *MobileCapabilities* object has the value html32.

The properties of the *MobileCapabilities* object are set to the appropriate values for the requesting device. For example, when a Pocket Internet Explorer browser makes a request, the *Browser* property of the *MobileCapabilities* object is set to Pocket IE, the *PreferredRenderingType* is set to html32, and the *ScreenPixelsWidth* and *ScreenPixelsHeight* properties are set to the correct values for the requesting device, which might be a Pocket PC, a Smartphone, or a Windows CE .NET device.

To work with Device Filters effectively, you need to know the property values of the *MobileCapabilities* object for the device or devices that you want to identify. The actual values assigned for a particular device are defined in the machine.Config or DeviceUpdate.config (if present) configuration files, which are in the /Microsoft.NET/Framework/*version*/CONFIG directory under the system root directory /WINNT or /Windows. (We look at the contents of these files and how you define configuration settings for new clients in Chapter 19.) To find the precise values that are assigned to *MobileCapabilities* object properties for a particular device, you could search these files. However, an easier method is to write a simple test application that writes *MobileCapabilities* properties to the screen, and call the application from the device that you are investigating.

> **Warning** Sometimes, properties of the *MobileCapabilities* object for a particular device might not be set to the value you expect. For example, when you test a mobile Web application using desktop Internet Explorer (which you will often do during development), you might expect the *PreferredRenderingType* to be set to *html40*.
>
> In fact, all flavors of Internet Explorer have a *preferredRenderingType* of *html32*. The ASP.NET mobile controls do not render HTML 4.0 markup, so all HTML browsers are sent HTML 3.2 markup.

Using Properties of the *MobileCapabilities* Class

The *MobileCapabilities* class has many properties, several of which are primarily of interest to developers writing custom controls. For a complete reference to all the properties of the *MobileCapabilities* class, refer to the online documentation for the ASP.NET mobile controls or MSDN. Table 9-1 describes the properties you'll most likely use with device filters.

Table 9-1 Selected Properties of the *MobileCapabilities* Object

Property	Description
Browser	The type of browser. Example values include *Pocket IE*, *Microsoft Mobile Explorer*, *Go.Web*, *i-mode*, *Nokia*, *Phone.com*, *Ericsson*, and *unknown*.
CanInitiateVoiceCall	Returns *true* if the device is capable of initiating a voice call.
CanSendMail	Returns *true* if the device or browser is capable of sending e-mail, using the *mailto* URL scheme.
HasBackButton	Returns *true* if the device has a dedicated Back button.
InputType	Returns the type of input supported on the device. Examples include *virtualKeyboard*, *telephoneKeypad*, and *keyboard*.
IsColor	Returns *true* if the device has a color display.
MaximumSoftkeyLabelLength	Returns the maximum supported length of text for a softkey label. This property will normally be 8 characters long.
MobileDeviceManufacturer	Returns the name of the manufacturer or *unknown*.
MobileDeviceModel	Returns the model name of the device or *unknown*.
NumberOfSoftkeys	Returns the number of softkeys the device supports.
PreferredImageMime	Returns the Multipurpose Internet Mail Extensions (MIME) type identifying the type of image content the device prefers. Typical values include *image/gif*, *image/jpeg*, *image/vnd.wap.wbmp*, and *image/bmp*.

Table 9-1 Selected Properties of the *MobileCapabilities* Object

Property	Description
PreferredRenderingMime	Returns the MIME type identifying the type of content the device prefers. Typical values include *text/html* and *text/vnd.wap.wml.*
PreferredRenderingType	Returns a string identifying the version and type of markup the device requires: *html32*, *wml11*, *wml12*, or *chtml10.*
ScreenBitDepth	Returns the depth of the display, in bits per pixel. Typical values include *8* for a Pocket PC and *1* for many WML browsers.
ScreenCharactersHeight	Returns the height of the display, in character lines. Typical values include *40* on Pocket PCs and *4* on mobile phones.
ScreenCharactersWidth	Returns the width of the display, in characters. Typical values include *80* on a Pocket PC and *20* or a similar value for a typical mobile phone with a small screen.
ScreenPixelsHeight	Returns the height of the display, in pixels. Typical values include *480* for a Pocket PC and *40* or a similar value for a typical mobile phone.
ScreenPixelsWidth	Returns the width of the display, in pixels. Typical values include *640* for a Pocket PC and *90* or a similar value for a typical mobile phone.
SupportsIModeSymbols	Returns *true* if the device supports the i-mode symbols. You can specify that an i-mode symbol be displayed using the *ImageUrl* property of the Image control, which we discussed in Chapter 4.
SupportsJPhoneSymbols	Returns *true* if the device supports the J-Phone-specific picture symbols. You can specify that a symbol be displayed using the *ImageUrl* property of the Image control.

The *Request* property of the *MobilePage* class exposes a *System.Web.HttpRequest* object, which is constructed on every client request. The *Browser* property of the *HttpRequest* object exposes the *MobileCapabilities* object for the current request. Consequently, you can test properties of the *MobileCapabilities* object in code, as shown here:

```
MobileCapabilities capabilities = (MobileCapabilities)Request.Browser;
if (capabilities.ScreenPixelsWidth > 120)
{
    // Code for larger screens
}
else
{
    // Code for smaller screens
}
```

In Microsoft Visual Basic .NET, use the *CType* function to cast the *Request.Browser* property to the correct type:

```
Dim capabilities As MobileCapabilities
capabilities = CType(Request.Browser, MobileCapabilities)
```

Defining Device Filters

To use DeviceSpecific/Choice constructs within your mobile Web Forms page, you must define device filters to test properties of the *MobileCapabilities* object. You define device filters in your application's Web.config file, in the *<deviceFilters>* section. Each *<filter>* element defines a device filter. Here's the syntax you use to define device filters:

```
<system.web>
    <deviceFilters>
        <filter
            name="filterName"
            compare="capabilityName"
            argument="comparisonString"/>
        <filter
            name="filterName"
            type="className"
            method="methodName"/>
    </deviceFilters>
</system.web>
```

As you can see, two forms of the *<filter>* child element exist. The first form is a *comparison evaluator*, which compares a string to a property of the *MobileCapabilities* object for simple equality. The attributes have the following meaning:

- ***name*** The name of the device filter. Note that device filter names are case sensitive. For example, *isHTML* and *IsHTML* denote two different device filters.
- ***compare*** The property of the *MobileCapabilities* object to test.
- ***argument*** The comparison string.

The second form is an *evaluator delegate*, which references a custom evaluator that you must write and place in a .NET assembly to which your application contains a reference. The attributes have the following meanings:

- ***name*** The name of the device filter. Note that device filter names are case sensitive.
- ***type*** The class name and assembly name where the custom evaluator is defined—for example: *mynamespace.myclass, myassemblyname.*
- ***method*** The name of the static method that performs the capability evaluation.

Defining simple comparison evaluator filters Comparison evaluators don't require any additional code; you can define the evaluation entirely in the *<deviceFilter>* element. For example, to add a device filter that tests whether a device supports HTML version 3.2, you add the following code to Web.config:

```
<system.web>
    <deviceFilters>
        <filter name="isHTML32"
            compare="PreferredRenderingType"
            argument="html32">
        </filter>
    </deviceFilters>
</system.web>
```

This code defines a device filter named *isHTML32*, which tests the *PreferredRenderingType* property of the *MobileCapabilities* object for equality with *html32*. You use this filter within a DeviceSpecific/Choice construct. You can also use a comparison evaluator in code, using the *HasCapability* method of the *MobileCapabilities* object, as the following code demonstrates. Be aware that you don't use the second parameter of the *HasCapability* method with comparison evaluators.

```
MobileCapablities cap = (MobileCapabilities)Request.Browser;
if ((cap.HasCapability ("isHTML32", null))
{
    // Do something.
}
```

> **Note** If you create a new project in Visual Studio .NET using the ASP.NET Mobile Web Application project type, the Web.config file that the IDE generates will already contain a number of comparison evaluator device filters. These include *isWML11*, *isHTML32*, *isCHTML10*, and many others that identify particular browsers or image file preferences. If you open the Web.config file, you can view the full set of available device filters.

Defining custom evaluator delegate filters If you want a device filter that performs a more sophisticated evaluation than simply testing a property of the *MobileCapabilities* object for a particular value, you can write an evaluator delegate. You write the evaluation logic in a static method (*Shared* in Visual basic .NET) that you create in an assembly that's accessible to your application.

The evaluator method takes the following form:

```
public static bool MethodName
(System.Web.Mobile.MobileCapabilities capabilities, String param)
```

The second parameter is optional, and you can use it as additional input to your capability evaluator method.

In the Web.config file, you can reference evaluator delegate filters using the second form of the *<filter>* element. For example, this is how you create a device filter named *isMMEonSony* that uses a custom capability evaluator method named *MMEandSony* in the *MyClass* class within the namespace *MyNameSpace* in the *MyEvaluators.dll* assembly:

```
<system.web>
    <deviceFilters>
        <filter name="isMMEonSony"
            type="MyNameSpace.MyClass, MyEvaluators.dll"
            method="MMEandSony">
        </filter>
    </deviceFilters>
</system.web>
```

This configuration sets the *type* attribute to the fully qualified name of the class: *namespace.method, assembly*. The *method* attribute names the actual method that the runtime will call.

Using an evaluator delegate from a DeviceSpecific/Choice construct is no different from using a simple comparison evaluator, as this next code snippet illustrates:

```
<mobile:Form id="Form1" runat="server">
    <mobile:Label id="Label1" runat="server"
                 Text="Client is NOT MME on Sony">
        <DeviceSpecific>
            <Choice Text="Client is MME on Sony"
                    Filter="isMMEonSony">
            </Choice>
        </DeviceSpecific>
    </mobile:Label>
</mobile:Form>
```

You can also employ the *MobileCapabilities.HasCapability* method to use an evaluator delegate within code. Doing so enables you to use the extra parameter of the custom evaluator method, which you can't do when using this kind of evaluator in a DeviceSpecific/Choice construct. Here's the syntax:

```
if (((MobileCapabilities)Request.Browser).HasCapability(
    "isMMEonSony",
    "Some Useful Client Information"))
```

```
{
    // Do something.
}
```

A good way to use the second parameter is to pass information known about the client device that the properties of the *MobileCapabilities* object don't specify. The *System.Web.HttpRequest* object that's accessed through the *Page.Request* property contains properties for other information that the client device passes to your application in HTTP headers. For example, *Request.UserLanguages* returns a string array containing the preferred content languages. If you write an evaluator delegate named *PrefersFrench*, you can call it from your code, passing the first item in the *UserLanguages* array associated with this client. The following code demonstrates this technique:

```
if (((MobileCapabilities)Request.Browser).HasCapability (
    "PrefersFrench",
    Request.UserLanguages[0]))
{
    // Display content in French.
}
```

Example of an evaluator delegate filter The example application in this section targets HTML browsers on devices with larger screens, such as the Pocket PC, and HTML browsers on devices with small screens, such as i-mode devices or phones with Microsoft Mobile Explorer. The application also targets WML browsers on small and larger screen devices, such as the Ericsson R380. The application uses custom evaluators to select the most appropriate graphics file to send to the requesting device. Each graphic has four versions: a small GIF, a large GIF, a small WBMP, and a large WBMP. The application must categorize each device that accesses it according to its image file requirements. In doing so, the application requires four device filters:

- ***UsesLargeGIF*** *True* if the device supports GIF files and has a larger screen
- ***UsesSmallGIF*** *True* if the device supports GIF files and has a smaller screen
- ***UsesLargeWBMP*** *True* if the device supports a Wireless Application Protocol (WAP) bitmap file and has a larger screen
- ***UsesSmallWBMP*** *True* if the device supports WAP graphics and has a smaller screen

The code to implement these capability evaluators uses two properties of the *MobileCapabilities* object: *PreferredImageMime* and *ScreenPixelsWidth*. To create the assembly for these evaluators, open Visual Studio .NET and follow these steps to create a new project:

1. In the New Project window, select Class Library as the project type. Type a suitable project name, such as **MyEvaluators**, and then click OK.

2. The Visual Studio .NET IDE opens the code for the class module. Delete the constructor *Class1*; you don't need this method because the class will contain only static methods. Give the class declaration a more meaningful name, such as *CustomEvals*.

3. The methods you define take a *MobileCapabilities* object as a parameter. You must add a reference to the new project so that the appropriate assemblies containing the *MobileCapabilities* class are accessible. Right-click References in Solution Explorer, and then click Add Reference. Select the .NET pane, locate the ASP.NET mobile controls assembly (*System.Web.Mobile.dll*) in the list, and double-click to select it.

4. As the *MobileCapabilities* object descends from the *System.Web.HttpBrowserCapabilities* object, which is found in the *System.Web* .NET assembly, you must also add a reference to that assembly. Locate *System.Web.dll* in the list and double-click it to select that assembly too. Click OK to close the window.

5. At the top of the class module, add the statement *using System.Web.Mobile*; so that you don't need to enter the full class definition for the *MobileCapabilities* class when you use it in your code. Now define the methods so that the module mirrors the one in Listing 9-1.

```
using System;
using System.Web.Mobile;

namespace MSPress.MobWeb.MyEvaluators
{
    /// <summary>
    /// Custom Device Capability Evaluators
    /// </summary>
    public class CustomEvals
    {
        public static bool UseSmallGif(
            MobileCapabilities caps,
            String notused)
```

Listing 9-1 Source file CustomEvals.cs in sample MyEvaluators

```
        {
            bool retval = false;
            if (caps.PreferredImageMime == "image/gif" &&
                (caps.ScreenPixelsWidth < 100))
                retval = true;
            return retval;
        }
        public static bool UseLargeGif(
            MobileCapabilities caps,
            String notused)
        {
            bool retval = false;
            if (caps.PreferredImageMime == "image/gif" &&
                !(caps.ScreenPixelsWidth < 100))
                retval = true;
            return retval;
        }
        public static bool UseSmallWBMP(
            MobileCapabilities caps,
            String notused)
        {
            bool retval = false;
            if (caps.PreferredImageMime == "image/vnd.wap.wbmp" &&
                (caps.ScreenPixelsWidth < 100))
                retval = true;
            return retval;
        }
        public static bool UseLargeWBMP(
            MobileCapabilities caps,
            String notused)
        {
            bool retval = false;
            if (caps.PreferredImageMime == "image/vnd.wap.wbmp" &&
                !(caps.ScreenPixelsWidth < 100))
                retval = true;
            return retval;
        }
    }
}
```

Compiling this code sample creates an assembly named *MyEvaluators.dll*, located in the /bin/debug directory of your project. To use these evaluators in a project, create a new project in Visual Studio .NET, like so:

1. Create a new project of type ASP.NET Mobile Web Application.
2. To use the new capability evaluators, you must add a reference to the assembly containing them to the project. Right-click References in Solution Explorer as you did before, but this time click Browse in

the Add Reference window. Browse to the *MyEvaluators.dll* assembly that you just created, and click Open to select it. After you click OK, the *MyEvaluators* assembly is added to your project references, as Figure 9-1 shows.

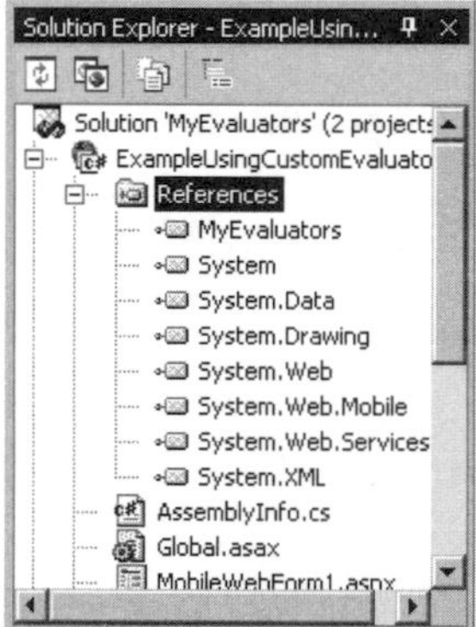

Figure 9-1 *MyEvaluators* in the References window of a new Visual Studio .NET project

3. Now open Web.config, and enter device filter definitions to access the custom capability evaluator methods. Enter these definitions after the device filters supplied by Visual Studio .NET, as shown here:

```
<deviceFilters>
    ⋮
    <filter name="UseLargeGIF"
            type="MyEvaluators.CustomEvals,MyEvaluators"
            method="UseLargeGif" />
    <filter name="UseSmallGIF"
            type="MyEvaluators.CustomEvals,MyEvaluators"
            method="UseSmallGif" />
    <filter name="UseLargeWBMP"
            type="MyEvaluators.CustomEvals,MyEvaluators"
            method="UseLargeWBMP" />
    <filter name="UseSmallWBMP"
            type="MyEvaluators.CustomEvals,MyEvaluators"
            method="UseSmallWBMP" />
</deviceFilters>
```

4. The final step is to reference the device filters from within DeviceSpecific/Choice constructs in the mobile Web Forms page. In this example, you don't use the *UseLargeGIF* evaluator method because it's the default choice that applies if none of the other device filters returns *true,* as this code illustrates:

```
<mobile:Form id="Form1" runat="server">
    <mobile:Image id="Image1" runat="server">
```

```
            <DeviceSpecific>
                <Choice Filter="UseLargeWBMP" ImageUrl="LargePic.wbmp"
                    AlternateText="Large WBMP">
                </Choice>
                <Choice Filter="UseSmallWBMP" ImageUrl="SmallPic.wbmp"
                    AlternateText="Small WBMP">
                </Choice>
                <Choice Filter="UseSmallGIF" ImageUrl="SmallPic.gif"
                    AlternateText="Small GIF">
                </Choice>
                <Choice ImageURL="LargePic.gif"
                    AlternateText="Large GIF">
                </Choice>
            </DeviceSpecific>
        </mobile:Image>
    </mobile:Form>
```

You can find this application in the sample ExampleUsingCustomEvaluators in the companion material on the book's Web site.

Defining Device Filters Using Visual Studio .NET Tools

The syntax for DeviceSpecific/Choice constructs and device filters described up to now in this chapter assumes that you're typing the syntax directly into the mobile page using the HTML view in Visual Studio .NET or editing the Web.config file directly. However, the Mobile Internet Designer provides graphical tools for defining device filters and DeviceSpecific/Choice constructs that you can use instead of editing the source files directly.

Note The Visual Studio .NET Toolbox contains a control named DeviceSpecific. The Mobile Internet Designer allows you to drag this control onto a Form or Panel control. When you do this, the Mobile Internet Designer inserts the syntax for a DeviceSpecific/Choice construct into the target Form or Panel, as you can see if you switch to the HTML view of the page you're editing. However, you can't drag this control onto any other control to implement a DeviceSpecific/Choice construct (which might seem confusing). Instead, the DeviceSpecific/Choice syntax is automatically added to a control when you define a property override or one of the list control templates. The DeviceSpecific control is used only to define templating options for a Form or Panel control when designing with the GUI tools. We'll discuss templates more in the section "Using Templated Controls" later in this chapter.

Creating and applying device filters You can access the Applied Device Filters dialog box by clicking on any mobile control in a form to select it and then clicking the ellipsis (…) button in the *(Applied Device Filters)* property shown in the Properties window. This tool's primary purpose is to apply device filters to the control whose properties you're editing. However, this editor also allows you to define new device filters. Any new device filter definitions you create apply to the whole application and are available for use with any control. The runtime stores these new device filters in the application's Web.config file.

Figure 9-2 shows how the Applied Device Filters dialog box will look.

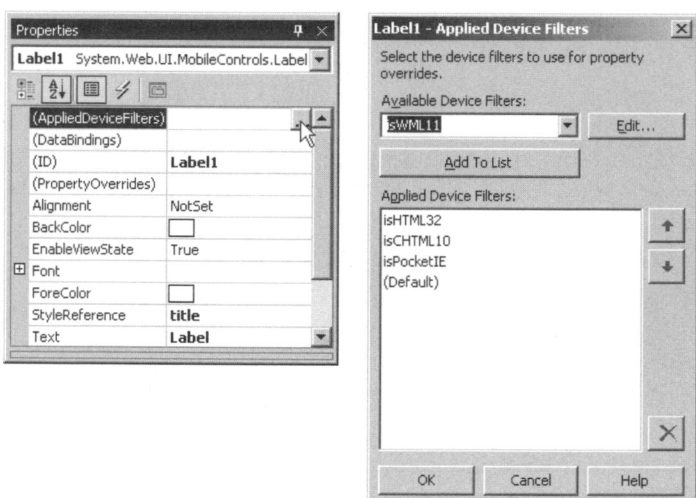

Figure 9-2 Using the Applied Device Filters dialog box

The Available Device Filters drop-down list displays all existing device filters that you haven't yet applied to the control whose properties you're editing. The Applied Device Filters list at the bottom of the dialog box shows the filters that you've applied to the control.

To create new device filters, click the Edit button. The Device Filter Editor dialog box will appear as shown in Figure 9-3. In this dialog box, you'll see a list of existing device filters. When you select a comparison evaluator item in the list, the attributes of the filter will be displayed in the Compare box and the Argument text box.

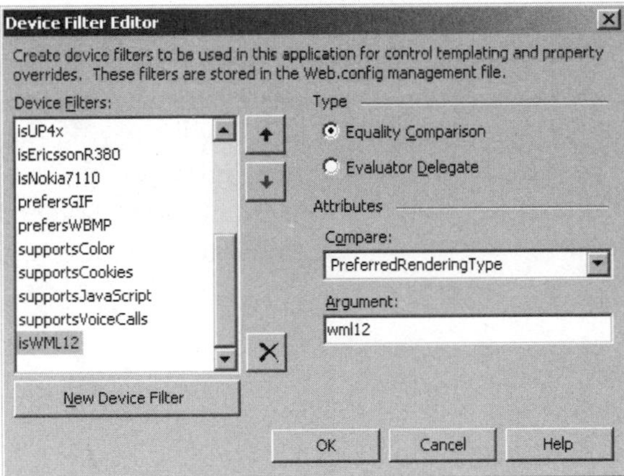

Figure 9-3 Equality comparison in the Device Filter Editor

To add a new comparison evaluator, follow these steps:

1. Click the New Device Filter button.
2. Type the name of your evaluator in the new list entry.
3. Select Equality Comparison as the Type choice.
4. In the Compare box, type or choose the property of the *MobileCapabilities* class that you want to compare with the value in the Argument text box.
5. Enter the Argument value. The comparison evaluator will return *true* when the specified property of a *MobileCapabilities* object equals this value.

The procedure to create a new evaluator delegate is the same, except instead of typing the comparison property and argument, you type values for the type of class that contains your evaluator and the name of the actual evaluator method. For the *UseLargeGIF* evaluator described earlier in this section, you'd type **MyEvaluators.CustomEvals,MyEvaluators** for the type and **UseLargeGif** for the method. After you've defined all the device filters you need for your application, apply them to each control on which you want to implement property overrides. Any new device filters you've defined will appear in the Available Device Filters drop-down list.

Applying a Device Filter to a Control In the Applied Device Filters dialog, select the device filter you want to apply to a control, and click Add To List to move the filter to the Applied Device Filters list box. Then use the up and down arrows to set the required order of evaluation. The device filter named *(Default)* is the default choice and will always return *true*. Therefore, *(Default)* should go at the bottom of your list. If you don't have a default choice, the properties that you specify directly in the control will provide the default settings when no *<Choice>* elements return *True*. Figure 9-4 shows the applied device filters for a Label control. This figure specifies that three device filters should apply to this control. The *<Choice>* elements will be evaluated in this order: *isHTML32*, *isWML11*, *(Default)*.

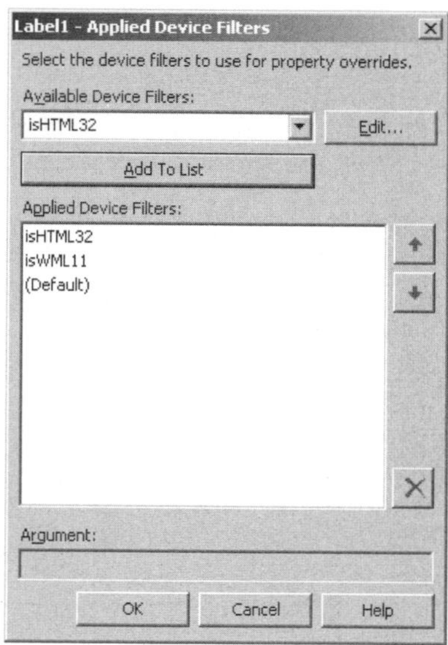

Figure 9-4 Device filters applied to a control prior to defining property overrides

Programming *<DeviceSpecific>* and *<Choice>* Elements

The server control syntax declaration of any control that inherits from *System.Web.UI.MobileControl* can contain a single *<DeviceSpecific>* element. As we've mentioned, a *<DeviceSpecific>* element can contain any number of *<Choice>* elements. You format a *<Choice>* element this way:

```
<Choice
    Filter="filterName"
    xmlns="urlToSchema"
    <!--Optional Property Overrides--!>
    >
    <!--Optional Templates--!>
</Choice>
```

Table 9-2 describes the usage of the attributes and child elements of *<Choice>*.

Table 9-2 Attributes and Child Elements of the *<Choice>* Element

Attribute/Child	Description
Filter	The *filterName* value must be the name of a valid device filter defined in the *<deviceFilters>* section of this application's Web.config file. Device filters are case sensitive. If you don't define this attribute, the *<Choice>* element will be the default choice. The default *<choice>* element should always be the last element in the list.
Property overrides	You can specify any attribute of the control that encloses the DeviceSpecific/Choice constuct. If the device filter returns *true*, the property of the enclosing control is set to the value specified here, overriding any setting defined for the enclosing control. You saw an example of this earlier, when we set the *ImageUrl* property of the Image control.
Template elements	The templated controls—Form, Panel, List, and ObjectList—allow you to define content that's incorporated into the control when rendered. (You'll learn more about templated controls later in this chapter, in the section "Using Templated Controls.")
xmlns	This attribute is not for general developer use. It is used by the Microsoft Visual Studio .NET Mobile Internet Designer to determine the type of markup inside templates. Visual Studio .NET inserts this attribute into *<Choice>* elements you create using the integrated development environment (IDE). Your application doesn't require this attribute to operate, and you don't need to supply a value.

You can specify one of the *<Choice>* elements within a *<DeviceSpecific>* element without a *Filter* attribute; this is the default *<Choice>* element. You don't have to define a default *<Choice>* element, but if you do, it should always be the last in the list. Because the runtime evaluates the *<Choice>* elements sequentially, it will apply the first element that returns *true* for the particular client requesting the mobile page. The default *<Choice>* element will always return *true*, so the runtime will apply this *<Choice>* element to the enclosing control unless a *<Choice>* element earlier in the list is applied first. If a default *<Choice>* element appears earlier in the list, you can't use any *<Choice>* elements below it.

Listing 9-2 illustrates the various ways you can use the *<Choice>* element—using it for property overrides and to define *<HeaderTemplate>* and *<FooterTemplate>* elements, which are templates used with the Form control.

```
<%@ Page Inherits="System.Web.UI.MobileControls.MobilePage"
    Language="C#" %>
<%@ Register TagPrefix="mobile"
    Namespace="System.Web.UI.MobileControls"
    Assembly="System.Web.Mobile" %>

<mobile:Form runat="server">
    <DeviceSpecific>
        <Choice Filter="isHTML32">
            <HeaderTemplate>
                <table width="100%" height="100%" cellspacing="1">
                <tr><td bgcolor="#003366">
                    <img src="sportsextra.gif">
                </td></tr>
                <tr><td bgcolor="#cccccc" valign="top" height="100%">
            </HeaderTemplate>
            <FooterTemplate>
                </td></tr>
                <tr><td bgcolor="#003366" height="4"></td></tr>
                </table>
            </FooterTemplate>
        </Choice>
        <Choice>
            <HeaderTemplate>
                <mobile:Label runat="server" StyleReference="title"
                              Text="SPORTS EXTRA!" />
            </HeaderTemplate>
        </Choice>
    </DeviceSpecific>
    <mobile:Label runat="server" Font-Size="Small" Font-Name="Arial">
         Welcome to our mobile Sports Extra Web site.
         Check here for up-to-the minute sports news as it happens!
        <DeviceSpecific>
            <Choice Filter="isWML11" Text="Welcome to LIVE results!"/>
            <Choice Filter="isCHTML10"
                    ForeColor="Red"
                    Text="Welcome to LIVE results!">
            </Choice>
        </DeviceSpecific>
    </mobile:Label>
</mobile:Form>
```

Listing 9-2 Source file DeviceSpecificExample.aspx

This example requires the following device filters in the application Web.config file:

```
<configuration>
  <system.web>
    <deviceFilters>
        <filter name="isHTML32"
             compare="PreferredRenderingType" argument="html32" />
        <filter name="isWML11"
             compare="PreferredRenderingType" argument="wml11" />
        <filter name="isCHTML10"
              compare="PreferredRenderingType" argument="chtml10" />
    </deviceFilters>
  </system.web>
</configuration>
```

The Form control contains a *<DeviceSpecific>* element that inserts a *HeaderTemplate* and a *FooterTemplate* if the client device supports HTML 3.2. Together these templates insert HTML markup to format the page as a table. This table has a graphic in the top row specified by using the HTML *<img>* tag.

The second *<Choice>* element in the Form control's DeviceSpecific/Choice construct has no *Filter* attribute, so this is the default *<Choice>* element. If the *isHTML32 filter* evaluates to *False* for the current request, the application uses a *<HeaderTemplate>* element that contains a single, mobile Label control.

The form defined in Listing 9-2 also contains a Label control with a DeviceSpecific/Choice construct, which is used to apply a property override. The default value for the Label control's *Text* property is the long string *Welcome to our mobile Sports Extra Web site. Check here for up-to-the minute sports news as it happens!* However, on smaller devices, such as those for which *isWML11* or *isCHTML10* is *true*, this text shortens to *Welcome to LIVE results!* And on the i-mode device, both the *Text* and the *ForeColor* properties have overrides as well.

These device-specific customizations yield an application that's visually appealing on Pocket Internet Explorer. Figure 9-5 shows an example of this display. In this example, the Openwave simulator accesses the application as a WML browser, and so the *isWML11* filter evaluates to *true*.

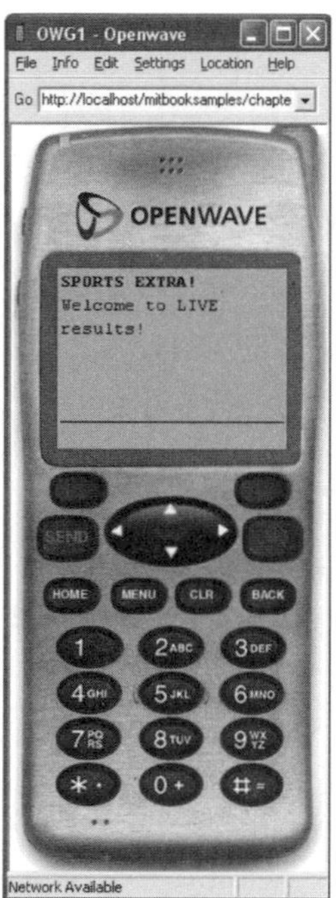

Figure 9-5 The DeviceSpecific/Choice construct used to customize presentation on Pocket Internet Explorer and a WML browser

Device-Specific Customization with Property Overrides

A property override is a technique that allows you to set control properties differently on various requesting devices by applying a DeviceSpecific/Choice construct to the control.

Each mobile control can contain a DeviceSpecific/Choice construct. Each *<Choice>* element within a *<DeviceSpecific>* element is evaluated in turn. The first *<Choice>* element that evaluates to *True* is applied to the control containing it. In Chapter 4, we used this technique with the Image control to test which graphics file format a client supports, as the following code illustrates:

```
<mobile:Image runat="server" id="myImages" AlternateText="Northwind Corp.">
    <DeviceSpecific>
      <Choice Filter="isHTML32" ImageUrl="Northwindlogo.gif"/>
      <Choice Filter="isWML11" ImageUrl="Northwindlogo.wbmp"/>
    </DeviceSpecific>
</mobile:Image>
```

When a client requests the mobile page that contains this Image control, the runtime uses the capabilities of the mobile device to evaluate the <*Choice*> elements. If the *isHTML32* filter returns *True*, the *ImageURL* property of the enclosing Image control is set to Northwindlogo.gif. If *isWML11* returns *True*, the control will use Northwindlogo.wbmp. If neither of these is *True*, the *ImageUrl* property remains undefined, which, for the Image control, means that *AlternateText* will be displayed instead. The two device filters used in this example are defined in the application Web.config file, as explained in the first part of this chapter.

This example demonstrates one common usage of DeviceSpecific/Choice constructs: to override properties of the enclosing control if a particular device filter is true. Property overrides have the following uses:

- **Using different graphics files** You do this when a client device supports different graphics formats.
- **Modifying text strings to account for differing display sizes** You might want to supply a longer version of a string on some devices but an abbreviated version on devices with smaller screens.
- **Supporting multilingual applications** You can set the *Text* properties differently depending on the preferred language of the client device.
- **Customizing style properties for particular devices** The Mobile Internet Controls Runtime does a good job of using the font and color support capabilities of each client device when rendering controls. However, sometimes you might want to apply different style attributes to a particular device.

You can also use the DeviceSpecific/Choice construct with the templated controls to apply additional ASP.NET controls or appropriate device-specific markup. You'll learn more about these additional features later in this chapter, in the section "Using Templated Controls."

Defining Property Overrides in Visual Studio .NET

Visual Studio .NET provides graphical tools for defining and applying device filters, and to define property overrides. You must apply a device filter to the control where you want to use a property override. The way you do this was described earlier in this chapter, in the section "Defining Device Filters using Visual Studio .NET Tools." To define which properties to override when one of the applied device filters returns *True*, you must open the Property Overrides

Editor. You access the Property Overrides Editor by clicking the ellipsis (…) button next to the *(Property Overrides)* entry in the control's Properties list, as Figure 9-6 shows.

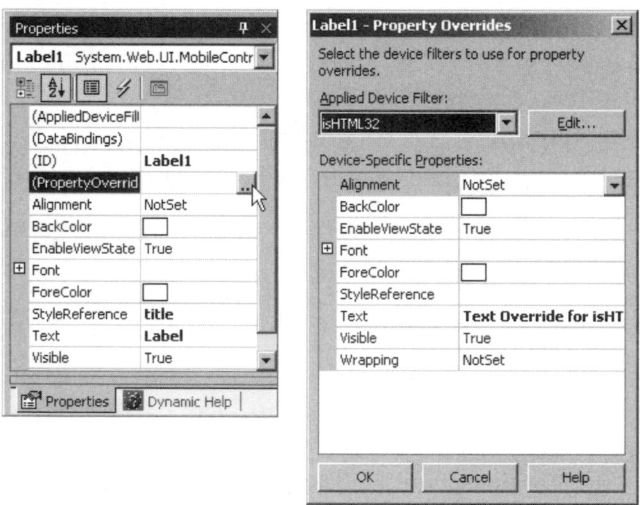

Figure 9-6 The Property Overrides Editor

Select each applied device filter from the drop-down list, and select the property overrides you want the filter to apply to the control when the filter is chosen. You can alter the list of applied device filters by clicking the Edit button.

Using Templated Controls

The templated controls—Form, Panel, List, and ObjectList—offer additional capabilities for customization. These controls enable developers to define additional content to insert into a control's rendered representation at defined points. You can define content within the templates described in Table 9-3.

Table 9-3 Templates Supported by the Templated Controls

Control	Template	Description
Form	*<HeaderTemplate>*	*<HeaderTemplate>* is rendered at the top of the form. When you enable pagination, this template is rendered at the head of each page.
	<FooterTemplate>	*<FooterTemplate>* is rendered at the foot of the form. When you enable pagination, this template is rendered at the foot of each page.

Table 9-3 Templates Supported by the Templated Controls

Control	Template	Description
	<ScriptTemplate>	*<ScriptTemplate>* is rendered at the top of the form. The content of *<ScriptTemplate>* is inserted directly after the *<head>* tag in HTML forms or after the opening *<card>* tag of a WML deck. When you enable pagination, this template is inserted at the head of each page.
Panel	*<ContentTemplate>*	You can use *<ContentTemplate>* to introduce blocks of device-specific markup. When specified, this template completely replaces any other contents of the Panel control.
List	*<HeaderTemplate>*	*<HeaderTemplate>* is rendered at the top of the list. When you enable pagination, the template is rendered at the head of the list on each page.
	<FooterTemplate>	*<FooterTemplate>* is rendered at the bottom of the list. When you enable pagination, the template is rendered at the foot of the list on each page.
	<ItemTemplate>	You use *<ItemTemplate>* to render each item.
	<AlternatingItemTemplate>	If specified, the application uses this template to render even-numbered items—the second item, the fourth item, and so on.
	<SeparatorTemplate>	The *<SeparatorTemplate>* is rendered between each item.
ObjectList (same templates as a List control, with the addition of *<ItemDetails-Template>*)	*<ItemDetailsTemplate>*	You use *<ItemDetailsTemplate>* to render the Details view in an ObjectList control.

You must define all templates in a mobile Web Forms page as the body inside one of the *<Choice>* … *</Choice>* tags in a DeviceSpecific/Choice construct, as the following example illustrates:

```
<mobile:Form> <!-- or Panel, List, ObjectList-->
    <mobile:DeviceSpecific>
        <Choice Filter="filterName"  OptionalPropertyOverrides go here >
            <HeaderTemplate> <!-- Templates Go Here-->
                ⋮
```

```
            </HeaderTemplate>
        </Choice>
    </mobile:DeviceSpecific>
</mobile:Form>
```

You can use the templates listed in Table 9-3 in many ways. First, you can customize the appearance of pages and lists on all mobile devices. For example, you can insert generic mobile controls into a template to specify running headers and footers and to modify list presentation. In this case, the templates will contain only literal text and mobile controls.

Second, you can customize what is displayed on specific devices. When you use these templates within DeviceSpecific/Choice constructs, you can define *template sets*, which are customizations targeted at specific devices. You could opt to use only literal text and mobile controls in these templates—literal text and mobile controls work with any client device. However, if you use appropriate device filters in your DeviceSpecific/Choice constructs, you can include native device markup for rendering on the appropriate devices. These markup languages include HTML 3.2, compact HTML (cHTML) 1.0, WML 1.1, WML 1.2 or XHTML. For example, if you use the *isHTML32* device filter, you can insert HTML 3.2 markup directly into the template, which the runtime then inserts into the markup sent to clients of the appropriate type.

Third, you can present data in tables on WML browsers. In their default rendering, the mobile controls don't present data in tables on WML browsers. Using the *<HeaderTemplate>*, *<ItemTemplate>*, and *<FooterTemplate>* elements of the List and ObjectList controls, you can specify the WML markup to present as a table on devices that support it.

Fourth, you can introduce whole blocks of client-side script or markup into your applications. Using the *<ScriptTemplate>* template of the Form control or the *<ContentTemplate>* of the Panel control, you can insert blocks of WML for execution on WML browsers, blocks of cHTML for use on i-mode devices, and blocks of HTML 3.2 for HTML browsers. You can also introduce blocks of JavaScript to execute on browsers that support it or calls to WMLScript resources on WAP devices.

Fifth, you can use regular (not mobile) ASP.NET controls. The ASP.NET controls can't operate with WML or cHTML browsers. But using a DeviceSpecific/Choice construct that selects HTML browsers enables you to apply nonmobile controls to devices that aren't mobile. And sixth, you can define your templates in a style defined in a style sheet and apply the templates to controls simply by setting the *StyleReference* property to the style containing the templates, just as you would with regular styles. This allows you to use a single style name to encapsulate a template set that combines templates for various devices.

Using the Form Control's *<HeaderTemplate>*, *<FooterTemplate>*, and *<ScriptTemplate>* Elements

You can use *<HeaderTemplate>* and *<FooterTemplate>* to specify content to appear at a page's top and bottom, respectively. If you set the *Form.Pagination* property to *True*, the templates will be rendered at the top and bottom of each page when pagination occurs. You can use *<ScriptTemplate>* to insert content directly after the *<head>* tag in HTML forms or after the opening *<card>* tag of a WML deck.

Implementing Running Headers and Footers

The simplest application of templates is to implement a basic running header and footer on each page. If you want all devices to support this functionality, you must use mobile controls, literal text, or a combination of the two. Listing 9-3 shows the code for this.

```
<%@ Register TagPrefix="mobile"
    Namespace="System.Web.UI.MobileControls"
    Assembly="System.Web.Mobile" %>
<%@ Page language="c#"
    Inherits="System.Web.UI.MobileControls.MobilePage" %>

<mobile:Form id="Form1" runat="server"
             Paginate="True" BackColor="Khaki">
    <mobile:TextView id="TextView1" runat="server">
  This TextView control is on this form to demonstrate how
  <b>&lt;HeaderTemplate&gt;</b> and <b>&lt;FooterTemplate&gt;</b>
  elements on a Form control are used at the top and the bottom of
  each page. <br/><br/>
  If your application uses pagination (that is you've set
  the <i>Paginate</i> property of the Form control to <i>true</i>),
  the header and footer appear at the top and bottom of all pages.
  <br/><br/>On HTML browsers, one thing you can do to enhance the
  layout is to format the page as a table. The table is initiated in the
  header template and closed in the footer template. Any content on the
  page then appears as a table row.
    </mobile:TextView>
    <mobile:DeviceSpecific id="DeviceSpecific1" runat="server">
        <Choice>
            <HeaderTemplate>
                <mobile:Label runat="server"
                              StyleReference="title"
                              ForeColor="Crimson">
```

Listing 9-3 Source file SimpleFormTemplateExample.aspx

```
                    This appears at the head of each page
                </mobile:Label>
            </HeaderTemplate>
            <FooterTemplate>
                <mobile:Label runat="server"
                              StyleReference="subcommand">
                    ..and this at the foot of each page
                </mobile:Label>
            </FooterTemplate>
        </Choice>
    </mobile:DeviceSpecific>
</mobile:Form>
```

In Listing 9-3, the Form control contains a single TextView control, which contains a block of text to display. A DeviceSpecific/Choice construct within the Form control contains a single *<Choice>* element with no device filter applied, meaning that it will apply to all clients. Within this *<Choice>* element, the *<HeaderTemplate>* and *<FooterTemplate>* elements each contain a mobile Label control. Figure 9-7 shows how the output of this example looks on a Pocket PC and on an Openwave WML browser.

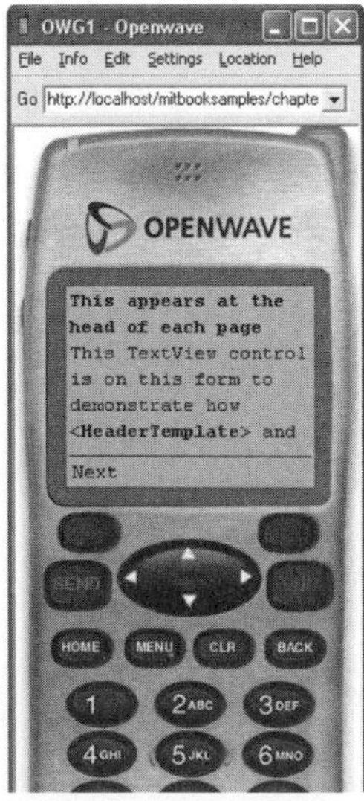

Figure 9-7 Content defined in the Form control *<HeaderTemplate>* and *<FooterTemplate>* elements rendered at the top and bottom of each page

Customizing Headers and Footers on Different Devices

To take this simple example a step further, we can introduce more *<Choice>* elements into the DeviceSpecific/Choice construct so that different *<Header-*

Template> and <*FooterTemplate*> elements apply to different devices. For example, you can easily enhance the DeviceSpecific/Choice construct used in Listing 9-3 to make the Label controls for the header and footer the default choice. Listing 9-4 is the same as Listing 9-3 except that it includes an additional <*Choice*> element in the DeviceSpecific/Choice construct, which, if the client browser is Pocket Internet Explorer, causes a GIF graphics file to be rendered for a header, instead of the Label controls defined in the default choice.

```
<%@ Register TagPrefix="mobile"
    Namespace="System.Web.UI.MobileControls"
    Assembly="System.Web.Mobile" %>
<%@ Page language="c#"
    Inherits="System.Web.UI.MobileControls.MobilePage"%>

<mobile:Form id="Form1" runat="server"
             Paginate="True" BackColor="Khaki">
    <mobile:TextView id="TextView1" runat="server">
  This TextView control is on this form to demonstrate how
  <b>&lt;HeaderTemplate&gt; </b>and <b>&lt;FooterTemplate&gt; </b>
  elements on a <i>Form </i>control are used at the top and bottom of
  each page. <br /><br />
  If your application uses pagination (that is, you have set
  the <i>Paginate </i>property of the <i>Form </i>control to true),
  then the header and footer appear at the top and bottom of all pages.
  <br /><br />On HTML browsers, one thing you can do to enhance the
  layout is to format the page as a table. The table is initiated in the
  header template and closed in the footer template. Any content on the
  page then appears as a table row.
    </mobile:TextView>
    <mobile:DeviceSpecific id="DeviceSpecific1" runat="server">
        <Choice Filter="isPocketIE">
            <HeaderTemplate>
                <mobile:Image runat="server" ImageUrl="AGoodHeader.gif"
                              AlternateText="A Good header">
                </mobile:Image>
            </HeaderTemplate>
        </Choice>
        <Choice>
            <HeaderTemplate>
                <mobile:Label runat="server"
                              StyleReference="title"
                              ForeColor="Crimson">
                    This appears at the head of each page
                </mobile:Label>
```

Listing 9-4 FormTemplateSetExample.aspx—a template set defining different <*HeaderTemplate*> elements for Pocket Internet Explorer and for the default choice

```
            </HeaderTemplate>
            <FooterTemplate>
                <mobile:Label runat="server"
                              StyleReference="subcommand">
                    This appears at the foot of each page
                </mobile:Label>
            </FooterTemplate>
        </Choice>
    </mobile:DeviceSpecific>
</mobile:Form>
```

Introducing Device-Specific Markup into a Template

If you use device filters to identify the particular markup that a client device requires (such as *isHTML32*, *isCHTML10*, and *isWML11)*, the template can contain markup that is inserted into the page.

If you use the Form control templates to insert HTML markup, the rendered page sent to an HTML browser takes the following form:

```
<html>
    <body>
        <form…>
            <!-- Content supplied in a ScriptTemplate goes here-->
            <!-- Content supplied in a HeaderTemplate goes here-->
            Rest of Form content
            <!-- Content supplied in a FooterTemplate goes here-->
        </form>
    </body>
</html>
```

If you use the Form control templates to insert markup for WML browsers, the runtime inserts the markup this way:

```
<wml>
    <card id=…>
        <!-- Content supplied in a ScriptTemplate goes here-->
        <p>
            <!-- Content supplied in a HeaderTemplate goes here-->
            Rest of Form content
            <!-- Content supplied in a FooterTemplate goes here-->
            <!-- Navigation <anchor> elements go here, if required.-->
        </p>
    </card>
</wml>
```

You saw this technique earlier, in Listing 9-2 where we used the *isHTML32* device filter to insert HTML markup into the header and footer. Doing so formatted the HTML page as a table and then assigned HTML style attributes. Listing 9-5 shows the HTML sent to a client for this application; the boldface markup is defined in the *<HeaderTemplate>* and *<FooterTemplate>* elements.

```
<html><body>
<form id="_ctl0" name="_ctl0" method="post"
 action="DeviceSpecificExample.aspx?__ufps=571483">
::
<table width="100%" height="100%" cellspacing="1">
<tr><td bgcolor="#003366">
    <img src="sportsextra.gif">
</td></tr>
<tr><td bgcolor="#cccccc" valign="top" height="100%">
<font size="-1" face="Arial">Welcome to our mobile Sports Extra Web site.
Check here for up-to-the-minute sports news as it happens!</font><br>
</td></tr>
<tr><td bgcolor="#003366" height="4"></td></tr>
</table>
</form></body></html>
```

Listing 9-5 HTML sent to the client for the DeviceSpecificExample.aspx shown in Listing 9-2

> **Important** When introducing device-specific markup into the content sent to the client, it's essential that you have a clear understanding of the markup language the client requires and that you study the structure of the markup that the ASP.NET mobile controls generate. You'll need to have access to tools that allow you to examine the source markup that the device receives. With HTML, this is easy—test with Internet Explorer, and click View and then Source to examine the markup. For WML testing, you must have access to a device emulator that offers the facility to view the source markup. Emulators from Nokia, Openwave, Yospace, and others offer this facility. Refer to Chapter 16 for details of available emulators and how to acquire them.

Using *<ScriptTemplate>*

This template allows you to insert markup directly after the *<head>* tag in HTML forms or after the opening *<card>* tag of a WML deck. Possible uses for this template are to add JavaScript functions defined within *<script>... </script>* tags in an HTML page, define *<do>* actions on a WML card, or take advantage of features such as the WML *<timer>* tag. The *<ScriptTemplate>* is ignored for XHTML clients.

Listing 9-6 shows an example application that inserts WML markup using the WML *<timer>* tag to display a splash screen graphic for 5 seconds, before the application continues. On non-WML clients, only the text enclosed in the Form control is displayed.

```
<%@ Page language="c#" Inherits="System.Web.UI.MobileControls.MobilePage"
    AutoEventWireup="false" %>
<%@ Register TagPrefix="mobile" Namespace="System.Web.UI.MobileControls"
    Assembly="System.Web.Mobile" %>

<mobile:Form id="Form1" runat="server">
This form contains a ScriptTemplate, which is
used to display a splash screen on WML clients.
    <mobile:DeviceSpecific id="DeviceSpecific1" runat="server">
        <Choice Filter="isWML11">
            <ScriptTemplate>
                    <onevent type="onenterforward">
                        <go href="#splash"/>
                    </onevent>
                </card>
                <card id="splash" ontimer="#MITcard">
                    <timer value="50"/>
                    <p align="center">
                        <big>Welcome</big>
                        <br/>
                        <img src="welcome.wbmp" alt="SportsExtra"
                          align="middle"/>
                    </p>
                </card>
                <card id="MITcard">
            </ScriptTemplate>
        </Choice>
    </mobile:DeviceSpecific>
</mobile:Form>
```

Listing 9-6 Source file ScriptTemplateExample.aspx

This application requires a Web.config file with the *isWML11* device filter defined in it (included as standard in mobile applications created in Visual Studio .NET). If this application didn't contain the *<ScriptTemplate>* element, the WML that the client receives is as shown in Listing 9-7.

```
<?xml version='1.0'?>
<!DOCTYPE wml PUBLIC '-//WAPFORUM//DTD WML 1.1//EN'
     'http://www.wapforum.org/DTD/wml_1.1.xml'>
```

Listing 9-7 WML sent to the client if no *<ScriptTemplate>* is defined

```
<wml>
<head>
<meta http-equiv="Cache-Control" content="max-age=0" />
</head>
<card>
    <p>
        This form contains a ScriptTemplate, which is
        used to display a splash screen on WML clients.
    </p>
</card>
</wml>
```

The application in Listing 9-6 inserts the contents of the *<ScriptTemplate>* element after the first *<card>* tag, resulting in the WML shown in Listing 9-8. The markup inserted by the *<ScriptTemplate>* is shown italicized.

```
<?xml version='1.0'?>
<!DOCTYPE wml PUBLIC '-//WAPFORUM//DTD WML 1.1//EN'
    'http://www.wapforum.org/DTD/wml_1.1.xml'>
<wml>
<head>
<meta http-equiv="Cache-Control" content="max-age=0" />
</head>
<card>
    <onevent type="onenterforward">
    <go href="#splash"/>
    </onevent>
</card>
<card id="splash" ontimer="#MITcard">
    <timer value="50"/>
    <p align="center">
        <big>Welcome</big>
        <br/>
        <img src="welcome.wbmp" alt="SportsExtra" align="middle"/>
    </p>
</card>
<card id="MITcard">
    <p>
        This form contains a ScriptTemplate, which is
        used to display a splash screen on WML clients.
    </p>
</card>
</wml>
```

Listing 9-8 WML sent to the client with the contents of the *<ScriptTemplate>* element inserted

Using the Panel Control's *<ContentTemplate>* Element

You can use the Panel control template to insert arbitrary blocks of markup into an application. You insert arbitrary markup into a page by using the *<HeaderTemplate>*, *<ScriptTemplate>*, and *<FooterTemplate>* elements of the Form control. However, the Panel control's *<ContentTemplate>* element completely replaces any other controls or content that you might have defined in the Panel control.

On HTML browsers, the markup you specify in a *<ContentTemplate>* element is inserted at whatever point you position your Panel control. For a Form control containing only a single Panel control, the contents of the *<ContentTemplate>* element will be inserted like this:

```
<body>
    <form…>
    <!--Markup supplied in a ContentTemplate goes here-->
    </form>
</body>
```

If you use the Panel control template to insert markup for WML browsers, the markup will be inserted this way:

```
<wml>
    <card id=…>
        <p>
            <!--Markup supplied in a ContentTemplate goes here-->
        </p>
    </card>
</wml>
```

Listings 9-9 and 9-10 depict a simple currency converter. For this example to work, you must place the WMLScript file currency.wmls into your application directory. This file is included in the companion material on the book's Web site, in the CurrencyConverter sample directory. You must also configure Internet Information Services (IIS) to serve WMLScript files, as will be described a little later. This example illustrates how you can call a function defined in WMLScript from within a *<ContentTemplate>* element, which will be rendered only on WML version 1.1 browsers.

```
<%@ Page language="c#" CodeBehind="CurrencyConverter.aspx.cs"
    Inherits="MSPress.MobWeb.CurrencyConverter.MyWebForm"
    AutoEventWireup="true" %>
<%@ Register TagPrefix="mobile"
    Namespace="System.Web.UI.MobileControls"
    Assembly="System.Web.Mobile" %>

<mobile:form id="Form1" title="Currency" runat="server">
```

Listing 9-9 Source file CurrencyConverter.aspx

```
    Enter Amount in cents/pence:
    <mobile:TextBox id="TextBox1" runat="server" Numeric="True">
    </mobile:TextBox>
    <mobile:Label runat="server">From:</mobile:Label>
    <mobile:SelectionList id="SelectionList1" runat="server">
        <Item Value="EUR" Text="Euro"></Item>
        <Item Value="GBP" Text="Sterling"></Item>
        <Item Value="USD" Text="Dollar"></Item>
    </mobile:SelectionList>
    <mobile:Label runat="server">To:</mobile:Label>
    <mobile:SelectionList id="SelectionList2" runat="server">
        <Item Value="EUR" Text="Euro"></Item>
        <Item Value="GBP" Text="Sterling"></Item>
        <Item Value="USD" Text="Dollar"></Item>
    </mobile:SelectionList>
    <mobile:Panel id="Panel1" runat="server">
        <mobile:DeviceSpecific id="DeviceSpecific1" runat="server">
            <Choice Filter="isWML11">
                <ContentTemplate>
                    <do type="accept" label="Convert">
                        <go href="currency.wmls#convert('$SelectionList1',
                             '$SelectionList2','$TextBox1')" />
                    </do>
                </ContentTemplate>
            </Choice>
        </mobile:DeviceSpecific>
    </mobile:Panel>
</mobile:Form>

<mobile:Form id="Form2" runat="server">
    <mobile:Label runat="server">
        I'm sorry. This function is not yet available on your device.
    </mobile:Label>
</mobile:Form>
```

```
using System;
using System.Web.Mobile;
using System.Web.UI.MobileControls;
Namespace MSPress.MobWeb.CurrencyConverter
{
public class MyWebForm : System.Web.UI.MobileControls.MobilePage
{
    protected System.Web.UI.MobileControls.Form Form2;

    protected void Page_Load(Object sender, EventArgs e)
    {
```

Listing 9-10 Code-behind file CurrencyConverter.aspx.cs

```
            MobileCapabilities cap = (MobileCapabilities)Request.Browser;
            if (!cap.HasCapability("isWML11", null))
            {
                //Not a WML device. We do not support this yet.
                ActiveForm = Form2;
            }
        }
    }
}
```

Enabling WMLScript in IIS

To execute a sample like the currency converter in Listings 9-9 and 9-10, you must enable IIS to serve WMLScript files. The same is true if you want to serve static WML files that have a .wml file extension (as distinct from WML created by an ASP.NET mobile controls application). To do so, follow these steps:

1. In Control Panel, double-click Administrative Tools, and open Internet Information Services, or open Internet Information Manager if you're running Microsoft Windows 2000.
2. Expand the tree view, right-click on Default Web Site, and then click Properties. (In Windows 2000, you right-click on the Web Server item to get to Properties.)
3. On the HTTP Headers tab, click the File Types button in the MIME Map section. (You'll find this button labeled Edit on the Internet Information Services tab in Windows 2000.)
4. Click New Type and type **.wmls** for the Associated extension and **text/vnd.wap.wmlscript** for the Content type (MIME). To serve static WML files, use the extension .wml and the MIME type text/vnd.wap.wml.

For this change to take effect, you must stop the IIS service and restart it again.

The CurrencyConverter application pulls together some of the features we've described in this chapter. In the *Page_Load* method, the *HasCapability* method of the *MobileCapabilities* object determines whether the requesting device supports WML version 1.1. If it doesn't, a form displaying an apology appears.

The *Form1* form uses standard mobile controls to accept input from the user. Then *<ContentTemplate>* inserts WML code for a *<do type="accept">* command, which is rendered as a softkey or another link with the legend *Convert*. When selected, the softkey calls the *convert* function in the WMLScript file named currency.wmls, which it fetches from the Web server. The convert function takes arguments that are the values the user entered (the variables *$SelectionList1*, *$SelectionList2*, and *$TextBox1*). Figure 9-8 shows the resulting WML markup.

```
Phone Information
POST Data:
__EVENTTARGET=cmdConvert&txbAmount=350&selFrom=3&selTo=1

------------------ DATA SIZE --------------------------
Uncompiled data from HTTP is 383 bytes.
...found Content-Type: text/vnd.wap.wml.
Compiled WAP binary is 136 bytes.
--------------------------------------------------------

********************************************** Current WML ******************
*************************
<!-- WBXML public ID number 0x0004: "-//WAPFORUM//DTD WML 1.1//EN" -->
<wml>
  <card id="frmCallWMLScript">
    <p>
      <do type="accept" label="Convert">
        <go href="currency.wmls#convert('USD','EUR','350')"/>
      </do>
    </p>
  </card>
</wml>
{}
******************************************************************************
```

Figure 9-8 WML markup created for the CurrencyConverter application

The WML client browser fetches the WMLScript module currency.wmls (not shown) from the Web server. The convert function contained within this script module calculates the result and displays it using a WMLScript *Dialog* function.

Using <ContentTemplate> to Run JavaScript on the Client

Certain HTML browsers, such as Pocket Internet Explorer on a Pocket PC, support the running of JavaScript functions embedded in the HTML page sent to the client. You can use the <ContentTemplate> to send JavaScript for execution on a client that can handle it.

In Listing 9-11 below, the contents of the <ContentTemplate> is a JavaScript function that executes when the Window *onLoad* event happens—which is when the Web page sent to the browser is loaded for display. This function calls the *Window.alert* JavaScript function to display a pop-up message window, and then sets input focus to *TextBox1*.

```
<%@ Page language="c#"
    Inherits="System.Web.UI.MobileControls.MobilePage" %>
<%@ Register TagPrefix="mobile"
    Namespace="System.Web.UI.MobileControls"
    Assembly="System.Web.Mobile" %>

<mobile:Form id="Form1" runat="server">
    <mobile:Panel id="Panel1" runat="server">
        <mobile:DeviceSpecific id="DeviceSpecific1" Runat="server">
            <Choice Filter="supportsJavaScript">
                <contenttemplate>
                    <Script for="window" event="onload"
                        language="jscript">
                        window.alert("Hello from JavaScript");
                        window.Form1.TextBox1.focus();
                    </Script>
                </contenttemplate>
            </Choice>
        </mobile:DeviceSpecific>
    </mobile:Panel>
    <mobile:TextBox id="TextBox1" runat="server" text="1st TextBox"/>
    <mobile:TextBox id="TextBox2" runat="server" text="2nd TextBox"/>
</mobile:Form>
```

Listing 9-11 Source file JavaScriptExample.aspx

Working with Controls in Form and Panel Templates

You're used to setting properties of controls on a mobile Web Forms page from within code. However, if you've placed a control in a template and you try to set a property of that control in code using its control ID to identify it, as you might normally do, a run-time error occurs.

For example, assume you have this simple template applied to a Form control:

```
<mobile:Form id="Form1" runat="server" >
    <mobile:DeviceSpecific id="DeviceSpecific1" runat="server">
        <Choice>
            <HeaderTemplate>
                <mobile:Label runat="server" id="Label1">
                    This appears at the head of each page
                </mobile:Label>
            </HeaderTemplate>
        </Choice>
    </mobile:DeviceSpecific>
</mobile:Form>
```

You might expect to be able to set properties of the Label control in code like so:

```
Label1.Text = "This label's Text property is set in code";
```

In fact, this returns a run-time error, stating that *Label1* is a null object.

Introduction to the *TemplateContainer* Object

This error is due to the way that the contents of templates are instantiated. Every control that supports templates has one or more child controls that are either *System.Web.UI.MobileControls.TemplateContainer* objects or objects descended from the *TemplateContainer* class. When you define a template, the contents of that template are instantiated as child controls of the *TemplateContainer* object, ASP.NET and mobile controls are instantiated as themselves (like the Label control in the example above), and any literal text (for example, native markup code) is instantiated as *System.Web.UI.MobileControls.LiteralText* objects. The controls defined in templates are not direct children of a standard container control like Form or Panel but are instead hidden down the control tree, so to address them in code you must use a different technique.

The Form control has *Footer*, *Header*, and *Script* properties that expose the *TemplateContainer* objects for the *<FooterTemplate>*, *<HeaderTemplate>*, and *<ScriptTemplate>* elements. The Panel control has a *Content* property that exposes the *TemplateContainer* object for the *<ContentTemplate>* element. You can use the *FindControl* method of *System.Web.UI.Control* (the parent class of *MobileControl*) to locate the specific child controls of one of these *TemplateContainer* objects.

Using *FindControl* to Locate Controls in the Control Tree

You use the *FindControl* method with any control that is a *Naming Container*. Naming Container objects are those that implement the *INamingContainer* interface, and they guarantee that any child controls they contain have a unique name within the mobile Web Forms page. *TemplateContainer* objects are Naming Containers. The Form and Panel controls expose the *TemplateContainer* object for a particular template through special properties: *Footer*, *Header*, *Script*, or *Content*. To get a reference to any control inside a template, you get a reference to the TemplateContainer object by getting the appropriate property of the Form and Template and then call the TemplateContainer object's *FindControl* method, passing the ID of the child control.

In Listing 9-12, the Form control's *<HeaderTemplate>* element contains a Label control with the ID *Label2*. In the *Page_Load* method in Listing 9-12, the *Header* property of *Form1* returns the *TemplateContainer* object for the *<HeaderTemplate>* element. Then the *FindControl* method locates *Label2* so that its properties can be set.

```
<%@ Register TagPrefix="mobile"
    Namespace="System.Web.UI.MobileControls"
    Assembly="System.Web.Mobile" %>
<%@ Page language="c#"
    Codebehind="TemplateControlsInCodeExample.aspx.cs"
    Inherits="MSPress.MobWeb.TemplateControlsInCode.MobileWebForm1"
    AutoEventWireup="true" %>

<mobile:Form id="Form1" runat="server">
    <mobile:Label id="Label1" runat="server">
        This control is in the Form
    </mobile:Label>
    <mobile:DeviceSpecific id="DeviceSpecific1" runat="server">
        <Choice>
            <HeaderTemplate>
                <mobile:Label id="Label2" runat="server">
                    This control is in the template
                </mobile:Label>
            </HeaderTemplate>
        </Choice>
    </mobile:DeviceSpecific>
</mobile:Form>
```

Listing 9-12 Source file TemplateControlsInCodeExample.aspx

```
using System;
using System.Web.UI;
using System.Web.UI.MobileControls;
namespace MSPress.MobWeb.TemplateControlsInCode
{
public class MobileWebForm1 : System.Web.UI.MobileControls.MobilePage
{
    protected System.Web.UI.MobileControls.Label Label1;
    protected System.Web.UI.MobileControls.DeviceSpecific DeviceSpecific1;
    protected System.Web.UI.MobileControls.Form Form1;

    override protected void OnInit(EventArgs e)
    {
        InitializeComponent();
        base.OnInit(e);
    }

    private void InitializeComponent()
    {
        this.Load += new System.EventHandler(this.Page_Load);
    }
    }
```

Listing 9-13 Code-behind file TemplateControlsInCodeExample.aspx.cs

```
    private void Page_Load(object sender, System.EventArgs e)
    {
        // The 'header' property exposes the Header template container
        Label LabelInTemplate = this.Form1.Header.FindControl("Label2")
                                    as Label;
        //Set property of the label in the template
        LabelInTemplate.Text = "Text reset in Code";
    }
}
```

Defining Templates Using Visual Studio .NET Tools

The Mobile Internet Designer provides graphical tools for defining templates that work in tandem with the tools for defining device filters and DeviceSpecific/Choice constructs. You can use these graphical tools as an alternative to editing the source files directly. These tools make it easy to create templates. However, you must perform the following six tasks in sequence:

1. Define device filters for your application.
2. Enable DeviceSpecific/Choice constructs on the desired controls.
3. Apply the device filters for templating.
4. Select each applied device filter, one at a time, to edit the templates.
5. Edit the templates.
6. Finish editing.

Let's take a closer look at each of these tasks.

Defining Device Filters for Your Application

You must define all templates within the context of a DeviceSpecific/Choice construct, even if this consists of only a single default *<Choice>* element that applies to all devices. Therefore, you must first define device filters for your application, as described earlier in this chapter, in the section "Defining Device Filters Using Visual Studio .NET Tools." If you need to add device filters later, you can access the Device Filter Editor from either the Applied Device Filters dialog box, or the Templating Options dialog box, which we will discuss shortly.

Enabling DeviceSpecific/Choice Constructs on the Desired Controls

How you apply templates depends on whether you're using the Form and Panel controls or the List and ObjectList controls. To apply templates to Form and Panel controls, drag a DeviceSpecific control from the Toolbox onto the

Form or Panel control. The Mobile Internet Designer will allow you to drag only one DeviceSpecific control onto a Form or Panel control. Like all other controls contained within the Form or Panel container controls, the List and ObjectList controls already support DeviceSpecific/Choice constructs. Therefore, you don't have to drag this capability onto those controls, as you do with the Form and Panel controls.

Applying Device Filters for Templating

As we described earlier in this chapter, in the section "Defining Device Filters using Visual Studio .NET Tools" the *(Applied Device Filters)* option within the Properties window provides access to the Device Filters Editor, and the *(Property Overrides)* option allows you to define property overrides using device filters that you've applied to the control.

You must define which device filters you want to use with your templates. In Design view, select the control for which you want to define templates by clicking it. At the bottom of the Properties window, you'll see a link to Templating Options. The same option is available from the context menu, which you can access by right-clicking the control, as Figure 9-9 shows.

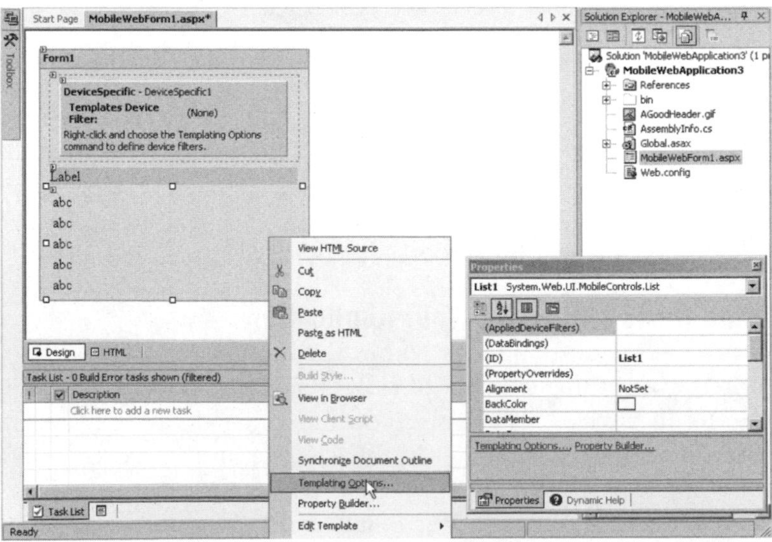

Figure 9-9 Applying device filters to templated controls through the Templating Options link

By selecting either the menu option, or the Properties window link, the Templating Options dialog box will appear. Initially, the Applied Device Filter drop-down list contains only the (None) option, indicating that you haven't yet applied any device filters to this control for templating, as Figure 9-10 shows. Be aware that if you've already applied device filters to create property overrides, by definition these filters will apply to templating as well. You'll see these device filters in the Applied Device Filter drop-down list.

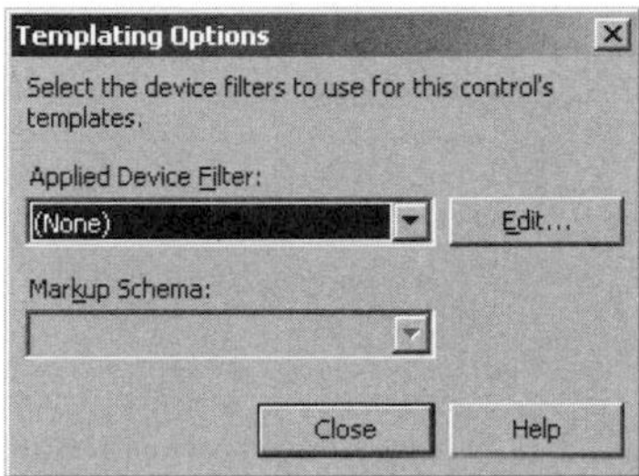

Figure 9-10 The Templating Options dialog box

Click the Edit button to access the Applied Device Filters dialog box. Select the device filters that you want to use with this control, just as you did for the property overrides. Remember, each device filter that you apply to this control has its own set of templates, and you need to edit the templates separately for each filter. You don't have to define all the available templates. Default control rendering applies to any function that a template doesn't override.

Selecting Each Applied Device Filter to Edit the Templates

After you've applied device filters to the control, select which filter to edit from the Applied Device Filter list. The Markup Schema option indicates which markup schema to apply to the content you enter into the template. This setting has no effect at run time; its only use is to provide assistance in the form of Microsoft IntelliSense and auto-completion while you edit within the HTML view of the Mobile Internet Designer. After making your selection for template editing, click Close.

Each time you want to switch to a different applied device filter to edit its associated templates, you must select that filter from the Templating Options dialog box. A quicker way to select an applied device filter for template editing is to choose it from the Template Device Filter dialog box in the Properties window.

Editing the Templates

Right-click the templated control once more, and click Edit Templates. Then click on the template you want to edit. The Mobile Internet Designer now presents a design area within each selected template. Figure 9-11 shows how such a design area looks.

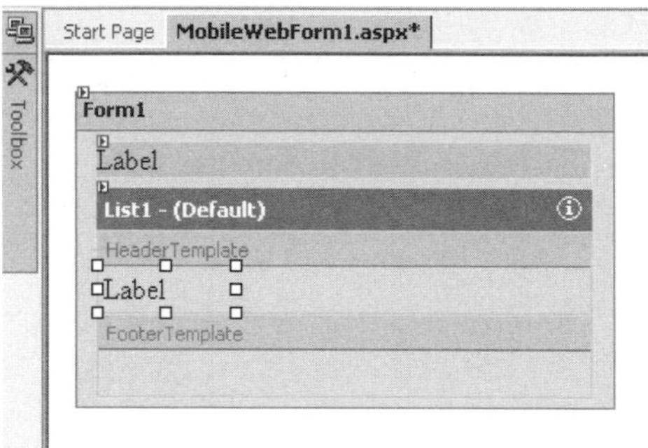

Figure 9-11 Editing in the design area in Mobile Internet Designer

You can type literal text into this design area or drag controls onto it from the Toolbox. When typing device-specific markup, we advise that you switch to HTML view to benefit from IntelliSense editing support.

Finishing Editing

When your changes are complete, right-click the control again and select End Template Editing. Note that switching between Design view and HTML view also terminates editing.

Defining Templates Within Style Sheets

The facilities for defining styles within style sheets and customizing the presentation of the Form, Panel, List, and ObjectList controls using templates enable extensive customization of your applications. Nonetheless, getting the presentation exactly as you want it often requires a great deal of time and effort. Once you've defined a presentation style you're happy with, you'll undoubtedly want to apply it to other projects.

As we described in Chapter 8, in the section "Programming Styles and Style Sheets," you can store styles in style sheets to apply them to multiple controls. You can also use external style sheets to encapsulate styles to apply to multiple projects. This encapsulation also extends to template sets. By placing styles and template sets under a named style within a style sheet, you can apply styles and templating options to different controls in multiple projects, just by setting the controls' *StyleReference* property to the appropriate external style.

Listing 9-14 shows an example using List control templates. We discuss the use of templates with the List and ObjectList controls in Chapter 10; however, the techniques demonstrated in the sample apply just as well to the templates of the Form and Panel controls. In this sample, the template set resides in the style named *MyListStyle* within the StyleSheet control. The List control in *Form1* accesses the template set by setting the *StyleReference* property to *MyListStyle*.

```
<%@ Page Language="c#" Inherits=
    "MSPress.MobWeb.TemplatesInStylesheetsExample.ExampleWebForm"
    CodeBehind="TemplatesInStylesheetsExample.aspx.cs"%>
<%@ Register TagPrefix="mobile"
    Namespace="System.Web.UI.MobileControls"
    Assembly="System.Web.Mobile" %>

<mobile:Stylesheet runat="server">
    <Style Name="MyListStyle" Font-Name="Arial">
        <DeviceSpecific>
            <Choice Filter="isHTML32">
                <HeaderTemplate>
                    <table width="100%">
                        <tr><td><img align="left"
                            src="title.gif"
                            width="440" height="70"/>
                        </td></tr>
                </HeaderTemplate>
                <ItemTemplate>
                     <tr><td bgcolor="#00c0c0"><font face="Arial">
                         <b><asp:LinkButton runat="server">
                             <%# ((MobileListItem)Container).Text %>
                         </asp:LinkButton></b>
                     </font></td></tr>
                </ItemTemplate>
                <AlternatingItemTemplate>
                     <tr><td bgcolor="#ffc080"><font face="Arial">
                         <b><asp:LinkButton runat="server">
                             <%# ((MobileListItem)Container).Text %>
                         </asp:LinkButton></b>
                     </font></td></tr>
                </AlternatingItemTemplate>
                <SeparatorTemplate>
                    <tr><td>
                        <img align="left" src="divider.gif"
                        width="440" height="10"/>
                    </td></tr>
                </SeparatorTemplate>
                <FooterTemplate>
                    <tr><td>
                        <img align="left" src="divider.gif"
                        width="440" height="10"/>
```

Listing 9-14 Source file TemplatesInStyleSheetsExample.aspx

```
                    </td></tr>
                    </table>
                </FooterTemplate>
            </Choice>
        </DeviceSpecific>
    </Style>
</mobile:Stylesheet>

<mobile:Form runat="server" id="Form1">
    <mobile:Label runat="server" StyleReference="title">
        Season 2003 results
    </mobile:Label>
    <mobile:List id="List1" runat="server"
        StyleReference="MyListStyle"
        OnItemCommand="ClickTeamSelection"
        DataTextField="TeamName"
        DataValueField="Stats">
    </mobile:List>
</mobile:Form>

<mobile:Form runat="server" id="Form2">
    <mobile:Label runat="server">Teams Full Stats:</mobile:Label>
    <mobile:Label runat="server" id="Label1" />
</mobile:Form>
```

```
using System;
using System.Collections;
using System.Web.UI.MobileControls;

namespace MSPress.MobWeb.TemplatesInStylesheetsExample
{
public class ExampleWebForm : System.Web.UI.MobileControls.Mobile Page
    {
        protected Label Label1;
        protected List  List1;
        protected Form  Form1;
        protected Form  Form2;

        override protected void OnInit(EventArgs e)
        {
            InitializeComponent();
            Base.OnInit(e);
        }
```

Listing 9-15 Code-behind file TemplatesInStylesheetsExample.aspx.cs

```
    private void InitializeComponent()
    {
        this.Load += new System.EventHandler(this.Page_Load);
        this.List1.ItemCommand +=
        new System.ListCommandEventHandler(this.ClickTeamSelection);
    }

    protected void Page_Load(Object sender, EventArgs e)
    {
        if (!IsPostBack)
        {
            ArrayList array = new ArrayList();
            array.Add(
                new TeamStats("Dunes", "Posn:1 Pl:38 Pts:80"));
            array.Add(
                new TeamStats("Phoenix", "Posn:2 Pl:38 Pts:70"));
            array.Add(
                new TeamStats("Eagles", "Posn:3 Pl:38 Pts:69"));
            array.Add(
                 new TeamStats("Zodiac", "Posn:4 Pl:38 Pts:68"));

            List1.DataSource = array;
            List1.DataBind();
        }
    }

    protected void ClickTeamSelection(
        Object source,
        ListCommandEventArgs args)
    {
        //Display the Stats page
        this.ActiveForm = Form2;
        Label1.Text =
            args.ListItem.Text + ": " + args.ListItem.Value;
    }
}

public class TeamStats
{
    private String teamName, stats;

    public TeamStats(String teamName, String stats)
    {
        this.teamName = teamName;
        this.stats = stats;
    }
```

```
        public String TeamName
        {
            get { return this.teamName; }
        }

        public String Stats
        {
            get { return this.stats; }
        }
    }
}
```

You can encapsulate Form and Panel control templates in style sheets in a similar way. Encapsulating styles and templates this way and placing them within an external style sheet allows you to reuse the styles you've developed in multiple applications. Thus, you can more easily apply a consistent appearance and shorten the development time needed to produce visually outstanding applications.

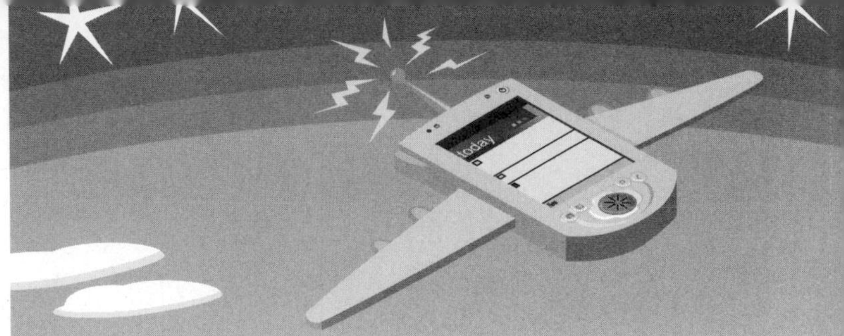

10

Advanced List Control Programming

You first encountered the SelectionList, List, and ObjectList controls in Chapter 6. In this chapter, you'll learn about some more advanced techniques for programming list controls. You'll learn how to data-bind the list controls to a data collection, how to override methods of the list controls to change what is displayed in the list, and how to use the template features of the List and ObjectList controls to override the default rendering of these controls.

Using the Advanced Data Binding Features of the List Controls

As described in Chapter 6, the Microsoft ASP.NET mobile controls include three controls that you can use to present lists of data items: SelectionList, List, and ObjectList. In this section, you'll learn how to take advantage of the data binding capabilities of these controls.

Defining Static List and SelectionList Items

The SelectionList and List controls allow you to define items statically in the ASP.NET server control syntax, using one or more *<Item>* elements. Here's an example:

```
<Item Text="Text" Value="Value" />
```

The *Text* attribute specifies the item displayed to the user, while the *Value* attribute specifies a hidden associated value.

List items defined this way create entries in a *System.Web.UI.MobileControls.MobileListItemCollection* object. Instead of using server control syntax to define items, you can use code to add, remove, and clear items in this collection. The following code excerpt shows how to define several items in code for display in a SelectionList control; it's taken from the sample StaticListItemsFromCode in the companion material on this book's Web site.

```
protected void Page_Load(Object sender, EventArgs e)
    {
        if (!IsPostBack)
        {
            SelectionList1.Items.Add(
               new MobileListItem("Dunes", "Posn:1 Pl:38 Pts:80"));
            SelectionList1.Items.Add(
               new MobileListItem("Phoenix", "Posn:2 Pl:38 Pts:70"));
            SelectionList1.Items.Add(
               new MobileListItem("Eagles", "Posn:3 Pl:38 Pts:69"));
            SelectionList1.Items.Add(
               new MobileListItem("Zodiac", "Posn:4 Pl:38 Pts:68"));
        }
    }
```

The *Items* property of the SelectionList and List controls exposes the *MobileListItemCollection* object of the list control. In code, you can access this collection, modify items, or hide individual list items by setting the *Visible* property of the item to *false*.

Binding to a Data Collection

Although static lists have their uses, invariably your applications will work with items from a data collection. With the ObjectList control, you can only bind it to a data collection as it doesn't support statically defined items.

You can bind the controls that support data binding to two types of data sources: those that implement the *IEnumerable* interface, and those that implement the *IListSource* interface. Many of the collection classes supplied in the Microsoft .NET Framework implement the *IEnumerator* interface and consequently can be used as a data source. Examples of collections that implement *IEnumerator* include *Array*, *ArrayList*, *Hashtable*, *ListDictionary*, and many of the collections associated with controls, such as *MobileListItemCollection,* the object the List control uses to contain *MobileListItem* objects (as described a moment ago).

> **Tip** If a class is enumerable, you can walk through it using the C# *foreach* statement or the Microsoft Visual Basic .NET *For Each... In...Next* statement.

You can also bind controls to collections that implement *IListSource*. A number of .NET classes support this interface, including *DataSet* and *DataTable*. These classes are part of the Microsoft ADO.NET architecture and represent an in-memory cache of data retrieved from a database. We'll offer a more detailed description of the *DataSet* class in Chapter 11, in the section "Using ADO.NET."

In the descriptions of list controls in Chapter 6, you saw many examples demonstrating the use of a .NET collection that supports *IEnumerable*. Listings 10-1 and 10-2, which are excerpts from the DataboundListExample contained in the companion material on this book's Web site, offer a variation on those examples. In Listing 10-1, you define the *TeamStats* class to use as the source data items. In Listing 10-2, the *Page_Load* method in the code-behind module of a mobile Web Forms page creates the *TeamStats* objects and inserts them into an *ArrayList* collection. The code then binds the List control (*List1*) to the collection of *TeamStats* objects.

```
namespace MSPress.MobWeb.DBListEx
{
    class TeamStats
    {
        private String  _teamName;
        private int _position, _played, _won, _drawn, _lost, _points;

        public TeamStats(String teamName,
            int position,
            int played,
            int won,
            int drawn,
            int lost,
            int points)
        {
            this._teamName = teamName;
            this._position = position;
            this._played = played;
            this._won = won;
            this._drawn = drawn;
```

Listing 10-1 *TeamStats* class definition

```
            this._lost = lost;
            this._points = points;
        }

        public String TeamName { get { return this._teamName; } }
        public int    Position { get { return this._position; } }
        public int    Played   { get { return this._played; } }
        public int    Won      { get { return this._won; } }
        public int    Drawn    { get { return this._drawn; } }
        public int    Lost     { get { return this._lost; } }
        public int    Points   { get { return this._points; } }
    }
}
```

```
using System;
using System.Collections;
using System.Web.UI.MobileControls;

namespace MSPress.MobWeb.DBListEx
{
  public class DataboundListExample : System.Web.UI.MobileControls.MobilePage
    {
        protected List  List1;

        override protected void OnInit(EventArgs e)
        {
            InitializeComponent();
            base.OnInit(e);
        }

        private void InitializeComponent()
        {
            this.Load += new System.EventHandler(this.Page_Load);
            this.List1.ItemCommand +=
                new ListCommandEventHandler(this.List1_OnItemCommand);
        }

        protected void Page_Load(Object sender, EventArgs e)
        {
            if (!IsPostBack)
            {
                ArrayList array = new ArrayList();
                array.Add(new TeamStats("Dunes",1,38,24,8,6,80));
                array.Add(new TeamStats("Phoenix",2,38,20,10,8,70));
                array.Add(new TeamStats("Eagles",3,38,20,9,9,69));
                array.Add(new TeamStats("Zodiac",4,38,20,8,10,68));
```

Listing 10-2 Code-behind module binding a List control to an *ArrayList* collection

```
                List1.DataSource = array;
                List1.DataTextField = "TeamName";
                List1.DataValueField = "Points";
                List1.DataBind();
            }
        }
        private void List1_OnItemCommand(
            Object source, ListCommandEventArgs args)
        {
            // Display the Stats page.
            this.ActiveForm = Form2;
            Label1.Text = args.ListItem.Text + ": " + args.ListItem.Value;
        }
    }
}
```

Understanding Data Binding and *ViewState*

If you look at the code listings in this chapter, you might notice that the *Page_Load* method in Listings 10-2, 10-4, and 10-6 builds the data collection and data-binds the List control only if *MobilePage.IsPostBack* is *false*—in other words, only during the processing of the initial request, but not on subsequent requests in this application, as shown here:

```
protected void Page_Load(Object sender, EventArgs e)
{
    if (!IsPostBack)
    {
        ArrayList array = new ArrayList();
        array.Add(new TeamStats("Dunes", "Posn:1 Pl:38 Pts:80"));
        array.Add(new TeamStats("Phoenix", "Posn:2 Pl:38 Pts:70"));
        array.Add(new TeamStats("Eagles", "Posn:3 Pl:38 Pts:69"));
        array.Add(new TeamStats("Zodiac", "Posn:4 Pl:38 Pts:68"));

        List1.DataSource = array;
        List1.DataBind();
    }
}
```

This is efficient code because the code that accesses the data (which is trivial in this example, but would likely be more complex and take longer to run in a real application) runs only on the first request. If you data-bind the control on every request, your application is performing unnecessary work. On subsequent requests, the List control "remembers" the contents of the list without having to bind to the data collection again because the *Text* and *Value* properties of the *MobileListItem* objects (the container objects for an item in the List control) are persisted in *ViewState* between requests. Similarly, with the

ObjectList control, each *ObjectListItem* object maintains a string collection of the values of each field from the data item that will be displayed in the initial list and in the Details view. This string collection is also persisted in *ViewState* between requests. This process is illustrated in Figure 10-1.

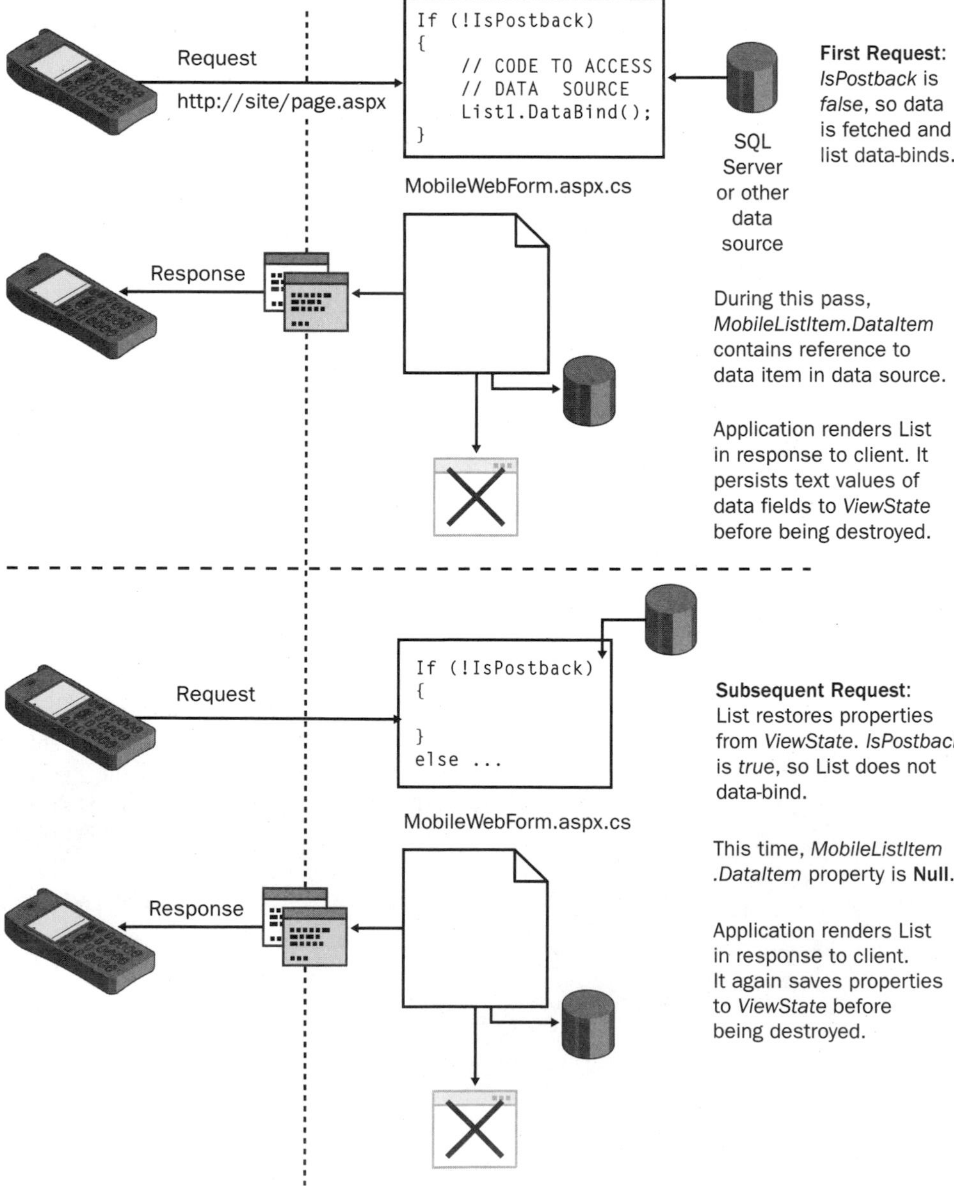

Figure 10-1 Saving list control data to ViewState

> **Caution** You might encounter a subtle problem if you data-bind the control on every request. Remember that the client browser posts back to the server whenever the user clicks on an item in a list, clicks a button, or engages in other similar interactive operations. Perhaps your application displays a list, allowing a user to select an item, whereupon you dispay a new screen that displays details of the selected item. Then the user clicks a button that causes your application to display the original list once more. If you data-bind on every request and the underlying data source has been updated in the meantime, the list you display to your user the second time will change, which is not always what you intended.
>
> Of course, this behavior might be exactly what you want, in which case you would be correct to data-bind on every request.

Using the *DataItem* Property to Access the Data Source

When a control is data bound, as with statically defined items, the individual list items are stored in a *MobileListItemCollection* object (or an *ObjectListItemCollection*, in the case of the ObjectList control) that's accessible through the control's *Items* property. However, the *DataItem* property of each *MobileListItem* in the collection is assigned a value that is a reference to the original item in the data source. This property is *null* if the control isn't data bound and if you have created statically defined list items.

In many applications, you do not need to access the source data item through the *DataItem* property after the control has been data bound. For example, the code just shown in Listing 10-2 does not make use of the *DataItem* property. In the *Page_Load* method, the *DataTextField* property of List1 is set to the name of the field in the data source to display in the list (*TeamName*) and the *DataValueField* is set to the name of the field that provides the hidden value (*Points*). Then the *List1.DataBind()* method is called, and the List control reads in its data from the data source. Farther down in Listing 10-2, the *List1_OnItemCommand* method is the *ItemCommand* event handler for the List control; the *ListCommandEventArgs* argument to this method has a *ListItem* property, which exposes the *MobileListItem* object for the selected item. As shown in Listing 10-2, this method contains the following code:

```
private void List1_OnItemCommand(
    Object source, ListCommandEventArgs args)
{
    // Display the Stats page.
```

```
        this.ActiveForm = Form2;
        Label1.Text = args.ListItem.Text + ": " + args.ListItem.Value;
    }
```

This code sets *Label1.Text* to a string constructed from the *args.ListItem.Text* and *args.ListItem.Value* properties of the selected item and then sets the active Form control to Form2 so that *Label1* is displayed. The *args.ListItem.Text* property, the data that is displayed in the list, is the *TeamName* field from the original data source. The *Value* property is the *Points* field, as set by the *DataValueField* property of the List control.

If we make use of the *DataItem* property, we have more flexibility concerning which fields we can use from the source data item. For example, you can modify the *List1_OnItemCommand* method in Listing 10-2 to fetch the *TeamName*, *Played*, *Points*, and *Position* fields from the data source and to display them in a TextView control instead of a Label control with the following code:

```
protected void List1_OnItemCommand(Object source,
                             ListCommandEventArgs args)
{
    this.ActiveForm = Form2;
    TextView1.Text = String.Format (
        "<b>{0}</b><br/>Played : {1}<br/>Points " +
        ": {2}<br/>Position : {3}",
        ((TeamStats)(args.ListItem.DataItem)).TeamName,
        ((TeamStats)(args.ListItem.DataItem)).Played,
        ((TeamStats)(args.ListItem.DataItem)).Points,
        ((TeamStats)(args.ListItem.DataItem)).Position);
}
```

Why the *DataItem* Property Is Sometimes *null*

It's important to remember that the *DataItem* property is set to the source data item only during the processing of the request, when data binding of the control takes place. It's a common mistake to data-bind a control within a *Page_Load* method but then to place that code within an *if (!IsPostBack)* statement. After the initial list is sent back to the requesting browser, your application running on the server closes down and is destroyed, as usual. When the user clicks an item in the list, the client browser posts back the next HTTP request, and the ASP.NET runtime restarts your ASP.NET application on the server. Display of the list data still occurs on later requests because the *Text* and *Value* properties of each *MobileListItem* are persisted in *ViewState*, however, the *DataItem* property is not persisted. The list is not data bound during this request processing because *IsPostBack* is *true*. When an *OnItemCommand* (or other) event handler method executes, it does so during the processing of a subsequent request. On this request, the control is not data bound, so code that gets the *DataItem* property fails at run time because the *DataItem* property is *null*. The control *must* be data bound on every request for this code to work.

Overriding Single-Field Display in the List Controls

You usually use the SelectionList and List controls to bind to only two properties of the data item: the displayed property set by the *DataTextField* property of the List control, and the hidden value field set by the *DataValueField* property.

The ObjectList control provides the *TableFields* property, through which you can specify more than one property to display in each row of the initial display list, provided that the client device has an HTML browser and has a large enough screen (such as a Pocket PC). However, on devices with a small screen, such as a mobile phone with a Wireless Markup Language (WML) browser, the ObjectList control is still rendered as a list consisting of a single property from the data source.

Overriding Single-Field Display in SelectionList and List Controls

You can make the SelectionList and List controls display more than one property by creating an *OnItemDataBind* event handler, in which you set the *ListItem.Text* property to a string that you build by concatenating the values of two or more individual fields.

Returning to the example shown in Listings 10-1 and 10-2, you add code to wire up the *ItemDataBind* event handler method in the *InitializeComponent* method, as shown in the following code. (Or you can use one of the other techniques described in Chapter 3.)

```
private void InitializeComponent()
{
    this.Load += new System.EventHandler(this.Page_Load);
    this.List1.ItemCommand += new
        ListCommandEventHandler(this.List1_OnItemCommand);
    this.List1.ItemDataBind += new
        ListDataBindEventHandler(this.List1_OnItemDataBind);
}
```

You can then code the event handler method as shown here:

```
private void List1_OnItemDataBind(
        Object sender,
        ListDataBindEventArgs e)
    {
```

```
        e.ListItem.Text = String.Format ("{0} : {1}",
            ((TeamStats)(e.ListItem.DataItem)).Position,
            ((TeamStats)(e.ListItem.DataItem)).TeamName);
    }
```

This code will cause the initial list to display a composite item composed of the *Position* and *TeamName* fields, rather than just the *TeamName* field. Figure 10-2 shows how this list appears on the Nokia simulator and a Pocket PC. The C# and Visual Basic samples ListDisplayMultipleFieldsExample in the companion material on this book's Web site are simple applications that use this technique.

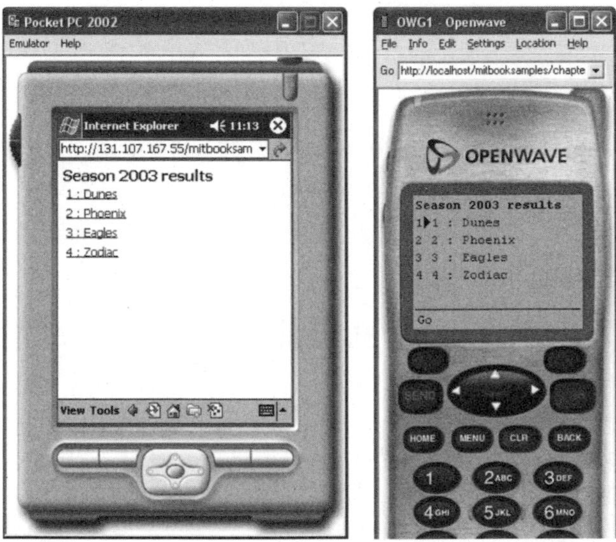

Figure 10-2 *OnItemDataBind* method implemented to override default display of a single property from a List control's data source

Overriding Single-Field Display in ObjectList

As we've just seen, to override single field display in the SelectionList and List controls, you implement an *OnItemDataBind* event handler method and set the *Text* property of the *MobileListItem* object to the new value you want to display. The ObjectList control's *ObjectListItem* object is more complex than the *MobileListItem*. The ObjectList control displays a single field from the data source in the initial list that displays and then displays many more fields from the source data in an item's Details view. To support this functionality, the *ObjectListItem* contains a collection of fields that represents each of these data fields, indexed by the field name. When using an *OnItemDataBind* method, you must name the field from this collection you want to reset. The following code presents an example of an *OnItemDataBind* method for an ObjectList control that resets the display of the *TeamName* field, making the new value to be displayed a composite of the values of the *Position* and *TeamName* fields from the data source:

```
private void ObjectList1_OnItemDataBind(
        Object sender,
        ObjectListDataBindEventArgs e)
    {
        // Get the data object being bound.
        TeamStats dataObj = (TeamStats)e.DataItem;
        // Get the list item being created.
        ObjectListItem item = (ObjectListItem)e.ListItem;
        // Modify the text displayed for a field.
        item["Posn-Team"] =
            String.Format ("{0} : {1}", dataObj.Position, dataObj.TeamName) ;
    }
```

This code extract is taken from the sample application ObjectListDisplay-MultipleFieldsExample, which is available in the companion material on this book's Web site.

Using Templates in List and ObjectList Controls

The templates that the List and ObjectList controls support differ from those that the Form and Panel controls support, which we discussed in Chapter 9. Instead of just using List and ObjectList to display a textual list of items, using templates you can completely replace the default rendering of the list's contents.

The List and ObjectList controls support the use of the templates described in Table 10-1:

Table 10-1 Templates Supported by the Templated Controls

<HeaderTemplate>	*<HeaderTemplate>* is rendered at the top of the list. When you enable pagination, the template is rendered at the head of the list on each page.
<FooterTemplate>	*<FooterTemplate>* is rendered at the bottom of the list. When you enable pagination, the template is rendered at the foot of the list on each page.
<ItemTemplate>	You use *<ItemTemplate>* to render each item.
<AlternatingItemTemplate>	If specified, the application uses this template to render even-numbered items—the second item, the fourth item, and so on.

Table 10-1 Templates Supported by the Templated Controls

<SeparatorTemplate>	The *<SeparatorTemplate>* is rendered between each item.
<ItemDetailsTemplate> (ObjectList only)	You use *<ItemDetailsTemplate>* to render the Details view in an ObjectList control.

You'll normally use templates to enhance the data presentation on a particular browser. To do this effectively, you need both an understanding of the markup that the client requires and the functionality that you want the list to provide.

Programming the *List* Control Templates

Back in Chapter 6 when we first looked at how to use the List control, Listing 6-7 in that section showed a simple application called ListItemCommandExample.aspx file that did not use templates. The application displays a simple list of team names. When the user selects an item from the list, additional details appear on a second form, as Figure 10-3 shows. Although not particularly eye-catching, the default rendering is functional.

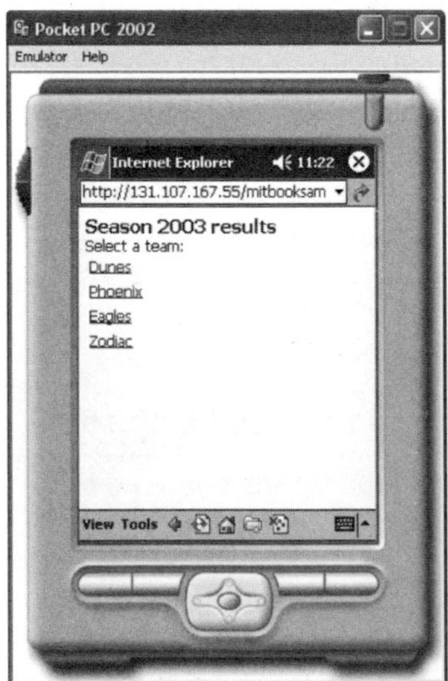

Figure 10-3 Default rendering of ListItemCommandExample.aspx

Using templates can greatly enhance your list presentation. In the following example, we use *<HeaderTemplate>* to output markup to open an HTML *<table>* and to display a graphic in the first row of the table. We use the *<ItemTemplate>* and *<AlternatingItemTemplate>* templates to inject the tags for

HTML table items (*<td>...</td>*) and rows (*<tr>...</tr>*) and to apply different colors and fonts. *<SeparatorTemplate>* creates a visually appealing divider bar, and *<FooterTemplate>* closes the HTML table. Listings 10-3 and 10-4 show how to implement these templates.

```
<%@ Page Inherits="MSPress.MobWeb.TemplateListEx.ExampleWebForm"
    Language="c#" CodeBehind="TemplatedListExample.aspx.cs"%>
<%@ Register TagPrefix="mobile"
    Namespace="System.Web.UI.MobileControls"
    Assembly="System.Web.Mobile" %>

<mobile:Form id="Form1" runat="server">
    <mobile:Label runat="server" StyleReference="title">
        Season 2003 results
    </mobile:Label>
    <mobile:List id="List1" runat="server"
        DataTextField="TeamName"
        DataValueField="Stats">
        <DeviceSpecific>
            <Choice Filter="isHTML32">
                <HeaderTemplate>
                    <table width="100%">
                        <tr><td><img align="left"
                            src="title.gif"
                            width="440" height="70"/>
                        </td></tr>
                </HeaderTemplate>
                <ItemTemplate>
                     <tr><td bgcolor="#00c0c0"><font face="Arial">
                         <b><asp:LinkButton runat="server">
                             <%# ((MobileListItem)Container).Text %>
                         </asp:LinkButton></b>
                     </font></td></tr>
                </ItemTemplate>
                <AlternatingItemTemplate>
                     <tr><td bgcolor="#ffc080"><font face="Arial">
                         <b><asp:LinkButton runat="server">
                             <%# ((MobileListItem)Container).Text %>
                         </asp:LinkButton></b>
                     </font></td></tr>
                </AlternatingItemTemplate>
                <SeparatorTemplate>
                    <tr><td>
                        <img align="left" src="divider.gif"
                        width="440" height="10"/>
                    </td></tr>
                </SeparatorTemplate>
```

Listing 10-3 Source file TemplatedListExample.aspx

```
                <FooterTemplate>
                    <tr><td>
                        <img align="left" src="divider.gif"
                        width="440" height="10"/>
                    </td></tr>
                    </table>
                </FooterTemplate>
            </Choice>
        </DeviceSpecific>
    </mobile:List>
</mobile:Form>

<mobile:Form runat="server" id="Form2">
    <mobile:Label runat="server">Teams Full Stats:</mobile:Label>
    <mobile:Label runat="server" id="Label1" />
</mobile:Form>
```

```
using System;
using System.Collections;
using System.Web.UI.MobileControls;

namespace MSPress.MobWeb.TemplateListEx
{
    public class ExampleWebForm : System.Web.UI.MobileControls.MobilePage
    {
        protected Label Label1;
        protected List  List1;
        protected Form  Form1;
        protected Form  Form2;

        override protected void OnInit(EventArgs e)
        {
            InitializeComponent();
            base.OnInit(e);
        }

        private void InitializeComponent()
        {
            this.Load += new System.EventHandler(this.Page_Load);
            this.List1.ItemCommand +=
                new ListCommandEventHandler(this.ClickTeamSelection);
        }

        protected void Page_Load(Object sender, EventArgs e)
        {
            if (!IsPostBack)
            {
                ArrayList array = new ArrayList();
```

Listing 10-4 Code-behind file TemplatedListExample.aspx.cs

```
            array.Add(new TeamStats("Dunes", "Posn:1 Pl:38 Pts:80"));
            array.Add(new TeamStats("Phoenix", "Posn:2 Pl:38 Pts:70"));
            array.Add(new TeamStats("Eagles", "Posn:3 Pl:38 Pts:69"));
            array.Add(new TeamStats("Zodiac", "Posn:4 Pl:38 Pts:68"));

            List1.DataSource = array;
            List1.DataBind();
        }
    }

    protected void ClickTeamSelection(
        Object source,
        ListCommandEventArgs args)
    {
        //Display the Stats page
        this.ActiveForm = Form2;
        Label1.Text = args.ListItem.Text + ": " + args.ListItem.Value;
    }
}

public class TeamStats
{
    private String teamName, stats;

    public TeamStats(String teamName, String stats)
    {
        this.teamName = teamName;
        this.stats = stats;
    }

    public String TeamName
    {
        get { return this.teamName; }
    }

    public String Stats
    {
        get { return this.stats; }
    }
}
}
```

Templates must always be coded inside *<Choice>* elements of a DeviceSpecific/Choice construct. The server control syntax in Listing 10-3 includes a DeviceSpecific/Choice filter so that the templates are used only for HTML 3.2 client devices; however, this application still works fine on other devices using the List control's default rendering. Figure 10-4 shows how this code output looks on an HTML 3.2 browser.

Figure 10-4 Presentation on an HTML 3.2 browser enhanced by using templates

If you want the template to apply to all devices, code the template inside the default *<Choice>* element, as in the following example:

```
<mobile:List id="List1" runat="server">
    <DeviceSpecific>
        <Choice>
            <HeaderTemplate>
                ⋮
            </HeaderTemplate>
        </Choice>
    </DeviceSpecific>
</mobile:List>
```

Displaying Data Values in Templates

The contents of *<ItemTemplate>* and *<AlternatingItemTemplate>* need more explanation. Let's examine the *<ItemTemplate>* template in Listing 10-3 in more detail:

```
<ItemTemplate>
     <tr><td bgcolor="#00c0c0"><font face="Arial">
         <b><asp:LinkButton runat="server">
             <%# ((MobileListItem)Container).Text %>
```

```
2           </asp:LinkButton></b>
1       </font></td></tr>
    </ItemTemplate>
```

This code displays the list item within the markup for an HTML table row, and consists of three distinct parts:

- The *1* lines (of the code) are just HTML markup that is used to format the list item as an HTML table cell, and to set the font to Arial.
- The first *2* line contains a *<b>* tag to start bold formatting, and then the tags for a regular (not mobile) ASP.NET LinkButton control. The second *2* line contains the closing tags for these elements. The ASP.NET LinkButton is there to maintain the interactivity of the list, so the user can click on an item to select it. We'll examine this in more detail in the section "Enabling *OnItemCommand* Events in Templates" later in this chapter.
- The *3* line contains special tags *<%# … %>* which indicates that this is an ASP.NET data binding statement; inside these tags you place program code that returns a data value. In this case the code is *((MobileListItem)Container).Text*; we'll look at what this is and how it works now.

When you define an item template, it completely replaces the normal default rendering of the list item. Inside the item template, you must include code to display the data item as a part of your template. In this particular example, you achieve this by using ASP.NET data binding syntax *<%# … %>*. We'll look at ASP.NET data binding syntax in more detail in the next chapter, but for now, all you need to know is that the runtime evaluates the contents of this syntax when the *DataBind* method of the containing list control executes (called within the *Page_Load* method in Listing 10-4). The data binding syntax used here extracts the underlying data item using the syntax *<%# ((MobileListItem)Container).Text %>*, which to the ASP.NET page parser means: get the *Container* property of this template item, cast it to a *MobileListItem* object, and then get the *Text* property of the *MobileListItem* object. The *Text* property of the *MobileListItem* returns the value of the data item to display. The *Container* variable has a special meaning in templates, as we'll explain shortly.

Understanding Template Containers A List control stores all the items in the list in a collection of *MobileListItem* objects. An ObjectList control stores its list items in a collection of *ObjectListItem* objects. Both the *MobileListItem* and the *ObjectListItem* objects are descended from the *System.Web.UI.MobileControls.TemplateContainer* class, which indicates that they can act as a container for templates. Whenever you define an *<ItemTemplate>* or *<Alternating-*

ItemTemplate> template, the contents of the template is instantiated as a child object of each *MobileListItem* or *ObjectListItem* object of that list control. In any ASP.NET data binding expression within a template, you can use the variable *Container*, which points to the containing *MobileListItem* or *ObjectListItem* object. In our example, you use the *Container* variable to access the enclosing *MobileListItem* object.

You must cast the *Container* variable to the correct type, *MobileListItem*. You can then use this variable to access properties of *MobileListItem*. The code accesses the *Text* property, *((MobileListItem)Container).Text*, which is the default display value of the *MobileListItem* object. In the example shown earlier in Listing 10-3 and 10-4, the List control is programmed to display the *TeamName* property of the underlying data class, and so the *Text* property of the *MobileListItem* returns the name of the team.

In Visual Basic, you need to use the *CType* function to perform the casting:

```
<ItemTemplate>
    <%# CType(Container, MobileListItem).Text %>
</ItemTemplate>
```

See the C# and Visual Basic samples DataBindingInTemplateExample in the companion materials on this book's Web site for applications that use this technique.

> **Tip** It's a common programming error to forget to call the *DataBind* method. To evaluate data binding expressions, you must call the *DataBind* method of the containing control. The previous example simply calls *DataBind* for the List1 control, but usually, calling the *DataBind* method of the mobile page within the *Page_Load* event handler is sufficient because doing so also calls the *DataBind* method of all enclosed controls. The following code illustrates this concept:
>
> ```
> protected void Page_Load(Object sender, EventArgs e)
>     {
>         this.DataBind();
>     }
> ```
>
> See the section "Using ASP.NET Declarative Data Binding" in the next chapter for more information.

Enabling *OnItemCommand* Events in Templates

When applying item templates, the final step is to ensure that the *OnItemCommand* capability remains intact. In the default rendering, the user clicks a list item to access another page. You can trap the *ItemCommand* event and execute code in your application as a result. However, if you write an *<ItemTemplate>* similar to the following, it simply displays the data value of the list item, and the templated version of the list becomes a static list display without any interactivity:

```
<ItemTemplate>
    <%# ((MobileListItem)Container).Text %>
</ItemTemplate>
```

The template for a list item must therefore incorporate an interactive control as well as the data to display. A mobile Command control might seem like a good choice, as it is rendered on all mobile clients; however, this control is rendered as a button. The perfect choice is the ASP.NET LinkButton control, which renders the item as a hyperlink, as required. The LinkButton control's *Click* event bubbles up to its parent control, allowing you to use the same event handler. The final version of the *<ItemTemplate>* template—excluding HTML markup to manipulate style attributes—now reads as follows:

```
<ItemTemplate>
    <tr><td>
        <asp:LinkButton runat="server" id="LinkButton1">
            <%# ((MobileListItem)Container).Text %>
        </asp:LinkButton>
    </td></tr>
</ItemTemplate>
```

Event Handling for Controls Embedded in Templates

Certain mobile control events support ASP.NET's event bubbling capability. For example, the mobile Command control supports two events: *Click* and *ItemCommand*. The *ItemCommand* event bubbles up; the *Click* event doesn't. Event handlers for events that can bubble up take an argument that descends from *System.Web.UI.WebControls.CommandEventArgs*. The event handler for the List control *ItemCommand* event takes an argument of type *ListCommandEventArgs*, which descends from *CommandEventArgs*. You can embed any control that raises an event that bubbles up, and the parent control's event handler can trap it.

If you have an event handler that handles events from a number of controls, you can identify the source of the event using the *CommandName* property of the *System.Web.UI.WebControls.CommandEventArgs* object. The *CommandName* property is set to *null* when an *ItemCommand* event of the List control is raised when no templates are used. However, if you embed a control such as the ASP.NET LinkButton control or the ASP.NET mobile controls Command control (which both support event bubbling), you can specify a *CommandName* property, which passes to the event handler in the *CommandEventArgs* argument object.

This way, your event handler code can distinguish between events raised through the default rendering (where the *CommandName* property is *null*) and those raised by controls contained within templates.

Programming the *ObjectList* Control Templates

Most of the techniques we have just seen for use with the List control, apply too to the ObjectList control. However, the List control is designed to display a listing of the values of a single field from the data source, whereas the ObjectList is used to display many fields for a data item, and this makes the programming of templates slightly different.

The ObjectList control supports the same templates as the List control, and it also supports the *<ItemDetailsTemplate>* for customizing the data item details view.

Displaying Data Values in ObjectList Control Templates

In general, the technique for displaying fields in the *<ItemTemplate>* and *<AlternatingItemTemplate>* templates with the ObjectList control is the same as the List control technique. In the previous example, you saw that the *MobileListItem* object that contains a single item in the list for a List control has *Text* and *Value* properties that expose the two fields used for the *DataTextField* and *DataValueField* properties, respectively.

The ObjectList control is designed to show multiple fields for a single data item, so the *ObjectListItem* object that contains a single item in the list actually contains a collection of strings, one for each field from the data source that the control will display. Consequently, to display a specific field inside an *<ItemTemplate>* or *<AlternatingItemTemplate>* template, you must index into that collection using the field name as the index, as shown here:

```
<ItemTemplate>
    <%# ((ObjectListItem)Container)["fieldname"] %>
</ItemTemplate>
```

Listings 10-5 and 10-6 show a simple application that uses an ObjectList control and templates. In fact, the use of the *<ItemTemplate>* in this example does not introduce any customization of the output of the ObjectList control, but it serves to illustrate how to program ObjectList templates.

```
<%@ Page language="c#" Codebehind="ObjectListTemplateExample.aspx.cs"
    Inherits="MSPress.MobWeb.ObjListTemplEx.ObjectListTemplateExample"
    AutoEventWireup="false" %>
<%@ Register TagPrefix="mobile" Namespace="System.Web.UI.MobileControls"
    Assembly="System.Web.Mobile" %>

<mobile:form id="Form1" runat="server">
    <mobile:Label id="Label1" runat="server" StyleReference="title">
    Season 2003 results</mobile:Label>
    <mobile:ObjectList id="ObjectList1" runat="server">
        <DeviceSpecific>
            <Choice>
                <ItemTemplate>
                    <asp:LinkButton id="LinkButton1" Runat="server">
                        <%# ((ObjectListItem)Container)["TeamName"] %>
                    </asp:LinkButton>
                    <br>
                </ItemTemplate>
            </Choice>
        </DeviceSpecific>
    </mobile:ObjectList>
</mobile:form>
```

Listing 10-5 Source file ObjectListTemplateExample.aspx

```
using System;
using System.Collections;
using System.Web.UI.MobileControls;

namespace MSPress.MobWeb.ObjListTemplEx
{
    public class ObjectListTemplateExample :
        System.Web.UI.MobileControls.MobilePage
    {
        protected System.Web.UI.MobileControls.ObjectList ObjectList1;
        protected System.Web.UI.MobileControls.Label Label1;
        protected System.Web.UI.MobileControls.Form Form1;

        override protected void OnInit(EventArgs e)
        {
            InitializeComponent();
```

Listing 10-6 Code-behind file ObjectListTemplateExample.aspx.cs

```
            base.OnInit(e);
        }

        private void InitializeComponent()
        {
            this.ObjectList1.ItemCommand += new
                ObjectListCommandEventHandler(this.ObjectList1_ItemCommand);
            this.Load += new System.EventHandler(this.Page_Load);

        }

        protected void Page_Load(Object sender, EventArgs e)
        {
            if (!this.IsPostBack)
            {
                ArrayList array = new ArrayList();
                array.Add(new TeamStats("Dunes",1,38,24,8,6,80));
                array.Add(new TeamStats("Phoenix",2,38,20,10,8,70));
                array.Add(new TeamStats("Eagles",3,38,20,9,9,69));
                array.Add(new TeamStats("Zodiac",4,38,20,8,10,68));

                ObjectList1.DataSource = array;
                ObjectList1.LabelField = "TeamName";
                this.DataBind();
            }
        }

        private void ObjectList1_ItemCommand
            (object sender, ObjectListCommandEventArgs e)
        {
            ObjectList1.SelectedIndex = e.ListItem.Index;
            ObjectList1.ViewMode = ObjectListViewMode.Details;
        }
    }

    class TeamStats
    {
        private String  _teamName;
        private int _position, _played, _won, _drawn, _lost, _points;

        public TeamStats(String teamName,
            int position,
            int played,
            int won,
            int drawn,
            int lost,
            int points)
```

```
        {
            this._teamName = teamName;
            this._position = position;
            this._played = played;
            this._won = won;
            this._drawn = drawn;
            this._lost = lost;
            this._points = points;
        }

        public String TeamName { get { return this._teamName; } }
        public int    Position { get { return this._position; } }
        public int    Played   { get { return this._played; } }
        public int    Won      { get { return this._won; } }
        public int    Drawn    { get { return this._drawn; } }
        public int    Lost     { get { return this._lost; } }
        public int    Points   { get { return this._points; } }
    }
}
```

Enabling *OnItemCommand* Events in Templates with the ObjectList Control

To make a templated ObjectList control raise a *Command* event, you use an ASP.NET LinkButton control, just as you do with the List control. However, if you want to retain the default behavior of the ObjectList control so that clicking an item in the list displays the Details view, you must write some more code.

In the example just shown in Listing 10-5, the *<ItemTemplate>* template contains the following code:

```
<ItemTemplate>
    <asp:LinkButton id="LinkButton1" Runat="server">
         <%# ((ObjectListItem)Container)["TeamName"] %>
    </asp:LinkButton>
    <br>
</ItemTemplate>
```

The ObjectList control raises the *ItemCommand* event when an item in the list is selected. Inside your event handler method, you must include the following code to switch the display to the Details view (as demonstrated in Listing 10-6):

```
private void ObjectList1_ItemCommand(
    object sender,
    System.Web.UI.MobileControls.ObjectListCommandEventArgs e)
{
    ObjectList1.SelectedIndex = e.ListItem.Index;
    ObjectList1.ViewMode = ObjectListViewMode.Details;
}
```

This code sets the *SelectedIndex* property of the ObjectList control to the item the user clicked, and it sets the *ViewMode* property so that the Details view is displayed.

Using the ObjectList Control's *<ItemDetailsTemplate>*

By default, the Details view of an item selected from an ObjectList control is displayed as a separate page, appearing as a table on HTML browsers and as a simple list of static text on WML browsers. When you specify an *<ItemDetailsTemplate>* template, you replace the entire details page rather than just a single row of a table, as occurs with the *<ItemTemplate>* template. Listings 10-7 and 10-8 show you how to do this.

```
<%@ Page Inherits="MSPress.MobWeb.ObLItemDetTemplate.MyWebForm"
    CodeBehind="ObjectListItemDetailsTemplateExample.aspx.cs"
    Language="c#" %>
<%@ Register TagPrefix="mobile" Namespace="System.Web.UI.MobileControls"
    Assembly="System.Web.Mobile" %>

<mobile:Form runat="server" id="Form1">
    <mobile:Label runat="server" StyleReference="title">
        Season 2003 results</mobile:Label>
    <mobile:ObjectList id="ObjectList1" runat="server"
        AutoGenerateFields="false">
        <Field Title="Team" DataField="TeamName"></Field>
        <Field Title="Won" DataField="Won"></Field>
        <Field Title="Drawn" DataField="Drawn"></Field>
        <Field Title="Lost" DataField="Lost"></Field>
        <Field Title="Points" DataField="Points" Visible="false"></Field>
        <DeviceSpecific>
            <Choice>
                <ItemDetailsTemplate>
                    <%# DataBinder.Eval(
    ((ObjectList)Container.NamingContainer).Selection.DataItem,
    "TeamName", "Team : {0}") %>
                    <br/>
                    <%# DataBinder.Eval(
    ((ObjectList)Container.NamingContainer).Selection.DataItem,
    "Won", "Won  : {0}") %>
                    <br/>
                    <%# DataBinder.Eval(
    ((ObjectList)Container.NamingContainer).Selection.DataItem,
    "Drawn", "Drawn: {0}") %>
                    <br/>
```

Listing 10-7 Source file ObjectListItemDetailsTemplateExample.aspx

```
                <%# DataBinder.Eval(
    ((ObjectList)Container.NamingContainer).Selection.DataItem,
    "Lost", "Lost : {0}") %>
                </ItemDetailsTemplate>
            </Choice>
        </DeviceSpecific>
    </mobile:ObjectList>
</mobile:Form>
```

```
using System;
using System.Collections;
using System.Web.UI;
using System.Web.UI.MobileControls;

namespace MSPress.MobWeb.ObLItemDetTemplate
{
    public class MyWebForm : System.Web.UI.MobileControls.MobilePage
    {
        protected ObjectList ObjectList1;

        override protected void OnInit(EventArgs e)
        {
            InitializeComponent();
            base.OnInit(e);
        }

        private void InitializeComponent()
        {
            this.Load += new System.EventHandler(this.Page_Load);
        }

        protected void Page_Load(Object sender, EventArgs e)
        {
            ArrayList array = new ArrayList();
            array.Add(new TeamStats("Dunes",1,38,24,8,6,80));
            array.Add(new TeamStats("Phoenix",2,38,20,10,8,70));
            array.Add(new TeamStats("Eagles",3,38,20,9,9,69));
            array.Add(new TeamStats("Zodiac",4,38,20,8,10,68));

            ObjectList1.DataSource = array;
            ObjectList1.LabelField = "TeamName";
            ObjectList1.DataBind();
        }
    }
```

Listing 10-8 Code-behind file ObjectListItemDetailsTemplateExample.aspx.cs

```
    public class TeamStats
    {
        private String  _teamName;
        private int _position, _played, _won, _drawn, _lost, _points;

        public TeamStats(String teamName,
            int position,
            int played,
            int won,
            int drawn,
            int lost,
            int points)
        {
            this._teamName = teamName;
            this._position = position;
            this._played = played;
            this._won = won;
            this._drawn = drawn;
            this._lost = lost;
            this._points = points;
        }

        public String TeamName { get { return this._teamName; } }
        public int    Position { get { return this._position; } }
        public int    Played   { get { return this._played; } }
        public int    Won      { get { return this._won; } }
        public int    Drawn    { get { return this._drawn; } }
        public int    Lost     { get { return this._lost; } }
        public int    Points   { get { return this._points; } }
    }
}
```

In this example, the *<ItemDetailsTemplate>* template contains the following ASP.NET data binding syntax to access the underlying data item the user selects. It uses the *DataBinder.Eval* method to simplify data binding syntax—see the sidebar later on for an explanation of how to use *DataBinder.Eval*.

```
<ItemDetailsTemplate>
    Played: <%# DataBinder.Eval(
  ((ObjectList)Container.NamingContainer).Selection.DataItem, "Played") %>
</ItemDetailsTemplate>
```

In the earlier example shown in Listing 10-5 that demonstrated the use of the *<ItemTemplate>*, the code used to access the data item cast the *Container* variable to an *ObjectListItem*:

```
<ItemTemplate>
    <asp:LinkButton id="LinkButton1" Runat="server">
        <%# ((ObjectListItem)Container)["TeamName"] %>
    </asp:LinkButton>
    <br>
</ItemTemplate>
```

The situation is different with the *<ItemDetailsTemplate>* of the ObjectList control. You use this template to format the "all fields'" form that's displayed after the user selects an item from the list. Here the display of the data item's field detail is a logically separate operation that occurs outside the data listing, after the user selects an item from the list. You can't cast to the *ObjectListItem* class to access the individual field items of the selected list entry; in the details view, there is no *ObjectListItem*. Instead, you must access the item through the parent control—in this case, the ObjectList control.

The way you obtain access to the parent control from within the *<ItemDetailsTemplate>* template requires some explanation. Controls in a mobile Web Forms page are organized hierarchically, and each control has a parent control. At the top of the hierarchy lies the instance of the *MobilePage* class that's created when the user first accesses the page. Each control on a mobile Web Forms page must have a unique ID. The parent control that implements the *System.Web.UI.INamingContainer* interface enforces the uniqueness of the child control's ID. (This parent control often is the underlying MobilePage control.) The control that implements *INamingContainer* creates a namespace that uniquely identifies the controls it contains. This is particularly important with list controls because the runtime creates many similar controls to present each line of data. For this reason, the List and ObjectList controls implement *INamingContainer*.

Every control inherits the *NamingContainer* property from the *System.Web.UI.Control* base class. This property returns a reference to the parent control above it in the hierarchy that provides its naming context. In an *<ItemDetailsTemplate>* template, you use the syntax *Container.NamingContainer* to reference the parent ObjectList control. This is because the *Container* variable references the *TemplateContainer* in which you've instantiated the template, and the *NamingContainer* property returns a reference to the parent ObjectList. You can then access properties and methods of the parent ObjectList, as shown in this example:

```
<ItemDetailsTemplate>
    Played: <%# DataBinder.Eval(
  ((ObjectList)Container.NamingContainer).Selection.DataItem, "Played") %>
</ItemDetailsTemplate>
```

Here's how the same example looks in Visual Basic:

```
<ItemDetailsTemplate>
    Played: <%# DataBinder.Eval(
CType(Container.NamingContainer,ObjectList).Selection.DataItem, "Played") %>
</ItemDetailsTemplate>
```

Using this technique, properties of the ObjectList control, such as *Selection*, are accessible and allow the individual fields of the selected data item to be accessed and displayed.

The output of this application is shown in Figure 10-5. This application illustrates a technique, so the output is less impressive than the default ObjectList rendering. With *<ItemDetailsTemplate>*, you have complete control over the content of the Details view.

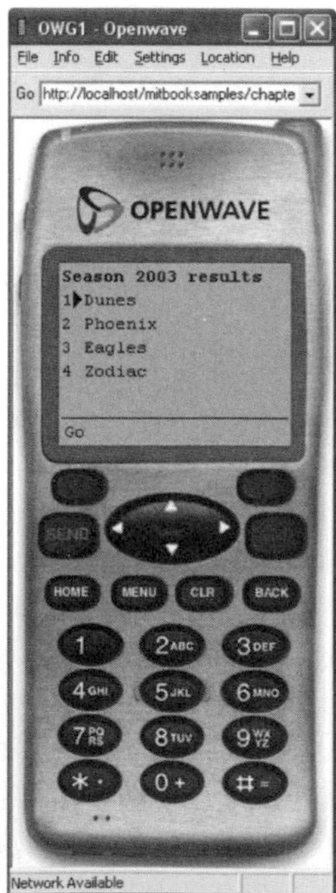

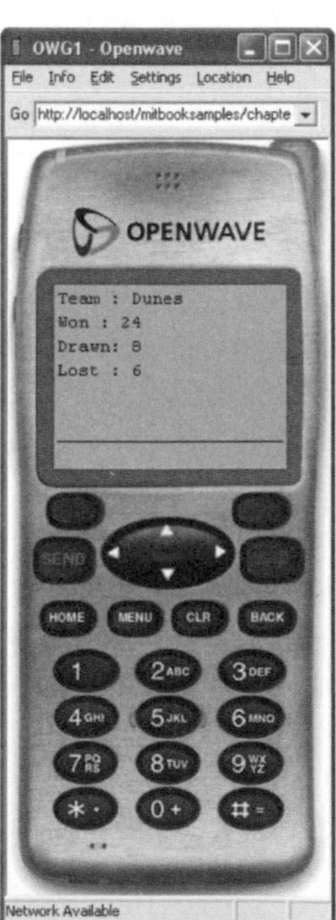

Figure 10-5 Output of the ObjectListItemDetailsTemplateExample application, with the Details view replaced by the contents of *<ItemDetailsTemplate>*

Simplifying Data Binding Syntax with *DataBinder.Eval*

The *DataBinder.Eval* statement in the example is a static method of the *System.Web.UI.DataBinder* class that eliminates much of the complicated explicit type casting that data binding syntax often requires. Although this static method is easier to use than explicit type casting, this usability comes at a price. *DataBinder.Eval* uses *late-bound reflection*, which is a technique that allows the type of an object to be determined at run time rather than explicitly casting the object to the correct type at compile time. The object is then converted to a string representation, consequently incurring a performance overhead.

The *DataBinder.Eval* static method is particularly useful when you're working with data items in templates. For example, consider an *<ItemTemplate>* template that retrieves an integer item from the underlying data source:

```
<ItemTemplate>
    <%# String.Format("{0:N2}",
     ((MobileListItem)Container).DataItem["Points"] %>
</ItemTemplate>
```

This syntax can be hard to remember. Using *DataBinder.Eval* simplifies the code a little:

```
<ItemTemplate>
    <%# DataBinder.Eval(((MobileListItem)Container).DataItem,
    "Points", "{0:N2}" ) %>
</ItemTemplate>
```

The first parameter is the *naming container* for the data item. (We'll talk about naming containers in the section "Working with Controls in Templates Programmatically.") The second parameter is the data field name, and the third parameter is an optional formatting string. If you omit the third parameter, *DataBinder.Eval* returns a result of type *object*.

Working with Controls in Templates Programmatically

In Chapter 9, in the "Working with Controls in Form and Panel Templates" section, you learned why it is not as simple as you might think to write code that sets or gets properties of controls placed in templates. For example, if you have a Label control inside a template with the ID *Label2*, you can't use code like this:

```
Label2.Text = "A suitable heading";
```

In fact, this returns a run-time error, stating that *Label2* is a null object. This is because controls inside templates are not child controls of the Form, but instead are instantiated inside each of the *MobileListItem* objects (or *ObjectListItem* objects in the case of the ObjectList control) that are created to contain the items in the list. The controls defined in templates are hidden down the control tree, so to address them in code, you must use the *System.Web.UI.Control.FindControl* method.

The situation is more complicated in the case of the list controls than it is with the templates of the Form and Panel controls. With lists, an *<ItemTemplate>*, an *<AlternatingItemTemplate>*, or a *<SeparatorTemplate>* template is instantiated each time it is used—in other words, for every item in the list. If you have a Label control inside one of these templates with an ID of *Label2*, you might expect a naming clash because a list of, say, five items would end up with five instances of a Label control with the same ID, which isn't allowed.

ASP.NET handles this situation by giving certain controls the ability to establish a naming context. Such a control has the ability to ensure that all child controls have a unique ID by prefixing the assigned ID of the child control with its own ID. For instance, in the previous example, the *TemplateContainer* child control of the List1 object can have a system assigned ID of *ctrl0*, so the Label control has a unique ID of *List1:ctrl0:Label2*. The *NamingContainer* object for the *<ItemTemplate>*, *<AlternatingItemTemplate>*, or *<SeparatorTemplate>* template of the List and ObjectList controls is the *MobileListItem* or *ObjectListItem* object that is present for each list item; you can access these objects through each control's *Items* collection. The *NamingContainer* object for the *<HeaderTemplate>* and *<FooterTemplate>* templates of the List and ObjectList controls is a *TemplateContainer* child control, which is also the *NamingContainer* object for the ObjectList control's *<ItemDetailsTemplate>*.

If you can find the object that provides the naming container, you can use the *FindControl* method of *System.Web.UI.Control* (the parent class of *MobileControl*) to locate specific child controls within that naming context.

> **Tip** If you're finding it difficult to understand the control hierarchy within a Web Forms page, turn on the trace facility, as described in Chapter 16. Part of the trace output is a listing of the full control hierarchy, which is a great help when you're working with child controls and naming contexts.

Accessing Controls in List and ObjectList Templates from Code

Consider the .aspx file shown in Listing 10-9, which uses an ObjectList control with an *<ItemTemplate>* template that contains a Label control with the ID *Label2*. We want to display the data as a numbered list, so we'll use the Label2 control that's included in the template to display the line number.

```
<%@ Register TagPrefix="mobile" Namespace="System.Web.UI.MobileControls"
    Assembly="System.Web.Mobile" %>
<%@ Page Codebehind="ObjectListTemplateControlsFromCode.aspx.cs"
    Inherits="MSPress.MobWeb.OblTemplateCtrlsEx.MyWebForm"
    language="c#" AutoEventWireup="false" %>

<mobile:form id="Form1" runat="server">
    <mobile:Label id="Label1" runat="server" StyleReference="title">
        Season 2003 results</mobile:Label>
    <mobile:ObjectList id="ObjectList1" runat="server"
        AutoGenerateFields="False">
        <DeviceSpecific>
            <Choice Filter="isHTML32">
                <HeaderTemplate>
                    <table width="90%">
                </HeaderTemplate>
                <ItemTemplate>
                    <TR><TD>
                        <mobile:Label id="Label2" Runat="server"/>
                    </TD><TD><B>
                        <asp:LinkButton id="LinkButton1" Runat="server">
                            <%# ((ObjectListItem)Container)["TeamName"] %>
                        </asp:LinkButton>
                   </B></TD></TR>
                </ItemTemplate>
                <FooterTemplate>
                    </table>
                </FooterTemplate>
            </Choice>
        </DeviceSpecific>
        <Field Title="Team" DataField="TeamName"></Field>
        <Field Title="Won" DataField="Won"></Field>
        <Field Title="Drawn" DataField="Drawn"></Field>
        <Field Title="Lost" DataField="Lost"></Field>
        <Field Title="Points" DataField="Points" Visible="False"></Field>
    </mobile:ObjectList>
</mobile:form>
```

Listing 10-9 Source file ObjectListTemplateControlsFromCode.aspx

You can't trap the *DataBind* event and set the *Text* property of the Label2 control to the required value because at the point in the control's life cycle when the *DataBind* event executes, the contents of the template have not yet been instantiated. Instead, let the control build the list of items, and then trap the *PreRender* event that's raised after all other processing on the server has completed and just before the output to be sent to the client is rendered.

In the *PreRender* event handler, we can enumerate the collection of *ObjectListItem* objects (exposed by the *ObjectList.Items* property). The contents of the template have by now been instantiated as child controls of the *ObjectListItem* object, so we use *FindControl* to locate the Label2 control and set its *Text* property to the required value. This process is illustrated in Listing 10-10:

```
using System;
using System.Collections;
using System.Web.UI.MobileControls;

namespace MSPress.MobWeb.OblTemplateCtrlsEx
{
    public class MyWebForm : System.Web.UI.MobileControls.MobilePage
    {
        protected System.Web.UI.MobileControls.Label Label1;
        protected System.Web.UI.MobileControls.ObjectList ObjectList1;
        protected System.Web.UI.MobileControls.Form Form1;

        override protected void OnInit(EventArgs e)
        {
            InitializeComponent();
            base.OnInit(e);
        }

        private void InitializeComponent()
        {
            this.ObjectList1.PreRender += new
                System.EventHandler(this.ObjectList1_PreRender);
            this.ObjectList1.ItemCommand += new
                ObjectListCommandEventHandler(this.ObjectList1_ItemCommand);
            this.Load += new System.EventHandler(this.Page_Load);
        }

        protected void Page_Load(Object sender, EventArgs e)
        {
            if (!this.IsPostBack)
            {
                ArrayList array = new ArrayList();
                array.Add(new TeamStats("Dunes",1,38,24,8,6,80));
```

Listing 10-10 Code-behind file ObjectListTemplateControlsFromCode.aspx.cs

```
            array.Add(new TeamStats("Phoenix",2,38,20,10,8,70));
            array.Add(new TeamStats("Eagles",3,38,20,9,9,69));
            array.Add(new TeamStats("Zodiac",4,38,20,8,10,68));

            ObjectList1.DataSource = array;
            ObjectList1.LabelField = "TeamName";
            this.DataBind();
        }
    }

    private void ObjectList1_PreRender(object sender, System.EventArgs e)
    {
        // Walk the Items collection of the ObjectList. This collection
        // contains the items that are displayed.
        int itemcounter =1;
        foreach (ObjectListItem item in ObjectList1.Items)
        {
            Label lblInTemplate = item.FindControl("Label2") as Label;
            if (lblInTemplate != null)
                lblInTemplate.Text = itemcounter.ToString();
            itemcounter++;
        }
    }

    private void ObjectList1_ItemCommand(
        object sender, ObjectListCommandEventArgs e)
    {
        // User has selected an item, so switch to details view.
        // You only need to do this switch manually because we are
        // using templates.
        ObjectList1.SelectedIndex = e.ListItem.Index;
        ObjectList1.ViewMode = ObjectListViewMode.Details;
    }
}

class TeamStats
{
    // Not shown - same as in listing 10-7
    :
}
}
```

This example uses the ObjectList control, but you can use the same technique with the List control where you enumerate the *List.Items* collection in the *PreRender* event handler, which is a collection of *MobileListItem* objects.

today

11

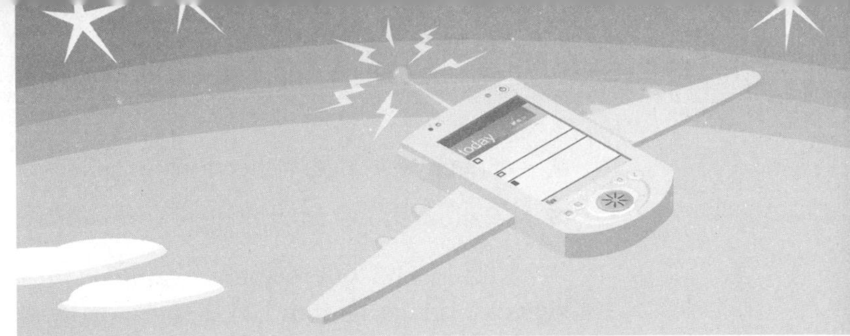

Accessing Data

Every Microsoft ASP.NET application works with some form of data. As you saw in Chapter 6, certain mobile Web Forms controls—such as the SelectionList, List, and ObjectList controls—can be data bound to a structured data source. This data source can be either one of the Microsoft .NET Framework collection classes, such as an *ArrayList*, or a Microsoft ADO.NET *System.Data.DataSet* or *System.Data.DataTable*.

ADO.NET is the latest generation of Microsoft data access technologies. It's not a replacement for Microsoft ActiveX Data Objects (ADO), the application programming interface familiar to many Microsoft Visual Studio 6.0 developers; ADO remains available for use alongside ADO.NET. Instead, ADO.NET provides a similar API, supporting data access in a way that's most appropriate for .NET Web-based applications.

In the previous chapter, you were introduced to ASP.NET's data binding syntax, and in this chapter we'll explore its use in more details. We'll also introduce you to ADO.NET programming and show you which Visual Studio .NET tools you can use to work with databases and datasets.

Using ASP.NET Declarative Data Binding

Many of the examples introduced in earlier chapters in this book included data expressions in the mobile Web Forms page, enclosed in these tags: <%#…%>. This ASP.NET declarative data binding syntax is particularly useful in templates when you want to access data items in the underlying data collection. However, you can also use this syntax to achieve the following results:

- Insert the values of public variables, page properties, or other controls into your Web page

- Specify the data collections to which controls are bound
- Call methods or evaluate expressions

Table 11-1 offers some examples of common uses for this data binding syntax. Listings 11-1 and 11-2 show many of these techniques in action.

Table 11-1 Examples of Declarative Data Binding Syntax

Source of Data	Example Usage	Explanation
Property	`<%# TopTitle %>`	The value that displays is the *TopTitle* property of the code-behind class.

Collection	`<mobile:ObjectList`
	`id="ObjectList1"`
	`runat="server"`
	`LabelField="TeamName"`
	`DataSource =`
	`<%# MyArray %>`
	`/>`
		The *DataSource* property of the ObjectList is set to the *MyArray* property of the code-behind class. The *MyArray* property exposes an instance of a collection class (such as *ArrayList)* or *DataTable*.

Expression	`<%# (TeamStats.Played`
	`+ " Pts: "`
	`+ TeamStats.Points) %>`
		The value that displays is constructed from an expression that concatenates properties of the *TeamStats* class and literal text.

Function execution	`<%# String.Format(`
	`"Position: {0}",`
	`TextBox1.Text.`
	`PadLeft(2,'0')) %>`
		Here the content of the page is the output of the *String.Format* function.

Method result	`<%# GetOdds(SelectionList1` `.Selection.Text) %>`	In this example, the *GetOdds* method is a method of the code-behind class. The return value of this method is inserted into the mobile page.

You can use declarative data binding code anywhere in a mobile Web Forms page, as long as the evaluated expression returns the correct object type for the context it's used in. For example, in the Collection item in Table 11-1, the *MyArray* variable must evaluate to an object that implements *IEnumerable* or *IListSource*.

To evaluate data binding expressions, you must call the *DataBind* method of the containing control. Usually, calling the *DataBind* method of the mobile page within the *Page_Load* event handler is sufficient because doing so also calls the *DataBind* method of all enclosed controls. The following code illustrates this concept:

```
protected void Page_Load(Object sender, EventArgs e)
{
    this.DataBind();
}
```

Sometimes calling the *DataBind* method of the *MobilePage* class isn't appropriate. If the data binding expressions reference objects that have a *null* value when the page first loads, calling the *MobilePage.DataBind* method this way will cause a run-time error. For example, referencing the *Selection* property of a SelectionList or an ObjectList control before the user makes a selection causes a run-time error. In this case, you might have to delay calling *DataBind* for all objects in the mobile page until you've defined the required items, as the following example demonstrates.

Listings 11-1 and 11-2 show an example application that uses an ObjectList control and declarative data binding wherever possible.

```
<%@ Page Inherits="MSPress.MobWeb.DeclDBEx.ExampleWebForm" Language="c#"
    CodeBehind="DeclarativeDataBinding.aspx.cs" AutoEventWireup="false" %>
<%@ Register TagPrefix="mobile" Namespace="System.Web.UI.MobileControls"
    Assembly="System.Web.Mobile" %>

<mobile:Form runat="server" id="Form1">
    <mobile:Label id="Label1" runat="server" StyleReference="title">
        <%# TopTitle %></mobile:Label>
    <mobile:ObjectList id="ObjectList1" runat="server"
        DefaultCommand="aSelection"
        LabelField="TeamName"
        DataSource = <%# MyArray %> >
        <Command Name="aSelection" Text="Show Details"/>
    </mobile:ObjectList>
</mobile:Form>

<mobile:Form runat="server" id="Form2">
    <mobile:Label id="Label2" runat="server" StyleReference="title">
        You selected <%# ObjectList1.Selection["TeamName"] %>
    </mobile:Label>
    <mobile:TextView id="txvDetail" runat="server">
    Played : <%# ObjectList1.Selection["Played"] %> <br>
    Points : <%# ObjectList1.Selection["Points"] %> <br>
    <%# String.Format("Position: {0}",
        ObjectList1.Selection["Position"].PadLeft(2,'0')) %>
    </mobile:TextView>
</mobile:Form>
```

Listing 11-1 Source file DeclarativeDataBindingExample.aspx

```
using System;
using System.Collections;
using System.Web.UI.MobileControls;

namespace MSPress.MobWeb.DeclDBEx
{
    public class ExampleWebForm : MobilePage
    {
        protected System.Web.UI.MobileControls.Form Form1;
        protected System.Web.UI.MobileControls.Form Form2;
        protected System.Web.UI.MobileControls.ObjectList ObjectList1;
        private   ArrayList  _myArray;

        protected ArrayList MyArray
        {
            get { return _myArray; }
        }

        public string TopTitle
        {
            get { return "Season 2003 results"; }
        }

        override protected void OnInit(EventArgs e)
        {
            InitializeComponent();
            base.OnInit(e);
        }

        private void InitializeComponent()
        {
            this.Load += new System.EventHandler(this.Page_Load);
            this.ObjectList1.ItemCommand += new
                ObjectListCommandEventHandler(this.OnTeamSelection);
        }

        private void Page_Load(Object sender, EventArgs e)
        {
            if (!this.IsPostBack)
            {
                _myArray = new ArrayList();
                _myArray.Add(new TeamStats("Dunes",1,38,24,8,6,80));
                _myArray.Add(new TeamStats("Phoenix",2,38,20,10,8,70));
                _myArray.Add(new TeamStats("Eagles",3,38,20,9,9,69));
                _myArray.Add(new TeamStats("Zodiac",4,38,20,8,10,68));
```

Listing 11-2 Code-behind file DeclarativeDataBindingExample.aspx.cs

```
            Form1.DataBind();
        }
    }

    private void OnTeamSelection(
        Object source,
        ObjectListCommandEventArgs args)
    {
        Form2.DataBind();
        this.ActiveForm = Form2;
    }
}

class TeamStats
{
    private String  _teamName;
    private int _position, _played, _won, _drawn, _lost, _points;

    public TeamStats(String teamName,
        int position,
        int played,
        int won,
        int drawn,
        int lost,
        int points)
    {
        this._teamName = teamName;
        this._position = position;
        this._played = played;
        this._won = won;
        this._drawn = drawn;
        this._lost = lost;
        this._points = points;
    }

    public String TeamName { get { return this._teamName; } }
    public int    Position { get { return this._position; } }
    public int    Played   { get { return this._played; } }
    public int    Won      { get { return this._won; } }
    public int    Drawn    { get { return this._drawn; } }
    public int    Lost     { get { return this._lost; } }
    public int    Points   { get { return this._points; } }
}
}
```

In Listing 11-2, the *ExampleWebForm* class gains two new public properties: a *TopTitle* string, and an *ArrayList* named *MyArray*. *MyArray* allows access to the private class member *_myArray*, which we've set up in the *Page_Load* event handler. In Listing 11-1, we bind the text value of the *Label1* label to the *TopTitle* property of the *ExampleWebForm* class in the code-behind module. We then access the *MyArray* property to provide the data source collection for the ObjectList control.

When the user selects an item from the list, the code calls the *OnTeamSelection* event handler. This sets the active form to *Form2*, in which you use further data binding expressions to access the *Selected* property of the ObjectList situated on the first form.

Note carefully the use of *DataBind* here. In the *Page_Load* method, we call *DataBind* only for *Form1* and, by implication, all controls that the form contains. If the application calls *DataBind* for the *MobilePage* at this point, a run-time error occurs because *Form2* contains data binding statements that reference the *ObjectList1.Selected* property, which remains *null* until the user makes a selection. The code resolves the data binding expressions for the second form by calling *Form2.DataBind* from within the *OnTeamSelection* event handler, which occurs after the user makes a selection.

Using ADO.NET

All the examples of data binding that you've seen so far have used .NET Framework collection classes, such as *ArrayList*. However, if your data is held in a database, you'll use ADO.NET classes such as *DataSet* and *DataView*.

As mentioned at the beginning of this chapter, ADO—ADO.NET's predecessor—will be familiar to developers with Visual Studio 6.0 experience. However, ADO.NET presents a new model for working with data that's well suited for distributed applications. In the past, developers based the design of data-driven applications on the fact that these applications were permanently connected to the database and that the database managed record locking, updates, and deletions.

Data access from server-side code in an ASP.NET application presents special challenges because a Web page is essentially stateless. The data you access during the application might require updating at a later point, by which time the program will have instantiated the Web page class a number of times. ADO.NET provides a model that's ideally suited for this type of access. In ADO.NET, the application works with a *DataSet* or DataReader (any class that implements the *System.Data.IDataReader* interface), which is a representation of the data that's disconnected from the database and works independently of the data source.

Understanding the ADO.NET Objects

DataSet objects represent the actual data that an application works with. Because a *DataSet* object is always disconnected from its source data, you can modify it independently. However, you can easily reconcile changes to a *DataSet* object with the original data. The internal structure of a *DataSet* object is similar to that of a relational database; it contains tables, columns, relationships, constraints, views, and so on. *DataSet* objects can result from a database query. You can also construct *DataSet* objects in code and serialize them to, and deserialize them from, an XML file. Because a *DataSet* object remains independent from its underlying data, you can work with a consistent programming model, regardless of the data source.

DataAdapters are classes that implement the *System.Data.IDataAdapter* interface, and are responsible for populating a *DataSet* object. DataAdapters also reconcile changes in the database with changes applied to the *DataSet*. *Connections* implement *System.Data.IDbConnection* and represent a physical connection to a data store, such as Microsoft SQL Server or an XML file. *Commands* are classes that implement the *System.Data.IDbCommand* interface, and contain the SQL commands used to actually access the data source.

As an alternative to the *DataSet*, you'll often use a DataReader, which is a set of classes that implement the *System.Data.IDataReader* interface and provide efficient, read-only data access to a data source. A DataReader doesn't contain the full functionality of a *DataSet* object, such as the ability to make changes or identify changed data rows, and only allows you to read forward through the contained data.

Choosing a Data Provider

The *IDataAdapter*, *IDataReader*, *IDbConnection* and *IDbCommand* interfaces together define how a managed application accesses a database. A *Data Provider* is a set of classes that implements these interfaces for a specific database. In .NET Framework 1.1, you have a choice of four data providers:

- SQL Server .NET Data Provider (in the *System.Data.SqlClient* namespace). The SQL data provider talks directly to Microsoft SQL Server.
- OLE DB .NET Data Provider (in the *System.Data.OleDb* namespace). You can use the OLE DB data provider to talk to any data source that offers an OLE DB interface
- Microsoft .NET Data Provider for Oracle (in the *System.Data.OracleClient* namespace). You can use the Oracle data provider to access Oracle databases.
- ODBC .NET Data Provider (in the *System.Data.Odbc* namespace). You can use the ODBC data provider to connect to any data source that implements an ODBC interface.

Each data provider implements its own Connection, Command, DataAdapter, and DataReader classes. For example, the SQL data provider implements the *SQLConnection*, *SQLCommand*, *SQLDataAdapter*, and *SQLDataReader* classes, and the OLE DB data provider implements the *OLEDbConnection*, *OLEDbCommand*, *OLEDbDataAdapter*, and *OLEDbDataReader* classes. The examples we'll look at next in this section will use the SQL data provider.

To use the ADO.NET objects, you must import the relevant namespaces:

```
using System.Data;
using System.Data.SqlClient;
```

If you're using the OLE DB data provider, the syntax will look like this:

```
using System.Data;
using System.Data.OleDb;
```

Note The examples that follow use the *pubs* database, which installs with the Microsoft .NET Framework SDK QuickStart samples. You do not need to install the SQL Server product on your development system. The setup for the .NET Framework QuickStart samples will install a stand-alone database server named the Microsoft SQL Server Desktop Engine (MSDE) on your system if necessary. To install the MSDE Server and the sample databases, go to the C:\Program Files\Microsoft.NET\Framework SDK\ folder or the C:\Program Files\Microsoft Visual Studio .NET\FrameworkSDK folder and click StartHere.htm. The Microsoft .NET Framework SDK welcome page will appear. Click on the QuickStarts, Tutorials, And Samples link. If you have not already installed the .NET Framework QuickStart samples, the page that's displayed shows two steps you must perform to install them onto your computer. First click Step 1: Install The .NET Framework Samples Database. When the database has been set up, click Step 2: Set Up The QuickStarts to install all the sample databases and set up the .NET Framework QuickStart tutorials. Note that if you are using SQL Server to run these samples, you'll need to change the DataSource element of the *SqlConnection* Connection string from *(local)\NETSDK* to *localhost*.

If you install SQL server or MSDE, make sure you install the latest service pack as well, which you can download from MSDN. Service pack 3 or later is necessary to guard against virus attacks such as the "slammer" virus that caused so much havoc in early 2003.

Using a *DataReader* Object for Read-Only Data Access

If you don't need to update the data you're fetching from a database, the DataReader offers a more efficient alternative to using a *DataSet*. To use a DataReader, you must first open a connection to the database, define the SQL command to fetch the data in a Command object, and then call the *ExecuteReader* method of the Command object. This returns a *DataReader* object containing the data that you can use as the data source for the control. Be aware that this transaction doesn't involve the use of a DataAdapter.

Listing 11-3 shows a simple code sample using a List control. In Listing 11-4, the *Page_Load* method accesses the database and builds the *SqlDataReader*, which then provides data to the control.

```
<%@ Register TagPrefix="mobile" Namespace="System.Web.UI.MobileControls"
    Assembly="System.Web.Mobile" %>
<%@ Page language="c#" Codebehind="DataReaderExample.aspx.cs"
    Inherits="MSPress.MobWeb.DataRdrEx.DataReaderMobileWebForm" %>

<mobile:Form id="Form1" runat="server" Paginate="True">
    <mobile:List id="List1" runat="server"></mobile:List>
</mobile:Form>
```

Listing 11-3 Source file DataReaderExample.aspx

```
using System;
using System.Data;
using System.Data.SqlClient;
using System.Web.UI.MobileControls;

namespace MSPress.MobWeb.DataRdrEx
{
    /// <summary>
    /// Use the DataReader for efficient read-only access to data.
    /// </summary>
    public class DataReaderMobileWebForm
        : System.Web.UI.MobileControls.MobilePage
    {
        protected System.Web.UI.MobileControls.List List1;
        protected System.Web.UI.MobileControls.Form Form1;

        override protected void OnInit(EventArgs e)
        {
            InitializeComponent();
            base.OnInit(e);
        }
```

Listing 11-4 Code-behind file DataReaderExample.aspx.cs

```
        private void InitializeComponent()
        {
            this.Load += new System.EventHandler(this.Page_Load);
        }

        private void Page_Load(object sender, System.EventArgs e)
        {
            // Use the DataReader to fetch a read-only dataset.
            String strConnectionString = "server=(local)\\NetSDK;" +
                "database=pubs;Trusted_Connection=yes";
            SqlConnection myConnection =
                new SqlConnection(strConnectionString);
            SqlCommand myCommand =
                new SqlCommand("select * from Authors", myConnection);

            myConnection.Open();

            SqlDataReader dr = myCommand.ExecuteReader();

            List1.DataSource = dr;
            List1.DataTextField="au_lname";
            List1.DataBind();

            myConnection.Close();
        }
    }
}
```

The output is a list of all the last names of entries in the authors table, as Figure 11-1 shows.

Using a *DataSet* Object for Data Binding

In many applications, the DataReader provides all the required functionality. However, for applications that involve long transactions or require you to update the database, the *DataSet* offers a number of advantages. A *DataSet* also has the benefit of containing information about the constraints defined in the underlying database. Therefore, you can make changes to the *DataSet* data and trap any constraint violations in your application (such as data field lengths or valid ranges) when you apply updates to the *DataSet*, rather than when you attempt the database update. When you update the database from the *DataSet*, the data remains consistent with any constraints defined in the database.

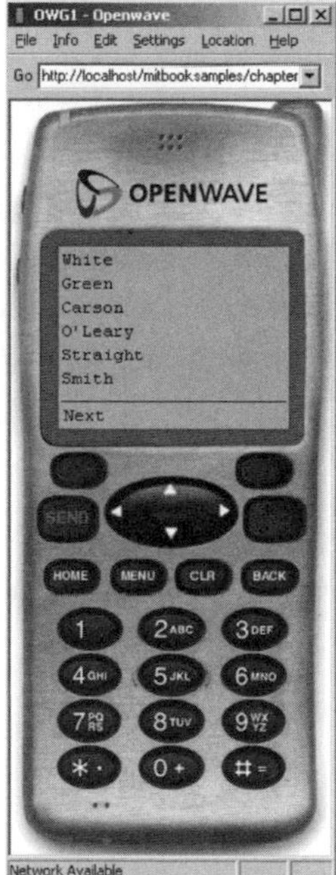

Figure 11-1 A List control bound to a database table

Accessing a database to populate a *DataSet* is very similar to fetching data using a DataReader. However, you define the SQL command to retrieve the data in a DataAdapter, rather than in a Command. Listing 11-5 shows the syntax for creating such a *DataSet*. See the C# and Visual Basic examples DatasetExample in the companion material on this book's Web site for applications that use a *DataSet* object.

```
// Use the DataAdapter to fill a dataset.
String strConnectionString =
    "server=(local)\\NetSDK;database=pubs;Trusted_Connection=yes";
SqlConnection myConnection =
    new SqlConnection(strConnectionString);
SqlDataAdapter myCommand =
    new SqlDataAdapter("select * from Authors", myConnection);

DataSet ds = new DataSet();
myCommand.Fill(ds, "Authors");
```

Listing 11-5 Creating a *DataSet* object, which is bound to the ObjectList control named *ObjectList1*

```
ObjectList1.DataSource = ds.Tables["Authors"].DefaultView;
ObjectList1.LabelField = "au_lname";
ObjectList1.AutoGenerateFields = true;
ObjectList1.DataBind();
```

A *DataSet* object contains *DataTable* objects, which in turn contain *DataRow* and *DataColumn* objects. Together, these classes offer a rich set of functionality for manipulating data. However, this functionality is too extensive to detail here. For more information, consult the .NET Framework SDK documentation.

Creating a Mobile Web Application to Update a Database

If your application requires the user to make a series of changes that must be applied to the database in a single transaction, the ideal approach is to programmatically alter a *DataSet* object, storing changes as they're made. You then apply these changes to the database using a DataAdapter.

If the user makes changes to a single record, which is more likely in a mobile application, you can adopt a simpler approach. In Listings 11-6 and 11-7 shown later in this section, the application uses an ObjectList control to display data from the authors table in the pubs database installed with the .NET Framework samples. The code defines an item command using the *<Command…>* syntax in the .aspx file, which allows the user to edit the details. When selected, *Form2* appears, displaying the current field values using editable controls, such as TextBox. To keep the example short, this application allows editing of only the *First Name* and *Last Name* fields. Figures 11-2 and 11-3 show how the user interface of this example will look.

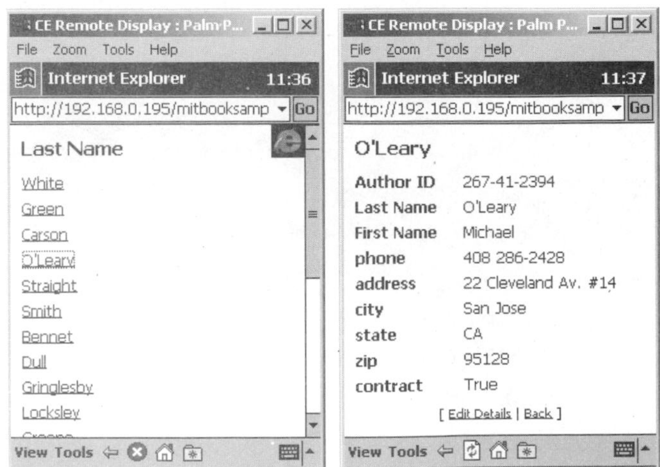

Figure 11-2 The ObjectList control on the first form lists the last names of entries in the authors table. When the user selects an entry, an additional Edit Details command appears.

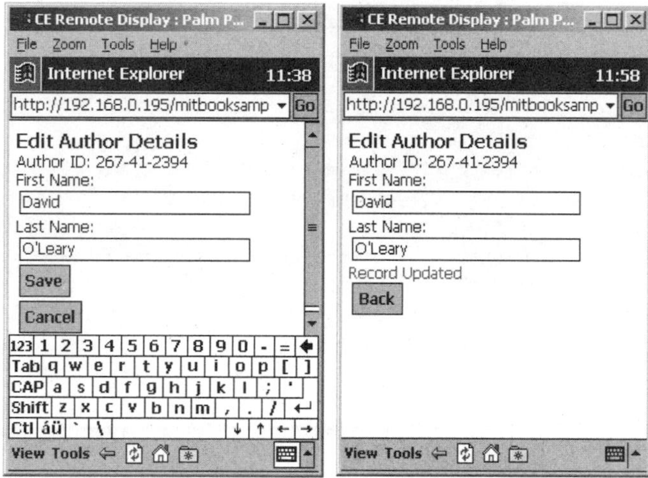

Figure 11-3 When the user makes changes and clicks Save, the database updates.

The Edit form, shown in Listing 11-6, employs a data binding syntax that inserts the values for the currently selected record into the TextBox controls ready for editing. This form also presents two command buttons: one to save any changes, and one to cancel without saving. The same *OnItemCommand* event handler, named *CancelConfirmEdit*, handles both these buttons.

If the user clicks the Save button, the runtime calls the *SaveChanges* event handler method (shown in listing 11-7). This method uses a parameterized SQL query string to update the required record. The parameters are set to the values the user enters into the text boxes on the form. Be aware that the user isn't allowed to edit the *au_id* field on the Edit form because this field is the primary key of the database item and isn't user assignable.

```
<%@ Page language="c#" Codebehind="DataUpdateExample.aspx.cs"
    Inherits="MSPress.MobWeb.DataUpdateEx.DataUpdateMobileWebForm" %>
<%@ Register TagPrefix="mobile"
    Namespace="System.Web.UI.MobileControls"
    Assembly="System.Web.Mobile" %>

<mobile:Form id="Form1" runat="server" Paginate="True">
    <mobile:ObjectList id="ObjectList1" runat="server">
        <Command Name="EditCommand" Text="Edit Details"/>
    </mobile:ObjectList>
</mobile:Form>

<mobile:Form id="Form2" runat="server">
    <mobile:Label id="Label1" runat="server"
```

Listing 11-6 Source file DataUpdateExample.aspx

```
        text="Edit Author Details" StyleReference="title"/>
    <mobile:Label runat="server">
        Author ID: <%# ObjectList1.Selection["au_id"] %>
    </mobile:Label>
    First Name:
    <mobile:TextBox id="TextBox1" runat="server" MaxLength="20"
        Text='<%# ObjectList1.Selection["au_fname"]%>' />
    Last Name:
    <mobile:TextBox id="TextBox2" runat="server" MaxLength="40"
        Text='<%# ObjectList1.Selection["au_lname"]%>' />
    <mobile:Label id=Label3 runat="server"
        StyleReference="error" Visible="false"/>
    <mobile:Command id="Command1" runat="server" Text="Save"
        CommandName="Save" />
    <mobile:Command id="Command2" runat="server" Text="Cancel"
        CommandName="Cancel" />
</mobile:Form>
```

```
using System;
using System.Data;
using System.Data.SqlClient;
using System.Web.UI.MobileControls;
using System.Web.UI.WebControls;

namespace MSPress.MobWeb.DataUpdateEx
{
    /// <summary>
    /// Use the DataReader to fetch the data.
    /// </summary>
    public class DataUpdateMobileWebForm
        : System.Web.UI.MobileControls.MobilePage
    {
        SqlConnection myConnection;

        protected System.Web.UI.MobileControls.ObjectList ObjectList1;
        protected System.Web.UI.MobileControls.Form       Form1;
        protected System.Web.UI.MobileControls.Form       Form2;
        protected System.Web.UI.MobileControls.Label      Label3;
        protected System.Web.UI.MobileControls.Command    Command1;
        protected System.Web.UI.MobileControls.Command    Command2;
        protected System.Web.UI.MobileControls.TextBox    TextBox1;
        protected System.Web.UI.MobileControls.TextBox    TextBox2;

        override protected void OnInit(EventArgs e)
        {
            InitializeComponent();
            base.OnInit(e);
        }
```

Listing 11-7 Code-behind file DataUpdateExample.aspx.cs

```
private void InitializeComponent()
{
    this.Load += new System.EventHandler(this.Page_Load);
    this.ObjectList1.ItemCommand += new
        ObjectListCommandEventHandler(this.OnEditCommand);
    this.Command1.ItemCommand += new
        CommandEventHandler(this.CancelConfirmEdit);
    this.Command2.ItemCommand += new
        CommandEventHandler(this.CancelConfirmEdit);
}

private void Page_Load(object sender, System.EventArgs e)
{
    // Use the DataReader to fetch a read-only data set.
    String strConnectionString = "server=(local)\\NetSDK;" +
        "database=pubs;Trusted_Connection=yes";
    myConnection = new SqlConnection(strConnectionString);

    if (!IsPostBack) BindList();
}

private void BindList()
{
    SqlCommand myCommand =
        new SqlCommand("select * from Authors", myConnection);
    myConnection.Open();
    SqlDataReader dr = myCommand.ExecuteReader();

    ObjectList1.DataSource = dr;
    ObjectList1.LabelField = "au_lname";
    ObjectList1.AutoGenerateFields = true;
    ObjectList1.DataBind();

    // The field names of au_id, au_lname, and au_fname
    // do not provide good titles, so change them in the
    // AllFields collection.
    ObjectList1.AllFields[ObjectList1.AllFields.IndexOf("au_id")]
        .Title = "Author ID";
    ObjectList1.AllFields[ObjectList1.AllFields.IndexOf("au_fname")]
        .Title = "First Name";
    ObjectList1.AllFields[ObjectList1.AllFields.IndexOf("au_lname")]
        .Title = "Last Name";
}

/// <summary>
/// Called when the user clicks the 'Edit Details' link
/// </summary>
```

```
protected void OnEditCommand(
    Object source,
    ObjectListCommandEventArgs args)
{
    // DataBind the form to insert the selected item details.
    Form2.DataBind();
    this.ActiveForm = Form2;

    Label3.Visible = false;
    Command1.Visible = true;
    Command2.Visible = true;
    Command2.Text = "Cancel";
}

/// <summary>
/// Called when a user clicks on either 'Save' or 'Cancel' button
/// on Edit screen
/// </summary>
private void CancelConfirmEdit(Object sender, CommandEventArgs e)
{
    if (e.CommandName == "Save") {
        SaveChanges();
    }
    else
    {
        // Go back to the List View.
        this.ActiveForm = Form1;
        ObjectList1.ViewMode = ObjectListViewMode.List;
    }

    BindList();
}

private void SaveChanges()
{
    String updateCmd = "UPDATE Authors SET au_lname = @LName, " +
        "au_fname = @FName where au_id = @Id";

    SqlCommand myCommand = new SqlCommand(updateCmd, myConnection);

    myCommand.Parameters.Add(
        new SqlParameter("@Id", SqlDbType.NVarChar, 11));
    myCommand.Parameters.Add(
        new SqlParameter("@LName", SqlDbType.NVarChar, 40));
    myCommand.Parameters.Add(
        new SqlParameter("@FName", SqlDbType.NVarChar, 20));
```

```
            myCommand.Parameters["@Id"].Value =
                ObjectList1.Selection["au_id"];
            myCommand.Parameters["@LName"].Value = TextBox2.Text;
            myCommand.Parameters["@FName"].Value = TextBox1.Text;

            myCommand.Connection.Open();

            try
            {
                myCommand.ExecuteNonQuery();
                Label3.Text = "Record Updated";
            }
            catch (SqlException)
            {
                Label3.Text = "ERROR: Could not update record";
            }

            myCommand.Connection.Close();

            Label3.Visible = true;
            Command1.Visible = false;
            Command2.Visible = true;
            Command2.Text = "Back";
        }
    }
}
```

The code that performs the actual database update resides in the *SaveChanges* method. ADO.NET denotes parameters in a SQL command by using a leading at sign (@), as illustrated here:

```
String updateCmd = "UPDATE Authors SET au_lname = @LName, " +
                   "au_fname = @FName where au_id = @Id";
SqlCommand myCommand = new SqlCommand(updateCmd, myConnection);
```

The code adds a *SQLParameter* object to the *SQLCommand* object for each variable quantity within the SQL command, configured with the appropriate data format, as shown here:

```
myCommand.Parameters.Add(new SqlParameter("@Id", SqlDbType.NVarChar, 11));
```

Then the code sets the actual value that you want to substitute into the SQL command for that parameter:

```
myCommand.Parameters["@LName"].Value = txtLName.Text;
```

After you've defined the SQL command, you can execute it in one of two ways. If you want the code to return a new *DataSet* object, you can call the

Execute method of the *SQLCommand* object. If you don't need a *DataSet* object returned, call *ExecuteNonQuery* like this:

```
myCommand.ExecuteNonQuery();
```

We gave this particular example a final polish by presenting a confirmation message, using the label *Label3*. This label has its *Visible* property set to *false* when *Form2* is first displayed. However, it's set to a result string and appears after the database update occurs (or fails). Similar program logic hides the Save button after the user saves the record, and it changes the legend on the Cancel button to Back.

You can achieve database inserts and deletions using similar logic. To do so, just set the SQL *Command* string to the appropriate SQL INSERT or DELETE command. Needless to say, a real application would require more extensive error checking to handle complex error situations, such as a duplicate key error when attempting an INSERT.

Building Data Components with Visual Studio .NET

Visual Studio .NET provides a number of useful tools that can greatly assist developers who work with data. The Database Designer allows you to interact with database objects using database diagrams, through which you can create database tables, rows, columns, keys, indexes, relationships, and constraints. The Table Designer is a visual tool that allows you to design a single database table. For details about these tools, consult the Visual Studio .NET SDK documentation. In this section, we'll look at two other useful tools in Visual Studio .NET, the Server Explorer and the Component Designer.

Using Server Explorer

Even if you don't consider yourself a database designer, Visual Studio .NET offers a number of useful features that allow you to view databases and create data components. One such feature is Server Explorer. Server Explorer allows you to navigate and access data sources that are available to your applications.

You can open Server Explorer by clicking the Server Explorer tab below the Toolbox tab in Visual Studio .NET. Alternatively, you can open the View menu and then click Server Explorer.

Using Server Explorer, you can perform the following tasks:

- Open data connections to SQL servers and other databases
- Connect to SQL servers and display their databases

- Connect to systems on your network and display their system services, including event logs, message queues, performance counters, system services, and SQL databases
- View information about available XML Web services and the methods and schemas they make available

For example, if you want to check the fields containing the names and characteristics of the authors table that we used in the previous section's examples, click Server Explorer and navigate to the authors table in the pubs database within SQL Server. Figure 11-4 shows what you'll see.

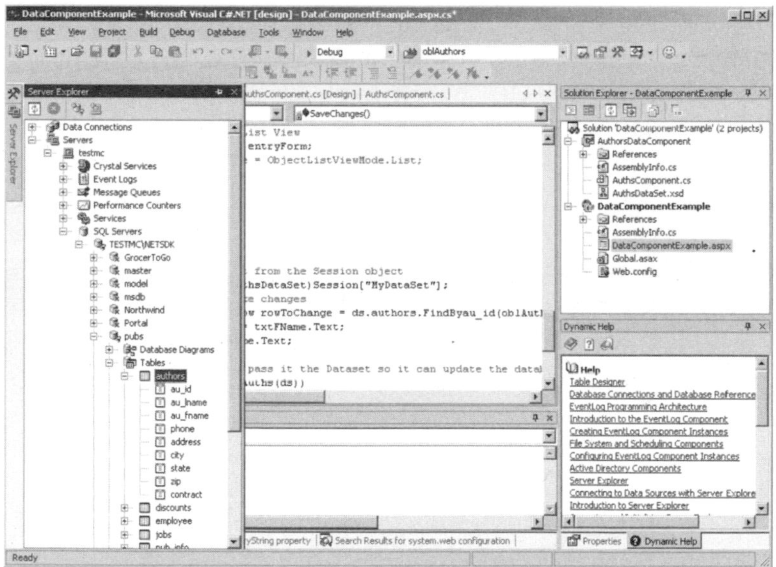

Figure 11-4 Using Server Explorer to examine database contents

Creating Data Components

Simple applications can access the database directly, as shown in the example in the previous section. However, it's often a good idea to adopt a two-tier or an *n*-tier model. In both these models, the classes that handle the user interface don't directly handle data; instead, they call components that perform data manipulation on their behalf. In an *n*-tier model, the user interface classes call components that enforce the business logic or business rules. These middle-tier components call other components that are responsible for fetching and updating data. In this architecture, a *DataSet* is the ideal object for transferring data between components because it's completely detached from the database. However, a *DataSet* object still knows about the relationships and constraints that apply to the database, and it enforces them when it is updated.

Visual Studio .NET offers a Component Designer that works with Server Explorer, making it easy to create data components. To demonstrate how to use these tools, you'll update the DataUpdateExample example from Listing 11-7 using a data component instead of embedded data handling logic.

First create a new project of type Visual C# Class Library and name it AuthorsDataComponent. This creates a project that will compile into an assembly, initially containing a class file named Class1.cs. Right-click this file in Solution Explorer, and click Delete. You don't need this file because you'll create a new class module using the Component Designer.

Next right-click the project file in Solution Explorer, click Add on the context menu, and then click Add Component. In the Add New Item window, click Component Class, enter the name **AuthsComponent.cs**, and click Open. Visual Studio .NET adds the AuthsComponent.cs file to your project and opens it in Design view. Now click Server Explorer, and navigate to the authors table in the pubs database. Drag the authors table from Server Explorer onto the AuthsComponent.cs Design view, as Figure 11-5 shows. This creates a *SqlConnection* object and a *SqlDataAdapter* object within the component class, both of which you'll see represented in the Design view. The code for the component class automatically sets up these objects with the appropriate connection string and the correct *SqlCommand* objects for selecting, deleting, inserting, and updating the authors table.

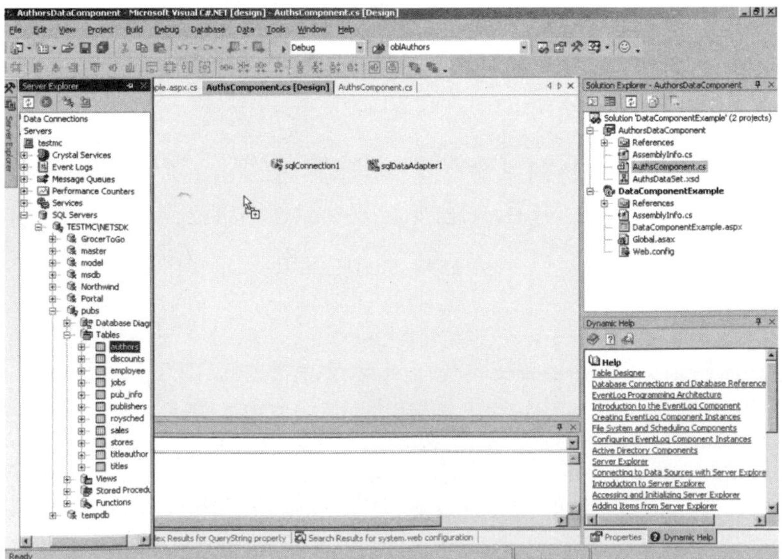

Figure 11-5 Dragging a database table from Server Explorer to the Component Designer to automatically set up *SqlConnection* and *SqlDataAdapter* objects

This component will communicate with other classes by sending and receiving *DataSet* objects. The Component Designer allows you to generate a *DataSet* object for the table you've selected. Click the Data menu in Visual Studio .NET, and then click Generate Dataset. In the Generate Dataset window, click New and enter the name **AuthsDataSet**, as shown in Figure 11-6. Verify that you've checked the authors table to include it in the *DataSet*, and check the "Add this dataset to the designer" check box. When you click OK, the runtime creates an XML schema file for the *DataSet*, named AuthsDataSet.xsd, and adds it to your project. The application then creates an instance of this new object, named *authsDataSet1*, and adds it to the Design view.

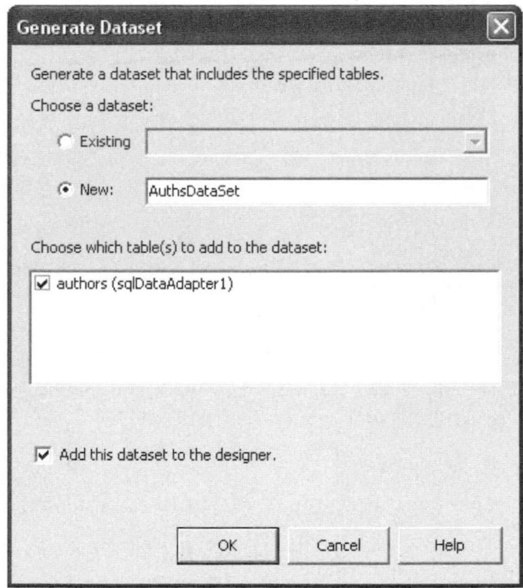

Figure 11-6 Generating the Typed DataSet in your component

As it stands, the data component contains all the low-level plumbing required to manipulate the authors table. If you right-click the Design view of the Component Designer and select View Code, you'll see that the runtime has created a class. If you then scroll down and click the plus sign (+) next to the code block labeled Component Designer Generated Code, you'll see all the code needed to connect to the pubs database and manipulate the authors table data. (Be sure that you don't alter any code in this region!) Aside from containing all this generated code, this component currently does nothing. Thus, you must add methods to populate the dataset and make it available externally.

Now add a public property to the class that fills the *authsDataSet1* private class member and returns the dataset to the caller, as shown here:

```
/// <summary>
/// Returns a dataset of all authors in the authors table of the pubs database
/// </summary>
public AuthsDataSet AllAuthors
{
    get
    {
        // Update class member dataset.
        this.sqlDataAdapter1.Fill(this.authsDataSet, "authors");
        return this.authsDataSet1;
    }
}
```

The *Fill* method of the *SqlDataAdapter* automatically opens a connection to the database, reads the data into the *DataSet* object, then closes the connection.

This component should also implement a method to update the database with any changes to the data. The code that the Component Designer has generated makes this update very easy to implement. The Component Designer has set up the *SqlDataAdapter* object with the appropriate *SqlCommand* objects to insert, update, and delete rows in the authors table. When you call the *Update* method of the *SqlDataAdapter* object, passing it a *DataSet* object that contains changes, the runtime applies the changes to the database for each row in the *DataSet* that you've added, updated, or deleted using the appropriate *SqlCommand*. Consequently, the code that you need to add in order to implement a public method to update the database is quite simple:

```
/// <summary>
/// Take a DataSet, including changes, and apply it to the database.
/// </summary>
public bool UpdateAuths(AuthsDataSet DataChanges)
{
    bool boolRetval;
    try
    {
        this.sqlDataAdapter1.Update(DataChanges, "authors");
        boolRetval = true;
    }
    catch(Exception)
    {
        boolRetval = false;
    }
    return boolRetval;
}
```

Now build your component. Creating a data component that offers basic functionality is that simple. However, a real application would undoubtedly require more complex error-handling code.

Using a Data Component in a Web Application

When you remove all the data-handling code from the component, the main application class becomes much cleaner and can focus on the logic required to drive the user interface.

To prepare a component for use in a Web application, open the DataUpdateExample project you used in the preceding example or use the Copy Project feature to make a copy, naming it DataComponentExample.

To use the data component, you must add a reference to it in your project. From the Project menu, click Add Reference. You can select the .NET assemblies or COM objects that your application uses from within the Add Reference window (shown in Figure 11-7). To add a reference to a custom component, click the Browse button and navigate to the assembly that the runtime built when you compiled your data component. Click the My Projects button, and then open the AuthorsDataComponent project folder. The AuthorsDataComponent.dll assembly resides in the /bin/debug directory. Click this assembly to select it, and then click OK.

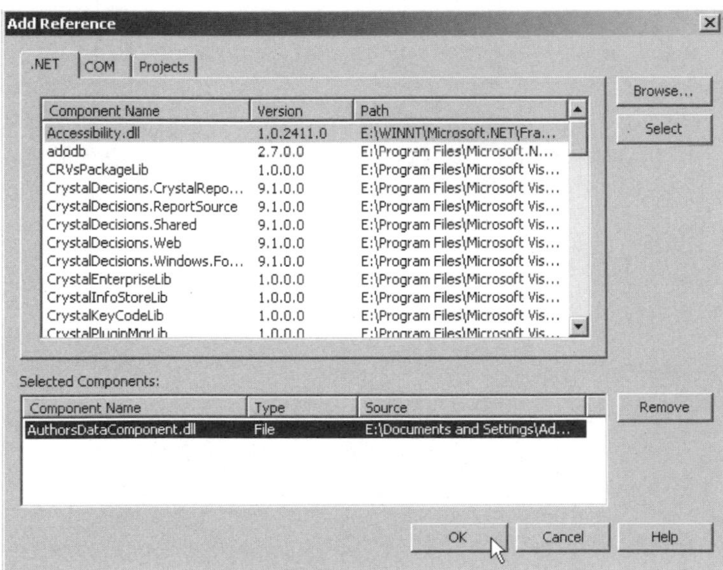

Figure 11-7 The Add Reference window

Now add a declaration for the *AuthorsDataComponent* namespace at the top of the DataComponentExample.aspx.cs code-behind module so that you don't have to enter the fully qualified name of the component every time you use it. Here's the declaration:

```
using MSPress.Mob.Web.AuthorsDataComponent;
```

Next create the data component as a private member of the class. This application actually instantiates the object in the *Page_Load* method each time you create the class. This instantiation occurs when the application first starts and each time the client posts back to the server. The *Page_Load* method no longer needs to open a connection to the database as before because the component handles this. Here's how the syntax looks:

```
private AuthsComponent myDataComp;

private void Page_Load(object sender, System.EventArgs e)
{
// Create the data component each time the application
// returns to the server.
myDataComp = new AuthsComponent();

if (!IsPostBack)
    BindList();
}
```

The *BindList* method has scarcely changed, apart from fetching the dataset to which the ObjectList control binds from the component and storing the *DataSet* in the *Session* object (an improvement over the method's previous incarnation). A *Session* object is used to store data across different HTTP request/response interactions; you'll learn more about the *Session* object in Chapter 12. *BindList* stores the *DataSet* in the *Session* object as a convenience to the *SaveChanges* method, which also requires access to the *DataSet* when it handles data changes later on in this appliction, during the processing of a later postback from the client. Let's take a look at the code:

```
public void BindList()
{
    // Use the DataComponent to fetch a dataset.
    AuthsDataSet ds = myDataComp.AllAuthors;

    ObjectList1.DataSource = ds.Tables["authors"].DefaultView;
    ObjectList1.LabelField = "au_lname";
    ObjectList1.AutoGenerateFields = true;
    ObjectList1.DataBind();

    // The field names of au_id, au_lname, and au_fname do not provide
    // good titles, so change them in the AllFields collection.
    ObjectList1.AllFields[ObjectList1.AllFields.IndexOf("au_id")].Title
        = "Author ID";
    ObjectList1.AllFields[ObjectList1.AllFields.IndexOf("au_fname")].Title
        = "First Name";
    ObjectList1.AllFields[ObjectList1.AllFields.IndexOf("au_lname")].Title
        = "Last Name";
```

```
    // Store the DataSource in a session variable so that
    // it can persist across multiple postbacks.
    Session["MyDataSet"] = ds;
}
```

The purpose of the *SaveChanges* method is to update the *DataSet* with the changes that the user makes and to pass the revised *DataSet* back to the data component. The data component will then apply the changes retrieved from the dataset to the original data in the database. With the *SaveChanges* method, the real utility of the *AuthsDataSet* class generated by the Component Designer comes to light. The *AuthsDataSet* class that the Component Designer creates is derived from *DataSet*. The *AuthsDataSet* class offers methods and properties tailored to the manipulation of data retrieved from the authors table in the database. These methods and properties make the developer's job much easier. For example, the *authors* property of *AuthsDataSet* contains the *authorsDataTable* object, which has a *FindByau_id* method that searches for a specific *authorsRow* object using the primary key value. The *authorsRow* object contains each of the individual fields as properties.

Figure 11-8 shows the *AuthsDataSet* class structure as seen in the Visual Studio .NET Object Viewer.

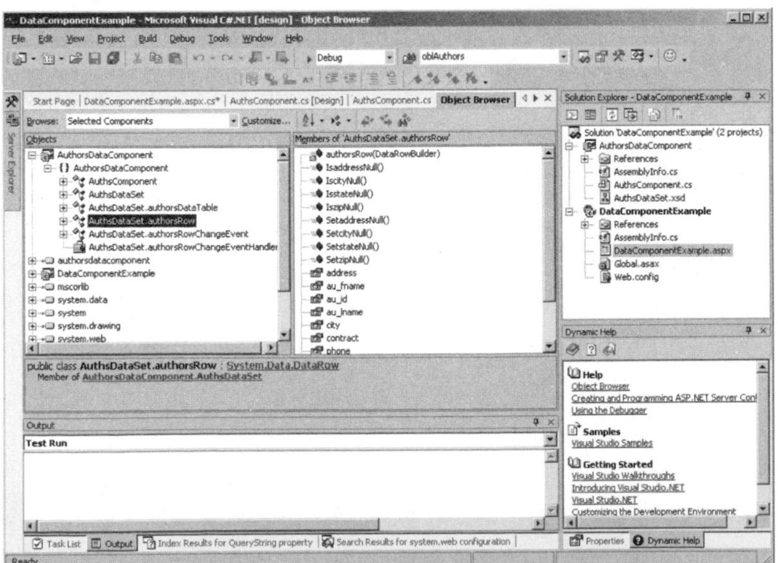

Figure 11-8 The structure of the *AuthsDataSet* class, which contains the *authorsRow* object, which in turn shows all the individual fields as properties

Using this component, the logic to update the *DataSet* and send it to the data component becomes quite simple:

```
private void SaveChanges()
{
    // Retrieve the dataset from the Session object.
    AuthsDataSet ds = (AuthsDataSet)Session["MyDataSet"];
    // Find the row and make changes.
    AuthsDataSet.authorsRow rowToChange =
        ds.authors.FindByau_id(ObjectList1.Selection["au_id"]);
    rowToChange.au_fname = TextBox1.Text;
    rowToChange.au_lname = TextBox2.Text;

    // Call the UpdateAuths method of data component.
    // Pass it the dataset so that it can update the database.
    if (myDataComp.UpdateAuths(ds))
        Label3.Text = "Record Updated";
    else
        Label3.Text = "ERROR: Could not update record";

    Label3.Visible = true;
    Command1.Visible = false;
    Command2.Visible = true;
    Command2.Text = "Back";
}
```

The application saves the *AuthsDataSet* object instance that we used to bind the ObjectList control in the *BindList* method's *Session* object to ensure that the *DataSet* persists across client requests. Then the runtime generates the markup for *Form2* and sends it to the client browser. After you've finished editing, the client posts back to the server, where the runtime instantiates the classes of the mobile Web Forms page once more. In the *SaveChanges* method, the code retrieves the same data that the user viewed and edited from the *Session* object and updates that data to reflect the user's changes.

Learning More About ADO.NET

This chapter has given you the briefest of introductions to ADO.NET and the ways in which you might use it in your mobile applications. Needless to say, ADO.NET and the Visual Studio .NET Database Tools possess far more capabilities than those described here. For more information about programming with ADO.NET and programming data components, consult the documentation and tutorials installed with Visual Studio .NET.

12

State Management

When you build dynamic Web applications, you usually need a mechanism to store information between client requests. Unfortunately, HTTP is effectively stateless, which means you must maintain state in some other way. In the past, developers often used cookies to track—and thus identify—a user with a session ID and to reconcile information stored on the server to that user. For example, Active Server Pages (ASP) used cookies to track users and stored information relevant to each user in a *Session* object. Although ASP's use of cookies was a powerful method for maintaining state, it isn't always appropriate with wireless devices because many of them don't support cookies.

On the other hand, Microsoft ASP.NET offers a range of mechanisms for maintaining state, some of them built on the foundations of ASP. In this chapter, you'll learn about four significant techniques ASP.NET offers for preserving state:

- **Session state** Allows you to maintain the variables and objects for a client over the course of multiple requests and responses.
- **Hidden variables** Allow you to persist objects between server round-trips by posting the data to the client as hidden fields.
- ***ViewState*** Allows you to maintain the values of a mobile Web Forms page on the server. The runtime stores this information in an instance of the *System.Web.UI.StateBag* class, which is itself stored within the Session. However, as you'll learn later in this chapter, in the section "*ViewState*," the server sends some information to the client.
- **Application state** Allows you to maintain the variables and objects of an application over multiple requests by multiple clients.

The first three of these techniques require that the server be able to identify the client so that it can track multiple request-response interactions between the server and the same client. This requires that some kind of unique token is sent to the client with each server response, which the client then returns to the server with its next request. With regular desktop browsers, this is usually done using HTTP cookies, but many small mobile devices do not support cookies. ASP.NET uses *munged URLs* for clients that don't support cookies. Munged URLs are URLs that the runtime modifies to contain a unique session ID. We'll discuss munged URLs later in this chapter, in the section "Using Munged URLs."

Session State

HTTP does provide a mechanism for maintaining persistent connections that allow you to identify and maintain user information. This mechanism involves using keep-alive messages to proxy servers. However, the technique is prone to error and has poor support. Therefore, as we mentioned, the HTTP protocol is effectively stateless—that is, it provides no mechanism for identifying or maintaining sessions between a Web server and a client.

Microsoft addressed this problem in ASP by providing a *Session* object that allowed you to uniquely identify a user and store information specific to his or her interactions with a Web server. ASP.NET offers an updated and improved version of the *Session* object. This object allows you to perform the following tasks:

- Identify a user through a unique session ID
- Store information specific to a user's session
- Manage a session's lifetime through event handler methods
- Release session data after a specified time-out

The ASP.NET session management facility also offers two particularly useful benefits for enterprise applications. The first of these benefits is a session state that you can maintain on a separate machine, which makes the facility suitable for deployment in multiple-machine and multiple-process scenarios. In a Web farm, the different incoming requests from a client can be processed on any machine in the Web Farm, which may be a different machine from the one that processed the previous request from the same client. If the session state is maintained on a specific machine, session is maintained regardless of which machine in the Web farm processes the request. The second benefit is the ability to store session state in a Microsoft SQL Server database. This separation provides a scalable solution and enables you to recover session state in the event of a system crash or a restart of IIS. In this chapter, we'll use the default configuration, which is to store session state on the same machine that handles the initial request from the client. For details of configuring your application to store session state on a specific machine, or in SQL Server, refer to the .NET Framework SDK documentation.

In ASP.NET, the *Session* object is a generic term for the *System.Web.SessionState.HttpSessionState* class object, which is constructed for every client session. The *Session* property of the *System.Web.HttpApplication* class (the parent class of the Global.asax page) and the *Session* property of the *MobilePage* class (the parent class of your mobile Web Forms page) both give access to the *Session* object. Table 12-1 shows the methods and properties of the *Session* object that you'll use most frequently.

Table 12-1 Common Methods and Properties of the *Session* Object

Name	Description
Methods	
Abandon	Abandons the current session.
Add	Adds an item to the session state.
Clear	Clears the session state, but doesn't abandon the current session.
Remove	Removes an object from the current session state.
RemoveAll	Removes all items from the current session state.
RemoveAt	Removes an item at a given index from the current session state.
Properties	
Count	Returns the number of items in the current session state.
IsCookieless	Returns a Boolean value that indicates whether the session is cookieless. (You'll learn about cookieless sessions later in this section.)
IsNewSession	Returns a Boolean value that indicates whether this request is the first of the session.
IsReadOnly	Returns a Boolean value that indicates whether the session is read-only.
IsSynchronized	Returns a Boolean value that indicates whether the session is thread-safe.
Item	Gets or sets individual session values. This is the indexer of the collection of items in the *Session* object, so you use this item by addressing items directly, as in this example: *Session["key-name"]=value; or Session[index]=value;*
Keys	Returns all the keys from the current *Session* object.

Using the *Session* Object

Typically, you'll manipulate the *Session* object either in the code-behind module of your application's Global.asax file or in the code-behind module of your mobile Web Forms page. Like mobile Web Forms pages, the Global.asax file supports a code-behind module. This module follows the naming convention Global.asax.*extension*, where *extension* indicates the programming language used. For example, you'd name a C# code-behind module Global.asax.cs.

The code in Listing 12-1 demonstrates two approaches for adding state data to the *Session* object. First, we use an indexer with a key of *UserStartTime* to add a string representing the user's session start time to the *Session* object. Second, we use the *Session.Add* method to define an entry with the key *HelpAccess*, which has an initial value of *false*.

```
using System;
using System.Collections;
using System.Web;
using System.Web.SessionState;

namespace MSPress.MobWeb.SessEx
{
    public class Global : System.Web.HttpApplication
    {
        protected void Session_Start(Object sender, EventArgs e)
        {
            Session["UserStartTime"]=DateTime.Now.ToLongTimeString();
            Boolean HelpAccess=false;
            Session.Add("HelpAccess",HelpAccess);
        }
    }
}
```

Listing 12-1 Global.asax.cs file for the SessionObjectExample project

The Global.asax file that references the code-behind module in Listing 12-1 consists of a single line containing just an @ *Application* directive:

```
<%@ Application Codebehind="Global.asax.cs"
    Inherits="MSPress.MobWeb.SessEx.Global" %>
```

The mobile Web Forms page shown in Listing 12-2 includes two Form controls. On *Form1*, there is a Command button and a Label named *Label1*. The *Text* property of *Label1* is not set here—it is set by code in the code-behind module (shown in Listing 12-3). On *Form2*, there are only two Label controls. One of these labels signifies that this is the Help page. The other Label control is blank—the runtime will assign its value in the code-behind module.

```
<%@ Register TagPrefix="mobile" Namespace="System.Web.UI.MobileControls"
    Assembly="System.Web.Mobile" %>
<%@ Page language="c#" Codebehind="MobileWebForm1.aspx.cs"
    Inherits="MSPress.MobWeb.SessEx.MobileWebForm1" %>

<mobile:Form id="Form1" runat="server">
    <mobile:Label id="Label1" runat="server"/>
    <mobile:Command id="Command1" runat="server">Go To Help</mobile:Command>
</mobile:Form>
<mobile:Form id="Form2" runat="server">
<mobile:Label id="Label2" runat="server">
       This is a help page.
    </mobile:Label>
    <mobile:Label id="Label3" runat="server"></mobile:Label>
</mobile:Form>
```

Listing 12-2 MobileWebForm1.aspx of the SessionObjectExample project

```
using System;
using System.Web.Mobile;
using System.Web.SessionState;

namespace MSPress.MobWeb.SessEx
{
    public class MobileWebForm1 : System.Web.UI.MobileControls.MobilePage
    {
        protected System.Web.UI.MobileControls.Label Label1;
        protected System.Web.UI.MobileControls.Label Label3;
        protected System.Web.UI.MobileControls.Command Command1;
        protected System.Web.UI.MobileControls.Form Form1;
        protected System.Web.UI.MobileControls.Form Form2;

        override protected void OnInit(EventArgs e)
        {
            InitializeComponent();
            base.OnInit(e);
        }

        private void InitializeComponent()
        {
            this.Load += new System.EventHandler(this.Page_Load);
            this.Command1.Click += new
                System.EventHandler(this.Command1_OnClick);
        }
```

Listing 12-3 MobileWebForm1.aspx.cs of the SessionObjectExample project

```
        private void Page_Load(object sender, System.EventArgs e)
        {
            Label1.Text = "Help accessed: ";
            Label1.Text += Session["HelpAccess"].ToString();
        }

        private void Command1_OnClick(object sender, System.EventArgs e)
        {
            //Switch to the Help form, set the flag in Session object
            Session["HelpAccess"] = true;
            Label3.Text = "Help accessed: ";
            Label3.Text += Session["HelpAccess"].ToString();
            ActiveForm = Form2;
        }
    }
}
```

When this simple application executes, the *HelpAccess* flag in the *Session* object is initialized as *false* in Global.asax.cs. When the Web Form is displayed, the code in the *Page_Load* method sets the label on *Form1* to display the current value of the *HelpAccess* flag. (The message is "Help accessed: False.") The server application sends the rendering for *Form1* to the client, and then terminates.

When the user clicks the Command control labeled Go To Help, the client browser posts back to the server, and during the processing of this request, the *Command1_Click* event handler in the code-behind module executes, fetches the *HelpAccess* item from the *Session* object and sets it to *true,* also setting the text of *Label3* to reflect this state. The *HelpAccess* item was persisted in the *Session* object between the end of the processing of the initial client request and the start of the processing of the next request that resulted from the user clicking the Command button.

Working with Cookies

ASP.NET identifies a session by setting a session ID in an HTTP cookie, which passes between the client and the Web server with each request and response. ASP.NET uses the session ID, which it parses from the cookie, to identify and then restore state information from the *Session* object. The session ID is the only way ASP.NET can identify a session. Therefore, it's crucial that the session ID is unique as well as inaccessible to malicious third parties. ASP.NET ensures this by using a random encryption key (changed each time the Web server restarts) and a 32-bit session ID mixed with random data that it then encrypts to create a 16-bit cookie string. This process ensures that each session ID has a unique value and prevents hackers from guessing the algorithm that ASP.NET uses to crcatc thc IDs.

Cookies provide an invaluable way for Web servers to identify wired clients such as HTML desktop browsers. However, the potential of cookies is limited with regard to applications for wireless clients. This is because many wireless devices, including some WAP and i-mode devices, don't support cookies. If you know that your target devices support cookies or that a proxy supports them on the client's behalf, as is the case with some WAP gateways, cookies provide an excellent way to track and identify sessions. However, if you think that devices that don't support cookies will access your application, you should disable the use of cookies and use munged URLs instead. We'll discuss munged URLs in the next section.

> **Note** NTT DoCoMo (the Japanese mobile communications company) classifies i-mode sites as either official (in other words, sanctioned by NTT DoCoMo) or unofficial. NTT DoCoMo makes the unique ID of each i-mode handset available to the developers of official sites. The developer can use this ID in place of a cookie to track a session on the server. No such mechanism exists for unofficial sites. The WAP 2.0 specifications offer a number of ways to work with sessions and user identification—for example, by providing a unique client ID. You can read these specifications at *http://www.wapforum.org/what/technical.htm*.

Using Munged URLs

You can use munged URLs to pass a session ID between the client and server, rather than using a cookie. As we mentioned, a munged URL is a URL that contains a session ID, such as *http://microsoft.com/myapp/(dcdb0uvhclb2b145ukpyrr55)/index.aspx*

When the Web server receives the request, it parses the session ID from the munged URL. The runtime then uses the session ID the same way it would use a session ID obtained from a cookie.

Earlier you learned that cookies are the default method of passing the session ID between the client and server. However, the runtime doesn't automatically use munged URLs if the client doesn't support cookies. Instead, you must explicitly disable cookies to make the runtime use munged URLs.

You can disable cookies quite simply by setting the *cookieless* attribute of the *sessionState* element within the Web.config file. The following code fragment shows how you can disable cookie use in the Web.config file.

```
<!-- configuration details -->
<sessionState
    mode="inProc"
    stateConnectionString="tcpip=127.0.0.1:42424"
    sqlConnectionString="data source=127.0.0.1;user id=sa;password="
    cookieless="true"
    timeout="20"
/>
<!-- more configuration details -->
```

Note that this code fragment is taken from a standard Web.config file, and it includes lines that have meaning only if you are not storing session state on the current machine. The *stateConnectionString* line is used if you are storing session state on a different machine (the mode attribute is set to StateServer), and the *sqlConnectionString* line is used only if you are storing session state in SQL Server (mode is set to SQLServer). The *timeout* attribute sets the time in minutes that a session can remain idle before the session expires; this is discussed further in the section titled "*ViewState*," later in this chapter.

You can test whether a session is cookieless by checking the value of the read-only *IsCookieless* property of the *Session* object, like so:

```
if (Session.IsCookieless)
{
    ⋮
}
```

To Cookie or Not to Cookie

Considering what you've learned about mobile devices and cookie support, you might be wondering why you should bother using cookies at all and what's stopping you from using munged URLs universally. In fact, there are several reasons munged URLs aren't always the ideal solution for passing a session ID.

First, some browsers can experience difficulties dealing with relative URLs after they have been redirected to a munged URL. For example, if a browser initially requests *http://servername/a.aspx* and the application is configured to be cookieless, the runtime redirects the client to a URL similar to *http://servername/(xyz123)/a.aspx*. If the application subsequently accesses a page at the relative URL *b.aspx*, the browser makes a request for the URL *http://servername/b.aspx*, failing to use the munged URL, which includes the session identifier. The standard mobile controls allow for this restriction and always render relative URLs as properly rooted URLs, so a reference to *b.aspx* is rendered as */(xyz123)/b.aspx* in the markup sent to the client. However, authors of custom mobile controls should be aware of this issue. The *MobilePage* class and *DeviceAdapter* base classes include helper methods that allow you to convert URLs to rooted URLs that take account of cookieless operations.

Second, ASP supports cookies but not munged URLs. Therefore, when backward compatibility is an issue, munged URLs aren't an acceptable solution. Although a developer writing an ASP application commonly included a session ID in a URL, he or she had to append the session ID to the URL to form a query string. The third disadvantage of using munged URLs is that many wireless browsers support URL lengths much shorter than those supported by desktop browsers. Thus, an application in a deeply nested hierarchy might require URLs with lengths that exceed what is supported by some browsers.

Hidden Variables

Sometimes you might want to pass small amounts of information between Web pages without using session state. For example, suppose you need to collect information from a multipart form that the user fills in. In HTML, you'd pass the information from one page to another using *input* tags with a *type* value of *hidden*. But in WML, you'd set variables in the browser's cache and then post all their values to the server when the user completed the forms. The *MobilePage* class's *HiddenVariables* property provides this type of functionality. This property allows you to store name-value pairs, which the runtime then passes back and forth between the server and the client as hidden fields.

You need to know when to use the *Session* object to store information and when to use the *HiddenVariables* property. In fact, you don't need to use the *HiddenVariables* property to store information. This property just offers an alternative way to retain information between requests and responses; you can easily use the *Session* object in its place. Furthermore, you should use *HiddenVariables* only for small amounts of information. There are a number of reasons for this, including the following:

- Many mobile devices have limited bandwidth. You don't need to use this bandwidth when you can easily store data on the server in the *Session* object.
- WAP devices support compiled deck sizes of only up to approximately 1.4 KB. (A *deck* is the outermost element of a file of WML content. Each WML file must support exactly one deck.)

Listings 12-4 and 12-5 show code that uses the *HiddenVariables* property to pass information between forms in a multipart form. The user accesses the first form and enters his or her name. The runtime then adds this information to the *HiddenVariables* collection, and *Form2* activates. The user then enters his or her e-mail address, which the runtime also adds to the *HiddenVariables* collection. Finally, *Form3* activates, causing data contained within the *HiddenVariables* collection to populate the TextView control and be displayed to the user.

> **Note** The WAP gateway compiles WML files before they arrive at the WML browser. The WML browser uses these compiled files instead of the raw WML files stored on the Web server. When you use ASP.NET, the runtime generates uncompiled WML code, which it then sends to the WAP gateway. The WAP gateway in turn compiles the WML and forwards it to the WML browser on the client.

```
<%@ Register TagPrefix="mobile"
    Namespace="System.Web.UI.MobileControls"
    Assembly="System.Web.Mobile" %>
<%@ Page language="c#" Codebehind="MobileWebForm1.aspx.cs"
    Inherits="MSPress.MobWeb.HidVarEx.MobileWebForm1"
    AutoEventWireup="false" %>

<mobile:Form id="Form1" runat="server">
    <mobile:Label id="Label2" runat="server">Your name:</mobile:Label>
    <mobile:TextBox id="TextBoxName" runat="server"></mobile:TextBox>
    <mobile:Command id="Command1" runat="server">
        Submit
    </mobile:Command>
</mobile:Form>

<mobile:Form id="Form2" runat="server">
    <mobile:Label id="Label1" runat="server">
        Your e-mail:
    </mobile:Label>
    <mobile:TextBox id="TextBoxEmail" runat="server"/>
    <mobile:Command id="Command2" runat="server">
        Submit
    </mobile:Command>
</mobile:Form>

<mobile:Form id="Form3" runat="server">
    <mobile:TextView id="TextView1" runat="server">
        TextView
    </mobile:TextView>
</mobile:Form>
```

Listing 12-4 MobileWebForm1.aspx from the HiddenVariablesExample project

```
using System;
using System.Collections;
using System.Web;
using System.Web.Mobile;
using System.Web.SessionState;

namespace MSPress.MobWeb.HidVarEx
{
    public class MobileWebForm1 : System.Web.UI.MobileControls.MobilePage
    {
        protected System.Web.UI.MobileControls.Form Form2;
        protected System.Web.UI.MobileControls.Command Command1;
        protected System.Web.UI.MobileControls.Command Command2;
        protected System.Web.UI.MobileControls.Form Form3;
        protected System.Web.UI.MobileControls.TextView TextView1;
        protected System.Web.UI.MobileControls.TextBox TextBoxName;
        protected System.Web.UI.MobileControls.TextBox TextBoxEmail;
        protected System.Web.UI.MobileControls.Form Form1;

        public MobileWebForm1()
        {
            Page.Init += new System.EventHandler(Page_Init);
        }

        private void Page_Init(object sender, EventArgs e)
        {
            InitializeComponent();
        }

        private void InitializeComponent()
        {
            this.Command1.Click +=
                new System.EventHandler(this.Command1_Click);
            this.Command2.Click +=
                new System.EventHandler(this.Command2_Click);
            this.Form3.Activate +=
                new System.EventHandler(this.Form3_Activate);
        }

        private void Command1_Click(object sender, System.EventArgs e)
        {
            HiddenVariables.Add(TextBoxName.ID,TextBoxName.Text);
            this.ActiveForm=Form2;
        }
```

Listing 12-5 The code-behind file MobileWebForm1.aspx.cs from the HiddenVariablesExample project

```
        private void Command2_Click(object sender, System.EventArgs e)
        {
            HiddenVariables.Add(TextBoxEmail.ID,TextBoxEmail.Text);
            this.ActiveForm=Form3;
        }

        private void Form3_Activate(object sender, System.EventArgs e)
        {
            String FormData="";
            foreach (Object o in HiddenVariables.Keys)
            {
                FormData+=o.ToString()+" "+HiddenVariables[o]+"<br>";
            }
            TextView1.Text=FormData;
        }
    }
}
```

Figure 12-1 shows how this code's output looks when viewed in the Nokia simulator.

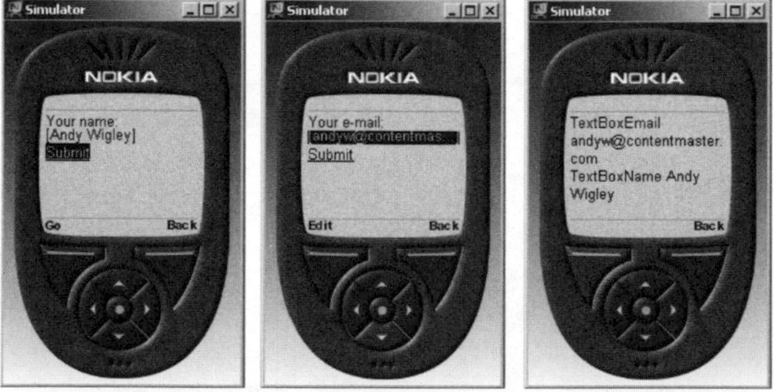

Figure 12-1 Output of the HiddenVariablesExample project displayed in the Nokia simulator

ViewState

ASP.NET gives the user the impression that the runtime maintains the state of pages over several server round-trips. The pages don't really exist over multiple requests and responses; instead, the runtime saves the properties of the page and each server control's *ViewState* to an instance of the *StateBag* class. When the user makes a request, the runtime automatically reconstructs the page using the property values persisted in the *StateBag* instance.

As a developer, you might find the automatic reconstruction of a page's state a useful feature. For example, if you define a property in your code-behind class, that property isn't automatically saved and restored each time the page is torn down and then reconstructed on the next request. If you set this property in code on one request, you might want to persist this value across server round-trips. You could add the property to the Session or even persist it by using hidden variables. However, if you use the *ViewState* property of the *MobilePage* class to maintain the property's value, the runtime will automatically save and restore that value on your behalf.

The *ViewState* property has the scope of the current *MobilePage* object (the current .aspx file plus any code-behind module). If your application moves from one *MobilePage* object to another, either by sending an HTTP redirect to the client (using *MobilePage.Response.Redirect("url")*) or by transferring control to another page at the server (using *MobilePage.Server.Transfer("url")*), in the new mobile page you can't retrieve properties and objects that were stored in *ViewState* in the first *MobilePage* object. Use the *Session* or *Application* objects to transfer objects between pages; we discuss the *Application* object in the next section.

Listing 12-6 shows how you might save a property in *ViewState* and then retrieve it later.

```
using System;
using System.Web;
using System.Web.Mobile;
using System.Web.UI.MobileControls;
using System.Web.UI;

public class MobileWebForm1 : System.Web.UI.MobileControls.MobilePage
{
    protected System.Web.UI.MobileControls.Command Command1;
    protected System.Web.UI.MobileControls.Label Label1;

    // MyMessage property get and set accessors
    // using the ViewState property
    public String MyMessage
    {
        get
        {
            // Explicit cast to String
            return (String) ViewState["MyMessage"];
        }
        set
        {
```

Listing 12-6 Using the *ViewState* property

```
            ViewState["MyMessage"]=value;
        }
    }

    private void Command1_Click(object sender, System.EventArgs e)
    {
        // Consume the persisted property.
        Label1.Text=this.MyMessage;
    }
}
```

By default, mobile pages and server controls have *ViewState* enabled. However, you can override this behavior and enable or disable a page or individual controls within that page. If you disable *ViewState* for a control that contains other controls, such as the Panel control, all child controls automatically will have their *ViewState* disabled.

To disable the *ViewState* of an individual control, you must set that control's *EnableViewState* property to *False*, either in code or in server control syntax, as the following code illustrates:

```
<mobile:Label id="Label1" runat="server" EnableViewState="False"/>
```

To disable the *ViewState* of an entire page, you can use the *MobilePage.ViewState* property in code or use the *EnableViewState* attribute of *@ Page* directive within the mobile page .aspx file, as shown here:

```
<%@ Page language="c#" Codebehind="MobileWebForm1.aspx.cs"
    Inherits="MobileWebForm1" EnableViewState="False" %>
```

When writing ASP.NET applications for wired clients, you'll often want to disable the *ViewState* to enhance your application's speed. The runtime distributes *ViewState* information to the client in a way that's similar to the hidden variables you learned about earlier, and sending large amounts of data between the client and server places a large overhead on the network. However, mobile applications are different. For applications built with the ASP.NET Mobile Controls, Microsoft changed the implementation of *ViewState* because of the extreme bandwidth limitations placed on those clients. For mobile Web applications, the runtime saves *ViewState* information in the *Session* object and *doesn't* send that information to the client; it sends the client only an identifier.

This unique approach to *ViewState* management means that you can forgo the performance-related considerations a developer working with standard ASP.NET would have. However, you do have to consider the effect of using the *Session* object to maintain *ViewState*—something that doesn't concern a developer of nonmobile applications.

When using the *Session* object to store *ViewState,* you have two important considerations. First, sessions can expire, which means that you can lose your *ViewState* information. The number of minutes allowed to elapse before a response is received from a client is set by the *timeout* attribute of the *sessionState* element in the application's Web.config file, as shown in the following code. (Twenty minutes is the default.)

```
<configuration>
    <system.web>
        <sessionState
            mode="inProc"
            cookieless="true"
            timeout="20"
        />
    </system.web>
</configuration>
```

If a user posts back data after a session expires, the runtime calls the page's *OnViewStateExpire* event handler method. By default, this method throws an exception; however, you can override this method in your code-behind class to implement different behavior. Your application could display a friendly page informing the user that the session has timed out and perhaps redirecting the user to a menu page in your application. In some circumstances, you could attempt recovery of the *ViewState* information manually by calling the *LoadViewState* method of the *MobilePage* object.

The second consideration is that the page displayed on the client and the current state of the session information held on the server can fall out of sync. This can occur when a user uses a Back feature on the browser to return to a page viewed previously—for instance, by clicking a Back button. For example, imagine that a user goes to the first page of an application and then clicks a link to go to the second page. If the user then navigates backward to the first page, the user views the first page while the server holds session data for the application's second page. The ASP.NET mobile controls overcome this issue by maintaining a small history of *ViewState* information in the user's session. When the user posts back to the server from the first page in the scenario just described (when the server "thinks" the user is on the second page), the runtime reconciles the identifier received from the client with the identifier of the *ViewState* information to pull the correct *ViewState* out of the history. You can configure the size of the *ViewState* history, meaning that you can modify it to suit your application. The default history size is 6. To change the history size, use the *sessionStateHistorySize* attribute of the *mobileControls* element within the Web.config file, as the following code shows.

```
<configuration>
    <system.web>
        <mobileControls sessionStateHistorySize="10"/>
    <system.web>
</configuration>
```

All items that use the *Session* object have to deal with the issues of state expiration; however, the automatic management that ASP.NET provides effectively hides these issues from you. The simplest way to avoid unforeseen problems is to ensure that you have a session expiration time and state history size appropriate to your application. For example, it's foolish to set a session expiration time of 1 minute for a shopping application because users often flit between applications or think about a product before making a purchase. Therefore, sessions should reflect your users' pace of browsing through pages, and the time-out should occur after a more realistic time frame, such as 20 minutes. In addition, the user might make significant use of the history stack when browsing through pages in this type of application. You should ensure that you increase the session state history size to reflect this pattern.

Application State

In ASP.NET, an *application* is the total of all the files that the runtime can invoke or run within the scope of a virtual directory and all its subdirectories. At times, you might want to instantiate variables and objects that have scope at an application level rather than at a session level. The *System.Web.HttpApplicationState* class allows you to do this. The *Application* object is the generic term for the instance of this class for your application, which is exposed through the *Application* property of the *System.Web.HttpApplication* class (the parent class of the Global.asax page) and the *Application* property of the *MobilePage* class (the parent class of your mobile Web Forms page).

The *Application* object represents the ASP.NET application itself and exists as soon as any client makes the first request for a file from the given virtual directory. Because the *Application* object contains methods and properties similar to those of the *Session* object, you use the *Application* object in a similar way. However, unlike session information, any information the *Application* object stores persists between the requests of various users and remains available to all users of the application. The *Application* object exists in the server's memory until the Web server stops or until you modify or refresh the Global.asax file.

Using Application State in Global.asax

You can manipulate information in application state in your program code, and in the Global.asax file, which always resides at the root of a virtual directory. For the moment, you'll use Global.asax to implement event handlers associated with application state, but remember that you can also use this file to store other information such as session state, as described earlier.

You define application state data within the code-behind module of Global.asax by writing code for the two event handler methods, *Application_Start* and *Application_End*. The *Application_Start* event fires the first time any client accesses your application after IIS has started, or the first time a client accesses your application after the Global.asax file has been updated. The *Application_End* event fires when the Global.asax file has been updated; the runtime detects that the file has been changed and effectively reboots the application, so the *Application_End* event fires in any instances of this application that are running.

The *Application* object contains a dictionary-like collection to which you add objects identified by a string key. Listing 12-7 shows how you can define a global variable and add it to the *Application* object in the Global.asax.cs file.

```
using System;
using System.Collections;
using System.ComponentModel;
using System.Web;

namespace MSPress.MobWeb.AppObjEx
{
    public class Global : System.Web.HttpApplication
    {
        protected void Application_Start(Object sender, EventArgs e)
        {
            // Declare and assign a value to the global variable.
            String AppStartTime = DateTime.Now.ToLongTimeString();
            // Add the global variable to the Application object.
            Application["AppStartTime"] = AppStartTime;
        }
    }
}
```

Listing 12-7 Global.asax.cs of the ApplicationObjectExample project

The Global.asax file that references the code-behind module in Listing 12-7 consists of a single line containing just an *@ Application* directive:

```
<%@ Application Codebehind="Global.asax.cs"
    Inherits="MSPress.MobWeb.AppStateEx.Global" %>
```

You can access the global variable by name through the *Application* object. Listing 12-8 illustrates how you can consume the global variable from the mobile Web Forms page of a project named ApplicationObjectExample.

```
using System;
using System.Collections;
using System.Web;
using System.Web.Mobile;
using System.Web.SessionState;

namespace MSPress.MobWeb.AppObjEx
{
    public class MobileWebForm1 : System.Web.UI.MobileControls.MobilePage
    {
        protected System.Web.UI.MobileControls.Label Label1;
        protected System.Web.UI.MobileControls.Form Form1;

        override protected void OnInit(EventArgs e)
        {
            InitializeComponent();
            base.OnInit(e);
        }

        private void InitializeComponent()
        {
            this.Load += new System.EventHandler(this.Page_Load);
        }

        private void Page_Load(object sender, System.EventArgs e)
        {
            Label1.Text = "Application started at: "
                + (Application["AppStartTime"]).ToString();
        }
    }
}
```

Listing 12-8 MobileWebForm1.aspx.cs of the ApplicationObjectExample project

Listing 12-9 shows the .aspx file for the ApplicationObjectExample project.

```
<%@ Register TagPrefix="mobile"
    Namespace="System.Web.UI.MobileControls"
    Assembly="System.Web.Mobile" %>
<%@ Page language="c#" Codebehind="MobileWebForm1.aspx.cs"
```

Listing 12-9 MobileWebForm1.aspx of the ApplicationObjectExample project

```
    Inherits="MSPress.MobWeb.AppObjEx.MobileWebForm1" %>

<mobile:Form id="Form1" runat="server">
    <mobile:Label id="Label1" runat="server">Label</mobile:Label>
</mobile:Form>
```

> **Note** Internally, the *Application* object is a collection of named items, similar in usage to the *Session* object. Methods of the *HttpApplicationState* class allow you to access and manipulate this collection, but by far the easiest way is to use the collection's built-in indexer to address objects in the collection directly, either by name, or by numeric index; for C#, the syntax is *Application["itemName"]* or *Application[*index*]*. Listing 12-8 shows how you can access a global variable from the *Application* object's collection using the code *Application["AppStartTime"]*. The *HttpApplicationState* object also has the *Contents* property, provided for backward compatibility with ASP. This property returns a reference to the *HttpApplicationState* object—in other words, to itself. Therefore, you can also access the value of the variable by using the syntax *Application.Contents["AppStartTime"]*, which is useful if you are porting old ASP code to ASP.NET.

When a user first requests the mobile Web Forms page, the runtime assigns the value of the current time to the global variable *AppStartTime*. Figure 12-2 illustrates how the value of this variable doesn't change as the runtime makes subsequent requests for the mobile Web Forms page.

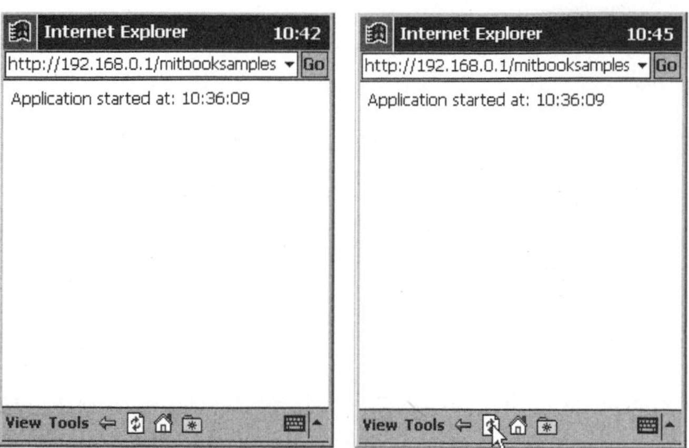

Figure 12-2 The start time of an application stored as a global variable

Whenever an instance of an application changes application state information, the runtime changes the information for all the application's users. This is demonstrated in Listings 12-10, 12-11, and 12-12, which together make up an application named SharedApplicationStateExample. In Listing 12-10, the *Application_Start* event handler creates a global variable in the *Application* object that represents a user's name.

```
using System;
using System.Collections;
using System.ComponentModel;
using System.Web;
using System.Web.SessionState;

namespace MSPress.MobWeb.SharedApplicationStateExample
{
    public class Global : System.Web.HttpApplication
    {
        protected void Application_Start(Object sender, EventArgs e)
        {
            Application["LastUser"]="Nobody";
        }
    }
}
```

Listing 12-10 Global.asax.cs file for the SharedApplicationStateExample project

The Global.asax file consists of the following code:

```
<%@ Application Codebehind="Global.asax.cs"
    Inherits="MSPress.MobWeb.SharedApplicationStateExample.Global" %>
```

The mobile Web Forms page that you use in this application consists of two forms. The first form prompts the user for his or her name, which the user then sends to the server by clicking the Command control. The second form consists of a label that displays the name of the last user to access the application.

```
<%@ Register TagPrefix="mobile"
    Namespace="System.Web.UI.MobileControls"
    Assembly="System.Web.Mobile" %>
<%@ Page language="c#" Codebehind="MobileWebForm1.aspx.cs"
    Inherits="MSPress.MobWeb.SharedApplicationStateExample.MobileWebForm1" %>
```

Listing 12-11 MobileWebForm1.aspx file for the SharedApplicationStateExample project

```
<mobile:Form id="Form1" runat="server">
    <mobile:TextBox id="TextBox1" runat="server"></mobile:TextBox>
    <mobile:Command id="Command1" runat="server">Enter</mobile:Command>
</mobile:Form>

<mobile:Form id="Form2" runat="server">
    <mobile:Label id="Label1" runat="server">Label</mobile:Label>
</mobile:Form>
```

Listing 12-12 depicts the code-behind module.

```
using System;
using System.Collections;
using System.Web;
using System.Web.Mobile;
using System.Web.SessionState;

namespace MSPress.MobWeb.SharedApplicationStateExample
{
    public class MobileWebForm1 : System.Web.UI.MobileControls.MobilePage
    {
        protected System.Web.UI.MobileControls.Command Command1;
        protected System.Web.UI.MobileControls.TextBox TextBox1;
        protected System.Web.UI.MobileControls.Form Form2;
        protected System.Web.UI.MobileControls.Label Label1;


        override protected void OnInit(EventArgs e)
        {
            InitializeComponent();
            base.OnInit(e);
        }

        private void InitializeComponent()
        {
            Command1.Click += new System.EventHandler(this.Command1_Click);
        }

        private void Command1_Click(object sender, System.EventArgs e)
        {
            ActiveForm = Form2;
            Label1.Text = "Previous User: " +
                Application["LastUser"].ToString();
            Application["LastUser"] = TextBox1.Text;
        }
    }
}
```

Listing 12-12 Code-behind file MobileWebForm1.aspx.cs for the SharedApplicationStateExample project

When the application first runs, the code in the *Application_Start* method in Global.asax.cs sets *Application["LastUser"]* to the value *Nobody*. The user enters his or her name and clicks the button. This causes the application to execute the *Command1_Click* method, which sets the text of *Label1* to the value stored in *Application["LastUser"]* which is the name of the previous user (currently *Nobody)*, and then stores in *Application["LastUser"]* the name the user has just entered in *TextBox1*. When the application is run again by a new user, the same process happens, but this time the name of the previous user that the application displays in *Label1* is not *Nobody*, it's the name that the previous user entered. Figure 12-3 illustrates this process.

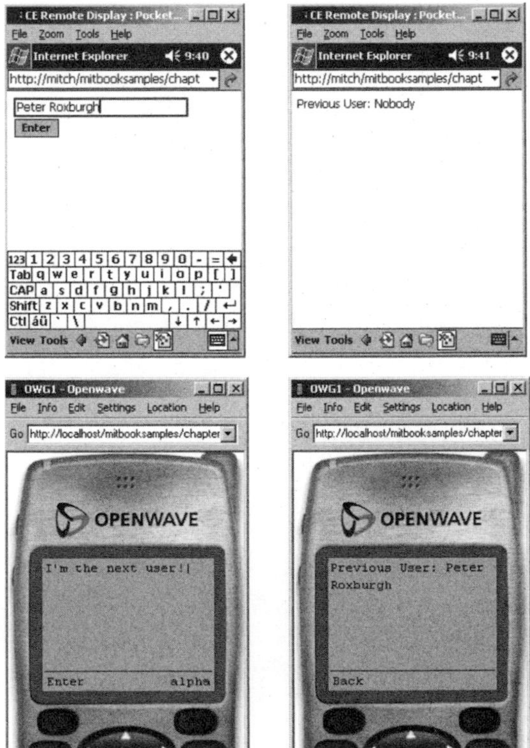

Figure 12-3 Displaying the previous user's name to the current user

The application object contains several methods for handling objects stored in collections. For full details about these methods, consult the ASP.NET documentation.

Things to Consider When Using Application State

At times, you might wonder whether to use session state or application state. Although application state allows you to build very powerful and flexible applications, there are several reasons you should use it with care.

First, information stored in application state is memory hungry. In other words, the application holds all application state information in memory and doesn't release the memory, even when a user exits an application. For example, you can easily make heavy demands on a server's memory by placing large datasets in application state. Second, all threads in a multithread application can access application data simultaneously because ASP.NET doesn't automatically lock resources. Therefore, if concurrent access from processes to some data stored in application scope could cause your application to fail, you should use the *Enter* and *Exit* methods of the *System.Threading.Monitor* .NET Framework class to ensure that a process wanting to update the data takes out an exclusive lock. (The C# *lock* statement is a quick way of doing the same thing.) Other than the obvious workload increase, this situation can easily affect scalability. This is because all the locks operate in a global context, meaning that the operating system blocks threads and could block all threads while waiting for a lock. Finally, unlike session state, application state doesn't persist across multiple-process or multiple-server environments. Therefore, application state is accessible only within the process in which you create it.

If you can't determine whether to use application state or session state, you should use session state. This will ensure that you avoid the problems we've just outlined.

today

13 Enhancing Application Performance

A compelling application is one that offers useful functionality in a way that's convenient and, one hopes, pleasurable to work with. The application should be intuitive and simple, requiring only enough user input to fulfill its function. This way, your application will more than reward your users' efforts, and they'll be happy to work with it again. Your application should perform well. No matter how cleverly designed your application is or how good its functionality is, if your application is slow, people won't like it.

In this chapter, we'll examine how to optimize the performance of your applications. We'll look at the programming and configuration techniques you can use to achieve the best performance, and we'll look at how to use Microsoft ASP.NET output caching, fragment caching, and data caching.

Programming and Configuration Techniques

You can optimize your application's throughput in a variety of ways. We'll now take a look at a number of different things you should consider; some or all of them will apply to your own mobile Web applications.

Turn Off Debug Support in Your Release Builds

The first technique for enhancing performance is to be sure to turn off debug support in your runtime builds. (It's easy to forget to disable this.) Remember that the runtime compiles each requested page using just-in-time compilers. If your application has debug support enabled, this can have a serious effect on response time. Here's how to ensure that debug support is disabled in the application's Web.config file:

```
<configuration>
  <system.web>
    ⋮
    <compilation debug="false"/>
    ⋮
  </system.web>
</configuration>
```

Disable *ViewState* If It's Not Required

ViewState enables the ASP.NET server controls to store all their property settings across HTTP requests. At the end of one request, the runtime stores the controls' property values in the *ViewState*. At the beginning of the next request, the runtime reinitializes the controls with values from the *ViewState*, thus restoring those controls to their state at the end of the previous HTTP request.

In many cases, this technique isn't necessary and wastes time. Consider a data bound List control. There's no point in this control saving its *ViewState* if the control is bound to its data source on every request. Saving the *ViewState* would just restore all the List control's properties from this state, only to have the runtime overwrite them again the next time the control is data bound.

To disable *ViewState* for a server control, set its *EnableViewState* property to *false*. Alternatively, you can disable *ViewState* for a whole page by setting the *EnableViewState* attribute of the *@ Page* directive to *false*:

```
<%@ Page EnableViewState="false" … %>
```

Disable Session State If It's Not Required

Your application can store data for a particular user and make it available throughout his or her session by using the *Session* object. If your application doesn't require this functionality, you should disable it completely. To disable session state for a whole page, set the *EnableSessionState* attribute of the *@ Page* directive to *false*:

```
<%@ Page EnableSessionState="false" %>
```

If a page requires access to variables stored in the *Session* object but doesn't create or modify them, set the value of the *EnableSessionState* attribute to *ReadOnly*. (We described the use of the *Session* object in Chapter 12.)

Cache Data in the *Application* Object

In many applications, you might have many Web clients running the same application, all accessing the same resources. An optimization technique that can yield real benefits is to open shared, read-only or infrequently modified resources in the *Application_Start* method in the Global.asax file and cache the data in the *Application* object. Each process servicing a client then accesses the data from there instead of retrieving it from the source again, which can benefit the performance of your application.

The following code in the Global.asax file uses the AuthsComponent data component that we developed in Chapter 11 to retrieve a *DataSet* object, which the code stores in the application state:

```
public void Application_Start()
{
    // Create the data component.
    AuthorsDataComponent.AuthsComponent myDataComp =
    new AuthorsDataComponent.AuthsComponent();

    // Use the data component to fetch a DataSet.
    AuthorsDataComponent.AuthsDataSet ds = myDataComp.AllAuthors;

    // Store the data source in the application state so that
    // the data source is available to all clients.
    Application["AuthsDataSet"] = ds;
}
```

Each request can then access the data source from the *Application* object in the *Page_Load* method, rather than fetch it from the database again:

```
void Page_Load(Object sender, EventArgs e)
{
    DataSet sourceDS = (DataSet)(Application["AuthsDataSet"]);
    ⋮
    List1.DataSource = sourceDS;
    List1.DataMember = "authors";
    ⋮
}
```

Use Custom Pagination with the List Controls

If you're loading large *DataSet* objects into the SelectList, List, and ObjectList controls, or the list contents require extensive computation time to build the row items, consider using custom pagination. (For a refresher on this technique, see Chapter 6.) The code supplies data to the control only when the control must be displayed, thus avoiding long delays during the initial load of a control.

Don't Perform Unnecessary Processing on Postback

Another optimization technique is to use the *MobilePage.IsPostBack* property to avoid unnecessary processing on a postback. You use the *IsPostBack* property to determine whether this is the first time the page is being displayed or whether it's loading as the result of a subsequent postback from the client. Often, the processing that the runtime must perform when the page first loads isn't required on subsequent loads. An example of this is binding a control to data.

Concatenate Strings Using *System.Text.StringBuilder*

You can also enhance your applications by concatenating string objects using *System.Text.StringBuilder.* If you use the addition operator (+) to concatenate string objects, the runtime must create a new *String* object to contain the result because strings are immutable. If your application performs a lot of string concatenation, it's much more efficient to use the *StringBuilder* object:

```
StringBuilder detailText = new StringBuilder();
detailText.Append("This block of text ");
detailText.Append("will be <b>displayed</b> in a ");
detailText.Append("TextView Control.");

TextView1.Text = detailText.ToString();
```

The performance benefits are particularly pronounced if you are concatenating large numbers of strings. In fact, in the example just shown, the performance advantage is negligible, but if your application needs to concatenate more than 9 or 10 different strings, the *StringBuilder* yields real performance benefits.

Optimize SQL Server Data Access

Using SQL-stored procedures for data access will help to optimize your mobile applications too. When you retrieve data from Microsoft SQL Server, it's much more efficient to compile stored procedures than ad hoc queries.

Using *SqlDataReader* or *OleDBDataReader* for data access can further optimize your applications. Use one of the DataReaders if you need just forward, read-only access to data retrieved from a database. Although using a DataReader provides better performance than using a *DataSet*, it doesn't support data updates.

Explicitly Declare Object Types in Visual Basic .NET

A final way you can help boost application performance is to explicitly declare data types when you're programming in Microsoft Visual Basic .NET. By default, ASP.NET doesn't enforce the explicit declaration of variable types. However, this flexibility has a performance cost. If possible, add the *Option Explicit* declaration at the head of your Visual Basic code-behind modules and other class modules. The *Option Strict* directive, which is even more stringent, permits you to set a variable to the value of a different type of variable only if there's no risk of truncation or loss of precision.

In your .aspx Web Forms page, you can enable *Option Strict* for any contained code by using the *Strict* attribute in the *@ Page* directive, as follows:

```
<%@ Page Language="VB" Strict="true" %>
```

Caching

ASP.NET provides three methods for caching that you can use to improve performance:

- **Output caching** The runtime caches the entire output of the page for a specific period of time.
- **Fragment caching** The runtime caches the output of a user control.
- **Data caching** Pages can use this dictionary-structured cache to store arbitrary objects across HTTP requests.

Let's take a look at each of these caching methods.

Using Output Caching

You can cache a page by using an *@ OutputCache* directive at the head of the mobile Web Forms page, as you see here:

```
<%@ OutputCache Duration="60" VaryByParam="none"%>
```

The *Duration* attribute specifies the number of seconds that IIS should cache the output of this page. The *VaryByParam* attribute is required but you disable it by setting it to *none*; we'll look at the use of this attribute in a moment.

With this statement placed at the top of the page, the runtime determines whether to send the cached version of the page or to regenerate the page by comparing the *HTTP_User_Agent* identification string. The *HTTP_User_Agent* identification string is sent in the HTTP headers with every request and identifies the type of browser that is on the client. Therefore, if a client requests a page and the runtime has a cached copy of the output for the same type of browser and it hasn't expired, the runtime serves that page from the cache instead of regenerating it. For example, if a device running Microsoft Internet Explorer for the Pocket PC requests a page, the runtime should cache the resulting output and return it only for other devices running Pocket Internet Explorer.

Listing 13-1 shows an example application that has output caching enabled.

```
<%@ OutputCache Duration="60" VaryByParam="none"%>
<%@ Register TagPrefix="mobile"
    Namespace="System.Web.UI.MobileControls"
    Assembly="System.Web.Mobile" %>
<%@ Page Inherits="System.Web.UI.MobileControls.MobilePage"
    Language="c#"%>

<html>
<head>
    <script language="c#" runat="server">
        public void Page_Load(Object sender, EventArgs e)
        {
            lblTime.Text = "Page Loaded at: " + DateTime.Now.ToLocalTime();
        }
    </script>
</head>

<body
<mobile:Form runat="server" id="frmMain">
    <mobile:Label id="lblTime" runat="server"/>
</mobile:Form>
</body>
</html>
```

Listing 13-1 Page with output caching enabled

When you run the application in Listing 13-1 from a browser and then refresh the display a few times or access it from another browser of the same type, the time displayed doesn't change until 60 seconds after the first access.

As we've said, by default the runtime makes the decision on whether to serve a cached copy of the page output by looking at the *HTTP_User_Agent* identification string of the request. You can change the default behavior using the *VaryByParam*, *VaryByHeader*, and *VaryByCustom* attributes of the *@ OutputCache* directive.

The *@ OutputCache* directive must include the *VaryByParam* attribute and can include the optional *VaryByHeader* and *VaryByCustom* attributes. These attributes have the following meanings:

- ***VaryByParam*** You use this mandatory attribute to specify one or more of the values that are posted back from the client to the server, either as a *POST* parameter or in the query string. If you've set *VaryByParam* to *none* (as in Listing 13-1), the runtime will cache only the initial *GET* request (because this has no POST parameters) or query string (unless the user explicitly enters the URL to fetch with a query string attached—that is, it ends with "?" followed by some data).

    In interactive mobile Web applications (the majority), your user typically enters some data, such as a search string or an item selected from a *SelectionList*, which is used in the server application to make a selection from data, and the selected data is sent back to the browser for display. You'll want to use *VaryByParam* to make sure that the output is cached based on the user's selections, so you'll enter the names of the POST parameters or query string variables that are used to postback the user's selection to the server. We'll look some more at this technique in the following section, "Using *VaryByParam* to Cache Based on User Input."

    To cache based on more than one parameter, separate the names with a semicolon, as shown here:

    ```
    <%@ OutputCache Duration="60" VaryByParam="selState;txtSearch" %>
    ```

    To make your cache selective based on every value specified in the query string or *POST* parameters rather than specific named items, specify an asterisk for the *VaryByParam* attribute:

    ```
    <%@ OutputCache Duration="45" VaryByParam="*" %>
    ```

- ***VaryByHeader*** This attribute enables you to cache based on an item in the HTTP headers. For example, to cache based on the *Accept-Language* header, specify the *OutputCache* directive this way:

    ```
    <%@ OutputCache Duration="60"
        VaryByHeader="Accept-Language"
        VaryByParam="none" %>
    ```

- ***VaryByCustom*** Use this attribute to vary caching based on the browser type (by using the special value *"browser")* or based on a custom string that you specify. By default, ASP.NET Mobile Controls automatically applies *VaryByCustom="browser"*, making all caching dependent on the type of browser that makes the request.

You can write custom cache selectors by specifying an arbitrary string for the *VaryByCustom* attribute and then overriding the *GetVaryByCustomString* method of the *HttpApplication* object in the Global.asax file. This method should return a string for the current request, which the runtime then uses to vary caching. For example, the *@ OutputCache* directive specifying a custom selector named *MySelector* is coded like this:

```
<%@ OutputCache Duration="60"
    VaryByCustom="MySelector"
    VaryByParam="none" %>
```

In Global.asax.cs, you would implement the custom selector like this:

```
public override string GetVaryByCustomString(
    HttpContext context, string arg)
{
    switch (arg){
        case "MySelector":
            // Send back the string that is used to distinguish
            // between client devices for output caching.
            return "MySelector=" + context.Request.Browser
                + context.Request.Frames;
        default:
            return "";
    }
}
```

Using *VaryByParam* to Cache Based on User Input

If you've set *VaryByParam* to *none*, the runtime will cache only the initial *GET* request. The application won't cache any subsequent *GET* requests that include a query string or any parameters on a *POST* request. In mobile Web applications, the initial *GET* request of the application is the only element that doesn't involve *POST* parameters or query strings. Thereafter, any server controls will return the result of user interaction as *POST* parameters, and the runtime will track sessions through munged URLs, *POST* parameters, and query strings. In these cases, if you want to enable caching beyond the initial *GET* request, you must use *VaryByParam* to specify a parameter or parameters to vary by.

To implement caching that works effectively, you need to identify the particular parameter or parameters that control the returned content—in other words, you must designate the particular server control used to manage the output to the user. Consider the application shown in Figure 13-1. The user selects a state, which the runtime passes back to the server. The server then generates the new output and sends it back to the client.

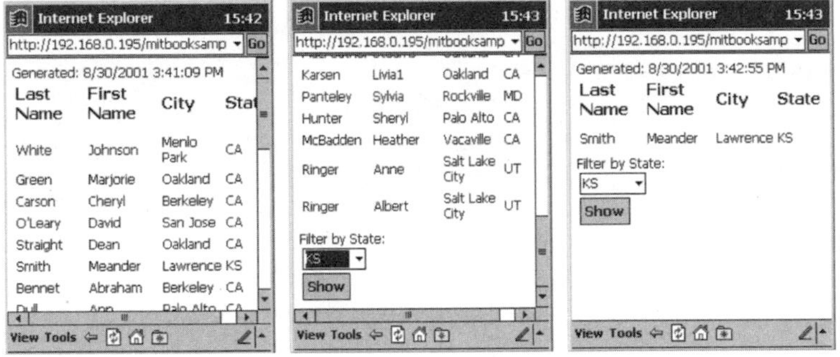

Figure 13-1 The state selected from the drop-down list that posts back to the server and ultimately creates the new data list

The *@ OutputCache* directive of this application should specify the *POST* parameter used to post back the value that the user entered in the SelectionList control. The ASP.NET mobile controls use the control ID when posting back values. In this case, where the SelectionList control has the ID *selState*, the *OutputCache* directive reads as follows:

```
<%@ OutputCache Duration="120" VaryByParam="selState" %>
```

This code is sufficient to yield the required results on a Pocket Internet Explorer browser. However, you must also specify the *__EVENTARGUMENT* parameter of the *@ OutputCache* directive to ensure that this application runs on smaller devices on which the length of the list triggers pagination. We'll explain the reason for this in the next section, "Design Considerations for Applications that Use Caching."

Listings 13-2 and 13-3 show the full source code for this example, named PageCacheByParam. This sample introduces some other objects that you've not met before in this book. First it uses an *ADO.NET DataView* object in the *BindToCachedData* method, which is very similar to a *DataTable* object that you met in Chapter 11. The *DataView* object is very useful because you can call the *Filter* method to create a subset of the data in a *DataTable*; in this application it selects rows from the master *DataTable* based on the state code the user enters. The second new feature is the use of the *Cache* object. This is nothing to do with output caching, but is an object that exposes the ASP.NET Data Cache, which is another optimization tool available to you. We describe the use of the Data Cache later in this chapter.

```
<%@ OutputCache Duration="10" VaryByParam="selState;__EVENTARGUMENT" %>
<%@ Register TagPrefix="mobile" Namespace="System.Web.UI.MobileControls"
    Assembly="System.Web.Mobile" %>
<%@ Page language="c#" Codebehind="PageCacheByParam.aspx.cs"
    Inherits="MSPress.MobWeb.PageCacheEx.MobileWebForm"
    EnableViewState="false"%>

<mobile:Form id="Form1" runat="server" Paginate="True">
    Generated:
    <mobile:Label id = "lblTimeMsg" runat="server"/>
    <mobile:ObjectList id="oblAuth" runat="server"
        AutoGenerateFields="false" LabelField="au_lname"
        TableFields="au_lname;au_fname;city;state">
        <Field title="Last Name" DataField="au_lname"/>
        <Field title="First Name" DataField="au_fname"/>
        <Field title="City" DataField="city"/>
        <Field title="State" DataField="state"/>
    </mobile:ObjectList>
    <mobile:Label runat="server" text="Filter by State:"/>
    <mobile:SelectionList id="selState" runat="server">
        <Item Text="All" Value="*" />
        <Item Text="CA" Value="CA" />
        <Item Text="IN" Value="IN" />
        <Item Text="KS" Value="KS" />
        <Item Text="MD" Value="MD" />
        <Item Text="MI" Value="MI" />
        <Item Text="OR" Value="OR" />
        <Item Text="TN" Value="TN" />
        <Item Text="UT" Value="UT" />
    </mobile:SelectionList>
    <mobile:Command runat="server" text="Show" />
</mobile:Form>
```

Listing 13-2 Source for PageCacheByParam.aspx

```
using System;
using System.Data;
using System.Data.SqlClient;
using System.Web.UI.MobileControls;

namespace MSPress.MobWeb.PageCacheEx
{
    public class MobileWebForm
        : System.Web.UI.MobileControls.MobilePage
    {
        protected System.Web.UI.MobileControls.ObjectList oblAuth;
        protected System.Web.UI.MobileControls.SelectionList selState;
        protected System.Web.UI.MobileControls.Label lblTimeMsg;
```

Listing 13-3 Code-behind module PageCacheByParam.aspx.cs

```
override protected void OnInit(EventArgs e)
{
    InitializeComponent();
    base.OnInit(e);
}

private void InitializeComponent()
{
    this.Load += new System.EventHandler(this.Page_Load);
}
private void Page_Load(object sender, System.EventArgs e)
{
    if (!this.IsPostBack)
    {
        CacheData();
        selState.SelectedIndex = 0;
    }

    BindtoCachedData();

    // Capture the time of the current request.
    // Subsequent requests that are cached will show the
    // original time.
    lblTimeMsg.Text = DateTime.Now.ToString("G");
}

private void CacheData()
{
    // Fetch a dataset.
    String strConnectionString =
     "server=(local)\\NetSDK;database=pubs;Trusted_Connection=yes";
    SqlConnection myConnection =
        new SqlConnection(strConnectionString);
    SqlDataAdapter myCommand =
        new SqlDataAdapter("select * from Authors", myConnection);

    DataSet ds = new DataSet();
    myCommand.Fill(ds, "Authors");

    // Save DataSet in the data cache; has application scope.
    Cache["DS"] = ds;
}

public void BindtoCachedData()
{
    DataSet ds;
    try
    {
        //Get the Dataset from the cache
```

```
                ds = (DataSet)(Cache["DS"]);
            }
            catch (NullReferenceException)
            {
                // Items in the Data Cache may be 'expired' by the system
                // so you get a NullreferenceException when you try
                // to cast the item. You have to code for this eventuality.
                CacheData();
                ds = (DataSet)(Cache["DS"]);
            }

            // Create a DataView based on the filter value.
            DataView dv = new DataView(ds.Tables["authors"]);
            if (selState.Selection != null)
               if (selState.Selection.Value != "*")
                  dv.RowFilter = "state='" + selState.Selection.Value + "'";
            oblAuth.DataSource = dv;
            oblAuth.DataBind();
        }
    }
}
```

Listing 13-3 retrieves a *DataSet* object from the database when the user first requests the page. Thereafter, in the *BindtoCachedData* method, the code builds a *DataView* object from the *DataSet* object it retrieves from the *Cache* object. (The *Cache* property exposes the data cache, which is described later in this chapter, in the section "Using Data Caching.")

Design Considerations for Applications that Use Caching

You must carefully design applications with which you use caching. You have to consider what will happen if a particular client receives its output from the server cache instead of running code that you've written to execute based on particular events. The PageCacheByParam example shown in Listing 13-3 incorporates solutions for three potential problems that you might encounter when designing applications that use caching.

First of all, you can't use *ViewState* when using output caching. If the ObjectList control saves its state between every request, the runtime tracks the session through an identifier added to the query string. If the first request fetches its output from the server cache, the runtime never establishes the session, and a runtime error results on a subsequent postback. Consequently, we designed the application in Listing 13-3 to be truly stateless. We included *EnableViewState = "false"* in the *@ Page* directive of the mobile Web Forms page, and we designed the application to build a *DataView* object and bind the ObjectList control to the data on every request.

The second issue in Listing 13-3 is that the application retrieves the data from the database only on the first access of this page, and caches the *DataSet* object to improve performance on subsequent requests. If the application caches the *DataSet* object in the *Session* object, a runtime error would again result when other clients attempt to access this page. If the server cache satisfies the initial page load, the *Page_Load* method won't execute and the runtime won't store the data for that session. Instead, the application uses the *Cache* object, which has application scope and is therefore available to all sessions. (We'll describe the *Cache* object in a moment, in the section "Using Data Caching.")

You'd expect that this application would require you to specify only *VaryByParam="selState"* to yield the desired result. However, if you've coded the application like this and you run it on a small device such as a WAP-enabled mobile phone, the third problem emerges.

The form in this application specifies *Paginate="true"*. Therefore, the code sends only the first part of the list to the client device and includes the Next and Previous hyperlinks on the page to let the user navigate through the paged list. Each time the user follows one of these links, a postback to the server occurs, fetching the next page to display. An ASP.NET mobile Web application tells the server which page to display by posting back a parameter named *__EVENTARGUMENT*. Figure 13-2 shows an emulator displaying the Next and Back pagination links.

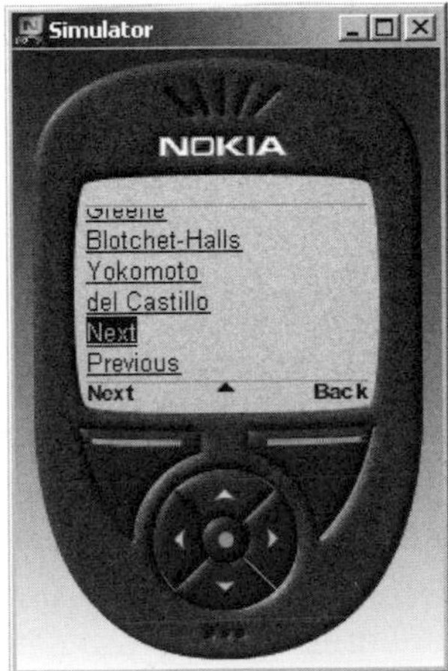

Figure 13-2 Next and Back pagination links on the Nokia simulator

Consequently, if you don't include this *@ OutputCache* directive parameter with those you use to determine whether to return a cached copy, when the user selects the Next or Previous link on a page and a cached version is available, the server will simply return the same page. However, specifying the *@ OutputCache* directive by using *VaryByParam="selState;__EVENTARGUMENT"* offers a viable solution.

Using Fragment Caching

Fragment caching is a technique you use with *user controls*; we'll look at user controls in detail in Chapter 20. User controls are a great way of creating reusable graphical components, which implement some piece of user interface functionality that you find yourself using over and over in your applications—for example, in headings, login screens, and user complaints forms(!). You use a user control in much the way as a regular mobile control; you drag it onto a Form and it generates part of the output of the Form, just as if it was a regular control.

You can use fragment caching to cache the output of a user control, which might be only a part of the whole page that is sent to the client. You should use fragment caching where the output of the user control is essentially static and doesn't need to be dynamically generated for each request. Good candidates for fragment caching are navigation links, headers, footers, and other code fragments that can be implemented as user controls and might benefit from the performance gains that are associated with having their output retrieved from a cache. Chapter 20 describes in detail how you can build user controls to encapsulate reusable elements of user interface functionality. You code these controls similarly to the way you code regular mobile Web Forms pages, but you store them in a file with an .ascx extension. You implement fragment caching for a user control by placing an *OutputCache* directive at the head of the .ascx file, in the same way as we just described for .aspx mobile Web forms pages. This directive applies caching to the output of the user control, independent of the mobile Web Forms page in which you're using the control.

The *@ OutputCache* directive you use in an .ascx file supports the *VaryByParam*, *VaryByHeader* and *VaryByCustom* attributes, just as when you use it in a .aspx file. However, you can specify one additional attribute in the *@ OutputCache* directive that applies to user controls: the *VaryByControl* attribute. This attribute is similar to *VaryByParam*, but it specifies a particular control within the user control you employ to vary caching. For example, if a user control includes a SelectionList control that has the ID *selState*, the following would be the *@ OutputCache* directive that enables caching depending on the value the user selects in the SelectionList:

```
<%@ OutputCache Duration="320"
    VaryByControl="selState"
    VaryByParam="none" %>
```

Using Data Caching

ASP.NET supports a memory-resident cache that you can use to store arbitrary objects across HTTP requests. We used this cache in Listing 13-3 to store a *DataSet* object across requests.

Because the data cache has application scope, it's accessible to different sessions. As noted earlier in this chapter, in the section "Design Considerations for Applications that Use Caching," and as implemented by the PageCacheByParam example, this accessibility helps ensure that cached objects remain available to sessions that don't execute setup code because the server cache satisfied their initial request. In Listing 13-3 of the PageCacheByParam example, the code retrieves the *DataSet* object from the database and stores it in the data cache any time that the *Page_Load* method executes. This method executes any time the *Page* cache can't satisfy a particular request for this page. A better solution might be to fetch the *DataSet* from within the *Application_Start* method in the Global.asax file.

The data cache is dictionary-structured; therefore, it's very easy to use programmatically:

```
// Save DataSet in the data cache; has Application scope.
  Cache["DS"] = myDataset;
  ⋮
  // Get the DataSet from the cache.
  DataSet ds = (DataSet)(Cache["DS"]);
```

The data cache is similar in scope and functionality to the *Application* object described in Chapter 12. However, the data cache offers this added functionality:

- **Scavenging** Because the cache is memory resident, it could become full if memory resources become scarce. In this case, ASP.NET removes objects that the runtime hasn't accessed for a while. Code defensively to allow for this. That way, if your application doesn't find an expected object in the cache, it can still access the required object from its original source. See the *BindToCachedData* method in Listing 13-3, which codes for the eventuality of the requested item not being present in the cache.
- **Object expiration** When you add objects to the cache using the *Cache.Insert* method, you can specify an absolute expiration time for objects in the cache. When the expiration time is reached, ASP.NET removes the object from the data cache. You can also specify a sliding expiration time that's dependent on an object's last use.

- **File and object dependencies** When entering objects into the cache, you can specify the path to a file or to another object. ASP.NET monitors that file or object, and if it's altered, the runtime invalidates any objects in the cache that have a declared dependency on that file or object.

Search the .NET Framework SDK documentation for the *Cache.Insert* methods and *CacheDependency* class for further details.

14

Multilingual and Multicultural Web Applications

In some applications, multilingual support will be required. Most browsers, including those commonly used on handheld devices, allow the user to specify a preference for content in a particular language. User preferences are passed to the content server in the HTTP headers of each request. Microsoft ASP.NET contains powerful, easy-to-use facilities for writing multilingual applications that can supply content according to a user's language preference. In this chapter, you'll learn how to build a multilingual mobile user interface.

Building Multilingual and Multicultural Mobile Web Applications

You can increase the usability of your application for users in different countries of the world by offering an interface that's translated into the user's preferred language as well as formatting currency and dates according to cultural norms. ASP.NET has a number of features to help you build applications that provide content appropriate for a specific culture.

When you're considering applications for users in different regions of the world, don't make the mistake of thinking that you need *only* to translate the user interface into various languages. Language is only one part of it; you also need to consider issues such as date, time, and currency formatting, and string sort ordering. By considering internationalization during the design phase of an application, you can produce a high-quality, internationalized application that you can easily extend to new target cultures. The alternative—developing your application in one language and then retrofitting support for other cultures—can be expensive and might not result in a quality solution.

In your design of a multilingual, multicultural application, you must consider a number of issues:

- **Display and support of input using different character sets** Use the *System.Resources.ResourceManager* class and resource files to present strings in different languages. Use the *responseEncoding* and *requestEncoding* attributes of the *<Globalization>* element in your Web.config file to configure Unicode character encodings such as *utf-8* for the transfer of characters between client and server.
- **Date and time formatting** Use the *System.Globalization.DateTimeFormatInfo* class for help with this.
- **Local conventions for formatting currency, weights, and measures** The *System.Globalization.NumberFormatInfo* class can help with this.
- **Alphabetic sort orders that conform to norms for the character set used by a culture** Use the *System.Globalization.SortKey* and *System.Globalization.CompareInfo* classes to help with sorting.

Globalization is the process of building in support for culture-specific date formats, character sets, currency formats, and units of measure. The management of string resources for different languages is called *localization*.

Defining Culture for Formatting Strings, Dates, and Times

By defining a culture, you influence the formatting style of methods that your application uses to output information, such as strings, dates, and number formats. If you don't specify any culture settings, the application uses the local settings of the Web server. However, it's good practice to specify culture settings explicitly.

You can define the culture settings for an application in three ways: in the Web.config application configuration file, in the @ *Page* directive, and in the code. The first two methods are appropriate for establishing an application's default settings. Defining *Culture* or *UICulture* in the @ *Page* directive overrides any settings in Web.config, as the following code demonstrates. Here's some code defining *Culture* and *UICulture* in Web.config:

```
<configuration>
   <system.web>
      <globalization
           culture="de-DE"
           uiCulture="de"
        />
   </system.web>
</configuration>
```

And here's the code defining culture settings in the @ *Page* directive:

```
<%@ Page UICulture="en" Culture="en-US"…%>
```

These two culture settings determine the formatting the runtime applies to dates, times and currencies, and where the application should look for localized strings:

- ***Culture* attribute** This setting ensures that the runtime formats information according to the appropriate conventions for the specified culture. You must set the specific culture identifier, such as *en-US* (English-United States) or *fr-CA* (French-Canada). You can't specify a neutral culture identifier such as *en* or *de* because these don't distinguish among different cultures, such as U.S. English (*en-US*) and U.K. English (*en-GB*). Search the Microsoft .NET Framework documentation for the *CultureInfo* class for a complete list of supported culture identifiers. In code, you shouldn't set the corresponding *MobilePage.Culture* property. Instead, set the *CurrentCulture* property of the *System.Threading.Thread* class, as shown in the next example.
- ***UICulture* attribute** As with the *Culture* attribute, this must be one of the culture identifiers supported by the *CultureInfo* class. Unlike *Culture*, however, with *UICulture* you're allowed to use neutral culture identifiers such as *de* or *fr* as well as specific culture identifiers. The Resource Manager uses the identifier at run time to select a resource file for accessing localized string values. For example, if you set *UICulture* to *en*, the Resource Manager accesses the Resourcesfile.en.resx resource file. If you set *UICulture* to " ", the empty quotation marks indicate the neutral culture, and the Resource Manager accesses the resources from Resourcesfile.resx. We'll describe the use of resource files and the *ResourceManager* class later in this section. In code, you set this feature by setting the *CurrentUICulture* property of the thread, as shown in the example below.

One approach to building multicultural applications is to develop a set of mobile Web Forms pages, each of which implements the user interface of your application—one for each supported locale. In this case, you define the *Culture* settings in the *@ Page* directive of each page.

However, you can also have a single mobile Web Forms page that sets the *Culture* in code at run time, depending on the user preferences defined in the client device's browser. Many handheld devices allow the user to specify the preferred language for content. Sophisticated browsers such as the desktop Internet Explorer allow the user to specify more than one preferred language, in order of preference. The devices then pass these preferences to the server in the HTTP headers of every request. For example, in Internet Explorer, click Tools and then Internet Options. Then click the Languages button to select your language preferences. Mobile phones usually allow the user to specify the preferred language in the Settings menu.

Testing Multicultural Applications with Mobile Phone Emulators

Internet Explorer is a useful tool for testing applications that respond to the language preference that the user sets in the client browser, and which is passed to the server in the HTTP headers, as we've described in this section.

If you want to test a multilingual application with a mobile phone emulator, you can use a real device or you can download one of the developer's toolkits available from a major mobile phone browser manufacturer. Emulators from Nokia, Openwave, Ericsson, and other manufacturers offer the capability to specify language preferences. For example, in the Openwave UP.Browser 4.1.1 emulator, click on the Settings menu, option Device settings; the dialog that displays allows you to define the Language and Charset to use. See Chapter 16 for more details on downloading and using emulators.

Within code, the client's preferred languages are available in the *UserLanguages* property of the *Request* object, which returns a string array of a user's specified preferences, normally in the order of preference. Be aware that the strings sent from the client browser can also include additional data such as a weighting factor (for example, *en-us;0.3*), which some applications can use to determine the relative preference weighting of each language in the list. Therefore, you need to process the array passed in the headers to extract the locale code for the user's preferred language. But be warned: browsers often allow you to specify language preferences by using neutral culture identifiers (such as *en* or *fr*), and you can't use these neutral identifiers to set the *CurrentCulture* property of *System.Threading.Thread* directly. Instead, use the *System.Globalization.CultureInfo.CreateSpecificCulture* method, which will accept as a parameter a neutral culture identifier and return the default *CultureInfo* object for the specified culture.

In your applications, you can choose how far you wish to fine-tune your support for different cultures. For example, perhaps you want to observe the cultural differences between French-Canadian, French-Algerian, and French-French, so you create string resource files for each of these cultures. Alternatively, you might wish to provide a single French language string resource to be used with any of these French-speaking cultures (and any others in the world), avoiding the effort of writing separate string resource files for each.

The example shown in Listing 14-1 shows how you implement this simplified approach. It extracts the first element of the *UserLanguages* array, strips off any weighting factor, and creates a new *CultureInfo* object, which it uses to set the *CurrentCulture* of the current thread. This makes use of a specific culture setting, such as *en-US*, or *fr-CA*. This setting determines date-time formats, currency formatting, and so on. The method then creates a new *CultureInfo* object which it uses to set the *CurrentUICulture* property for the current thread, but this time using only the first two characters of the culture specifier the client has passed, which equates to a neutral culture specifier, such as *en*, *fr* or *de*. The *CurrentUICulture* property determines where the application gets its string resources from—for example, it will fetch resource strings for the *en* culture from Resources.en.resx, for *fr* from Resources.fr.resx, and for *de* from those you define in the Resources.de.resx file. We'll make use of this method in the LocalizingExample sample application, shown later in this chapter in Listing 14-2. You'll learn how to create and use string resource files in the next section, "Creating and Using Resource Files."

```
private void setCulture()
{
    // Extract first element of languages array
    String lang = Request.UserLanguages[0])
    // Strip off any weighting appended to the string.
    String langOnly = lang.Split(new Char[] {';'})[0];

    // Set Culture - sets date-time, currency formats etc
    System.Globalization.CultureInfo ci =
        System.Globalization.CultureInfo.CreateSpecificCulture(langOnly);
    System.Threading.Thread.CurrentThread.CurrentCulture = ci;
```

Listing 14-1 Setting *Culture* and *UICulture* by examining the preferences sent from the client browser. This method is part of Default.aspx.cs of the LocalizingExample project.

```
    // Set the UICulture - defines string resource file
    // We support string resources for 'main' language only
    // such as en, fr or de
    ci = CultureInfo.CreateSpecificCulture(langOnly.Substring(0,2));
    System.Threading.Thread.CurrentThread.CurrentUICulture = ci;
}
```

> **Tip** You might be wondering what happens if the client requests a culture for which you have not written a resource file. You'll learn in the next section about the *ResourceManager* object, which you use to access resources from resource files. If the *ResourceManager* cannot find a resource file for the requested culture, it falls back on resources for the neutral culture. You define resources for the neutral culture in the file Resources.resx.

Creating and Using Resource Files

Any application displays a lot of text. Not only is there the text that you define in Label and TextView controls, there's also many other properties of mobile controls that display text to the user, such as page headings, navigation prompts to move forward or backward through the application, menu links, and so on. The following are some of the most common sources of text in any application:

- You set static text displayed in the Label and TextView controls at run time by using the *Text* property.
- The *Title* property of the Form control displays on the head of a page in many browsers.
- When you enable a Form control for pagination, you set the text displayed for the forward and backward links through the *NextPageText* and *PreviousPageText* properties of that control's *PagerStyle* object.
- Various controls contain properties you can display only on a specific type of device. An example of this is the *SoftkeyLabel* property of the Link and Command controls.
- You use the *Text* property of the *MobileListItem* object to display static text in a listing using the SelectionList and List controls.

- When displaying a list of data objects using the ObjectList control, the column heading that displays for data fields is defined by the *Title* property of the *ObjectListField* object.
- You set the menu prompt for an ObjectList item command using the *Text* property of an *ObjectListCommand* object.
- You use the *MoreText* property of the ObjectList control to set the text displayed for the link used to view the details of an item.

The normal way to set these strings (and the method used by 99 percent of the examples in this book) is simply to use the properties window of the Mobile Internet Designer to set the properties of mobile controls that take textual values, or to set properties in code using embedded literal strings. That's fine if you're supporting only a single culture in your application, but if you're producing internationalized applications, you should separate the definition of strings from the code, and store all string definitions in resource files.

As we described in the previous section, you set the *UICulture* property at run time to define which resource file should be used to provide the string values to be used with the current request. For example, if you want your application to support localized content for English, French, and French-Canadian, you'd set the *UICulture* property to a *CultureInfo* object for the requested language, *en*, *fr*, or *fr-CA* when a request comes in from a client requesting one of those languages. Then in code you use a *System.Resources.ResourceManager* object to fetch strings from the selected resource file.

Microsoft Visual Studio .NET makes adding resource files easy. As a simple exercise, create a mobile application that has a single Form control on it as well as three Label controls. Figure 14-1 shows how this application might appear in the Mobile Internet Designer.

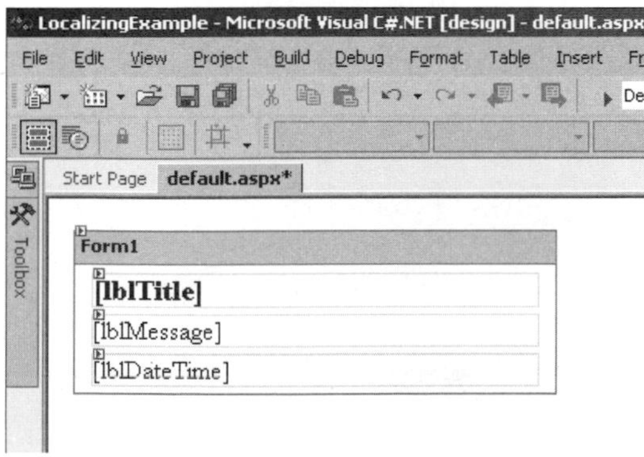

Figure 14-1 Form to be localized

In this example, you'll provide translations in English, German, and French, identified by the *UICulture* settings of *en*, *de*, and *fr*, respectively. In fact, we won't create a Resources.en.resources file for the English language because we will place English translations into the default (invariant) culture resources file, Resources.resx.

One of the great things about the way that resource files are managed in .NET is that you can add support for new languages later on, without recompiling the main application. If you set the *UICulture* property to a particular culture, and at run time no resource file for that culture is found, the client just gets the string resources defined for the invariant culture. You can deploy a resource assembly for a new culture later on, and the application will start to use it without having to recompile the application. See the sidebar "Resource Manager and Satellite Assemblies" for a more detailed explanation of how the .NET Resource Manager uses resources at run time. You have to define string resources in the invariant culture resources file using one language or another; in this application, the language used is English.

To create a resources file in Visual Studio.NET, right-click the project in Solution Explorer, point to Add, and then click Add New Item. In the Add New Item window, scroll down the Templates pane, select Assembly Resource File, and give it a suitable name, such as MyResources.resx. This first resource file is for the neutral culture, and this application uses this file for any clients that don't specify a preference for French or German.

The XML Designer allows you to create strings in the resource file, add a comment to them, and identify those strings with a name. You must add the text to be displayed on each of the three controls on the mobile Web Forms page, as Figure 14-2 shows.

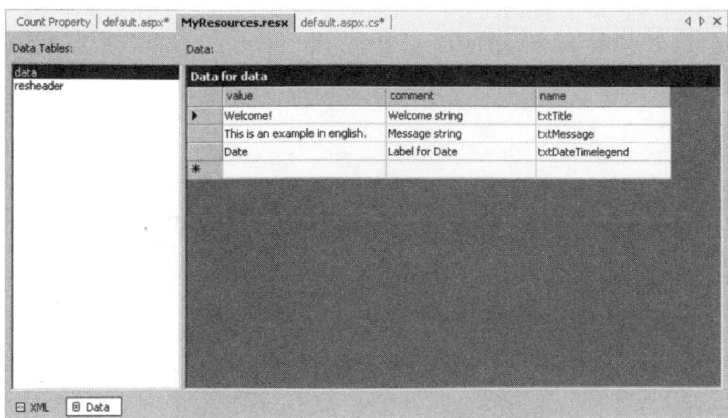

Figure 14-2 Defining strings for localization using the Visual Studio .NET Resource Editor

Resource Manager and Satellite Assemblies

.NET resource files are compiled into special assemblies known as *satellite assemblies*. Satellite assemblies contain only resources and no executable code. These assemblies have a number of advantages. The most important advantage is that satellite assemblies allow you to deploy resources for a new language separately from the main application so that you can update resources or add support for new languages without the need to recompile and distribute your entire application. Another benefit is that a satellite assembly is a dynamic-link library (DLL) which is shadow-copied by each process that accesses it, meaning that you can update the satellite assembly even if it's in use.

Resources for the default culture are compiled into the main application assembly. Resources for other cultures are compiled into a satellite assembly and deployed in a directory beneath the \bin folder in your application that has the name of the culture code. For example, default culture resources for the application LocalizingExample go into \bin\LocalizingExample.dll, French resources into \bin\fr\LocalizingExample.resources.dll, and German resources go into \bin\de\LocalizingExample.resources.dll. If you use Visual Studio .NET to build your applications, it does so without your having to take any special steps.

If you set the culture at run time to a particular locale code and the Resources Manager can't find a satellite assembly containing resources for that locale, the resources in the default culture resources file (which are in English in this application) are used. You can use this behavior to release an application that initially supports only one or a few cultures and then add support for more cultures without having to recode your main application. Even if *setCulture* sets the *Culture* and *UICulture* properties of the application to a culture for which no resources are found at run time, the client will get the default culture. But if you create the resources file for a culture later and compile it, you can just deploy the satellite assembly for that culture onto the Web server, and the application will automatically start using it.

If you are deploying satellite assemblies later, you do have to make sure that the satellite assembly has the same version number as the main assembly. See Chapter 17 for details of how to set the version number of an assembly.

Create two more assembly resource files with the same prefix, MyResources, but ending with .de.resx for the German translation and .fr.resx for the French version. In the Resource Editor, add entries for the three strings using the same name as you did for the English version.

When you compile this application, it creates a satellite DLL named *projectName*.resources.DLL in a subdirectory under the /bin directory for each of the culture-specific resource files you've created. In other words, the German resources reside in /bin/de, and the French reside in /bin/fr. The default culture resources (in this case, the English version) reside in the main application assembly in /bin.

Create a *ResourceManager* object which you use to access these resources at run time using the name you gave to each resource string. The form of the constructor you'll want to use takes two parameters, as shown here:

```
ResourceManager  LocRM =
    new ResourceManager("MSPress.MobWeb.LocalizingEx.MyResources",
                        typeof(MobileWebForm1).Module.Assembly);
```

- The first parameter is the root name of the resources. For example, the root name for the resource file named "MyResource.en-US.resources" is "MyResource". You should prefix this with the namespace name, as previously shown.
- The second parameter is the main assembly for the resources.

Once you have a ResourceManager, use the *GetString(*"resource_string_name") method to fetch strings from the resource file:

```
Label1.Text = LocRM.GetString("Title");
```

The ResourceManager uses the current *UICulture* setting to determine which resource assembly to access. For example, this application uses the *setCulture* method shown in Listing 14-1 to define the *Culture* and *UICulture* properties and then creates a *ResourceManager* object to set the strings, as Listing 14-2 shows. This example also uses the *DateTime.Now.ToString* method to return the *LongDateTimeFormat* (format identifier *F*). This identifier formats the date in the appropriate language and layout as defined in the current *Culture* setting.

```
using System;
using System.Web.UI.MobileControls;
using System.Resources;
using System.Threading;
using System.Globalization;
```

Listing 14-2 Code-behind file Default.aspx.cs of the LocalizingExample project demonstrates using localized string resources.

```
namespace MSPress.MobWeb.LocalizingEx
{
    public class MobileWebForm1 : System.Web.UI.MobileControls.MobilePage
    {
        protected System.Web.UI.MobileControls.Label Label1;
        protected System.Web.UI.MobileControls.Label Label2;
        protected System.Web.UI.MobileControls.Form Form1;
        protected System.Web.UI.MobileControls.Label Label3;
        protected ResourceManager LocRM;

        override protected void OnInit(EventArgs e)
        {
            InitializeComponent();
            base.OnInit(e);
        }

        private void InitializeComponent()
        {
            this.Load += new System.EventHandler(this.Page_Load);
        }

        private void Page_Load(object sender, System.EventArgs e)
        {
            setCulture();

            LocRM = new ResourceManager(
                        "MSPress.MobWeb.LocalizingEx.MyResources",
                        typeof(MobileWebForm1).Module.Assembly);
            Label1.Text = LocRM.GetString("Title");
            Label2.Text = LocRM.GetString("Message");

            Label3.Text = LocRM.GetString("DateTimelegend") + ": " +
                DateTime.Now.ToString("F");
        }

        private void setCulture()
        {
            // Extract first element of languages array
            String lang = Request.UserLanguages[0])
            // Strip off any weighting appended to the string.
            String langOnly = lang.Split(new Char[] {';'})[0];

            // Set Culture - sets date-time, currency formats etc
            CultureInfo ci = CultureInfo.CreateSpecificCulture(langOnly);
            System.Threading.Thread.CurrentThread.CurrentCulture = ci;
```

```
                // Set the UICulture - defines string resource file
                // We support string resources for 'main' language only
                // such as en, fr or de
                ci = CultureInfo.CreateSpecificCulture(langOnly.Substring(0,2));
                System.Threading.Thread.CurrentThread.CurrentUICulture = ci;
            }
        }
    }
```

When you build this application and run it with a browser set to each of the supported languages, the output appears as shown in Figure 14-3.

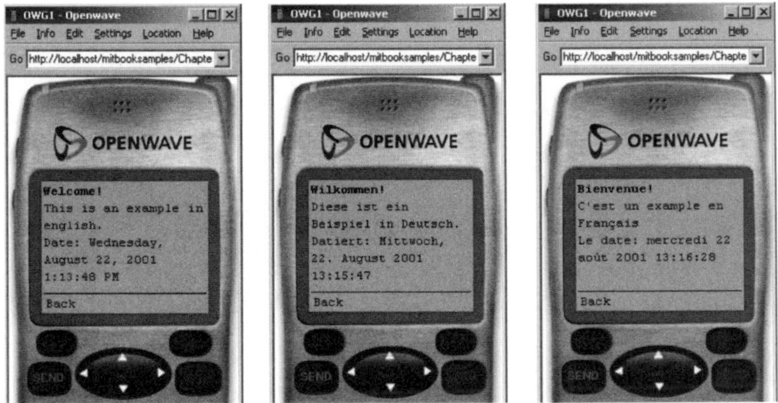

Figure 14-3 Setting the Openwave simulator to different language preferences provides this output for the LocalizingExample application.

Defining Character Set Encodings

ASP.NET uses Unicode internally and objects such as the *String* class to ensure that Web applications can operate with any displayable characters. Network entities such as WAP gateways and the client browsers themselves need to know what encoding you've used to transfer the character data across the Web in order to interpret it correctly.

You can define character set encodings in the Web.config file, as shown here:

```
<configuration>
   <system.web>
      <globalization
           responseEncoding="utf-8"
```

```
            requestEncoding="utf-8"
            fileEncoding="utf-8"
        />
    </system.web>
</configuration>
```

You set the *responseEncoding* attribute to set the encoding that the server uses to send data to the client—for example, *UTF-8*. A definition of this attribute also appears in the HTTP headers to inform recipients of the encoding used. You set the *requestEncoding* attribute to indicate the assumed encoding of incoming requests. The default if not specified is *UTF-8*. If the client defines an *Accept-Charset* value in the HTTP headers sent with the request, the encoding specified in there is used instead of the value you enter in the *requestEncoding* attribute.

The *FileEncoding* attribute specifies the encoding that's used to interpret the data included in the .aspx file when the ASP.NET page parser reads it in order to compile it. If you have written string literals into your page that use non-US-ASCII characters (perhaps in setting the *Text* property of a control), you must save the page to disk using the character encoding that supports those characters. When saving such a file in Visual Studio .NET, you must click the File menu and choose Advanced Save Options. You set the *FileEncoding* attribute in Web.config to record the encoding used to save the mobile Web Forms page so that when the runtime parses it at run time, it knows what encoding to use to interpret the page.

You can also define character set encodings in the *@ Page* directive which apply to that page only and override settings in the Web.config file:

```
<%@ Page ResponseEncoding="utf-8" RequestEncoding="utf-8" …%>
```

> **Note** When you're working with multilingual applications, you might find the Microsoft Windows Character Map application useful. To open the Character Map application, click Start and then click Run. Next type **charmap** in the Open box and click OK. This application offers one way to access characters that aren't available from your keyboard so that you can copy them into files and documents.

today

15

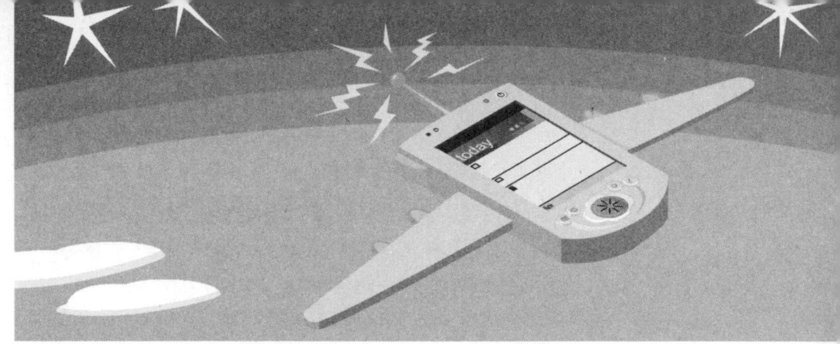

XML Web Services

XML Web services offer an exciting new way to provide remote access to software components. If you're a traditional Web developer, you'll need to undergo a paradigm shift to really understand XML Web services. If you're a programmer who uses existing forms of remote procedure calls, you're in for a pleasant surprise. You can think of an XML Web service as a special kind of Web site; one designed for programmatic access rather than interactive access through a browser.

This chapter is a brief introduction to how you can use XML Web services in mobile Web applications. You'll learn how to create an XML Web service using Visual Studio .NET and how to consume an XML Web service from a .NET application. We'll also explain how to create and modify Web service description documents and work with *DataSet* objects. And finally, we'll present some design considerations for using XML Web services in applications for mobile devices.

For a detailed analysis of XML web services, readers are advised to consult books dedicated to this subject, such as *Microsoft .NET XML Web Services Step by Step* by Adam Freeman and Allen Jones (Microsoft Press, 2002), or *Building XML Services for the Microsoft .NET Platform* by Scott Short (Microsoft Press, 2002).

Introduction to XML Web Services

XML Web services differ immensely from earlier distributed component technologies, such as CORBA or DCOM. For one thing, they're platform independent and language independent; programs written in any language (not just the Microsoft .NET Framework languages) and running on any platform can consume them. For another, they're based on existing, open protocols: XML Web services run over protocols, such as HTTP; use the lightweight, XML-based Simple Object Access Protocol (SOAP) to communicate; and return data defined using XML Schema Definition (XSD) data types packaged into XML messages. Because they are constructed using these established standards, XML Web services can navigate today's Internet firewall landscape, unlike other remote access methods. Firewalls that allow the passage of regular Web traffic over HTTP also allow the passage of data passing to and from an XML Web service. The use of XML as a means both to describe the service (to describe to client software how to access the service) and to communicate data between a client and an XML Web service makes this powerful component architecture truly cross-platform.

Using XML Web Services in Web Applications

XML Web services provide data or services that can be accessed by client programs situated elsewhere on the Web. A good example of an XML Web service is the Microsoft MapPoint .NET Web service (see *http://www.microsoft.com/mappoint/net/*). This service is a great way of building location-based mobile Web applications. For example, you can build an application using ASP.NET mobile controls designed to give driving directions. Your application would accept input from users giving their starting location and their destination, and in the code of your application you call the MapPoint .NET Web service, passing it the two locations. The Web service returns the driving directions to your Web application, which displays the directions using standard ASP.NET mobile controls.

Messages that your application sends to an XML Web service and the response that comes back from the Web service must be written in XML using the SOAP protocol. Fortunately, unless you are a developer who is deeply involved in the intricacies of XML Web services, you do not need to know much about how SOAP works. Using the .NET Framework tools or Microsoft Visual Studio .NET, you can add to your Microsoft ASP.NET project automatically generated code that handles formatting of messages and communication with the XML Web service and transparently parses the XML response so that calling an XML Web service is no more complicated than calling a method of a local object.

XML Web services are easy to write, especially because doing so requires skills that you probably already possess. XML Web services written using the .NET Framework are also easy to deploy and consume. Furthermore, the supporting files an XML Web service requires are easy to produce using the powerful command-line tools provided in the .NET Framework SDK or through Microsoft Visual Studio .NET.

Although simple to write, deploy, and consume, XML Web services allow you to work with complex data types, such as classes, enumerations, and structures. You can even pass Microsoft ADO.NET *DataSet* objects back and forth. XML Web services written for ASP.NET have access to the *Session* and *Application* objects like any other ASP.NET Web application, which you should now be familiar with. Thus, you can maintain both application and session state for your XML Web service.

Managing Session and Application State

A surprising yet very useful feature of XML Web services built with ASP.NET is their state management capability. Like any other ASP.NET application, an XML Web service provides access to both the *Session* object and the *Application* object, which you learned about in Chapter 12. You use the *Session* object and the *Application* object within an XML Web service the same way you use them in a mobile Web Forms page. You should refer to Chapter 12 for details of how to make use of these objects.

Creating an XML Web Service

This first example will show you just how easy creating an XML Web service is. In keeping with tradition, you'll write a "Hello World" XML Web service. You'll do this first with the powerful command-line tools the .NET Framework provides and then by using Visual Studio .NET, which provides helpful wizards to ease the development process.

Creating an XML Web Service Using a Text Editor

You store XML Web services in files that have an .asmx extension in a virtual directory on your Web server, just like standard mobile Web pages. Create a virtual directory, and name it MyFirstWebService. Using a text editor, create a new file named MyWebService.asmx. Listing 15-1 shows the code you should write and save in the file.

```
<%@ WebService Language="c#" Class="MyWebService" %>

using System;
using System.Web.Services;

[WebService(Namespace="http://127.0.0.1/MyFirstWebService/")]

class MyWebService : System.Web.Services.WebService
{
    [WebMethod]
    public string HelloWorld()
    {
        return "Hello World";
    }
}
```

Listing 15-1 Source file MyWebService.asmx

Although this code resembles a typical ASP.NET "Hello World" program, it has a few important differences:

- The first line declares that the code is an XML Web service. You must include this declaration in all XML Web services.
- You import *System.Web.Services*, which contains the *WebService* class your class will extend.
- The *[WebService...]* attribute declares that the class that follows it describes a Web service. This attribute is optional and doesn't affect the operation of the class as a Web service. However, it does allow you to change the namespace, the name, and the description of the Web service. The XML namespace declaration should declare the unique namespace for the Web service to distinguish it from other Web services. The namespace usually takes the form of a URL but can be any name that is unique.
- Your XML Web service class (*MyWebService*) extends the *System.Web.Services.WebService* class. You can inherit some useful methods and properties of this class; however, you don't have to inherit from this class to create an XML Web service.
- The *[WebMethod]* attribute that precedes the *HelloWorld* method signifies that the *HelloWorld* method is accessible as an XML Web service. To make the method available as an XML Web service, you must declare it *public*.

That's it! You've completed your first XML Web service. Now you can either learn how to create this application in Visual Studio .NET or skip the next section to learn how to deploy and consume this XML Web service.

Creating an XML Web Service Using Visual Studio .NET

You can use Visual Studio .NET to easily create XML Web services. To create a new XML Web service, follow these steps:

1. Open Visual Studio .NET.
2. Click the File menu, then New... Project.
3. In the New Project dialog box, select your preferred language in the Project Types pane and then select the ASP.NET Web Service template from the Templates pane.
4. Give the project a name, such as MyWebService, and click OK. The main window will then change to display a Design view, as Figure 15-1 shows.

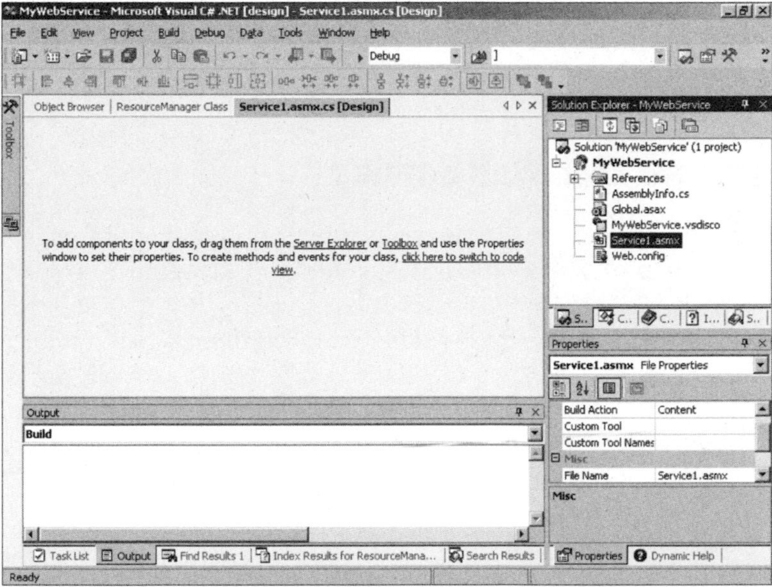

Figure 15-1 Visual Studio .NET Design view

5. Click the Click Here To Switch To Code View link. The window will update to show the XML Web service code-behind module.

6. Depending on your version of Visual Studio .NET, you might have a presupplied *HelloWorld* method. If so, you can just uncomment this method. If no *HelloWorld* method exists, add the following method to the code:

```
[WebMethod]
public string HelloWorld()
{
    return "Hello World";
}
```

That's it! You've now created your first XML Web service using Visual Studio .NET. The source files you create in Visual Studio .NET are very similar to the solution we created in Listing 15-1 with a text editor. The primary difference is that Visual Studio .NET structures the XML Web service source files as an .asmx file (containing only an @ *WebService* directive), such as Service1.asmx, and a code-behind module (Service1.asmx.cs).

Your XML Web service is now ready to use, running on the IIS Web server on your development computer. You deploy XML Web services that you build using Visual Studio .NET to production Web servers in exactly the same way as an ASP.NET application, either by using the Copy Project facility or by building a Visual Studio .NET setup and deployment project. (This technique will be described in Chapter 17.)

Consuming an XML Web Service

You can test any XML Web service by simply calling it from a Web browser and accessing its Web methods. Just enter the URL of the Web service—for example, *http://localhost/MyWebService/Service1.asmx*. For Web Services hosted on an IIS server that has the .NET Framework installed, what is returned is a page that describes the service and allows you to invoke it from the page, as shown in Figure 15-2. However, in real life, you'll probably integrate the XML Web service into a program you're writing. This section describes how to consume an XML Web service programmatically.

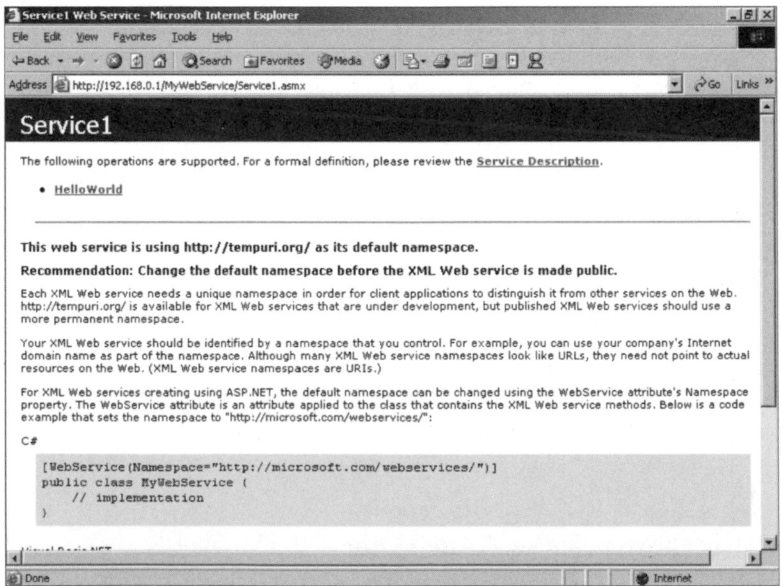

Figure 15-2 Directly calling an XML Web service from a Web browser

Consuming XML Web Services Using Visual Studio .NET

You typically consume an XML Web service by calling methods of a local proxy class that in turn accesses the Web methods within the remote XML Web service. In a Visual Studio .NET project, you generate the proxy class by using the Add Web Reference feature.

Create a new mobile Web application, and name it ConsumeMyFirstWebService. This application will contain the mobile Web Forms page that will consume the XML Web service you created earlier. Create a mobile Web Forms page with a single Label control. The Label control should have a blank *Text* property. The process of consuming an XML Web service has two stages. The first stage entails adding a Web reference to the XML Web service you want to consume to your Visual Studio .NET project:

1. In the Solution Explorer, right-click on the project to select it.
2. Select Add Web Reference from the menu.
3. When the Add Web Reference dialog box appears, click the Web Reference On Local Web Server link (Visual Studio .NET 2002) or the Web Services On The Local Machine link (Visual Studio .NET 2003). Figure 15-3 shows the Add Web Reference dialog box from Visual Studio .NET 2003.

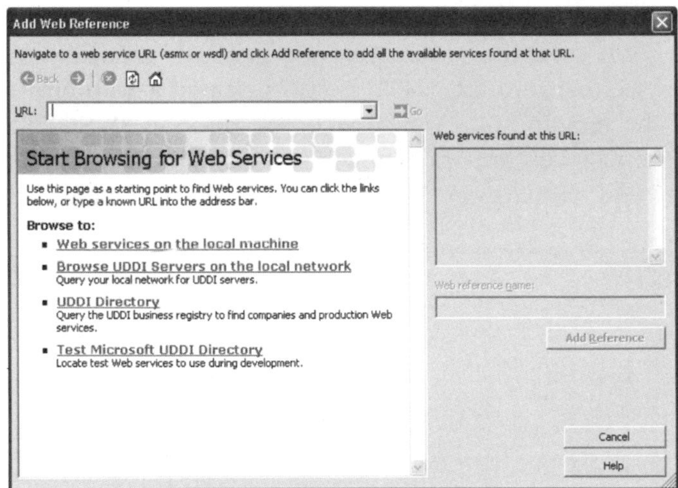

Figure 15-3 Add Web Reference dialog box

4. Wait a few seconds for the list of available XML Web services to be displayed. Select the XML Web service you want to consume.
5. The display changes to show a description of the XML Web service you selected. You'll learn how to alter this description in the section "Defining XML Web Service Behavior," later in this chapter. Click the Add Reference button.

You've now added a Web reference to the XML Web service you want to consume. Visual Studio .NET has automatically downloaded the WSDL document that describes the Web service (see the sidebar WSDL Documents for more information) and used that information to create the proxy class you use to access the XML Web service, and this proxy class is now part of your application.

WSDL Documents

Every XML Web service publishes a Web Service Description Language (WSDL) document written in XML alongside the actual Web service itself. The document is known as a *service description* and is accessible by clients who want to use your XML Web service. The purpose of the document is to describe how an XML Web service acts. For example, a WSDL document might specify which methods an XML Web service provides, what parameters these methods accept, and what data types they return. In other words, this document tells a user what to expect from HTTP or SOAP method calls. You can think of a service description as a contract between an XML Web service and its potential users that says, "Here I am, this is what I do, and this is how I do it."

You can view the service description of any publicly accessible XML Web service that supports HTTP. To do so, open a Web browser, type the URL of the remote XML Web service, and append **?WSDL** to the URL to call the service description. Figure 15-4 shows the service description of a "Hello World" application like the one you've just written.

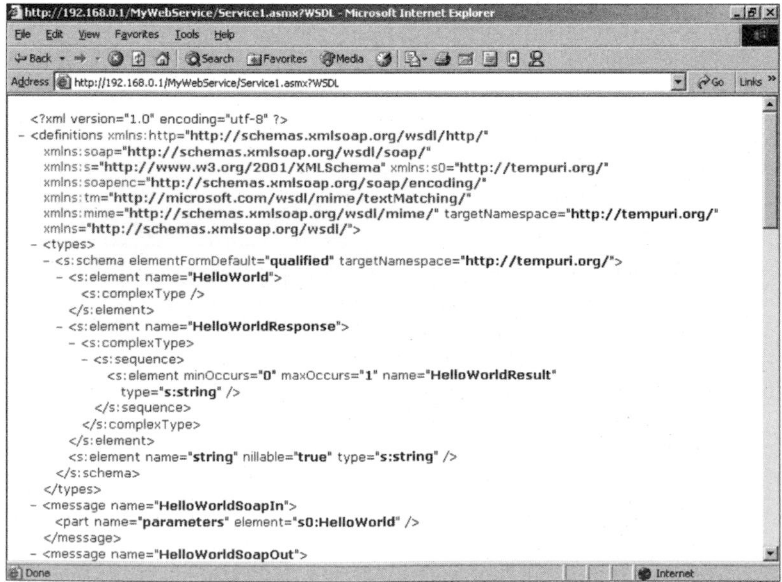

Figure 15-4 Internet Explorer displaying a service description

The proxy class has been generated using the namespace ConsumeMy-FirstWebService.localhost. To keep your code concise when you use the methods of this class, you should import this namespace into your code-behind module. Here's the syntax:

```
using ConsumeMyFirstWebService.localhost;
```

Tip When you add a Web reference to your project using Visual Studio .NET (the 2002 release), the generated proxy class is placed into a namespace in the form *projectNamespace.remoteHostName*. For example, if you add a Web reference to an XML Web service on your local machine, Visual Studio .NET defines the generated proxy in the *projectNamespace*.localhost namespace. The namespace Visual Studio .NET selects is not a meaningful name for the XML Web service, but you can change this by renaming the Web service reference using Solution Explorer.

In Visual Studio .NET 2003, you can set the namespace for the proxy from the Add Web Reference dialog box. Simply enter the required name in the Web Reference Name box in this dialog box and then click the Add Reference button.

Through the proxy class you can use any of the methods of the XML Web service as though it were a local object. In this example, you can access the *HelloWorld* method of the XML Web service. You can use the result to set the value of the Label control's *Text* property in the mobile Web Forms page you created earlier by adding this syntax to the code-behind module:

```
private void Form1_Load(Object sender, System.EventArgs e)
{
    // Create a new instance of the Web Service proxy class.
    Service1 service1 = new Service1();

    // Call the HelloWorld method.
    String msg = service1.HelloWorld();

    // Assign the result to the Text property of the Label.
    Label1.Text = msg;
}
```

Tip If you're unsure of a class name or method name, you can find it by viewing the WSDL file for the XML Web service. To do so, you either access the service description by using a browser (as described previously) or view the WSDL document within Visual Studio .NET. You can access the document through Solution Explorer. If you don't see a file with a .wsdl extension, click the Show All Files icon to ensure that all the project's files appear.

When you execute the code, the *Form1_Load* method creates a new instance of the *Service1* class, which is the proxy object. You then can call the *HelloWorld* method on this object. Next the proxy object makes a request to the remote XML Web service, which returns an XML response. The proxy object parses the response and returns the data value to the caller of the *HelloWorld* method. The consumer application then sets the *Text* property of the Label control to the value fetched from the XML Web service. Figure 15-5 shows the output of this code, as viewed in a the Nokia emulator.

Figure 15-5 Output of the Web service consumption code

Web Service Discovery

You might be wondering how Visual Studio .NET knows which XML Web services are available for you to consume. You might also be wondering how you can find those XML Web services. The answer to both questions is *Web service discovery*.

Web service discovery is the process of locating the URLs of XML Web services on a remote server. This process accesses discovery (.disco) files, which are files that contain links to resources that describe an XML Web service. When you add a Web reference to your project, Visual Studio .NET performs a Web service discovery. However, you can perform a Web service discovery from the command line by using the Disco.exe tool, which performs a search and saves the results to your local machine. For more information about this tool and Web service discovery, refer to the .NET Framework SDK documentation.

Defining XML Web Service Behavior

When you created your first XML Web service, you placed a *WebMethod* attribute before the method you wanted to make publicly accessible as a Web method. This directive accepts a number of optional arguments that allow you to define certain behaviors and characteristics of the XML Web service method. Table 15-1 outlines the most common arguments of this attribute.

Table 15-1 Common Properties of the *WebMethod* Attribute

Property	Type	Description
BufferResponse	*Bool*	When the value is *True*, the IIS runtime buffers the output from the XML Web service in memory until the response is complete. The runtime then sends this buffered response to the client. If the value is *False*, the IIS runtime still buffers the output, but the size of the buffer is limited to 16KB. The default value is *True*.
CacheDuration	*int*	The length of time for which a server caches the response. This can be useful if the Web service is likely to handle several requests for the same information in a short period of time. The caching engine caches responses according to the parameters used to call the Web method. You probably won't need to enable caching; the default value of 0 seconds disables caching.

Table 15-1 Common Properties of the *WebMethod* Attribute

Property	Type	Description
Description	*String*	Describes the Web method. This description is displayed in the service description for the XML Web service.
EnableSession	*Bool*	Indicates whether session state is enabled or disabled. The default value is *False*, which means that the session state is disabled. You'll learn more about using session state with XML Web services in the next section.
MessageName	*String*	The name or alias for the Web method. You can use this attribute to provide a publicly callable alias for a method as an alternative to its actual name. You might find this useful when a class contains more than one publicly accessible method with the same name (method overloads).

You'll likely use the *Description* and *EnableSession* attributes more than any of the others. You'll learn about session management in the next section. The following code fragment shows how to use the *Description* attribute:

```
[WebMethod (Description="Method returns a Hello World String" )]
public String HelloWorld() {
    return "Hello World";
}
```

When you created your first XML Web service using command-line tools, you used a *WebService* attribute. This type of attribute is similar to a *WebMethod* attribute, except that it applies to the XML Web service as a whole rather than a single method. Table 15-2 shows the properties of this attribute that you'll use most frequently.

Table 15-2 Common Properties of the *WebService* Attribute

Property	Type	Description
Description	*String*	Describes the XML Web service. This description is displayed in the service description for the XML Web service.
Name	*String*	Defines the name of the XML Web service. Its default value is the name of the class implementing the service. You use this name within the service description, and the service's Help page displays the name.

Table 15-2 Common Properties of the *WebService* Attribute

Property	Type	Description
Namespace	*String*	Defines the XML namespace to which the XML Web service belongs. You must provide a namespace for all XML Web services that you write. The XML namespace uniquely identifies the Web methods it contains. When you create a Web service with Visual Studio .NET, the Web service gets the default namespace of *http://tempuri.org*. You should change this to your own unique namespace before putting your Web service into production.

You used the *Namespace* argument of the *WebService* attribute when you wrote your first application in this chapter. The other two arguments allow you to provide information that might be helpful to potential users of your XML Web service. You should always give these argument values. Doing so enhances the usability of the XML Web services you write.

Listing 15-2 shows the "Hello World" XML Web service you wrote earlier in the chapter—only now this service uses the *WebService* and *WebMethod* attributes to enhance its usability.

```
<%@ WebService Language="c#" Class="WebService1.MyWebService" %>

using System;
using System.Web.Services;

namespace WebService1
{
    [WebService(Namespace="http://127.0.0.1/MyFirstWebService/",
    Name="Quotes",
    Description="Provider of quite useless quotes and phrases." )]

    class MyWebService : System.Web.Services.WebService
    {
        [WebMethod(EnableSession=true,
         Description="Returns the venerable Hello World string")]
        public string HelloWorld()
        {
            return "Hello World";
        }
    }
}
```

Listing 15-2 "Hello World" XML Web service using attributes

Figure 15-6 shows the output that appears on a desktop Web browser when you view this new version of "Hello World" Web service.

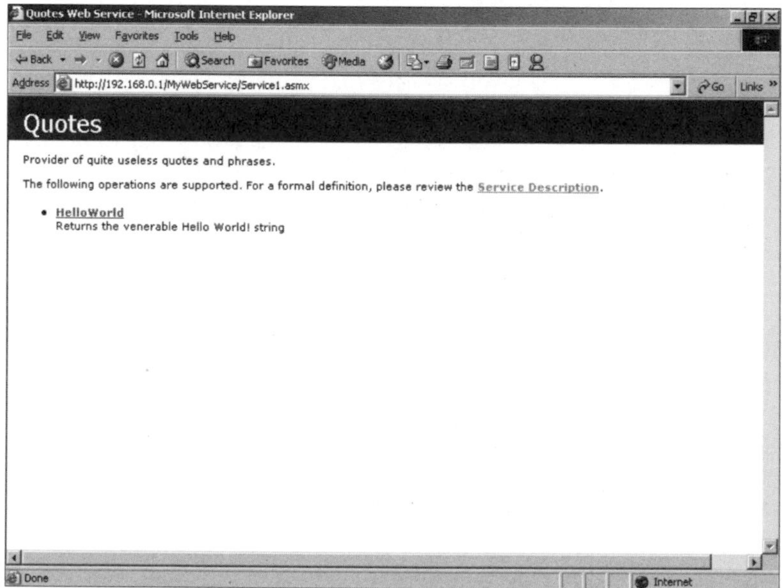

Figure 15-6 MyFirstWebServiceWithAttributes—our new version of "Hello World" with added attributes values

Working with Data Types

Each of the XML Web service examples that we've looked at so far have returned strings. However, XML Web services can return—and accept as parameters—a wide range of data types. These data types include classes, enumerations, datasets (discussed in the next section), various arrays, and the standard value types, such as *Char* and *Int32*. All these have to be encoded in XML for transfer between client and server. Value types translate directly to primitive types in the XML Schema Definition (XSD) type system, whereas the .NET XML Serializer class is used to serialize classes and complex data types. Table 15-3 shows a brief summary of the permitted data types. For a complete list of the data types XML Web services can return, refer to the .NET Framework SDK documentation.

Table 15-3 Permitted XML Web Service Data Types

Type	Description
Arrays	Arrays of *any* of the types mentioned in this table.
Classes and structures	An XML Web service will return the public properties and fields of classes or structures.
DataSet	You can include *DataSet* objects as fields in classes or structs. We'll discuss *DataSet* objects in the next section.
Enumerated types	The values of enumerations.
Primitive types	You can use any of the standard data types: *String*, *Char*, *Byte*, *Boolean*, *Int16*, *Int32*, *Int64*, *UInt16*, *UInt32*, *UInt64*, *Single*, *Double* and *Decimal*.
Reference Types	You can use certain .NET Framework reference types: *Guid* (globally unique identifier), *DateTime* (as XML's *timeInstant*, *date*, or *time*), and *XmlQualifiedName* (as XML's *QName*).
XMLNode	An XML node is an XML fragment held in memory. (See the following note for more details.)

> **Note** You can pass fragments of XML to a Web method. You store these fragments within an *XMLNode* object. For example, you can store *<myxml>Here it is!</myxml>* in an *XMLNode*. You can pass an *XMLNode* as a parameter to an XML Web service, and an XML Web service can return an *XMLNode*.

Although simple, the code in Listing 15-3 illustrates how you pass data types other than strings to an XML Web service and how that service returns different data types. More specifically, an array of floating-point values is passed to the XML Web service, with the values representing two sides of a right triangle. The *GetHypotenuse* method calculates the length of the hypotenuse and returns a floating-point value that equates to the length of the hypotenuse. In addition, the XML Web service offers a *GetTriangleStats* method, which accepts an array of lengths as a parameter and returns a user-defined *Statistics* object.

```
using System;
using System.Collections;
using System.ComponentModel;
using System.Data;
using System.Diagnostics;
```

Listing 15-3 Code-behind file Service.asmx.cs of DataTypesWebService example that uses array parameters and returns a class

```
using System.Web;
using System.Web.Services;

namespace MSPress.MobWeb.DataTypesWebService
{
    public class Service1 : System.Web.Services.WebService
    {
        [WebMethod]
        public double GetHypotenuse(double[] sides)
        {
            return Math.Sqrt(Math.Pow(sides[0],2)+ Math.Pow(sides[1],2));
        }

        [WebMethod]
        public Statistics GetTriangleStats(double[] sides)
        {
            // Create a new Statistics object.
            Statistics myStats=new Statistics();

            // Calculate the area.
            double s1=Math.Min(sides[0],sides[1]);
            double s2=Math.Min(Math.Max(sides[0],sides[1]),sides[2]);
            myStats.area=(s1*s2)/2;

            // Calculate the perimeter.
            myStats.perimeter=sides[0]+sides[1]+sides[2];

            // Return the properties of the class instance.
            return myStats;
        }
    }

    public class Statistics
    {
        // Declare fields.
        public double area;
        public double perimeter;
    }
}
```

To consume the XML Web service, you might want to write a mobile Web Forms page that collects input from a user and then passes that input to the service. However, for the sake of brevity, this example will use hard-coded values in a mobile Web Forms page code-behind module. The mobile Web Forms page (whose code isn't shown here but that you can find in the ConsumeDataTypesWebService sample in the companion material on this book's Web site) simply consists of three Label controls. Listing 15-4 shows the code-behind module for this page.

```
using System;
using System.Web;
using System.Web.Mobile;
using System.Web.UI;
using System.Web.UI.MobileControls;
using ConsumeDataTypesWebService.localhost;

namespace MSPress.MobWeb.ConsumeDataTypesWebService
{
    public class MobileWebForm1 : System.Web.UI.MobileControls.MobilePage
    {
        protected System.Web.UI.MobileControls.Form Form1;
        protected System.Web.UI.MobileControls.Label Label2;
        protected System.Web.UI.MobileControls.Label Label3;
        protected System.Web.UI.MobileControls.Label Label1;

        public MobileWebForm1()
        {
            Page.Init += new System.EventHandler(Page_Init);
        }

        private void Page_Load(object sender, System.EventArgs e)
        {
            // Create a new instance of the XML Web service.
            Service1 service1=new Service1();

            // Create an array of values.
            double[] sides=new double[3];
            sides[0]=10;
            sides[1]=10;

            // Pass to the XML Web service.
            sides[2]=s.GetHypotenuse(sides);

            // Get statistics.
            Statistics myStats = service1.GetTriangleStats(sides);

            // Set three labels to show the return values.
            Label1.Text="Hypotenuse length: " + sides[2].ToString();
            Label2.Text="Area: " + myStats.area.ToString();
            Label3.Text="Perimeter:" + myStats.perimeter.ToString();
        }
```

Listing 15-4 MobileWebForm1.aspx.cs of the ConsumeDataTypes-WebService sample

```
        private void Page_Init(object sender, EventArgs e)
        {
            InitializeComponent();
        }

        private void InitializeComponent()
        {
            this.Load += new System.EventHandler(this.Page_Load);
        }
    }
}
```

Be aware that in Listing 15-4, an instance of the *Statistics* class (the instance created in the XML Web service) doesn't actually return to the client. Instead, the properties and fields of that instance return to the client. The runtime creates a new object on the client and populates that object with the properties the XML Web service returns. Although this new object might look like an instance of the original *Statistics* object, it isn't. You can only access the properties and fields of the original object, not its methods.

Figure 15-7 shows the output this code yields.

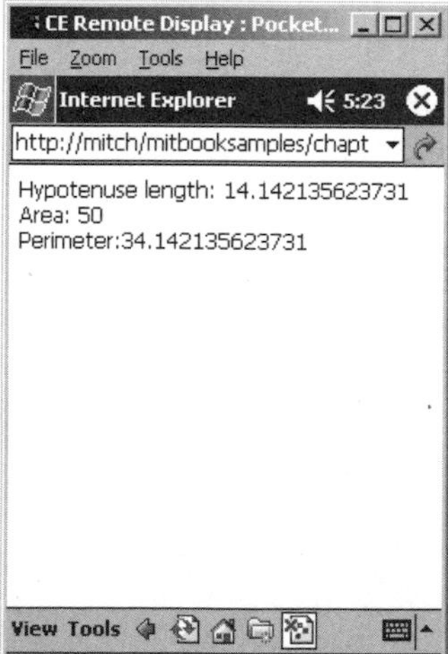

Figure 15-7 The three Label controls display values from the *Statistics* object fetched from the Web service.

Accessing Data

The example in the previous section might have led you to deduce that you can pass ADO.NET *DataSet* objects to XML Web services, which can also return

DataSet objects. The *DataSet* object is transferred between an application and an XML Web service. The ability to transfer disconnected *DataSet* objects like this allows you to manipulate data in ways that aren't possible in applications where a persistent connection to a database is required. For example, you now can perform the following tasks:

- Receive a large quantity of data in a single *DataSet* object and format the data to best suit the display characteristics of mobile devices
- Perform queries within an application on a *DataSet* that an XML Web service returns and then display only the application-level query results to the client
- Update a *DataSet* with a user's input and pass this to an XML Web service, which can then update the remote data store
- Pass *DataSet* objects obtained from a local source to an XML Web service for remote processing

DataSet objects passed to or returned from XML Web services provide an incredibly flexible approach to designing and writing data-driven mobile Web applications. This flexibility is best illustrated through an example. Listing 15-5 shows how to create an XML Web service named DataAccessWebService that returns a *DataSet*. Notice that the XML Web service is no different from any you've already created, except that it returns a *DataSet*. If you need a refresher on working with ADO.NET and *DataSet* objects, you should go to Chapter 11.

```
using System;
using System.Collections;
using System.ComponentModel;
using System.Data;
using System.Diagnostics;
using System.Web;
using System.Web.Services;
using System.Data.OleDb;

namespace MSPress.MobWeb.DataAccessWebService
{
    public class Service1 : System.Web.Services.WebService
    {
        [WebMethod]
        public DataSet GetHeights()
        {
            //Change the path to the database if it isn't installed at
            //the location defined here.
```

Listing 15-5 DataAccessWebService XML Web service, which returns a *DataSet* object

```
            string strMyConnection =
             "Provider=Microsoft.Jet.OLEDB.4.0;Data Source=" +
             "'C:\\Inetpub\\wwwroot\\DataAccessWebService\\Mountain.mdb'";
            string strMySelect = "SELECT * FROM Mountains";

            // Create a new connection.
            OleDbConnection connection =
                new OleDbConnection(strMyConnection);

            // Create the DataSet.
            DataSet myDataSet = new DataSet();

            // Create a new adapter.
            OleDbDataAdapter mycommand =
                new OleDbDataAdapter(strMySelect,connection);

            // Fill the DataSet.
            mycommand.Fill(myDataSet,"Mountains");

            return myDataSet;
        }
    }
}
```

You'll now write a mobile Web Forms page that consumes the XML Web service. The page in Listing 15-6 initially displays a list of choices to the user as well as a Command control. The code-behind module shown in Listing 15-7 accesses the XML Web service, which then returns a *DataSet*. Next you write a *switch* statement, which tests the SelectedIndex value of the SelectionList. Based on the user's input, the *switch* statement sets the string *myQuery* to a filter statement that you apply to a *DataView* object that you build from the *DataSet*. You can't apply filters directly to a *DataSet*, so you must first create a *DataView* object, as we do here.

```
<%@ Register TagPrefix="mobile"
    Namespace="System.Web.UI.MobileControls"
    Assembly="System.Web.Mobile" %>
<%@ Page language="c#"
    Codebehind="MobileWebForm1.aspx.cs"
    Inherits="MSPress.MobWeb.ConsumeDataAccessWebService.MobileWebForm1" %>

<mobile:form id="Form1" runat="server">
    <mobile:SelectionList id="SelectionList1" runat="server">
        <Item Text="All mountains"></Item>
```

Listing 15-6 MobileWebForm1.aspx of the ConsumeDataAccessWeb-Service sample application

```
        <Item Text="Above 1000m"></Item>
        <Item Text="Below 1000m"></Item>
    </mobile:SelectionList>
    <mobile:Command id="Command1" runat="server">View</ mobile:Command>
</mobile:form>

<mobile:form id="Form2" runat="server">
    <mobile:List id="List1" runat="server"></mobile:List>
</mobile:form>
```

```
using System;
using System.Collections;
using System.Data;
using System.Web;
using System.Web.Mobile;
using System.Web.UI;
using System.Web.UI.MobileControls;
using ConsumeDataAccessWebService.localhost;

namespace MSPress.MobWeb.ConsumeDataAccessWebService
{
    public class MobileWebForm1 : System.Web.UI.MobileControls.MobilePage
    {
        protected System.Web.UI.MobileControls.SelectionList SelectionList1;
        protected System.Web.UI.MobileControls.Command Command1;
        protected System.Web.UI.MobileControls.Form Form2;
        protected System.Web.UI.MobileControls.List List1;
        protected System.Web.UI.MobileControls.Form Form1;

        public MobileWebForm1()
        {
            Page.Init += new System.EventHandler(Page_Init);
        }

        private void Page_Init(object sender, EventArgs e)
        {
            InitializeComponent();
        }

        private void InitializeComponent()
        {
            this.Command1.Click += new
                System.EventHandler(this.Command1_Click);
        }

        private void Command1_Click(object sender, System.EventArgs e)
```

Listing 15-7 Code-behind module MobileWebForm1.aspx.cs of the ConsumeDataAccessWebService sample

```
        {
            String myQuery="";

            // Create a new instance of the XML Web service.
            Service1 myService = new Service1();

            // Get a DataSet from the XML Web service.
            DataSet myDataSet = myService.GetHeights();

            // Build a query.
            switch (SelectionList1.SelectedIndex)
            {
                case 0: myQuery="";
                    break;
                case 1: myQuery="HeightMeters > 1000";
                    break;
                case 2: myQuery="HeightMeters < 1000";
                    break;
            }

            // Create a new DataView using the Mountains table.
            DataView dv= new DataView(myDataSet.Tables["Mountains"]);

            // Run the filter to get the desired results.
            dv.RowFilter=myQuery;

            // Set the datasource of the list to the DataView.
            List1.DataSource=dv;

            // The name of the field to display
            List1.DataTextField="Mountain";

            // Bind
            List1.DataBind();

            // Set the active form.
            this.ActiveForm=Form2;
        }
    }
}
```

Figure 15-8 shows the output that appears after this code executes.

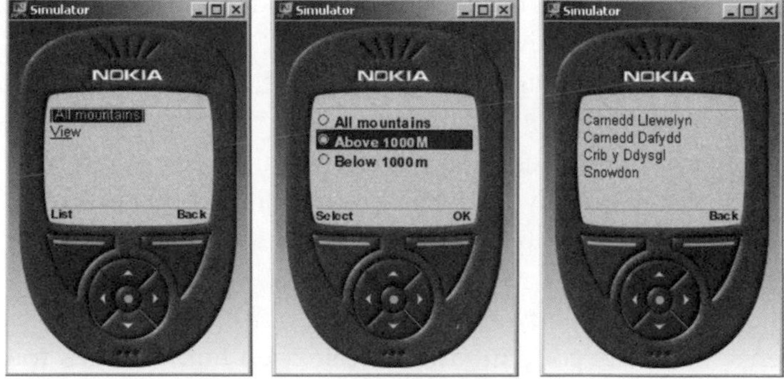

Figure 15-8 Output of a mobile Web application that consumes an XML Web service that passes data as *DataSet* objects

Considerations for Mobile Devices

You might find the title of this section a little strange. In an object-oriented framework, shouldn't XML Web services be loosely coupled with the applications that consume them and remain independent of the Web applications client? Although this is true, XML Web services offer such a flexible way to provide remote services that they're vulnerable to misuse, which can cause problems for a mobile client. That's why we thought this section was warranted.

You call XML Web services from your application code, such as an ASP.NET Mobile Controls application, and often the output from the Web service will be used to load a List control or to set the *Text* property of a TextView control, and hence is sent to be displayed in the client browser. For example, consider a stock price Web service: an application might allow the user to enter a code that indicates whether he or she requires the price of an individual stock or the prices of an entire sector, and this code is passed in the call to the stock price Web service. If the stock price Web service returns a response containing the prices of an entire sector, a desktop browser could easily display a page containing all that data. In fact, most desktop browsers could display all the prices of stocks that an individual exchange quotes. However, an application that displays on a mobile client can't display all the information the service returns, even though it can call the service.

This scenario even extends to situations in which you provide a mobile Web Forms page that formats and paginates information on behalf of the user. Imagine an application that displays 100 pages of information. This would certainly test the patience of even the most understanding user. As a developer, it's your responsibility to ensure that a mobile client gains the most benefit from a mobile application. To write usable applications that access XML Web services, you should always keep a few things in mind.

First, when you write an XML Web service, you should *not* make it provide data that's optimized for a particular client. For example, the idea of providing information in small chunks might appeal to you. However, this breaks the whole design philosophy of .NET applications. You should treat XML Web services as objects that simply return data from some processing function with no regard for the client.

Second, you should always consider the potential limitations of many mobile clients and write code in your mobile Web Forms pages to compensate for them. For example, the stock quote service mentioned earlier can return information in a *DataSet* object, which can contain the ticker symbol, current price, day high, day low, yield, gearing, and so forth. A desktop browser can easily display all this information. However, if you display all this information as a whole on a mobile client, the application will effectively be unusable. Restructure the information by providing a list of ticker symbols with links to further detail pages. It makes more sense to break this information up and to initially offer the user only the more important parts.

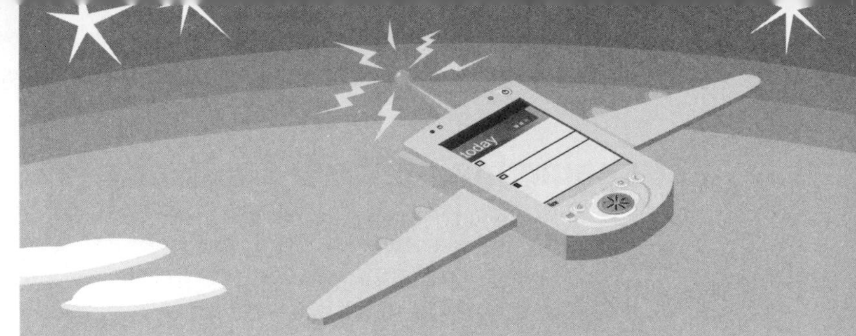

16

Debugging, Testing with Emulators, and Handling Run-Time Errors

As developers, we all want to write perfect code all the time. Of course, in the real world, although perfect code is the ideal, it's never the reality. Fortunately, Microsoft ASP.NET and ASP.NET Mobile Controls offer lots of help with tracking down the bugs and analyzing the errors that are the symptoms of imperfect code. If you're using Microsoft Visual Studio .NET, the integrated debugger serves as a valuable tool for examining applications while they're executing. The Microsoft .NET Framework SDK also includes a lightweight debugger that you can use when working outside Visual Studio .NET.

In this chapter, you'll learn how to configure your applications to support debugging with Visual Studio .NET or the debugger that ships with the .NET Framework SDK. You'll see how to use the ASP.NET Trace facility, a valuable tool that allows you to monitor execution time and the order of execution of methods, examine HTTP headers, and write your own debug output. You'll also find out how to trap run-time errors and implement custom error pages to display to your users instead of using the developer-oriented error display. And finally, you'll learn how to set up different mobile device emulators for testing.

Debugging Mobile Web Applications

When you build an application, the compiler ensures that the code defined in code-behind modules and other classes compiles correctly. Despite this compile-time syntax checking, several other types of errors can occur when you run your application:

- **Configuration errors** Parsing errors that occur in one of the configuration files: machine.config in the C:/WINNT/Microsoft.NET/Framework/*version*/CONFIG directory, the server-wide Web.config file in the Web server root directory, or Web.config in the application directories.
- **ASP.NET parser errors** Occur when the server control syntax in an .aspx file is malformed.
- **Compilation errors** Occur when a coding error exists in code modules included with an .aspx file.
- **Run-time errors** Caused by unexpected behavior of your application logic, or situations you have not anticipated, such as the existence of null object references or division by zero.

By default, if a run-time error occurs in an ASP.NET application during execution, the runtime tries to report as much information about the error as possible on the requesting browser screen. The ASP.NET Mobile Controls Runtime ensures that the markup language the error page uses is appropriate for the client device. The runtime provides a shorter version of the error page on WML devices, as Figure 16-1 shows. A WML device that has a large display area displays a usable amount of error feedback on a single screen. However, if you use a device or an emulator that has only a small display, paging through the information to get the error details you need becomes tedious. For this reason, we advise using Microsoft Internet Explorer to perform initial application testing.

Figure 16-1 Detailed error reporting in Internet Explorer vs. a shorter version of the same report on the Openwave simulator

Configuring Applications to Support Debugging

If you've configured an application to support debugging, the ASP.NET error display offers details about the source line where the error occurred. A debugger process must be able to link executable code to its source to give detailed error reports and to perform other debugging functions, such as pausing at the code line where the developer has set a breakpoint.

Compiling the source code with debug symbols enables this link between the source and the executable code. Because many parts of an ASP.NET application dynamically compile at run time, you configure the application to compile for debugging by setting the *debug* attribute to *true* in the *<compilation>* element within Web.config, the application configuration file in the application root directory. Listing 16-1 shows the syntax for this technique.

```
<?xml version="1.0" encoding="utf-8" ?>
<configuration>
  <system.web>

    <!--  DYNAMIC DEBUG COMPILATION
          Set compilation debug="true" to enable ASPX debugging.
          Otherwise, setting this value to
          false will improve runtime performance of this application.
    -->
    <compilation debug="true"/>
        ⋮
  </system.web>
</configuration>
```

Listing 16-1 Web.config file, including support for debug compilation

As the comment in Listing 16-1 suggests, when your application goes live, you should set the *debug* attribute to *false*. Leaving this attribute on creates a substantial performance overhead.

> **Note** In Visual Studio .NET, you can edit the Web.config file for an application directly. Double-click the Web.config file in Solution Explorer, and Visual Studio .NET opens an editor window. Another convenient way to make changes in this file is to view a mobile Web Forms control in Design view in the Mobile Internet Designer. If you click on the background outside any Form control, the Properties window displays properties of an item it calls DOCUMENT. Many of the properties displayed here, such as *debug*, *trace*, and *errorPage*, are settings that are stored in Web.config. Changing the property of the DOCUMENT element causes the Web.config file to be updated automatically.

Visual Studio .NET has an integrated debugger that allows you to set breakpoints, step through code, and watch variables. This integrated debugger makes it easy to step into components and even into code running on remote machines, such as XML Web services, to examine the operation of your applications. If you're not using Visual Studio .NET, you can use the Common Language Runtime Debugger (cordbg.exe) that comes with the .NET Framework. You can run this debugger from the command line. Consult the .NET Framework SDK documentation for details on using these debuggers.

Using the ASP.NET Trace Facility

The ASP.NET Trace facility is an easy-to-use tool that helps you debug applications by reporting lots of useful information about your application. Figure 16-2 shows an example of the kinds of information reported. This information includes execution times at various points in the application life cycle and details about the HTTP headers, and it shows the entire control tree for the application and gives information about cookies and *ViewState*.

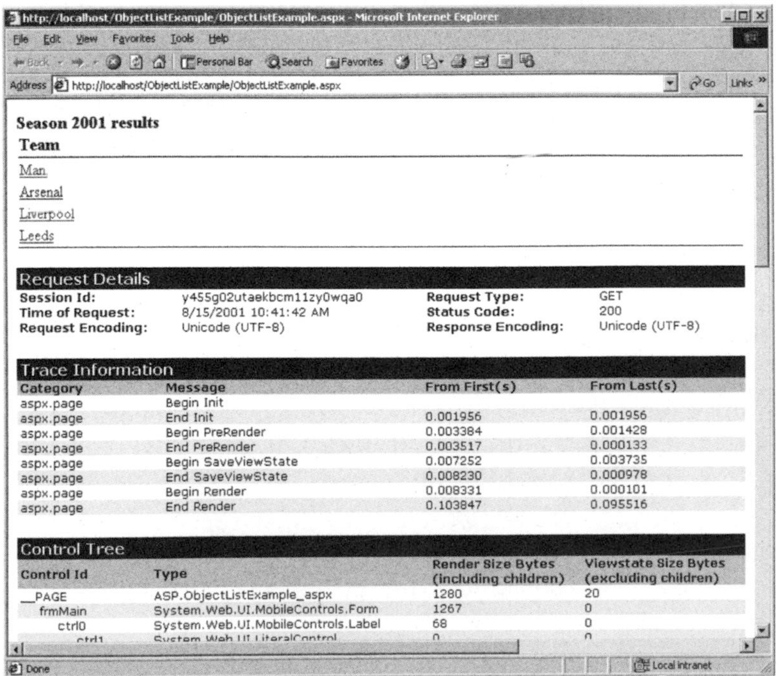

Figure 16-2 Example of page-level trace output

There are two ways of generating and examining trace output:

- **Page-Level Tracing** In this mode, the application's normal output is shown at the top of the page, and below it is appended the trace output, as shown in Figure 16-2.

> **Warning** The runtime always writes trace output in HTML. If you turn on page-level tracing and test with WML clients, the output from the *Trace* statements is still HTML. WML browsers cannot display a mixture of WML and HTML, so the client browser won't be able to display the page. Consequently, you can use page-level tracing only when testing with an HTML browser.

- **Application-Level Tracing** When you use application-level tracing, instead of including the trace output in the client output stream, the runtime writes the logging output to disk and retrieves it separately by using an HTML Web browser to access the specially mapped Trace.axd URL from the application root. For example, if your application resides at *http://localhost/MyMobileApp*, fetching *http://localhost/MyMobileApp/Trace.axd* retrieves the trace output.

You can also add your own custom messages into the trace output. You can insert debugging statements in your code to print out the value of variables and structures, test assumptions in your code, or assert that you've met specific conditions. The *Trace* property of the *MobilePage* class exposes a *System.Web.TraceContext* object. You can use the *Trace.Write* and *Trace.Warn* methods to print out debug messages. You can leave trace statements in place in production code because you can turn off tracing at the page level or the application level. If you do turn off tracing at either level, the methods of the *TraceContext* object won't execute.

Enabling Page-Level Tracing

To enable *page-level* trace logging, include the *Trace* attribute set to *true* within the *@ Page* directive at the top of the page:

```
<%@ Page Trace = "true" Inherits = … %>
```

In this mode, output from *Trace* debug messages is displayed as HTML statements appended to the output of the current page. As we've already mentioned, do not use page-level tracing with WML clients because the client browser will not be able to interpret the mixture of WML and HTML markup that it receives.

Enabling Application-Level Tracing

To enable *application-level* trace logging, include the following configuration code in the Web.config application configuration file in the application root directory:

```
<configuration>
  <system.web>
    <trace enabled="true"/>
  </system.web>
</configuration>
```

This code turns on page-level tracing for every page within the application, but instead of including the trace output in the client output stream, the runtime writes the logging output to disk. You must use application-level trace logging when tracing applications with a WML client.

View the trace output by using an HTML Web browser to access the specially mapped Trace.axd URL from the application root. For example, if your application resides at *http://localhost/MyMobileApp*, fetching *http://localhost/MyMobileApp/Trace.axd* retrieves the trace output. When you fetch the trace.axd page, you see a listing of the trace output from recent requests, as shown in Figure 16-3. It's important to understand that there is one trace entry for each request, not one for the complete set of HTTP requests that a client makes as it runs through your application.

There are a number of attributes you can set on the *<trace>* element to modify default application tracing behavior. The following code shows the full syntax for this, including all attributes:

```
<configuration>
  <system.web>
    <trace
      enabled="true"
      traceMode="SortByCategory"
      requestLimit="15"
      pageOutput="false"
      localOnly="true"
    />
  </system.web>
</configuration>
```

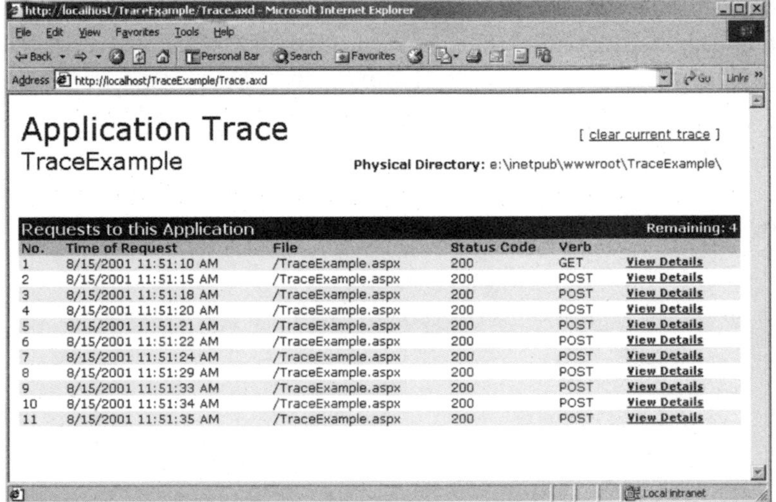

Figure 16-3 Accessing application-level traces from a desktop Web browser using the specially mapped URL Trace.axd

Table 16-1 describes the attributes of the *<trace>* element.

Table 16-1 Trace Attributes

Attribute	Description
enabled	Set to *true* or *false*. This attribute indicates whether tracing is enabled for the application. The default is *true* when a *<trace>* element is present. Therefore, you must set this attribute to *false* when you deploy the application, or you must remove the *<trace>* element from the Web.config file. Even if application-level tracing is enabled, you can disable tracing for an individual page if that page specifies the *<%@ Page Trace="false" ... %>* directive.
traceMode	Set to *SortByTime* or *SortByCategory*. This attribute dictates how the runtime sorts trace messages on output. The default is *SortByTime*.
requestLimit	Application-level tracing stores details of the last *requestLimit* requests to the application. The default is 10 requests. When you access the trace output by accessing Trace.axd from the application root, the runtime lists the stored requests so that you can select which one to examine. The display includes a Clear Current Trace link that clears cached request traces. Figure 16-3 shows this list.
pageOutput	Set to *true* or *false* (default). If *false*, trace output is accessible only through the Trace.axd URL. If *true*, the trace output is rendered (in HTML) at the end of each page's output as well. A word of caution: do not set this attribute to *true* when testing with WML clients.
localOnly	Set to *true* (default) or *false*. If *true*, the trace log is viewable only from the local machine. If *false*, any machine can access the trace log.

Be aware that enabling application-level tracing doesn't automatically disable page-level tracing. You can turn off tracing in individual pages in your application by including a *<%@ Page Trace = "false" … %>* directive in them.

Table 16-2 describes the effects of combining application-level trace settings and page-level settings.

Table 16-2 Combining Application-Level and Page-Level Settings

Page Directive	Application Tracing	Result
No trace setting defined	*enabled = "true"*	Trace output for that page goes only to the application trace log, Trace.axd.
trace="true"	*enabled = "true"*	Trace output goes to the application log and is also appended (in HTML) to the normal application page sent to the client.
trace="false"	*enabled = "true"*	Trace output disabled for that page.
trace="true"	*<trace>* element not specified	HTML trace output is appended to the normal application page sent to the client.
Any value	*enabled = "false"*	Trace output is disabled.

Adding Your Own Trace Statements

As we've mentioned, the *MobilePage.Trace* property exposes a *TraceContext* object. You can use this object to add statements of your own that write to the trace output. *Trace.Write* and *Trace.Warn* both print to the trace output; the only difference is that *Trace.Warn* appears in red. In its simplest usage, you insert these statements into your code to output trace messages tracking passage through a section of code or to print out values:

```
// Trace message
Trace.Write("Beginning Validation Code...");
```

Overloads of the *Warn* and *Write* methods take parameters of a user-defined category name as well as the string to output, as the following syntax shows:

```
// Trace message
Trace.Warn("arrayContents", "Creating data array");
```

Categories can be useful when you want to group trace output statements or ensure that the code lists your own trace messages together, rather than interspersing them with the default trace messages. The *TraceMode* attribute of the *Page* directive is *TraceMode="SortByTime"* by default. If you want to sort by category, modify the *@ Page* directive as shown in the following code:

```
<%@ Page Trace="true" TraceMode="SortByCategory" ... %>
```

This code causes the runtime to sort the Trace Messages section of the output by category. The *axpx.page* category identifies the default trace messages, while the category that you've defined contains the trace messages that you've written. Figure 16-4 shows trace messages sorted by category.

Trace Information			
Category	**Message**	**From First(s)**	**From Last(s)**
arrayContents	Creating data array	0.005193	0.002884
arrayContents	Name: Dunes	0.009203	0.004009
arrayContents	Name: Phoenix	0.009315	0.000113
arrayContents	Name: Eagles	0.009367	0.000052
arrayContents	Name: Zodiac	0.009420	0.000052
aspx.page	Begin Init		
aspx.page	End Init	0.002310	0.002310
aspx.page	Begin PreRender	0.010127	0.000707
aspx.page	End PreRender	0.010372	0.000245
aspx.page	Begin SaveViewState	0.010996	0.000624
aspx.page	End SaveViewState	0.011933	0.000938
aspx.page	Begin Render	0.012015	0.000082
aspx.page	End Render	0.049350	0.035693
SessionViewState	/mitbooksamples/chapter16/cs/TraceExample/TraceExample.aspx(1)	0.013658	0.001643

Figure 16-4 Trace messages sorted by category

Executing Blocks of Code in Trace Mode

Occasionally, you might need to execute some code to generate the output that you want to send to the trace output. The *TraceContext* object includes the *IsEnabled* property, which you can use in your application to determine whether the trace facility is enabled. This property is useful when you want to output more complicated trace information, such as listing the members of a collection, as shown here:

```
if ( Trace.IsEnabled )
{
    if (array.Count == 0)
    {
        Trace.Warn("arrayContents", "No entries!");
    }
    else
    {
        foreach (TeamStats aTeam in array)
            {
                Trace.Write("arrayContents", "Name: " + aTeam.TeamName);
            }
    }
}
```

Handling Errors

No matter how rigorous your testing process, sometimes your application will fail after going live. During development, the detailed error reports that are displayed are a valuable aid to debugging. But in a live application, you probably won't want your users to see these detailed error reports.

Implementing Custom Error Pages

In the *<system.web>* section of the *<configuration>* settings in Web.config, you can specify that the code deliver custom error pages to your clients. In the following example, the code reports all errors for remote clients through a custom error page named GenericError.aspx, situated in the root directory of the application:

```
<?xml version="1.0" encoding="utf-8" ?>
<configuration>
    <system.web>
        <!--  CUSTOM ERROR MESSAGES
          Set mode="On" or "RemoteOnly" to enable custom error messages,
          "Off" to disable.
          Add <error> tags for each of the errors you want to handle.
        -->
        <customErrors
            defaultRedirect="genericerror.aspx"
            mode="RemoteOnly">
        </customErrors>

        <httpRuntime useFullyQualifiedRedirectUrl="true" />

    </system.web>
</configuration>
```

For custom error pages to work with all mobile clients, you must set the *useFullyQualifiedRedirectUrl* attribute of the *<httpRuntime>* element to *true* as the code shows because some clients don't handle relative URLs correctly. Table 16-3 describes the attributes of the *<customErrors>* element.

Be sure to code your custom error page using mobile controls so that it can be displayed on all clients.

You can provide different error pages for specific HTTP status codes, such as error 500, Internal Server Error, and error 403, Access Denied. Here's the syntax you'd use for these status codes:

```
<?xml version="1.0" encoding="utf-8" ?>
<configuration>
    <system.web>
        <customErrors
```

```
            defaultRedirect="../genericerror.aspx"
            mode="RemoteOnly">
            <error statusCode="500" redirect="/error/interror.aspx"/>
            <error statusCode="404" redirect="/error/notfound.aspx"/>
            <error statusCode="403" redirect="/error/noaccess.aspx"/>
        </customErrors>
    </system.web>
</configuration>
```

You can use the custom error page to provide a much more user-friendly message to your remote users. Although your application might have failed, using such a message allows it to fail with some style!

Table 16-3 Attributes of the *customErrors* Element

Attribute	Settings
mode	Set to *On*, *Off*, or *RemoteOnly*. ■ ***On*** The runtime enables custom error pages and sends them to all clients. ■ ***Off*** The runtime disables custom error pages and sends standard detailed ASP.NET error pages to both localhost and remote clients. ■ ***RemoteOnly*** Clients running on the ASP.NET server get detailed error reports, while remote clients get custom error pages.
defaultRedirect	The URL of the default custom error page.

The runtime redirects the client to a custom error page passing the URL of the page where the error originated in the query string in the *aspxerrorpath* parameter. Listing 16-2 shows an example of a custom error page that makes use of the *aspxerrorpath* parameter to display the URL of the page where the error occurred in the message to the user. This error page is designed to display a suitable message when the code traps an error 404 (Resource Not Found). In the <script> block on this page, there is code that defines the *errorSource* property, which exposes the *aspxerrorpath* parameter from the query string. The *Page_Load* method simply calls the *DataBind* method to ensure that all ASP.NET data binding statements are resolved. In the text the TextView control displays are the data binding statements (<%# *errorSource* %>), which display the value of the *errorSource* property.

```
<%@ Page Inherits="System.Web.UI.MobileControls.MobilePage"
    Language="c#" %>
<%@ Register TagPrefix="mobile" Namespace="System.Web.UI.MobileControls"
    Assembly="System.Web.Mobile" %>

<html>
    <head>
        <script language="c#" runat="server">

        public String errorSource {
            get { return (
              (NameValueCollection)Request.QueryString)["aspxerrorpath"];
            }
        }

        void Page_Load(object sender, System.EventArgs e)
        {
            DataBind();
        }

        </script>
    </head>

    <body>
        <mobile:Form runat="server" id="frmMain">
            <mobile:Label runat="server" StyleReference="title" id="lbl1">
                An Error Has Occurred</mobile:Label>

            <mobile:TextView runat="server">
            We could not locate the page you requested...
            <p>The URL was: <br>
            <a href='<%# errorSource %>'><%# errorSource %></a>
            <br><br>
            Please try again, or visit our search page for help.
            </mobile:TextView>
        </mobile:Form >
    </body>
</html>
```

Listing 16-2 Source for notfound.aspx, a custom error page that is displayed when the code traps an HTTP error 404

Figure 16-5 shows the output of this error message on Pocket Internet Explorer. The sample application CustomErrorPageExample, included in the companion material on this book's Web site, illustrates this technique.

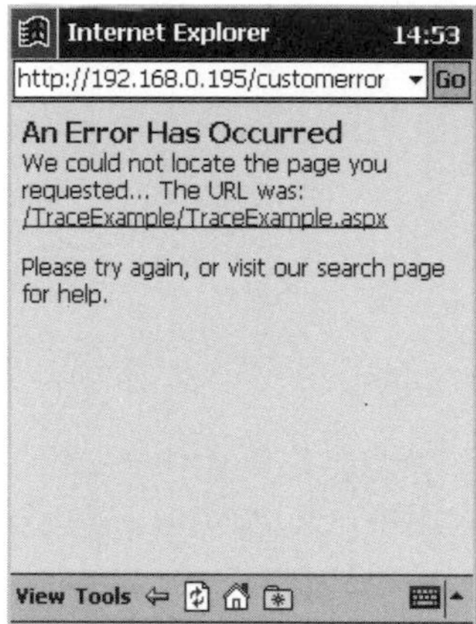

Figure 16-5 Output of the notfound.aspx custom error page on Pocket Internet Explorer

Handling Errors Programmatically

Another way to handle errors is to trap them in code. The *Page* base class contains the *Page_Error* method, which you can override in your mobile page. You'll see an example of this in a moment, in Listing 16-4. The code calls the *Page_Error* method whenever an untrapped run-time exception occurs. You must disable *<customErrors>* in Web.config if you want to trap errors in code.

Alternatively, you can trap errors at the application level by trapping the *Application_Error* event in Global.asax. This event has the following signature:

```
void Application_Error(Object sender, EventArgs e)
{
    //Do something here.
}
```

Handling errors in code allows you to perform additional functions, such as write to an application error log, send e-mail to a support account, page personnel (if an application is critical), or write to the Windows system event log.

CustomErrorInCode.aspx (shown in Listing 16-3) and its code-behind module, CustomErrorInCode.aspx.cs (shown in Listing 16-4), cause an error in the *Page_Load* method by trying to perform a *ToString* method on a *null* object. The code traps this object in the *Page_Error* method, where it sends an e-mail message to the system administrator and then redirects the request to a different mobile Web Forms page, Errorforms.aspx. The ErrorForms.aspx page displays an apology form. In Listing 16-5, the first Web Forms page where the error occurred stores data in the *Session* object. The error page retrieves the data from the *Session* object and uses it to set the *LabelSource* label.

> **Note** For this sample to operate, SMTP mail must be enabled on your Web server. Enter **File:\\%systemroot%\help\mail.chm** in your browser address bar to access help for the SMTP mail service built into Microsoft Windows.

```
<%@ Page Inherits="MSPress.MobWeb.CustomError.MyWebForm" Language="c#"
    CodeBehind="customerrorincode.aspx.cs"%>
<%@ Register TagPrefix="mobile" Namespace="System.Web.UI.MobileControls"
    Assembly="System.Web.Mobile" %>

<mobile:Form runat="server" id="Form1">
    <mobile:Label runat="server" id="Label1"/>
</mobile:Form>
```

Listing 16-3 Source file CustomErrorInCode.aspx

```
using System;
using System.Collections;
using System.Web.Mail;
using System.Web.UI.MobileControls;

namespace MSPress.MobWeb.CustomError
{
    public class MyWebForm : System.Web.UI.MobileControls.MobilePage
    {
        protected Label Label1;

        override protected void OnInit(EventArgs e)
        {
            InitializeComponent();
            base.OnInit(e);
        }

        private void InitializeComponent()
        {
            this.Load += new System.EventHandler(this.Page_Load);
        }

        protected void Page_Load(Object sender, EventArgs e)
        {
            String foo = null;
            Label1.Text = foo.ToString();
```

Listing 16-4 Code-behind module CustomErrorInCode.aspx.cs

```
        }

        void Page_Error(Object sender, EventArgs e)
        {
            String message = Request.Url.ToString()
                + "<font color='red'>" + Server.GetLastError().ToString()
                + "</font>";

            MailMessage mail = new MailMessage();
            mail.From = "applicationErrorTrapper@yourservername.com";
            mail.To = "administrator@yourservername.com";
            mail.Subject = "Mobile Web Site Error";
            mail.Body = message;
            mail.BodyFormat = MailFormat.Html;
            SmtpMail.Send(mail);

            Server.ClearError();

            Session["Errorsource"] = Request.Url.ToString();
            Response.Redirect("ErrorForms.aspx");
        }
    }
}
```

```
<%@ Page Inherits="System.Web.UI.MobileControls.MobilePage"
    Language="c#" %>
<%@ Register TagPrefix="mobile" Namespace="System.Web.UI.MobileControls"
    Assembly="System.Web.Mobile" %>

  <head>
      <script runat="server" language="c#">
          void Page_Load(object sender, System.EventArgs e)
          {
              LabelSource.Text = "Error occurred at URL "
                  + Session["Errorsource"];
          }
      </script>
  </head>

  <body>
      <mobile:Form runat="server" id="Form1" BackColor="Khaki">
          <mobile:Label runat="server" StyleReference="title">
```

Listing 16-5 The ErrorForms.aspx mobile Web Forms page that is displayed as a result of the redirect in Listing 16-4

```
            An Error Has Occurred</mobile:Label>
        <mobile:Label runat="server" id="LabelSource"
           StyleReference="error"/>
        <mobile:TextView runat="server">
        We're sorry!
        <p>
        Our support team has been notified and will be working to
        resolve the problem as soon as possible.
        <br><br>
        Please try again later.
        </mobile:TextView>
    </mobile:Form>
</body>
```

Figure 16-6 shows an Openwave simulator displaying this error form.

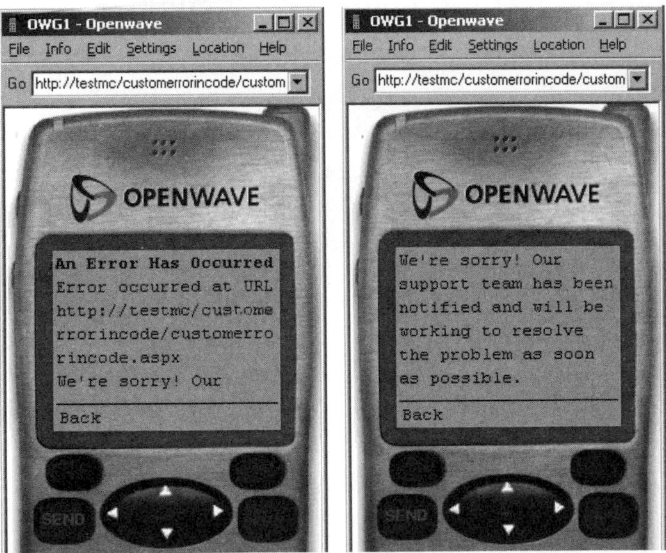

Figure 16-6 Openwave simulator output of the error form shown in Listing 16-5

Testing with Emulators and Real Devices

In Chapter 2, you learned how to test your applications using Internet Explorer and the Openwave simulator. The use of the WML, cHTML, or XHTML browser of your choice alongside Internet Explorer might prove sufficient for much of your initial application testing. However, if you expect your users to access your application from different devices, you should test with emulators of those devices and, ultimately, with the actual devices. Although the software emulator tools often use the same browser software used in the actual device, there's no substitute for testing with the real device. Emulators operate as Windows processes, which clearly isn't the situation when the browser runs on a mobile phone or handheld device. The other major difference between an emulator and a real device is in the response speeds. A real device operating over a wireless network uses network links that operate much slower than an emulator operating over your local area network (LAN). Real wireless network links also experience much higher *latency*—the delay introduced by network components. You must test with real devices to get a realistic feel for the performance of your application.

Using Pocket Internet Explorer for Application Testing

The Pocket PC is a very popular and versatile handheld device. Pocket Internet Explorer, an HTML 3.2 browser that runs on devices with the Pocket PC 2000 and Pocket PC 2002 operating systems, is one of the browsers that ASP.NET mobile controls support. From a developer's point of view, Pocket Internet Explorer is one of the more interesting clients because it supports a large screen and color display, allowing more flexibility in content design.

Pocket PC Phone Edition devices include integrated telephony support, enabling you to connect to the Internet by signing up with a wireless Internet service provider (ISP). Other devices are equipped with 802.11 support, allowing them to connect to a wireless LAN (WLAN) or to a WLAN hot spot in public spaces such as airports, coffee shops, and meeting halls. Devices without integrated wireless network connectivity can still connect to the Web through a fixed line when equipped with an appropriate modem. Alternatively, if you have a mobile phone that's Internet enabled and supports infrared communications, you can use the infrared (IR) link of the Pocket PC to connect to the mobile phone and thus connect to the Web.

As a developer, you'll do much better to connect to your development Web server over the LAN, without connecting over external wireless or fixed-line networks. Connecting to your development Web server over a secure and private LAN will promote rapid and cost-efficient coding without requiring you to debug in a live environment.

When you place your Pocket PC in its desktop cradle and connect it to your PC using a serial or USB connection, you can use Microsoft ActiveSync software to connect the two components and thus synchronize your contacts, e-mail, data, and cached Web content. In versions of Pocket PC software prior to Pocket PC 2002, Pocket Internet Explorer was unable to connect to the Web over an ActiveSync connection, although that restriction is now removed.

As an alternative to accessing the Web over an ActiveSync connection, you can equip your Pocket PC with an Ethernet card, such as those from Socket Communications (*http://www.socketcom.com*). This card is essential for power users such as mobile application developers. An Ethernet card connects your Pocket PC to your LAN and enables you to use Pocket Internet Explorer to connect to applications on any Web server—including development servers on your LAN.

The Microsoft Pocket PC Web site offers a tool that allows you to remotely control your Pocket PC from your desktop. This tool is called Remote Display Control, and it's invaluable when testing with a real device. You can download this tool from *http://www.microsoft.com/mobile/pocketpc/downloads/powertoys.asp*. This unsupported tool opens a window on your desktop PC that's a copy of the current display on the remote Pocket PC connected to your network. You can also enter data using your PC keyboard as though you were inputting it directly into the Pocket PC, which can save you time during development testing.

Using a Pocket PC Emulator

If you don't have access to a real Pocket PC, a solution for testing with a Pocket PC is to use the Pocket PC 2002 emulator included in Microsoft Visual Studio .NET 2003. (Visual Studio .NET 2003 also includes an emulator of a Microsoft Windows CE .NET device.) This emulator is intended for developing applications for smart devices using the Microsoft .NET Compact Framework, but it's also invaluable for testing mobile Web applications. The Microsoft .NET Compact Framework is a "lite" version of the full .NET Framework, which supports the execution of .NET applications running on Pocket PC or Windows CE .NET devices. .NET Compact Framework applications are "rich-client" applications that run on the device, as compared with ASP.NET Mobile Controls applications that run on Web servers and communicate with Web browsers on the devices. The Pocket PC 2002 emulator runs the Windows CE operating system and includes all the standard bundled applications, including Pocket Internet Explorer.

> **Note** If you don't have Visual Studio .NET 2003, you can still get the Pocket PC emulators if you install eMbedded Visual Tools 3.0 (or later) on your PC. You can access this free download from *http://www.microsoft.com/mobile/developer/default.asp* or order it on CD. eMbedded Visual Tools 3.0 includes eMbedded Microsoft Visual Basic and eMbedded Microsoft Visual C++, both of which you can use to develop native applications for the Pocket PC. More important for the ASP.NET developer, eMbedded Visual Tools 3.0 also includes a full software emulation of a Pocket PC 2000 device. (You can download the Pocket PC 2002 SDK from the same source to "upgrade" the standard eMbedded Visual Tools emulator to the Pocket PC 2002 emulator, similar to the one bundled with Visual Studio .NET 2003.)
>
> To run the emulator, go to Start, point to Microsoft Windows Platform SDK For Pocket PC, and then click Desktop Pocket PC Emulation.

> **Warning** The Pocket PC 2000 emulator that's shipped in eMbedded Visual Tools 3.0 doesn't include Microsoft JScript support by default, which is required for some ASP.NET mobile controls applications. You must download emulation support from the MSDN download center. See *http://support.microsoft.com/support/kb/articles/Q296/9/04.ASP* for details.

To start the emulator in Visual Studio .NET 2003, click the Tools menu, choose Connect To Device, select Pocket PC in the Platform drop-down list, select Pocket PC 2002 Emulator in the Devices list, and then click Connect.

If you haven't worked with a Pocket PC before, you'll notice that the Start button appears in the upper left corner of the screen instead of the lower left corner, as on a desktop PC. Click Start in the emulation, and click Internet Explorer in the menu that appears. To use Pocket Internet Explorer for development testing, you'll need to enter your own URLs. To do so, click View, and then click Address Bar to make the address bar visible, as shown in Figure 16-7. Make sure that the Fit To Screen option on this menu is checked.

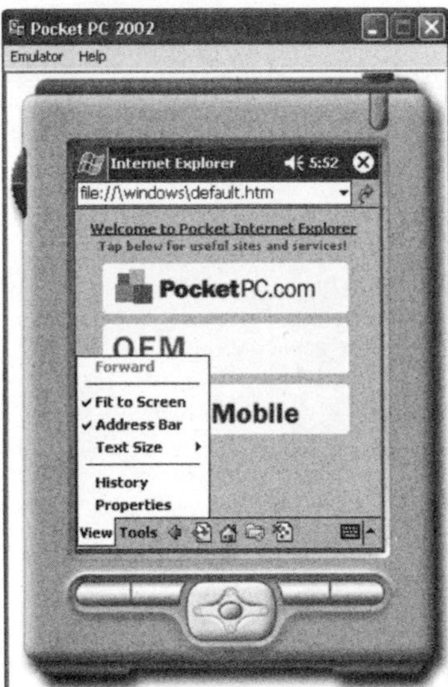

Figure 16-7 Make the address bar visible in Pocket Internet Explorer to enter application URLs

Testing with a Microsoft Smartphone Emulator

The Smartphone Emulator for Windows CE is supported by Device Update 2 for ASP.NET, which you can download from the Microsoft ASP.NET Web site at *http://www.asp.net/mobile/testeddevices.aspx?tabindex=6*. (There are two versions of Device Update 2 available for download: one for Visual Studio .NET 2002 and one for Visual Studio .NET 2003.) The emulator is shown in Figure 16-8. This emulator is available for free, but you must first download and install Microsoft eMbedded Visual Tools (also free), which is the integrated development environment (IDE) you use to develop applications for Smartphone. Download eMbedded Visual Tools from *http://www.microsoft.com/mobile/developer/default.asp*, or order it on CD. When you install the eMbedded Visual Tools, you have the option of installing the Handheld PC SDK, Palm-Size PC SDK, and Pocket PC SDK, but you don't need these to use the Smartphone emulator.

After you have installed eMbedded Visual Tools, you must download and install the Smartphone 2002 SDK, again from *http://www.microsoft.com/mobile/developer/default.asp*. When you have done so, you can start up the emulator. Start eMbedded Visual C++ 3.0 from the Start menu, click Tools, choose Configure Platform Manager, double-click Smartphone 2002 Emulation, and then click Test.

To use the Smartphone for testing mobile Web applications, click the left softkey, marked Programs, and then enter the number in the Programs list for Internet Explorer (number 4 by default). Click the right softkey, marked Menu, and then click the center of the main control pad to select the GoTo option. You can enter URLs on this page, as shown in Figure 16-8.

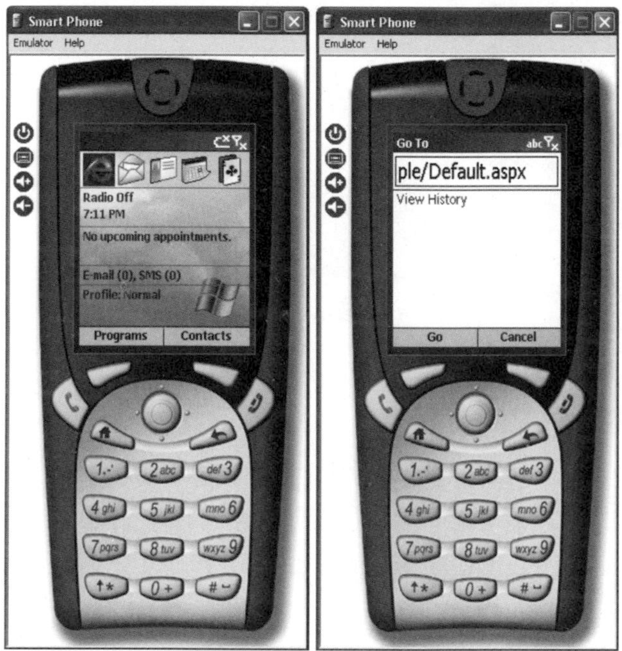

Figure 16-8 The Microsoft Smartphone 2002 emulator, which uses Pocket Internet Explorer to enter application URLs

Testing with Mobile Phone Emulators

ASP.NET supports mobile Web applications on a large number of mobile devices, including the following:

- Pocket Internet Explorer used on Pocket PC and Smartphone devices
- 11 different Nokia devices, plus the 3.0 (WML) and 3.1 (XHTML) emulators from the Nokia Mobile Internet Toolkit
- Samsung and Sprint devices using Openwave UP.Browser
- Sanyo and Sony devices, and the Openwave simulator with the Mitsubishi T250 skin that uses the Openwave UP.Browser version 3.2
- Alcatel, Samsung, Sanyo, Sony, Siemens, LG, Motorola, and the UP.Browser 4.1 emulator with default skin that uses the Openwave UP.Browser version 4.1

- Microsoft Mobile Explorer on Sony handsets
- RIM BlackBerry 950 and 957 two-way pagers with the Go.America browser
- Palm VIIx, Palm V, and m505 devices with Blazer, AvantGo, Go.America, Palm, AU-Systems, and Omnisky browsers
- Mitsubishi and NEC 502i i-mode mobile phones
- Ericsson T20, T29, T39, T65, T68, R320 and R380 devices, plus the R380 emulator and WAP Toolkit 3.2 emulator

Check the Microsoft ASP.NET Web site, at *http://www.asp.net/mobile/testeddevices.aspx?tabindex=6*, for an updated list of the supported devices. Also check the same site and the Microsoft mobile devices Web site (*http://www.microsoft.com/mobile*) for any new Device Update packs. If Microsoft doesn't support the particular device that you want to use, you might want to add support for it yourself. You'll learn more about Device Update packs and how to add support for new devices in Chapter 19.

If you expect users to access your application with a number of different devices, you should plan to test with real examples of those devices. However, it's often more convenient—and less expensive—to test with emulators. Most of the major mobile phone suppliers and a number of other companies provide emulators that you can download for testing. The following is a list of some of the more popular emulators you can download:

- **Nokia** Nokia frequently updates its Nokia Mobile Internet Toolkit, which includes an emulator. Version 3.1 supports XHTML markup. You can also download emulators for many Nokia phones, including the 6210/6290 phone and a WML version 1.2 phone emulator, with more models added as they're released. You can download this toolkit for free from *http://forum.nokia.com*.
- **Openwave** You can download Openwave's simulator for free from *http://developer.openwave.com*, with version 3.2, 4.1.1, 5.0, 6.1, and 6.2 SDKs available at the time of writing. Version 6.1 and later includes a browser that supports XHTML markup, whereas version 4.1.1 includes an excellent WML 1.2 emulator. The emulator in the Openwave SDK version 4.1.1 and later has the advantage that it can be run from the command line, passing the URL to open as a command-line parameter. This allows integration of the emulator into Visual Studio .NET as a test tool, as described in the section "Integrating an Emulator into Visual Studio .NET," later in this chapter.

- **Ericsson** You can download Ericsson's WapIDE 3.2.1, which includes phone emulators, from *http://www.ericsson.com/mobilityworld/sub/open/tools-all.html*. This site offers additional R380 emulations, including one that supports Chinese character sets. Downloads are free to developers.
- **Go.America** The Go.America browser includes an emulation of a RIM BlackBerry 950 or 957 device. After you register with Go.America's Web site, you can download this emulator for free from *http://www.goamerica.net/partners/developers/index.html*.
- **Yospace Smartphone Emulator, Developer Edition** This is one of the best tools available for testing applications on a number of WML devices at once. Unfortunately it's not free, but you can download the evaluation edition to try it out before parting with any money! To download this emulator, go to *http://www.yospace.com/spede.html*. This tool emulates the Nokia, Ericsson, and Openwave browsers and includes emulations of the Nokia 7110, 6210, 3330, 5210, 8310, and 7650 phones; Ericsson T68, T68i, R320, and R380 models; Motorola Timeport, V70 and V60; Siemens C35; and a Yospace concept personal digital assistant (PDA) called the Yopad. Best of all, you can enter a URL to fetch, and the emulator can test your mobile application on all these devices simultaneously.
- **WinWAP** Desktop WML browser available from *http://www.winwap.org*. A fee is payable after the initial 30-day evaluation period. This desktop browser looks like an Internet Explorer window, but a menu option allows the screen to be configured to the same size as some popular mobile phones.

Check the manufacturers' Web sites for emulators we haven't mentioned here. You'll find developer-oriented Web sites such as Palo Wireless (*http://www.palowireless.com*), which lists many available tools and emulators, another good source of information.

One advantage of the toolkits such as those from Nokia or Openwave is that they include a WML encoder—functionality that normally resides in the WAP gateway in a live configuration. With a WML encoder, you can display the source WML markup that the ASP.NET mobile controls generate. This feature is very valuable to advanced developers who create device adapters and custom controls like the ones described in Chapter 21 and Chapter 22. Using this tool, developers can quickly verify that the generated markup is correct. This feature is also valuable to developers who use the templated controls where the code generates device-specific markup. If an error occurs at run time, the built-in WML compilers in these toolkits will show you where the error lies in the source code.

Verifying Support for an Emulator

Whenever you use an emulator, you shouldn't assume that ASP.NET mobile controls have been configured to support it. There are two ways in which it can become apparent that support for the emulator isn't present:

- The real device works, but an emulator of that device does not.
- The emulator appears to work, but formatting problems are apparent with mobile pages.

The first of these problems is easier to identify and to fix. ASP.NET identifies browsers by examining the User Agent string the client sends in the HTTP headers with every request. Normally, an emulator returns the same User Agent string as the real device it is emulating, but this is not always true (particularly if the emulator has been produced by a different company from the manufacturer of the real device). If the emulator specifies an unrecognized User Agent string in the HTTP headers, the ASP.NET runtime classifies it as an "unknown" HTML 3.2 device. If the emulator expects to receive WML and instead gets HTML 3.2, the browser can't understand the markup it has received and displays an Unrecognized Content Type error. The next section, "Verifying Emulator Identification," describes how to resolve this problem for the Yospace emulator.

The second problem, formatting problems, can also result because the emulator isn't a supported device. However, the configuration XML that ASP.NET uses to recognize devices sometimes results in a device receiving the correct kind of markup but in a form that isn't optimized for that device. The way that ASP.NET identifies what kind of device is making the request is fully explained in Chapter 19. On rare occasions, ASP.NET might correctly identify the manufacturer of the device but not identify the specific model. As a result, the *MobileCapabilities* object that the ASP.NET runtime builds to identify the capabilities of the device is not optimized for that particular model, resulting in the ASP.NET mobile controls not rendering optimum markup for that particular browser. You might find that an ASP.NET Mobile Web application appears to work with the device's emulator, but you might later realize that pages aren't formatted correctly or that navigation buttons or softkeys don't work as expected. You might conclude incorrectly that your application isn't working for some reason; but the reason for the problem might just be that your device is getting only the basic level of support for a browser from that manufacturer.

This is a subtle problem that can be hard to identify. The next section presents a useful application named WhoAmI that can help you to verify whether ASP.NET correctly identifies the browser you are trying to use. You can specify a number of configuration settings to fully support a new device so that ASP.NET Mobile Web applications work optimally on that device; these settings are described in Chapter 19.

Verifying Emulator Identification

If you encounter the situation in which your application works fine with a real device but doesn't work with an emulation of the same device, the reason is probably that the emulator is not sending the same User Agent string as the real device. For example, the ASP.NET mobile controls support the Ericsson R380 mobile phone. However, when you try to access a mobile ASP.NET application with the Ericsson R380 emulation in the Yospace Smartphone emulator, the runtime reports an error, saying that it can't display the page. Similarly, the Motorola Timeport emulation in the Yospace Smartphone emulator reports error 406 (Unrecognized Content Type). However, the emulations of the Nokia 7110 and 6210 phones work fine with this emulator.

The way that ASP.NET identifies these browsers at run time accounts for these discrepancies. If you're using .NET Framework 1.0, when you install the ASP.NET Mobile Controls, it updates the main configuration file, machine.config, which resides in the /WINDOWS/Microsoft.NET/Framework/v1.0.3705/CONFIG directory. If you're using .NET Framework 1.1, device configuration is found in the machine.config file, and might also be found in the file deviceupdate.config in the /WINDOWS/Microsoft.NET/Framework/v1.1.4322/CONFIG directory.

If you examine the machine.config file or deviceupdate.config file, you'll see that it contains browser identification logic within a section enclosed by the following tags:

```
<browserCaps> … </browserCaps>
```

ASP.NET identifies browsers by using regular expressions to match the *HTTP_USER_AGENT* string that the client browser sends with every request. Once ASP.NET identifies a browser, the runtime extracts all the values for its capabilities from the *<browserCaps>* element and uses them to initialize the *MobileCapabilities* object. In Chapter 9, we introduced you to the *MobileCapabilities* object and the way it defines the characteristics and capabilities of a mobile device. You define each of the properties that you can query through the *MobileCapabilities* object, including *ScreenPixelsHeight*, *IsColor*, and *MobileDeviceModel*, in the *<browserCaps>* section of the configuration file. For example, the section that identifies the Ericsson R380 mobile phone looks like this:

```
<!-- Ericsson -->

<case
    match=
"R380 (?'browserMajorVersion'\w*)(?'browserMinorVersion'\.\w*) WAP 1\.1">
    browser = "Ericsson"
    type = "Ericsson R380"
    version = ${browserMajorVersion}.${browserMinorVersion}
    majorVersion = ${browserMajorVersion}
    minorVersion = ${browserMinorVersion}
    isMobileDevice = "true"
    preferredRenderingType = "wml11"
    preferredRenderingMIME = "text/vnd.wap.wml"
    preferredImageMIME = "image/vnd.wap.wbmp"
    inputType = "virtualKeyboard"
    canInitiateVoiceCall = "true"
    mobileDeviceManufacturer = "Ericsson"
    mobileDeviceModel = "R380"
    screenPixelsWidth = "310"
    screenPixelsHeight = "100"
    screenCharactersHeight = "7"
    screenBitDepth = "1"
    isColor = "false"
</case>
```

If the runtime can't match the *HTTP_USER_AGENT* string for a particular browser, the settings within the *<default>* device definition in *<browserCaps>* apply. These settings define the client browser as an HTML 3.2 browser, of browser type *Unknown*. The Yospace R380 emulator doesn't work because it sends a different *HTTP_USER_AGENT* string from the real device, and the regular expression used to identify an R380 model as defined in machine.config doesn't recognize it. Consequently, ASP.NET defines the device as an HTML 3.2 device and formats the page in HTML. The WAP browser can't render HTML, which explains the error message that appears when you access the application through this emulator.

You can easily verify whether there is a device identification problem using the trace output you learned about earlier in this chapter, in the section "Using the ASP.NET Trace Facility." The WhoAmI application, shown in Listing 16-6, simply outputs a few of the properties defined in the *MobileCapabilities* object to mobile Label controls, including the *MobileCapabilities.Browser* property, which it also writes to the trace log. More important, the runtime configures the Web.config file for application-level tracing, as Listing 16-7 shows.

```
<%@ Page Inherits="System.Web.UI.MobileControls.MobilePage"
    Language="c#" %>
<%@ Register TagPrefix="mobile" Namespace="System.Web.UI.MobileControls"
    Assembly="System.Web.Mobile" %>
<%@ Import Namespace="System.Web.Mobile" %>

<head>
    <script language="c#" runat="server">
    void Page_Load(object sender, System.EventArgs e)
    {
        MobileCapabilities cap=((MobileCapabilities)Request.Browser);
        lblBrowser.Text = "Browser: " + cap.Browser;
        lblManu.Text = "Manufacturer: "+ cap.MobileDeviceManufacturer;
        lblModel.Text = "Model: " + cap.MobileDeviceModel;
        lblContent.Text = "Content: " + cap.PreferredRenderingType;
        lblHeight.Text = "PxlsHeight: " + cap.ScreenPixelsHeight;
        lblWidth.Text = "PxlsWidth: " + cap.ScreenPixelsWidth;

        // Output MobileCapabilities. Browser property to Trace.
        Trace.Write("Browser: " + cap.Browser);
    }
    </script>
</head>

<body>
    <mobile:Form runat="server" id="frmMain">
        <mobile:Label runat="server" StyleReference="title">
            ASP.NET Mobile Controls Client Identification</mobile:Label>
        <mobile:Label runat="server" id="lblBrowser"/>
        <mobile:Label runat="server" id="lblManu"/>
        <mobile:Label runat="server" id="lblModel"/>
        <mobile:Label runat="server" id="lblContent"/>
        <mobile:Label runat="server" id="lblHeight"/>
        <mobile:Label runat="server" id="lblWidth"/>
    </mobile:Form>
</body>
```

Listing 16-6 Default.aspx mobile Web Forms page of the WhoAmI application

```
<?xml version="1.0" encoding="utf-8" ?>
<configuration>
    <system.web>
        <!--  APPLICATION-LEVEL TRACING -->
        <trace enabled="true" />
    </system.web>
</configuration>
```

Listing 16-7 Application-level tracing in the Web.config file of the WhoAmI application

If you run this application on a supported device, it displays the values of some of the properties of the *MobileCapabilities* object, as shown in Figure 16-9 for the Openwave 6.1 browser. However, if you try to access *http://localhost/whoami* from the Yospace R380 emulator, the application fails to display the output for the reasons just described.

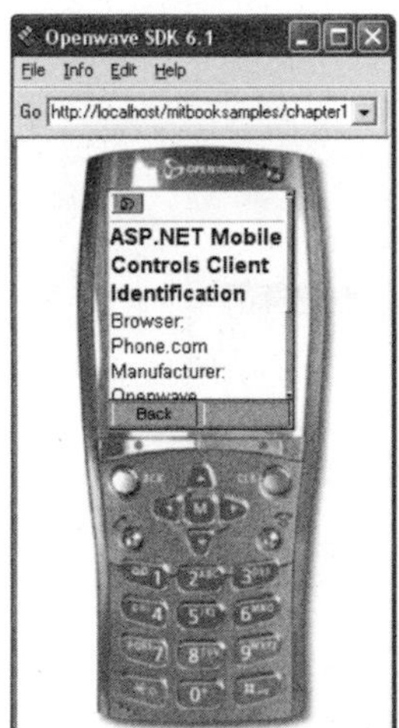

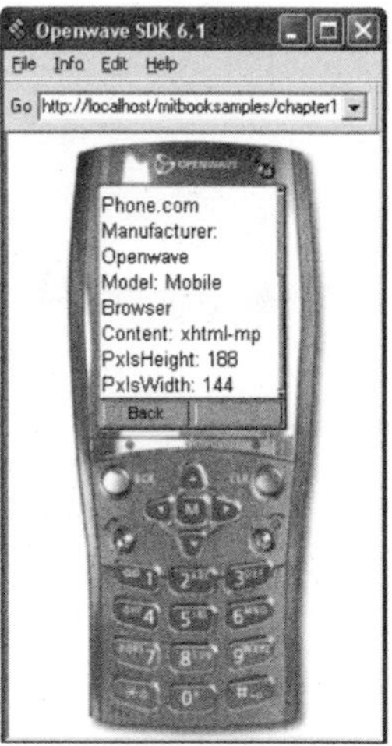

Figure 16-9 WhoAmI application displaying ASP.NET device capabilities settings for this device

If you then use Internet Explorer to access the application-level trace file at *http://localhost/whoami/trace.axd* and select the most recent trace, you'll see that the *MobileCapabilities.Browser* property is set to *Unknown*, as shown in the Trace Information section. You'll also notice that, in the Headers Collection section of the trace, the *HTTP_USER_AGENT* string for the Yospace R380 emulation appears as *Ericsson R380 version 0.0 (compatible; Yospace SmartPhone Emulator Developer Edition 2.0)*. Figure 16-10 shows this trace output.

Here we see the root of the problem! The existing code in *<browserCaps>* that identifies the R380 model looks for an *HTTP_USER_AGENT* string that matches *R380 majorVersion.minorVersion WAP 1.1*, while the Yospace emulator actually identifies itself as *Ericsson R380 version 0.0 (compatible; Yospace SmartPhone Emulator Developer Edition 2.0)*.

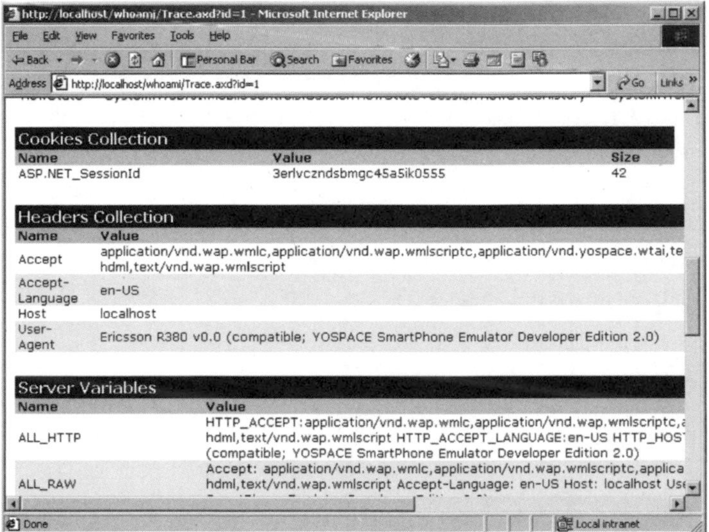

Figure 16-10 Trace output showing the HTTP headers sent by the client browser

> **Note** Chapter 19 describes the full procedure for extending support to a new device. We advise you to read that chapter before getting too deeply involved in making changes in *<browserCaps>* and device adapters, particularly if you're trying to add support for a device that wasn't previously supported. In this case, however, the change required is very minor, since the runtime already supports the device that the Yospace emulator is simulating.

To make this change, create or edit your application's Web.config file and write the tags for a *<browserCaps>* section in a similar way to that in the device configuration file in the /WINDOWS/Microsoft.NET/Framework/*version*/CONFIG directory. Remember to include the *<use var="HTTP_USER_AGENT" />* and *<filter>* tags to enable browser matching. The basic structure of the code you need is shown here:

```
<?xml version="1.0" encoding="UTF-8"?>

<configuration>
    <system.web>
        <browserCaps>
```

```
            <use
                var="HTTP_USER_AGENT" />
            <filter>
<!--  Insert your own browser definitions here. -->

            </filter>
        </browserCaps>
    </system.web>
</configuration>
```

Locate the section that identifies the R380 model in the device configuration file, copy it, and paste it into the Web.config file you're writing. Modify the matching string used in the regular expression as shown in boldface type in the following example:

```
<?xml version="1.0" encoding="utf-8" ?>
<configuration>
    <system.web>
<!--
BEGIN Browser support for Yospace emulations
-->
        <browserCaps>
            <use
                var="HTTP_USER_AGENT" />
            <filter>
                <!-- YOSPACE Emulations -->
                <case match=".*YOSPACE.*">
                    <filter>
                        <!-- Ericsson -->
                        <case
                            match=
"Ericsson R380 v(?'browserMajorVer'\w*)(?'browserMinorVer'\.\w*) .*" >
                            browser = "Ericsson"
                            type = "Ericsson R380"
                            version =
                               ${browserMajorVer}.${browserMinorVer}
                            majorVersion = ${browserMajorVer}
                            minorVersion = ${browserMinorVer}
                                preferredRenderingType = "wml11"
                                preferredRenderingMime = "text/vnd.wap.wml"
                                preferredImageMime = "image/vnd.wap.wbmp"
                                inputType = "virtualKeyboard"
                                canInitiateVoiceCall = "true"
                                mobileDeviceManufacturer = "Ericsson"
                                mobileDeviceModel = "R380"
                                screenPixelsWidth = "310"
                                screenPixelsHeight = "100"
                                screenCharactersHeight = "7"
```

```
                                    screenBitDepth = "1"
                                    isColor = "false"
                                    maximumRenderedPageSize = "3000"
                                </case>
                            </filter>
                        </case> <!-- End YOSPACE emulations -->
                    </filter>
                </browserCaps>
            </system.web>
        </configuration>
```

This match will work with the Yospace *HTTP_USER_AGENT* string and set the device up as an R380. You can then save this new Web.config file in your /Inetpub/wwwroot directory, where it will apply to all applications on that server, or you can save the file in the application root directory, where it will apply only to that application. You could even just add this new browser definition to the *<browserCaps>* section in the deviceupdate.config file (.NET Framework 1.1) or machine.config file (.NET Framework 1.0) alongside the existing definitions supplied by Microsoft.

Remember that if you install a new Device Update issued by Microsoft in the future, the *<browserCaps>* section in deviceupdate.config or machine.config will be updated to include settings for newly supported devices. Browser definitions in a Web.config file in the wwwroot directory or in the application root directory override any settings for the same browser in machine.config (if any exist). Whenever you install a new Device Update, you should review any custom browser definitions you've implemented because official support for the affected browsers might be included in the device update, in which case you should remove the corresponding custom definition.

With this modification in place, the Mobile Internet Controls Runtime will recognize the Yospace emulation as an R380 and correctly format the response in WML 1.1.

Integrating an Emulator into Visual Studio .NET

You can run some software emulators from the command line, specifying the URL to fetch as a command-line parameter. An example is the Openwave simulator. You can integrate an emulator with this capability into the Visual Studio .NET IDE to make your testing easier. To do so, follow these steps:

1. Open any ASP.NET project, and right-click any .aspx file in Solution Explorer. Click Browse With on the context menu.
2. In the Browse With window, click the Add button.

3. In the Add Program window, browse to the file location of the emulator executable, and click Open. After the file location, add any command-line parameters the emulator requires. Visual Studio .NET automatically sends the URL of the page you are testing as the first command-line parameter, but you can use the *%URL* variable to insert the location of the starting page elsewhere in the command-line parameters. The Openwave simulator in the SDK 4.1.1 requires the command-line parameters *–reload %URL*, whereas the simulator in SDK 5.0 and later needs only the URL. For example, to use the WML 1.2 simulator from the Openwave SDK 4.1.1, in the file location, type **"C:\Program Files\Openwave\UPSDK411 \upsim411.exe" -reload %URL**. (Note carefully the position of the quotation marks.) To use the XHTML-MP browser in the simulator from the Openwave SDK 6.1, in the file location, type **C:\Program Files\Openwave\SDK 6.1\program\http \OSDK61http.exe**. (Here quotation marks are not needed.)
4. Type a friendly name for the browser, such as **Openwave SDK 4.1.1 simulator**, to add to the list of browsers available through the Browse With window.
5. Click the OK button to accept your changes. If Visual Studio .NET displays the error message *File name does not exist, is invalid, or contains parameters that cannot be validated. Do you want to change your entry?*, click No.
6. If you want, you can make this the default browser for the Browse option by selecting the newly added emulator in the list and clicking Set As Default.

You must change a project property to enable your Web application projects to use a browser other than Internet Explorer when you run them for debugging. To change this property, follow these steps:

1. Right-click the project name in Solution Explorer, and click Properties on the context menu.
2. Click the Configuration Properties folder in the tree on the left to expand it. Then click the Debugging suboption.
3. For Visual Basic projects, clear the Always Use Internet Explorer When Debugging Web Pages check box. In a C# project, set the Always Use Internet Explorer option to *false*. Click OK.

Visual Studio .NET will now use the browser specified as the default in the Browse With window for debugging for *all* projects.

Alternatively, you can specify debugging with a particular emulator just in a specific project by modifying the project properties as follows:

1. Open the project properties and set the Always Use Internet Explorer to *True* so that other projects debug using Internet Explorer as usual.
2. Set the Debug Mode property to *Program*.
3. Set the Start Application property to the full path of the Openwave SDK 4.1.1 executable. If you installed the 4.1.1 SDK in the default location, the path name is: C:\Program Files\Openwave\UPSDK411\upsim411.exe.
4. Set the Command Line Arguments property to *-reload*, followed by the absolute URL of the start page of your application—for example, **http://localhost/MobileWebApplication1/MobileWebForm1.aspx**. You need the URL only and not the *–reload* command-line parameter if you're using Openwave SDK 5.0 or later.
5. Click the OK button to accept your changes.

Visual Studio .NET will now use the Openwave browser for debugging in this project but will still use Internet Explorer for other projects.

17

Packaging and Configuration

Designing a mobile Web application and writing its code is only part of what it takes to build complete solutions. You must also package and then deploy the mobile Web application to your production environment. Often, executing these tasks means performing the roles of both system administrator and application developer. This chapter focuses on the tasks most application developers will need to perform to get their mobile Web applications published. Specifically, this chapter covers the following topics:

- **Packaging and deploying a mobile Web application** You'll learn how to copy an application using Microsoft Visual Studio .NET, create a Microsoft Installer using Visual Studio .NET, and understand how the .NET Framework versions assemblies.
- **Using configuration files to configure an application** You'll also see how to capitalize on Web.config files that inherit configuration settings and use the Web.config configuration handlers. Configuring applications with .NET is simple because it relies on a configuration system that uses text files based on Extensible Markup Language (XML) that you can edit in a text editor.

Also in this chapter, we'll look at one aspect of application design that relates to deployment—how to write a redirect page so that your users can use the same URL to access both desktop and mobile versions of your application.

Packaging and Deploying an Application

Once you write an ASP.NET application, you must deploy it to a production system. The way you deploy the application depends on a number of factors, including the following:

- The visibility of the production system from the development environment
- Whether the application depends on other assemblies that haven't previously been installed on the production system
- Whether the application depends on assemblies of a different version than those already on the production system
- Whether you've developed the application for internal or external use

You don't need to create a special installation package for an application in simple situations—for example, when an application doesn't depend on any other assemblies. In this case, you can deploy the application by copying it to the remote system using either the Visual Studio .NET Copy Project facility or the Xcopy command. In more complex situations or when the application requires packaging for installation on a Web server to which you do not have direct network access, you can create a Microsoft Windows Installer application using Visual Studio .NET and run this installer on the remote system.

Copying an Application

Imagine a stand-alone "Hello World" application with no dependencies on shared assemblies. (See the sidebar "Referencing Assemblies in .NET" for an explanation of references to shared and private assemblies.) You could simply copy this program to another computer with the .NET Framework installed and it would run. Similarly, you can write a simple mobile Web application with a code-behind module; when you compile it, you get a DLL for the code-behind module. And if your application added a reference to any other assemblies (such as components you've written to access data), in the /bin directory you'll also have private copies of the DLLs of the referenced assemblies. As long as you have installed .NET Framework 1.1 (or .NET Framework 1.0 and the Mobile Internet Toolkit) on your production system, you can simply use Visual Studio .NET to copy the mobile Web application to the production environment and it will run.

Referencing Assemblies in .NET

Sharing components has been problematic in the past. In fact, before .NET, the sharing of components sometimes resulted in problems that became known as DLL hell. Applications would share a component, and if developers updated that component, existing applications would attempt to use the component's new version. Because backward compatibility was intended but wasn't guaranteed, developers could easily find their applications in an inoperable state.

The .NET Framework overcomes the problem of shared components—or more specifically, *assemblies*, as they're called in .NET applications. Each assembly is self-describing through the inclusion of a *manifest*. The manifest contains information such as the assembly's identity, the list of files that make up the assembly, the identity of other assemblies that the assembly references, exported types and resources, and permission requests. The use of a manifest negates the need for this kind of information to be stored in the Windows registry.

One of the key features that help you to avoid the problems of shared components is the .NET use of private copies of referenced assemblies. If you create components that implement business logic, for example, and then add a reference to the component in your Visual Studio .NET project, a copy of the referenced assembly is made and copied to the /bin directory of your application. The application manifest is updated to record the specific filename of the referenced assembly, its version number, and if it is digitally signed, the hash of the public key of its digital certificate. The copy of the referenced assembly is private to your application, and your application runs forever using the exact same copy of the referenced assembly that it was built with. Other applications that reference the same business logic assembly make their own private copy of that assembly. If you want to upgrade the referenced assembly at some time in the future—perhaps to fix bugs—you must update the reference to the assembly in your project, which takes a new copy of the now updated assembly, and then rebuild and redeploy your application.

In many instances, deploying all assemblies as private wastes resources; it makes more sense to share some assemblies. The .NET Framework still allows the use of single copies of assemblies that are shared by many applications, analogous to the old ways of storing DLLs in the \Windows directory. Such assemblies are stored in a special repository called the global assembly cache (GAC). In fact, all the assemblies that contain the .NET Framework base classes and all the ASP.NET classes are in the GAC. The GAC has significant advantages over the old way of storing a single copy of a DLL and hoping that new revisions are backward-compatible with the previous version. It uses four-part version numbers and digital certificates to uniquely identify different versions of the same assembly. This allows you to store multiple versions of an assembly on the same machine and run the versions side by side. Thus, if you install new software that uses a new version of a shared assembly, the newer applications use the new version of the assembly in the GAC, but your existing applications won't break because they'll continue to use the older versions of that assembly.

The first deployment scenario we'll examine shows you how to copy an application across a network from one machine to another.

1. Create a new "Hello World" mobile Web application, and name it FirstDeployment. Assume that you want to copy this application to a production Web server. To copy the project, you must first access the Copy Project dialog box. Do this by selecting Project and then Copy Project from the Visual Studio .NET menu. The Copy Project dialog box shown in Figure 17-1 appears.

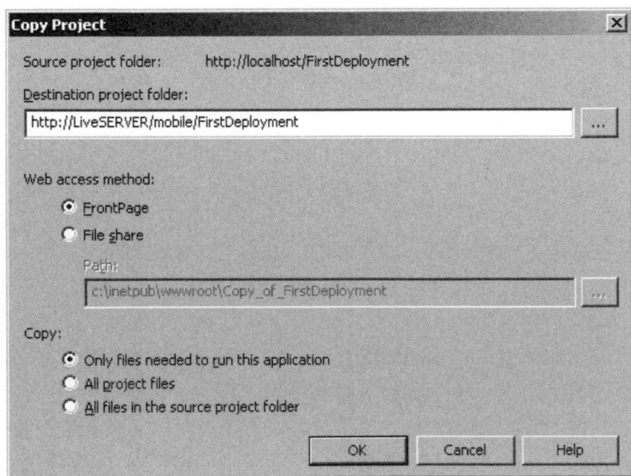

Figure 17-1 The Copy Project dialog box

2. Enter the URL of the destination project folder, and then select FrontPage or File Share as the Web access method. If you select FrontPage, Visual Studio .NET uses Microsoft FrontPage Server

Extensions to transfer files to the remote server over HTTP. To use this method, the server must have FrontPage Server Extensions installed. Alternatively, you can use the File Share method, which doesn't require FrontPage Server Extensions. Instead, this method allows you to access the remote server through a file share, so you must be able to connect to the local area network (LAN) in which the target server is situated.

3. After you select an appropriate Web access method, you must choose which files to copy. There are three possible options:

   - **Only Files Needed To Run This Application** Copies only the files the runtime requires to run the application. These include Global.asax, Web.config, all .aspx files, and any built output files (assemblies contained in the \bin folder).
   - **All Project Files** Copies all the project files. These include those mentioned in the previous list item, as well as Visual Studio .NET project files and source files. Using this approach allows the project to be opened from the target folder using Visual Studio .NET and for further development to be carried out.
   - **All Files In The Source Project Folder** Copies all the project files and any other files in the project folder or its subdirectories.

In most cases, you'll copy only the files required to run the application. Once you choose which files to copy, simply click OK and Visual Studio .NET copies the files to the remote server.

> **Tip** Another way to copy a mobile Web application to another server is to use Xcopy from a command prompt. This command allows you to copy your application files and directory structure to another location. Xcopy provides similar functionality to the Visual Studio .NET Copy command. However, it doesn't set up virtual directories in Internet Information Services (IIS), register files, verify the location of assemblies, or prevent you from overriding existing files and directories. In addition, you must have access to a network share on the target server; Xcopy cannot use FrontPage Server Extensions to copy the files to the target server. To learn more about Xcopy, open a command prompt and type **Xcopy /?**.

Creating a Web Setup Project

In many instances, simply copying an application from one server to another is inappropriate. For example, the production environment might not be accessible from the development machine, or you might have written the application for use by some external entity, such as another business. In these instances, Visual Studio .NET offers an alternative for packaging and distributing an application: creating a Windows Installer package.

To create a Windows Installer package for your application, you must first create a new Web Setup Project. Start the process of creating a new project as you would for a mobile Web application. However, instead of selecting ASP.NET Mobile Web Application, select Setup And Deployment Projects from the Project Types list, and choose Web Setup Project from the Templates pane, as shown in Figure 17-2. Give your deployment project a suitable name.

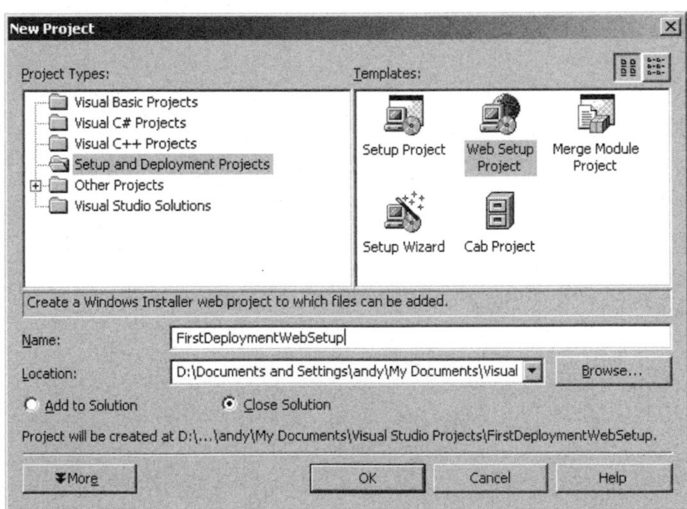

Figure 17-2 The New Project dialog box showing the Web Setup Project icon

You must now add to the solution any existing projects you want to deploy. To do this, follow these steps:

1. From the File menu, select Add Project.
2. Choose Existing Project from the submenu.
3. The Add Existing Project dialog box appears. From this, select the project you want to deploy (the project file for a Web project is in the application directory, typically something like C:\inetpub\wwwroot\myApplicationName).

Now add the output from the existing project to the deployment project. To do so, follow these steps:

1. Click Web Application Folder in the File System window, as shown in Figure 17-3.

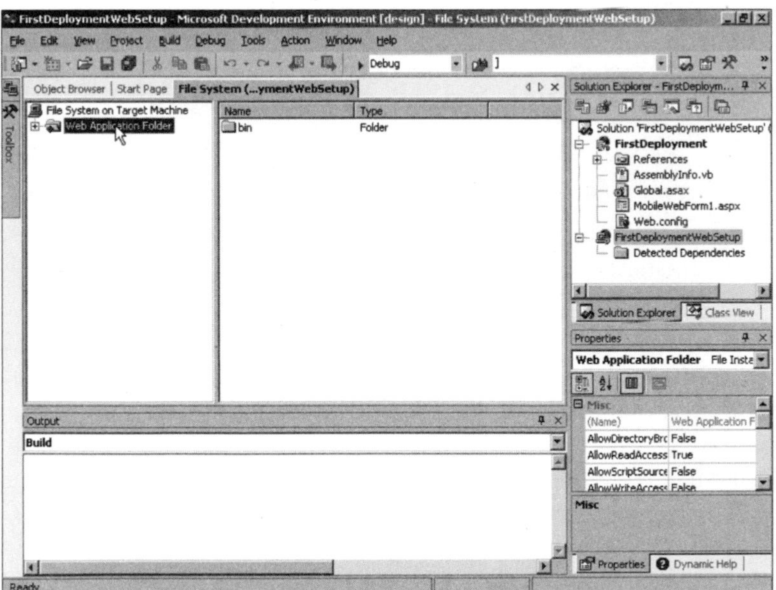

Figure 17-3 File System editor of a Setup and Deployment project

2. Open the Project menu, and click Add.
3. Choose Project Output from the submenu. The Add Project Output Group dialog box appears, as shown in Figure 17-4.

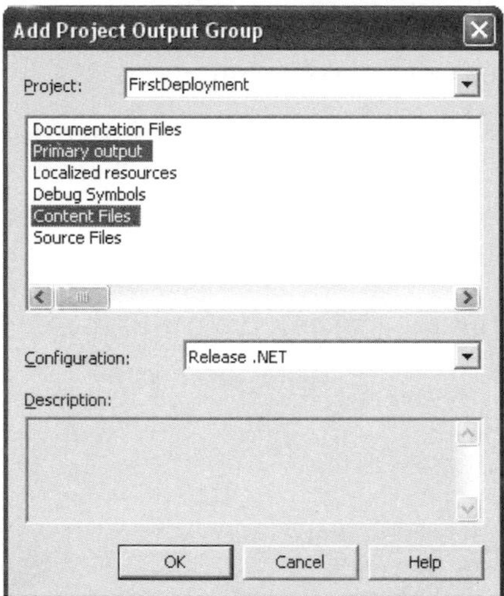

Figure 17-4 Add Project Output Group dialog box

4. Select both the Primary Output and Content Files options.
5. The Configuration options allow you to determine whether release or debug output is contained in the deployment package. In this instance, choose Release .NET.
6. Click OK.

Now that you've added the output from the existing project to the deployment project, you might want to know what the various options in the Add Project Output Group dialog box do. These options allow you to specify which of the project outputs Visual Studio .NET adds to the installer package. Table 17-1 lists these options and the type of output they include in the installer.

Table 17-1 Add Project Output Group Options

Option	Description
Documentation Files	Contains the project's Intellidoc documentation files. Intellidoc is the name for documentation files that can be automatically generated from C# projects using specially tagged comments in your code. The generated file can then be used to display prompts in IntelliSense. Look up the topic "Recommended Tags for Documentation Comments" in the Visual Studio .NET Help for more details.
Primary Output	Contains the application's DLLs.

Table 17-1 Add Project Output Group Options

Option	Description
Localized Resources	Contains each culture's satellite resource assemblies. (See Chapter 14 for more information about cultures and localization.)
Debug Symbols	Contains the project's debugging files. (See Chapter 16 for more information about debugging.)
Content Files	Contains the project's content files. These are your .aspx, .asmx, and .ascx files. You must include these files for the project to be able to run after deployment.
Source Files	Contains the project's source files, such as your .aspx.cs or .aspx.vb files. These files are compiled into DLLs, so you do not need to include these to ensure the application can run after deployment.

You must build the deployment project to finish creating the installer package. To do this, choose Build projectName (the name of your Deployment project name) from the Build menu. Visual Studio .NET now builds the project. Be aware that this might take a few minutes on machines with lower specifications.

> **Tip** If the Web Setup Project build fails, it means that the project output you included in the build has a Debug build only. To rectify the problem, choose Configuration Manager from the Build menu, and verify that all the projects it lists have a configuration setting of *Release*. After you've rebuilt your mobile Web application, add its output to your Web Setup project as detailed earlier in this section.

When Visual Studio .NET finishes building the project, you can locate the installer file in the Release folder of your Web Setup Project folder. You can now copy this file to any remote location. When you double-click this file, your application and its correctly versioned dependencies will be installed.

Deploying Applications to Servers Running Different Versions of the .NET Framework

If you're developing on a machine that has Visual Studio .NET 2002 and the Mobile Internet Toolkit installed, your application references .NET Framework 1.0 and Mobile Internet Toolkit shared assemblies (assemblies in the GAC). If you're using Visual Studio .NET 2003, you're using .NET Framework 1.1, which requires no Mobile Internet Toolkit add-on because the ASP.NET mobile controls are a fully integrated part of the .NET Framework 1.1. You might be wondering what run-time components must be present on the Web server to which you wish to deploy and whether the choice of components is dependent on the version that was used to build the application.

The assembly versioning capabilities of the .NET Framework mean that there are surprisingly few complications involved in deploying to servers running different versions of the .NET Framework. Consider an application built with .NET Framework 1.0 and the Mobile Internet Toolkit. If you deploy your application to a Web server that has the .NET Framework 1.0 runtime and the Mobile Internet Toolkit, unsurprisingly your application will run. If you have .NET Framework 1.1, but not the earlier version, installed on the target Web server, your application will still run without your having to recompile it because the new version of the .NET Framework is backward-compatible. If you have both the .NET Framework 1.1 runtime and .NET Framework 1.0 with the Mobile Internet Toolkit installed on the target server, again your application will run, and in fact it will use the .NET Framework 1.0 and Mobile Internet Toolkit shared assemblies in preference to the 1.1 versions.

The only difficulty comes with an application that is built using Visual Studio .NET 2003. By default, this application will run on a Web server that has the .NET Framework 1.1 runtime installed. If you deploy to a Web server that has only version 1.0 and the Mobile Internet Toolkit installed, the application will not run because the configuration system of the .NET Framework 1.0 is not able to redirect requests for version 1.1 assemblies to the version 1.0 assemblies.

The possible combinations of compiled version and runtime support are summarized in Table 17-2.

Table 17-2 .NET Framework Runtime Version Requirements

Application Built Using	Runtime Version(s) on Web Server	Result
.NET Framework 1.0 + Mobile Internet Toolkit 1.0	.NET Framework 1.0 + Mobile Internet Toolkit 1.0	Application runs.
	.NET Framework 1.0 + Mobile Internet Toolkit 1.0 and .NET Framework 1.1	Application runs using version 1.0 assemblies and ignores presence of version 1.1.
	.NET Framework 1.1 only	Application runs using the version 1.1 shared assemblies. The .NET Framework redirects requests for version 1.0 assemblies to version 1.1 assemblies.
.NET Framework 1.1	.NET Framework 1.0 + Mobile Internet Toolkit 1.0	Application cannot run. It requires version 1.1 assemblies.
	.NET Framework 1.0 + Mobile Internet Toolkit 1.0 and .NET Framework 1.1	Application runs using version 1.1 shared assemblies.
	.NET Framework 1.1 only	Application runs.

If you must build applications using Visual Studio .NET 2003 that must be deployed to servers that have only version 1.0 and the Mobile Internet Toolkit 1.0 installed, you can configure the application that you build with Visual Studio .NET 2003 to run with .NET Framework 1.0 assemblies. To configure this option, go to the Project Properties window, select the General tab, and select Supported Runtimes. The .NET Framework Version window that appears allows you to choose between Microsoft .NET Framework version 1.1 (the default) or both .NET Framework versions 1.1 and 1.0, as shown in Figure 17-5. When you select the option to support both versions, Visual Studio .NET adds an *<assemblyBinding>* XML tag to the Web.config file so that requests for any of the .NET version 1.1 assemblies are redirected to the version 1.0 assemblies if the version 1.1 assemblies aren't found at run time.

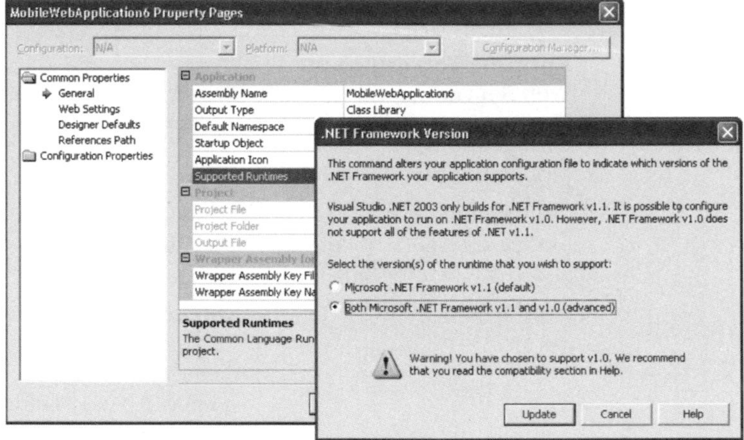

Figure 17-5 Configuring an application to run with either runtime in Visual Studio .NET 2003

Installing .NET Framework Runtime on a Web Server

When you install Visual Studio .NET on a development computer, one of the first things the installation procedure does is to install the .NET Framework runtime components, if they're not already installed. On the Web server where the applications you build are to run, you do not need to install Visual Studio .NET, but you must install the .NET Framework runtime components. You can install the .NET Framework runtime components from the Visual Studio .NET installation CDs, just select the Install Server Components option from the start page that displays when you insert the installation CD into your CD-ROM drive. Alternatively, you can download the .NET Framework redistributable and the current Service Pack from MSDN at the following URLs:

- **.NET Framework 1.0 and 1.1 Redistributables** *http://msdn.microsoft.com/library/default.asp?url=/downloads/list/netdevframework.asp*
- **.NET Framework Service packs** *http://msdn.microsoft.com/netframework/downloads/updates/default.asp*

For .NET Framework 1.0 installations, you also need the Mobile Internet Toolkit, which doesn't have a separate redistributable for use on Web servers. Instead, you use the same installer you use to update Visual Studio .NET 2002, available from *http://msdn.microsoft.com/library/default.asp?url=/downloads/list/netdevmit.asp*. At the time of this writing, there are no service packs, but there is a single hot fix for Mobile Internet Toolkit 1.0, available from *http://msdn.microsoft.com/vstudio/downloads/updates/mobileinternet.asp*.

Device Update Packs

You should always install new Device Update packs on your Web servers when they become available, as well as on your development machines. These Device Update packs ensure that your mobile Web applications work with the greatest number of current devices available. Download Device Update packs from MSDN, either by following the links from *http://www.asp.net* or directly from *http://msdn.microsoft.com/library/default.asp?url=/downloads/list/netdevmit.asp*. Be careful to download the correct version for the particular runtime installed on your Web server; there are different downloads for .NET Framework 1.0 /Mobile Internet Toolkit and for .NET Framework 1.1.

Configuring Applications

Some of the preceding chapters introduced you to configuring mobile Web applications. For example, in Chapter 12, you learned how to enable or disable cookies using the Web.config file. In this section, you'll learn about some of the specifics of application configuration, such as the format of XML configuration files. You'll learn how to use multiple configuration files through configuration inheritance. We'll also show you how ASP.NET uses configuration files and how you can change the contents of a configuration file.

The ASP.NET configuration system offers a new way to configure Web applications. The system uses multiple, XML-based text files that inherit configuration system settings from one another. This hierarchical configuration file framework allows you to precisely define the behavior of an entire machine, groups of applications, or individual applications.

With this new approach to system configuration, you can easily modify configuration settings using simple tools such as Notepad. Another important feature is that you can modify a configuration file at run time, and have the changes take effect, without having to restart the Web server. Furthermore, ASP.NET creates a cache in memory of each individual application's configuration settings. The runtime then uses this cache for each request to an application. Another significant feature is that you can extend the configuration system by writing your own configuration file section handlers.

Understanding the .NET Configuration Files

You can configure an entire machine using the machine.config file, or you can configure individual applications or groups of applications using Web.config files. The machine.config file typically resides at C:\WINNT\Microsoft.NET\Framework*versionNumber*\CONFIG. (If you're running a clean install of Windows XP, the WINNT directory might be named Windows on your machine.) You use the machine.config file to configure machine-wide settings, such as security policies. You can lock these settings to enforce policies on users, or your Web.config files can extend or override these settings at an application level.

You use a Web.config file to configure an individual application or, through inheritance, a group of applications. You place a Web.config file in the virtual directory that houses your application. The settings of this file will cascade to any subdirectories, as Figure 17-6 shows.

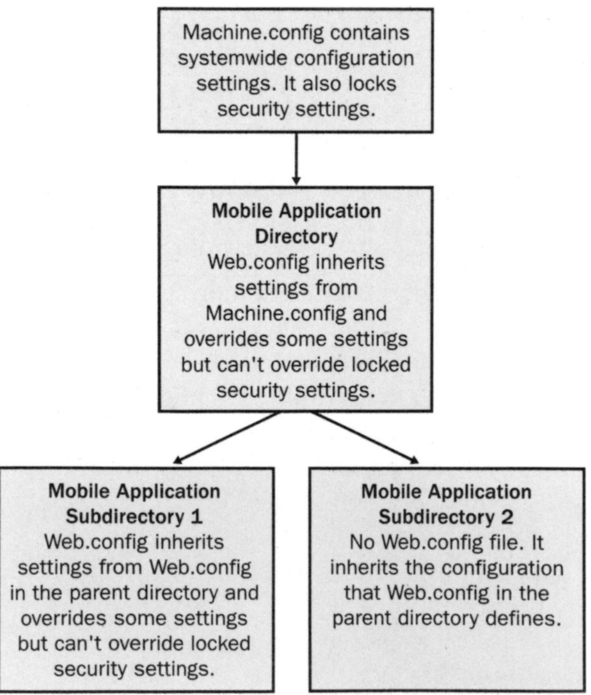

Figure 17-6 Extending and overriding configuration settings

> **Caution** When using virtual directories, you might find that your application won't inherit the configuration settings you assume it will. For example, suppose you have a physical directory named PD1, which contains a configuration file and has a subdirectory named PD2. You then map a virtual directory named VD1 to PD2. If you call a page using the URL *http://127.0.0.1/PD1/PD2/MobilePage1.aspx*, the application will inherit the configuration settings in PD1, as you'd expect. However, if you call that same file using the URL *http://127.0.0.1/VD1/MobilePage1.aspx*, the application *won't* inherit the configuration settings. To avoid this issue, you shouldn't create virtual directories this way.

Both the machine.config and Web.config files start with a *<configuration>* tag. Web.config files then contain a single child element of *<system.web>*; machine.config contains *<system.web>* as well as a number of other child elements. Table 17-3 shows the configuration sections you can include in the *<system.web>* element of your Web.config files.

Table 17-3 Configuration Sections of Web.config

Configuration Section	Description
<authentication>	Defines authentication support settings—for example, password hash algorithms. You can learn more about this tag in Chapter 18.
<authorization>	Defines the setting for authorizing application users. For example, you can authorize user roles to access an application. You'll learn more about this tag in Chapter 18.
<browserCaps>	Defines the settings of the browser capabilities component. You'll learn more about this tag in Chapter 19.
<compilation>	Defines the compilation settings—for example, defining the default compilation language. For more information about how to set this tag to support debugging, see Chapter 16. For additional details, consult the .NET Framework SDK documentation.
<customErrors>	Defines custom errors and redirects the user in the event of an error. For more information about this tag, see Chapter 16.

Table 17-3 Configuration Sections of Web.config

Configuration Section	Description
<globalization>	Defines an application's globalization or localization settings, such as language or character encoding. For more information about this tag, see Chapter 14.
<httpHandlers>	Maps incoming requests to a *System.Web.IHttpHandler* or *System.Web.IHttpHandlerFactory* class. You can define which class the request maps to—and which assembly or DLL contains that class—depending on the HTTP transaction method.
<httpModules>	Allows you to add *HttpModules* to or remove them from an application. *HttpModules* are assemblies that contain classes that implement the *IHttpHandler* interface.
<httpRuntime>	Defines the runtime's configuration settings. For example, you can define the maximum length of time that an application can execute before the runtime shuts it down, or you can set the maximum duration for which the runtime will make a request.
<identity>	Defines the application identity of the ASP.NET application thread executing your mobile Web application. Normally, an ASP.NET application thread runs with the identity of an unprivileged local account named ASPNET. Instead, you can use impersonation by setting *<identity impersonate="true">*, whereby the ASP.NET process runs with the identity (and security context) of the authenticated user. Access to resources is then controlled through normal NTFS access controls. If you do use impersonation, you can specify a fixed account to be used for authenticated users by specifying values for the *username* and *password* attributes. Whether you use a fixed account or the identity of the authenticated user, you must apply access controls to allow them read/write access to the %installroot%\ASP.NET Temporary Files directory and to the application directory. The account must also have read access to the %systemdrive%\inetpub\wwwroot and the %windir%\assembly directories. You'll learn more about this topic in Chapter 18.
<machineKey>	Defines how ASP.NET encrypts and decrypts authentication cookie data. You can allow ASP.NET to automatically generate keys for you, or you can set your own keys.
<pages>	Defines page-specific configuration settings. You'll learn more about this configuration section in the example following this table.

Table 17-3 Configuration Sections of Web.config

Configuration Section	Description
<processModel>	Configures the ASP.NET process model settings on IIS. For example, you can set the number of requests that IIS accepts before ASP.NET launches a new worker process to replace the current one. Unlike most of the configuration settings, changes to *<processModel>* don't take effect until IIS is restarted.
<securityPolicy>	Maps security levels to policy files.
<sessionState>	Defines settings for session state, such as the time-out period of a session or whether a session supports cookies. For more information about this tag, see Chapter 12.
<trace>	Configures the ASP.NET Trace facility. For more information about tracing, see Chapter 16.
<trust>	Configures the code access security permissions that ASP.NET applies to an application.
<webServices>	Defines the settings of XML Web services. For more information about XML Web services, see Chapter 15.

Web.config Configuration Example

The code in Listing 17-1 shows a simple Web.config file that contains some of the configuration sections Table 17-3 describes. The comments in the listing explain the use of these various configuration sections.

```
<?xml version="1.0" encoding="utf-8" ?>

<configuration>
    <system.web>
        <!-- Set the default language to C# and enable compilation of
             debug binaries. -->
        <compilation defaultLanguage="c#" debug="true"/>

        <!-- Use Passport for authentication. -->
        <authentication mode="passport"/>

        <!-- Disable the trace service. -->
        <trace enabled="false"/>

        <!-- Enable session state and view state, and disable page
            events. -->
        <pages enableSessionState="true" enableViewState="true"
```

Listing 17-1 Sample Web.config file

```
            autoEventWireup="false"/>

        <!-- Configure state to be stored on a SQL server and to use
            a munged URL instead of a cookie. -->
        <sessionState mode="SqlServer" cookieless="true"
            sqlConnectionString="data source=127.0.0.1;user id=sa;
            password=""/>
    </system.web>
</configuration>
```

Building ASP.NET Applications with Integrated Desktop and Mobile Access

The final topic in this chapter is a subject that is related to deployment and implementation on a Web server but that is actually about design and coding that should take place during application development. In many cases, a mobile Web application is developed to allow access from mobile devices to an application that has already been implemented for desktop browsers. Perhaps the application has proven so useful that users have requested access to it when they're away from their desks or away from the office. This scenario poses significant design problems because a desktop Web application is typically much too rich to implement successfully on a mobile device. You can't just take the desktop application and build a new GUI for mobile devices using mobile Web Forms. You must analyze the application to determine which transactions make sense as a mobile Web application and distill the application down to the essential functionality that you want to make available to your mobile users.

When you're designing ASP.NET applications, it's good object-oriented practice to separate the code responsible for handling the user interface from code that implements business logic or handles data access. In Chapter 11, you saw a simple example of this when you built a component that retrieves and updates data from a database. The code in the .aspx file and its code-behind module is entirely concerned with the manipulation of the user interface; the data-handling code is implemented in external classes; and beneath that is the database where the data is stored. This approach is called *three-tier design*.

This design tactic yields particular benefits when you build an application that offers a desktop browser interface constructed with Web Forms and a user interface for mobile clients built with mobile Web Forms. If you move the business logic this application requires to external classes, both user interfaces can make use of it. This ensures that business rules are applied and data is accessed consistently, regardless of whether the client uses the desktop or mobile device versions of the application.

Tailoring Functionality to the Client Device

The functionality available in an application's desktop version is rarely available in its entirety in the mobile version. Often the screen display size makes this impossible. Some of the most successful integrated applications of this type regard the mobile channel as a way to provide the most crucial functions of the desktop application to users who aren't near their PCs. Users welcome the ability to access the most important functionality remotely but still view the desktop browser as the primary version of the application.

This approach has additional benefits. Perhaps the desktop application offers a great many options to users. Different users might employ varied subsets of the available options. Thus, they should be able to access a corresponding subset of options in the mobile version. A function in the desktop application that allows users to register their preferences for the mobile application can be used by your application to tailor menus and options when the users access the application from a mobile device.

Implementing a Redirect Page for the Mobile Web Site

Each .aspx Web Forms page has its own URL. Therefore, you can offer desktop and mobile versions of your Web site using different URLs. However, it's easier for your users if they use the same URL, regardless of the client accessing it.

One way to achieve this is to create a default page that performs a redirect to the Web Forms page or the mobile Web Forms page, depending on the client type. This redirect page can be a mobile Web Forms page or an ASP.NET Web Forms page; it uses the *IsMobileDevice* property of the *MobileCapabilities* class, which is set to *true* if the requesting browser is recognized as a supported mobile device. (See Chapter 19 for details on how the ASP.NET configuration system recognizes devices.) Listing 17-2 shows an example of a redirect page. You'll find this page in the RedirectExample project in the companion material on this book's Web site.

```
<%@ Page language="c#" Codebehind="default.aspx.cs" AutoEventWireup="false"
        Inherits="System.Web.UI.Page" %>
<!DOCTYPE HTML PUBLIC "-//W3C//DTD HTML 4.0 Transitional//EN" >
<HTML>
  <HEAD>
    <script language="C#" runat="server">
      public void Page_Load(Object sender, EventArgs e)
      {
          if (Request.Browser["IsMobileDevice"] == "true")
```

Listing 17-2 Redirect page to route clients to a Web Forms page or a mobile Web Forms page as appropriate

```
            {
                Response.Redirect("http://MyWebServer/MobileMain.aspx");
            }
            else
            {
                Response.Redirect("Main.aspx");
            }
        }
    </script>
  </HEAD>
  <body>
    <p>If you are not redirected, click <A href="Main.aspx">here</A>.</p>
  </body>
</HTML>
```

If this page is named Default.aspx and IIS recognizes that name as a default document (as it does by default), users need only enter the URL up to the application name—for example, *http://MyWebServer/MyApplication*. Another convenience of this design approach!

You might be tempted to make the initial page a mobile Web forms page and then redirect desktop clients to a directory beneath. For example, the mobile Web application could be at *http://Myserver/MyApplication/default.aspx*, and the redirect page at that URL could then send desktop clients to the relative URL */Desktop/Main.aspx*. However, it's better to redirect to a *fully qualified* URL elsewhere on the server; otherwise, your desktop application will inherit the configuration settings from the Web.config file at *http://Myserver/MyApplication/default.aspx*. Typically, the Web.config for a mobile Web application configures the application to operate cookieless, and if you put the desktop version of the application in a child directory, the configuration for cookieless session tracking will then be inherited by the desktop application. (For an explanation of cookieless applications, see Chapter 12.) Once an application has been configured for cookieless session tracking, the setting can't be undone in the Web.config file of a child directory (although the reverse isn't true—you can configure an application in a child directory to start using cookieless session tracking).

For desktop applications, this behavior might give unexpected results: most desktop applications will operate fine using the munged URLs (for example, *http://Myserver/MyApplication/(shjj44633k2)/default.aspx*) that ASP.NET uses to support cookieless clients, but the developers of the desktop application will probably expect their application to operate using cookies, and preventing the use of cookies might introduce unexpected problems.

Response.Redirect and Cookieless Session Tracking

For a redirect from the start page of an application, you can use the *Response.Redirect* method with a relative *or* absolute URL to redirect to your mobile Web site. If you are using *Response.Redirect* elsewhere in your application and you've configured your application to operate as cookieless, you must specify a relative URL as the redirect location. This is because in a cookieless application, the runtime tracks the session ID by munging the URL with an embedded token. If you specify an absolute URL, you will lose the munged URL and the cookieless session tracking. (For more information about cookieless applications, see Chapter 12.)

Also be sure to set *UseFullyQualifiedRedirectURL* to *True* in the Web.config application file. Some mobile devices can't handle redirects specifying relative URLs. And by making this configuration setting, you cause the runtime to convert the URL specified in *Response.Redirect* to a full URL before sending it to the client (but without losing the munged URL if your application is cookieless).

today

18

ASP.NET Application Security

Building a secure Web application is a complex task. If you build a simple, open-to-all mobile Web application that publishes information, it "just works." As soon as you want to restrict access to specific users or classes of users, or allow certain functions in your application to be available to some users but not to others, you must start to consider how you determine the identity of the remote user and how you use access controls to limit access to resources. A complete analysis of the topic of securing Microsoft ASP.NET applications requires a book all its own, rather than just one chapter in this book. Fortunately, such a resource exists and is available for free download from MSDN: see the paper "Building Secure ASP.NET Applications: Authentication, Authorization, and Secure Communication," which is available at *http://msdn.microsoft.com/library/default.asp?url=/library/en-us/dnnetsec/html/secnetlpMSDN.asp*. This chapter provides an introduction to the topic of ASP.NET security. In this chapter, you'll learn specific techniques for securing ASP.NET mobile Web applications, including how to program Forms, Passport, and Windows authentication.

Encrypting Data Transfers Between Client and Server

Securing an ASP.NET application can be a significant undertaking that requires the skills of several people. The ASP.NET application running on the Web server is only one part of a chain of computers and networks that are involved in the running of an application. In a typical secure enterprise mobile Web application, data is transferred over an encrypted data link between the mobile client and the Web server, as shown in Figure 18-1. The Web server sits inside a demilitarized zone (DMZ), separated from the enterprise backbone by a firewall, and connects to an application server, where business logic components are located. There might be an additional hop from the application server to the database server.

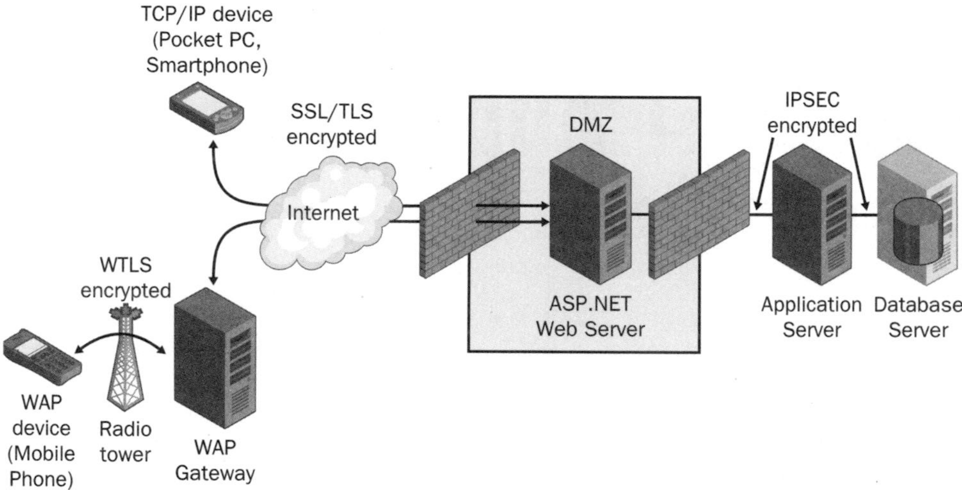

Figure 18-1 A typical secure Web application, which involves many systems with different security policies applied to each system

As you can see in Figure 18-1, a crucial part of the mobile Web application that must be protected is data flowing between the mobile client and the Web server. Applications that transfer sensitive data such as personal details, usernames and passwords, financial data, or business-critical data must protect that data from being accessed by unauthorized people.

Fortunately, the techniques for securing data transfers between Web browsers and servers are well established. High-end mobile devices, such as personal digital assistants (PDAs) and smart phones, support TCP/IP communications from the device to the server. When you have end-to-end TCP/IP, you can use Secure Sockets Layer (SSL) or Transport Layer Security (TLS) encryption to protect the data from unauthorized access. TLS is a protocol that encrypts data that transfers between a client and a server over the Internet, ensuring that it cannot be understood or altered if the data is intercepted by a malicious third-party. TLS is based on an earlier protocol called SSL 3.0; most modern browsers support SSL and TLS. The browser sets up a channel encrypted using TLS when you enter **https://** as the scheme of the destination URL. The Web server must be set up as a secure server, which means that it is equipped with a server cer-

VeriSign or Entrust. The client browser verifies this server certificate when the connection is negotiated to ensure that the certificate offered by the server is valid and has not expired. If there's a problem with the certificate, the browser either drops the connection or informs the user of the problem giving them the option to continue or to cancel the connection request.

With WAP 1.x devices, the situation is slightly more complex. WAP 1.x devices do not use HTTP over TCP/IP as the data transport from the device. Instead, they use a stack of optimized wireless protocols including Wireless Session Protocol (WSP), Wireless Transaction Protocol (WTP), Wireless Transport Layer Security (WTLS), and Wireless Datagram Protocol (WDP). As with TCP/IP devices, entering as the scheme of the destination URL causes an encrypted session to be set up, but this time using WTLS protocols. This encrypts the data between the device and a network end point called a *WAP Gateway*. Normally, the WAP Gateway resides inside the network operator's domain, but in some cases, large corporations have deployed their own WAP Gateway inside their own secure domain. At the WAP Gateway, the encrypted data must be momentarily decrypted to clear text and then reencrypted using SSL/TLS for its onward journey through the Internet to the Web server. Although this decryption/encryption takes place only in the memory of the WAP Gateway and network operators can generally be considered to be trustworthy organizations that operate secure computer facilities, this break in end-to-end security between device and Web server is enough to deter some organizations from using WAP devices for secure Web applications.

In WAP 2.0, devices now use standard Internet communications standards, so you can use HTTP with SSL/TLS directly from the device, eliminating this problem. The WAP 1.x protocols were devised for devices running on very slow, low-bandwidth networks, but with the emergence of faster digital wireless technologies such as GPRS and CDMA2000, the need for the WAP 1.x protocols is removed. (For more information about security in WAP 2.0, refer to *http://rr.sans.org/wireless/WAP2_sec.php*.)

Providing Authentication

Authentication is the process of identifying a user, ensuring that the user is who he or she claims to be. If you successfully authenticate a user, you can apply access controls to a given resource that determine whether the user is authorized to access that resource. In addition to using authentication and authorization to determine whether a user can access a particular resource, you can customize the content you serve to the user based on the user's identity and the roles he or she performs. ASP.NET provides authentication services in conjunction with Internet Information Services (IIS).

Any request that comes into an IIS server from a browser must first pass through IIS authentication mechanisms, as shown in Figure 18-2. Having successfully passed this hurdle, the request is then passed to ASP.NET, where you can apply additional authentication mechanisms. After it has successfully passed through ASP.NET authentication, the request will have an assigned identity (meaning that the request executes under the guise of a particular Microsoft Windows user) and might have an assigned role (a Windows account belongs to one or more Windows groups). You then configure access controls using NTFS permissions, Windows access control lists (ACLs), or SQL Server Access controls to allow or deny access to a file or database, depending on the identity or role of the requester.

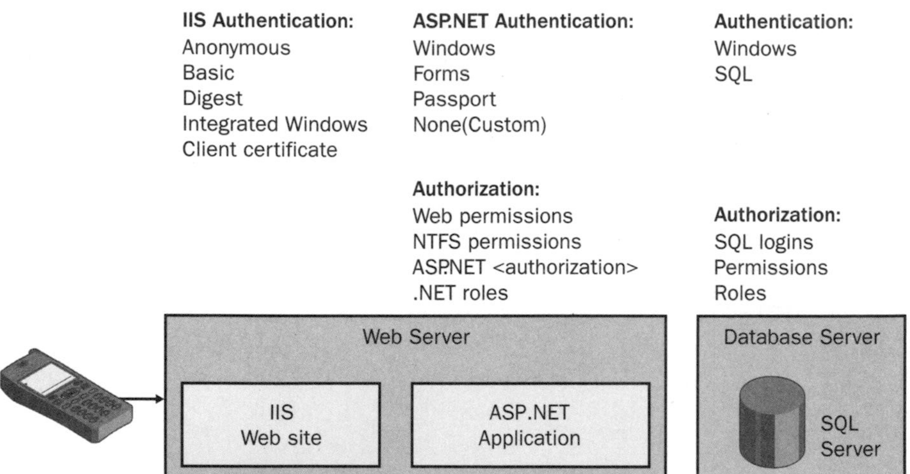

Figure 18-2 Requests from browsers must pass through IIS authentication, ASP.NET authentication, and then authorization to access resources

IIS Authentication

You configure IIS authentication for the virtual directory of an individual Web site using Internet Services Manager in the Administrative Tools section of the Windows control panel. To configure the security settings of your application's root directory in IIS, follow these steps:

1. Open Internet Services Manager.
2. Select the virtual directory you want to configure.

3. Choose Properties from the Action menu. A Properties dialog box appears.
4. Select the Directory Security tab, and click the Edit button in the Anonymous Access And Authentication Control section of the dialog box.
5. Configure the necessary settings in the Authentication Methods dialog box. For example, to configure Basic authentication, make sure that Anonymous Access is unchecked, and then select Basic Authentication. We describe each of the available authentication mechanisms next.
6. Click OK to close the Authentication Methods dialog box, and then click OK to complete the IIS configuration.

Figure 18-3 shows the Internet Services Manager interfaces used to configure IIS authentication.

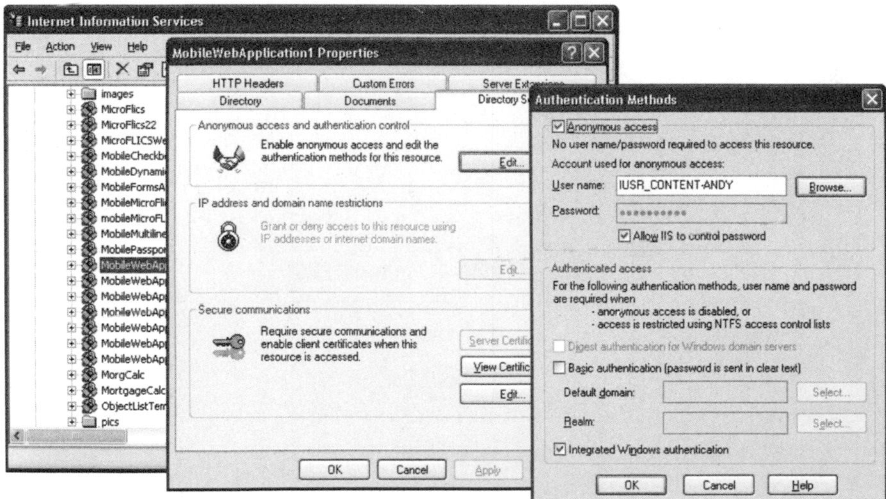

Figure 18-3 IIS Authentication Methods editor

You can configure Anonymous, Basic, Digest, Integrated Windows, or Certificate authentication, as described in Table 18-1. For mobile Web applications, only Anonymous and Basic can be used with any confidence, as the other forms of authentication are generally not supported by mobile browsers.

Table 18-1 IIS Authentication Types

Authentication Type	Description
Anonymous	Use this mode if you do not need to authenticate your clients. For anonymous access, IIS creates a Windows access token for the guest account. By default, this access token is named IUSR_*MACHINENAME* where *MACHINENAME* is the NetBIOS name of the computer.
Basic	Basic authentication requires users to supply a username and password to prove their credentials. This mechanism is a proposed Internet standard (RFC 2617) and is supported by nearly all browsers, including the majority of mobile browsers. IIS validates the username and password against a Windows account and creates a Windows access token for that account.
Digest	This is similar to Basic authentication, but instead of the username and password, it transmits a hash of the credentials. As a result, it is more secure. However, Digest authentication is not widely supported by mobile browsers.
Integrated Windows	This technique is supported only by Microsoft Internet Explorer browsers and is consequently of little use for mobile Web applications.
Certificate	Some devices allow you to install a client certificate, which the browser presents to the server to identify itself. As with Integrated Windows authentication, this technique is of little use with the majority of mobile browsers.

The IIS authentication mechanism you use drives the ASP.NET authentication mechanism, which we describe in the next section. You must decide on which type of ASP.NET authentication you need to use and implement the ISS authentication mechanism necessary to support that.

> **Warning** Most mobile devices on the market support only credential exchange via Basic authentication. When using Basic authentication, the browser transmits the username and password in an unencrypted Base64-encoded form to the server. Therefore, you should use Basic authentication only over an SSL/TLS or a WTLS-SSL encrypted channel to avoid revealing these details to hackers armed with network sniffers.

ASP.NET Authentication

ASP.NET allows four main types of authentication, described in Table 18-2.

Table 18-2 Authentication Types ASP.NET Supports

Authentication Type	Description
Forms	ASP.NET performs authentication by presenting a mobile Web Forms page you create, on which the user enters his or her credentials (typically a username and password). You write code to validate the credentials, and then an authentication ticket is generated that is round-tripped to and from the client on each subsequent request. You should set IIS authentication to *Anonymous* when using ASP.NET Forms authentication.
Passport	ASP.NET can use Microsoft's Web-based Passport .NET authentication service. You must install the Microsoft Passport SDK on the Web server; you can then use the centralized Passport authentication services to authenticate your users. This works with mobile clients as well as desktop browsers, as described in the section "Passport Authentication," later in this chapter.
Windows	In this mode, ASP.NET delegates authentication to IIS, so your application relies on one of the IIS authentication mechanisms described in the previous section.
None	This setting indicates that you don't want to authenticate users or that you're using a custom authentication scheme. To implement a custom authentication scheme, you must write a custom HTTP module to perform authentication. (This topic is outside the scope of this book; refer to the .NET Framework SDK documentation for more information.) With this authentication setting, any IIS authentication setting will still apply to an application.

Warning When you're using Forms authentication, the browser sends the username and password to the server in clear text. Therefore, you should use Forms authentication only over an SSL/TLS or WTLS-SSL encrypted channel to avoid revealing these details to hackers armed with network sniffers.

You use the *<system.web>* configuration section of Web.config files to define the type of authentication required. Here are the elements and attributes you can configure:

```
<configuration>
    <system.web>
        <authentication mode="Windows|Forms|Passport|None">
            <forms name="name" loginUrl="aURL"
                protection="All|None|Encryption|Validation"
                timeout="intSeconds" path="aPath"
                requireSSL="true|false"
                slidingExpiration="true|false" >
                <credentials passwordFormat="Clear|SHA1|MD5">
                    <user name="username" password="password"/>
                </credentials>
            </forms>
            <passport redirectURL="internal"/>
        </authentication>
    </system.web>
</configuration>
```

Most of the elements and attributes in this configuration file sample are specific to ASP.NET Forms or Windows authentication. Let's take a closer look at each of these authentication types now.

Forms Authentication

Forms authentication allows you to provide your own mobile Web Forms page as a logon page. Forms authentication uses client-side redirection to forward unauthenticated users to a specified logon form that allows them to enter their credentials (typically, username and password), as illustrated in Figure 18-4. These credentials are then validated, and an authentication ticket is generated and returned to the client, which is used to maintain the user identity for the duration of the user's session. In ASP.NET applications for desktop browsers, this authentication ticket is in the form of a cookie that the client returns with every request. In mobile Web applications that are usually configured to be cookieless, the authentication ticket is encoded into the query string appended to the URL that the client returns with each request.

> **Important** Forms authentication sends the username and password to the Web server in plain text. As a result, you should use Forms authentication in conjunction with a channel secured by SSL or WTLS-SSL. The authentication ticket is transmitted on subsequent requests, so you should consider using encryption for all pages within your application, not just the logon page, to protect the ticket from hackers using network monitoring tools.

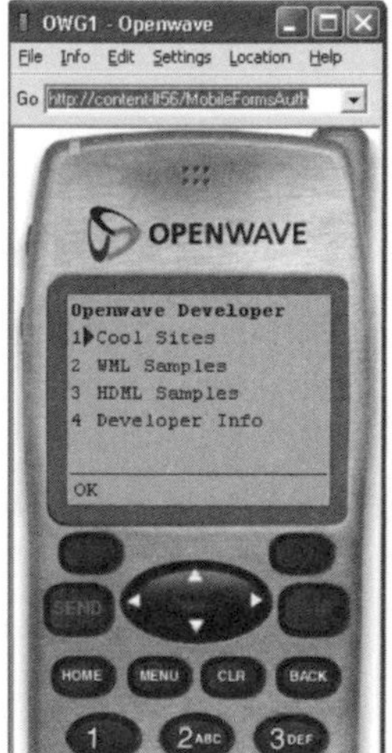

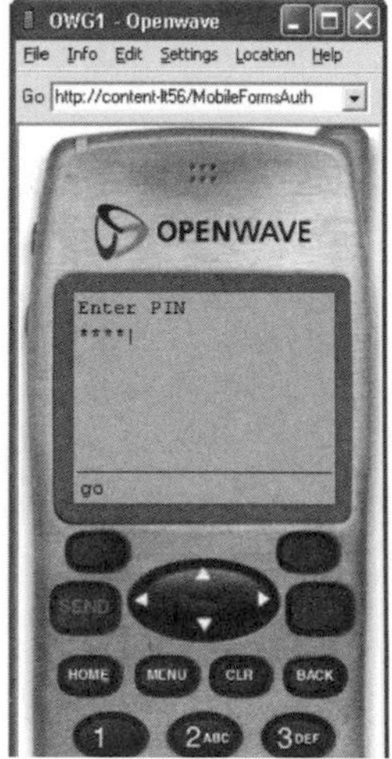

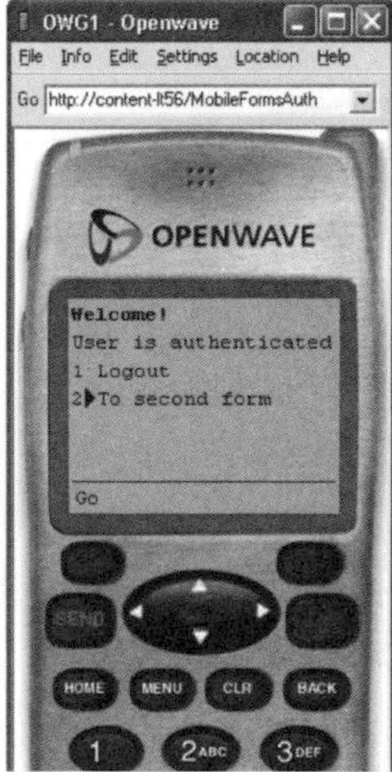

Figure 18-4 A mobile Web application redirected to a logon page by Forms authentication

Configuring Forms Authentication

You add a *<forms>* element to your Web.config application configuration files to protect access to your application, and if a user tries to access any page, he or she is automatically redirected to the login page. The following XML from an application's Web.config file shows how you can configure an application to use Forms authentication:

```
<configuration>
    <system.web>
        ⋮
        <authentication mode="Forms">
            <forms loginUrl="Login.aspx"
```

```
                name="nameOfAuthCookie"  timeout="10" path="/" >
                <credentials passwordFormat="Clear">
                    <user name="05678912" password="0284"/>
                    ⋮
                </credentials>
            </forms>
        </authentication>
        <authorization>
            <deny users="?"/>
        </authorization>
        ⋮
        <sessionState cookieless="true"
        ⋮
        </sessionState>
    </system.web>
</configuration>
```

Note that when you're using the *<forms>* element to configure Forms authentication for ASP.NET applications targeting desktop browsers, you can also use the *requireSSL* and *slidingExpiration* attributes. These attributes affect the way that cookies are used with browsers that support them. However, in this example, the *<sessionState cookieless="true" …>* element configures the application to operate without using cookies (which is how you will configure the majority of mobile Web applications), so the *requireSSL* and *slidingExpiration* attributes do not affect the way that Forms authentication operates with cookieless browsers.

The *<authorization>* tag has an important role in the implementation of Forms authentication: the *<deny users="?"/>* element denies all anonymous users access to any application resources. The optional *<credentials>* child element of the *<forms>* element allows you to define a set of username and password credentials. You define each set of credentials in a *<user>* element. The *<user>* element accepts two attributes, *name* and *password*, which represent the user's login name and password, respectively. The *credentials* element has one attribute, *passwordFormat*, which defines the type of hashing algorithm ASP.NET uses for the passwords stored in this Web.config file. The three possible values for the *passwordFormat* attribute are *Clear* (as shown in this example), *MD5*, and *SHA1*. For example, if the passwords are hashed using the SHA1 hash digest, the password sent from the client is hashed by the server and the hash value compared with the value stored in this file. An intruder can't derive the original password by inspecting the hash value. The following *<credentials>* element defines two users named Kim and John. The *passwordFormat* attribute of the *<credentials>* element specifies the use of the SHA1 algorithm for password hashing, and the *password* attributes for Kim and John contain hashed versions of their passwords.

```
<credentials passwordFormat="SHA1" >
      <user name="Kim" password="9611E4F94EC4972D5A537EA28C69F89AD28E5B36"/>
      <user name="John" password="BA7157A99DFE9DD70A94D89844A4B4993B10168F"/>
</credentials>
```

To authenticate against usernames and passwords stored in the configuration file, use the *FormsAuthentication.Authenticate* method in the logic of your logon page, as shown in Listings 18-1 and 18-2.

> **Note** Using the Web.config file to store usernames and passwords is only one way of implementing a credentials store. Most applications would store user credentials in SQL Server or Active Directory. In either of those cases, the code in Login.aspx would change to validate the username and password that the client has sent against the external credentials store, instead of using the *FormsAuthentication.Authenticate* method.

```
<%@ Register TagPrefix="mobile" Namespace="System.Web.UI.MobileControls"
    Assembly="System.Web.Mobile" %>
<%@ Page language="c#" Codebehind="Login.aspx.cs"
    Inherits="MSPress.MobWeb.MobileFormsAuth.Login"
    AutoEventWireup="false" %>

<mobile:form id="Form1" title="Login" runat="server">
    <mobile:Label id="messageLabel" runat="server" visible="false"
        StyleReference="error"></mobile:Label>
    <mobile:Label id="IDLabel" runat="server">
        Your Phone Number:</mobile:Label>
    <mobile:TextBox id="Usernametxt" title="Phone Number" runat="Server"
        Numeric="True"></mobile:TextBox>
    <mobile:Label id="PasswordLabel" runat="server">
        Enter PIN</mobile:Label>
    <mobile:TextBox id="Passwordtxt" title="PIN Number" runat="Server"
        Numeric="True" Password="True"></mobile:TextBox>
    <mobile:Command id="LoginCommand" runat="Server" SoftkeyLabel="go">
        Go</mobile:Command>
</mobile:form>
```

Listing 18-1 Mobile Web Forms page of Login.aspx for Forms authentication

```
using System;
using System.Web.Mobile;
using System.Web.Security;
using System.Web.UI.MobileControls;

namespace MSPress.MobWeb.MobileFormsAuth
{
    /// <summary>
    /// Login form for Forms Authentication
    /// </summary>
    public class Login : System.Web.UI.MobileControls.MobilePage
    {
        protected System.Web.UI.MobileControls.Label IDLabel;
        protected System.Web.UI.MobileControls.Label PasswordLabel;
        protected System.Web.UI.MobileControls.Command LoginCommand;
        protected System.Web.UI.MobileControls.TextBox Usernametxt;
        protected System.Web.UI.MobileControls.Label messageLabel;
        protected System.Web.UI.MobileControls.TextBox Passwordtxt;
        protected System.Web.UI.MobileControls.Form Form1;

        override protected void OnInit(EventArgs e)
        {
            InitializeComponent();
            base.OnInit(e);
        }

        private void InitializeComponent()
        {
            this.LoginCommand.Click +=
                new System.EventHandler(this.LoginCommand_Click);
        }

        private void LoginCommand_Click(object sender, System.EventArgs e)
        {
            if(IsAuthenticated(Usernametxt.Text, Passwordtxt.Text))
            {
                MobileFormsAuthentication.RedirectFromLoginPage
                   (Passwordtxt.Text,true);
            }
            else
            {
                messageLabel.Text = "Check your credentials";
                messageLabel.Visible = true;
            }
        }
```

Listing 18-2 Code-behind module Login.aspx.cs for Forms authentication

```
        private bool IsAuthenticated(String user, String password)
        {
            //Check the values against forms authentication store.

            if(FormsAuthentication.Authenticate(user, password))
            {
                return true;
            }
            else
            {
                return false;
            }
        }
    }
}
```

You can also configure five attributes and one child element of the *<forms>* element to define how ASP.NET performs authentication. Most of these attributes relate to the use of cookies to support Forms authentication. This is rarely the case with mobile Web applications, which usually operate cookieless (by setting *<sessionState cookieless="true"/>* in the Web.config file). Table 18-3 describes these five attributes.

Table 18-3 Attributes of the *<forms>* Element

Attribute	Description
name	Name of the cookie that ASP.NET uses for authentication. The default name is .ASPXAUTH. When the application is configured to operate cookieless, ASP.NET uses this name for the parameter in the query string that is used to pass the authentication token between client and server.
loginUrl	URL of the page to which ASP.NET redirects the user if they have not yet been authenticated. The default value is Default.aspx.
path	The path for cookies. The default value is / (forward slash).
protection	The level of protection that ASP.NET gives the cookie it uses in the authentication process. This attribute has four possible values: ■ ***All*** ASP.NET uses both validation and encryption to protect the cookie. ■ ***None*** ASP.NET *doesn't* validate or encrypt the cookie. ■ ***Encryption*** ASP.NET only encrypts the cookie. ■ ***Validation*** ASP.NET only validates the cookie.

Table 18-3 Attributes of the *<forms>* Element

Attribute	Description
requireSSL	Specifies whether a secure connection is required to transmit the authentication cookie. The default is *false*, which means a secure connection is not required to transmit the cookie. If *true*, a compliant client browser will not transmit the cookie unless an SSL/TLS channel is being used. This parameter does not have any effect when the application is configured to operate cookieless.
sliding-Expiration	Specifies whether sliding expiration is enabled. Sliding expiration resets an active authentication cookie's time to expiration upon each request during a single session. If *false* (the default), the cookie expires *timeout* minutes after it was first issued. If *true*, the expiration time on the cookie is reset to *timeout* minutes on every request. This parameter does not have any effect when the application is configured to operate cookieless.
timeout	The time in integer minutes after which the cookie expires. The default value is 30 minutes.

Forms Authentication Example

One benefit of using Forms authentication is that very little code is required in your application. Once configured, the ASP.NET runtime takes care of checking the authentication ticket passed by the client in the query string and redirects the caller to the logon form if the ticket has expired or is invalid. A simple application is shown in Listings 18-3, 18-4, 18-5, and 18-6, which you can use with the Login.aspx form shown earlier in Listing 18-1 and Listing 18-2. (The output of this application was shown in Figure 18-4.)

This application demonstrates how Forms authentication works. When the browser makes an initial request for the main page of this application, default.aspx, it is automatically redirected by the Forms Authentication system to the Login.aspx page. Listing 18-3 shows the Web.config file for this application, which includes within it the credentials store which is set to only allow a username of 05678912 with a password of 1284. When the user has entered the correct username and password, the logic in Login.aspx calls *MobileForms-Authentication.RedirectFromLoginPage*, as shown in Listing 18-2, which instructs the runtime to redirect the client back to the page they originally requested.

> **Note** For any readers who are used to Forms Authentication in ASP.NET applications for desktop browsers, be careful to use the *RedirectFromLoginPage* method from the MobileFormsAuthentication class, not the method of the same name in the *FormsAuthentication* class that you may have used before. You must use the implementation in the *MobileFormsAuthentication* class which knows how to operate with cookieless mobile clients.

```
<?xml version="1.0" encoding="utf-8" ?>
<configuration>

  <system.web>

    <compilation
         defaultLanguage="c#"
         debug="true"
    />

    <!--  AUTHENTICATION
          This section sets the authentication policies of the
          application.Possible modes are "Windows", "Forms",
          "Passport" and "None"
    -->
        <authentication mode="Forms">
            <forms loginUrl="Login.aspx"
                name="nameOfAuthCookie" timeout="10" path="/">
                <credentials passwordFormat="Clear">
                    <user name="05678912" password="1284"/>
                </credentials>
            </forms>
        </authentication>
        <authorization>
            <deny users="?"/>
        </authorization>

    <!--  SESSION STATE SETTINGS  -->
    <sessionState
          mode="InProc"
          cookieless="true"
          timeout="20"
    />
```

Listing 18-3 Configuration file Web.config for the Forms authentication example

```
    <!--  GLOBALIZATION
          This section sets globalization settings of the application.
    -->
    <globalization
           requestEncoding="utf-8"
           responseEncoding="utf-8"
    />

    <!-- FULLY QUALIFY URL FOR CLIENT REDIRECTS
          Some mobile devices require that the URL for client
          redirects be fully qualified.
    -->
    <httpRuntime
           useFullyQualifiedRedirectUrl="true"
    />

    <!-- SPECIFY COOKIELESS DATA DICTIONARY TYPE
        This will cause the dictionary contents to appear in
        the local request url querystring.
        This is required for forms authentication to work on
        cookieless devices.
    -->
    <mobileControls
        cookielessDataDictionaryType="System.Web.Mobile.CookielessData" />

  </system.web>

</configuration>
```

The main form for this application is shown in Listing 18-4 and 18-5. This simple form contains a button labeled Logout and a link to a second mobile Webform called SecondForm.aspx, which is shown in Listing 18-6. When you run this application and you have successfully passed through the logon form, you can click on the link which displays the text To second form, and your browser redirects to that Form. You can then use the Back key or button on your browser to view Default.aspx once again. If you now click on the Logout button, the code in the *Command1_Click* method executes, shown in Listing 18-5. This method calls *MobileFormsAuthentication.SignOut*, which signs you out of the application. If you then try the link to the second page, the runtime detects that the client is no longer authenticated and redirects the client to the logon page once more.

```
<%@ Register TagPrefix="mobile" Namespace="System.Web.UI.MobileControls"
    Assembly="System.Web.Mobile" %>
<%@ Page language="c#" Codebehind="default.aspx.cs"
    Inherits="MSPress.MobWeb.MobileFormsAuth._default" %>

<mobile:Form id="Form1" runat="server">
    <mobile:Label id="Label1" runat="server" StyleReference="title">
        Welcome! </mobile:Label>
    <mobile:Label id="isAuthenticatedLabel" runat="server">
        User is authenticated</mobile:Label>
    <mobile:Command id="Command1" runat="server">Logout</mobile:Command>
    <mobile:Link id="Link1" runat="server" NavigateUrl="SecondForm.aspx">
        To second form</mobile:Link>
</mobile:Form>
```

Listing 18-4 Source file Default.aspx that demonstrates Forms authentication

```
using System;
using System.Collections;
using System.Web.Mobile;
using System.Web.Security;
using System.Web.UI.MobileControls;

namespace MSPress.MobWeb.MobileFormsAuth
{
    public class _default : System.Web.UI.MobileControls.MobilePage
    {
        protected System.Web.UI.MobileControls.Label Label1;
        protected System.Web.UI.MobileControls.Label isAuthenticatedLabel;
        protected System.Web.UI.MobileControls.Link Link1;
        protected System.Web.UI.MobileControls.Command Command1;
        protected System.Web.UI.MobileControls.Form Form1;

        override protected void OnInit(EventArgs e)
        {
            InitializeComponent();
            base.OnInit(e);
        }

        private void InitializeComponent()
        {
            this.Command1.Click +=
                new System.EventHandler(this.Command1_Click);

        }
```

Listing 18-5 Code-behind module Default.aspx.cs

```
        private void Command1_Click(object sender, System.EventArgs e)
        {
            // Logout of the application

            MobileFormsAuthentication.SignOut();
            isAuthenticatedLabel.Text = "User is Logged Out";
        }
    }
}
```

The file SecondForm.aspx is extremely simple and just displays a label to show you that you've got there. When this is displayed, use the Back key or button on your browser to return to Default.aspx, and then exercise the Logout functionality, as explained in the previous paragraph.

```
<%@ Page language="c#" Inherits="System.Web.UI.MobileControls.MobilePage" %>
<%@ Register TagPrefix="mobile" Namespace="System.Web.UI.MobileControls"
    Assembly="System.Web.Mobile" %>
<mobile:Form id="Form1" runat="server">
    <mobile:Label id="Label1" runat="server">
        This is the second Mobile Web Form in this application
    </mobile:Label>
</mobile:Form>
```

Listing 18-6 Source file SecondForm.aspx

Passport Authentication

Many large Web sites allow the use of Microsoft Passport .NET Single Sign-In. Many readers will be familiar with the .NET Sign-In button that you see when you access facilities such as MSN Messenger from a desktop browser. With Passport, you can sign in once, and this automatically signs you in to all other sites you access that have integrated Passport authentication without your having to repeat the entry of credentials.

You can extend these benefits to mobile Web applications also. Microsoft Passport 2.1 extends Single Sign-In capability to mobile Web sites. Users of your application must register their phone number and PIN on the Passport Member Services page, as shown in Figure 18-5.

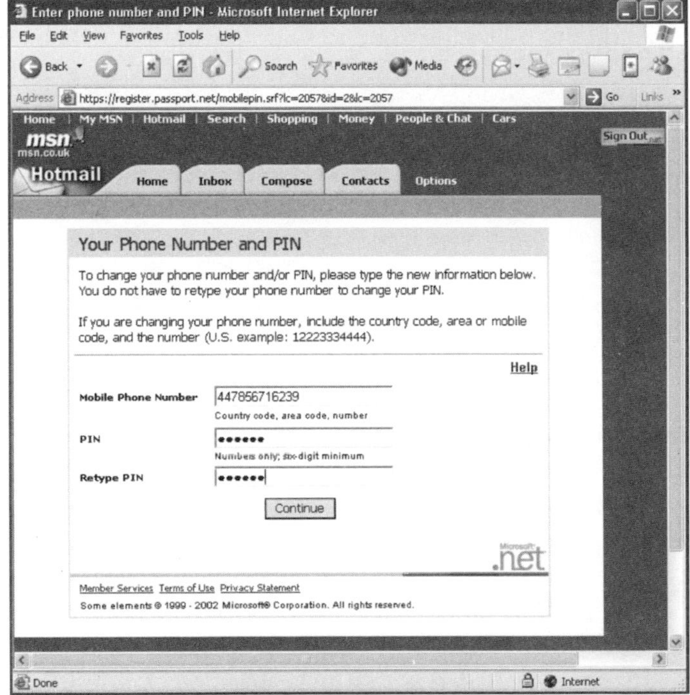

Figure 18-5 Registering a phone number and PIN in Passport .NET

Configuring Passport Support

The first stage is to download the Passport SDK from MSDN and to install it on your development system and Web server. You should then review the documentation. There are a number of requirements for Web sites that use Passport, such as the need to display certain logos. However, these requirements are relaxed for mobile devices due to the lack of screen size and the inability of certain devices to display JPEG graphics.

Passport's usage policy permits Web sites to use either a *soft sign-in* or a *hard sign-in*. You can design your mobile Web site to allow a soft sign-in, which permits the user to browse the Web site without being logged into the Passport system. The alternative is a hard sign-in, which requires the user to be logged in before accessing any part of the Web site. In the following example, we will use the hard sign-in method.

To configure your application for Passport authentication with cookieless mobile clients, add the following code to your application's Web.config file:

```
<configuration>
    <system.web>
        ⋮
        <authentication mode="Passport" />
        ⋮
        <sessionState cookieless="true"
            ⋮
        </sessionState>
    </system.web>
</configuration>
```

As with Forms authentication, the ASP.NET runtime supports cookieless clients by encoding the authentication ticket into the query string in the URL. This query string is passed back to the server with each request from the client, to stop the client being redirected to the Passport sign-in page again on each request. Normally, you would have to manage this query string yourself, but ASP.NET provides a mechanism called the cookielessDataDictionary, which was designed to support cookieless clients by managing cookies that have been encoded into the URL. However, the standard version of cookielessDataDictionary needs to be replaced with a new implementation that supports the Passport parameters.

Implementing a cookielessDataDictionary for Passport

You must write an implementation of *System.Collections.IDictionary* that analyzes the incoming request, extracts the Passport authentication ticket from it, and stores it inside the dictionary. This ensures that the authentication ticket is passed back to the client in the query string of the return URL when the response is constructed and sent back to the client.

The Passport authentication ticket is always in a parameter named "*t*", so you must get the item from the page's *Request.Params* collection (which stores items in the query string for an incoming request) using the key "*t*" and then copy it into your implementation of the dictionary. Unfortunately, it's not always quite that simple. Some mobile devices—notably, Openwave's UP.Browser—return the Passport parameters inside an HTTP *Authorization* header rather than as a query string in the URL, so you must also use a regular expression to analyze the HTTP headers to search for the Passport parameter there.

A full implementation of a cookielessDataDictionary is shown in Listing 18-7. You must save the "*t*" value in the constructor and you must also implement the *RemoveCookies* method, which clears the collection.

```
using System.Collections.Specialized;
using System.Text.RegularExpressions;
using System.Web;

namespace MSPress.MobWeb.MobilePassport
{
   class PassportDictionary : HybridDictionary
   {
      public PassportDictionary()
      {
         GetT(HttpContext.Current.Request.Params);
      }

      public void GetT(NameValueCollection parameters)
      {
         string t = parameters["t"];
         if(t != null)
         {
            this["t"] = t;
            return;
         }
         GetEmbeddedT(parameters);
      }

      /// <summary>
      /// The T value might be embedded inside a returned parameter
      /// depending on the device used. This function looks for 't'
      /// inside a parameter by looking at the following pattern   t=XXXXX
      /// Where the size of XXXX is 90 characters long.
      /// </summary>
      public void GetEmbeddedT(NameValueCollection parameters)
      {
         string t_pattern = @"^(.*[^\w])?t=(.{90})(.*)";
         string t_value = @"$2";
         foreach(string key in parameters)
         {
            string value = parameters[key];
            if(Regex.IsMatch(value,t_pattern))
            {
                string temp = Regex.Replace(value,t_pattern,t_value);
                this["t"] = temp;
                return;
            }
         }
      }
```

Listing 18-7 *cookielessDataDictionary* class to support mobile Passport

```
        public void RemoveCookies()
        {
            this.Clear();
        }
    }
}
```

When you have compiled the assembly containing the new dictionary, switch to the project for your mobile Web application, and add a reference to the new assembly. Then modify the *mobileControls* section of the application's Web.config file so that it makes use of the new assembly:

```
<mobileControls
   sessionStateHistorySize="6"
   cookielessDataDictionaryType=
       "MSPress.MobWeb.MobilePassport.PassportDictionary, MobilePassport"
/>
```

The *cookielessDataDictionaryType* attribute is set to a string consisting of the full name of the class comma-separated from the name of the assembly in which the class is contained (MobilePassport.dll in this case).

Programming Passport Authentication

All that remains is to program the call to the Passport authentication module at the appropriate point. You must write an *OnAuthenticate* event handler in your Global.asax.cs file to trap the Passport *Authenticate* event, as shown here. This method uses the *PassportIdentity.AuthUrl2* method to format the URL to which the mobile client redirects, with the required information encoded in the query string. See the Passport SDK documentation and the .NET Framework SDK for more information on this method.

```
public void PassportAuthentication_OnAuthenticate(Object sender,
    PassportAuthenticationEventArgs e)
{
    System.Web.Security.PassportIdentity id = e.Identity;

    if(!id.IsAuthenticated)
    {
        System.Web.UI.MobileControls.MobilePage mobile_page =
            new System.Web.UI.MobileControls.MobilePage();
        mobile_page.RedirectToMobilePage(
            id.AuthUrl2(
            "http://YourServer/YourSite/MainPage.aspx",
            -1,             // Default time limit since last log-on
            true,           // Force a logon if time-limit passes
            String.Empty,   // String to append to co-branding URL
```

```
                -1,            // Use default language for page display
                String.Empty,  // Use default domain to create passport
                -1,            // Use default data collection policies
                false          // Do not use https for logion UI
                )
                );
        }
    }
```

To log out of a Passport session, call the *SignOut* method of your *PassportIdentity* instance, calling *Session.RemoveAll* to clear the instance of the dictionary—which has the effect of clearing the query string of Passport information—and then redirect to another page without the parameters:

```
id.SignOut();
Session.RemoveAll();
mobile_page.RedirectToMobilePage("LogoutForm");
```

Windows Authentication

ASP.NET, in conjunction with IIS, provides Windows authentication services. Although Windows authentication doesn't offer the same flexibility as Forms authentication, it does give you programmatic access to authentication information. The most common usage of Windows authentication with mobile clients will be to use HTTP Basic authentication to get the login credentials from the client.

The first step in implementing Basic authentication for an application is to configure the security settings of your application's root directory in IIS. To do this, edit the IIS authentication settings as described earlier in this chapter, in the section "IIS Authentication." Verify that Anonymous Access is unchecked, and then select Basic Authentication. After you configure IIS, you can configure your application. You must first modify the application's Web.config file so that the *<authentication>* tag uses Windows authentication. The following code demonstrates this:

```
<?xml version="1.0" encoding="utf-8" ?>
    <configuration>
        <system.web>
            <authentication mode = "Windows"/>
        </system.web>
    </configuration>
```

The configuration of Windows authentication is now complete. To test the authentication, you can write a small application that uses information IIS passes to ASP.NET. Create a new mobile Web Forms page containing a single

Label control that has no value for its *Text* property. In the code-behind module, include the following code within the *Page_Load* method:

```
if (User.Identity.IsAuthenticated)
{
    Label1.Text=User.Identity.Name+" is authenticated!";
}
else
{
    Label1.Text="Authentication Failed";
}
```

The *Name* property is a property of the *System.Security.Principal.IIdentity* interface, which defines the basic functionality of identity objects. The interface has three public instance properties: *AuthenticationType*, *IsAuthenticated*, and *Name*. To learn more about this interface and the objects that implement it, refer to the Microsoft .NET Framework SDK documentation.

When you access the application that you've just built, the program asks you for a username and password. Once you submit these, IIS authenticates you and the mobile Web Forms page is displayed, as shown in Figure 18-6.

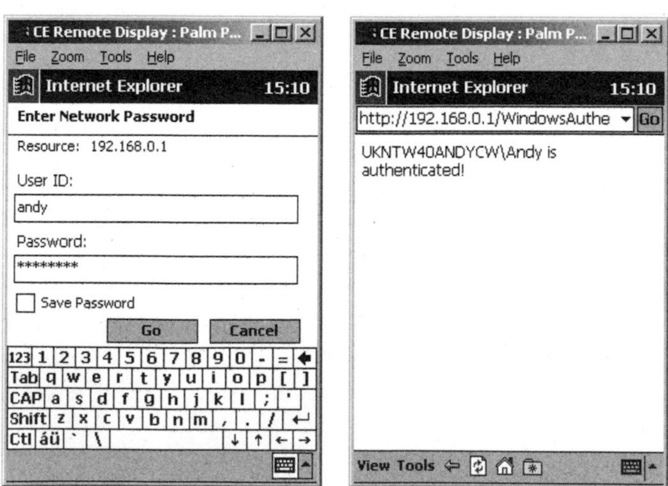

Figure 18-6 Using Pocket Internet Explorer to access an application configured for Windows authentication

User Authorization

Once you have transferred an HTTP request from the mobile device over an encrypted channel to the Web server and you have authenticated the client's identity, you must then put your mind to deciding what that user is allowed to do—that is, you *authorize* the user. Central to this is determining the identity of the process that is running your application. This identity depends on the form of authentication you have chosen.

Whenever your mobile Web application runs on the Web server, it does so using a Windows identity. Effectively, your process (which is running the ASP.NET worker process *aspnet_wp.exe)* logs on as a Windows user. By default, an ASP.NET application runs using the *machineName*\ASPNET identity. This default ASPNET account is specially configured to run with the minimum possible set of privileges. For example, you'll find that by default your application can access only specific folders that are required to run a Web application, such as the \bin directory in which a Web application stores compiled files, it cannot create new processes, or create new event log categories.

The account that ASP.NET Web applications run under is configured in the machine.config file in \Windows*(or Winnt)*\Microsoft.NET\Framework*version*\config by the *<processModel>* element:

```
<processModel username="machine" password="AutoGenerate" />
```

The machine username indicates the ASPNET account. The password is maintained and secured by the system. If your application is running under the ASP-NET account, you will need to configure NTFS permissions and Windows ACLs to allow access to specific resources. If you access resources over the network, you will have to set the ASPNET password to a specific value, record it in the *<processModel>* element, and then create an account also named ASPNET with the same password on the remote system.

If you set the *username* attribute of *<processElement>* to *"system"*, the ASP.NET worker process runs as the local SYSTEM account. This is not recommended, as it makes your machine vulnerable to attack if your Web application is compromised.

Impersonating a User

Instead of running under the nonprivileged ASPNET account, you can use impersonation by setting *<identity impersonate="true">* in the application's Web.config file, whereby the ASP.NET process runs with the identity (and security context) of the authenticated user. Access to resources is then controlled through normal NTFS access controls.

The *<identity>* element has two usages:

```
<identity impersonate="true"/>
<identity impersonate="true" username="Andy" password="P455w0rd"/>
```

Use the first form to run the ASP.NET process under the identity of the user as authenticated by IIS. This could be a Windows user account if HTTP Basic authentication is used. If Anonymous access is configured in IIS, it could be the IUSR_*MACHINENAME* account, where *MACHINENAME* is the NetBIOS name of the computer specified at install time.

Using the second form, you can specify a fixed account to be used for authenticated users by specifying values for the *username* and *password* attributes. This is not recommended in .NET Framework 1.0 because you had to grant the ASPNET process identity the "Act as part of the operating system" privilege, which makes your Web server more vulnerable to attack from hackers. In .NET Framework 1.1, the ASPNET account does not need this privilege. Also, in .NET Framework 1.1, you are able to store the username and password in the Windows registry in encrypted form. See the .NET Framework SDK documentation for the *<Identity>* element for details of how to do this.

Whether you use a fixed account or the identity of the authenticated user, you must apply access controls to allow the account read/write access to the %installroot%\ASP.NET Temporary Files directory and to the application directory. The account must also have read access to the %systemdrive%\inetpub\wwwroot and the %windir%\assembly directories, so that ASP.NET can access the content files and can monitor file changes.

URL Authorization

Once you have determined the identity that your application is running under, you can authorize access to secure resources. You use the *<authorization>* element in the *<system.web>* section of a Web.config file to control which users and groups of users should have access to the application.

The *<authorization>* element has two child elements that you use to allow or deny access to resources. The two elements are *<allow>* and *<deny>*, which both have three attributes. Table 18-4 describes these three attributes.

Table 18-4 Attributes of the *<allow>* and *<deny>* Tags

Attribute	Description
Users	The users that have permission to access the resource. The attribute's value is a comma-separated list of users. You can substitute names with wildcard characters. You can use a question mark (?) to refer to anonymous users and an asterisk (*) to refer to all users.

Table 18-4 Attributes of the *<allow>* and *<deny>* Tags

Attribute	Description
Roles	The .NET roles that have permission to access the resource. The attribute's value is a comma-separated list of roles.
Verbs	The HTTP methods that have permission to access the resource. The attribute's value is a comma-separated list of methods, in which the possible values include GET, HEAD, POST, and DEBUG.

If you're using ASP.NET Windows authentication (*<authentication mode="Windows"/>*), you are authorizing against Windows accounts and groups, so usernames and roles take the forms *DomainName\Username* and *DomainName\WindowsGroup*, respectively, as shown in the following code. (With Windows authentication, .NET roles map one-to-one with Windows groups.)

```
<allow users="MyDomainName\Bob"/>
<allow roles="MyDomainName\Administrators"/>
```

If you're using Forms authentication, you are authorizing against the username that you validated against, regardless of whether that username was configured in the *<credentials>* elements in Web.config or whether you validated against a database or Active Directory. Specify just the name for users or roles, as shown here:

```
<allow users="Bob"/>
```

If you're using Passport authentication, you are authorizing against the Passport User ID (PUID) or against roles mapped to the PUID that your application has retrieved from a database.

At run time, the authorization module iterates through all the *<allow>* and *<deny>* tags until it finds the first match for the requesting user. This is then used to allow or deny access to the URL. The following XML from an application's Web.config file shows how you can configure an application to authorize users:

```
<configuration>
    <system.web>
        ⋮
        <authorization>
            <deny verbs="GET,HEAD"/>
            <allow users="josh@adatum.com,max@adatum.com"/>
            <allow roles="Admins"/>
            <deny users="*" />
        </authorization>
        ⋮
    </system.web>
</configuration>
```

This code instructs ASP.NET to deny all GET and HEAD requests. If the request comes from a permitted method, such as POST, the users *josh@adatum.com* and *max@adatum.com* and the Admins role can access the resource. ASP.NET will deny access to all other users.

Usually, *<authorization>* settings in Web.config refer to all the files in the current directory and all subdirectories (unless a subdirectory contains its own Web.config file with an *<authorization>* element—in which case, the settings in the subdirectory override those of its parent). However, you can use the *<location>* tag to apply authorization settings to a particular file or directory. The following example shows how you can apply authorization to a specific page:

```
<location path="admin.aspx" />
    <authorization>
        <allow users="josh@adatum.com,max@adatum.com"/>
        <allow roles="Admins"/>
        <deny users="*" />
    </authorization>
</location>
```

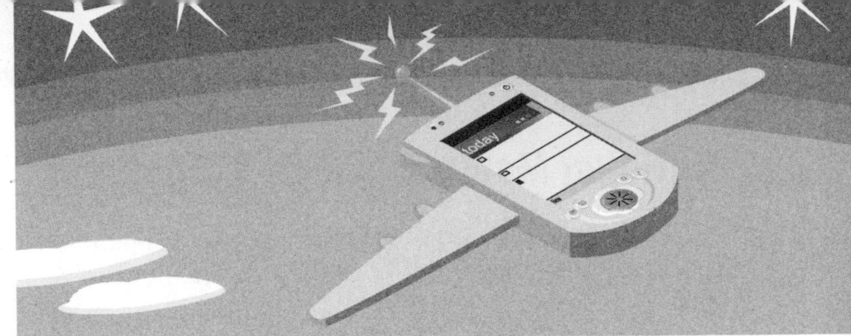

19

Supporting New Clients

In most instances, Microsoft ASP.NET delivers your mobile Web Forms pages to clients the way you expect. However, this isn't always the case. Your handheld device might report an error when you try to access an application, or the application might not be displayed correctly on the device. The most likely reason is that the runtime isn't configured to support the device in question. Think about how many browsers (and versions of them) run on such a wide variety of devices; it probably won't surprise you that the ASP.NET mobile controls don't support them all. Periodically, Microsoft releases Device Update packs to add support for new devices that they have tested. Go to *http://www.asp.net/mobile/deviceupdate.aspx?tabindex=6* to find the latest device update and to review the list of devices currently supported. You might find that you want to use a device that is not yet one of the officially supported devices. Fortunately, ASP.NET has an extensible configuration architecture that allows you to add support for new mobile clients.

In this chapter, we'll show you how to identify the type of a new device, identify its capabilities, and configure support for it. In Chapter 22, you'll learn how to write *device adapters*, which are plug-in mobile control components that handle the rendering of markup for a particular control on a particular type of mobile device. In this chapter, you'll come to understand the role of device adapter sets and learn how to use Extensible Markup Language (XML)–based configuration files to map device adapters to mobile controls. You'll also learn how to use the extensible configuration architecture to support new client devices, how device adapter sets are configured, how the correct device adapter set is selected for a device, and how to extend device adapter functionality to support new versions of markup languages. In addition, you'll learn more about the *System.Web.Mobile.MobileCapabilities* class and how the runtime identifies a client and serves the markup best suited to it.

Defining Mobile Devices in Configuration Files

To add support for a new client, you must understand how the runtime identifies a client and renders the markup most suitable for it. Figure 19-1 illustrates the process the runtime undertakes to determine the client type and to make the client identification available to your application.

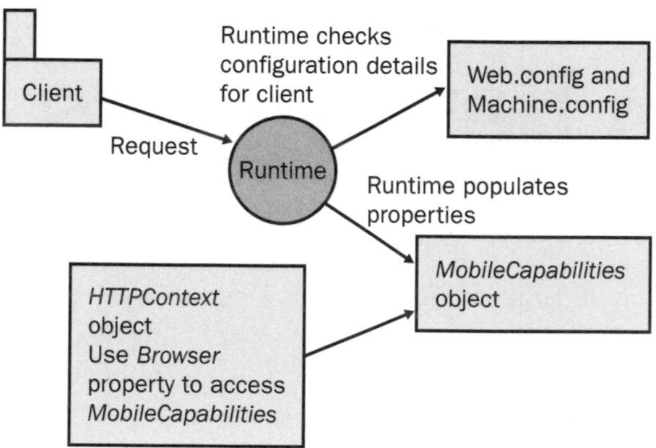

Figure 19-1 Identifying a client

In Figure 19-1, the client makes a request for a mobile Web Forms page. When the runtime receives the request, it creates an instance of the *HttpRequest* class. This object exposes a *MobileCapabilities* object (through the *Browser* property), which the runtime uses to store information about the capabilities of the requesting device. The runtime then checks the application configuration file (Web.config) and the system configuration file (machine.config) for *<browserCaps>* sections. If you have installed Device Update 2 or later and you are running .NET Framework 1.1, there is also a *<browserCaps>* section in the file DeviceUpdate.config. The files machine.config and DeviceUpdate.config (if present) are in the /Microsoft.NET/Framework/*version*/CONFIG directory under the system root directory /WINNT or /Windows.

Listing 19-1 provides an extract from one of these files. In this listing, the *<browserCaps>* section contains a large number of *<case>* sections, one for each supported client browser. These sections use a regular expression to match the *HTTP_USER_AGENT* environment variable, which the requesting browser originally passes as an HTTP request header. If a match occurs, the runtime successfully identifies the device type. The runtime then uses the information in the *<case>* section of the configuration file to populate the *MobileCapabilities* object.

```
<browserCaps>
    <use var="HTTP_USER_AGENT" />
        <filter>
            <!-- Nokia -->
            <case
                match="Nokia.*">
                browser = "Nokia"
                mobileDeviceManufacturer = "Nokia"
                preferredRenderingType = "wml11"
                preferredRenderingMime = "text/vnd.wap.wml"
                preferredImageMime = "image/vnd.wap.wbmp"
                defaultScreenCharactersWidth = "20"
                defaultScreenCharactersHeight = "4"
                defaultScreenPixelsWidth="90"
                defaultScreenPixelsHeight="40"
                screenBitDepth = "1"
                isColor = "false"
                inputType = "telephoneKeypad"
                numberOfSoftkeys = "2"
                hasBackButton = "false"
                rendersWmlDoAcceptsInline = "false"
                rendersBreaksAfterWmlInput = "true"
                requiresUniqueFilePathSuffix = "true"
                maximumRenderedPageSize = "1397"
                canInitiateVoiceCall = "true"
                requiresPhoneNumbersAsPlainText = "true"
                rendersBreaksAfterWmlAnchor = "true"
                canRenderOneventAndPrevElementsTogether = "false"
                canRenderPostBackCards = "false"
                canSendMail = "false"

                <filter>
                    <case
                        match="Nokia7110/1.0 \((?'versionString'.*)\)">
                        type = "Nokia 7110"
                        version = ${versionString}
                        <filter
                            with="${versionString}"
                            match=
        "(?'browserMajorVersion'\w*)(?'browserMinorVersion'\.\w*).*">
                            majorVersion = ${browserMajorVersion}
                            minorVersion = ${browserMinorVersion}
                        </filter>
                        mobileDeviceModel = "7110"
                        optimumPageWeight = "800"
```

Listing 19-1 Sample *<case>* section for a Nokia 7110 within the *Browser Capabilities* section of an ASP.NET configuration file

```
                    screenCharactersWidth="22"
                    screenCharactersHeight="4"
                    screenPixelsWidth="96"
                    screenPixelsHeight="44"
                </case>
            </filter>
        </case>
    </filter>
:
</browserCaps>
```

If the runtime doesn't successfully match the requesting device to one of the *<case>* sections, it populates the *MobileCapabilities* object with the default settings, which are found at the beginning of the *<browserCaps>* section in machine.config, which classifies the requesting device as an HTML 3.2 browser of type *Unknown*.

In most instances, you can successfully add support for a new client by adding a new *<case>* section in the *<browserCaps>* element. This element defines a suitable regular expression to match the *HTTP_USER_AGENT* string the device sends, and it contains information defining the device's capabilities. You'll learn how to identify the characteristics of a new device and provide support for it in the section "Supporting a New Client," later this chapter.

When the runtime searches for a device in the *<browserCaps>* sections, it does so in the following order: machine.config, then DeviceUpdate.config, and then Web.config (the application configuration file). If there are duplicate device definitions in any of these files, the runtime merges the different sections together so that the resulting *MobileCapabilities* object combines the settings for that device in each of the files. If there are duplicates for individual settings for a particular device in different configuration files (for example, *maximumRenderedPageSize* is set to 1397 for the Nokia 7110 in machine.config, but set to a different value in Web.config), the value that is used is the last one the runtime reads (the value in Web.config in this example).

Device Configuration Files in .NET Framework 1.1

In the first release of the .NET Framework, version 1.0, when you installed the Mobile Internet Toolkit to add support for ASP.NET mobile controls, all the device configuration XML was inserted into machine.config. When Device Update 1 was released, these definitions too went into machine.config. If you install Device Update 2 or later into a .NET Framework 1.0 installation, these updates also go into machine.config.

The machine.config file is of critical importance to a .NET Framework installation and defines many crucial settings in addition to device capabilities. Many companies like to keep this file under tight version control, so it's better to remove the comparatively volatile device update configuration to another file.

If you install Device Update 2 or later onto a .NET Framework 1.1 system and then examine the machine.config file, you'll still find the device definitions that were in the Mobile Internet Toolkit 1.0, but at the head of that section of the file is the following XML:

```
<browserCaps>
    <result type="System.Web.Mobile.MobileCapabilities, System.Web.Mobile,
        Version=1.0.5000.0, Culture=neutral,
        PublicKeyToken=b03f5f7f11d50a3a" />
    <file src="deviceupdate.config" />
    <use var="HTTP_USER_AGENT" />
        ⋮
```

The line *<file src="deviceupdate.config" />* is a link to the separate file containing device updates. When you install Device Update 2 on a system that has .NET Framework 1.1 installed, it places its browser definitions into this file, and it's recommended that you add any custom definitions to DeviceUpdate.config also. Be aware that the contents of this file will be replaced when you install future device updates, so be sure to keep a copy of any custom definitions and reapply them to DeviceUpdate.config after future upgrades.

Supporting a New Client

ASP.NET's XML-based configuration files make adding support for a new client relatively simple. You can modify the machine.config file or DeviceUpdate.config file to provide support for a new client in all your applications on that system. To provide support on an application-by-application basis, you can use an application's Web.config file.

> **Warning** You'll lose the modifications you've made to machine.config if you reinstall the .NET Framework, and if you've applied Device Update 2 and have added your customizations to DeviceUpdate.config, you'll lose those changes if you install a new Device Update pack. To ensure that your modifications persist between installs, it's safer to apply your changes to Web.config files, although you'll have to do so on an application-by-application basis.

Regardless of the configuration file you use, you must take three steps to add support for a new device:

1. Provide a regular expression that allows the runtime to identify the device.
2. Identify the capabilities of the device.
3. Enter these capabilities into the configuration file.

After you complete these steps, you of course will have to perform tests to ensure that the runtime correctly identifies your device and that the controls are rendered on the client as you expect.

Identifying the Device

The most common way to identify a device is to test the HTTP User-Agent request header with a regular expression. However, you can use any valid HTTP request header when determining the type of a new client. For example, some devices host dual-mode browsers that can handle both WML and HTML, so filtering on the User-Agent header is sufficient to distinguish between them. However, if the User-Agent string is the same, you can first use the User-Agent header to determine the type of device and then filter on the Accept-Type header to establish which type of content the browser is requesting.

In a mobile Web application, the value of the User-Agent header is accessible through the *MobilePage.Request* property. Of course, to find out the value of the User-Agent header for a new device, you can't just write an application that displays the value of *MobilePage.Request* in a Label control because your ASP.NET mobile controls application won't run because the client remains unsupported. However, you can use an ASP.NET application that uses the Trace facility to provide output—as demonstrated in the WhoAmI application we examined in Chapter 16. As an alternative to WhoAmI, you can write a simple mobile Web Forms page that has no graphical representation. The sample project WriteHTTPHeaders writes the value of the relevant headers to a local log file, as shown in Listing 19-2.

The code in Listing 19-2 writes the value of the User-Agent request header to the Header.log file. You'll need to ensure that the NTFS permissions on the application directory grant write access to the account that is used to run the application, which for a default application is the ASPNET account.

In this chapter, we'll use the EZOS EzWAP 2.1 browser to demonstrate the entire process of supporting a new client. (Go to *http://www.ezos.com* for a trial download.) EzWAP is a WML browser that's available for many devices, including the Pocket PC and the Palm personal digital assistant (PDA). When EzWAP accesses the application shown in Listing 19-2, the value of the User-Agent header is found to be *EZOS – EzWAP 2.1 for Pocket PC*.

```
<%@ Import Namespace="System.IO" %>
<%@ Page language="c#" Inherits="System.Web.UI.MobileControls.MobilePage"%>
<%@ Register TagPrefix="mobile"
    Namespace="System.Web.UI.MobileControls"
    Assembly="System.Web.Mobile" %>

<script runat="server" language="C#">
    public void Page_Load(object sender, System.EventArgs e)
    {
        FileStream fs = new FileStream(Request.PhysicalApplicationPath +
                                       "header.log",
                                       FileMode.Append,
                                       FileAccess.Write);
        StreamWriter log = new StreamWriter(fs);

        //Write the user agent to the log file.
        log.WriteLine(Request.UserAgent);
        log.Flush();
        log.Close();
    }
</script>
<mobile:Form id="Form1" runat="server">
</mobile:Form>
```

Listing 19-2 Writing HTTP header values to a local file

> **Note** At the time of writing, there are two versions of EzWAP available for download from the EZOS site. EzWAP 2.5 is the latest version of this browser; it is supported in Device Update 2. This new version is an XHTML browser. The discussion in this chapter concerns EzWAP 2.1, which is a WML browser and is not supported in Microsoft-supplied device configuration XML.

After you've found the value of the User-Agent request header, you must construct a regular expression in your Web.config file that you'll use to identify a client that uses this particular User-Agent identification. Although you use regular expressions, the syntax is quite simple in most cases. For example, to test whether a device is an EzWAP browser, you first instruct the runtime to use the User-Agent header and then provide a regular expression using the *match* attribute of the *<case>* element. Here's the syntax:

```
<browsercaps>
    <use var="HTTP_USER_AGENT"/>
    <filter>
        <case match="EZOS - EzWAP 2.1 for Pocket PC">
            ⋮
        </case>
    </filter>
</browsercaps>
```

However, you can expand the regular expression to capture the browser version information, which you can then use to populate the properties of the *MobileCapabilities* object. The following code identifies that the browser is EzWAP and captures information about the major and minor versions of the browser:

```
<case match=
    "EZOS - EzWAP (?'majorVersion'\d+)(?'minorVersion'\.\d+)(\w*)"
>
```

If you aren't familiar with regular expressions, Figure 19-2 will help you understand how the runtime uses the information in the User-Agent header. For details on the syntax of regular expressions, consult the .NET Framework SDK documentation.

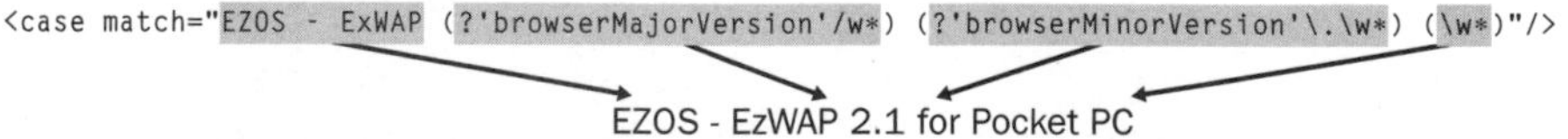
<case match="EZOS - ExWAP (?'browserMajorVersion'/w*) (?'browserMinorVersion'\.\w*) (\w*)"/>
EZOS - EzWAP 2.1 for Pocket PC

Figure 19-2 Identifying a device by using a regular expression

After you add the regular expression to your configuration file, ASP.NET can identify the new device. However, ASP.NET can't render the correct content to the device. To enable this, you must provide values, which the runtime uses to populate the properties of the *MobileCapabilities* object. You must define these capability values as accurately as possible because the runtime and device adapter classes use them to provide the correct markup for that client device.

Identifying Device Capabilities

The *MobileCapabilities* object has a large number of properties that describe the characteristics of a mobile device. Table 19-1 shows the properties you'll use most frequently when providing the minimum set of capabilities for a new device. For a full list of properties, refer to the .NET Framework SDK documentation.

Table 19-1 ***MobileCapabilities* Class Properties**

Property	Type	Default Value	Description
Browser	String	*Unknown*	The name of the browser.
CanInitiateVoiceCall	Boolean	*false*	Set to *true* if the device can initiate a voice call. Note that different browsers don't necessarily initiate voice calls the same way. For more information, refer to Chapter 5.
CanSendMail	Boolean	*true*	Set to *true* if the device can send e-mail using the *mailto* scheme.
HasBackButton	Boolean	*true*	Set to *true* if the device has a Back button, such as those found on many mobile phones.
InputType	String	*telephone-Keypad*	Describes the type of input capability the device possesses. Possible values include *telephoneKeypad*, *virtualKeyboard*, and *keyboard*.
IsColor	Boolean	*false*	Set to *true* if the device supports color.
IsMobileDevice	Boolean	*true*	Set to *true* if the device is supported by ASP.NET Mobile Controls.
MaximumRenderedPageSize	int	*2000*	The maximum length in bytes of the page that the device can display. This property is particularly useful when you're working with WML devices because many have quite restrictive maximum page sizes.
MaximumSoftkeyLabelLength	int	*5*	The maximum length of the text that a softkey label can display.
MobileDeviceManufacturer	String	*Unknown*	The name of the device manufacturer.
MobileDeviceModel	String	*Unknown*	The model name of the device.
NumberOfSoftkeys	int	*0*	Sets the number of softkeys supported on the device.

Table 19-1 *MobileCapabilities* Class Properties

Property	Type	Default Value	Description
PreferredImageMime	String	*image/gif*	The preferred Multipurpose Internet Mail Extensions (MIME) type of images that the device can display.
PreferredRenderingMime	String	*text/Html*	The preferred MIME type of the content that the device can display.
PreferredRenderingType	String	*html32*	The preferred type of content that the device can display. Possible values include *html32*, *wml11*, *wml12*, and *chtml10*.
ScreenBitDepth	int	*1*	The depth of the display in bits per pixel. A value of *1* indicates a monochrome device.
ScreenCharactersHeight	int	*6*	The approximate number of lines of text the device can display.
ScreenCharactersWidth	int	*12*	The approximate number of characters the device can display on each line.
ScreenPixelsHeight	int	*72*	The height of the screen in pixels.
ScreenPixelsWidth	int	*96*	The width of the screen in pixels.

If these values are set correctly in the device configuration, ASP.NET Mobile Controls applications will be rendered acceptably on your new device. However, the *MobileCapabilities* object has many other properties that are not listed in Table 19-1, and you might want to set them as well to optimize the support for your new device. These include the *CanRender** and *Renders** categories of properties (for example, *CanRenderPostBackCards* and *RendersBreaksAfterWMLAnchor*), which define specific behaviors related to WML rendering; the *Requires** category of properties (for example, *RequiresLeadingPageBreak*), which define specific requirements of a particular browser; and the *Supports** category of properties (such as *SupportsIModeSymbols*), which define unique capabilities of the browser. In most cases, the default values for these properties will be suitable, although in some cases you might need to set some of them to optimize rendering on your device. The majority of these properties are required by code in the device adapter classes to fine-tune the markup that is sent to the client.

To support your new device, you must identify the capabilities it possesses so that you can define the correct values for these properties. There are three ways you can do this. First, you can refer to your device's documentation. You can determine many of the capabilities of your device from this information. For example, you might determine whether the device supports color and discover the type of markup language it supports.

Second, you can write an application in a markup language that the device supports. You can then use this application to test the device's capabilities. Of course, you must know the syntax of the markup language to use this approach. Third, you can list all the mobile capabilities of your device in your configuration file. Then, one by one, change the values of the capabilities and view the results in your browser. Although effective, this approach can be quite time consuming.

> **Tip** In many cases, a new mobile phone from a manufacturer will simply be an upgrade to an existing model that the ASP.NET mobile controls already support. The browser of the new model usually operates much like its predecessors. The browser might even be the same one as in an existing model. In this case, it's quite easy to add support for the new model. A good starting point is to copy all the settings that define the characteristics of the older device and then modify the few properties that have changed. For example, you might need to update only the regular expression that identifies the browser and properties representing the width and height of the screen or the *MobileDeviceModel* property.

In reality, you'll use a combination of at least two of the approaches we just described, as well as a little of your own knowledge. For example, you might know that a device supports compact HTML (cHTML) and color without referring to the product documentation. But you might refer to the documentation to discover the size of the device's screen and the features specific to the device, such as whether it can send e-mail and initiate a voice call. Finally, you might determine the device's additional capabilities either by using native markup or by adjusting the values and viewing the results in your browser.

Using Markup to Identify Capabilities

Earlier in this section, you learned how to use a regular expression to test whether a browser was an EzWAP browser. Now you'll use WML code to test some of the capabilities of an EzWAP browser.

As described, some properties of the *MobileCapabilities* class relate to the way a specific markup language is rendered on a given device. An example of this is the *RendersBreaksAfterWMLAnchor* property. The default value for this property is *false*. When the ASP.NET mobile controls generate the markup code for the mobile Link control on WML devices, they generate a WML anchor element. On some WML browsers, such as the Nokia browser on the 7110 mobile phone, the browser automatically renders a break after an anchor, so on these devices, *RendersBreaksAfterWMLAnchor* is set to *true*. Other browsers don't automatically render a break. The rendering logic in the *System.Web.UI.MobileControls.Adapters.WMLLinkAdapter* device adapter class checks this property in the *MobileCapabilities* object for the requesting device and inserts a break into the output stream after an anchor only if *RendersBreaksAfterWMLAnchor* is *false* and the *BreakAfter* property of the Link control is *true*. You can easily ascertain the values of such properties by writing code in the native markup language that tests the properties. However, unless you're proficient in the markup language, it's quicker and simpler to establish a device's capabilities through testing. (You'll learn how to use this approach momentarily.)

In this example, you'll write WML code to test five properties: *MaximumSoftkeyLabelLength*, *RendersBreaksAfterWMLAnchor*, *RendersBreaksAfterWMLInput*, *RendersWMLDoAcceptsInline*, and *RendersWMLSelectAsMenuCards*. To test these properties, write a WML deck that contains two cards. The first card displays an input box and two ways to navigate to the second card, which contains a selection list. To link to the second card, provide a normal link using an anchor and then provide the second link using a *<do>* element. Listing 19-3 shows an Active Server Pages (ASP) page containing the WML code for these two cards.

```
<% Response.ContentType= "text/vnd.wap.wml" %>
<?xml version="1.0"?>
<!DOCTYPE wml PUBLIC "-//WAPFORUM//DTD WML 1.1//EN"
    "http://www.wapforum.org/DTD/wml_1.1.xml">

<wml>
    <card id="card1" title="Card #1" newcontext="true">
        <do type="accept" label="Softkey label">
            <go href="#card2"/>
        </do>
        <p align="center">
            <input type="text" name="test"/>
            Text after input box.
            <br/>
            <a href="#card2" title="anchor label">Next</a>
            Text after anchor
        </p>
```

Listing 19-3 TestBrowserCapabilities.asp sends raw WML to test browser capabilities.

```
    </card>

    <card id="card2" title="Card #2">
        <p align="center">
            <select>
                <option>One</option>
                <option>Two</option>
                <option>Three</option>
            </select>
        </p>
    </card>
</wml>
```

Figure 19-3 shows the EzWAP browser displaying the two WML cards.

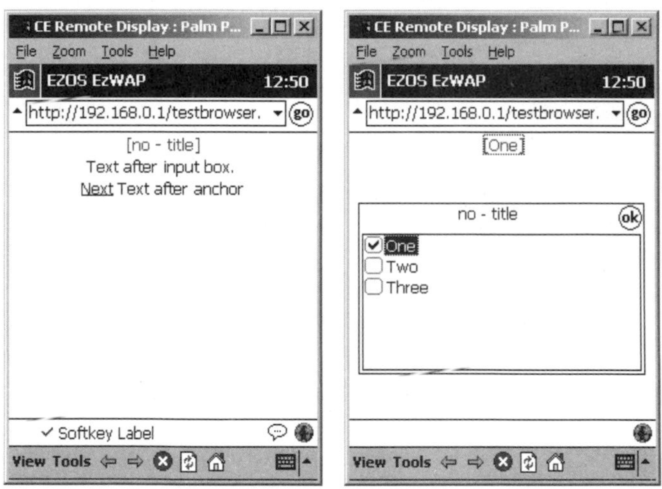

Figure 19-3 EzWAP browser displaying two WML cards that test a device's mobile capabilities

The browser renders a break after the input box but not after the anchor. In addition, the *label* attribute of the *<do>* element is displayed at the foot of the screen, like a softkey. The maximum length of the softkey's label is longer than the string you supplied. In fact, the EzWAP browser supports a very long string as its softkey label value. However, a value of *20* is suggested for ASP.NET mobile Web applications to maintain usability. When you access the second card, a link is displayed. When selected, this link displays a pop-up window that lists the select options. Thus, this simple piece of WML code establishes the values for the *MobileCapabilities* class properties listed in Table 19-2.

Table 19-2 EzWAP Browser Properties

Property	Value
MaximumSoftkeyLabelLength	*20*
RendersBreaksAfterWMLAnchor	*false*
RendersBreaksAfterWMLInput	*true*
RendersWMLDoAcceptsInline	*false*
RendersWMLSelectAsMenuCards	*false*

Although this example uses WML, you can just as easily test another device by using cHTML or HTML. The most important factor in using markup to identify device capabilities is that you carefully consider which capabilities you want to determine and then design your test code to exercise those capabilities.

Establishing Capabilities Through Testing

As mentioned, another way to establish a device's capabilities is to change the value of each property within the configuration file and view the results in the device's browser. Although subject to a little trial and error, this approach is simple, and it doesn't require any knowledge of specific markup languages.

You'll now establish some of the capabilities of the EzWAP browser through testing. In this particular instance, you find the values of the *RendersBreaksAfterWMLAnchor* and *RendersBreaksAfterWMLInput* properties. To do this, you must start with a configuration section in the application's Web.config file that supplies at least the bare minimum of details the runtime needs to identify the device and then attempt to render output. Listing 19-4 shows an example that starts configuration for the EzWAP browser.

```
<browserCaps>
    <use var="HTTP_USER_AGENT" />
    <filter>
        <case
            match=
    "EZOS - EzWAP (?'majorVersion'\d+)(?'minorVersion'\.\d+)(\w*)"
        >

            <!--start with previously established properties -->
            browser="EzWAP"
            type="EzWAP"
            version= ${majorVersion}.${minorVersion }
            majorVersion= ${majorVersion}
            minorVersion =${minorVersion }
            isMobileDevice="true"
```

Listing 19-4 Configuration through testing

```
            mobileDeviceModel="Pocket PC"
            preferredRenderingType="wml12"
            preferredRenderingMIME="text/vnd.wap.wml"
            preferredImageMIME="image/vnd.wap.wbmp"
            inputType="virtualKeyboard"

            <!--Test with default values for these properties first -->
            rendersBreaksAfterWMLAnchor="false"
            rendersBreaksAfterWMLInput="false"
        </case>
    </filter>
</browserCaps>
```

Now you must create a mobile Web Forms page for the new device to access. Because you're currently testing only the display characteristics of anchors and input dialog boxes, the mobile Web Forms page can be simple. Listing 19-5 shows an example of such a mobile Web Forms page.

```
<%@ Register TagPrefix="mobile"
    Namespace="System.Web.UI.MobileControls"
    Assembly="System.Web.Mobile" %>
<%@ Page language="c#" Codebehind="MobileWebForm1.apsx.cs"
    Inherits="MSPress.MobWeb.TestBrowserCapabilities.MobileWebForm1"
    AutoEventWireup="false" %>

<mobile:Form id="Form1" runat="server">
    <mobile:TextBox id="TextBox1" runat="server"/>
    <mobile:Label id="Label1" runat="server">
        Text After Input
    </mobile:Label>
    <mobile:Link id="Link1" runat="server">
        Link
    </mobile:Link>
    <mobile:Label id="Label2" runat="server">
        Text After Link
    </mobile:Label>
</mobile:Form>
```

Listing 19-5 Mobile Web Forms page to test new device configuration

Figure 19-4 shows the output the browser renders. Notice that a blank line appears between the text box and the text following it. From this, you can deduce that the browser does render a break after an input box. The text after the anchor appears on the very next line—clearly the browser doesn't automatically insert a break after anchors. Thus, you can deduce that the *RendersBreaksAfterWMLInput* property must be changed to *true* and the *RendersBreaksAfterWMLAnchor* property should stay set to *false*.

Figure 19-4 EzWAP browser displaying output from Listing 19-5

Configuration File Inheritance

When you define the capabilities of a device in a configuration file, you don't have to repeat the process for every application that the client will use. This is because Web.config files inherit and override settings, which you define in either a Web.config file, a machine.config file, or if present, a DeviceUpdate.config file. Remember, you'll only have a DeviceUpdate.config file if you are running .NET framework 1.1, and you have installed Device Update 2 or later.

When the runtime receives a request from a client, it determines the *MobileCapabilities* settings by searching each of the configuration files for a regular expression that matches for the requesting device. If the device is found in more than one file, the *MobileCapabilities* settings from each match are merged together. If any properties are defined in more than one file, the order of precedence is, from lowest to highest machine.config, DeviceUpdate.config, and then Web.config. As always Web.config files inherit from each other, so if you have a child folder that has a Web.config, it inherits settings from any Web.config file in the parent folder.

For example, you include a *<browserCaps>* section within the Web.config file for your application, and that section provides support for the EzWAP 2.1 browser. When an EzWAP browser makes a request, the runtime checks your application's Web.config file. It finds a match for the EzWAP browser, and so it uses that entry. If you use Microsoft Internet Explorer to make a subsequent request, the settings for Internet Explorer are taken from machine.config.

Configuring Device Adapters

Device adapters provide the device-specific implementation of a mobile control, as Figure 19-5 shows. You group these adapters into sets (known as *device adapter sets*), and the runtime establishes which of these sets to apply to a specific device. In Chapter 22, you'll learn how to write device adapter code for custom controls and how to add them to existing device adapter sets. In this section, you'll review the role of device adapters, discover how the runtime selects a device adapter set for the requesting device, and learn how to extend an existing device adapter set to add support for custom device adapters that support new devices or new markup languages.

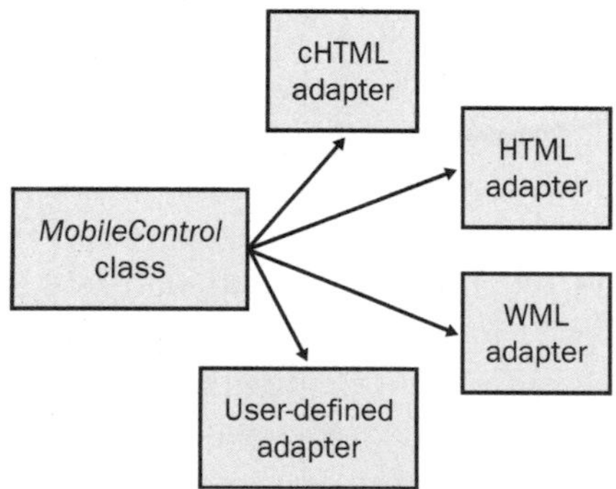

Figure 19-5 Several device adapters mapping to a single mobile control

The Role of Device Adapters

After the runtime successfully identifies a device and populates the *MobileCapabilities* object for a request, it must render the most appropriate markup for the device. By now, you're familiar with the idea that mobile controls are abstract—in other words, their physical appearance on the page isn't fixed across all devices. For example, a Command control can appear as a textual hyperlink on one device, while on another it maps to a softkey.

Device adapter classes are the counterparts of mobile control classes that implement the rendering of a mobile control on a given device. Think of device adapter classes as the bridge between an abstract control and a client. Figure 19-6 illustrates the relationship between the client, control, and adapter. Notice that for any given client request, the control has a unique adapter. Also, each new instance of a control binds to a new instance of that control's adapter.

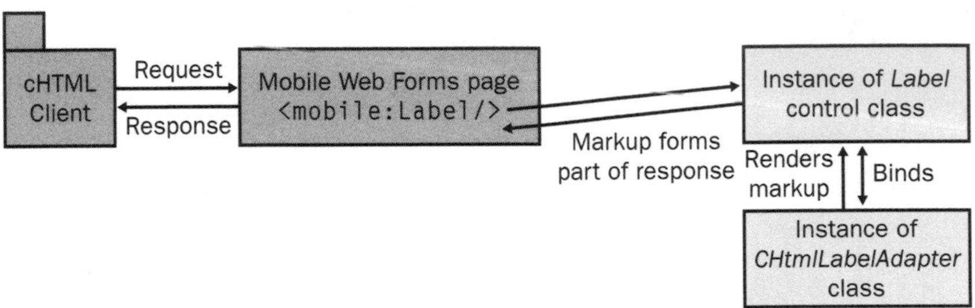

Figure 19-6 The relationship between client, control, and adapter

When creating the output that a client displays, the device adapter class generates content optimized for the requesting device by tailoring it based on the properties of the *MobileCapabilities* object for the current request. For example, the device adapter class for the TextBox mobile control outputs markup for a text box that is rendered consistently on different WML browsers by checking the *RendersBreaksAfterWMLInput* property. If the device automatically renders a break (*RendersBreaksAfterWMLInput* is *true*), the MobilePage and the TextBox device adapters create markup that consists solely of an *<input>* element. If the device doesn't insert a break, these classes ensure that the rendered markup contains both an *<input>* element and a *
* element. Because the device adapter classes determine the device capabilities from the *MobileCapabilities* object, changes in the *<browserCaps>* configuration settings for a given client type can result in changes in how information is displayed on that client.

ASP.NET Mobile Controls supports a broad family of WML 1.1, WML 1.2, cHTML 1.0, HTML 3.2, and XHTML clients. The existing device adapters yield good results on most handheld devices available at the time of this writing. Microsoft included the device adapter sources in the Mobile Internet Toolkit release to encourage extensibility and to prompt developers to create device adapters for use with current and future mobile devices. With the release of ASP.NET Mobile Controls, which supersedes the Microsoft Mobile Internet Toolkit, device adapter sources are no longer shipped with the product, but instead are available for separate download. Go to *http://go.microsoft.com/fwlink/?LinkId=6350* to download the ASP.NET 1.1 Device Adapter source code. If you want to make substantial changes to the way a mobile control is rendered on a particular client, you can create a new device adapter class to do so.

You might also want to create new device adapters to support a new custom control, modify the output that the runtime returns to an existing client, and add support for a new markup language or version of an existing language. If you need more details on how to write device adapters, see Chapter 22.

Using Device Adapter Sets

You define, or map, the relationship between device adapters and mobile Web Forms controls in either Web.config or machine.config. More specifically, you group together control adapters, and these groups form named device adapter sets. For example, the ASP.NET mobile controls come presupplied with three types of device adapter sets, which are defined as elements of the machine.config file: *<HtmlDeviceAdapters>*, *<WmlDeviceAdapters>*, and *<ChtmlDeviceAdapters>*, and Device Update 2 adds support for *<XHTMLDeviceAdapters>*.

Each device adapter set maps each mobile control to an appropriate device adapter, which renders the correct markup for a client. When the runtime receives a client request, it assigns one of the device adapter sets to that request, thus defining which control–device adapter pairings will service the request.

You define device adapter sets within a *<mobileControls>* element in either the Web.config file or the machine.config file. The *<mobileControls>* element supports multiple child *<device>* elements, which you use to declare device adapter sets. Table 19-3 shows the five attributes that the *<device>* element supports.

Table 19-3 Attributes of the *<device>* Element

Attribute	Description
name	The name of the device adapter set.
predicateClass	The name of the class containing the predicate method. (See next table entry.)
predicateMethod	The name of the adapter set's predicate method. The predicate method is a static method that the runtime uses to ascertain whether the device adapter set is suitable for the current client device.
pageAdapter	The name of the page adapter class that corresponds to the device adapter set.
inheritsFrom	An optional attribute that you can use to inherit configuration settings from another device adapter set. You'll learn more about device adapter set inheritance later in the section "Device Adapter Set Inheritance."

The *<device>* element supports multiple child *<control>* elements, which you use to map specific control adapters to mobile controls. For example, you can map a *WMLPanelAdapter* control adapter to the mobile Web Forms Panel control. The *<control>* element has two attributes: *name* and *adapter*. You set *name* to a mobile control class name, and you give *adapter* a name value of an adapter class for the specified mobile control. Listing 19-6 shows the mapping between controls and adapters in a Web.config file.

```
<?xml version="1.0" encoding="utf-8"?>
<configuration>
    <system.web>

        <!-- Other Web.config settings -->

        <mobileControls>
            <device
                name="HtmlDeviceAdapters"
                predicateClass=
                  "System.Web.UI.MobileControls.Adapters.HtmlPageAdapter"
                predicateMethod="DeviceQualifies"
                pageAdapter=
                  "System.Web.UI.MobileControls.Adapters.HtmlPageAdapter">

                <control name="System.Web.UI.MobileControls.Panel" adapter=
                    "System.Web.UI.MobileControls.Adapters.HtmlPanelAdapter"/>

                <control name="System.Web.UI.MobileControls.Form" adapter=
                    "System.Web.UI.MobileControls.Adapters.HtmlFormAdapter"/>
                ⋮
                <!--Adapter mappings continue ->
                ⋮
            </device>
        </mobileControls>
    </system.web>
</configuration>
```

Listing 19-6 Extract from Web.config that illustrates the configuration of a device adapter set

Defining a Device Adapter Set

We mentioned that you might want to write new device adapter classes for a number of reasons. For example, you might want to replace the standard device adapter with a customized version, or you might want to add device adapters that support custom controls. (As you'll learn in Chapter 20 and Chapter 21, user controls and custom controls built by inheritance or by composition use the device adapters of the standard controls from which they derive, and they rarely have custom device adapters. Controls built from scratch do have device adapters, as described in Chapter 22.)

If you're replacing a standard device adapter with a customized version, or adding configuration for a new custom mobile control and its adapters, you can update the existing device adapter set definitions in machine.config by replacing the standard device adapter class name with the custom version or by adding new lines into an existing device adapter set definition to include support for device adapters for new custom controls. Alternatively, you can define a new device adapter set that inherits all settings from an existing device adapter set using the *inheritsFrom* attribute of the *<device>* element. In the child device adapter set, control-adapter mappings defined in *<control>* elements override those of the same name in the parent, and you can define additional control-adapter mappings for custom controls.

You can define your own adapter sets in a Web.config file in the application directory (applies only to that application), in the Web server wwwroot directory (applies to all applications in that Web server), or in machine.config.

Device Adapter Set Inheritance

As mentioned, you can create a new device adapter set by inheriting from an existing device adapter set using the *inheritsFrom* attribute of the *<device>* element. The new device adapter set inherits all the mappings its parent defines, and you can then add new mappings or override the ones that already exist. This technique is used in Chapter 22, where a new device adapter set is defined to add support for the custom CMTable control created in that chapter. The parent adapter set can reside in the same Web.config file, a parent Web.config file, or machine.config. If the application doesn't find the named device adapter set in the current Web.config file, the runtime checks the parent and progresses upward through the configuration file hierarchy until it does find the parent. Listing 19-7 shows an example of device adapter set inheritance within a Web.config file.

There are a few important points to note about Listing 19-7. First, the device adapter set inherits from the *WmlDeviceAdapters* set. Therefore, all the mappings *WmlDeviceAdapters* defines also apply to the new device adapter set, apart from those that you override in the new set. Also, the predicate class and predicate method are exactly the same as the ones defined in the configuration of the *WmlDeviceAdapters* device adapters set in machine.config. The runtime calls the predicate method to determine which adapter set to use with the requesting device. As it searches through the configuration files for the device adapter set to use, it evaluates the predicate method of each adapter set until one returns a value of *true*. Using the default device adapter sets, the predicate method of the *WmlDeviceAdapters* device adapters set returns *true* for any device that requires WML markup. When you introduce the customizations shown in listing 19-7, the same predicate method is used to select WML browsers, but these devices will now use the *NewWmlDeviceAdapters* device adapters set instead of the *WmlDeviceAdapters* device adapters set.

```
<?xml version="1.0" encoding="utf-8"?>
<configuration>
    <system.web>
        :
        <!-- Other Web.config settings-->
        :
        <mobileControls>
            <device
                name="NewWmlDeviceAdapters"
                inheritsFrom="WmlDeviceAdapters"
                predicateClass=
                    "System.Web.UI.MobileControls.Adapters.WmlPageAdapter"
                predicateMethod="DeviceQualifies"
                pageAdapter=
                    "System.Web.UI.MobileControls.Adapters.WmlPageAdapter">

                <control
                    name="System.Web.UI.MobileControls.MyControl"
                    adapter=
                "System.Web.UI.MobileControls.Adapters.WmlMyControlAdapter"/>

            <!-- Place any new mappings here -->

            </device>
        </mobileControls>
    </system.web>
</configuration>
```

Listing 19-7 Creating a new device adapter set through inheritance

> **Warning** Where both child and parent device adapter sets use the same predicate method, the child adapter set supersedes the parent adapter set and is used instead of the parent, as long as it is evaluated and thus selected first. If the child and parent adapter set are in the same configuration file and use the same predicate method, be sure to place the definition of the child above its parent; otherwise, it will never be selected.

Writing Predicate Methods

Creating a new predicate method is something you might do only occasionally—for example, if you want to provide support for a new markup language. In ASP.NET Mobile Controls in version 1.1 of the .NET Framework and with Device

Update 2 applied, the standard device adapter sets choose between HTML, cHTML, XHTML, Openwave WML, and non-Openwave WML devices. The Openwave set (*UpWmlDeviceAdapters*) inherits from *WmlDeviceAdapters* but has Openwave-specific device adapters for some of the controls. If you want to create a new device adapter set that selects a new group of client devices—different from these five existing groupings—you must write a custom predicate method. For example, some devices on the market support an enhanced version of WML version 1.2.1, known as WML version 1.3. (The official next version after WML 1.2.1 is version 2.0, which uses XHTML, but some suppliers implemented version 1.3 as an interim solution offering enhanced usability.) This version of WML is backward compatible with versions 1.1 and 1.2, so you don't have to create a new adapter set to support these devices. However, if you want to customize some of the device adapter classes so that you can take advantage of new features in WML version 1.3 on those devices that support it, you might consider creating a new device adapter set that inherits from the existing set but that overrides some or all of the existing device adapters with custom versions that render WML 1.3 markup. This adapter set needs to have a predicate method that returns *true* for devices that support WML 1.3.

Predicate methods, described in Table 19-3, are static methods that the runtime calls to evaluate whether the device adapter set is appropriate for the current device. The method can be in any class—existing implementations are in the page adapter class for the device adapter set. The predicate method takes one argument of the *System.Web.HttpContext* type and returns a Boolean value that indicates whether the device adapter set suits the current device. Within this method, you can write code that tests the capabilities of the client device. You access these capabilities through the *Browser* property of the *HttpContext* object because the *Browser* property returns a *MobileCapabilities* object.

Consider the example of a predicate method that evaluates whether a WML 1.3 adapter set is suitable for a client device, shown in Listing 19-8 below. The predicate method in this example is placed within a custom class called *Wml13PageAdapter*, which inherits from the standard *WmlPageAdapter* class. (The Page adapter class is responsible for formatting the output for a complete page of output for a particular device, incorporating the rendered output of all the individual mobile controls on the page.) The *DeviceQualifies* predicate method accepts an *HttpContext* object as a parameter and returns a Boolean value. The predicate method must return *true* if the requesting device can accept WML 1.3. To test whether the device can read this markup, the code gets the *Browser* property of the *MobileCapabilities* object for the requesting client device. If the device has the value *Openwave13* for the *Browser* property, this predicate method returns *true*.

```
public class Wml13PageAdapter : WmlPageAdapter
{
    public static bool DeviceQualifies(HttpContext context)
    {
        MobileCapabilities capabilities =
            ((MobileCapabilities)context.Request.Browser);
        bool qualifies = capabilities.Browser == "Openwave13";
        return qualifies;
    }
}
```

Listing 19-8 Predicate method example

> **Note** This example tests for a specific value in the *Browser* property of the *MobileCapabilities* object of *Openwave13*. This is a string value that's set by the device configuration you define for the requesting device in the *<browserCaps>* configuration section, as described in the section "Defining Mobile Devices in Configuration Files" earlier in this chapter. It would be more logical to test the *PreferredRenderingType* for a value of *wml13*; however, at the time of this writing, the only permissible values for this property are *html32*, *wml11*, *wml12*, *chtml10*, *wml20*, *xhtml-mp*, and *xhtml-basic*.
>
> If you decide to implement some custom versions of controls that take advantage of WML 1.3 features and you configure a *WML13DeviceAdapterSet* to use the custom controls, you'll use the predicate method shown in this example. You'll also need to ensure that you update the device configuration files so that devices that support WML 1.3 set the *Browser* property to the value *Openwave13* so that they get to use the *WML13DeviceAdapterSet* when they make a request.

That's it! You've now written the predicate method for the WML 1.3 device adapter set. To use this method as the selector for the device adapter set, compile it into an assembly containing your custom device adapters, named in this example Custom13Adapters, and set the *<device>* element attributes like so:

```
<mobileControls>
    <device
        name="Wml13DeviceAdapters"
        inheritsFrom="WmlDeviceAdapters"
        predicateClass="Custom13Adapters.Wml13PageAdapter"
        predicateMethod="DeviceQualifies"
        pageAdapter="Custom13Adapters.Wml13PageAdapter">

        ⋮
```

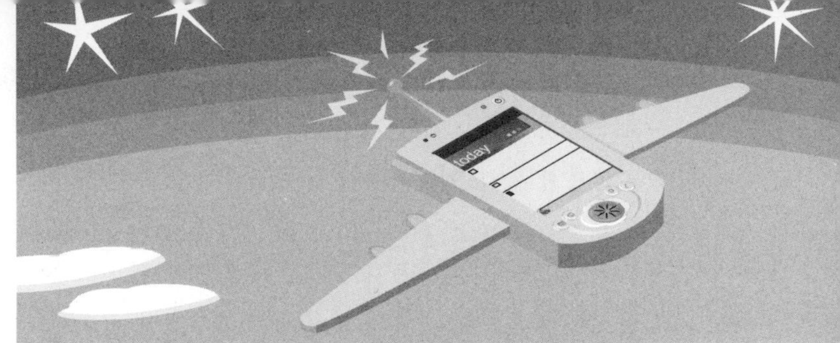

20

Building a Reusable User Interface as User Controls

Microsoft ASP.NET Mobile Controls provide a rich selection of mobile controls that offer the functionality you need to build compelling mobile Web applications. However, you might find yourself repeatedly implementing the same piece of user interface functionality, using the same combination of controls. By encapsulating this user interface functionality in a reusable component, you can take advantage of a major strength of ASP.NET: *user controls*. In this chapter, you'll learn how to build user controls.

Building a User Control

User controls are very easy to build. In fact, they aren't any harder to build than regular mobile Web Forms pages, and they look identical to mobile Web Forms pages except for the header declarations. Like mobile Web Forms pages, user controls can consist of a single file containing ASP.NET declarative syntax and code, or they can consist of an ASP.NET page and a code-behind module. By convention, you name a user control with the .ascx extension to distinguish it from a regular mobile Web Forms page.

User controls offer several advantages. They're quick and easy to develop using ASP.NET declarative syntax and script blocks (or a code-behind module). They offer a convenient way to reuse pieces of user interface functionality because converting an existing mobile Web Forms page to a user control is a simple matter. And you can cache user controls using page fragment caching, as described in Chapter 13.

Creating a Simple User Control

To begin, create a new mobile Web application project in Microsoft Visual Studio .NET, and name it SimpleUserControl. Click Project, click Add New Item, and then click Mobile Web User Control in the Templates pane of the Add New Item dialog box. Name this user control HelloWorldUserControl.ascx. Click Open, and Visual Studio .NET creates a mobile Web user control and adds it to your project.

In Design view of the user control, drag controls onto the user control just as if you were developing a mobile Web Forms page, the main difference being that with a user control you're not required to position controls within a Panel or Form container control. For this simple example, drag a Label onto the user control and change its text to **Hello User Control.**

Now double-click on MobileWebForm1.aspx in Solution Explorer to display the form in Design view. To use the user control you just created, simply click on HelloWorldUserControl.ascx in Solution Explorer and drag it onto Form1 in Design view. That's it! If you run this application, the output of the user control is displayed as part of the output of MobileWebForm1.aspx. However, the HelloWorldUserControl.ascx file is a component that you can reuse in your other mobile Web applications (although, in this example, the control isn't very useful).

Coding a User Control Module

If you examine the files that Visual Studio .NET creates for a mobile Web user control, you'll find that they look very much like a regular mobile Web Forms control. In fact, converting an existing mobile Web Forms page to a user control can be simple: change the file extension to .ascx, change the declarative statements at the head of the .ascx file, and change the base class from which the control is inherited to *System.Web.UI.MobileControls.MobileUserControl.*

The declarative statements at the head of a user control consisting solely of an .ascx file must use the following format. (These examples are for C#, but you can specify any .NET-supported language.)

```
<%@ Control "System.Web.UI.MobileControls.MobileUserControl"
    Language="C#" %>
<%@ Register TagPrefix="mobile"
    Namespace="System.Web.UI.MobileControls"
    Assembly="System.Web.Mobile" %>
```

If the user control has a code-behind module, the *@ Control* declaration consists of the following directives:

```
<%@ Control CodeBehind="modulename.ascx.cs" Language="c#"
    Inherits="namespace.classname" %>
```

These directives are very similar to those of a mobile Web Forms page, except that you use the *@ Control* directive instead of the *@ Page* directive. The *Inherits* attribute can point to the *System.Web.UI.MobileControls.MobileUserControl* class or to any other class that inherits directly or indirectly from the *MobileUserControl* class, such as one defined in a code-behind module.

Using a User Control in a Web Forms Page

Working with a user control in an application is quite simple. You place the .ascx file and its code-behind file (if one exists) in the application directory or another accessible directory. Then you declare the *TagPrefix* and *TagName* that you'll use to represent the user control within the page, as well as the path to the file containing the user control source. You place the *TagPrefix* and *TagName* declarations at the head of the mobile Web Forms page, alongside the usual declarative statements. Here's the syntax:

```
<%@ Page language="c#" Codebehind="MobileWebForm1.aspx.cs"
    Inherits="MSPress.MobWeb.UserControlExample.MobileWebForm1"
    AutoEventWireup="false" %>
<%@ Register TagPrefix="mobile"
    Namespace="System.Web.UI.MobileControls"
    Assembly="System.Web.Mobile" %>
<%@ Register TagPrefix="custom"
    TagName="ShortDateUC"
    Src="ShortDateControl.ascx" %>
```

Next you employ the user control in the same way as you would a standard mobile control, but you use the declared *TagPrefix* and *TagName*:

```
<mobile:Form id="Form1" runat="server">
    <custom:ShortDateUC runat="server" id="ucShortDate" />
</mobile:Form>
```

When you dragged the user control onto the Form control, as described in the section "Creating a Simple User Control," earlier in this chapter, Visual Studio .NET inserted this syntax into the mobile Web Forms page.

User Control Example

You've already created a simple user control that displays only a Label control. In this section, you'll create a more complex example. The Calendar control is ideal for applications in which the user needs to select a date. However, this control provides a rich user interface that takes up a lot of space on a Pocket PC and can span many screens on a mobile phone.

To see an example of a user control, let's build a more compact date selector that is rendered as three drop-down lists on an HTML browser and as a single input box on a WML browser. We'll call this control the Short Date control. Short Date allows a user to select a date between 01-Jan-2003 and 31-Dec-2010. You can build the bare bones of this control by using server control tags, as Listing 20-1 shows.

```
<%@ Control CodeBehind="ShortDateControl.ascx.cs"
    Inherits="MSPress.MobWeb.UserControlExample.ShortDateControl"
    Language="c#" AutoEventWireup="false" %>
<%@ Register TagPrefix="mobile"
    Namespace="System.Web.UI.MobileControls"
    Assembly="System.Web.Mobile" %>

<mobile:Panel id="Panel1" runat="server">
    <mobile:DeviceSpecific id="DeviceSpecific1" runat="server">
        <Choice Filter="isWML11">
            <ContentTemplate>
                <mobile:Label id="Label1" runat="server">
                    Enter date (MMDDYY):</mobile:Label>
                <mobile:TextBox id="TextBox1" runat="server"
                    numeric="true" Text="010103" MaxLength="6"
                    wmlFormat="NN\/NN\/NN">
                </mobile:TextBox>
            </ContentTemplate>
        </Choice>
        <Choice Filter="isHTML32">
            <ContentTemplate>
                <table>
                    <tr>
                        <td>
                            <mobile:Label id="Label2" runat="server"
                                BreakAfter="false">
                                Day:</mobile:Label>
                        </td>
                        <td align="right">
                            <mobile:SelectionList id="SelectionList1"
                                runat="server" BreakAfter="false">
                                <Item Text="01" />
                                ⋮
                            Intervening items not shown
                                ⋮
```

Listing 20-1 Source file ShortDateControl.ascx

```
                        <Item Text="31" />
                    </mobile:SelectionList>
                </td>
            </tr>
            <tr>
                <td>
                    <mobile:Label id="Label3" runat="server"
                        BreakAfter="false">
                        Month:</mobile:Label>
                </td>
                <td align="right">
                    <mobile:SelectionList id="SelectionList2"
                        runat="server" BreakAfter="false">
                        <Item Text="Jan" Value="01" />
                        ⋮
                    Intervening items not shown
                        ⋮
                        <Item Text="Dec" Value="12" />
                    </mobile:SelectionList>
                </td>
            </tr>
            <tr>
                <td>
                    <mobile:Label id="Label4" runat="server"
                        BreakAfter="false">
                        Year:</mobile:Label>
                </td>
                <td align="right">
                    <mobile:SelectionList id="SelectionList3"
                        runat="server" BreakAfter="false">
                        <Item Text="2003" />
                        ⋮
                    Intervening items not shown
                        ⋮
                        <Item Text="2010" />
                    </mobile:SelectionList>
                </td>
            </tr>
        </table>
      </ContentTemplate>
    </Choice>
  </mobile:DeviceSpecific>
</mobile:Panel>
```

When you include the Short Date control on a Form control, the DeviceSpecific/Choice construct inside *Panel1* tests whether *isWML11* is *true*. If it is, the device is a Wireless Application Protocol (WAP) handset, and the control is displayed as a text box that accepts a six-digit number. On HTML devices, this control outputs a *<table>* element containing three drop-down lists with prompt labels. However, to be really useful, this control needs to have additional functionality defined in its code-behind module. (We'll describe how to add this functionality in the following sections.) As it stands, the control displays the default date *Jan 1, 2003*. The user can enter a different date, but there's no way to access his or her selection.

Note that this user control has an external dependency. You must define the following *isWML11* and *isHTML* capability evaluators in the Web.config file of any application in which you want to use this control.

```
<?xml version="1.0" encoding="utf-8" ?>
<configuration>
  <system.web>
    <deviceFilters>
      <filter name="isHTML32" compare="PreferredRenderingType"
        argument="html32" />
      <filter name="isWML11" compare="PreferredRenderingType"
        argument="wml11" />
    </deviceFilters>
  </system.web>
</configuration>
```

If you use Visual Studio .NET to create your mobile Web applications, the runtime will include *isWML11* and *isHTML* in Web.config by default. See Chapter 9 for more information about capability evaluators.

Implementing Properties in a User Control

To make the Short Date user control useful, you must give it a public property through which you can set the starting date and can retrieve the user's selection after the control executes. You implement this functionality in the code-behind module. You add a private data member to the class of type *System.DateTime*, named *_currentdate*. A public property named *SelectedDate* allows clients to get or set the control's *_currentdate* member. The *set* accessor for *SelectedDate* validates the date values passed in, ensuring that they're within range. Finally, in the class constructor, the application initializes *_currentdate* to today's date and defines the minimum and maximum dates allowed in the control. The application then uses the minimum and maximum dates in the *set* accessor's validation code. Listing 20-2 shows this code sequence. The other methods in this example are *OnInit*, *InitializeComponent*, and *Page_Load*; *OnInit* calls *InitializeComponent*, which declares *Page_Load* to be an event handler for the *MobilePage.OnLoad* event. In *Page_Load*, the *MobilePage.AllowCustom-*

Attributes property is set to *true*, which allows us to use the *wmlFormat* custom attribute with the TextBox control. (See Chapter 4 for more information about custom attributes and the *wmlFormat* attribute of the TextBox control.)

```
using System;
using System.Web;
using System.Web.Mobile;
using System.Web.UI.MobileControls;

namespace MSPress.MobWeb.UserControlExample
{

    /// <summary>
    /// Compact date selector
    /// </summary>
    public abstract class ShortDateControl :
        System.Web.UI.MobileControls.MobileUserControl
    {
        protected System.Web.UI.MobileControls.Panel Panel1;
        private DateTime _currentdate;
        private DateTime _minDate;
        private DateTime _maxDate;

        /// <summary>
        /// Gets and sets the date displayed in System.DateTime format.
        /// </summary>
        public System.DateTime SelectedDate
        {
            get
            {
                return _currentdate;
            }
            set
            {
                if ((value < _minDate) || (value > _maxDate))
                {
                    // Invalid date
                    throw(new ArgumentOutOfRangeException
                        ("SelectedDate",
                        value.ToString("d-MMM-yyy"),
                   "Date out of supported range 01-Jan-2003 to 31-Dec-2010"
                        ));
                }
                _currentdate = value;
            }
        }
        public ShortDateControl()
```

Listing 20-2 Code-behind module ShortDateControl.ascx.cs

```
        {
            _currentdate = DateTime.Now;
            _minDate = new DateTime(2003,1,1);
            _maxDate = new DateTime(2010,12,31);
        }

        override protected void OnInit(EventArgs e)
        {
            InitializeComponent();
            base.OnInit(e);
        }

        private void InitializeComponent()
        {
            this.Load += new System.EventHandler(this.Page_Load);
        }

        private void Page_Load(object sender, System.EventArgs e)
        {
            // Allow custom attributes so we can use the wmlFormat attribute.
            ((MobilePage)Page).AllowCustomAttributes = true;
        }
    }
}
```

Displaying the Properties of the User Control

The *SelectedDate* property defines the currently selected date of the user control. However, you must set the child controls in this user control to display that date. This seems like a simple task; just set the *Text* property of *TextBox1* if the client is a WML client, or set the *SelectedIndex* property of each of the SelectionList controls if it's an HTML client. However, this relatively simple task is complicated in this particular user control by the fact that it uses a *<ContentTemplate>* element within a Panel control. Thus, the controls you need to set aren't top-level controls; instead, they are child controls inside a TemplateContainer control, which is itself a child of *Panel1*.

As described in Chapter 9, you must use the *FindControl* method of *System.Web.UI.Control* to search through the control tree in the user control to find controls that have been instantiated as children of a template. The *Content* property of the Panel control exposes the *TemplateContainer* that contains the controls inside the template. Call the *FindControl* method of this *TemplateContainer*, passing the ID of the child controls to locate them.

> **Tip** If you're finding it difficult to understand the control hierarchy in a mobile Web Forms page, turn on the Trace facility described in Chapter 16. Part of the trace output is a listing of the full control hierarchy, which is a great help when you're working with child controls and with naming contexts.

For example, to find the *SelectionList* control with an ID of *SelectionList1*, you use the following code:

```
protected System.Web.UI.MobileControls.Panel Panel1;
private System.Web.UI.MobileControls.SelectionList SelDay;

private void Page_Load(object sender, System.EventArgs e)
{
    // Find the SelectionList control in the template
    SelDay = Panel1.Content.FindControl("SelectionList1") as SelectionList;
    ⋮
```

Notice that the protected class member *Panel1* is a reference to the top-level control *Panel1*, which is declared in the .ascx file shown in Listing 20-1. The class member *SelDay* is declared as private because it has scope only within this module. Its value is set by the return value of the *FindControl* method.

In Listing 20-3, enhancements to the ShortDateControl.ascx.cs code-behind module required to display the *SelectedDate* property are shown in boldface. *Page_Load* uses the technique just described to locate the controls inside *ContentTemplate*. You use the *HasCapability* method of the *MobileCapabilities* object in code to determine whether the *isWML11* device filter is *true*, and thus which controls should appear. The call to the *EnsureTemplatedUI* method at the beginning of *Page_Load* ensures that all child controls within templates have been instantiated at the time this method executes. The code that sets the display properties of the TextBox or SelectionList control is implemented in the *Page_PreRender* event handler, which is the last event to be fired before the control is rendered. (See Table 21-1, in Chapter 21, for more details on the life cycle of a control.) The *PreRender* event handler is wired up by the addition to the *InitializeComponent* method.

```
public abstract class ShortDateControl :
        System.Web.UI.MobileControls.MobileUserControl
    {
        protected System.Web.UI.MobileControls.Panel Panel1;
        private System.Web.UI.MobileControls.SelectionList SelDay;
        private System.Web.UI.MobileControls.SelectionList SelMonth;
        private System.Web.UI.MobileControls.SelectionList SelYear;
        private System.Web.UI.MobileControls.TextBox WMLDate;
        private DateTime _currentdate;
        private DateTime _minDate;
        private DateTime _maxDate;

        /// <summary>
        /// Gets and sets the date displayed in System.DateTime format.
        /// </summary>
        public System.DateTime SelectedDate
        {
            get
            {
                return _currentdate;
            }
            set
            {
                if ((value < _minDate) || (value > _maxDate))
                {
                    // Invalid date
                    throw(new ArgumentOutOfRangeException
                        ("SelectedDate",
                        value.ToString("d-MMM-yyy"),
                    "Date out of supported range 01-Jan-2003 to 31-Dec-2010"
                        ));
                }
                _currentdate = value;
            }
        }

        public ShortDateControl()
        {
            _currentdate = DateTime.Now;
            _minDate = new DateTime(2003,1,1);
            _maxDate = new DateTime(2010,12,31);
        }

        override protected void OnInit(EventArgs e)
```

Listing 20-3 Listing of ShortDateControl.ascx.cs, showing enhancements required to set properties of the visual elements so that they display the currently selected date

```
{
    InitializeComponent();
    base.OnInit(e);
}

private void InitializeComponent()
{
    this.Load += new System.EventHandler(this.Page_Load);
    this.PreRender += new System.EventHandler(this.Page_PreRender);
}

private void Page_Load (object sender, System.EventArgs e)
{
    // Allow custom attributes so we can use the wmlFormat attribute.
    ((MobilePage) Page).AllowCustomAttributes = true;

    Panel1.EnsureTemplatedUI();

    if (((MobileCapabilities)(Request.Browser))
        .HasCapability("isWML11",""))
    {
        // Set for WML
       WMLDate = Panel1.Content.FindControl("TextBox1") as TextBox;
    }
    else
      {
        // Set for HTML and cHTML
        SelDay = Panel1.Content.FindControl("SelectionList1")
        as SelectionList;
        SelMonth = Panel1.Content.FindControl("SelectionList2")
        as SelectionList;
        SelYear = Panel1.Content.FindControl("SelectionList3")
        as SelectionList;
    }
}

private void Page_PreRender(object sender, System.EventArgs e)
{
    if (((MobileCapabilities)(Request.Browser))
        .HasCapability("isWML11",""))
    {
        // Set display properties for the WML version
        if (WMLDate != null)
            WMLDate.Text = _currentdate.ToString("MM/dd/yy");
    }
    else
    {
```

```
                // Set for HTML and cHTML
                if (SelDay != null)
                    SelDay.SelectedIndex = _currentdate.Day - 1;
                if (SelMonth != null)
                    SelMonth.SelectedIndex = _currentdate.Month - 1;
                if (SelYear != null)
                    SelYear.SelectedIndex = _currentdate.Year - 2003;
            }
        }
    }
}
```

Responding to Events in a User Control

With this code, you can use the Short Date user control in a mobile Web Forms page, and you can initialize the control to a particular date by using the *SelectedDate* property. All that remains is to trap the user's input so that your *SelectedDate* property can discover which date the user selected. You achieve this the same way as you do in a mobile Web Forms page.

You define an event handler method for the *SelectedIndexChanged* event for each of the three SelectionList controls the client uses to enter the day, month, and year. However, you define an event handler for the *TextChanged* event for the text box used for WML clients, as Listing 20-4 shows.

```
private void Page_Load(object sender, System.EventArgs e)
        {
            // Allow custom attributes so we can use the wmlFormat attribute.
            ((MobilePage)Page).AllowCustomAttributes = true;

            Panel1.EnsureTemplatedUI();

            if (((MobileCapabilities)(Request.Browser))
                .HasCapability("isWML11",""))
            {
                WMLDate = Panel1.Content.FindControl("TextBox1") as TextBox;
                // Set event handler for the WML version
                WMLDate.TextChanged +=
                    new System.EventHandler(this.ChangeWMLDate);
            }
            else
            {
                // Set for HTML and cHTML
                SelDay = Panel1.Content.FindControl("SelectionList1")
                    as SelectionList;
```

Listing 20-4 Modified *Page_Load* method of ShortDateControl.ascx.cs, showing the declaration of event handlers

```
            SelMonth = Panel1.Content.FindControl("SelectionList2")
                as SelectionList;
            SelYear = Panel1.Content.FindControl("SelectionList3")
                as SelectionList;
            SelDay.SelectedIndexChanged +=
               new System.EventHandler(this.ChangeDate);
            SelMonth.SelectedIndexChanged +=
               new System.EventHandler(this.ChangeDate);
            SelYear.SelectedIndexChanged +=
               new System.EventHandler(this.ChangeDate);
        }
    }
```

Listing 20-5 shows the event handler routines that you need to use to save the user action results to the *currentdate* member variable of the class.

```
private void ChangeDate(object sender, System.EventArgs e)
{
    SelectedDate = new DateTime(
    SelYear.SelectedIndex + 2003,
    SelMonth.SelectedIndex + 1,
    SelDay.SelectedIndex + 1);
}

private void ChangeWMLDate(object sender, System.EventArgs e)
{
    // Date may be in MM/DD/YY format from WML clients
    String InputDate = WMLDate.Text.Replace("/", "");
    SelectedDate = new DateTime(
        int.Parse(InputDate.Substring(4,2)) + 2000,
        int.Parse(InputDate.Substring(0,2)),
        int.Parse(InputDate.Substring(2,2)));
}
```

Listing 20-5 Event handlers saving user action results to the class member variable

This user control is now functional, but there's still much room for improvement. For example, the control could offer standard style properties, such as *ForeColor*, *BackColor*, and *Font*. You handle these properties by directly setting the corresponding properties of one or more of the child controls in the user control. In this case, doing so is easy. This is because setting the property in the Panel control causes all the child controls to inherit that setting. The following code illustrates this concept:

```
/// <summary>
        /// Gets and sets the date field's ForeColor.
        /// </summary>
```

```
public System.Drawing.Color ForeColor
{
    get
    {
        return Panel1.ForeColor;
    }
    set
    {
        Panel1.ForeColor = value;
    }
}
```

To significantly improve this solution, you could make the control sensitive to the current setting of the enclosing page's *Culture* property. To do this, you make the format for date input appropriate for the current culture. (See Chapter 14 for a description of the *Culture* setting and culture-specific formatting.) You can then internationalize the control, which could display a drop-down list and labels in various languages.

You can use the current control in a mobile Web Forms page, as Listing 20-6 demonstrates. This example sets the selected date of the control to *March 02, 2004*.

```
<%@ Register TagPrefix="mobile"
    Namespace="System.Web.UI.MobileControls"
    Assembly="System.Web.Mobile" %>
<%@ Page language="c#" Inherits="System.Web.UI.MobileControls.MobilePage" %>
<%@ Register TagPrefix="custom" TagName="ShortDateUC"
    Src="ShortDateControl.ascx" %>

<head>
    <script runat="server" language="C#">
    public void Button_OnClick(Object sender, EventArgs e)
    {
        Label1.Text = "You selected: "
            + ucShortDate.SelectedDate.ToLongDateString();
        this.ActiveForm = Form2;
    }
    </script>
</head>
<body>
    <mobile:form id="Form1" runat="server">
        <custom:ShortDateUC id="ucShortDate" runat="server"
            SelectedDate="02-Mar-2004" ForeColor="Firebrick">
        </custom:ShortDateUC>
        <mobile:Command id="Command1" Runat="server"
```

Listing 20-6 Default.aspx of sample UserControlExample—mobile Web Forms page that uses the Short Date user control

```
            onclick="Button_OnClick" Text="Next">
        </mobile:Command>
    </mobile:form>

    <mobile:Form ID="Form2" Runat="Server">
        <mobile:Label id="Label1" Runat="Server" />
    </mobile:Form>
</body>
```

After the user selects a date and clicks the Next button, the second form displays the new selected date of the user control, as Figure 20-1 shows.

Figure 20-1 Output of the Short Date user control on the Openwave simulator

today

21

Creating Custom Controls by Inheritance and Composition

As you saw in Chapter 20, user controls are easy to build and to use. But for more flexibility, advanced developers will want to create custom controls that inherit from and extend an existing control class, or they'll want to build these controls from scratch by inheriting from the *System.Mobile.UI.MobileControl* class.

In this chapter, you'll learn how to build a custom control by inheriting from an existing mobile control and how to extend new controls with custom properties and events. You'll also learn how to build a custom control by *composition*, meaning that the custom control creates one or more child mobile controls that implement the user interface.

Building Controls in Code

User controls offer a powerful and relatively easy way to create custom controls and reusable pieces of user interface functionality. A user control also can be an appropriate solution for rapidly developing a reusable component.

Building controls entirely in code is a step up from simply working with user controls. Because you build controls entirely in a run-time-compliant language and compile them into assemblies, they generally offer better performance and more flexible functionality than user controls.

Developing controls in code is appropriate in a number of scenarios. First, you can use this technique when an existing control more or less does what you want but you want to change its behavior or add certain properties or events. This is control development by simple inheritance.

Second, you might want to develop a *composite control*, which combines two or more existing mobile controls into a single control that performs some function. Think of this as the programmatic version of a user control. In rare cases, you also might want to override the default rendering of the child controls and write device adapter classes to provide custom rendering of the composite control.

Finally, if none of the existing controls do what you want, you can develop a control from scratch by inheriting from the *MobileControl* class. This base class provides all the basic functionality a control requires to operate within the Mobile Internet Controls Runtime. You add properties, methods, and events, and then write device adapter classes to render your control on a particular device. We describe this scenario in Chapter 22.

Understanding the Control Life Cycle

Before you can write controls, you must have a clear understanding of the phases a control goes through and which methods it calls at which time. When the Microsoft ASP.NET runtime receives a request from a client, it performs the following steps:

1. Loads the mobile page
2. Parses the server control syntax in the .aspx page and uses it to build the control tree
3. Restores the controls to the state they were in at the end of the previous request (if there was one)
4. Accesses data and binds any data bound controls
5. Executes the code you've written
6. Constructs the response and sends it to the client

After that, the runtime destroys the page and discards it along with all the controls. However, using a Web application involves many request-response interactions. Each time the runtime returns a response to the browser, it renders the response, allows the user to interact with the response, and posts the results back to the server. The ASP.NET page framework and server controls maintain an illusion of continuity. Although the runtime builds and discards the page on every request, the user isn't aware of this. Moreover, before the runtime discards the page, it saves the current state of the page and controls so that at the next application request, it can restore the page and controls to the same state. This process is illustrated in Figure 21-1.

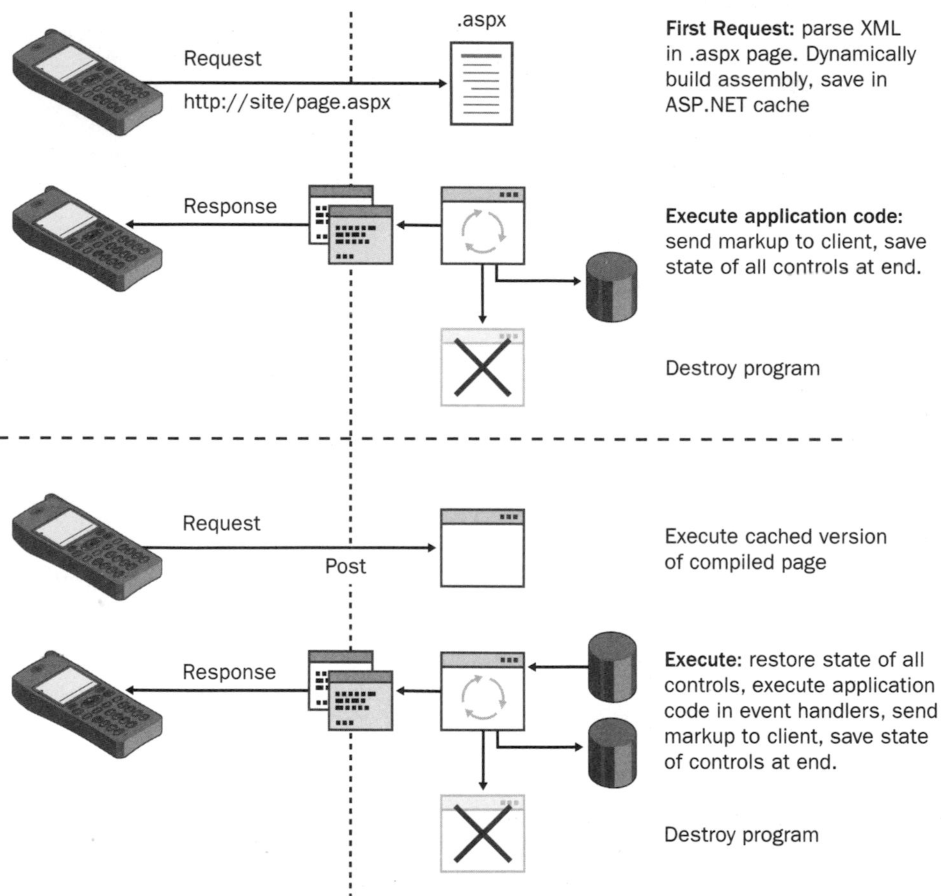

Figure 21-1 Life cycle of the mobile Web Forms page

To participate in the life cycle, a mobile control undergoes a number of phases. During each cycle, the runtime calls certain methods that you can override to implement your own custom functionality. Table 21-1 describes the control life cycle.

Table 21-1 Control Life Cycle

Phase	What Happens	Control Method or Event Executed by Runtime
Initialize	Settings needed during the current Web request are initialized. Properties of the control are set from values declared in server control syntax in the .aspx page.	*OnInit* (*Init* event) The MobileControl base class implementation of the *OnInit* method raises the *Init* event. Custom control authors may wish to override *OnInit* to implement the setup logic for your control.
Load *ViewState*	*ViewState* of the control is loaded from the persistence format saved at the end of the previous request.	*LoadViewState* The base class implementation of *LoadViewState* will be appropriate for most cases. However, override *LoadViewState* if you need to customize state restoration.
Process postback data	Data posted back from the client is analyzed.	*LoadPostData* The result of client interaction with your control is posted back to the server. Analyze the postback data, and update the appropriate properties of the control. Only controls that implement *IPostBackDataHandler* take part in this phase.
Load	Actions that should occur on every request, such as opening database connections, are performed.	*OnLoad* (*Load* event) At the end of this method, the control is fully built; state has been restored and updated as a result of postback data. Other resources the control requires, such as data from a database, have been fetched. The *MobileControl* base class implementation of the *OnLoad* method raises the *Load* event. Custom control authors may wish to override *OnLoad* to perform additional processing.

Table 21-1 Control Life Cycle

Phase	What Happens	Control Method or Event Executed by Runtime
Send postback change notifications	Change events are raised if required—that is, if data posted back has caused a change in the control's state.	*RaisePostDataChangedEvent* Change events are raised if state has changed between previous and current postbacks. One example is the *TextChanged* event of the TextBox control. Only controls that implement *IPostBackDataHandler* participate in this phase.
Handle postback events	Events that correspond to client-side events as a result of client interaction are raised.	*RaisePostBackEvent* This event occurs after any change events. An action the user performs on the client browser translates to a control event that is raised on the server during this phase. For example, when the user clicks a mobile Command control, a postback occurs. The resulting *Click* event is raised here. Only controls that implement *IPostBackEventHandler* participate in this phase.
Prerender	Any updates are performed prior to the control being rendered.	*OnPreRender* (*PreRender* event) A developer can write an event handler for the *PreRender* event to make any final updates to the state of the control, just prior to it being rendered. The *MobileControl* base class implementation of the *OnPreRender* method raises the *PreRender* event. Custom control authors may wish to override *OnPreRender* to perform additional processing.
Save state	*ViewState* property of the control is persisted to a string object.	*SaveViewState* The base class implementation of *SaveViewState* will be appropriate for most cases. However, override *SaveViewState* if you need to customize state restoration.

Table 21-1 Control Life Cycle

Phase	What Happens	Control Method or Event Executed by Runtime
Render	Methods in the associated device adapter class are called to generate output to be sent to the client.	*Render* Calls the *Render* method of the associated device adapter class to output the required markup.
Unload	Control releases any resources.	*OnUnload* (*UnLoad* event) Releases expensive resources such as database connections before destruction. The *MobileControl* base class implementation of the *OnUnload* method raises the *UnLoad* event. Custom control authors may wish to override *OnUnLoad* to perform additional processing.
Dispose	Any logic that should be executed prior to the control being torn down is executed.	*Dispose* Final cleanup before the control is released from memory.

Table 21-1 doesn't illustrate the role of *device adapters*—classes that work in tandem with the control classes and provide the device-specific functionality of a control, such as outputting the required markup. Unless you're building controls from scratch, you probably won't need to provide new device adapter classes. Controls you create through inheritance and by composition will use the rendering support of their parent controls, and in most cases, you won't need to make any modifications. If the standard rendering doesn't yield the result you want, you can implement a new device adapter for the control and override the control's *Render* method. However, with controls built by inheritance or by composition, you'll need to do this only occasionally. You'll learn how to program device adapter classes in Chapter 22.

Building Controls by Inheritance

In this scenario, an existing mobile control provides most of the functionality you need. However, you can extend that control to provide additional properties and events. Or you can make the control specialized, such as a List control that's designed to read news reports from a database, display the headlines as a list of links, and display the news text when the user selects a headline from the display list.

As a simple example, consider a specialized List control that lists data from an XML file. To build this control, you need to create a new control that inherits and extends the standard List control by performing the following steps:

1. Create a new property named *XMLsource* that specifies the path and file name of the data source.
2. Use the *DataMember* property inherited from the base *List* class to specify the XML node to read from the source. Use the *DataTextField* and *DataValueField* properties to specify the attributes to extract from and insert into the list.
3. Override the *OnLoad* method so that it uses the *System.Xml.XmlTextReader* class from the Microsoft .NET Framework to parse the XML input and build the list.

To build a custom mobile control in Microsoft Visual Studio .NET, select the Web Control Library project template in the New Project dialog box. After Visual Studio .NET creates the project, click the Project menu, then click Add Reference, and add the Mobile Internet Controls Runtime to your project—the assembly file name you need to reference is named *System.Web.Mobile.dll*. This particular example requires the .NET Framework classes that manipulate XML resources. Because these classes reside in the *System.Xml.dll* assembly, you must add a reference to that assembly as well.

The code for this control is quite simple, as Listing 21-1 shows. The control overrides the *OnLoad* method of the parent List control and uses the *XMLTextReader* object to parse the input file that you specify through the *XMLSource* property. The runtime creates a *MobileListItem* object for each element in the XML source that has the same name as the *DataMember* property. The code sets the *Text* property of the *MobileListItem* object to the value of the attribute whose name matches the *DataTextField* property and sets the *Value* property to the value of the attribute whose name matches the *DataValueField* property. We've kept the error handling very rudimentary in this example.

```
using System;
using System.Xml;
using System.Web.UI.MobileControls;

namespace MSPress.MobWeb.CustomControls
{
    public class xmlList : System.Web.UI.MobileControls.List
    {
```

Listing 21-1 Source file CustomMobileControlLibrary.cs implements the custom xmlList control

```
private String _xmlSource;

/// <summary>
/// Get and set the file containing the XML data to be parsed.
/// </summary>
public String XMLsource
{
    get
    {
        return _xmlSource;
    }
    set
    {
        _xmlSource = value;
    }
}
protected override void OnLoad(EventArgs e)
{
    if (!Page.IsPostBack)
    {
        base.OnLoad(e);

        // Get the path to the source on the local Web server.
        String strFullPath = Page.Server.MapPath(_xmlSource);

        XmlTextReader xmlreader = null;
        try
        {
            xmlreader = new XmlTextReader(strFullPath);
            while (xmlreader.Read())
            {
                if (xmlreader.NodeType == XmlNodeType.Element)
                {
                    if (xmlreader.Name == this.DataMember)
                    {
                        MobileListItem item =
                            new MobileListItem();
                        while (xmlreader.MoveToNextAttribute())
                        {
                            if (xmlreader.LocalName ==
                                this.DataTextField)
                            {
                                item.Text = xmlreader.Value;
                            }
                            if (xmlreader.LocalName ==
                                this.DataValueField)
                            {
                                item.Value = xmlreader.Value;
```

```
                                    }
                                }
                                Items.Add(item);
                            }
                        }
                    }
                }
                catch
                {
                    if (xmlreader != null) xmlreader.Close();
                }
            }
        }
    }
}
```

For example, suppose that the XML source file contains the data shown in Listing 21-2 and that you set the *DataMember*, *DataTextField*, and *DataValueField* properties of an xmlList control to *Team*, *TeamName*, and *Coach*, respectively. The control will then display a list of the values of the *TeamName* attribute and set the hidden list item value to the value of the *Coach* attribute.

```
<?xml version="1.0"?>
<Premiership>
    <Team TeamName="Dunes"
          Played="3"
          Won="3"
          Drawn="0"
          Lost="0"
          Points="9"
          Coach="Robert Brown"/>
    <Team TeamName="Toffees"
          Played="3"
          Won="2"
          Drawn="1"
          Lost="0"
          Points="7"
          Coach="Jeff Price"/>
    <Team TeamName="Phoenix"
          Played="3"
          Won="2"
          Drawn="1"
          Lost="0"
          Points="7"
          Coach="Robert O'Hara"/>
</Premiership>
```

Listing 21-2 Contents of the TeamData.xml file, which is XML-encoded data used as the data source for the xmlList custom control

Property or Public Data Member?

The xmlList control shown in Listing 21-1 defines the *XMLsource* property. In this example, this property is coded using *get* and *set* accessors, which don't implement any extra logic. You could just as easily make the *XML-source* property a public data member of the class without any visible difference to the control's users. Whether or not you implement properties of a class that have no associated validation logic as public data members is up to you. However, it's good practice to get into the habit of implementing properties using *get* and *set* accessors, because they are more visible in the source and allow you to include validation logic. You saw an example of this in Chapter 20, in Listing 20-2, where the *set* accessor for the *SelectedDate* property in the user control example included validation logic that verified that the date was within permissible boundaries.

Using a Compiled Custom Control

Any controls you build in code compile into an assembly with a .dll file extension. To use an assembly containing custom controls, you must add a reference to the assembly in your Visual Studio .NET project, just as you would with any other .NET assembly. This makes a private copy of the referenced assembly in the application's \bin directory. Then you add a *Register* directive to the head of the mobile Web Forms page to associate a *TagPrefix* with the classes in the assembly that contains the custom controls, just as you would to associate the *TagPrefix* "mobile" with the ASP.NET Mobile Controls in their assembly. Here's the syntax:

```
<%@ Page language="c#"
    Inherits="System.Web.UI.MobileControls.MobilePage"%>
<%@ Register TagPrefix="mobile"
    Namespace="System.Web.UI.MobileControls"
    Assembly="System.Web.Mobile" %>
<%@ Register TagPrefix="CMcustom"
    Namespace="MSPress.MobWeb.CustomControls"
    Assembly="CustomMobileControlLibrary" %>
```

To use the control, reference it in the ASP.NET server control syntax by using the declared *TagPrefix* and the control's class name:

```
<CMcustom:xmlList id="lstTeamList" runat="server"
    DataValueField="Coach" DataTextField="TeamName"
    DataMember="Team" xmlSource="TeamData.xml" >
</CMcustom:xmlList>
```

In every way, this particular control remains a List control—but it's a List control with particular capabilities that you've programmed. For example, you can still implement an *OnItemCommand* event handler to execute when the user selects an item from this List control. And, unless you override them, this List control still possesses the properties of its parent List control.

Listing 21-3 provides a full example of using the xmlList control. This example requires you to place the TeamData.xml XML source file in the application directory.

```
<%@ Page language="c#"
    Inherits="System.Web.UI.MobileControls.MobilePage"%>
<%@ Register TagPrefix="mobile"
    Namespace="System.Web.UI.MobileControls"
    Assembly="System.Web.Mobile" %>
<%@ Register TagPrefix="CMcustom"
    Namespace="MSPress.MobWeb.CustomControls"
    Assembly="CustomMobileControlLibrary" %>

<head>
    <script runat="server" language="C#">
    public void SelectItem(
            Object source,
            ListCommandEventArgs args)
        {
            // Display the second page.
            this.ActiveForm = Form2;
            Label1.Text = "You selected: " + args.ListItem.Text
                                + ":" + args.ListItem.Value;

        }
    </script>
</head>

<body>
    <mobile:Form id="Form1" runat="server">
        <CMcustom:xmlList id="lstTeamList" runat="server"
            DataValueField="Coach" DataTextField="TeamName"
            DataMember="Team" xmlSource="TeamData.xml"
            OnItemCommand="SelectItem">
        </CMcustom:xmlList>
    </mobile:Form>

    <mobile:Form id="Form2" runat="server">
        <mobile:Label id="Label1" runat="server"></mobile:Label>
    </mobile:Form>
</body>
```

Listing 21-3 Source file Default.aspx demonstrates the use of the xmlList control

When the user selects an item in the List control, the second form is displayed, as shown in Figure 21-2.

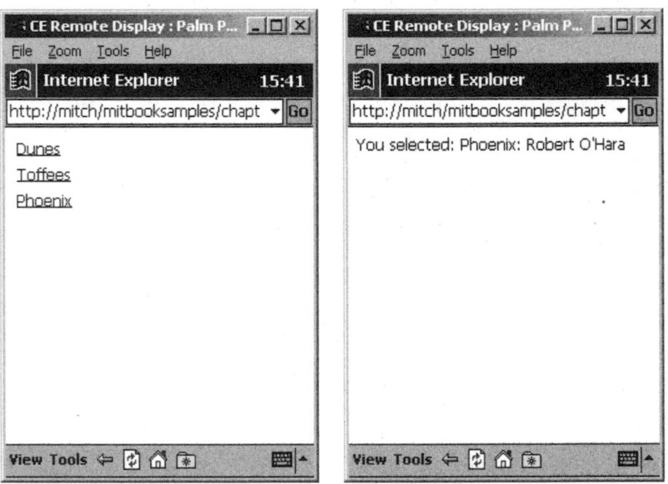

Figure 21-2 Using the XML-parsing custom List control in Pocket Internet Explorer

Building Controls by Composition

You build a composite control by creating a class that inherits directly or indirectly from *System.Web.UI.MobileControls*, and you implement the composite control's user interface by instantiating one or more mobile controls as child controls within it. You define properties and events to give your control the capabilities you need. The controls you build this way are analogous to user controls. The principal difference between user controls and composite controls is that you define the former declaratively using ASP.NET tag syntax. User controls consist of a text file with an .ascx extension that contains ASP.NET server control syntax and which may also have a code-behind module. Composite controls consist entirely of code and are compiled into assemblies, consequently offering improved performance over user controls.

It's generally a good idea to inherit from the Panel control instead of directly from *MobileControl*. This is because the .NET Framework tries to avoid splitting child controls of a Panel control across multiple pages. Device adapters for the *MobileControl* class and the *Panel* class render child controls by default. Because you construct the interface by using existing mobile controls (or custom controls built by inheriting a standard control, as described earlier), you don't have to write any new device adapter classes to handle rendering.

Composite controls and controls that provide data binding must implement the *System.Web.UI.INamingContainer* interface. This interface doesn't have any methods, but it serves as a marker to the .NET Framework and guarantees any child controls a unique ID. You declare a class that inherits from *Panel* and implements the *INamingContainer* interface in C# as shown here:

```
public class MyCompositeControl : Panel, INamingContainer
```

Creating the Child Controls in a Composite Control

When you create a composite control, you must override the *CreateChildControls* method of the *System.Web.UI.Control* base class. In this method, you must create the child controls, which implement the user interface, and add them to the custom control's *Controls* collection. By default, the runtime calls the *CreateChildControls* method after *OnLoad*. Therefore, any initialization of the controls must occur in the *CreateChildControls* method. The runtime can call *CreateChildControls* many times during various phases of a control's life. To stop the runtime from executing *CreateChildControls* more than once, set the *ChildControlsCreated* property to *True* at the end of this method.

Other methods requiring that the child controls already exist can call the *EnsureChildControls* method, which causes the runtime to call *CreateChildControls* if it hasn't done so already. For example, you might have a public property that gets or sets a property or properties of a child control directly.

Listing 21-4 illustrates all these techniques and demonstrates the essential functionality of a composite control. This composite control provides functionality very similar to the user control example shown in Listings 20-1 and 20-2 in Chapter 20, and in fact it even has the same name, CMShortDate. However, unlike the user control in Chapter 20, all the functionality of this control is defined in code. To keep things simple, this listing doesn't implement a different user interface depending on whether the client is HTML or WML, although it could easily be extended to do so. We'll build this control in three steps, increasing the functionality each time. The first step of this control, shown here, simply displays a date specified through the *SelectedDate* property. This listing hasn't yet implemented any logic that returns the user's selection after a date has been selected using the control.

```
using System;
using System.Web.UI;
using System.Web.UI.MobileControls;

namespace MSPress.MobWeb.CustomControls
{
    /// <summary>
    /// Example of a composite control
    /// </summary>
    public class CMShortDate : Panel, INamingContainer
    {
        private SelectionList _selDay;
        private SelectionList _selMonth;
        private SelectionList _selYear;
        private Label         _lblPrompt;

        private DateTime _currentdate;
        private DateTime _minDate;
        private DateTime _maxDate;

        /// <summary>
        /// Gets and sets the date displayed in System.DateTime format
        /// </summary>
        public System.DateTime SelectedDate
        {
            get
            {
                return _currentdate;
            }
            set
            {
                if ((value < _minDate) || (value > _maxDate))
                {
                    // Invalid date
                    throw(new ArgumentOutOfRangeException
                        ("SelectedDate",
                        value.ToString("d-MMM-yyy"),
                    "Date out of supported range 01-Jan-2002 to 31-Dec-2012"
                        ));
                }
                _currentdate = value;
            }
        }
        /// <summary>
        /// Gets and sets the text displayed for a prompt
        /// </summary>
```

Listing 21-4 CMShortDate.cs—step 1: the source of a composite control

```
public String Text
{
    get
    {
        this.EnsureChildControls();
        return _lblPrompt.Text;
    }
    set
    {
        this.EnsureChildControls();
        _lblPrompt.Text = value;
    }
}

public CMShortDate()
{
    _currentdate = DateTime.Now;
    _minDate = new DateTime(2002,1,1);
    _maxDate = new DateTime(2010,12,31);
}

protected override void CreateChildControls()
{
    // Create child controls.
    Label label;
    MobileListItem item;

    _lblPrompt = new Label();
    _lblPrompt.Text = "Select a date:";
    Controls.Add(_lblPrompt);

    label = new Label();
    label.Text = "Day: ";
    Controls.Add(label);

    _selDay = new SelectionList();
    for (int intDay=1; intDay < 32; intDay++ )
    {
        item = new MobileListItem();
        item.Text = intDay.ToString();
        _selDay.Items.Add(item);
    }
    Controls.Add(_selDay);

    label = new Label();
    label.Text = "Month: ";
    Controls.Add(label);
```

```
            _selMonth = new SelectionList();
            for (int intMonth=1; intMonth < 13; intMonth++ )
            {
                item = new MobileListItem();
                DateTime dt = new DateTime(1,intMonth,1);
                item.Text = dt.ToString("MMM");
                item.Value = intMonth.ToString();
                _selMonth.Items.Add(item);
            }
            Controls.Add(_selMonth);

            label = new Label();
            label.Text = "Year: ";
            Controls.Add(label);

            _selYear = new SelectionList();
            for (int intYear=2002; intYear < 2011; intYear++ )
            {
                item = new MobileListItem();
                item.Text = intYear.ToString();
                _selYear.Items.Add(item);
            }
            Controls.Add(_selYear);

            //Set the controls for the currentdate
            _selDay.SelectedIndex = _currentdate.Day - 1;
            _selMonth.SelectedIndex = _currentdate.Month - 1;
            _selYear.SelectedIndex = _currentdate.Year - 2002;

            ChildControlsCreated = true;
        }
    }
}
```

The code implements only two properties directly. But because this custom control descends from *Panel*, which itself descends from *MobileControl*, it already possesses all the standard properties, such as *UniqueID*, *Font*, and *ForeColor*.

The *Text* property sets and gets the *Text* property of the child *_lblPrompt* Label control; before it does so, the accessor methods call *EnsureChildControls* to verify that the child controls exist. This example simply produces three drop-down lists with accompanying prompts, as Figure 21-3 shows.

Figure 21-3 Selecting a date in the CMShortDate user control

Processing Postback Data

The CMShortDate control must act on the data that the client posts back to the server to determine which date the user selected and update its *SelectedDate* property accordingly. To do so, capture the appropriate *PostDataChangedEvent* of the control's child controls—in this case, the *SelectedIndexChanged* event of the three SelectionList controls. In the *CreateChildControls* method, set the *SelectedIndexChanged* property of each SelectionList control to the CMShort-Date control's *OnSelectionChanged* event handler method. Listing 21-5 depicts the changes you make to the control code.

```
using System;
using System.Web.UI;
using System.Web.UI.MobileControls;

namespace MSPress.MobWeb.CustomControls
{
    public class CMShortDate : Panel, INamingContainer
    {
        ⋮

        protected void OnSelectionChanged(object sender, EventArgs e)
        {
            _currentdate = new DateTime(
                _selYear.SelectedIndex + 2002,
```

Listing 21-5 CMShortDate.cs—step 2: modifications to capture change events from the child controls

```
                _selMonth.SelectedIndex + 1,
                _selDay.SelectedIndex + 1);
        }

        protected override void CreateChildControls()
        {
                :

            //Set the controls for the currentdate
            _selDay.SelectedIndex = _currentdate.Day - 1;
            _selMonth.SelectedIndex = _currentdate.Month - 1;
            _selYear.SelectedIndex = _currentdate.Year - 2002;

            // Capture the change events of the child controls.
            _selDay.SelectedIndexChanged +=
                new EventHandler(this.OnSelectionChanged);
            _selMonth.SelectedIndexChanged +=
                new EventHandler(this.OnSelectionChanged);
            _selYear.SelectedIndexChanged +=
                new EventHandler(this.OnSelectionChanged);

            ChildControlsCreated = true;
        }
    }
}
```

With these changes in place, the control now provides the same functionality as the user control you developed in Chapter 20, in Listings 20-1 and 20-2. You can use the *SelectedDate* property to set the start date and to retrieve the user's selection after postback.

Raising Custom Events

After you've trapped the change events of the child controls in order to update the custom control's state, you can raise a change event, offering additional functionality to the page developer who is building applications using your custom control. We'll change the CMShortDate control so that if the application's user changes the date set in the control, the composite control raises the *DateChanged* event on the server. You implement this by making some simple additions to the *CMShortDate* class. First, you declare the event name in the class:

```
public class CMShortDate : Panel, INamingContainer
{
    public event EventHandler DateChanged;
    :
```

In *OnSelectionChanged*, the method we wrote in the previous section to capture the change events of the three SelectionList child controls, the application raises the event if the page developer has declared a *DateChanged* event handler. The updated *OnSelectionChanged* method is listed here with the modifications in bold.

```
protected void OnSelectionChanged(object sender, EventArgs e)
{
    _currentdate = new DateTime(
        _selYear.SelectedIndex + 2002,
        _selMonth.SelectedIndex + 1,
        _selDay.SelectedIndex + 1);

    // The'DateChanged' event property of this control is null
    // until the page developer has registered an event handler
    // for the event
    EventHandler onDateChanged = DateChanged;
    if (onDateChanged != null)
    {
        // Call any user-declared event handlers.
        onDateChanged(this, new EventArgs());
    }
}
```

Event handler methods always take a first parameter of the originating control and a second parameter of an *EventArgs* object or a class descended from *EventArgs*. In this example, the code sets the second parameter to an empty *EventArgs* instance. In other applications, you might want to define your own class with custom properties that you deliver with the event.

The page developer can now write his or her own event handler method and wire it up so that it is called when the control raises the event. This is done in exactly the same way as with standard controls, either by setting *DateChanged* to the developer's own event handler in code or by wiring up the event handler declaratively. The following code shows how to do the latter:

```
<CMcustom:CMShortDate runat="server" OnDateChanged="HasChanged" />
```

This particular control needs a refinement to make it work correctly. At the moment, if the user changes only one part of the date, such as the day, the runtime calls *OnSelectionChanged* only once. However, if the month or year changes too, the runtime calls *OnSelectionChanged* two or three times. Because you want the runtime to call the *DateChanged* event only once when any part of the date changes, you must add a *private bool* data member to act as a flag. The code initializes this flag to *false* in the class constructor (each time the code builds the control, at the beginning of processing of each request) and sets this flag the first time the runtime calls *OnSelectionChanged*. The runtime then uses this flag to block repeat processing in any one request. Listing 21-6 shows the full code changes needed for this event.

```
public class CMShortDate : Panel, INamingContainer
{
    private bool _DateChangeProcessed; // Flag to stop repeat events
    public event EventHandler DateChanged; // Event declaration

     // Other property declarations not shown
     ⋮
    public CMShortDate()
    {
        _currentdate = DateTime.Now;
        _minDate = new DateTime(2002,1,1);
        _maxDate = new DateTime(2010,12,31);
        _DateChangeProcessed = false;
    }

    protected void OnSelectionChanged(object sender, EventArgs e)
    {
        if (!_DateChangeProcessed)
        {
            _currentdate = new DateTime(
                _selYear.SelectedIndex + 2002,
                _selMonth.SelectedIndex + 1,
                _selDay.SelectedIndex + 1);

            EventHandler onDateChanged = DateChanged;
            if (onDateChanged != null)
            {
                onDateChanged(this, new EventArgs());
            }

            _DateChangeProcessed = true;
        }
    }
     ⋮

}
```

Listing 21-6 CMShortDate.cs—step 3: implementation of the *Date-Changed* event

The CMShortDate control now possesses a lot of useful functionality. Listing 21-7 shows how you can use this control in a mobile Web Forms page. This example also demonstrates how properties such as *Font-Bold* and *ForeColor* inherit from the containing Panel control.

```
<%@ Register TagPrefix="mobile"
    Namespace="System.Web.UI.MobileControls"
    Assembly="System.Web.Mobile" %>
<%@ Page language="c#"
    Inherits="System.Web.UI.MobileControls.MobilePage" %>
<%@ Register TagPrefix="CMcustom" Namespace="MSPress.MobWeb.CustomControls"
    Assembly="CustomMobileControlLibrary" %>

<head>
    <script runat="server" language="C#">
    public void DateHasChanged(Object sender, EventArgs e)
    {
        Label1.Text = "You selected: "
            + CMShortDate1.SelectedDate.ToLongDateString();
        this.ActiveForm = Form2;
    }
    </script>
</head>

<body>
    <mobile:Form id="Form1" runat="server">
        <CMcustom:CMShortDate id="CMShortDate1" runat="server"
            OnDateChanged="DateHasChanged" SelectedDate="01-Jan-2002"
            Font-Bold="true" ForeColor="Red" >
        </CMcustom:CMShortDate>
        <mobile:Command id="Command1" Text="Next" Runat="server"/>
    </mobile:Form>

    <mobile:Form id="Form2" runat="server">
        <mobile:Label id="Label1" runat="server"></mobile:Label>
    </mobile:Form>
</body>
```

Listing 21-7 Source file Default.aspx, which uses the CMShortDate custom control

Figure 21-4 shows the code output when accessed from the Nokia simulator.

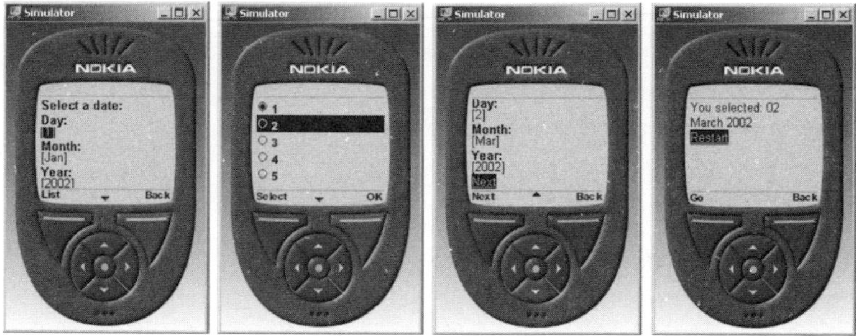

Figure 21-4 Output from Listing 21-7 on the Nokia simulator

Managing *ViewState*

Currently the CMShortDate control has a problem that will surface if your application displays it at a later stage of execution. For example, try modifying the sample application shown in Listing 21-7 by placing a Command control on *Form2*. When the user clicks the button shown in the client browser, this causes a postback to the server, where the Command control's click is raised. The event handler for the *Click* event that we now add to this application is called Return, which sets the *ActiveForm* to *Form1* again. Listing 21-8 shows the code and highlights the changes.

```
<%@ Register TagPrefix="mobile"
    Namespace="System.Web.UI.MobileControls"
    Assembly="System.Web.Mobile" %>
<%@ Page language="c#"
    Inherits="System.Web.UI.MobileControls.MobilePage" %>
<%@ Register TagPrefix="CMcustom" Namespace="MSPress.MobWeb.CustomControls"
    Assembly="CustomMobileControlLibrary" %>

<head>
    <script runat="server" language="C#">
    ⋮
    public void Return(Object sender, EventArgs e)
    {
        this.ActiveForm = Form1;
    }
    </script>
</head>

<body>
    ⋮
```

Listing 21-8 Source file Default.aspx—demonstrating loss of control state

```
    <mobile:Form id="Form2" runat="server">
        <mobile:Label id="Label1" runat="server"></mobile:Label>
        <mobile:Command id="Command2" Text="Return" Runat="server"
            OnClick="Return"/>
    </mobile:Form>
</body>
```

When *Form1* is displayed again as a result of the user clicking the Command button, the CMShortDate control displays the date it has initialized within the server control syntax (*"1-Jan-2002")*, rather than the date the user set. Figure 21-5 illustrates this problem.

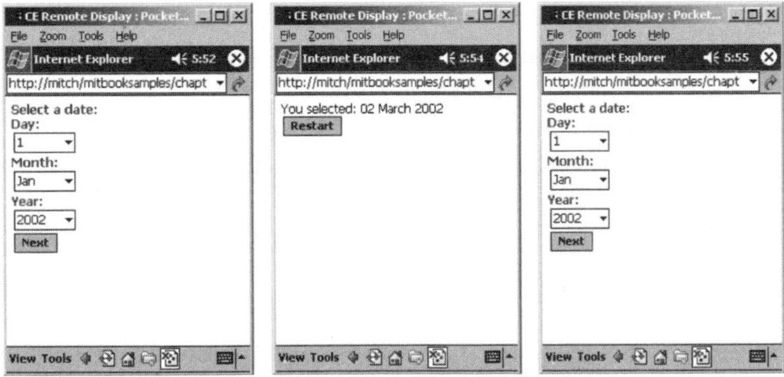

Figure 21-5 The CMShortDate control doesn't retain its settings across subsequent requests and doesn't implement *ViewState* correctly.

On each postback, the mobile page loads and the runtime creates all the controls. The application sets the *_currentdate* property of the CMShortDate control in the class constructor to *DateTime.Now*—in other words, the default value is today's date. Then the ASP.NET Runtime initializes properties of all controls according to the values declared in the .aspx file's server control syntax. In this instance, the code sets the CMShortDate control's *SelectedDate* property to "*1-Jan-2002*". Soon after, the runtime calls the *CreateChildControls* method. This method creates the SelectionList controls that implement CMShortDate's user interface and sets them to display the control's current date.

If you revisit the stages of a control's life shown in Table 21-1, you'll see that after the control initializes, its *LoadViewState* method executes. This updates properties from settings stored in the control's *ViewState* at the end of the previous request. Then the *LoadPostData* method executes, causing the control to analyze the data posted back from the client. If the user entered a value or selected an item that changes the control's state, the postback translates the user's instructions into action. (In this case, the code must update the

SelectedDate property.) Just before rendering the output that's sent back to the client, the runtime calls the *SaveViewState* method to persist any properties or other settings that must be restored at the beginning of the next request.

Clearly, you want the CMShortDate control to retain its date setting across requests, which means storing the *_currentdate* property in *ViewState*. Saving the *_currentdate* value in the control's *ViewState* collection rather than as a private data member easily achieves this. Because the *ViewState* collection is dictionary structured, you can store and retrieve objects by specifying a string key value, as shown here:

```
// Save a value.
ViewState["currentdate"] = value;
⋮
// Restore a value.
DateTime datefromViewState = (DateTime)ViewState["currentdate"];
```

Once you store values in the control's *ViewState* collection, the *LoadViewState* and *SaveViewState* methods of the control base class persist that *ViewState* across requests. You can store most simple types and arrays in the *ViewState* collection. However, if you have a complex object that you can't save by default in the persisted *ViewState* collection, you must override *SaveViewState* and *LoadViewState* to handle the serialization and deserialization of this object.

Listing 21-9 shows the changes the *CMShortDate* class requires.

```
using System;
using System.Web.UI;
using System.Web.UI.MobileControls;

namespace MSPress.MobWeb.CustomControls
{
    /// <summary>
    /// Example of a composite control
    /// </summary>
    public class CMShortDate : Panel, INamingContainer
    {

        private bool _DateChangeProcessed; // Flag to stop repeat events
        public event EventHandler DateChanged; // Event declaration

        private SelectionList _selDay;
        private SelectionList _selMonth;
        private SelectionList _selYear;
        private Label         _lblPrompt;
```

Listing 21-9 CMShortDate.cs—final version: storing properties to save across requests in the *ViewState* object rather than storing them as class member variables

```
// private DateTime _currentdate;  - no longer required
private DateTime _minDate;
private DateTime _maxDate;
private bool _DateChangeProcessed;

/// <summary>
/// Gets and sets the date displayed in System.DateTime format
/// </summary>
public DateTime SelectedDate
{
    get
    {
        return (DateTime) ViewState["currentdate"] ;
    }
    set
    {
        if ((value < _minDate) || (value > _maxDate))
        {
            // Invalid date
            throw(new ArgumentOutOfRangeException
                ("SelectedDate",
                value.ToString("d-MMM-yyy"),
    "Date out of supported range 01-Jan-2002 to 31-Dec-2012"
                ));
        }
        ViewState["currentdate"] = value;
    }
}
⋮
public CMShortDate()
{
    ViewState["currentdate"] = DateTime.Now;
    _minDate = new DateTime(2002,1,1);
    _maxDate = new DateTime(2010,12,31);
    _DateChangeProcessed = false;
}

protected void OnSelectionChanged(object sender, EventArgs e)
{
    if (!_DateChangeProcessed)
    {
        ViewState["currentdate"] = new DateTime(
            _selYear.SelectedIndex + 2002,
            _selMonth.SelectedIndex + 1,
            _selDay.SelectedIndex + 1);

        EventHandler onDateChanged = DateChanged;
```

```
                if (onDateChanged != null)
                {
                    onDateChanged(this, new EventArgs());
                }

                _DateChangeProcessed = true;
            }
        }

        protected override void CreateChildControls()
        {
            ⋮
            Controls.Add(_selYear);

            // Set the controls for the current date.
            DateTime currentdate = (DateTime) ViewState["currentdate"];
               _selDay.SelectedIndex = currentdate.Day - 1;
               _selMonth.SelectedIndex = currentdate.Month - 1;
               _selYear.SelectedIndex = currentdate.Year - 2002;

            // Capture the change events of the child controls.
            _selDay.SelectedIndexChanged +=
                new EventHandler(this.OnSelectionChanged);
            ⋮
        }
    }
}
```

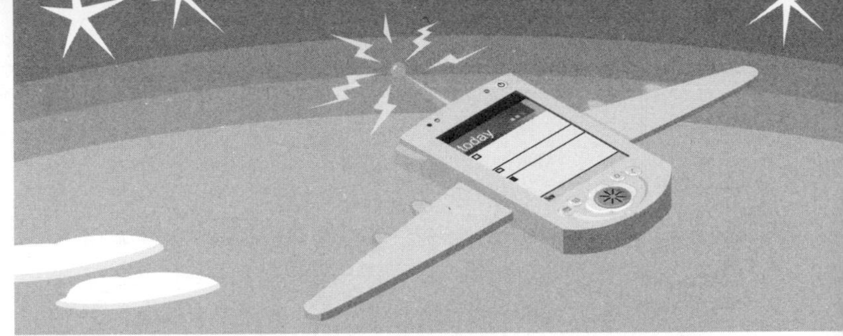

22

Programming Device Adapters and Building Controls from Scratch

In Chapter 20 and Chapter 21, you learned how to build user controls and how to build custom controls in code by inheritance and by composition. User controls are easy to build and employ. Custom controls can be quite simple to build using inheritance or composition, and these controls rarely require you to create new device adapter classes.

If you want complete control over the functionality of a custom control, however, you should build it from scratch by inheriting from a base class, such as *System.Mobile.UI.MobileControl*. This technique presents challenges you will not encounter when using other forms of custom controls. You need to understand the interactions between a control class, which implements the methods and properties of a mobile control and defines the control as the application developer views it, and device adapter classes, which implement device-specific behavior of the control such as rendering the markup that is sent to the client. It also requires an in-depth knowledge of the markup languages the devices use.

In this chapter, you'll come to understand the life cycle of a mobile control. You'll learn how to program device adapter classes to render a control and implement its device-specific logic. You'll see how to build a custom control from scratch by inheriting from the *MobileControl* class and implementing device adapter classes to render the user interface. You'll discover how to build controls that support data binding, handle *ViewState*, cause postback from the client to the server, and support templates. Also, you'll see how to implement a custom *System.Web.UI.MobileControls.MobileControlBuilder* object that allows you to parse ASP.NET server control syntax from an .aspx file.

Building Controls from Scratch

If none of the existing mobile controls do what you want, you can develop a control from scratch by inheriting from the *MobileControl* class or an appropriate mobile control class that functions as a base class, such as the *PagedControl* class or the *Panel* class. These classes provide all the basic functionality a control requires to operate as an ASP.NET mobile control.

Building controls from scratch involves more work than building controls by inheritance or composition. When you create a new control by inheriting from an existing control, you are simply modifying the behavior of the existing control, and often this can be as simple as adding new properties or methods, or overriding existing properties or methods. Similarly, when you create a new control by composition—taking two or more existing controls and combining them into a new composite control—the programming effort may not be too complex. Because you inherit the existing control's functionality, you also inherit the device adapter classes, which implement the device-specific logic. However, when you create a control from scratch, you must not only write the control class, you must also write a set of device adapter classes to handle rendering duties for all the different classes of device your control will support, such as WML 1.1 browsers, HTML 3.2 browsers, or compact HTML (cHTML) 1.0 browsers.

The Control Life Cycle

Before you start to write controls, you must have a clear understanding of the phases a control undergoes and which methods it calls at which time. When a client requests a Microsoft ASP.NET page, the *page framework* (the ASP.NET Mobile Controls runtime, which manages the handling of a request and the generation and delivery of the response) has many tasks to perform. Using a Web application involves many request-response interactions. Each time the user of a mobile browser requests a page from the Web, the page framework returns a response to the browser and the browser renders it. The user interacts with this data and then posts the results back to the server in a new request. The ASP.NET page framework and server controls work to maintain an illusion of continuity. To provide this continuity, the page framework saves the state of the pages and controls before discarding each page after each response. On the next request, the page framework restores the pages and controls to their previous state. This process can be summarized by the following steps:

1. Loads the mobile page and builds the controls
2. Restores the control's state if the runtime saved any at the end of the previous request to the application
3. Processes data posted back from the client and updates the control's state
4. Raises server events and executes event handlers
5. Saves the control's state for the next request
6. Constructs a response and sends it to the client
7. Tears down and discards the page as well as all the controls

As we've mentioned, a mobile control undergoes a number of phases during this process. During each phase, the page framework calls certain methods that you can override to implement your own custom functionality. Table 22-1 describes this control life cycle.

Table 22-1 Control Life Cycle

Phase	What Happens	Method or Event Executed	Device Adapter Method
Initialize	Settings needed during the current Web request are initialized. Control properties are set from the values defined in server control syntax on the .aspx page.	*OnInit* (*Init* event) The *OnInit* method raises the *Init* event, and calls *OnInit* in the device adapter class. Override this method to implement the setup logic for your control.	*OnInit* Soon after the control is instantiated, the appropriate device adapter class for the request is selected. *OnInit* in the *MobileControl* base class calls *OnInit* in the device adapter.
Load the contents of the *ViewState*	The contents of the control's *ViewState* are loaded from the persisted object saved at the end of the previous request.	*LoadViewState* Override *LoadViewState* if you need to customize state restoration. *LoadPrivateViewState* Loads internal state that was round-tripped to the client.	*LoadAdapterState* If the device adapter saves any device-specific *ViewState*, it is loaded here. The *LoadPrivateViewState* method of the *MobileControl* base class calls this method.

Table 22-1 Control Life Cycle

Phase	What Happens	Method or Event Executed	Device Adapter Method
Process postback data	Data posted back from the client is analyzed.	*LoadPostData* The result of client interaction with your control is posted back to the server as part of the current request. Analyze the postback data, and update the appropriate properties of the control. Only controls that implement *IPostBackDataHandler* take part in this phase.	By default, there are no device adapter class methods that participate in this phase.
Load	Actions that should occur on every request, such as opening database connections, are performed.	*OnLoad* (*Load* event) The *OnLoad* method raises the *Load* event, and calls *OnLoad* in the device adapter class. At the end of this method, the control is fully built, state has been restored and updated as a result of postback data, and other resources the control requires, such as data from a database, have been retrieved.	*OnLoad* *OnLoad* in the *MobileControl* base class calls *OnLoad* in the device adapter class.
Send postback change notifications	Change events are raised if required—that is, if data posted back has caused a change in the control's state.	*RaisePostDataChangedEvent* Change events are raised if state has changed between previous and current postbacks. For example, the *TextChanged* event of the TextBox control is one such event. Only controls that implement *IPostBackDataHandler* participate in this phase.	By default, there are no device adapter class methods that participate in this phase.
Handle postback events	Events that correspond to client-side events as a result of client interaction are raised.	*RaisePostBackEvent* This event occurs after any change events. A "client-side" event is raised on the server here. For example, when the user clicks on a mobile Command control, a postback occurs. The resulting *Click* event is raised here. Only controls that implement *IPostBackEventHandler* participate in this phase.	*HandlePagePostBackEvent* If events sent to the control can vary depending on the target device, the control must call *HandlePagePostBackEvent* to give the device adapter the opportunity to handle the postback event.

Table 22-1 Control Life Cycle

Phase	What Happens	Method or Event Executed	Device Adapter Method
Prerender	Any updates are performed prior to the control being rendered.	*OnPreRender* (*PreRender* event) The *OnPreRender* method raises the *PreRender* event, and calls *OnPreRender* in the device adapter class. Any final updates to the state of the control are performed.	*OnPreRender* *OnPreRender* in the *MobileControl* base class calls *OnPreRender* in the device adapter class.
Save state	The *ViewState* property of the control is persisted to a string object.	*SaveViewState* The base class implementation of *SaveViewState* will be appropriate for most cases. However, override *SaveViewState* if you need to customize state management. The *SaveViewState* method calls the *SavePrivateViewState* method, which saves internal state that is round-tripped to the client. Normally, because of mobile device bandwidth limitations, *ViewState* is stored in the Session on the server, as explained in Chapter12. However, the developer can disable *ViewState*. *PrivateViewState* is different; it does round-trip to the client (so use sparingly!) and cannot be disabled. See "Using *PrivateViewState*" later in this chapter for more details.	*SaveAdapterState* The device adapter can save any device-specific *ViewState* here. The *SavePrivateViewState* method of the *MobileControl* base class calls this method.
Render	Output to be sent to the client is generated.	*Render* Calls the *Render* method of the associated device adapter class.	*Render* This method uses the *MobileTextWriter* object to output the required markup for the control on the client device.

Table 22-1 Control Life Cycle

Phase	What Happens	Method or Event Executed	Device Adapter Method
Unload	The control releases any resources.	*OnUnload* (*UnLoad* event) The *OnUnload* method raises the *UnLoad* event, and calls *OnUnload* in the device adapter class. Tidies up prior to destruction. This phase should include releasing expensive resources such as database connections.	*OnUnLoad* *OnUnLoad* in the *MobileControl* base class calls *OnUnLoad* in the device adapter class.
Dispose	Any logic that should be executed prior to the control being torn down is disposed of.	*Dispose* Final cleanup before the control is released from memory.	

The Role of Device Adapters

The ASP.NET Mobile Controls technology extends ASP.NET. ASP.NET controls and mobile controls operate in a similar way, and both implement a similar set of methods and behaviors. This becomes clear as you climb the class inheritance tree because both sets of controls inherit much of their functionality from a common base class, *System.Web.UI.Control*. However, the mobile controls differ substantially from ASP.NET controls in that they use device adapter classes.

If you develop a custom control for ASP.NET, one of the first methods you'll write is *Render*, which outputs the markup that's sent to the client. The *MobileControl* class has a *Render* method as well, but you don't implement code in it to output any markup. Instead, the *MobileControl* implementation of *Render* calls the *Render* method in the associated device adapter class, which generates the output.

Control and device adapter classes completely depend on each other. A control class can't fulfill its function if a device adapter class doesn't accompany it. And a device adapter class exists solely to perform the rendering and device-specific duties for a control. Together the control class and the device adapter class comprise a mobile control. In fact, there is more than one device adapter class for each control class. Every control consists of the control class that implements device-independent logic and a set of device adapter classes. Each device adapter class provides support for operating the mobile control on a particular class of device. If you decide to write a custom control from scratch that supports the same broad subset of mobile devices as the standard ASP.NET mobile controls (after you've added XHTML support by installing Device Update 2), you'll have to create at least three device adapter classes to work with it: one for WML clients, one that supports HTML 3.2 and cHTML 1.0 clients, and one for XHTML clients. If the rendering output for HTML 3.2 clients isn't compatible with i-mode devices, you'll have to write a separate device adapter class for cHTML 1.0 clients as well.

Figure 22-1 demonstrates the interaction of a List control and its associated adapter classes.

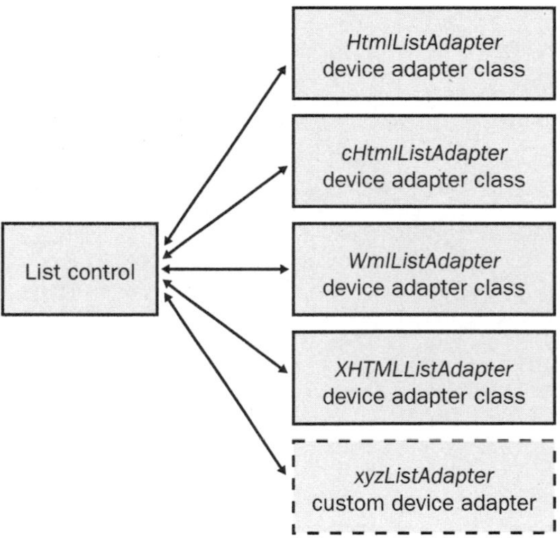

Figure 22-1 The control class works with a set of device adapter classes

When a particular client request reaches the server, the ASP.NET Mobile Controls Runtime identifies the client by examining the User-Agent string passed in the HTTP headers. The runtime looks up the device in the list of supported devices and assigns the appropriate *device adapter set* to the request. A device adapter set contains one device adapter class for each of the mobile controls. All device adapter classes in one set are related in that they support the same type of client device, such as WML 1.1, HTML 3.2, cHTML 1.0, or XHTML. Figure 22-2 shows the device adapters grouped in device adapter sets.

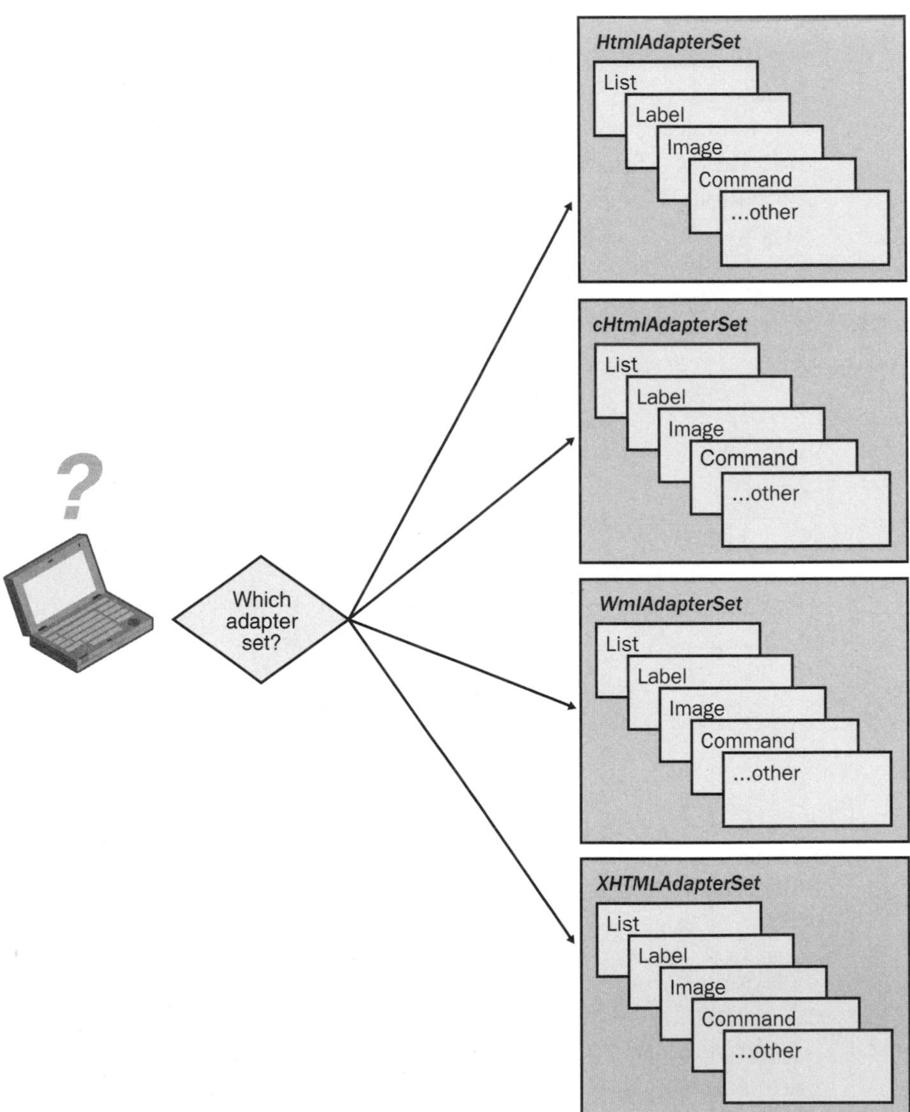

Figure 22-2 After receiving the client request, the runtime identifies the client browser and assigns the appropriate device adapter set to it.

When you write controls from scratch, you must write device adapters for each type of device you want to support and configure your application to include them in the appropriate device adapter set. When the runtime receives a client request, it identifies the client browser and assigns the appropriate device adapter set. During the processing of the request, each mobile control used in the mobile page will work with its device adapter in the selected set to create the markup that returns to the client, as shown in Figure 22-3. The *Adapter* property of the control class references the currently selected adapter class, and the *Control* property of the adapter points the other way. (Refer to Chapter 19 for additional details about configuring device adapter sets and device support.)

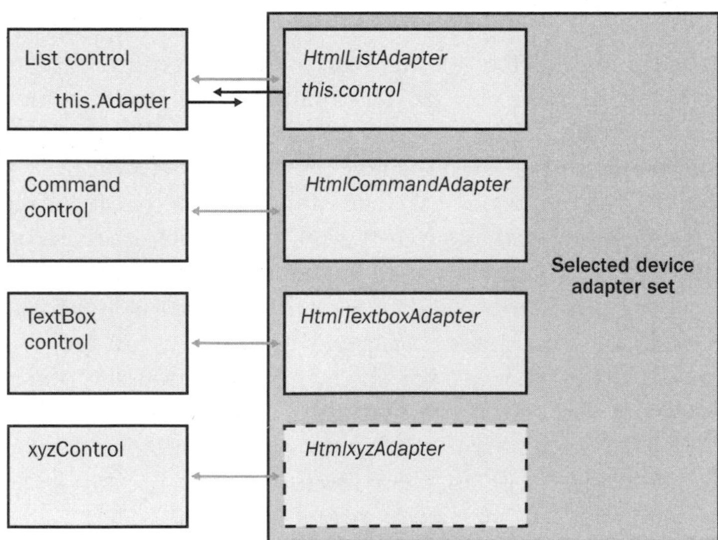

Figure 22-3 Each control creates the markup to return to the client by working with its device adapter in the selected device adapter set.

A device adapter class can be very simple, consisting of little more than a *Render* method that outputs the required markup. However, there is no limit on the device-specific logic that you can implement in a device adapter class. You can also build complex device adapters that create new child controls or paged output on one device but not another. For example, consider the differences in rendering and using a Calendar control on a WML device and on an HTML 3.2 device. On an HTML device with a large screen, the calendar control displays in a single screen of output, but on small-screen devices, the process of selecting a date involves many screens of output and numerous client-server interactions. The device adapter class for the Calendar control implements part of the relatively complex logic required to make this happen.

Extensible Device Support Architecture

The first release of ASP.NET Mobile Controls—the Microsoft Mobile Internet Toolkit—supported a number of WML 1.1 and WML 1.2 devices, HTML 3.2 clients such as Pocket Internet Explorer, and cHTML 1.0 devices. ASP.NET's device support architecture is extensible. Therefore, updates to ASP.NET Mobile Controls will support additional genres; Device Update 2 adds support for XHTML-MP and WML 2.0. If you don't want to wait for Microsoft to release support for a new class of device, you can add the necessary support yourself.

Custom device adapters aren't always required for every new device. Microsoft-supplied device adapters often will yield good results for new devices, particularly with new models in an existing family of devices from a particular manufacturer. Most new devices that come out use browsers that support exactly the same markup language as other devices on the market. However, with the relentless pace of change of mobile internet technology, devices appear fairly frequently that support new markup languages, or variants of existing ones. If the default rendering implemented by the device adapters provided for a particular class of client isn't suitable, Microsoft encourages developers to build custom device adapters to take advantage of the unique capabilities of the new devices. For this reason, Microsoft shipped the source of all the standard device adapters with the Mobile Internet Toolkit. If you're using Microsoft Visual Studio .NET 2002 and the Mobile Internet Toolkit, you'll find these sources in the Program Files/Mobile Internet Toolkit/Adapter Sources folder on your system. Device adapter sources for ASP.NET 1.1 are very similar to those that were shipped with the Mobile Internet Toolkit and are available online; go to *http://go.microsoft.com/fwlink/?LinkId=6350* to download the ASP.NET 1.1 Device Adapter source code.

> **Tip** New versions of markup languages are generally backward compatible with their predecessors. Therefore, if you have a new client that supports a more recent version of markup than your application supports, you don't necessarily have to write a new device adapter class. For example, WML 1.3 and 2.0 browsers still support WML 1.1 markup. Therefore, if you want to use your existing applications with a new WML 1.3 device, you can use existing device adapter classes. However, if you want to take advantage of the new features available in a new markup, you might need to write a new device adapter specifically for that version.

Working with the Device Adapter Sources

Creating a new project in Microsoft Visual Studio .NET is the easiest way to work with device adapters. You add the existing Microsoft-supplied device adapter sources to the project, modify the source code, and optionally add your own new device adapter classes. You then compile all the code into a new assembly that you can deploy on your Web server and use in your applications. Here are the steps you need to take:

1. In Visual Studio .NET, create a new Microsoft Visual C# project of type Class Library. Name the project Custom Adapters (or a different name, if you prefer).

2. Delete the Class1.cs class file that Visual Studio .NET creates for you. Right-click the project in Solution Explorer, and choose Add, then Add Existing Item. In the Add Existing Item dialog box, navigate to the folder where you have stored the device adapter sources, and add to your project all the C# files shown there.

3. Right-click the project in Solution Explorer, and choose Add Reference. In the .NET pane, locate the Mobile Internet Controls Runtime (*System.Web.Mobile.dll*) and the *System.Web.dll* components, and add these to your project.

4. The device adapter sources are the same sources used to compile the device adapters defined in the *System.Web.UI.MobileControls.Adapters* namespace in the runtime assembly, and these sources use the same class names. If you compile an assembly containing all these sources and you try to use it, the runtime will report a namespace clash. This is because the runtime can't distinguish between the two classes—for example, it can't differentiate between *System.Web.UI.MobileControls.Adapters.HtmlFormAdapter* and the same class in the same namespace in your own assembly.

5. Fortunately, the supplied sources use conditional compilation to define the namespace to which the classes belong. If the application defines the COMPILING_FOR_SHIPPED_SOURCE compilation constant, the runtime declares the device adapter sources in the *System.Web.UI.MobileControls.ShippedAdapterSource* namespace instead. In Visual Studio .NET, you define this constant by right-clicking the project in Solution Explorer and choosing Properties. Select the Configuration Properties folder in the left tree of the Property Pages window, choose the Build option, and enter **;COMPILING_FOR_SHIPPED_SOURCE** after any existing constants in the Conditional Compilation Constant box.

6. Create any new device adapters for your custom controls, or modify the source for existing controls. You can create these new adapters in the *System.Web.UI.MobileControls.ShippedAdapterSource* namespace or in a namespace of your own. When you've finished, compile the project. Doing so will build a new assembly containing all the device adapters.

7. To use the new assembly, create a new mobile Web project, right-click on the project in Solution Explorer, and choose Add Reference. Browse to the dynamic-link library (DLL) containing the custom adapters, and add it to your project. You'll also need to configure the project to use custom adapters by updating the Web.config file. To make this easy, Microsoft supplies the Web.config-shippedAdapters file along with the device adapter sources. Paste the contents of this file into the Web.config file of your mobile Web application. You'll need to add lines to each adapter set defined in Web.config for each new custom control that you create. You'll find examples of these code lines in the description of the simple custom control in the next section. Refer to Chapter 19 for the complete details of the format of this configuration data.

> **Note** You don't have to compile your own device adapters into the same assembly as the device adapter sources. However, doing so gives you an advantage when starting out because you'll frequently refer to existing device adapter sources when developing your own. Adding the supplied sources into the same Visual Studio .NET project makes this easier.

Building Simple Custom Controls and Device Adapters

Throughout the rest of this chapter, you'll build a custom control that works much like a List control. As you increase the complexity of this control, you'll learn many of the techniques you'll use as a custom control developer.

By default, the List control is rendered as an HTML table on devices such as the Pocket PC and as a list of static text (or anchors) on WML devices. The first control you'll build in this section is a dedicated table control. This control is rendered as a two-column table on HTML and WML devices. Note that you can create a list that is rendered as a two-column table on WML devices if you use the standard List control and an appropriate template. However, the custom control we're building achieves this functionality without using a template.

A Simple Control with Device Adapters for HTML and WML

The CMTable control shown in Listing 22-1 allows the page developer to specify the column 1 and column 2 text values as properties: *Item1Text* and *Item2Text*. The *Title* property allows you to specify a title string, which some WML browsers display at the head of a table. At present, you can output only a single table row. This control inherits from *System.Web.UI.MobileControls.MobileControl* and needs very little code to provide basic functionality.

```
using System;
using System.Web.UI.MobileControls;

namespace MSPress.MobWeb.CustomControls
{
    /// <summary>
    /// Simple example of a custom control built from scratch
    /// </summary>
    public class CMTable : MobileControl
    {
        private String _title, _item1Text, _item2Text;
        public CMTable()
        {
            Title = "";
            Item1Text = "";
            Item2Text = "";
        }

        /// <summary>
        /// Gets and sets the text that
        /// can be displayed as a title
        /// </summary>
        public String Title
        {
            get { return _title; }
            set {_title = value; }
        }

        /// <summary>
        /// Gets and sets the text displayed in column 1
        /// </summary>
        public String Item1Text
```

Listing 22-1 Simple custom control that allows you to specify a *Title* property as well as two properties that represent the items in a two-column table with only one row

```
        {
            get { return _item1Text; }
            set {_item1Text = value; }
        }
        /// <summary>
        /// Gets and sets the text displayed in column 2
        /// </summary>
        public String Item2Text
        {
            get { return _item2Text; }
            set { _item2Text = value; }
        }
    }
}
```

To build the assembly containing this control, use Visual Studio .NET to create a project of type Class Library. Give the project a suitable name, such as CustomMobileControlLibrary. Then add a reference to the ASP.NET Mobile Controls Runtime assembly (System.Web.Mobile.dll) as well as System.Web.dll, and add a class file to the project that contains the source that Listing 22-1 shows. Finally, compile the class file.

Two device adapter classes contain the rendering logic for this control. One class applies to HTML and cHTML clients, and the other applies to WML clients. These two classes appear in Listings 22-2 and 22-3, respectively.

```
using System;
using System.Web.UI.MobileControls;
using System.Web.UI.MobileControls.Adapters;
using MSPress.MobWeb.CustomControls;

namespace MSPress.MobWeb.CustomControls.Adapters
{
    public class HtmlCMTableAdapter : HtmlControlAdapter
    {
        protected new CMTable Control
        {
            get
            {
                return (CMTable)base.Control;
            }
        }

        public override void Render(HtmlMobileTextWriter writer)
        {
            String tableSuffix = "";
```

Listing 22-2 Device adapter for the CMTable control for HTML and cHTML browsers

```
            Alignment alignment =
                (Alignment)Style[Style.AlignmentKey, true];
            if(alignment != Alignment.NotSet && alignment != Alignment.Left)
            {
                writer.Write("<div align=\"");
                writer.Write(alignment.ToString());
                writer.WriteLine("\">");
                tableSuffix = "\r\n</div>";
            }

            writer.AddAttribute("width","90%");
            writer.AddAttribute("cellpadding", "3");
            writer.RenderBeginTag("table");
            writer.WriteLine("");
            writer.Write("<tr><td>");
            writer.EnterFormat(Style);
            writer.WriteEncodedText(Control.Item1Text);
            writer.ExitFormat(Style);
            writer.WriteLine("</td>");
            writer.Write("<td>");
            writer.EnterFormat(Style);
            writer.WriteEncodedText(Control.Item2Text);
            writer.ExitFormat(Style);
            writer.WriteLine("</td></tr>");
            writer.RenderEndTag();
            writer.WriteLine(tableSuffix);
        }
    }
}
```

```
using System;
using System.Web.UI.MobileControls;
using System.Web.UI.MobileControls.Adapters;
using MSPress.MobWeb.CustomControls;

namespace MSPress.MobWeb.CustomControls.Adapters
{
    public class WmlCMTableAdapter : WmlControlAdapter
    {
        protected new CMTable Control
        {
            get
            {
                return (CMTable)base.Control;
            }
        }
```

Listing 22-3 Device adapter for the CMTable control for WML browsers

```
public override void Render(WmlMobileTextWriter writer)
        {
            Alignment alignment =
                (Alignment)Style[Style.AlignmentKey, true];
            String alignID;
            switch (alignment)
            {
                case Alignment.Center:
                    alignID = "C";
                    break;
                case Alignment.Right:
                    alignID = "R";
                    break;
                default:
                    alignID = "L";
                    break;
            }

            //Write beginning of table
            writer.EnterLayout(Style);
            writer.EnterFormat(Style);
            writer.RenderText("<table", false, false);
            if (Control.Title.Length > 0)
                writer.WriteAttribute("title", Control.Title);
            writer.WriteAttribute("align", alignID + alignID);
            writer.WriteAttribute("columns", "2");
            writer.WriteLine(">");

            //First datacell
            writer.Write("<tr><td>");
            writer.RenderText(Control.Item1Text, true);
            writer.RenderText("</td><td>", false, false);
            //second datacell
            writer.RenderText(Control.Item2Text, true);
            writer.RenderText("</td></tr>", false, false);
            writer.WriteLine("</table>");

            //close table and output a trailing break
            writer.ExitFormat(Style);
            writer.ExitLayout(Style, true);
        }
    }
}
```

You must compile these classes into an assembly the same way you do for the control classes. You can place these classes in their own assembly, or you can include them in the same project as the control classes and compile everything into one assembly.

Listings 22-2 and 22-3 demonstrate a requirement of all device adapters: that they have a strongly typed property named *Control*. This property returns a *Control* object that's cast to the type of the control class for this adapter. The page framework uses this property to associate a device adapter class with its corresponding control class.

Writing Device Markup with the *MobileTextWriter* Classes

The page framework calls the *Render* method, passing as a parameter a class that descends from the *System.Web.UI.MobileControls.Adapters.MobileTextWriter* class. Specifically, the method passes an instance of *WmlMobileTextWriter* for device adapters that inherit from *WmlControlAdapter*, and *HtmlMobileTextWriter* for those that inherit from *HtmlControlAdapter*. You use *MobileTextWriter*-derived classes to output the markup that is sent to the client.

These *MobileTextWriter*-derived classes have many methods that simplify outputting the markup you need. For example, *WriteBeginTag("tagName")* starts a new element, and *WriteAttribute("name", "value")* outputs an attribute in an element. *WriteBreak* outputs a break tag. *WriteText("text")* and *WriteEncodedText("text")* write text to the output stream, with the option of encoding the text to represent special characters correctly for the target device. *WriteLine("text")* does the same thing, but it appends a carriage return so that the generated markup formats agreeably for a human reader. Furthermore, many methods make it easier to output specific elements such as *<anchor>* tags or to output text using emphasis elements. By using these methods, you'll be less likely to make errors that are hard to spot in the output markup.

Handling Style Attributes in Device Adapters

All mobile controls support the same set of style properties, such as *ForeColor*, *BackColor*, *Font* and so on, as explained back in Chapter 4. Most style attributes are advisory—that is, text output to a client will honor these attributes only if the client device supports them. It is the code in the device adapter class that must decide whether a style property that the developer has set on the control is translated to emphasis elements in the markup that is sent to the client. Clearly, setting *ForeColor* to *Red* should work with a color HTML browser but have no effect on a monochrome WML 1.1 browser. Fortunately, the *MobileTextWriter* classes make it very easy to output the emphasis elements you want in the appropriate device markup language. Below is a list of the *MobileTextWriter* methods you'll use most. All these methods take a parameter of type *Style*. All the style-related properties that the page developer sets on a mobile control are encapsulated in a *Style* object, which is exposed by the *Style* property of the *ControlAdapter* class, the base class of all the device adapter classes you'll write.

- ***EnterLayout(Style style)*** Starts a new paragraph block, applying style attributes encapsulated in a Style object.
- ***ExitLayout(Style style)*** Closes a paragraph block.
- ***EnterStyle(Style style)*** Writes character-formatting start tags.
- ***ExitStyle(Style style)*** Writes character-formatting end tags.

If you create a new device adapter for a WML device, your class should inherit from *System.Web.UI.MobileControls.WmlControlAdapter*. If you create a device adapter for an HTML device, it inherits from *System.Web.UI.MobileControls.HtmlControlAdapter*. The implementations of the *EnterLayout*, *ExitLayout*, *EnterStyle,* and *ExitStyle* methods in the *WmlControlAdapter* and *HtmlControlAdapter* classes know about the limitations of the class of device for which they are intended, so they return only appropriate markup without embedding emphasis attributes that would not work on those devices. In most cases, to ensure that the correct style attributes are set when outputting markup to the device, just call the appropriate *MobileTextWriter* method, passing it the *Style* property of the device adapter class, for example:

```
writer.EnterLayout(this.Style);  // can leave off the 'this.' for brevity
```

Rendering Text After *EnterLayout* and *EnterStyle*

In WML device adapters, you should always use the *RenderText* method to output markup immediately after calls to *EnterLayout* and *EnterStyle*. Don't use *Write** methods or *RenderBeginTag* because the *EnterLayout* and *EnterStyle* methods of *WmlMobileTextWriter* tell the rendering logic only that you would like paragraph and character formatting tags to be output; they don't actually render the tags. The *RenderText* method calls methods that are responsible for emitting the formatting tags, if they have been requested.

For example, the following code doesn't output paragraph and formatting tags as you might expect:

```
writer.EnterLayout(Style);
writer.EnterFormat(Style);
writer.WriteBeginTag("table");
```

Instead, use the *RenderText* method:

```
writer.EnterLayout(Style);
writer.EnterFormat(Style);
writer.RenderText("table", false, false);
```

HtmlMobileTextWriter doesn't have the same restrictions.

In addition to these methods, you can query individual style attributes from the control's *Style* object. The *Style* object defines some constants, such as *Style.AlignmentKey*, *Style.BoldKey*, and *Style.ItalicKey*. You use these constants to index the *Style* object's properties. The *WmlCMTableAdapter* shown in Listing 22-3 uses the *Style* object to determine the alignment that you requested for this control. Here's the syntax:

```
Alignment alignment =
                (Alignment)Style[Style.AlignmentKey, true];
```

The second parameter in this code is a Boolean that indicates whether the page framework should retrieve style attributes that apply directly to the control (*false*) or whether it should use style inheritance (*true*). If the page framework uses style inheritance to determine the style attribute, it applies the styles attributes inherited from the control's container, such as a Panel or Form control.

Using Custom Controls and Device Adapters

The procedure for using a custom control built from scratch is essentially the same as the procedure for using controls built by inheritance or composition. You add references to the assemblies that contain the custom controls and device adapters to your mobile Web project. And you use and declare custom mobile controls in the same way, as Listing 22-4 shows.

```
<%@ Register TagPrefix="CMcustom" Namespace="MSPress.MobWeb.CustomControls"
    Assembly="CustomMobileControlLibrary" %>
<%@ Register TagPrefix="mobile"
    Namespace="System.Web.UI.MobileControls"
    Assembly="System.Web.Mobile" %>
<%@ Page language="c#"
    Inherits="System.Web.UI.MobileControls.MobilePage" %>

<mobile:form id="Form1" runat="server" Alignment="Center">
    <CMcustom:CMTable id="CmTable1" title="A title" runat="server"
        StyleReference="title" Font-Size="Small"
        Item1Text="Simple" Item2Text="Table" >
    </CMcustom: CMTable>
    <CMcustom: CMTable id="CmTable2" runat="server"
        Item1Text="second" Item2Text="table"
        Font-Size="Large" Font-Bold="False" Font-Italic="True"
        Alignment="Left">
    </CMcustom: CMTable>
</mobile:form>
```

Listing 22-4 Mobile Web Forms page using the CMsimple one-row table control

For this application to run, you must configure new device adapter set definitions in the application's Web.config file. Edit (or add if it's not already there) the *<mobileControls>...</mobileControls>* section in the Web.config file. You must define new adapter sets that inherit from the standard device adapter sets (which are defined in the machine.config file in \Windows\microsoft.NET\Framework\version\CONFIG) and add in the configuration for the new custom control and its corresponding device adapters, as Listing 22-5 shows.

```
<configuration>
  <system.web>
    ⋮
    <mobileControls
        sessionStateHistorySize="6"
        cookielessDataDictionaryType="System.Web.Mobile.CookielessData">
        <device name="CMcustomHtmlDeviceAdapters"
                inheritsFrom="HtmlDeviceAdapters">
           <control
name="MSPress.MobWeb.CustomControls.CMTable,CustomMobileControlLibrary"
adapter="MSPress.MobWeb.CustomControls.Adapters.HtmlCMTableAdapter,
 CustomMobileControlLibrary" />
       </device>
       <device name="CMcustomcHtmlDeviceAdapters"
               inheritsFrom="ChtmlDeviceAdapters">
           <control
name="MSPress.MobWeb.CustomControls.CMTable,CustomMobileControlLibrary"
adapter="MSPress.MobWeb.CustomControls.Adapters.HtmlCMTableAdapter,
 CustomMobileControlLibrary" />
       </device>
       <device name="CMcustomUpWmlDeviceAdapters"
               inheritsFrom="UpWmlDeviceAdapters">
           <control
name="MSPress.MobWeb.CustomControls.CMTable,CustomMobileControlLibrary"
adapter="MSPress.MobWeb.CustomControls.Adapters.WmlCMTableAdapter,
 CustomMobileControlLibrary" />
       </device>
       <device name="CMcustomWmlDeviceAdapters"
               inheritsFrom="WmlDeviceAdapters">
           <control
name="MSPress.MobWeb.CustomControls.CMTable,CustomMobileControlLibrary"
adapter="MSPress.MobWeb.CustomControls.Adapters.WmlCMTableAdapter,
 CustomMobileControlLibrary" />
       </device>
     </mobileControls>
  </system.web>
</configuration>
```

Listing 22-5 Configuration of custom device adapter sets in Web.config, with long lines wrapped for readability (from `<control` to next closing `/>` tag)

You define each mapping of a control and a device adapter by using this syntax:

```
<control name= "controlName, assembly" adapter="adapterName, assembly" />
```

In this listing, the control class and the device adapters reside in the same assembly named *CustomMobileControlLibrary.dll*. Each *<device>...</device>* section defines a device adapter set. You must give these sets a unique name—our example uses the names *CMcustomHtmlDeviceAdapters, CMcustomcHtmlDeviceAdapters, CMcustomUpWmlDeviceAdapters and CMcustomWmlDeviceAdapters*. Add to each adapter set a line mapping your custom control to a device adapter. The *Html* and *cHtml* device adapter sets are configured to use the CMTable control with the *HtmlCMTableAdapter* device adapter, and the *UpWml* device adapter set (for Openwave Wml browsers) and the *Wml* device adapter set are configured to use the CMTable control with the *WmlCMTableAdapter* device adapter.

With this Web.config file in place, the application will run and will yield the results shown in Figure 22-4.

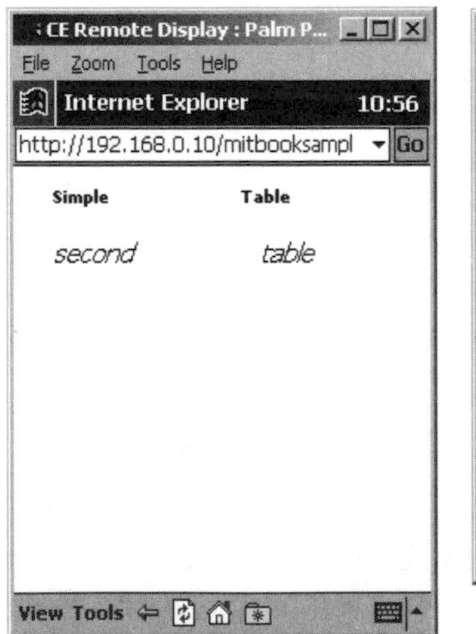

Figure 22-4 The mobile Web Forms page in Listing 22-4 outputs two single-row tables using a variety of style attributes.

A version of the CMTable control named CMSimple in the companion material on this book's Web site implements the functionality described so far.

Building a Data Bound Custom Control

A table control that displays only a single row isn't very useful. A table control becomes truly useful when you can data-bind it so that items from an array or a collection provide the data listed. We'll now enhance the CMTable control to implement data binding in a similar fashion to a SelectionList or List control. In the companion material on this book's Web site, you'll find a custom control named CMTableDB that implements the functionality described in this section.

To support data binding, perform the following steps:

1. Add a property of type *ICollection* in which you specify the data source. Name this property *DataSource* to remain consistent with existing data bound controls.
2. If you want to support binding to data sources of type *IListSource* (such as Microsoft ADO.NET datasets), add a property of type *String*, conventionally named *DataMember*. Through this property, you can specify the name of the data member (or data table) to extract from the source. Be aware that the example given here supports only data sources of type *IEnumerable*. Therefore, the code doesn't implement a *DataMember* property.
3. Add *String* properties that specify which data items to extract from each row of the data source. The CMTableDB control contains the *DataTextField1* and *DataTextField2* properties, which specify the items to display in column 1 and column 2. The control also contains the *DataValueField* property (to remain consistent with the SelectionList and List controls). This property specifies a hidden data value that the application stores with each list item.
4. When this control reads through the source data as it is data-binding, it must extract the data items indicated by the *DataTextField1*, *DataTextField2*, and *DataValueField* properties and store them in an object. The list items in the CMTableDB control are very similar to the *MobileListItem* objects the SelectionList and List controls use. The *MobileListItem* object has *DataItem*, *Text*, and *Value* properties. These three properties store a reference to the data row, the display value, and the hidden value, respectively. In the CMTableDB control, you must also store the value that the second column displays (the value of the *DataTextField2* field). Thus, you must create a new class named *CMTableListItem*, which inherits from *MobileListItem*. This class implements the additional property *Text2*, which you use to store the second column value. Listing 22-6 shows this class.

5. Store the *CMTableListItem* objects that represent the list entries in a collection (which the *CMTableDB* class exposes as a property) so that you can access and manipulate them. Like the existing List controls, the CMTableDB control has a property named *Items*, which grants access to the *MobileListItemCollection* that contains the *CMTableListItem* objects.

6. The *DataBind* method performs the actual process of reading the data source, building the *CMTableListItem* objects, and inserting the objects into the *MobileListItemCollection* object. This method, shown in Listing 22-7, uses reflection to determine the field names of the data item at runtime. If the data item possesses a field with a name that matches any of the field names that the *DataTextField1*, *DataTextField2*, or *DataValueField* properties specify, it stores the values in the *Text*, *Text2*, and *Value* properties of a *CMTableListItem* object.

Listing 22-7 shows the source code for this control. This listing also includes support for pagination, which we'll explain in the next section.

```
using System;
using System.Web.UI.MobileControls;

namespace MSPress.MobWeb.CustomControls
{
    /// <summary>
    /// Stores details of items displayed in the CMTableDB control.
    /// </summary>
    public class CMTableListItem : MobileListItem
    {
        // Add a property to hold text displayed in column 2.
        private String _text2;

        public String Text2
        {
            get { return _text2; }
            set { _text2 = value; }
        }

        public CMTableListItem() : base()
        {
            Text2 = "";
        }
```

Listing 22-6 The *CMTableListItem* class that stores the list item details inherits most of its functionality from *MobileListItem* but adds the *Text2* property to store the item that the second column uses.

```
        public CMTableListItem(
            System.Object dataItem,
            System.String text,
            System.String text2,
            System.String value)
            : base (dataItem, text, value)
        {
            Text2 = text2;
        }
    }
}
```

```
using System;
using System.Collections;
using System.Reflection;
using System.Web.UI.MobileControls;

namespace MSPress.MobWeb.CustomControls
{
    /// <summary>
    /// Custom control built from scratch using data binding.
    /// This control inherits from PagedControl rather than MobileControl.
    /// </summary>
    public class CMTable : PagedControl
    {
        private ICollection _dataSource = null;
        private MobileListItemCollection _items =
            new MobileListItemCollection();
        private String _title, _dataTextField1, _dataTextField2,
            _dataValueField;

        public CMTable()
        {
            Title = "";
            DataTextField1 = "";
            DataTextField2 = "";
            DataValueField = "";
        }

        public ICollection DataSource
        {
            get { return _dataSource; }
            set { _dataSource = value; }
        }
```

Listing 22-7 The CMTable control enhanced to support data binding

```
/// <summary>
/// Gets and sets the field displayed in the first column.
/// </summary>
public String DataTextField1
{
    get { return _dataTextField1; }
    set { _dataTextField1 = value; }
}
/// <summary>
/// Gets and sets the field displayed in the second column.
/// </summary>
public String DataTextField2
{
    get { return _dataTextField2; }
    set { _dataTextField2 = value; }
}

/// <summary>
/// Gets and sets the field stored as a hidden value.
/// </summary>
public String DataValueField
{
    get { return _dataValueField; }
    set { _dataValueField = value; }
}

/// <summary>
/// Gets the collection of items displayed in the table.
/// </summary>
public MobileListItemCollection Items
{
    get { return _items; } }

//InternalItemCount and ItemWeight are necessary to
//support pagination.
protected override int InternalItemCount
{
    get { return Items.Count; }
}

// This method can be implemented in the device adapter
// classes if the representation differs from device to device.
// However, an item in this control always takes up one line.
protected override Int32 ItemWeight
{
    get { return ControlPager.DefaultWeight; }
}

/// <summary>
/// Gets and sets the title displayed on some WML devices.
```

```
        /// </summary>
        public String Title
        {
            get { return _title; }
            set { _title = value; }
        }

        // Override DataBind method of base class to implement
        // data binding logic.
        public override void DataBind()
        {

            // Evaluate data binding expressions on the control itself.
            base.OnDataBinding(EventArgs.Empty);

            if (DataSource != null)
            {
                // Iterate DataSource.
                IEnumerator dataEnum = DataSource.GetEnumerator();
                while(dataEnum.MoveNext())
                {
                    // Create new item for each data item.
                    CMTableListItem item =
                        new CMTableListItem(dataEnum.Current,"","","");

                    System.Type objectType = dataEnum.Current.GetType();
                    PropertyInfo aProp =
                        objectType.GetProperty(this.DataTextField1);
                    if (aProp != null)
                        item.Text =
                      aProp.GetValue(dataEnum.Current,null).ToString();
                    aProp = objectType.GetProperty(this.DataTextField2);
                    if (aProp != null)
                        item.Text2 = aProp.GetValue
                                       (dataEnum.Current,null).ToString();
                    aProp = objectType.GetProperty(this.DataValueField);
                    if (aProp != null)
                        item.Value = aProp.GetValue
                                       (dataEnum.Current,null).ToString();

                    // Add item to the MobileListItemCollection.
                    _items.Add(item);

                    // Add the TableListItem as a Child control
                    this.Controls.Add(item);
                }
            }
        }
    }
}
```

In the *Render* method of the device adapter classes, you use the *Items* property of the CMTable control class to iterate through the *MobileListItemCollection*, which outputs the markup for each item in the list. Listing 22-8 shows the source for *HtmlCMTableAdapter*. The device adapter for Wml clients, *WmlCMTableAdapter* isn't shown here, but implements similar logic to *HtmlCMTableAdapter*. Notice that the adapter uses the *Control.FirstVisibleItemIndex* and *Control.VisibleItemCount* properties, set by the page framework at run time, to support pagination. You must use these properties to specify which items to output during rendering. How you support pagination is explained fully in the next section. You can find the source for the *CMTableDB*, *CMTableListItem*, *HtmlCMTableDBAdapter*, and *WmlCMTableDBAdapter* classes in the companion material on this book's Web site, along with all the other sample code.

```
using System;
using System.Web.UI;
using System.Web.UI.MobileControls;
using System.Web.UI.MobileControls.Adapters;
using MSPress.MobWeb.CustomControls;

namespace MSPress.MobWeb.CustomControls.Adapters
{
    /**
     * HtmlCMTableAdapter class
     */
    public class HtmlCMTableAdapter : HtmlControlAdapter
    {
        protected new CMTable Control
        {
            get { return (CMTable)base.Control; }
        }

        public override void Render(HtmlMobileTextWriter writer)
        {
            MobileListItemCollection items = Control.Items;
            if (items.Count == 0)
            {
                return;
            }

            int pageStart = Control.FirstVisibleItemIndex;
            int pageSize = Control.VisibleItemCount;
            if (items.Count < pageSize) pageSize = items.Count;
```

Listing 22-8 HTML device adapter for the CMTable control that supports data binding. The *Render* method walks the items held in the control's *MobileListItemCollection* and outputs the appropriate markup for each.

```
            String tableSuffix = "";
            Alignment alignment =
                (Alignment)Style[Style.AlignmentKey, true];
            if(alignment != Alignment.NotSet && alignment != Alignment.Left)
            {
                writer.Write("<div align=\"");
                writer.Write(alignment.ToString());
                writer.WriteLine("\">");
                tableSuffix = "\r\n</div>";
            }

            writer.AddAttribute("width","90%");
            writer.AddAttribute("cellpadding", "3");
            writer.RenderBeginTag("table");
            writer.WriteLine("");
            for (int i = 0; i < pageSize; i++)
            {
                CMTableListItem item =
                    (CMTableListItem)(items[pageStart + i]);
                writer.Write("<tr><td>");
                writer.EnterFormat(Style);
                writer.WriteEncodedText(item.Text);
                writer.ExitFormat(Style);
                writer.Write("</td><td>");
                writer.EnterFormat(Style);
                writer.WriteEncodedText(item.Text2);
                writer.ExitFormat(Style);
                writer.WriteLine("</td></tr>");
            }
            writer.RenderEndTag();
            writer.WriteLine(tableSuffix);
        }
    }
}
```

Supporting Internal and Custom Pagination

Any control that can produce a large amount of output should support pagination. If you use a large data collection with the data bound CMTable control and the containing Form control has its *Paginate* property set to *True*, you should allow the control to output a subset of items so that it pages across multiple screens.

Implementing support for pagination is easy, if you follow these steps:

1. The control class must inherit from *PagedControl* rather than *Mobile-Control*, as the CMTable control now does. This class automatically implements the features that you'll use for custom pagination, such as the *ItemCount* public property and the *LoadItems* public event.

2. Override the *InternalItemCount* method to return the number of items currently in the control.

   Override the *ItemWeight* property to return a value that indicates to the page framework how much display area a single line from the control consumes. When determining how many controls and list items to fit on a single display screen, the framework queries each control for its *ItemWeight* property. The framework does this before assigning each control and list item to a display page. A single display line consumes a nominal weight of 100 units in the default unit system that the page framework uses. This quantity is available in the *ControlPager.DefaultWeight* constant. The *ItemWeight* property of the CMTable control returns this constant, as each item in the list occupies one display line.

3. The page framework sets the control's *Control.FirstVisibleItemIndex* and *Control.VisibleItemCount* properties to indicate the first item the control must display and how many items it should display, respectively. The code you write for the *Render* method in device adapter classes must use this information to determine which items to output, as Listing 22-8 shows.

This is how you declare a mobile Web Forms page to use this control:

```
<mobile:form id="Form2" runat="server" Paginate="True">
    <CMcustom:CMTable id="CmTableDB1" runat="server" />
</mobile:form>
```

In the *Page_Load* method, the runtime builds the array and the control binds to it. Here is the code-behind class.

```
public class MobileWebForm1 : System.Web.UI.MobileControls.MobilePage
{
    protected System.Web.UI.MobileControls.Form Form1;
    protected CMTable CmTableDB1;

    private void Page_Load(object sender, System.EventArgs e)
    {

        // Create large array to illustrate pagination.
        ArrayList array = new ArrayList();
        array.Add(new TeamStats("Dunes",1,38,24,8,6,80));
        array.Add(new TeamStats("Phoenix",2,38,20,10,8,70));
        array.Add(new TeamStats("Eagles",3,38,20,9,9,69));
        array.Add(new TeamStats("Zodiac",4,38,20,8,10,68));
        array.Add(new TeamStats("Arches",5,38,20,6,12,66));
        array.Add(new TeamStats("Chows",6,38,17,10,11,61));
```

```
        array.Add(new TeamStats("Creation",7,38,15,12,11,57));
        array.Add(new TeamStats("Illusion",8,38,13,15,10,54));
        array.Add(new TeamStats("Torpedo",9,38,14,10,14,52));
        array.Add(new TeamStats("Generals", 10,38,14,10,14,52));
        array.Add(new TeamStats("Reaction",11,38,14,9,15,51));
        array.Add(new TeamStats("Peanuts",12,38,13,10,15,49));
        array.Add(new TeamStats("Caverns",13,38,14,6,18,48));
        array.Add(new TeamStats("Eclipse",14,38,9,15,14,42));
        array.Add(new TeamStats("Dragons", 15,38,10,12,16,42));
        array.Add(new TeamStats("Cosmos",16,38,11,9,18,42));

        CmTableDB1.DataSource = array;
        CmTableDB1.DataTextField1 = "TeamName";
        CmTableDB1.DataTextField2 = "Points";
        CmTableDB1.DataValueField = "Position";
        CmTableDB1.DataBind();
    }
    class TeamStats
    {
        private String  _teamName;
        private int _position, _played, _won, _drawn, _lost, _points;

        public TeamStats(String teamName,
            int position,
            int played,
            int won,
            int drawn,
            int lost,
            int points)
        {
            this._teamName = teamName;
            this._position = position;
            this._played = played;
            this._won = won;
            this._drawn = drawn;
            this._lost = lost;
            this._points = points;
        }

        public String TeamName { get { return this._teamName; } }
        public int    Position { get { return this._position; } }
        public int    Played   { get { return this._played; } }
        public int    Won      { get { return this._won; } }
        public int    Drawn    { get { return this._drawn; } }
        public int    Lost     { get { return this._lost; } }
        public int    Points   { get { return this._points; } }
    }
}
```

On a small handheld device, this class produces the output shown in Figure 22-5.

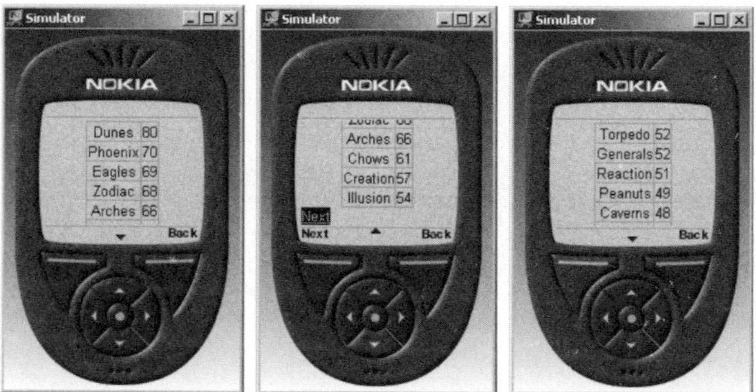

Figure 22-5 Paged output of the CMTable data bound control on the Nokia Simulator

Implementing the *OnDataBind* Event

You add public events to your control the same way you do for controls built by inheritance or composition. The standard data bound controls expose the *ItemDataBind* event, which an application developer can trap to implement custom data binding. It makes sense to implement this event for our custom control.

To implement the *ItemDataBind* event, declare a public delegate for the event handler. You declare this delegate in a source file, inside the namespace but outside any class definitions:

```
public delegate void CMTableListItemEventHandler(
    object sender,
    CMTableListItemEventArgs e);
```

The event handler takes a parameter of type *CMTableListItemEventArgs*. Here's how you define this object:

```
public sealed class CMTableListItemEventArgs : EventArgs
{
    private CMTableListItem item;

    public CMTableListItemEventArgs(CMTableListItem item)
    {
        this.item = item;
    }

    public CMTableListItem Item
```

```
    {
        get { return item; }
    }
}
```

You then declare the *ItemDataBind* event in the CMTable control class:

```
// Declare a static read-only object that will own the list of registered
// event handlers
private static readonly object EventItemDataBind = new object();

public event CMTableListItemEventHandler ItemDataBind
{
    add
    {
        Events.AddHandler(EventItemDataBind, value);
    }
    remove
    {
        Events.RemoveHandler(EventItemDataBind, value);
    }
}
```

Notice that this event uses the *MobileControl.Events.AddHandler* and *RemoveHandler* methods. This way to add and remove event handlers is an alternative to the technique we used in Chapter 21.

A mobile Web application developer using this control can write his or her own event handler method for the *ItemDataBind* event. You use the *OnItemDataBind* method to call out to the event handlers that the application developer declares:

```
protected virtual void OnItemDataBind(CMTableListItemEventArgs e)
    {
        CMTableListItemEventHandler onItemDataBindHandler =
            (CMTableListItemEventHandler)Events[EventItemDataBind];
        if (onItemDataBindHandler != null)
            onItemDataBindHandler(this, e);
    }
```

Finally, you call the *OnItemDataBind* method from within the *DataBind* method each time a new *CMTableListItem* is built while your control is reading through the data source, as shown in the following code. You must create a new *CMTableListItemEventArgs* object from the *CMTableListItem* and pass it as the argument to *OnItemDataBind*. By this mechanism, the control calls an *OnItemDataBind* event handler method that the application developer declares, providing an opportunity to customize the data binding behavior for a list item.

```
public override void DataBind()
{
    // Evaluate any data binding expressions on the control itself.
    base.OnDataBinding(EventArgs.Empty);

    if (DataSource != null)
    {
        // Iterate DataSource, creating a new item for each data item.
        IEnumerator dataEnum = DataSource.GetEnumerator();
        while(dataEnum.MoveNext())
        {
            // Create item
            CMTableListItem item =
new CMTableListItem(dataEnum.Current,"","","");
            ⋮
            //  intervening code not shown
            ⋮
            // Add item to the MobileListItemCollection of the control.
            _items.Add(item);

          // Add the TableListItem as a Child control
          this.Controls.Add(item);

            CMTableListItemEventArgs e = new CMTableListItemEventArgs (item);
            OnItemDataBind(e);
            // After any ItemDataBind events have been called, the
            // DataItem property has no purpose and is not relevant
            // on postback, so clear it.
            item.DataItem = null;
        }
    }
```

The sample files in the companion material on this book's Web site contain a version of the custom table control, CMTableEvents, which implements the *OnItemDataBind* event. The CustomControlExample sample is a mobile Web application that exercises all the controls in this chapter; it includes an example of the use of an *OnItemDataBind* event handler.

Supporting *ViewState* in a Custom Control

In its current stage of development, the custom Table control doesn't save *ViewState*. Therefore, to display the data from the data source, the runtime must data-bind the control on every request. We'll now develop the CMTable control further to save *ViewState*; this version of the control is called CMTableViewState in the samples available in the companion material on this book's Web site.

When you set the *EnableViewState* property of any ASP.NET server control to *true* (the default), you expect the control to retain its properties across HTTP request–response cycles—for example, the data the CMTable control displays should be saved across these cycles.

As a final stage before the page is rendered and the runtime sends the markup to the client, the page framework calls the *SaveViewState* method of every control for which *EnableViewState* is set to *true*. The control returns an object to the page framework, which contains all values and properties that it will save across requests. The page framework amalgamates all *ViewState* objects for all controls on the page and saves the state on the server in the *Session* object, as discussed in Chapter 12. The markup sent to the client includes a string token identifying the cached *ViewState*. Then the page framework tears down and discards the mobile page and all its controls on the server.

When the client posts back to the server for the next request, it posts back the *ViewState* token so that the page framework can retrieve the cached *ViewState* object from the *Session* object as part of rebuilding the mobile page and its controls. The page framework calls the *LoadViewState* method of every control, causing each control to restore its saved state from the *ViewState* cached at the end of the previous request.

Saving Control Properties to the *ViewState* Object

As with all the other forms of custom controls, if you want to save simple types (such as strings, integers, and simple arrays), you just store their value in the *ViewState* object. For example, the following code shows how you save the *Title* property of the CMTable custom control in *ViewState*:

```
public String Title
{
    get
        {
            return (String)ViewState["Title"];
        }
    set
        {
            ViewState["Title"] = value;
        }
}
```

If you save all states of your custom control this way, you don't need to do anything else to implement support for *ViewState*. The base class implementation of the *SaveViewState* and *LoadViewState* methods handles the saving and restoration of the contents of the *ViewState* object.

However, if you try to save a more complex object, such as the control's *MobileListItemCollection* object or the *CMTableListItem* object the control contains, the page framework generates an error. This is because the object isn't a simple type and doesn't support the *System.Runtime.Serialization.ISerializable* interface. (In other words, the object doesn't contain methods that save and restore the class to a format suitable for persistence). To save complex objects such as these, you must either implement *ISerializable* on the object you want to store, or override *SaveViewState* and *LoadViewState* in your control to implement custom *ViewState* handling.

Understanding the *IStateManager* Interface

SaveViewState and *LoadViewState* are required methods of the *System.Web.UI.IStateManager* interface. A third method of this interface is *TrackChanges*, which you call to instruct a server control to track changes to its state. The *IsTrackingViewState* property returns a Boolean value to indicate whether the control is tracking state. Together, these methods and this property make up the *IStateManager* interface. The page framework uses this interface to handle the saving and restoration of *ViewState* for all server controls on a page, as long as *EnableViewState* is *true* for that page and that control.

In the case of the CMTableViewState control, when the control binds to the data source, the runtime builds the *CMTableListItem* objects used to contain the items the list displays as we explained previously. After postback, the table should display the same data—meaning that you must save the *Text*, *Text2*, and *Value* properties of every *CMTableListItem* object in *ViewState*. You don't need to save the *DataItem* property. If you want the page framework to restore the control's state from *ViewState* on postback, the control won't bind to the data source again; because the data source is assumed not to be present on this request, you can't set the *DataItem* property to a meaningful value. Therefore, you should set the *DataItem* property, which points back to the source data item, to *Null*.

To correctly save *ViewState* for the CMTable control, perform the following steps. You can find the full source code in the CMTableViewState sample file in the companion material on this book's Web site.

1. Save properties of the CMTable control directly in the *ViewState* object, as we explained earlier when discussing the *Title* property.

2. Override the *SaveViewState* method. In your implementation of *SaveViewState*, first call the *SaveViewState* implementation of the *MobileControl* base class. This returns an object containing all objects stored directly in the *ViewState* object, such as the control properties

like *Title*. Then the code calls the *SaveViewState* method of all the *CMTableListItem* objects (implemented in step 5) to obtain their state. The application returns the resulting array of objects to the caller (the page framework) to store between requests. Here's the syntax, in the following code. For this and the *LoadViewState* method discussed next, you will need to import the *System.Web.UI* namespace to support the use of the *IStateManager* interface.

```
protected override object SaveViewState()
{
    // Customized state management saving state of
    // contained objects, such as a CMTableListItem
    object baseState = base.SaveViewState();

    // Create an array of objects to store the base
    // ViewState and the contained items.
    object[] myState = new object[Items.Count+1];
    myState[0] = baseState;

    int count = 1;
    foreach (CMTableListItem item in Items)
    {
        myState[count] =
        ((IStateManager)item).SaveViewState();
        count++;
    }

    return myState;
}
```

3. The *LoadViewState* method reverses the process. Remember that when the runtime builds the page for the very first request, no *ViewState* exists. Therefore, the *savedState* parameter is *Null*. On postback, however, the page framework calls this method, passing the state that the *SaveViewState* method saved.

   The first thing this method does is restore the *ViewState* of the base control. You use one property this method restores, *ViewState["NumItems"]*, to create the required number of *CMTableListItem* objects. The method then calls the *LoadViewState* method of each *CMTableListItem*, passing to the method the saved state extracted from the *savedState*. The following code illustrates this procedure:

```
protected override void LoadViewState(object savedState)
{
    // Customized state management restoring saved state
    if (savedState != null)
```

```
        {
            object[] myState = (object[])savedState;

            if (myState[0] != null)
            {
                // This restores ViewState["NumItems"] (amongst others)
                base.LoadViewState(myState[0]);
            }

            object o = ViewState["NumItems"];
            if (o != null)
            {
                int numItems = (int)o;
                for (int i=0; i < numItems; i++)
                {
                    // Create item.
                    CMTableListItem item =
                        new CMTableListItem();

                    // add item to the MobileListItemCollection
                    _items.Add(item);
                   // Add the TableListItem as a Child control
                   this.Controls.Add(item);
                    // Restore its state.
                    ((IStateManager)item).LoadViewState
                        (myState[i+1]);
                }
            }
        }
    }
```

4. The *LoadViewState* method restores state when the application builds the control during postback. As described in step 3, *LoadViewState* uses *ViewState["NumItems"]*, which it retrieves from the cached *ViewState* object. The *DataBind* method stores this value at the end of data binding the control while processing the previous request, as shown below.

    Although you're enhancing this control to give it the ability to data-bind only on the first request and then reload its display items from *ViewState* on subsequent requests, you must still handle the situation in which the application developer has coded the application so that the control data-binds on every request. When the page framework builds a control in a postback situation, it calls the *LoadViewState* method before the *DataBind* method. The *LoadViewState* method restores all the data items stored in *ViewState* at the end of the previous request, and the *DataBind* method adds new items all over again from the data source. Consequently, the *DataBind* method must clear the control's *Items* collection; otherwise, it will just add new items to the ones already built in *LoadViewState*. This next code snippet illustrates this concept, with the changes to the *DataBind* method highlighted in boldface.

```
public override void DataBind()
{
    base.OnDataBinding(EventArgs.Empty);

    if (DataSource != null)
    {
        // Empty any objects currently defined in
        // the collection.
        Items.Clear();
        // Clear any previous ViewState for existing child controls
        ClearChildViewState();
        // Clear any existing child controls.
        Controls.Clear();

        // Iterate DataSource; create a new item for each data item
        IEnumerator dataEnum = DataSource.GetEnumerator();
        int count = 0;
        while(dataEnum.MoveNext())
        {
            // Create item.
            CMTableListItem item =
                new CMTableListItem(dataEnum.Current,"","","");
            ⋮
            // Add item to the MobileListItemCollection.
            _items.Add(item);
           // Add the TableListItem as a Child control
           this.Controls.Add(item);
            count++;
        }

        // Store the number of items created in ViewState
        // for postback scenarios.
        ViewState["NumItems"] = count;
    }
}
```

5. You must now implement the *SaveViewState* and *LoadViewState* methods in the CMTableListItem class, which the CMTable control methods of the same name call, as shown in steps 2 and 3. The *SaveViewState* method simply returns a *String* array containing the three properties to save: *Text*, *Text2*, and *Value*. The *LoadViewState*

method restores the properties from the stored state. Here's the syntax; again, the changes are highlighted in bold. Remember to import the *System.Web.UI* namespace to support the use of the *IStateManager* interface.

```
namespace MSPress.MobWeb.CustomControls
{
    /// <summary>
    /// Summary description for MobileTableListItem
    /// </summary>
    public class CMTableListItem : MobileListItem, IStateManager
    {
        ⋮

        protected override void LoadViewState(object savedState)
        {
            // Customized state management to reload saved state.
            if (savedState != null)
            {
                String[] props = (String[])savedState;
                Text = props[0];
                Text2 = props[1];
                Value = props[2];
            }
        }

        protected override object SaveViewState()
        {
            String[] props = new String[3];
            props[0] = Text;
            props[1] = Text2;
            props[2] = Value;
            return props;
        }
    }
}
```

Using *PrivateViewState*

The handling of *ViewState* we've described so far is the same for ASP.NET server controls and mobile server controls. However, mobile controls have an additional capability for internal state management. In addition to *SaveViewState* and *LoadViewState*, the framework calls the *SavePrivateViewState* and *LoadPrivateViewState* methods of classes that inherit from *MobileControl*.

The difference between *ViewState* and *PrivateViewState* is quite simple. *SaveViewState* and *LoadViewState* act on the control's regular *ViewState*. You can turn off this feature by setting *EnableViewState* to *false* on the control or on the page. The runtime stores this *ViewState* on the server, and a token makes the round-trip to and from the client as a tracking mechanism.

SavePrivateViewState and *LoadPrivateViewState* act on the control's internal, private *ViewState*. You can't disable this functionality. The runtime stores *PrivateViewState* in the page sent to the client, which it subsequently posts back to the server. You shouldn't try to store large amounts of data in *PrivateViewState* because you might exceed client capabilities.

A control should use *PrivateViewState* to store internal control values that must persist across requests. An example of such a value is the current display page in a control that is rendered across multiple pages, such as the ObjectList or Calendar control.

Implementing a Custom *MobileControlBuilder* Class

At the beginning of processing each request, the page framework parses the mobile Web Forms page and creates instances of every control you declare within that page. Controls you define inside the start and end tags of another control are children of the enclosing control. The page framework adds these children to that control's *Controls* collection—for example, all the controls you declare inside the *<mobile:Form> ... </mobile:Form>* tags are in the *Controls* collection of the Form control.

The page framework uses a *System.Web.UI.MobileControls.MobileControlBuilder* object to perform this parsing. By default, this class creates enclosed controls as children of the enclosing control and creates LiteralText controls for any text you declare between nested control tags.

Sometimes, however, you'll want to override this default behavior. For example, in the custom CTable control we've been building, you can define items by binding to a data collection. We'll now add useful new functionality to the CMTable control so that it accepts list items that you statically declare in the server control syntax, such as the following:

```
<CMcustom:CMTable id="CmTableCB" runat="server" Alignment="Left">
    <Item Text="Apples" Text2="34.50" Value="static1" />
    <Item Text="Oranges" Text2="26.25" Value="static2" />
    <Item Text="Lemons" Text2="12.00" Value="static3" />
</CMcustom:CMTable>
```

If the standard *MobileControlBuilder* parses this code, it returns an error because the *<Item>* element doesn't represent a mobile control. To avoid this, define a custom *MobileControlBuilder* class and override the *GetChildControlType* method. The following example shows a custom *MobileControlBuilder* object that maps the *<Item>* element to a *CMTableListItem* object:

```
using System;
using System.Collections;
using System.Web.UI.MobileControls;

namespace MSPress.MobWeb.CustomControls
{
    public class CMTableCustomControlBuilder : MobileControlBuilder
    {

        public override Type GetChildControlType(
            String tagName,
            IDictionary attributes)
        {
            // Compare, ignoring case
            if (String.Compare(tagName, "item", true) == 0)
            {
                return typeof(MSPress.MobWeb.CustomControls.CMTableListItem);
            }
            return null;
        }
    }
}
```

Whenever the page framework identifies an object while parsing the server control syntax, it calls the *GetChildControlType* method of *CMTableCustomControlBuilder*. If that method returns a valid type instead of *Null*, it instantiates an object of that type. In addition, the method uses any attributes you declare in the server control syntax (in this case, *Text*, *Text2*, and *Value*) to set the corresponding properties of the new object.

Be aware that the code example shown here limits the allowable enclosed tags to <*Item*> only. If you want to expand the range of allowable enclosed tags, you must return the appropriate object type for those tags. For example, you might want to program the <*DeviceSpecific*> tag to allow property overrides or templates.

To configure a control to use a custom *MobileControlBuilder*, apply a *System.Web.UI.ControlBuilderAttribute* attribute to the control class, specifying the type of the custom *MobileControlBuilder* class. You must also override the *AddParsedSubObject* method. After the *MobileControlBuilder* builds any contained objects, it calls this method so that any logic associated with the addition of the child object to the control executes. In this case, the attribute adds the new *CMTableListItem* to the *Items* collection of the control. The following code shows in boldface the changes needed to the CMTable control to implement a custom control builder.

```
namespace MSPress.MobWeb.CustomControls
{
    [ControlBuilderAttribute(typeof(CMTableCustomControlBuilder))]
```

```
    public class CMTable : PagedControl
    {
        ⋮
        /// <summary>
        /// Statically defined list items are added here.
        /// CustomMobileControlBuilder parsed these from .aspx page.
        /// </summary>
        protected override void AddParsedSubObject(Object obj)
        {
            if (obj is CMTableListItem)
            {
                _items.Add((CMTableListItem)obj);
            }
        }
        ⋮
    }
}
```

In the companion material on this book's Web site, you'll find the CMTableControlBuilder sample code, which implements the functionality described in this section.

Enabling Client Postback in a Custom Control

A few of the standard mobile controls—Command, List, ObjectList, and in some cases, Link—render markup that causes postback to the server when the user clicks a command button or link. Other standard controls, such as the SelectionList and TextBox controls, also implement user interface elements with which users interact. However, these other standard controls don't cause postbacks; instead, they rely on one of the aforementioned controls to cause a postback, after which the runtime analyzes the postdata and raises any change events. We'll examine how to analyze postdata in the next section of this chapter.

If a custom control wants to generate a postback and raise events as a result, it must implement the *System.Web.UI.IPostBackEventHandler* interface. This tells the page framework that the control wants notification of a postback event. We'll develop the custom CTable control some more to implement this interface now. The CMTablePostback sample in the companion material on this book's Web site implements the functionality described in this section.

The *IPostBackEventHandler* interface consists of the *RaisePostBackEvent* method that the page framework calls when this control is responsible for a postback. In this method, you raise any events for this control that result from the postback. Additionally, the *Render* method in the device adapter class must write the link that provides the postback. The method must do this by using the *RenderPostBackEventAsAnchor* or *RenderPostBackEventAsAttribute* methods of the *HtmlControlAdapter* or *WmlControlAdapter* classes.

The control class implementation of *RaisePostBackEvent* can call the *HandlePagePostBackEvent* method in the adapter class. In some cases, the rendering of a control on different classes of device can vary and the postbacks associated with a control can differ, typically between WML devices and HTML devices. The *HandlePagePostBackEvent* of the adapter can handle events that are specific to the control's usage on a particular type of device.

Implementing Postback for the CMTable Control

Now we'll implement an event and property in the CMTable custom control so that the page developer programs postback with this control in the same way as with the standard List control: by implementing the *ItemCommand* event and the *HasItemCommandHandler* property. When the application developer using the CMTable control writes an *OnItemCommand* event handler and sets the *ItemCommand* property of the control to that event handler, the items in column 1 will be rendered as links, which cause postbacks to the server when they're selected. We'll also implement the *HasItemCommandHandler* in the CMTable control, which is a *Boolean* property that returns *true* when the application developer specifies an *ItemCommand* event handler. The device adapter class requires this property to easily determine whether to render a postback link.

To add this functionality, modify the class declaration to state that it implements *IPostbackEventHandler*, and define the *ItemCommand* event in the CMTablePostback control class. Also define the *HasItemCommandHandler* helper method, as shown here:

```
namespace MSPress.MobWeb.CustomControls
{
    public class CMTable : PagedControl, IPostBackEventHandler
    {
    ⋮
        private static readonly object EventItemCommand = new object();

        protected virtual void OnItemCommand(CMTableCommandEventArgs e)
        {
            CMTableCommandEventHandler onItemCommandHandler =
               (CMTableCommandEventHandler)Events[EventItemCommand] ;
            if (onItemCommandHandler != null) onItemCommandHandler(this, e);
        }

        public event CMTableCommandEventHandler ItemCommand
        {
            add
```

```
            {
                Events.AddHandler(EventItemCommand, value);
            }
            remove
            {
                Events.RemoveHandler(EventItemCommand, value);
            }
        }

        public bool HasItemCommandHandler
        {
            get { return (Events[EventItemCommand] != null); }
        }
    ⋮
    }
}
```

The code for the *OnItemCommand* method just described calls any *ItemCommand* event handlers the application developer declares. This method takes as a parameter an object of type *CMTableCommandEventArgs*. Because this object is very similar to *ListCommandEventArgs*, it inherits from that class. This object has two constructors that simply call the similar constructors of the base class. Furthermore, the *ListItem* property overrides the similarly named property of the base class and returns the *CMTableListItem* that corresponds to the item in the list that the user clicks. The following code illustrates this class:

```
using System;
using System.Web.UI.MobileControls;

namespace MSPress.MobWeb.CustomControls
{
    public sealed class CMTableCommandEventArgs : ListCommandEventArgs
    {
        public CMTableCommandEventArgs(
            CMTableListItem item,
            Object commandSource)
                :base(item, commandSource)
        {
        }

        public CMTableCommandEventArgs(
            CMTableListItem item,
            Object commandSource,
            System.Web.UI.WebControls.CommandEventArgs args)
                :base(item, commandSource, args)
        {
        }
```

```
        public new CMTableListItem ListItem
        {
            get  { return (CMTableListItem)(base.ListItem); }
        }
    }

    public delegate void CMTableCommandEventHandler(
        object sender,
        CMTableCommandEventArgs e);
}
```

Back in the *CMTable* class, the *RaisePostBackEvent* method, which implements the *IPostBackEventHandler* interface, must call the *OnItemCommand* method, which is responsible for calling event handlers the application developer declares, as shown in the following code. Note that *RaisePostBackEvent* takes a *String* parameter: *eventArgument*. The *eventArgument* parameter is the value that is posted back from the client to the server. In this case, the argument is the index into the list of items that the user clicks. You define what the argument value is when you generate the user interface in the *Render* method of the device adapter classes, as you'll see in a moment.

```
/// <summary>
/// Raises the ItemCommand event
/// </summary>
/// <param name="eventArgument">
/// Index (as string) into the CMTableListItems of the selected item
/// </param>
public void RaisePostBackEvent(String eventArgument)
{
    CMTableListItem item =
        (CMTableListItem)(this.Items[System.Int32.Parse(eventArgument) ]);
    OnItemCommand(new CMTableCommandEventArgs(item, this));
}
```

Next you rewrite the code in the *WmlCMTableAdapter* class that renders the item in column 1. Use the *RenderPostBackEvent* method, the second parameter of which defines the parameter that posts back when the user selects this item. When the page framework calls the *RaisePostBackEvent* in the main control class, the runtime passes this parameter as the *eventArgument* parameter:

```
// Render column 1.
if(!Control.HasItemCommandHandler)
{
    writer.WriteText(item.Text, true);
}
```

```
else
{
    RenderPostBackEvent(writer, (pageStart + i).ToString(),
        null, true, item.Text, true);
}
```

You use similar logic in the HTML device adapter, as shown in the following code:

```
public override void Render(WmlMobileTextWriter writer)
{
    MobileListItemCollection items = Control.Items;
    if (items.Count == 0)
    {
        return;
    }

    int pageStart = Control.FirstVisibleItemIndex;
    int pageSize = Control.VisibleItemCount;
    if (items.Count < pageSize) pageSize = items.Count;

    Alignment alignment = (Alignment)Style[Style.AlignmentKey, true];
    String alignID;
    switch (alignment)
    {
        case Alignment.Center:
            alignID = "C";
            break;
        case Alignment.Right:
            alignID = "R";
            break;
        default:
            alignID = "L";
            break;
    }

    writer.EnterLayout(Style);
    writer.RenderText("<table", false, false);
    if (Control.Title.Length > 0)
        writer.WriteAttribute("title", Control.Title);
    writer.WriteAttribute("align", alignID + alignID);
    writer.WriteAttribute("columns", "2");
    writer.WriteLine(">");

    for (int i = 0; i < pageSize; i++)
    {
        CMTableListItem item = (CMTableListItem)(items[pageStart + i]);
        writer.Write("<tr><td>");
```

```
            if(!Control.HasItemCommandHandler)
            {
                writer.WriteText(item.Text, true);
            }
            else
            {
                RenderPostBackEvent(writer, (pageStart + i).ToString(),
                    null, true, item.Text, true);
            }
            writer.Write("</td><td>");
            writer.WriteText(item.Text2, true);
            writer.WriteLine("</td></tr>");
        }
        writer.WriteLine("</table>");

        writer.ExitLayout(Style, true);
    }
```

Now the application developer can write *OnItemCommand* event handlers that this control calls when the user selects an item from column 1 of the table. Figure 22-6 shows an example of the output from a test application. In this example, the form contains a Label control (which initially sets *Visible="false")* and a CMTable control. The event handler method sets the text of a Label control to the name of the selected item and makes the Label visible.

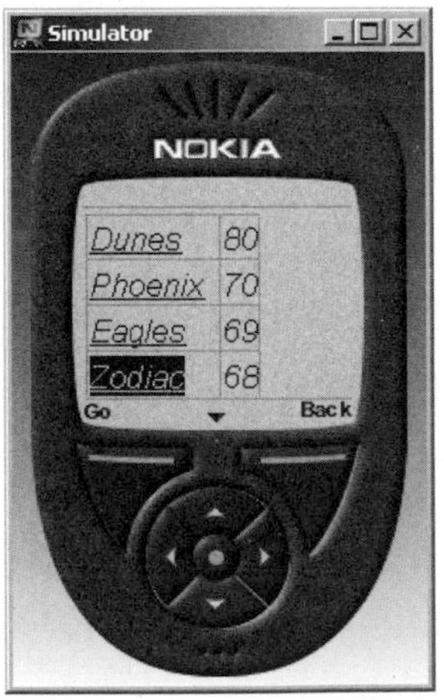

Figure 22-6 Specifying an *OnItemCommand* event handler method, which the runtime calls when the user selects an item from the first column

Processing Postdata

A number of the mobile controls, such as the SelectionList and TextBox controls, allow the user to interact with them at the client level but don't cause postback directly. Instead, you must accompany these controls with a control that does cause postback to the server, such as Command. The data that is posted back includes the results of interactions with the interactive controls. When it is processing the data posted back to the server, the page framework must notify each interactive control when a postback occurs. The control must examine the data posted back, update its own state if the user has utilized the control, and then raise the appropriate events (such as the *TextChanged* event that the TextBox control raises).

To do this, the class must implement the *System.Web.UI.IPostBackDataHandler* interface, which tells the page framework to call the control's *LoadPostData* method, passing all data posted back as key/value pairs. Classes that implement *IPostBackDataHandler* must also provide the *RaisePostDataChangedEvent* method. To raise an event as the result of a property's change in value, you put the code in this method. The framework calls *RaisePostDataChangedEvent* if *LoadPostData* returns *true*.

If the implementation of the user interface differs among the control's various device adapter classes, the data posted back might differ. The *LoadPostData* method of the control class can call the corresponding method of the device adapter to analyze the postdata and act on it there, instead of in the control class. In a moment, you'll see a code sample that illustrates this concept. The CMTablePostdata sample in the companion material on this book's Web site implements the functionality described in this section.

Implementing Postdata Processing in the CMTable Control

To illustrate the concepts just described, you'll equip the CMTable with a crude *AddNew* capability. If the *AddNewEnabled* property is set to *true*, the control is rendered with two input boxes. These input boxes allow the user to enter two text values that the control adds to the existing data in the table as a new row, after the changes are posted back. When the class adds a new row, the control raises the *ItemAdded* event.

First modify the class declaration to state that the class implements *IPostBackDataHandler*, define the *AddNewEnabled* property that switches this new functionality on and off, and initialize *AddNewEnabled* in the class constructor:

```
namespace MSPress.MobWeb.CustomControls
{
    public class CMTable : PagedControl,
        IPostBackEventHandler,
```

```
        IPostBackDataHandler
    {

        /// <summary>
        /// Gets and sets whether the user gets user interface for new item.
        /// </summary>
        public bool AddNewEnabled
        {
            get
            {
                return (bool)ViewState["AddNewEnabled"];
            }
            set
            {
                ViewState["AddNewEnabled"] = value;
            }
        }

        public CMTablePostdata()
         {
                Title = "";
                DataTextField1 = "";
                DataTextField2 = "";
                DataValueField = "";
                ItemsAsLinks = false;
                AddNewEnabled = false;
         }
```

Next define the *ItemAdded* event the same way that you define the other events for this control. The runtime calls *ItemAdded* event handlers with a parameter that passes a reference to the newly added *CMTableListItem* object. The *CMTableListItemEventArgs* class you wrote in the section "Building a Data Bound Custom Control," earlier in this chapter, for the *ItemCommand* event is perfect for this, so we'll reuse it for the *ItemAdded* event. Here's the syntax:

```
private static readonly object EventItemAdded = new object();

protected virtual void OnItemAdded(CMTableListItemEventArgs e)
{
    CMTableListItemEventHandler onItemAddedHandler =
             (CMTableListItemEventHandler)Events[EventItemAdded];
    if (onItemAddedHandler != null) onItemAddedHandler(this, e);
}

public event CMTableListItemEventHandler ItemAdded
{
    add  { Events.AddHandler(EventItemAdded, value); }
    remove { Events.RemoveHandler(EventItemAdded, value); }
}
```

Implement the two methods of the *IPostBackDataHandler* interface. In this example, *LoadPostData* calls the *LoadPostData* methods of the device adapter class because the implementation of the user interface for this feature differs between WML and HTML devices and the data posted back differs. Using *LoadPostData* in the device adapter class sets *dataChanged* to *true* if the data posted back caused the method to update the control's properties or state, and this value returns to the caller. If *LoadPostData* returns *true*, the page framework subsequently calls *RaisePostDataChangedEvent*, where the runtime raises the *ItemAdded* event. The following code lists the *LoadPostData* and *RaisePostDataChangedEvent* methods. You will need to import the *System.Collections.Specialized* namespace to support the use of the *NameValueCollection* class.

```
public virtual bool LoadPostData(
    string postDataKey,
    NameValueCollection postCollection)
{
    // Call the LoadPostData methods of the device adapters.
    bool dataChanged;
    this.Adapter.LoadPostData
        (postDataKey, postCollection, null, out dataChanged);
    return dataChanged;
}

public virtual void RaisePostDataChangedEvent()
{
    // Send an OnItemAdded with the new item (which is the last item
    // in the collection) passed in the arguments.
    // Reuse the CMTableListItemEventArgs used for OnItemDataBind.
    CMTableListItem aNewItem =
         (CMTableListItem)(this.Items[Items.Count-1]);
    OnItemAdded(new CMTableListItemEventArgs(aNewItem));
}
```

Providing Different User Interfaces in the *DeviceAdapter* Classes

HTML and WML have different capabilities for storing data in the cells of a table. The HTML *<input>* elements that allow you to enter text values can be rendered directly into a table's cells. But WML markup doesn't allow this, so the class must render the input elements differently.

You update the *Render* method in the *HtmlCMTableAdapter* class this way:

```
public override void Render(HtmlMobileTextWriter writer)
{
    ⋮
    Output of table list items not shown
    ⋮
```

```
        // Add user interface for new item entry, if requested.
        if (Control.AddNewEnabled)
        {
            writer.Write("<tr><td>");
            writer.WriteBeginTag("input");
            writer.WriteAttribute("name", Control.UniqueID);
            writer.WriteAttribute("type", "text");
            writer.WriteAttribute("value", "");
            writer.WriteAttribute("size", "12");
            writer.Write("/>");
            writer.Write("</td><td>");
            writer.WriteBeginTag("input");
            writer.WriteAttribute("name", Control.UniqueID);
            writer.WriteAttribute("type", "text");
            writer.WriteAttribute("value", "");
            writer.WriteAttribute("size", "12");
            writer.Write("/>");
            writer.WriteLine("</td></tr>");
        }
        writer.WriteLine(tableSuffix);
    }
```

The *name* attribute you specify for the *<input>* HTML element serves an important function. When all the data is posted back, the runtime identifies each value by the name of the generating user interface element. When the page framework calls the *LoadPostData* method, the second parameter will be a dictionary object containing all the data that the application has posted back. Consequently, you must give the user interface element a name that allows you to identify it in the dictionary collection. Usually, the control's *UniqueID* property provides a suitable value, since it's guaranteed to be unique among all the controls on the page. In this case, both *<input>* elements get the same name, which means that the data that is posted back includes two values of the same name. It's easy to extract these values from the dictionary collection, as this code sample shows:

```
// Parse the HTML posted data appropriately.
public override bool LoadPostData(
    String key,
    NameValueCollection data,
    Object controlPrivateData,
    out bool dataChanged)
{
    // The key parameter is the control's client ID.
    String[] newItems = data.GetValues(key);

    // Case where nothing is entered
    if((newItems[0] == String.Empty) && (newItems[1] == String.Empty))
```

```
    {
        dataChanged = false;
    }
    else
    {
        CMTableListItem item =
        new CMTableListItem(null, newItems[0], newItems[1], "");
        Control.Items.Add(item);
        dataChanged = true;
    }

    return true;
}
```

> **Note** The *NameValueCollection* object you use to pass the posted data into the *LoadPostData* method resides in the *System.Collections.Specialized* namespace. Therefore, you should add this namespace to your *using* statements in the device adapter source.

Listing 22-9 shows a mobile Web Forms page that you can use to test this control.

```
<%@ Register TagPrefix="CMcustom" Namespace="MSPress.MobWeb.CustomControls"
    Assembly="CustomMobileControlLibrary" %>
<%@ Register TagPrefix="mobile" Namespace="System.Web.UI.MobileControls"
    Assembly="System.Web.Mobile" %>
<%@ Page language="c#"
    Inherits="System.Web.UI.MobileControls.MobilePage" %>

<head>
<script runat="server" language="c#">
   public void TableItemAdded(object sender, CMTableListItemEventArgs  e)
   {
       Label1.Text =
          "You entered Col1: " + e.Item.Text + " Col2: " + e.Item.Text2;
       Label1.Visible = true;
       CMTable1.AddNewEnabled = false;
       Command1.Visible = false;
   }
</script>
</head>
```

Listing 22-9 Mobile Web Forms page that tests the ability of the CMTable control to analyze postdata and raise the *ItemAdded* event

```
<body>
    <mobile:Form id="Form1" runat="server">
        <mobile:Label id="Label1" runat="server" Visible="False"/>
        <CMcustom:CMTable id="CMTable1" runat="server"
            OnItemAdded="TableItemAdded" AddNewEnabled="true">
            <Item Text="Apples" Text2="10" />
            <Item Text="Oranges" Text2="4" />
            <Item Text="Lemons" Text2="6" />
            <Item Text="Grapefruit" Text2="2" />
         </CMcustom:CMTable>
        <mobile:Command id="Command1" Text="Update" runat="server"/>
    </mobile:Form>
</body>
```

Figure 22-7 shows the output on the HTML browser of a Pocket PC.

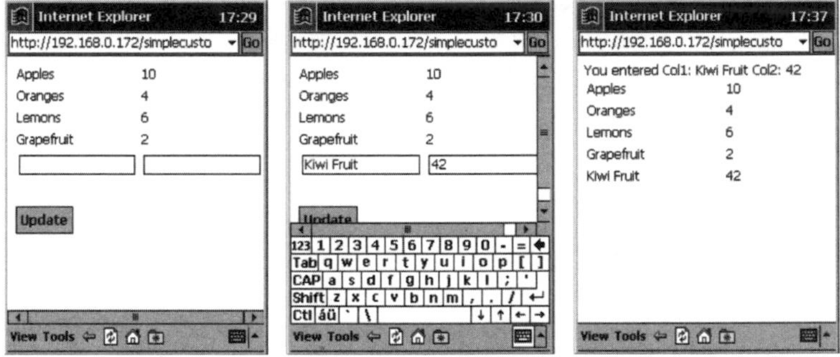

Figure 22-7 Implementing the *AddNewEnabled* feature on HTML devices by rendering two input elements into the table

Adding Child Controls in a Device Adapter Class

The approach we just described doesn't work with WML adapters. This is because the ASP.NET mobile controls don't support postback from two input elements that use the same name on the same WML card. Instead, you implement the user interface to accept the new entries by creating child controls of the CMTable control. The page framework ensures that all the child controls have unique *UniqueID* properties. Consequently, the adapter generates the WML markup of input elements that use different names. You identify the input values that post back by using a name that's the same as the child control's *UniqueID*.

Whenever a custom control creates child controls, the initial control must implement the *System.Web.UI.INamingContainer* interface. Although this interface has no methods, it tells the page framework to ensure unique names for any contained controls. Then the page framework assigns each of its child controls a *UniqueID* in the form *parentID:ctrl_n*. To implement this, simply add the interface name to the class description, as follows:

```
public class CMTable : PagedControl,
    IPostBackEventHandler,
    IPostBackDataHandler,
    INamingContainer
{
    ⋮
```

The *OnLoad* method of the *WmlCMTableAdapter* class creates the child controls. The child controls require a prompt string and an input box for each value that the user can enter. You use a LiteralText control and a TextBox control to create these elements:

```
public override void OnLoad(EventArgs e)
{
    base.OnLoad(e);
    if (Control.AddNewEnabled)
    {
        LiteralText lt1 = new LiteralText();
        lt1.Text = "New Col1 Value:";
        TextBox tb1 = new TextBox();
        LiteralText lt2 = new LiteralText();
        lt2.Text = "New Col2 Value:";
        TextBox tb2 = new TextBox();

        Control.Controls.Add(lt1);
        Control.Controls.Add(tb1);
        Control.Controls.Add(lt2);
        Control.Controls.Add(tb2);

        //Register for update on postback
        Page.RegisterRequiresPostBack(Control);
    }
}
```

The last line of code in this *OnLoad* method demands more explanation. Normally, these child TextBox controls are the ones that would be called by the page framework to process postdata, so they can update their state with the values entered at the client browser. But in this case, we want the parent control to process the postdata, so we call the *RegisterRequiresPostBack* method of the *Page* class to declare to the page framework that *Control* (that is, the parent control, CMTable) needs to process data posted back from the client.

Why Trapping Change Events of Child Controls Is Dangerous

You might be wondering why we don't just hook the *TextChanged* events of the TextBox controls and update the state of the CMTable control that way. Why do we need to process the postdata in the CMTable control, rather than just implement an *OnTextChanged* method for these child controls to find out what data has been posted back?

To answer these questions, you must understand how the runtime handles the "Load post data" and "Send postback change notifications" phases described in Table 22-1. During the "Load post data" phase, the runtime calls the *LoadPostData* method of all controls on the page that want to process the postdata. If as a result of this a control needs to raise a change event (for example, a TextBox control wants to raise a *TextChanged* event), it returns *true* from *LoadPostData*. The runtime later calls the *RaisePostDataChanged* event of the control to allow it to raise its change events, but not until all controls have completed processing postdata. The result of this is that all controls on the page have completed updating their state before any change events are raised. Change events can be raised in any order, but an event handler can query properties of any other control on the page knowing that that control has already updated its state.

If we simply hook the *TextChanged* events of the child TextBox controls, the state of the CMTable control will not be updated until the *OnTextChanged* event handler executes, which is sometime in the "Send postback change notifications" phase. If the application developer has written event handlers in the application for the change events of other controls on the page, there is no telling whether the event will execute before or after the state of the CMTable control is updated. If the code queries properties of CMTable before it has updated its state, they might get the old property value, not the current value following the postback. This would be a very difficult bug to track down! For this reason, it's important to process the postdata in the parent control during the "Load post data" phase.

Rendering Child Controls and Processing Postdata

In the *Render* method of *WmlCMTableAdapter*, the child controls must be rendered after the runtime outputs the table. Because these are the CMTable control's only child controls, you can easily achieve this by calling the *RenderChildren* method:

```
public override void Render(WmlMobileTextWriter writer)
    {
        ⋮
        // Add user interface for new item entry, if requested.
        if (Control.AddNewEnabled)
        {
            writer.BeginCustomMarkup();
            this.RenderChildren(writer);
            writer.EndCustomMarkup();
        }
    }
```

In the *LoadPostData* method, you can identify the values that post back for the child TextBox controls by their *UniqueID* name, which takes the form *parentID:childID*. The application passes the *ClientID* of the parent into the method in the *key* parameter. Thus, you can easily identify the posted data for the child controls and act upon it:

```
// Parse the WML posted data appropriately.
public override bool LoadPostData(String key,
    NameValueCollection data,
    Object controlPrivateData,
    out bool dataChanged)
{
    if (!Control.AddNewEnabled)
        dataChanged = false;
    else
    {
        String[] newItems = {"",""};
        int count = 0;
        foreach (string childkey in data.Keys)
        {
            //Child controls have ID in the form 'parent:ctrl_n'
            //'key' identifies parent.
            if (childkey.StartsWith(key))
            {
                newItems[count++] = data[childkey];
            }
        }

        // Case where nothing is entered.
        if((newItems[0] == String.Empty) && (newItems[1] == String.Empty))
        {
            dataChanged = false;
        }
        else
        {
            CMTableListItem item =
```

```
                new CMTableListItem(null, newItems[0], newItems[1], "");
                Control.Items.Add(item);
                dataChanged = true;
            }
        }

        return true;
    }
```

Developing a Templated Custom Control

In Chapter 9, you learned how to use DeviceSpecific/Choice constructs to apply property overrides to any control or to replace part of a templated control's user interface. If your control doesn't use a custom *MobileControlBuilder*, it supports property overrides by default. If your control does use a custom *MobileControlBuilder*, all you need to do to support property overrides is to ensure that its *GetChildControlType* method returns a *Type* of *System.Web.UI.MobileControls.DeviceSpecific* when passed the *<DeviceSpecific>* tag. (See the section "Implementing a Custom *MobileControlBuilder* Class," earlier in this chapter, for more details on this topic.)

To support templates, you must do some programming work in the control class. But first you must decide how to apply templates to your control. You have two options:

- Some controls, such as Panel, replace their entire user interface with the contents of the template. The runtime will ignore any other controls defined inside the Panel control.
- Other controls, such as List and ObjectList, allow templates to replace part of the control's user interface. Together, the *HeaderTemplate*, *FooterTemplate*, *ItemTemplate*, *AlternatingItemTemplate*, and *ItemSeparatorTemplate* represent the various parts of a List control's user interface. As an application developer, you're free to use any or all of these parts.

Implementing Support for Templates

To add support for templates, you first must ensure that the control class implements the *System.Web.UI.MobileControls.ITemplateable* interface. Although this interface has no methods, it alerts the page framework that the control supports templates.

The *MobileControl* base class implements the *IsTemplated* property. When the runtime processes a request from a client device, it evaluates any DeviceSpecific/Choice constructs you've specified for any controls. If this results in the runtime selecting a template for that request, *IsTemplated* returns *true*. This property is useful when implementing logic for handling templates.

Your custom control must test *IsTemplated*, and if it returns *true*, the control must call the base class implementation of *CreateTemplatedUI*. Typically, you'll do this in one of the *OnInit*, *CreateChildControls*, or *DataBind* methods. The base class implementation of *CreateTemplatedUI* calls the *CreateTemplatedUI* method of the device adapter class:

By default, the device adapter base class implementation of *CreateTemplatedUI* simply calls the *CreateDefaultTemplatedUI* method in the control class. However, if the implementation of the user interface for the templated elements is device specific, you should override *CreateTemplatedUI* in the device adapter class and instantiate the templates there. If your control implements support for templates that is generic to all client devices, you should override the *CreateDefaultTemplatedUI* method in the control class to instantiate the templates there.

The *GetTemplate* method of the *MobileControl* base class retrieves the content that the application developer defines for a particular template. This method takes a parameter that's the tag name of the template—for example, *ItemTemplate*. If this method doesn't return *Null*, the application has defined and selected a template of that name after the evaluation of choice filters.

You must then instantiate the template contents inside a container control derived from *System.Web.UI.MobileControls.TemplateContainer*. The *InstantiateIn* method of *TemplateContainer* instantiates the contents of the template as child controls of the *TemplateContainer*. A template can contain native markup or other server controls; these are instantiated as LiteralText or server controls, respectively. Finally, the runtime can call *DataBind* to evaluate any data binding syntax on the child controls:

```
TemplateContainer container = new TemplateContainer();
ITemplate itemTemplate = GetTemplate(Constants.ItemTemplateTag);
if (itemTemplate != null)
{
    itemTemplate.InstantiateIn(container);
    if (doDataBind)
       container.DataBind();
}
```

In the *Render* method in the device adapter, the runtime renders the child controls of the *TemplateContainer* at the appropriate point:

```
// If an ItemTemplate has been defined, render that.
if (Control.IsTemplated)
{
    // First control in the control's Controls collection
    // is the TemplateContainer, which in this case is a MobileListItem.
    ((MobileListItem)(Control.Controls[0])).RenderChildren(writer);
}
else
:
```

Implementing Template Support for a Data Bound List Control

To illustrate the concepts just described, you'll equip the CMTable custom control with support for the *<ItemTemplate>*. In this control, we've decided that an *<ItemTemplate>* replaces the contents of the table cell in the left column. Listing 22-10 shows the mobile Web Forms page you use to test this new functionality, and Listing 22-11 depicts the *Weather* class you use to create the source data for testing the templated CMTable control.

```
<%@ Register TagPrefix="CMcustom" Namespace="MSPress.MobWeb.CustomControls"
    Assembly="CustomMobileControlLibrary" %>
<%@ Register TagPrefix="mobile" Namespace="System.Web.UI.MobileControls"
    Assembly="System.Web.Mobile" %>
<%@ Page language="c#"
    Inherits="System.Web.UI.MobileControls.MobilePage"%>

<head>
<script runat="server" language="c#">
    public void Page_Load(object sender, System.EventArgs e)
    {
        // Set up data for templated CMTable example.
        ArrayList array = new ArrayList();
        array.Add(new
            Weather("Seattle", "Sunny", "Sun.gif", "sun"));
        array.Add(new
            Weather("Calgary", "Snow", "Snow.gif", "snowflake"));
        array.Add(new
            Weather("San Frans.", "Cloudy", "Cloud.gif", "cloudy"));

        CMTableTemplate.DataSource = array;
        CMTableTemplate.DataTextField1 = "Summary";
        CMTableTemplate.DataTextField2 = "CityName";
        CMTableTemplate.DataBind();
    }
```

Listing 22-10 Mobile Web Forms page that exercises the templating capability of the CMTable custom control

```
</script>
</head>

<body>
    <mobile:form runat="server">
        <CMcustom:CMTable id="CMTableTemplate"
            runat="server" Font-Bold="true">
            <DeviceSpecific>
                <Choice Filter="isUP4x">
                    <ItemTemplate>
                        <mobile:Image runat="server"
                            AlternateText=
'<%# DataBinder.Eval(((CMTableListItem)Container).DataItem, "Summary")%>'
                            ImageURL='Symbol:
<%# DataBinder.Eval(((CMTableListItem)Container).DataItem, "WmlImage")%>'>
                        </mobile:Image>
                    </ItemTemplate>
                </Choice>
                <Choice>
                    <ItemTemplate>
                        <mobile:Image runat="server"
                            AlternateText=
'<%# DataBinder.Eval(((CMTableListItem)Container).DataItem, "Summary")%>'
                            ImageURL=
'<%# DataBinder.Eval(((CMTableListItem)Container).DataItem, "HtmlImage")%>'>
                        </mobile:Image>
                    </ItemTemplate>
                </Choice>
            </DeviceSpecific>
        </CMcustom:CMTable>
    </mobile:form>
</body>
```

```
using System;

namespace MSPress.MobWeb.CustomControls
{
    public class Weather
    {
        private String  _cityName, _summary, _HtmlImageURL, _WmlImage;

        public Weather(String CityName,
            String Summary,
            String HtmlImage,
            String WmlImage)
```

Listing 22-11 Class used to create the source data for testing the templated CMTable control

```
        {
            this._cityName = CityName;
            this._summary = Summary;
            this._HtmlImageURL = HtmlImage;
            this._WmlImage = WmlImage;
        }

        public String CityName { get { return this._cityName; } }
        public String Summary { get { return this._summary; } }
        public String HtmlImage { get { return this._HtmlImageURL; } }
        public String WmlImage { get { return this._WmlImage; } }
    }
}
```

Listing 22-12 shows the significant methods for the templated version of the CMTable control. There's one important thing to note before looking at this code: if you've been building this control as you worked through this chapter, you'll have the CMTable control implementing the *INamingContainer* interface. This interface has no methods; it's just a marker for the ASP.NET runtime, so you just add it to the class name declaration. In the templated control, you need to make the *CMTableListItem* objects implement *INamingContainer* because that is the container object for anything the page developer puts inside the template. Remove *INamingContainer* from the *CMTable* class declaration, and add it into *CMTableListItem* instead:

```
public class CMTableListItem : MobileListItem,
     IStateManager, INamingContainer
{
     ⋮
}
```

In CMTable, also remove the *[ControlBuilderAttribute(typeof(CMTableCustomControlBuilder))]* attribute on the *CMTable* class. The custom control builder you built earlier in this chapter is not sophisticated enough to handle templated content, and rather than enhance it to do so, we'll simply remove it from this example. Now here are the code changes for CMTable:

```
using System;
using System.Reflection;
using System.Web.UI;
using System.Web.UI.MobileControls;

namespace MSPress.MobWeb.CustomControls
```

Listing 22-12 Important methods involved in the instantiation of content defined in the CMTable control's templates

```
{
    /// <summary>
    /// Custom control allows templating.
    /// </summary>
    public class CMTable: PagedControl,
//      INamingContainer,  REMOVE THIS!! Apply to CMTableListItem instead
        ITemplateable,
        IPostBackEventHandler,
        IPostBackDataHandler
    {
        :
        // Intervening properties, events, methods as in earlier examples
        :

        public override void DataBind()
        {
            // Evaluate any data binding expressions on the control itself.
            base.DataBind();

            if (DataSource != null)
            {
                // Empty any objects currently defined in the collection.
                Items.Clear();
                // Clear any previous ViewState for existing child controls
                ClearChildViewState();
                // Clear any existing child controls.
                Controls.Clear();

                // Iterate DataSource; create a new
                // item for each data item.
                IEnumerator dataEnum = DataSource.GetEnumerator();
                int count = 0;
                while(dataEnum.MoveNext())
                {
                    // Create item
                    CMTableListItem item =
                        new CMTableListItem(dataEnum.Current,"","","");

                    System.Type objectType = dataEnum.Current.GetType();
                    PropertyInfo aProp =
                        objectType.GetProperty(this.DataTextField1);
                    if (aProp != null)
                        item.Text = aProp.GetValue(
                                        dataEnum.Current,null).ToString();
                    aProp = objectType.GetProperty(this.DataTextField2);
                    if (aProp != null)
                        item.Text2 = aProp.GetValue(
                                        dataEnum.Current,null).ToString();
                    aProp = objectType.GetProperty(this.DataValueField);
```

```
                if (aProp != null)
                    item.Value = aProp.GetValue(
                                    dataEnum.Current,null).ToString();

                // Add item to the MobileListItemCollection.
                Items.Add(item);
                // Also add the item to the
                // child control's collection.
                this.Controls.Add(item);

                count++;
            }

            if (this.IsTemplated)
            {
                CreateTemplatedUI(true);
            }

            // Prevent child controls from being created again.
            ChildControlsCreated = true;
            // Store the number of items created in ViewState.
            ViewState["NumItems"] = count;
        }
    }

    protected override void CreateChildControls()
    {
        if (this.IsTemplated)
        {
            // The parameter here is doDataBind;
            // it should be set to true only
            // on first request. Set it to false
            // if state should be restored from
            // ViewState. CreateChildControls is called on postback.
            CreateTemplatedUI(false);
        }
    }

    public override void CreateDefaultTemplatedUI(bool doDataBind)
    {
        foreach (CMTableListItem item in this.Items)
        {
            // Normally we would instantiate a TemplateContainer here,
            // but a CMTableListItem inherits from MobileListItem, which
            // inherits from TemplateContainer.
            ITemplate itemTemplate =
                GetTemplate(Constants.ItemTemplateTag);
            if (itemTemplate != null)
            {
```

```
                itemTemplate.InstantiateIn(item);
                if (doDataBind)
                    item.DataBind();
            }
        }
    }
}
}
```

Note that the CMTable control uses *CMTableListItem* objects to store the data for each row of the table. *CMTableListItem* inherits from the standard *MobileListItem* class, which itself inherits from *TemplateContainer*. You must instantiate templates inside an instance of a class that descends from *TemplateContainer*. Thus, in this control, the templates instantiate inside the *CMTableListItem* objects.

In the *DataBind* method, you create a *CMTableListItem* object for each data item in the data source, as you did before. But unlike earlier examples, you add each *CMTableListItem* object to the control's *Controls* collection. If you execute the sample shown in Listing 22-10 on an HTML browser and set *Trace="true"* in the *@ Page* directive, you can view the resulting control hierarchy in the trace output. Each *CMTableListItem* is a child of the CMTable control. And within each *CMTableListItem*, which is the *TemplateContainer*, you'll find the controls that the template defines—in this case, the mobile Image controls.

> **Note** Using the code described here, the CMTable control doesn't support *ViewState* for items in the template. You need to write additional code in the *SaveViewState* and *LoadViewState* methods of the *CMTableListItem* class to save and restore the state of any child controls that you create from the template. You can find a full implementation of this in the companion material on this book's Web site.

The change that the device adapter requires is very simple. In the *Render* method, where the item in column 0 is rendered, the contents of the *TemplateContainer* are rendered instead. Listing 22-13 shows this procedure.

Figure 22-8 shows the output of this listing on Pocket Internet Explorer. In the first image, the runtime defines the output without applying changes through templates. In the second image, the application uses a template to display an Image control in the first column.

```
public override void Render(HtmlMobileTextWriter writer)
    {
        :

        writer.AddAttribute("width","90%");
        writer.AddAttribute("cellpadding", "3");
        writer.RenderBeginTag("table");
        writer.WriteLine("");
        for (int i = 0; i < pageSize; i++)
        {
            CMTableListItem item = (CMTableListItem)(items[pageStart + i]);
            writer.Write("<tr><td width=500>");

            //If an ItemTemplate has been defined, render that.
            if (Control.IsTemplated)
            {
                ((CMTableListItem)(Control.Controls[i]))
                    .RenderChildren(writer);
            }
            else
            {
                //Render nontemplated table data cell contents.
                writer.EnterFormat(Style);
                writer.WriteEncodedText(item.Text);
                writer.ExitFormat(Style);
            }

            //Close first row item and render second.
            writer.Write("</td><td width=500>");
            :
```

Listing 22-13 Changes to the *Render* method of the device adapter to render the contents of the template

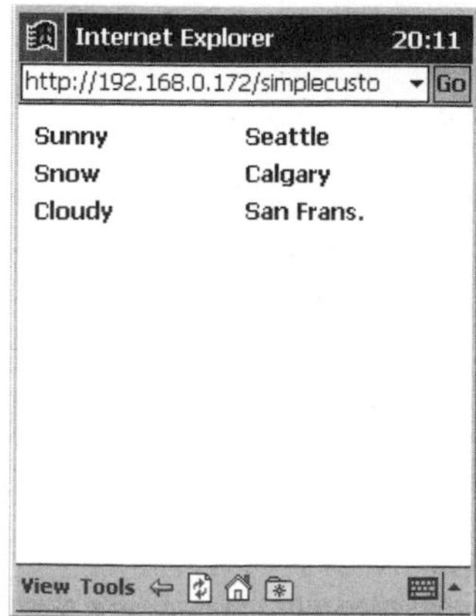

Figure 22-8 Templated CMTable output

Index

B

C

E

F

G

H

I

J

N

O

T

X

Y

Z

Andy Wigley

Andy Wigley is a Principal Technologist at Content Master. He works exclusively with mobile technologies and particularly loves researching, programming, and writing about applying Microsoft .NET to mobility solutions. This interest has led him to devise and coauthor two books: the one you are holding now, and *Microsoft .NET Compact Framework (Core Reference)* with Stephen Wheelwright (Microsoft Press, 2003), which focuses on building rich client .NET applications for Pocket PC and Microsoft Windows CE .NET devices. He has contributed to MSDN and other publications and regularly appears at conferences, presenting on applications of mobile technology. He's a member of the Microsoft .NET Code Wise Community, supporting the developer community with help and advice on mobility issues.

He lives with his wife, Caroline, and their two daughters, Frances and Claire, in North Wales. When he's not at a computer, you'll find him rock climbing and walking in the mountains.

PowerTools

At Microsoft Press, we use tools to illustrate our books for software developers and IT professionals. Tools very simply and powerfully symbolize human inventiveness. They're a metaphor for people extending their capabilities, precision, and reach. From simple calipers and pliers to digital micrometers and lasers, these stylized illustrations give each book a visual identity, and a personality to the series. With tools and knowledge, there's no limit to creativity and innovation. Our tagline says it all: *the tools you need to put technology to work.*

The manuscript for this book was prepared and galleyed using Microsoft Word. Pages were composed by Microsoft Press using Adobe FrameMaker+SGML for Windows, with text in Garamond and display type in Helvetica Condensed. Composed pages were delivered to the printer as electronic prepress files.

Cover Designer:	Methodologie, Inc.
Interior Graphic Designer:	James D. Kramer
Principal Compositor:	Paula Gorelick
Interior Artist:	Joel Panchot
Copy Editor:	Jennifer Harris
Proofreader:	nSight, Inc.
Indexer:	Julie Hatley

Get a **Free**

e-mail newsletter, updates, special offers, links to related books, and more when you

register on line!

Register your Microsoft Press® title on our Web site and you'll get a FREE subscription to our e-mail newsletter, *Microsoft Press Book Connections.* You'll find out about newly released and upcoming books and learning tools, online events, software downloads, special offers and coupons for Microsoft Press customers, and information about major Microsoft® product releases. You can also read useful additional information about all the titles we publish, such as detailed book descriptions, tables of contents and indexes, sample chapters, links to related books and book series, author biographies, and reviews by other customers.

Registration is easy. Just visit this Web page and fill in your information:

http://www.microsoft.com/mspress/register

Microsoft

Proof of Purchase

Use this page as proof of purchase if participating in a promotion or rebate offer on this title. Proof of purchase must be used in conjunction with other proof(s) of payment such as your dated sales receipt—see offer details.

Building Microsoft® ASP.NET Applications for Mobile Devices, Second Edition

0-7356-1914-X

CUSTOMER NAME

Microsoft Press, PO Box 97017, Redmond, WA 98073-9830